Urban Issues

Urban Issues

2013

SIXTH EDITION

Los Angeles | London | New Delhi
Singapore | Washington DC

SELECTIONS FROM **CQ RESEARCHER**

Los Angeles | London | New Delhi
Singapore | Washington DC

FOR INFORMATION:

CQ Press
An Imprint of SAGE Publications, Inc.
2455 Teller Road
Thousand Oaks, California 91320
E-mail: order@sagepub.com

SAGE Publications Ltd.
1 Oliver's Yard
55 City Road
London EC1Y 1SP
United Kingdom

SAGE Publications India Pvt. Ltd.
B 1/I 1 Mohan Cooperative Industrial Area
Mathura Road, New Delhi 110 044
India

SAGE Publications Asia-Pacific Pte. Ltd.
3 Church Street
#10-04 Samsung Hub
Singapore 049483

Printed in the United States of America

Library of Congress Control Number: 2012945756

ISBN 978-1-4522-2678-1

This book is printed on acid-free paper.

MIX
Paper from
responsible sources
FSC® C014174

Acquisitions Editor: Elise Fraser
Production Editor: Laura Stewart
Typesetter: C&M Digitals (P) Ltd.
Cover Designer: Candice Harman
Marketing Manager: Jonathan Mason

12 13 14 15 16 10 9 8 7 6 5 4 3 2 1

Contents

Annotated Contents

EDUCATION

School Reform

With international tests showing that the United States no longer leads in school achievement, a bipartisan coalition of reformers is advocating the creation of more charter schools and a system of basing pay and firing decisions for teachers on students' standardized test scores. Conservatives have long recommended such businesslike approaches for schools, and Republican lawmakers and politicians are pushing for laws to weaken unions' ability to defend teachers against charges of incompetency. Teachers' unions remain opposed to market-oriented reforms, but the philosophy has new adherents among education-reform groups and centrist Democrats such as President Obama, whose administration is providing funding to states to develop data-driven teacher assessments. Meanwhile, some education scholars point out that poorly performing students are concentrated in low-income districts, where funding shortfalls, bad teaching conditions and poverty make educating students more difficult.

Fixing Urban Schools

African-American and Hispanic students — largely in urban schools — lag far behind white students, who mostly attend middle-class suburban schools. Critics argue that when Congress reauthorizes the 2002 No Child Left Behind Act (NCLB), it must retarget the legislation to help urban schools tackle tough problems, such as encouraging the best teachers to enter and remain in high-poverty schools, rather than focusing on tests and sanctions. Some advocates propose busing students across district lines to create more socioeconomically diverse student bodies. But conservative analysts argue that busing wastes students' time and that permitting charter schools to compete with public schools will drive improvement. Meanwhile, liberal analysts point out that successful charter programs are too costly for most schools to emulate, and that no one has yet figured out how to spread success beyond a handful of schools, public or private.

LAND USE AND URBAN DEVELOPMENT

Blighted Cities

Dozens of cities, including Detroit, Flint, Mich., and Youngstown, Ohio, have been ravaged by staggering declines in population and vast neighborhood blight. Some planners are advocating controversial "shrinking-cities" strategies aimed at demolishing thousands of derelict structures, converting blighted blocks to open space or other uses and providing incentives for residents of decrepit neighborhoods to move to healthier ones, in part to save on municipal-service costs. But critics say demolishing parts of cities is the wrong way to save them, and they point to failed urban-renewal efforts of the 1960s as evidence. Meanwhile, progress is slow in cities that are trying to remake themselves. Funds for demolition and cleanup are tight, and residents fear being forced to relocate — a practice city officials deny advocating. Moreover, intractable urban problems such as poverty and unemployment make the prospect of reducing blight especially daunting.

Downtown Renaissance

After World War II, suburban job and population growth in the United States far outstripped that of cities, leading many to worry that downtowns were doomed. In recent years, however, many cities have revived their fortunes by fashioning downtowns that are attractive and — for the first time in decades — drawing in new residents. Once-forlorn urban centers from San Diego to Philadelphia are now busy construction zones that are filling up with trendy shops and restaurants. But despite the good news, downtowns are still grabbing only a tiny fraction of metropolitan growth. Some skeptics worry that the downtown renaissance is fragile, largely built on upscale shopping and entertainment — relatively new trends that could easily change. But others believe downtowns, having once again become the most vital parts of many cities, will provide a model for future development — even in the suburbs.

Attracting Jobs

Tax-supported subsidies aimed at luring companies to relocate or retain offices and factories in specific locations have proliferated. Local and state governments, engaged in fierce competition for jobs, are giving businesses up to $70 billion annually in tax breaks, new roads and training facilities and other incentives. Economic-development officials and companies that have relocated for subsidies say the incentives have spurred employment growth and helped some businesses stay profitable. But critics, who include many economists, argue that the incentives generate relatively few new jobs and instead lead many companies merely to shift operations from one place to another, depending on where they can broker the best deal. Among the most controversial subsidies are those supporting professional-sports stadiums. Supporters say new sports facilities help cities raise their profile and attract growth, while critics charge the subsidies fail to pay for themselves.

Rapid Urbanization

About 3.3 billion people — half of Earth's inhabitants — live in cities, and the number is expected to hit 5 billion within 20 years. Most urban growth today is occurring in developing countries, where about a billion people live in city slums. Delivering services to crowded cities has become increasingly difficult, especially in the world's 19 "megacities" — those with more than 10 million residents. Moreover, most of the largest cities are in coastal areas, where they are vulnerable to flooding caused by climate change. Many governments are striving to improve city life by expanding services, reducing environmental damage and providing more jobs for the poor, but some still use heavy-handed clean-up policies like slum clearance. Researchers say urbanization helps reduce global poverty because new urbanites earn more than they could in their villages. The global recession could reverse that trend, however, as many unemployed city dwellers return to rural areas. But most experts expect rapid urbanization to resume once the economic storm has passed.

Aging Infrastructure

The deadly collapse in August 2007 of Minneapolis' Interstate I-35 West bridge over the Mississippi River tragically underscored the condition of the nation's highways, dams, wastewater treatment systems, electrical transmission networks and other infrastructure. Many facilities and systems are 50-100 years old, and engineers say they have been woefully neglected. Decades ago taxpayers, lawmakers and private companies found it relatively easy to ante up the huge sums needed to build vital infrastructure, but money for repairs and maintenance has been far tougher to come by in recent years. Federal and state lawmakers today often prefer to spend public dollars on high-profile convention centers and sports arenas, and anti-tax groups often fight tax hikes or utility-rate increases to pay for maintenance. But now lawmakers are debating whether aging infrastructure merits higher taxes or other measures, such as turning more highways into privately run toll roads.

High-Speed Trains

The Obama administration has designated $8 billion in stimulus funds for high-speed passenger rail, buoying hopes that supertrains will operate throughout the American landscape as they do in Europe and Asia. The money, most likely to be divided among multiple corridors, won't buy a single fast-rail system. But supporters say it will help traditional trains run faster and pay for planning to make true high-speed rail networks a reality. Washington's support signals a transformation in federal policy that has long favored highway and air travel, experts say. Some argue that money should be focused first on building true high-speed service in the busy Northeast Corridor. But supporters in the Midwest, Florida, California and elsewhere are expected to vie for a portion of the rail funds. So far, California appears furthest ahead in planning for fast rail, aided by a $9.95 billion bond issue. But critics say the plan's benefits are exaggerated.

LAW ENFORCEMENT

Police Misconduct

The U.S. Department of Justice is stepping up its oversight of local police departments, pressuring them to limit the use of force in civilian encounters and eliminate racial profiling during traffic stops and other enforcement. The Justice Department's civil rights division has criticized long-troubled police agencies in such places as New Orleans, Seattle and Maricopa County, Ariz., which includes Phoenix. The department's power stems from a 1994 law allowing the federal government to identify a "pattern or practice" of constitutional violations and threaten court action to force police agencies to adopt changes. Seattle officials have proposed a detailed plan to answer the government's criticisms, but negotiations are stalled in New Orleans and Maricopa County, where Sheriff Joe Arpaio is balking at the government's demand for court supervision of policy changes. Meanwhile, the racially charged shooting death of a Florida teenager by a neighborhood watch volunteer focused attention on police handling of the case.

RACE, CLASS, AND ETHNICITY

Domestic Poverty

Despite sweeping welfare reforms in the 1990s and generally healthy economic growth in recent years, domestic poverty remains intractable. Moreover, signs are emerging that so-called deep poverty is growing sharply — most significantly among children. U.S. poverty is fueled by a long list of problems, including Katrina's devastation, immigration, the growing income gap between rich and poor, the subprime mortgage fallout and education disparities. Conservatives say solutions must emphasize personal responsibility, higher marriage rates and fewer out-of-wedlock births. Liberals focus on the negative effects of government budget cuts for anti-poverty programs, tax cuts benefiting the wealthy and the need for more early-childhood-development programs.

Immigration Conflict

Americans are very concerned about illegal immigration but ambivalent about what to do about it — especially the 11 million aliens currently in the United States illegally. Frustrated with the federal government's failure to secure the borders, several states passed laws allowing state and local police to check the immigration status of suspected unlawful aliens. Civil rights organizations warn the laws will result in ethnic profiling of Latinos. The Obama administration has sued to block several of the laws for infringing on federal prerogatives. Advocates of tougher enforcement say undocumented workers are taking jobs from U.S. citizens, but many business and agricultural groups say migrant workers are needed to fill jobs unattractive to U.S. workers. In 2010, the U.S. Supreme Court upheld an Arizona law providing stiff penalties for employers that knowingly hire illegal aliens. In 2012, the justices heard arguments on the controversial, new Arizona law that inspired other states to crack down on illegal immigration.

Child Poverty

One in five American children lives in a household with income below the poverty line — $22,050 for a family of four. Not only are the daily lives of poor children difficult, but experts worry that many will suffer lifelong effects from early deprivation. Concern about child poverty has grown especially strong amid a push in Congress for sweeping budget cuts, including reductions in spending on food stamps and other anti-poverty programs. As child poverty continues to rise amid the nation's persistent economic woes and high unemployment, a long-simmering debate over the problem's root causes is heating up. Liberals argue that fewer children would fall into poverty if the government safety net were stronger and more jobs were available for struggling parents. Conservatives, on the other hand, say child poverty largely stems from parental behavior — particularly a growing tendency to have children out of wedlock.

Preface

As the daily news constantly reminds us, coming to terms with the full complexity and variety of issues that confront America's urban areas is no small feat. Is a new approach needed to help the poorest Americans? Is demolishing parts of cities the way to save them? Does the United States need supertrains? In order to promote change and hopefully reach viable resolution, scholars, students and policymakers must strive to understand the context and content of each of these urban issues. It is such understanding that eventually enables students to define their roles as active participants in urban policy.

With the view that only an objective examination that synthesizes all competing viewpoints can lead to sound analysis, this sixth edition of *Urban Issues* provides comprehensive and unbiased coverage of today's most pressing policy problems. This book is a compilation of 12 recent reports from *CQ Researcher*, a weekly policy backgrounder that brings into focus key issues on the public agenda. It enables instructors to fairly and comprehensively uncover opposing sides of each issue, and illustrate just how significantly they impact citizens and the government they elect. *CQ Researcher* fully explains difficult concepts in plain English. Each article chronicles and analyzes past legislative and judicial action as well as current and possible future maneuvering. Each report addresses how issues affect all levels of government, whether at the local, state or federal level, and also the lives and futures of all citizens. *Urban Issues* is designed to promote in-depth discussion, facilitate further research and help readers think critically and formulate their own positions on these crucial issues.

This collection is organized into four subject areas that span a range of important urban policy concerns: Education; Land Use and Urban Development; Law Enforcement; and Race, Class and Ethnicity. These pieces were chosen to expose students to a wide range of issues, from the current state of U.S. infrastructure to the efficacy of cities' eminent domain powers. We are gratified to know that *Urban Issues* has found a following in a wide range of departments of political science, sociology, public administration and urban planning, and hope that this new edition continues to meet readers' needs.

CQ RESEARCHER

CQ Researcher was founded in 1923 as *Editorial Research Reports* and was sold primarily to newspapers as a research tool. The magazine was renamed and redesigned in 1991 as *CQ Researcher*. Today, students are its primary audience. While still used by hundreds of journalists and newspapers, many of which reprint portions of the reports, the *Researcher's* main subscribers are now high school, college and public libraries. In 2002, *Researcher* won the American Bar Association's coveted Silver Gavel award for magazine excellence for a series of nine reports on civil liberties and other legal issues.

Researcher staff writers — all highly experienced journalists — sometimes compare the experience of writing a Researcher report to drafting a college term paper. Indeed, there are many similarities. Each report is as long as many term papers — about 11,000 words — and is written by one person without any significant outside help. One of the key differences is that writers interview leading experts, scholars and government officials for each issue.

Like students, staff writers begin the creative process by choosing a topic. Working with the *Researcher's* editors, the writer identifies a controversial subject that has important public policy implications. After a topic is selected, the writer embarks on one to two weeks of intense research. Newspaper and magazine articles are clipped or downloaded, books are ordered and information is gathered from a wide variety of sources, including interest groups, universities and the government. Once the writers are well informed, they develop a detailed outline, and begin the interview process. Each report

requires a minimum of ten to fifteen interviews with academics, officials, lobbyists and people working in the field. Only after all interviews are completed does the writing begin.

CHAPTER FORMAT

Each issue of *CQ Researcher*, and therefore each selection in this book, is structured in the same way. Each begins with an overview, which briefly summarizes the areas that will be explored in greater detail in the rest of the chapter. The next section chronicles important and current debates on the topic under discussion and is structured around a number of key questions, such as "Has No Child Left Behind helped minority students? and "Do tax breaks for business spur employment?" These questions are usually the subject of much debate among practitioners and scholars in the field. Hence, the answers presented are never conclusive but detail the range of opinion on the topic.

Next, the "Background" section provides a history of the issue being examined. This retrospective covers important legislative measures, executive actions and court decisions that illustrate how current policy has evolved. Then the "Current Situation" section examines contemporary policy issues, legislation under consideration and legal action being taken. Each selection concludes with an "Outlook" section, which addresses possible regulation, court rulings, and initiatives from Capitol Hill and the White House over the next five to ten years.

Each report contains features that augment the main text: two to three sidebars that examine issues related to the topic at hand, a pro versus con debate between two experts, a chronology of key dates and events and an annotated bibliography detailing major sources used by the writer.

CUSTOM OPTIONS

Interested in building your ideal CQ Press Issues book, customized to your personal teaching needs and interests? Browse by course or date, or search for specific topics or issues from our online catalog of over 500 *CQ Researcher* issues at http://custom.cqpress.com.

ACKNOWLEDGMENTS

We wish to thank many people for helping to make this collection a reality. Thomas J. Billitteri, managing editor of *CQ Researcher,* gave us his enthusiastic support and cooperation as we developed this sixth edition. He and his talented staff of editors and writers have amassed a first-class library of *Researcher* reports, and we are fortunate to have access to that rich cache. We also thankfully acknowledge the advice and feedback from current readers and are gratified by their satisfaction with the book.

Some readers may be learning about *CQ Researcher* for the first time. We expect that many readers will want regular access to this excellent weekly research tool. For subscription information or a no-obligation free trial of *CQ Researcher,* please contact CQ Press at www.cqpress .com or toll-free at 1-866-4CQ-PRESS (1-866-427-7737).

We hope that you will be pleased by the sixth edition of *Urban Issues.* We welcome your feedback and suggestions for future editions. Please direct comments to Charisse Kiino, Publisher, College Division CQ Press, 2300 N Street, N.W., Suite 800, Washington, DC 20037, or *ckiino@cqpress.com.*

—*The Editors of CQ Press*

Contributors

Thomas J. Billitteri is managing editor of the *CQ Researcher*. He has more than 30 years' experience covering business, nonprofit institutions and public policy for newspapers and other publications. He holds a BA in English and an MA in journalism from Indiana University.

Charles S. Clark is a veteran Washington freelancer who writes for The Washington Post, National Journal and other publications. He previously served as a staff writer at the *CQ Researcher* and writer-researcher at Time-Life Books. He graduated in political science from McGill University.

Staff writer **Marcia Clemmitt** is a veteran social-policy reporter who previously served as editor in chief of *Medicine & Health* and staff writer for *The Scientist*. She has also been a high school math and physics teacher. She holds a liberal arts and sciences degree from St. John's College, Annapolis, and a master's degree in English from Georgetown University. Her recent reports include "Genes and Health" and "Animal Intelligence."

Roland Flamini is a Washington-based correspondent who specializes in foreign affairs. Fluent in six languages, he was *Time* bureau chief in Rome, Bonn, Beirut, Jerusalem and the European Common Market and later served as international editor at United Press International. While covering the 1979 Iranian Revolution for *Time*, Flamini wrote the magazine's cover story — in which Ayatollah Ruhollah Khomeini was named Man of the Year — and was promptly expelled because authorities didn't like what they read. His books include a study of Vatican politics in the 1960s,

Pope, Premier, President. His most recent report for *CQ Global Researcher* was "Rising Tension Over Iran."

Alan Greenblatt covers foreign affairs for National Public Radio. He was previously a staff writer at *Governing* magazine and *CQ Weekly*, where he won the National Press Club's Sandy Hume Award for political journalism. He graduated from San Francisco State University in 1986 and received a master's degree in English literature from the University of Virginia in 1988. For the *CQ Researcher*, his reports include "Confronting Warming," "Future of the GOP" and "Immigration Debate." His most recent *CQ Global Researcher* reports were "Attacking Piracy" and "Rewriting History."

Associate Editor **Kenneth Jost** graduated from Harvard College and Georgetown University Law Center. He is the author of the *Supreme Court Yearbook* and editor of *The Supreme Court from A to Z* (both *CQ Press*). He was a member of the *CQ Researcher* team that won the American Bar Association's 2002 Silver Gavel Award. His previous reports include "States and Federalism" and "Bilingual Education vs. English Immersion." He is also author of the blog *Jost on Justice* (http://jostonjustice.blogspot.com).

Reed Karaim, a freelance writer living in Tucson, Arizona, has written for *The Washington Post, U.S. News & World Report, Smithsonian, American Scholar, USA Weekend* and other publications. He is the author of the novel, *If Men Were Angels*, which was selected for the Barnes & Noble Discover Great New Writers series. He is also the winner of the Robin Goldstein Award for Outstanding Regional Reporting and other journalism honors. Karaim is a graduate of North Dakota State University in Fargo.

Peter Katel is a *CQ Researcher* staff writer who previously reported on Haiti and Latin America for *Time* and *Newsweek* and covered the Southwest for newspapers in New Mexico. He has received several journalism awards, including the Bartolomé Mitre Award for coverage of drug trafficking, from the Inter-American Press Association. He holds an A.B. in university studies from the University of New Mexico. His recent reports include "Prisoner Reentry" and "Downsizing Prisons."

Bill Wanlund is a freelance writer in the Washington, D.C., area. He is a former foreign service officer, with service in Europe, Asia, Africa and South America. Previously, he was a Washington-based editor and reporter. He holds a degree in journalism from The George Washington University.

Jennifer Weeks is a Massachusetts freelance writer who specializes in energy, the environment and science. She has written for *The Washington Post, Audubon, Popular Mechanics* and other magazines and previously was a policy analyst, congressional staffer and lobbyist. She has an A.B. degree from Williams College and master's degrees from the University of North Carolina and Harvard. Her recent *CQ Researcher* reports include "Gulf Coast Restoration" and "Energy Policy."

1

School Reform

Marcia Clemmitt

Thousands of young college graduates teach in urban schools through Teach for America, a nonprofit group that receives support from venture philanthropy groups such as the Bill & Melinda Gates Foundation. Above, Erin Gavin conducts a discussion with her seventh-graders in Brooklyn Center, Minn., on Feb. 4.

AP Photo/Andy King

From *CQ Researcher*,
April 29, 2011.

Karen Caruso, a third-grade teacher in Los Angeles, read the embarrassing news last August in the *Los Angeles Times*: She was in the bottom 10 percent of city elementary teachers, according to the paper's analysis of seven years of students' performance on standardized math and English tests.

Yet, that poor showing didn't fit Caruso's profile. A 26-year classroom veteran, she was among the district's first teachers certified by the prestigious National Board for Professional Teaching Standards, and her principal had named her one of the best teachers at Hancock Park Elementary School, which serves a mainly upper-middle-class neighborhood.

Caruso was taken aback by the *Times*' findings but told the newspaper she was determined to do better. "If my student test scores show I'm an ineffective teacher," she said, "I'd like to know what contributes to it. What do I need to do to bring my average up?"[1]

It's a question teachers nationwide may soon be asking. With international tests showing that the United States no longer leads in K-12 learning, an emerging coalition of reformers is aiming to use market-based ideas to improve the nation's 99,000 public schools.[2] The ideas include paying teachers based on student performance and creating more publicly funded, privately run, charter schools to compete with public institutions.

Conservative analysts have long recommended such measures. But now they are joined by Democratic politicians, including President Barack Obama, and "venture philanthropists," led by Microsoft cofounder Bill Gates, who are bringing the ideas they

U.S. Lags Behind Asia in Math Scores

U.S. eighth-graders rank ahead of those in several European countries but behind students in England, Japan, South Korea and Taiwan.

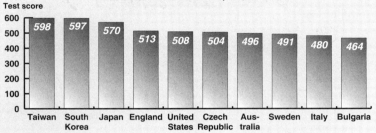

Average Math Scores of 8th-Grade Students by Selected Countries, 2007*

Test score

Taiwan 598, South Korea 597, Japan 570, England 513, United States 508, Czech Republic 504, Australia 496, Sweden 491, Italy 480, Bulgaria 464

* Scores are based on an 800-point scale. Top-scoring countries average about 600.

Source: Patrick Gonzales, et al., "Highlights From Trends in International Mathematics and Science Study 2007: Mathematics and Science Achievement of U.S. Fourth- and Eighth-Grade Students in an International Context," National Center for Education Statistics, September 2009, nces.ed.gov/pubs2009/2009001.pdf.

used to achieve business success to the domain of public education. Gates, Los Angeles insurance magnate Eli Broad and other wealthy donors have poured billions of dollars into market-oriented reform efforts, arguing that failing schools jeopardize the nation's economic competitiveness in the global market.

International data comparing K-12 student achievement across many nations clearly show that U.S. schools are failing, according to Eric Hanushek, a senior fellow at the Hoover Institution, a conservative think tank based at Stanford University in California. "While many people want to be reassured that things are going just fine, ignoring the real message" of these comparisons "actually imperils our economic future," he wrote.[3]

Key to gaining elusive public support for large-scale educational changes is persuading families, who generally support their local schools, that past strategies have been costly failures. Reformers have not been shy about making that case.

"Over the past four decades, the per-student cost of running our K-12 schools has more than doubled, while our student achievement has remained virtually flat," Gates wrote recently. "To build a dynamic 21st-century economy . . . we need to flip the curve."[4]

But teachers and many education scholars argue that reformers seek a simple fix for a complex problem. Low-performing students are concentrated in the lowest-income districts, where inadequate funding, teacher turnover and the ravages of poverty make it difficult for students to excel, critics of market-based reforms say.

"Achievement differences between students are overwhelmingly attributable to factors outside of schools," wrote Matthew Di Carlo, a senior fellow at the Albert Shanker Institute, a research and advocacy group affiliated with the American Federation of Teachers (AFT), the nation's second-largest teachers' union. Research shows that about 60 percent of variation in students' school achievement is "explained by student and family background characteristics," many related to income, Di Carlo wrote. Only 10 or 15 percent of achievement differences can be laid to teachers, he argued.[5]

Reform critics also argue that the emphasis on rising educational costs is misplaced.

For one thing, said Richard Rothstein, a research associate at the liberal Economic Policy Institute, a large chunk of the cost increase Gates mentions has been used to educate children with disabilities. That segment of K-12 school spending has swelled from 4 percent to 21 percent over the past four decades, he said. Previously, schools largely ignored the special needs of children with disabilities, he said.[6]

Henry Levin, a professor of economics and education at Columbia University in New York, says, too, that "no other country has to include [teachers'] health-care costs and pensions" in school-cost calculations. (Health insurance and retiree benefits add at least 20 percent in costs beyond salary for a public-sector worker, such as a teacher, according to the Bureau of Labor Statistics.)[7]

"Our per-pupil expenditures are the highest in the world," Levin acknowledges. But he argues that it isn't fair to criticize schools for this because of the vast difference in employee costs between countries.

None of these arguments, however, are persuasive to reform proponents, who say ample evidence exists to show that parental choice, school competition and data-based decision-making are needed to drive improvement.

New York Federal Reserve Bank economist Rajashri Chakrabarti found "unambiguous improvement in public school performance" in Florida and Wisconsin as a result of offering parents a choice of schools, according to the Center for Education Reform, in Washington, D.C. The center also cites research by the Manhattan Institute, a conservative think tank in New York, concluding that all students in a Florida program that offered wide school choice to students with disabilities "made greater academic improvements" as their school options expanded — and that included students who stuck with their neighborhood schools.[8]

In recent school-reform battles, such as last winter's hot dispute in Wisconsin over newly elected Republican Gov. Scott Walker's plan to drastically limit teachers' collective-bargaining rights, unions have been heavily criticized for running up costs while allowing poor teaching to flourish.[9]

"The unions have been pushing the case that there is a war against teachers, but I don't think that's true," says the Hoover Institution's Hanushek. "There is a war against teachers' unions" that unions have brought on themselves by opposing reform proposals such as basing firing decisions on student achievement, he says.

Linking teacher evaluations and student performance on standardized tests is indeed among the most contentious topics in public education.

Earlier this month, the Los Angeles Unified School District announced that it will privately inform individual teachers of their ratings on a so-called "value-added" success scale that it uses to link teacher performance and

Reading Proficiency Highest in Northeast

Connecticut ranks first in eighth-grade reading ability followed closely by other Northeastern states, including Massachusetts and New Jersey. The District of Columbia ranks below all 50 states.

State Rankings by 8th-Grade Reading Level, 2009		
1. Connecticut	18. Wyoming	35. Tennessee
2. Massachusetts	19. Idaho	36. Alaska
3. New Jersey	20. Illinois	37. Arizona
4. Vermont	21. Kansas	38. Arkansas
5. Pennsylvania	22. Kentucky	39. Georgia
6. New Hampshire	23. New York	40. Texas
7. Minnesota	24. Oregon	41. Oklahoma
8. Montana	25. Utah	42. Alabama
9. Ohio	26. Colorado	43. South Carolina
10. South Dakota	27. Florida	44. California
11. Maryland	28. Indiana	45. Hawaii
12. Washington	29. Iowa	46. Nevada
13. Maine	30. Virginia	47. New Mexico
14. Nebraska	31. Delaware	48. West Virginia
15. Missouri	32. Michigan	49. Louisiana
16. North Dakota	33. North Carolina	50. Mississippi
17. Wisconsin	34. Rhode Island	51. District of Columbia

Source: "8th Grade Reading 2009 National Assessment of Education Progress," Federal Education Budget Project, New America Foundation, febp.newamerica.net/k12/rankings/naep8read09.

test scores. The approach is a favorite of many reform advocates, and it was the L.A. district's data that the *Los Angeles Times* plumbed to create its rankings of Caruso and other teachers in the city.

The district is negotiating with the local teachers' union, the United Teachers Los Angeles, which is affiliated with both the AFT and the nation's largest teachers' union, the National Education Association, to include the measurements in formal performance reviews, a move the union strongly opposes.[10]

Times reporters argue that opposition is unwarranted because a "value-added" analysis compares teachers by evaluating the progress of each individual student in their classrooms against that student's own progress in earlier school years. By comparing a student's achievement only to his or her own record, the "value-added" approach takes into account such factors as poverty and learning disabilities, over which an individual teacher has

Putting Teachers to the Effectiveness Test

"Whether someone is capable or not is way more complex than it may seem."

Earlier this year, the Bill & Melinda Gates Foundation — one of the nation's biggest funders of school-reform projects — announced it would use the Memphis and Pittsburgh school districts, among others, as laboratories for developing "teacher effectiveness" programs using data on student achievement and teachers' classroom behaviors.

The idea is to figure out the connection between student achievement and actions of individual teachers and use the linkage to make "high-stakes" educational decisions — decisions, for example, on which teachers to fire, which to reward with merit pay or other recognition and which teaching practices to replicate.[1]

Microsoft cofounder Bill Gates told *The Wall Street Journal* that he will deem the project a success if "10 years from now . . . we have a very different personnel system that's encouraging effectiveness [in teaching] and our spending has contributed to that."

He went on to say that education-improvement efforts have suffered because data on teacher and school performance haven't been available. Contrast that situation, he said, to "professions like long-jump or tackling people on a football field or hitting a baseball," where "the average ability is so much higher today because there's this great feedback system, measurement system."[2]

Many education analysts agree that traditional teacher-evaluation practices haven't been of much use. "A principal sitting in the back of the room checking off things on a list" of recommended teacher behaviors "made almost no sense," partly because "it's bound to involve many very subjective judgments," says Aaron Pallas, a professor of sociology and education at Columbia University in New York. "Almost everybody does well" on such evaluations, proving that the approach isn't very accurate or useful, he says.

Nevertheless, Pallas maintains, while old-style evaluations "provide almost no guidance about what to do" to improve one's teaching, new data-oriented evaluation systems don't either — at least so far.

Yet, rejecting the data approach means "sticking our heads in the sand," says Valerie E. Lee, an education professor at the University of Michigan in Ann Arbor. "These things can be good so long as they're done right," she says.

no control. Thus, it is a fair way to judge teachers' success, the *Times* argued.[11]

Opponents maintain, however, that inciting teachers to compete with one another for pay is the wrong way to go about improving education.

Diane Ravitch, a research professor of education at New York University who recently disavowed her long-time support for market-based reforms, noted that legendary business-improvement consultant W. Edwards Deming believed that merit pay for workers was even "bad for corporations."

"It gets everyone thinking about what is good for himself," Ravitch wrote, "and leads to forgetting about the goals of the organization."[12]

Columbia's Levin argues that teaching requires collaboration more than competition. For example, he says, teachers who want their students to improve "need to talk to the teachers at lower grades about whether they're teaching" skills on which higher grades' lessons are based

and seek their cooperation to do so, he says. "It's hard to say that the future really is in competition."

As policymakers, schools and families debate how to improve schools, here are some questions they are asking:

Are the public schools failing?

Behind the push to reform K-12 education lies the proposition that wide-scale failure of American schools bears significant responsibility for a lagging economy. But critics of that view argue that reform enthusiasts ignore data showing progress alongside problems. What's more, they argue, it makes no sense to hold schools responsible for the nation's economic woes.

"American education is in a state of crisis," according to the Heritage Foundation, a conservative think tank in Washington. "Millions of children pass through America's schools without receiving a quality education that prepares them . . . to compete in the increasingly competitive global economy."[13]

That means including other measures besides standardized-test scores and being careful not to jump at untested teacher-evaluation approaches, she says. If developed and used judiciously, Lee says, a good system could control for individual differences in students, such as attendance and home life, over which a teacher has no influence. And that, she says, would make for fairer teacher-to-teacher comparisons than those that simply look at student test scores.

Donald B. Gratz, an education professor at Curry College in Milton, Mass., cited a bit of history in arguing that programs linking teacher merit pay and student test scores are ill-conceived. "In the mid-1800s, British schools and teachers were paid on the basis of the results of student examinations, for reasons much like" those cited by today's reformers, Gratz wrote. After about 30 years, however, "the testing bureaucracy had burgeoned, cheating and cramming flourished" and, with public opposition swelling "dramatically," the practice "was abandoned as a failure."[3]

Basing pay on test scores poses another problem, too, Gratz says: Fewer than half of teachers teach subjects whose material is contained in standardized tests.

Furthermore, Gratz notes, at grades six and up, students typically have six or seven teachers during a given year. "Who gets the credit or the blame" for a student's success or failure?" he asks. "It looks like a field day for labor lawyers."

Offering merit pay for good teaching hasn't been shown to improve instruction either, Gratz argues. Instituting merit-pay programs "assumes that teachers know what to do and just aren't doing it," but that's likely not the case, he says. "We do know a lot about how to teach," but teaching is an extremely complex task, and it's not as easy as it may seem for teachers to change their behavior to incorporate research findings about student learning, for example, he says.

Complicating matters is the fact that educators' and education administrators' ability to succeed relates to the situation in which they're working, says Jeffrey Henig, a professor of education at Columbia. "We have superintendents and principals, for example, who succeed in one school, then go somewhere else and fail," he notes. "So the question of whether someone is capable or not is way more complex than it may seem on the surface."

— *Marcia Clemmitt*

[1] Stephanie Banchero, "Bill Gates Seeks Formula for Better Teachers," *The Wall Street Journal online*, March 22, 2011, http://online.wsj.com/article/SB10001424052748703858404576214593545938506.html.

[2] Quoted in *ibid.*

[3] Donald B. Gratz, "The Problem with Performance Pay," *Educational Leadership*, November 2009, pp. 76-79.

Reform critics cite international PISA (Programme for International Student Assessment) tests, which compare student performance in dozens of countries, in arguing that U.S. teachers are, by and large, doing a good job. But the Hoover Institution's Hanushek dismisses that claim as "largely wrong."

It's true, Hanushek wrote, that recent PISA tests find U.S. 15-year-olds "above the developed-country average in reading, at the average in science, and below average in math," results that make it seem that "perhaps we are not doing so badly." But that's a faulty conclusion, he argued, because "reading is very difficult to assess accurately in the international tests. And reading scores have proven less important than math and science for both individual and national success."[14]

Furthermore, "international performance on these tests is very closely related to . . . economic growth," so that small score differences among countries may add up to big differences in economic well-being over time, Hanushek wrote.[15]

In an article co-authored with two other scholars, one of them German, Hanushek argued that economic productivity depends on "developing a highly qualified cadre of scientists, engineers, entrepreneurs and other professionals." International tests show, for example, that the United States produces fewer top scorers in math than countries it competes with, the scholars said.[16]

Furthermore, school failure is not confined to low-income neighborhoods, Hanushek says in an interview. "Some suburban schools seem to be great," he says, "but it's because of things parents are providing" for their children, which may mask the fact that the schools themselves do a poor job.

But many education scholars say that while some individual schools are in trouble, claims of widespread failure in American education are false.

The Economic Policy Institute's Rothstein wrote that the National Assessment of Educational Progress (NAEP), which tracks math and reading skills by following groups of students from fourth through 12th grades, shows that "American students have improved substantially, in some cases phenomenally," over the past two decades.[17]

Both black and white fourth- and eighth-graders have improved in math, the Economic Policy Institute's Rothstein wrote. What's more, he said, African-American students have, at the fourth-, eighth- and 12th-grade levels, improved their math and reading skills the most, achieving "a rate of progress that would be considered extraordinary in any area of social policy."[18]

The Organisation for Economic Cooperation and Development (OECD), an international intergovernmental group that manages the PISA tests, also cites U.S. educational improvement. Since 2006, "the United States has seen significant performance gains" on international science assessments, mainly because America's lowest-scoring students have been closing the gap that separates them from the top scorers, the OECD said.[19]

"Overall, the American public school system is pretty decent," says Katrina Bulkley, an associate professor of education at New Jersey's Montclair State University. "It's just that in pockets, it's served badly."

Those pockets are mainly in urban and rural districts with the greatest poverty.[20]

In low-poverty schools — where fewer than 10 percent of students qualify for free or reduced-price lunches — 15-year-old American students score above the international average in reading on the PISA assessment, according to Stephen Krashen, a professor emeritus of education at the University of Southern California. By contrast, in schools where low-income students make up more than 75 percent of enrollment, 15-year-old students scored second to last among the 34 OECD nations.[21]

The U.S. education system doesn't provide enough classroom resources to overcome the disadvantages wrought by poverty, analysts from the OECD argue. "The United States is one of only three OECD countries" in which class sizes in high-poverty schools are routinely much larger than in schools in higher-income districts, said a recent report. As a result, disadvantaged American students are at risk of receiving fewer educational resources, including teacher time, than richer students, the analysts said.[22]

Poverty imposes often-overlooked handicaps. "I can guarantee you right now that at least 20 percent of our kids need glasses," said Ramón González, principal of a public middle school in New York City's South Bronx who struggles to get private funding for vision tests and glasses. "They're in their classrooms right now, staring at blackboards with no idea what they're looking at," said González. "You can have the best teachers, the best curriculum and the greatest after-school programs in the world, but if your kids can't see, what does it matter?"[23]

Educational reformers such as former New York City school Chancellor Joel Klein "have said that to fix poverty you have to fix education," says Aaron Pallas, a professor of sociology and education at Columbia University. "Schools can partner with others to help do this," Pallas says. "But the idea that schools are going to transform poverty on their own is just giving schools too much credit."

Many school reformers argue that Americans are losing jobs to oversees competition because the United States isn't adequately educating its students, says Donald B. Gratz, an education professor at Curry College in Milton, Mass. But the real reason is that "American workers are expensive," he says. American workers' productivity has soared in the past 20 years, demonstrating that graduating good employees is not the problem, he says.

At the same time, universities — not the public schools — are the real culprits in failing to prepare students to compete in the emerging globalized economy, some critics contend.

"The quality of teaching in higher education is worse than at the lower levels, terrible," but "that's going unnoticed," says Richard Ingersoll, a professor of education and sociology at the University of Pennsylvania. "Professors lead the ranks of those who want to impose [standardized-test-based] evaluations on K-12 teachers, but nobody's asking for similar tests to be used on them. The double standard is striking."

But the higher-education scene is changing. In a study of 2,300 students at 24 U.S. universities, Richard Arum, a New York University professor of sociology and education, found that more than a third showed no improvement in critical thinking and writing skills after four years of college.[24] Their professors may soon find themselves on the test-score hot seat, Arum said.

concentrated effects of poverty

Beginning in 2016, the OECD will use the same test he used to compare college achievement internationally.

Said Arum, "The U.S. higher-education system has been living off its . . . reputation," but professors "will increasingly be held accountable."[25]

Are teachers' unions a major barrier to improving schools?

Many reform advocates say teachers' unions are blocking change by being obsessed with job protection. They point to sensational cases, such as the infamous "rubber rooms" in which hundreds of New York City teachers deemed unfit for the classroom by school administrators sat for months, or even years, drawing their salaries, while their cases awaited due-process hearings.[26]

But teacher advocates argue that, despite their flaws, such due-process protections are needed to shield teachers from politically motivated firings or firings based on prejudice.

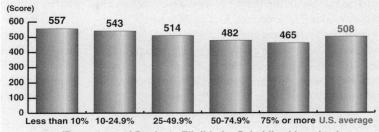

Lower Math Scores Tied to Poverty

Students who qualify for free or reduced-price lunches tend to score lower in mathematics than those whose family income is high enough to make them ineligible for subsidized lunches. The correlation suggests poverty contributes to lower achievement.

Average Mathematics Scores of 8th-Grade Students Eligible for Free or Reduced-price Lunches, 2007*

(Score)

Less than 10%	10-24.9%	25-49.9%	50-74.9%	75% or more	U.S. average
557	543	514	482	465	508

(Percentage of Students Eligible for Subsidized Lunches)

* Scores are based on an 800-point scale. Top-scoring countries average about 600.

Source: Patrick Gonzales, et al., "Highlights From Trends in International Mathematics and Science Study 2007: Mathematics and Science Achievement of U.S. Fourth- and Eighth-Grade Students in an International Context," National Center for Education Statistics, September 2009, nces.ed.gov/pubs2009/2009001.pdf.

They also say that reform proposals are drastic enough to warrant caution. What's more, they point out that unions are not uniformly opposed to reforms.

Because of union contracts, "it takes two years, $200,000 and 15 percent of the principal's total time to get one bad teacher out of the classroom," said Terry M. Moe, a senior fellow at the Hoover Institution. "If we figure that maybe 5 percent of the teachers . . . are bad teachers nationwide, that means that 2.5 million kids are stuck . . . with teachers who aren't teaching them anything," said Moe. "The unions are largely responsible."[27]

School systems in cities such as Chicago that have tried to pioneer substantial reforms have not been able to produce evidence confirming their value because unions and others "have nipped them in the bud," said Hanushek.[28]

In districts with strong unions, policy change takes longer, according to Katharine O. Strunk, an assistant professor of education and policy at the University of Southern California, and Jason A. Grissom, an assistant professor of public affairs at the University of Missouri. "Stronger unions are better able . . . to negotiate contracts that constrain districts' flexibility in policy setting," they wrote.[29]

Yet, unions aren't the only ones who make it hard to implement change in schools, some analysts argue. They point to resistance by school boards to expanding charter schools, which compete with regular public schools but are exempt from many regulations public schools must follow. "Local school boards have been as great a roadblock, and in some cases even fiercer opponents" of reforms, than unions, wrote PBS education reporter John Merrow. "They go to court to keep charter schools from opening or expanding. Why? It's about money and control."[30]

Blasting unions as driven solely by self-interest ignores facts, union supporters say.

For one thing, "there is no research . . . that correlates student achievement to collective bargaining rights," despite many reformers' claims that ending bargaining rights will improve schools, said Kate McLaughlin, executive vice president of the United Teachers of Lowell, the AFT local in Lowell, Mass. Massachusetts students, for example, "perform higher than anybody else in this country academically. Yet we have the strongest collective bargaining rights," she said.[31] Massachusetts teachers bargained for and won the right of every teacher to have "a qualified and trained mentor" during the first three years on the job to help them improve, a clear instance of unions working for students, McLaughlin said.[32]

Even many teachers agree that the most commonly used method of teacher evaluation — classroom evaluation by a school administration — usually doesn't work well, and some unions are trying to lead development of new methods, says Gratz of Curry College.

The Massachusetts Teachers Association (MTA) proposes basing evaluations on multiple measures that can be "validated against one another." Under the plan, the MTA says, "no high-stakes decisions" such as firing or raising pay would be based solely on test scores or any other single factor, such as expert evaluation of teachers' classroom and planning practices. Instead, if apparently good practices aren't matched by good scores or vice versa, evaluators would be "required to find out why" before acting.[33]

Union-management partnerships have "fostered reform" in places such as Toledo, Ohio, and Norfolk, Va., according to researchers led by David Lewin, a management professor at the University of California, Los Angeles. In those cities, administrators and unions emphasize professional development, teacher evaluation and mentoring to improve teacher quality. As an apparent result, school districts experience "very low levels of voluntary teacher turnover," the group wrote. Unions and administrators collaboratively make "difficult decisions to not retain ineffective teachers," they reported.[34]

Countries whose students regularly surpass U.S. students on international tests "without exception have strong unions," observed Dennis Van Roekel, president of the National Education Association (NEA). Teachers must implement administrators' policies, so a collaborative environment matters, he said.[35]

Green Dot, a nonprofit organization founded in 1999, operates 17 charter high schools and one middle school in high-poverty areas of Los Angeles and one high school in New York City, all unionized. "I've seen what happens to working people when they don't have . . . somebody fighting for them," said founder Steve Barr, a Democratic political activist and fundraiser who in 1990 cofounded the nonprofit, nonpartisan Rock the Vote group that aims to increase young people's political participation. When disagreements surface, Barr recommends that administrators and unions ask, "Is there 75 percent of this issue we all agree on?"[36]

The University of Pennsylvania's Ingersoll says that while the current reform movement "has a punitive cast toward teachers" that unions understandably resent, he doesn't absolve unions altogether. "Many unions aren't helping much," he says. "It would be good for them to get out in front on defining what a good, medium and bad teacher" is, but unions have done little of that. "Sometimes I think the unions are their own worst enemies."

Whatever the case, school management plays a huge role — negative or positive — in improving schools, says David Menefee-Libey, a professor of politics at Pomona College, in Claremont, Calif. There is "very strong research support" for five specific factors that underlie school improvement, "and, surprise! Those five factors frequently aren't present in schools where low-income students are," he says.

The five factors — which were validated in research by Anthony S. Bryk, president of the Carnegie Foundation for the Advancement of Teaching — are, according to Menefee-Libey:

- Support systems to guide teachers in what and how to teach;
- Good working conditions;
- Strong ties between the school and community;
- Safe, orderly environments, and
- Principals who prioritize learning.[37]

Is business-style competition a good model for improving schools?

Evidence shows that market-style competition and performance-measurement statistics can improve education, reform advocates say. But skeptics argue that reshaping education to operate like a business is, at best, an unproven strategy that may in fact be contrary to the goals of schooling.

Using data to figure out who is best at vital tasks — such as educating teachers — is crucial, says Gregory McGinity, managing director for education policy at the Los Angeles-based Broad Foundation, one of a small group of philanthropies making grants aimed at spurring education reforms and measuring their results.

Rather than propping up all teacher-training programs, he says, "governors and school superintendents must be more aggressive in using data to determine which schools of education are doing a good job" and then "put the dollars into the schools that provide the best teachers."

Critics focus too much on proposals for firing unsuccessful teachers while ignoring plans to use merit pay and public recognition to reward teachers whose students improve, McGinity says.

Some researchers have found data that links improved education to market-oriented changes, such as providing families with a wider choice of schools.

For example, a school-choice program in Chicago produced modest improvement in on-time high-school graduation rates for students who exercised the option to switch from their assigned neighborhood schools, reported Douglas Lee Lauen, an assistant professor of public policy at the University of North Carolina, Chapel Hill. Students who were high achievers and those from neighborhoods with low poverty rates benefited most, Lauen found.[38]

In a school system overhauled along market lines, schools would be closed and replaced rather than tinkered with in hopes of improvement, wrote Andy Smarick, a visiting fellow at the conservative Thomas B. Fordham

How U.S. Teacher Salaries Compare

Compared with salaries of other college-educated workers, U.S. teacher salaries are further behind than teacher salaries in many other countries.

Ranking of Selected Countries in Teacher Pay Compared with Other College-educated Workers

Spain
Germany
Australia
Finland
Sweden
France
England
South Korea
United States
Italy

Source: "Building a High-Quality Teaching Profession: Lessons From Around the World," Organisation for Economic Co-operation and Development, 2011, www2.ed.gov/about/inits/

Institute, an education-policy think tank. In other words, schools would be treated like businesses — those that fail or consistently produce losses are shuttered, and competition fills the gap.

"Once persistently low performing, the majority of schools will remain low performing despite being acted upon in innumerable ways," Smarick said. In what he calls an "alarming" record, only 14 percent of California schools restructured under the 2002 No Child Left Behind Act (NCLB), a major education-reform measure signed into law by President George W. Bush, achieved "adequate yearly progress" in the first year after the changes. The proportions for schools in Maryland (12 percent) and Ohio (9 percent) were even worse, Smarick wrote.[39]

(Under NCLB, "restructuring" means firing and replacing a school's principal and most of its teachers and/or reopening the school as a charter school or under the management of a private school-management company or the state government.)[40]

Frederick M. Hess, director of education policy at the conservative American Enterprise Institute, argues that the public-school system is too stodgy, rule-burdened and old-fashioned to improve. Furthermore, efforts to "scale up" and apply small improvements to many schools routinely fail, he says.

Thus, he argues, "instead of taking this 19th-century box called school and making it better, we ought to" scrap the traditional school system altogether and "think about how to help people get what they need." The way to do that, Hess says, is by harnessing entrepreneurs' energy to provide students and teachers with education products and services geared to their individual needs, such as instructional computer programs based on new brain research, and creating "virtual schools" that students can attend online.

But New York University's Ravitch said she saw "no reason to believe that closing a school and opening a new one would necessarily produce superior results." In fact, she wrote, half of New York City's 10 worst-performing schools on 2009 state math tests "were new schools that had been opened to replace failing schools."[41]

Firing teachers is also a dicey strategy, says Columbia's Pallas. "We know that new teachers, no matter where they come from, often are foundering" for at least a few years, he says. A more realistic approach would be to focus on improving "how we prepare teachers, both in school and once they get on the job," he contends.

Do reformers "think there's a huge army of new teachers to jump in to replace" those who are pushed out? asks Menefee-Libey, of Pomona College. "We haven't seen them."

Kenneth J. Saltman an associate professor of education at DePaul University in Chicago, worries that in the race to require schools to produce measurable outcomes, "the value of intellectual curiosity," among other things, will be lost. "What happens to the country when the curriculum gets narrowed" to exclude skills like deep reading and detailed debate of issues "because these skills aren't easily testable?" he asks.

"All of these reforms have been advanced as accomplishing really big stuff — bringing low-income kids fully into the mainstream," where they'll achieve on a par with higher-income students, says Columbia's Levin. But even studies that show positive effects of market-oriented strategies "show quite small effects," he says.

In Washington, D.C., schools recorded gains in test scores under the direction of Chancellor Michelle Rhee, a hard-nosed reformer best known for firing hundreds of low-performing teachers before resigning — possibly under pressure from a newly elected mayor — a mere three years into her tenure. But as Levin says, reading scores that apparently soared in the second year of Rhee's tenure "disappeared in the third year."

He adds, "If you're only looking for tiny gains, then you've evaded the original argument" for market-based reform.

BACKGROUND
Engine of Opportunity

Today's school-reform debates are the latest in a long line of disputes over public education dating back to the 19th century.

For two centuries, many have hoped that the public schools could help the United States break the historical mold of nations stratified by class. America's excellent universal education promises that "the rail-splitter . . . at 20 years of age may become the chief magistrate of 50 millions of free people before he is 50," declared William A. Mowry (1829-1917), a school administrator in Rhode Island and Massachusetts.[42]

Expectations for what schools should accomplish have continuously risen.

In 1870, only 2 percent of Americans graduated from high school, and 30 years later the rate was only 6.4 percent.[43] By 1940, however, fully half of American students graduated from high school, and in 1969 the graduation rate peaked at 77 percent.[44]

Despite the seemingly much greater progress made by American schools than in the past, however, the 20th century also saw virtually constant calls for improvement and reform, according New York University's Ravitch. Notwithstanding the remarkable gains in American students' educational attainment, "it is impossible to find a period in the 20th century in which education reformers, parents and the citizenry were satisfied with the schools," although few agreed about what should be done to improve them, she wrote.[45]

Beginning in the 1970s, oil shocks, recessions and a globalizing economy shook Americans' confidence in what had seemed an endlessly bright economic future. The schools came under new criticism as the United States found its world-beating school-completion rates surpassed by other nations. By the late 1980s, high-school graduation rates declined to just under 70 percent and leveled off. In 2007, the rate stood at 68.8 percent.[46]

Current reform projects aimed at retooling schools as an engine of economic prosperity trace their history at least as far back as 1957, when the Soviet Union launched *Sputnik*, the first spacecraft to orbit the earth, says Curry College's Gratz. *Sputnik*, he says, sparked worries that the United States might be losing its global technological superiority, and schools came under sharp criticism for not doing enough to prepare students in math and

CHRONOLOGY

1990s *Interest in school-reform grows, with limited results. Republicans push for expanded school choice; Democrats support developing compatible curriculum and nationwide learning standards.*

1990 Wisconsin legislature establishes nation's first school-voucher pilot program, to help 1,100 low-income Milwaukee students attend nonreligious private schools. . . . Princeton graduate Wendy Kopp turns her 1989 senior-thesis idea on eliminating education inequities into Teach for America, which recruits elite-college graduates to teach for two years in low-income districts.

1991 Minnesota enacts first charter-school law.

1992 First charter school opens in St. Paul, Minn. . . . California enacts second charter law.

1993 Tennessee adopts "value-added assessment system" to measure how much individual teachers increase or decrease students' test scores.

1994 President Bill Clinton signs Goals 2000: Educate America Act, creating the National Education Standards and Improvement Council with authority to approve states' academic standards; short-lived effort effectively ends when Republicans win control of the House in November. . . . Microsoft cofounder Bill Gates and his wife establish Bill & Melinda Gates Foundation, soon to become a major funder of school-reform projects.

1995 Teach for America alumni Michael Feinberg and David Levin launch Knowledge Is Power Program (KIPP) charter schools. . . . Ohio state legislators pilot a voucher program for low-income Cleveland students to use at either religious or nonreligious schools. . . . Illinois legislature hands control of Chicago public schools to Democratic Mayor Richard Daley.

1999 Florida establishes first statewide school voucher program.

2000s *No Child Left Behind law focuses attention on "failing" schools. Reformers seek to weed out teachers who don't raise students' achievement scores and reward those who do.*

2002 U.S. Supreme Court rules in favor of Ohio's voucher program. . . . Broad Foundation's first annual Broad Prize of $1 million, for an urban district that reduces achievement gaps for low-income students, goes to Houston.

2003 Gates Foundation awards millions to Boston and other cities to break large high schools into smaller units, based on the theory that a more personal environment aids learning.

2007 Newly elected Democratic Mayor Adrian Fenty of Washington is the latest official to wrest control of schools from the local school board; he appoints high-profile reformer Michelle Rhee as school chancellor. . . . New York City school Chancellor Joel Klein says he will fire principals of schools with lagging test scores. . . . Teach for America, which placed 500 teachers its first year, receives 18,000 applications for 2,900 positions.

2009 Citing disappointing results, Gates Foundation ends small-school program after awarding $2 billion in grants. . . . President Barack Obama announces Race to the Top grants for states to develop student-achievement databases, expand charter schools and improve teacher retention and recruitment.

2010 Using previously confidential school data, *Los Angeles Times* names L.A. elementary-school teachers who score high and low on "value-added" teacher assessments. . . . Fenty loses re-election after many residents protest Chancellor Rhee's teacher and principal firings; Rhee resigns. . . . Gates Foundation will fund development of databases to assess teachers' achievement.

2011 Newly elected Republican governors and legislators in states including Wisconsin, Ohio, Indiana, Idaho, New Jersey and Florida propose bills to lower costs and improve education by ending tenure, limiting teachers' union collective bargaining rights, instituting merit pay and firing teachers based on student-achievement assessments. . . . *USA Today* reports possible evidence of cheating on standardized tests at D.C. schools that former Chancellor Rhee praised as successful examples of school reform.

Charter Schools Draw Mixed Reviews

Education experts say only a few have merit.

The nation's 5,000 charter schools — taxpayer-funded institutions freed of some rules that public schools must follow — figure big in school reformers' plans to improve American education. But education experts say that while some individual charter schools have merit, the charter movement as a whole is not a panacea for what ails the nation's public-school system.

That assessment has not discouraged education-reform advocates from embracing charter schools. So-called venture philanthropies such as the Bill & Melinda Gates Foundation generously fund charter school-management organizations, such as San Francisco-based Knowledge Is Power Program (KIPP). Moreover, the Obama administration's school-reform funding program, Race to the Top, encourages states to make their school laws friendlier to charter development.

But information on how well charter schools perform is only gradually emerging. So far, the results are mixed, with some charter schools producing impressive learning results compared with demographically similar public schools, some lagging at the bottom on many measures and most ensconced somewhere in the middle of the pack on student achievement.

Valerie E. Lee, a professor of education at the University of Michigan in Ann Arbor, says that only "a few charter schools are really good" at improving student achievement, while "a few are absolutely awful, and the rest are no different" from traditional public schools. "Is this research solid enough to use as a basis for a large expansion of many of these schools?" she asks. "I'd probably say, 'No.'"

Charter schools are not covered by laws in some states that require a unionized teaching staff. What's more, they do not have to follow state and school-district requirements on curriculum and mode of instruction. While most charter schools operate similarly to traditional public schools, others use longer school days or avant-garde teaching methods, such as curricula built around music education or experiential learning.

While reformers' interest in charter schools has grown sharply in recent years, the charter-school movement isn't new. Minnesota's charter-school law, the first in the nation, is 20 years old this year. And with charter-school laws in effect in 40 states and the District of Columbia, the number of students enrolled in such schools tripled to 1.3 million between 2000 and 2008. [1]

Some of the newest research shows that while few charter schools seem to substantially improve students' test scores, "they do produce much higher graduation rates" — in other words, they instill students with motivation, says John Witte, a professor of public affairs and political science at the University of Wisconsin, Madison. "This parallels the old research on Catholic schools," showing that their students also were more likely than comparable public-school students to persist through graduation, Witte says.

In a 2010 analysis of 22 of the 99 schools managed by the San Francisco-based KIPP charter school-management organization, most of the schools had "positive, statistically significant and educationally substantial" effects on students' scores on state mathematics and reading tests. Furthermore, while KIPP schools serve smaller numbers of students for whom English is a second language and fewer special-education students, they also enroll "a

science. But he says efforts to blame the schools for the nation's large economic and technological challenges have an air of "unreality" because schools can't possibly be held responsible for globalization, growing income inequality and other such factors that shape the economy.

Even as Americans have had high hopes for schools, they've been skeptical about teachers.

Over the 20th century, national magazines regularly "fretted about teacher hygiene, perversion, patriotism and competence," wrote Hess of the American Enterprise Institute.[47]

The first U.S. teachers' union, the Chicago Teachers Foundation, was established in 1897.[48] At the time, many teachers faced unfair treatment, wrote Ravitch. The New York City Board of Education fired female teachers if they married and, after teachers successfully fought for the right to wed, it fired those who became pregnant. As late as the mid-20th century, in Texas, a "right to disproportionate share of low-income students" compared to other local schools, analysts wrote. [2]

A 2009 Stanford University study, meanwhile, found that charter-school students outperformed their public-school counterparts in Arkansas, Louisiana, Missouri, Denver and Chicago. But charter students significantly lagged in achievement in Arizona, Florida, Minnesota, New Mexico, Ohio and Texas and performed on a par with public-school students in California, Georgia, North Carolina and the District of Columbia. Nationwide, 17 percent of charter schools improved students' math achievement significantly, compared with public schools, but 37 percent lagged behind public schools on math achievement, according to the analysis. [3]

Furthermore, while reformers push to close low-achieving public schools, researchers have also found that, like public schools, low-achieving charter schools are extremely difficult to shut down. "Are bad schools immortal?" lamented researchers at the conservative Fordham Institute in a 2010 analysis. In follow-up research on both public and charter schools found to be low achievers in 2003-2004, a foundation analyst found that 72 percent of the low-achieving charters were still operating — and still "bad" — five years later. (Eighty percent of low-achieving public schools in the study also remained in operation.) [4]

The bottom line, say many scholars: Don't count on charter schools to drastically improve education.

Originally, many hoped that the freedom granted to charter schools would allow them to develop new modes of instruction that other schools could adopt. But so far, "there's not much evidence of charters serving as incubators for innovation," says Aaron Pallas, a professor of sociology and education at Columbia University in New York. "I can't say there's one reform that's come out that can be widely adopted," he says. Some charter-management organizations such as KIPP have significantly raised student achievement after lengthening

the school day and school year, he says. "But when it comes to the curriculum and ways of teaching, they're not looking much, if any, different from the public schools."

The number of charter schools "is always going to be limited because they require entrepreneurial people at the center," says Wisconsin's Witte.

That means that the existence of even the best charter schools in low-income districts does not let the community off the hook for making its public schools as good as they can be, says Lee. She says many families lack the time or knowledge to compete for the limited number of slots typically available in local charter schools. Parents usually must participate in a lottery for available seats.

Concern also exists among civil rights groups about the very large numbers of minority children enrolled in charter schools, which often don't have the same ties to the community or public accountability as do public schools, says Janelle Scott, an assistant professor of education at the University of California, Berkeley. Civil rights organizations and charter-management organizations "haven't been terribly involved with each other," she says. "So there's some concern about who's shaping education for people of color."

— *Marcia Clemmitt*

[1] "Fast Facts," National Center for Education Statistics, U.S. Department of Education, http://nces.ed.gov/fastfacts/display.asp?id=30.

[2] Christina Clark Tuttle, *et al.*, "Student Characteristics an Achievement in 22 KIPP Middle Schools," Mathematica Policy Research, Inc., June 2010, www.mathematica-mpr.com/publications/pdfs/education/kipp_fnlrpt.pdf.

[3] "Multiple Choice: Charter School Performance in 16 States," CREDO, Stanford University, 2009, http://credo.stanford.edu/reports/MULTIPLE_CHOICE_CREDO.pdf.

[4] David A. Stuit, "Are Bad Schools Immortal?" Fordham Institute, December 2010, www.edexcellence.net/publications-issues/publications/are-bad-schools-immortal.html.

work" state where teachers' unions have had little success in organizing and thus enjoy little clout, "an ultraconservative group called the Minute Women . . . would drop in unannounced to observe classes . . . to find out whether teachers expressed any unacceptable political opinions," such as support for desegregation, Ravitch wrote.[49]

Organized teachers won passage of the first tenure law in 1909, in New Jersey, to protect against firings based

on race, gender or unpopular political opinions or to make way for cronies of school management.[50]

Public and Private

As early as the mid-19th century, charities used private money to try to reshape the nation's public schools.

After the Civil War, abolitionist charity groups who feared that Southern states would not provide education to freed slaves took on the job themselves, notes Janelle Scott, an

Teaching Is a Prestige Profession in Some Countries

"There are few occupations with higher status" in Finland.

Today's U.S. school reformers, alarmed at what they see as widespread failure in the classroom, tend to focus on removing bad teachers, reducing the collective bargaining power of teacher unions and reducing the authority of teachers to stray from standardized curricula.

But in some other countries where students outpace American pupils on international tests, the focus is on giving teachers greater autonomy and elevating them to a professional status often reserved for lawyers and doctors.

"Finland has raised the social status of its teachers to a level where there are few occupations with higher status," states a report prepared for an international education summit organized by U.S. Education Secretary Arne Duncan in March.[1]

Test scores in Finland were below the international average 25 years ago but have recently risen to the top of the global rankings.

Finland focuses on bringing the best students into teaching and ensuring that the job confers respect in society, according to the report, prepared by the Organisation for Economic Cooperation and Development (OECD). In contrast to the United States, where elementary-school teachers, especially, come from the lower half of college classes, top students in Finland battle for primary-school teaching spots. In 2010, for example, "over 6,600 applicants competed for 660 available slots in primary-school preparation programs . . ., making teaching one of the most sought-after professions," the OECD said.[2]

Finnish teachers' unions play a key role in shaping education policy, too. "It's a totally different situation in Finland" than in the United States when it comes to the relationship between unions and school administrators, said Henna Virkunnen, the country's minister of education. "Our teachers' union has been one of the main partners — We are working very much together with the union," she said. "Nearly all of the teachers are members. I think we don't have big differences in our thinking."[3]

Virkunnen acknowledged that comparing education policies is not easy. Schooling is "very much tied to a country's own history and society, so we can't take one system from another country and put it somewhere else," she said. Still, national differences aside, paying close attention to teachers' pre-service and in-service training, developing teachers who "are experts of their own work," respecting their professional autonomy and knowledge and providing good workplace conditions are key, Virkunnen said.[4]

assistant professor of education at the University of California, Berkeley. For example, the American Missionary Association, a nondenominational Protestant group, opened more than 500 schools for freed slaves.[51]

Many private fortunes have helped shape U.S. education. The Carnegie Foundation for the Advancement of Teaching, established in 1905 by industrialist Andrew Carnegie, helped found the Educational Testing Service (ETS), for example. The ETS developed and to this day manages standardized tests that include the SAT. In addition, the Carnegie Foundation led the fight for federal Pell grants for low-income college students.[52]

In 1955, Milton Friedman, a University of Chicago libertarian economist and 1976 Nobel Prize winner, introduced a new twist to the idea of linking the public and private sectors on schooling. As part of his overarching theory that all public-sector enterprises overspend and underperform because they are not disciplined by market supply and demand, Friedman proposed that public funds should be directed to private schools.

The government should fund education but should not, in general, run schools, because government, by nature inefficient, should run as few institutions as possible, Friedman theorized. His plan would offer parents vouchers

Singapore also assigns high status to the teaching profession. It "carefully selects young people from the top one-third of the secondary-school graduating class whom the government is especially interested in attracting to teaching and offers them a monthly stipend, while still in school," the OECD said. The stipend, it said, is competitive with salaries for new graduates in other professional fields. In exchange, recipients must make a three-year commitment to teaching. They get a choice of career paths: becoming master instructors who train others, curriculum and research specialists or future administrators. [5]

Some have noted an irony in the fact that Education Secretary Duncan not only organized the international summit but co-authored a newspaper column with the top official of the event's host: Fred van Leeuwen, general secretary of 30-million-member Education International, the largest international teachers' union.

The Obama administration has vocally supported many of the principles of the U.S. school-reform movement, including the championing of charter schools, most of which employ nonunionized teachers and are intended to compete with traditional public schools.

Yet Duncan and his co-authors wrote that "increasing teacher autonomy" is "vital" for improving the schools. Contrary to arguments of many current U.S. school reformers, "many of the world's top-performing nations have strong teacher unions that work in tandem with local and national authorities to boost student achievement," they said. "These high-performing nations illustrate how tough-minded collaboration more often leads to educational progress than tough-minded confrontation." [6]

— *Marcia Clemmitt*

Finland focuses on bringing the best students into teaching. Above, a second-grade class in Vaasa.

[1] "Building a High-Quality Teaching Profession: Lessons from Around the World," Organisation for Economic Co-operation and Development, 2011, p. 11, www.oecd.org/document/53/0,3746 ,en_21571361_44315115_47386549_1_1_1_1,00.html.

[2] *Ibid.*

[3] Quoted in Justin Snider, "An Interview With Henna Virkunnen, Finland's Minister of Education," *The Hechinger Report*, March 16, 2011, http://hechingerreport.org/content/an-interview-with-henna-virkkunen-finlands-minister-of-education_5458.

[4] Quoted in *ibid.*

[5] "Building a High-Quality Teaching Profession," *op. cit.*, p. 9.

[6] Arne Duncan, Angel Gurría and Fred van Leeuwen, "Uncommon Wisdom on Teaching," Dept. of Education website, March 16, 2011, www.ed.gov/blog/2011/03/uncommon-wisdom-on-teaching.

"equal to the estimated cost of . . . a government school" to send children to private schools. Such a scheme would "permit competition to develop" and "not least . . . , make the salaries of school teachers responsive to market forces," Friedman wrote. [53]

Little noticed at first, the idea was promoted in the 1980s by a burgeoning network of conservative think tanks such as the American Enterprise Institute. [54]

The New Reformers

A wealth boom in the 1990s built fortunes for entrepreneurs in such fields as electronics and finance and gave rise to a new breed of school reformers, typified by Gates, the Microsoft cofounder, and Broad, who made his first fortune in Detroit real estate development before turning to insurance. This group has been dubbed "venture philanthropists" for their efforts to fuse business methods with their social activism.

Venture philanthropists' "critique of traditional philanthropy is that it's been far too incremental" in achieving goals, says the University of California's Scott. As a result, while old-style foundations generally announced broad funding areas, then solicited grant applications from experts in those fields, "venture philanthropists often don't ask you to apply." Instead, they "seek you out, if you're doing specific work that they support, because they tend to believe they already know" what works in a given field, Scott says.

But the venture philanthropists' ideas don't always pan out in practice.

For example, one of the Gates Foundation's early initiatives — running from 2001 to 2009 — funded the breakup of large high schools into small ones of a few hundred pupils each, on the theory that better education occurred in a more personal environment, Scott says. At the time, research showed that medium-sized high schools of 500 to 1,200 students got the best results. But Gates poured money into tiny schools anyway. Then, after several years, when the small schools didn't produce improvement, the foundation quietly dropped the program, says Scott. One person involved with the initiative told Scott that "researchers had told us" that medium-sized, rather than very small, high schools showed the best results, "but we didn't listen," she says.

On the positive side, the episode demonstrates that the Gates Foundation, at least, is willing to learn from poor results, says Scott. But it also illustrates the potential danger of privately funding a crucial public resource, she says. What happens to schools created with private dollars when that money is withdrawn? Should taxpayers support them? Scott asks.

Still, venture philanthropists are gaining power as they support mainly market-oriented school reforms in concert with like-minded politicians, such as New York City Mayor Michael Bloomberg and Chicago Mayor Richard Daley. Also working with the philanthropists are "education entrepreneurs" such as Wendy Kopp, the Princeton graduate who founded Teach for America, a nonprofit group that has placed thousands of young graduates of elite colleges into temporary teaching slots in urban schools.

Scott says venture philanthropists have "followed the lead of conservative funders" who in the 1970s began to build a network of professors, academic research centers and think tanks that today buttresses the powerful conservative movement. By funding multiple groups and individuals and providing multiyear funding to cover operating costs, rather than making single-project grants, the venture philanthropists have formed a coherent philosophical network with lasting power, she says.

"There's power because people aren't working at cross-purposes."

In recent years, "joint grant making" by education funders has increased, says Sarah Reckhow, an assistant professor of education at Michigan State University in East Lansing. While many cities and organizations get no venture-philanthropy cash, those that do — including the New York City and Los Angeles school districts and groups such as Teach for America —"get a lot," from multiple sources, which helps them make large-scale, high-profile changes, Reckhow says.

"Historically, education politics has been local," with reformers focusing on change in a single district, says Jeffrey Henig, a professor of political science and education at Columbia University. Today's "coalition is focused on changing the national system," such as by persuading the federal government to add public dollars for programs that echo foundation initiatives. "I don't think this would have been possible without the growing role" that states and the federal government have played in education policy, Henig says.

(Beginning in the 1970s, most states began creating statewide school-funding formulas to replace purely local ones. The 2002 No Child Left Behind law helped increase federal involvement in assessing student achievement.)

Compared to a school system's annual budget, philanthropy dollars are "a drop in the bucket," says Reckhow. However, since most school-district money is tied up in salaries, "the funding actually provides powerful leverage" because it's "nearly the only money available for new initiatives."

Wealthy investment-fund managers who pump money into school-reform efforts such as charter schools "honestly think they're doing good. Plus, it's a very strong goodwill builder" for an industry whose reputation has suffered from the financial crash and recession, says Columbia's Levin. A few million dollars "is a rounding error for a wealthy investor." But it "is huge for a school." Such funding, Levin says, can make a school highly influential by providing extra resources that may help achieve better results and allow adoption of interesting programs that gain public and media attention.

Education Entrepreneurs

Conservative reformers and venture philanthropists tend to stress different aspects of and reasons for school reform, says Montclair State's Bulkley.

Conservatives, who tend to be skeptical of public systems of any kind, often argue that reform's greatest value is to offer families free choice and to create a market where none existed, she says. By contrast, she continues, venture philanthropists "tend to believe in public purposes" for schools and often stress the importance of building a public system better equipped to produce a skilled workforce.

The Broad Foundation, for example, awards an annual prize to districts that improve disadvantaged students' achievement, citing as a key motivation the need to restore "the public's confidence in . . . public schools by highlighting" success.[55]

With their focus on freedom and individual choice, many conservative reformers are as supportive of small one-of-a-kind charter schools as they are of multischool charter-school groups, says Bulkley. But venture philanthropists "have their DNA in entrepreneurship" — having launched small companies that grew into giants — and this background translates into a strong interest among venture philanthropists in so-called "charter-management organizations" that seek to run many individual schools based on a single school-management philosophy, Bulkley says.

Venture philanthropy dollars have spurred development of numerous entrepreneurial groups. New Leaders for New Schools is a New York City-based private training program for aspiring urban-school principals. The Brooklyn-based New Teacher Project — founded in 1997 by Rhee before she became D.C. school chancellor — aims to change school practices to allow more hiring of teachers without traditional certifications.[56]

Venture philanthropists favor working with cities where mayors, not school boards, are in control. Both Chicago and New York, where schools have been under mayor control since 1995 and 2002, respectively, receive substantial private funding.[57]

"Old-style industrial-based foundations tended to work within institutional constraints," taking local politics into account, for example, Henig says. But "Silicon Valley-influenced" philanthropists inhabit a fast-moving world.

"I do understand the frustration" that leads them to prefer the one-stop shop of mayoral control, Henig says. "Why would you want to wait two generations to implement change incrementally, in part because it's hard to get top-heavy bureaucracies to move?" Nevertheless, incremental change that seeks widespread buy-in is probably the best path to lasting improvement, he suggests.

CURRENT SITUATION
Budget Battles

Several newly elected conservative governors are bringing school reform to the front pages this spring. Recession-triggered budget problems in such states as Wisconsin, Ohio, Idaho, Florida and New Jersey have opened the way for battles over teachers' benefits and unions' cherished right to bargain collectively.

Conservative reformers, especially, have welcomed the reform efforts. "Except for one year during the Great Depression," public-school funding "has gone up every year for 100 years," says the Hoover Institution's Hanushek. Much of the money "went into salaries and retirement" plans for teachers and for "reducing class sizes," neither of which improves education, he argues.

The budget battles provide an entry point for ensuring "accountability for every dollar and every child," wrote former Washington school chancellor Rhee, who continues to enjoy heavy venture-philanthropy backing. To save money, wrote Rhee, "districts must shift new employees from defined-benefit pension programs" — traditional pensions that promise retired workers a specific benefit level for the rest of their lives —"to portable, defined-contribution plans" whose payout depends on investment returns. And because "the budget crisis inevitably requires layoffs," she said, states can take the opportunity to begin basing firing decisions "on teachers' effectiveness, not on their seniority," as most districts do today.[58]

In March, Florida Republican Gov. Rick Scott, who has hired Rhee as a consultant, signed legislation to gradually eliminate tenure and base firings and pay raises on teachers' performance in raising student test scores.[59] In April, Republican Gov. C.L. "Butch" Otter of Idaho signed a measure ending tenure for new teachers, instituting merit pay and banning unions from bargaining over workload and class size.[60]

"There have also been lots of state-law proposals for school choice" this year, says John Witte, a professor of public affairs and political science at the University of Wisconsin, Madison. In the past, Republican lawmakers have pushed bills to bolster charter schools but haven't often

Has spending on public schools risen too high?

YES
Adam B. Schaeffer
Policy Analyst, Cato Institute

Written for *CQ Researcher*, April 2011

Real, per-pupil spending, adjusted for inflation, has more than doubled over 40 years, while test scores have remained flat at the end of high school. That's around $12,000 or $13,000 per student every year.

We've spent more every decade with no return in student performance. That's not investment — defined as getting a positive return on your money. It's just spending.

This poses a particularly difficult problem for state and local governments who bear most of the burden. State and local education spending consumes 46 percent of all tax revenue, or two-and-a-half times what's spent on Medicaid/CHIP.

It's also taking a bigger *share* of tax revenue. State education spending as a share of tax revenue has increased 90 percent in two decades. It's increased over 70 percent as a share of local revenue.

It's time to replace the "spending" model of education policy with an "investment" model.

We can make public education a lot more efficient. The number of public school staff per student increased 70 percent since 1970; cutting back on unnecessary personnel will bring significant savings.

But school choice, particularly through education tax credits, is the best way to *invest* in education. It's a proven way to improve *public* school performance, save money and increase choice. It's an effective, efficient investment in education.

Choice is the most intensively studied education reform there is, and the verdict is clear: It works. Decades of evidence and dozens of studies provide proof. It works in Chile and Sweden, and it works in Florida and Wisconsin and a dozen other states.

The vast majority of studies analyzing private choice policies demonstrate positive impacts on participants and children who remain in public schools. None have shown negative impacts. And choice programs are far less costly to taxpayers.

According to a 2008 fiscal analysis by the state Office of Program Policy Analysis and Government Accountability in Florida, the state gained $1.49 in savings for every $1 it lost in tax revenue to its education tax credit program. David Figlio, a Northwestern University researcher and official analyst of the program, found it significantly boosted performance in Florida's public schools.

Citizens and businesses want to invest directly in our education system. We should encourage them to do so.

Let's stop just *spending* money on education. Let's really start *investing* in it.

NO
Richard Rothstein
Research Associate, Economic Policy Institute

Written for *CQ Researcher*, April 2011

States' education spending varies widely, even after adjustment for purchasing-power differences. Real costs also vary, because disadvantaged students need more support than those whose early-childhood, after-school, home-literacy and cultural experiences supplement their schooling.

For decades, spending nationwide increased, largely for children with disabilities. Their individualized attention accounts for much of the staff increases. Nonetheless, achievement for regular students also improved, substantially so for the disadvantaged: On the "gold standard" National Assessment of Educational Progress, black 12th-graders gained nearly two-thirds of a standard deviation in math and reading since 1980.

Some states clearly spend too little. Others may spend more than needed for graduates' workplace success, because wealthier taxpayers choose to provide more fulfilling (and expensive) experiences for their children. Mississippi spends less per pupil — about $8,500 — than almost any state. Its percentage of low-income children is higher, test scores are lower and capacity to fund education (per-capita personal income) is less.

Massachusetts spends more — about $14,500 — with proportionally fewer low-income children than elsewhere. Its test scores are highest of all. Its fiscal capacity is greater than most states'.

Then there is California, spending less — about $10,000 — than most, with many low-income children, low scores and high income. It chooses not to tax itself to educate disadvantaged youth well, spending instead on prisons for those who fail.

More money should not be spent unwisely, but Mississippi cannot spend what's needed without greater federal aid. California should spend more, but with greater state effort. Both should invest in early childhood. Children from less literate homes have worse verbal skills than middle-class children — by age 3. This early gap cannot be overcome by more spending later, but better schools can sustain benefits from early investments. Well-qualified (and better-paid) teachers in smaller primary-grade classes for low-income children would be wise.

Massachusetts should also invest more in early childhood for disadvantaged students, but it need not boost average spending. Wealthy taxpayers should contribute more, choosing whether to do so by reducing suburban expenditures.

Today, federal aid exacerbates inequality. Subsidies for low-income students are proportional to existing state spending, so Massachusetts inexcusably gets more federal dollars per child than Mississippi. The question is not whether we overspend but whether we spend on the right programs for children most in need. The answer is "no".

sought voucher expansions, partly because their mostly suburban constituents like their local schools and wouldn't seek vouchers. "But now something on the right has changed," and voucher-expansion proposals are on the table "all around the country," Witte says.

Wisconsin's Gov. Walker has proposed repealing enrollment caps both for vouchers and for the number of students who can attend so-called "virtual" — or online — schools. He also wants to phase out income limits for voucher eligibility.[61] "That's a huge change" because voucher programs have previously assisted only the poor, says Witte.

Walker also proposes ending a requirement that students who use vouchers at private and online schools take state achievement tests. But that would be contrary to the stated principles of some venture-philanthropy reformers.

"If you're going to have a system of choice," then a common set of learning and achievement standards — preferably nationwide — is crucial for all schools, not just public ones, says Broad Foundation policy director McGinity. Otherwise, "you're not going to have a transparent market in which people can make comparisons." Ultimately, the standards would include both test scores and comparative information to help parents choose a school "with the best arts program," for example, he says.

Such developments cast doubt on just how much reforms backed by conservatives and venture philanthropists actually coincide, says Columbia's Henig. "There's also cleavage on how much money should be spent," he says. Venture philanthropists "have learned from charters and cities with mayoral control that it's expensive to do this," while conservatives stress cutting education spending.

Racing to the Top?

The Obama administration has worked in concert with reformers since taking office in 2009. Obama's Secretary of Education, Arne Duncan, was CEO of Chicago's public schools and gained reformers' favor through his strategy of closing down chronically low-performing schools and reopening them with new staff.[62]

Under Obama's Race to the Top program, states have pledged to:

- Adopt statewide learning standards and assessments;
- Build data systems to measure achievement;
- Recruit, retain and reward effective teachers and principals through measures such as merit pay and retention bonuses;

- Foster education innovation through such means as laws encouraging charter-school development; and
- Focus on turning around the lowest-performing schools.

Last year, 11 states and the District of Columbia won $4.35 billion in Race to the Top grants, including $350 million to support joint work among states on student assessment.[63]

This year, states are pushing forward with these projects. For example, Rhode Island is field-testing a teacher-evaluation program in two districts and a charter school. Delaware will pilot in-school expert coaches to help staff members analyze achievement data and adjust instruction to individual needs. Massachusetts will establish career ladders to encourage teachers to remain in the profession.[64]

Yet, some reformers have hit bumps in the road in recent months, at least partly because of public skepticism.

Last October, Rhee resigned from her post in Washington after then- mayor Adrian Fenty, who appointed her in 2007, lost his reelection bid, in large part because many city residents were fed up with Rhee. Some teachers and parents complained, for example, that teacher firings Rhee claimed she based on merit actually occurred before her new teacher-assessment plan had even gone into operation.[65]

Much of Rhee's "impatience was merited," says Columbia's Levin. "The idea that the school system is an employment agency for my friends" is a bad feature of many districts, including Washington, and needs changing, he says. "But I would try to build community support before doing that," he says. Rhee "has a big ego, and she instead took pride in her tactics."

Levin and others also say that Rhee's so-called "IMPACT" teacher-evaluation plan has merit. The plan is a useful, multifaceted attempt to produce an overall picture of teachers, including not just test scores "but evaluations by master teachers," who would seek "to recognize good teacher practices both in the classroom and in planning" lessons, says Columbia's Pallas.

Ultimately, external funders helped cause the "mischief" in Washington, says Levin. Through their venture-philanthropy ties, Rhee and Fenty "were getting national attention, funding and chances to air their views, so they took their eye off the local population" and viewed funders "as their constituency," Levin says. They failed to "strike the needed balance between getting external funding and then using it to build capacity" for improvement from within, he says.

Earlier this month, New York City Mayor Bloomberg's hand-picked chancellor, Cathleen P. Black, resigned under pressure after less than four months on the job. Black had been a top publishing executive, heading both Hearst Magazines (publisher of *Cosmopolitan* and *Popular Mechanics*, among others) and *USA Today*. But she had no education-management or teaching experience.[66] Black quickly ran afoul of teachers and parents by making what many considered insensitive jokes about school problems. "Could we just have some birth control for a while? It could really help us all out a lot," Black quipped at a parents' meeting to discuss school overcrowding.[67]

"Those kinds of comments show a lack of understanding of what parents are going through," said one parent.[68]

But McGinity, of the Broad Foundation, argues that Black's ouster actually makes "a great case" for one school-management principle reformers consider key — mayoral control. Unlike in districts where school-board politics dominate, Black and Bloomberg "could see that the situation wasn't working and made a change quickly" before problems worsened, he points out.

OUTLOOK
Common Standards

American education will change in the coming decades, but the shape of what's to come is hard to discern.

Some reform critics fear that private interests could dismantle the public schools Americans once prized.

The United States has long had a two-tier system, with schools in higher-income areas having many more resources, observes DePaul's Saltman. "But what you're seeing now is a new kind of two-tier system being created, in which schools in the bottom tier will be privately managed," he predicts.

"In poor city and rural areas," reform advocates are "quickly turning public distrust into short-term profit-making industries" that will seek some quick bucks from taxpayer-supported schools and get out, he warns. "Most Americans don't realize how far along this privatization agenda has gone." But with many Democratic politicians now agreeing "that public schools need to compete with the private sector, privatization has largely won," he says.

There's little doubt that databases tracking student performance will be established everywhere fairly soon. But while unions fear that teachers will lose their job security to overly simplified interpretation of standardized test scores, even some reform critics see possible long-term upsides to data tracking.

Databases now under construction will include school data only, but down the line databases from multiple social-service agencies might link information about health, poverty, homelessness and more to school records, muses Columbia's Henig. Such data could be "revolutionary" in revealing all factors that contribute to students' achievement, or lack thereof, and help propel holistic solutions, he says.

With Republicans and many Democrats now backing school choice, the national learning standards some have recommended for decades will appear at last, some analysts say.[69]

Prior to 2002's No Child Left Behind law, "everybody said they met standards because they could make up their own rules," says Kenneth K. Wong, an education professor at Brown University. But as assessments increasingly become comparable across state lines, this convenient mode of hiding failure is evaporating, he says. In addition, while accountability requirements so far apply only to public schools, with nearly 5,000 charter schools now in operation, "we must think about how we know they are meeting standards, too," Wong says. "If we are going to move toward school choice," the nation must confront the highly contentious question of "whether we're going to have something like a national examination," he says.

"My hope is that there will soon be a strong set of core [learning] standards with a common assessment" for all schools nationwide, says the Broad Foundation's McGinity.

Expansion of school choice to allow out-of-district enrollments and virtual schools will accelerate a "revolutionary" trend — delinking schooling from one's neighborhood, says Wisconsin's Witte. "For a hundred years people went to their neighborhood schools, and 90 percent still do. But until 20 years ago, everybody did," he says. Ultimately, "this change will affect everything" in schools, he says. For example, "We govern public schools through an elected school board, so should open-enrollment people [from out-of-district] also have seats on the board?"

Before the nation simply lets such large changes happen, however, "I think people need to ask themselves, 'What are our goals for our children?'" says Curry College's Gratz.

NOTES

1. Jason Felch, Jason Song and Doug Smith, "Who's Teaching L.A.'s Kids?" *Los Angeles Times*, Aug. 14, 2010, www.latimes.com/news/local/la-me-teachers-value-20100815,0,258862,full.story, p. A1.

2. "Public elementary and secondary schools by type of school," *Digest of Education Statistics*, National Center for Education Statistics, http://nces.ed.gov/programs/digest/d09/tables/dt09_093.asp.

3. Eric A. Hanushek, "Feeling Too Good About Our Schools," Education Next website, Jan. 18, 2011, http://educationnext.org.

4. Bill Gates, "How Teachers Development Could Revolutionize Our Schools," *The Washington Post*, Feb. 28, 2011, www.washingtonpost.com.

5. Matthew Di Carlo, "Teachers Matter, But So Do Words," *Shanker blog*, July 14, 2010, http://shanker-blog.org/?p=74.

6. Richard Rothstein, "Fact-Challenged Policy," *Economic Policy Institute website*, March 8, 2011, www.epi.org/analysis_and_opinion/entry/fact-challenged_policy.

7. "Employer Costs for Employee Compensation," press release, Bureau of Labor Statistics, March 9, 2011, www.bls.gov/news.release/ecec.nr0.htm.

8. "Fact-Checking School Choice Research," The Center for Education Reform, October 2010, www.edreform.com/_upload/No_More_Waiting_School_Choice.pdf.

9. For background, see Kenneth Jost, "Public-Employee Unions," *CQ Researcher*, April 8, 2011, pp. 313-336.

10. Jason Song and Jason Felch, "L.A. Unified Releases School Ratings Using 'Value-Added' Method," *Los Angeles Times*, April 12, 2011, www.latimes.com, p. A1.

11. *Ibid.*

12. Diane Ravitch and Deborah Meier, "Bridging Differences," *Education Week blogs*, March 29, 2011, http://blogs.edweek.org.

13. "Education, Leadership for America," Heritage Foundation website, www.heritage.org/Initiatives/Education.

14. Hanushek, *op. cit.*

15. *Ibid.*

16. Eric A. Hanushek, Paul E. Peterson and Ludger Woessmann, "Teaching Math to the Talented," *Education Next*, Winter 2011, http://educationnext.org. Peterson is a government professor at Harvard University; Woessmann is an economics professor at the University of Munich.

17. Rothstein, *op. cit.*

18. *Ibid.*

19. "Strong Performers and Successful Reformers in Education: Lessons from PISA for the United States," Organisation for Economic Co-operation and Development, 2011, p. 26, www.oecd.org/dataoecd/32/50/46623978.pdf.

20. For background, see Marcia Clemmitt, "Fixing Urban Schools," *CQ Researcher*, April 27, 2007 (update, Aug. 5, 2010), pp. 361-384.

21. Cited in Richard Kahlenberg, "Debating Michelle Rhee," *Taking Note blog*, Century Foundation, Feb. 25, 2011, http://takingnote.tcf.org/2011/02/debating-michelle-rhee.html.

22. "Strong Performers and Successful Reformers in Education," *op. cit.*, p. 28.

23. Quoted in Jonathan Mahler, "The Fragile Success of School Reform in the Bronx," *The New York Times Magazine*, April 6, 2011, p. 34. See also Joe Nocera, "The Limits Of School Reform," *The New York Times*, April 26, 2011, p. A23.

24. "A Lack of Rigor Leaves Students 'Adrift' in College," NPR website, Feb. 9, 2011, www.npr.org.

25. Quoted in Timothy J. Farrell, "Arum Research Calls Out 'Limited Learning' on College Campuses," *New York University blogs*, March 25, 2010, http://blogs.nyu.edu/blogs/dbw1/ataglance/2010/03/arum_research_calls_out_limite.html.

26. For background, see Jennifer Medina, "Teachers Set Deal with City on Discipline Process," *The New*

York Times, April 15, 2010, www.nytimes.com/2010/04/16/nyregion/16rubber.html.

27. "Don't Blame Teachers Unions for our Failing Schools," debate transcript, *Intelligence Squared U.S.*, March 16, 2010, http://intelligencesquaredus.org/wp-content/uploads/Teachers-Unions-031610.pdf.

28. Quoted in Carlo Rotella, "Class Warrior," *The New Yorker*, Feb. 1, 2010, p. 28.

29. Katharine O. Strunk and Jason A. Grissom, "Do Strong Unions Shape District Policies?: Collective Bargaining, Teacher Contract Restrictiveness, and the Political Power of Teachers' Unions," *Educational Evaluation and Policy Analysis*, December 2010, p. 389.

30. John Merrow, "The Road Not Traveled: Tracking Charter Schools Movement," *Taking Note blog*, Dec.1, 2009, http://takingnote.learningmatters.tv.

31. "Don't Blame Teachers Unions for our Failing Schools," *op. cit.*

32. *Ibid.*

33. "A Stronger Evaluation System," Massachusetts Teachers Association, March 22, 2011, http://massteacher.org/news/archive/2011/03-22.aspx; "MTA's Reinventing Educator Evaluation: Answers to Frequently Asked Questions," www.seateachers.com/HTMLobj-1742/MTAReinventing_Educator Eval12011.pdf.

34. David Lewin, *et al.*, "Getting It Right: Empirical Evidence and Policy Implications from Research on Public-Sector Unionism and Collective Bargaining," Employment Policy Research Network, March 16, 2011, www.employmentpolicy.org/sites/www.employmentpolicy.org/files/EPRN%20PS%20draft%203%2016%2011%20PM%20FINAL tk-ml4%20edits.pdf.

35. Quoted in Liana Heitin, "16 Nations Meet to Discuss Improving Teaching," *Education Week blogs*, March 17, 2011, http://blogs.eduweek.org.

36. Quoted in Bill Turque, "Green Dot's Barr: Unions Part of Solution," *The Washington Post*, Sept. 8, 2009, http://voices.washingtonpost.com.

37. For background, see Anthony S. Bryk, "Organizing Schools for Improvement," *Phi Delta Kappan*, April 2010, pp. 23-30.

38. Douglas Lee Lauen, "To Choose or Not to Choose: High School Choice and Graduation in Chicago," *Educational Evaluation and Policy Analysis*, September 2009, p. 179.

39. Andy Smarick, "The Turnaround Fallacy," *Education Next*, Winter 2010, http://educationnext.org/the-turnaround-fallacy; For background, see Kenneth Jost, "Revising No Child Left Behind," *CQ Researcher*, April 16, 2010, pp. 337-360.

40. "School Restructuring Options Under No Child Left Behind," *Education.com*, www.education.com/reference/article/Ref_School_Restructuring.

41. Diane Ravitch, *The Death and Life of the Great American School System* (2010), pp. 86-87.

42. Quoted in Diane Ravitch, *Left Back: A Century of Battles Over School Reform* (2000), p. 19.

43. Christopher B. Swanson, "U.S. Graduation Rate Continues Decline," *Education Week online*, June 2, 2010, www.edweek.org/ew/articles/2010/06/10/34swanson.h29.html?qs=historical+graduation+rates.

44. *Ibid.*

45. Ravitch, *The Death and Life, op. cit.*, p. 13.

46. Swanson, *op. cit.*

47. Frederick M. Hess, "A Policy Debate, Not an Attack," *Room for Debate blogs*, *The New York Times online*, March 6, 2011, www.nytimes.com.

48. "Chicago Teachers Federation," *Encyclopedia of Chicago*, www.encyclopedia.chicagohistory.org/pages/271.html.

49. Ravitch, *The Death and Life, op. cit.*, p. 174.

50. Trip Gabriel and Sam Dillon, "Teacher Tenure Targeted by GOP Governors," *The New York Times*, Jan. 31, 2011, p. 1, www.nytimes.com/2011/02/01/us/01tenure.html.

51. "American Missionary Association," *Encyclopedia Britannica online*, 2011, www.britannica.com/EBchecked/topic/19996/American-Missionary-Association.

52. "About Carnegie," *Carnegie Foundation for the Advancement of Teaching website*, www.carnegiefoundation.org/about-us/about-carnegie.

53. Milton Friedman, "The Role of Government in Education," *School Choices website*, www.schoolchoices.org/roo/fried1.htm.

54. For background, see Kenneth Jost, "School Voucher Showdown," *CQ Researcher*, Feb. 15, 2002, pp. 121-144, and Charles S. Clark, "Charter Schools," *CQ Researcher*, Dec. 20, 2002, pp. 1033-1056.

55. For background, see "Frequently Asked Questions," *The Broad Prize for Urban Education website*, www.broadprize.org/about/FAQ.html#2.

56. "Overview," The New Teacher Project website, http://tntp.org/about-us.

57. For background, see Ruth Moscovitch, Alan R. Sadovnik, *et al.*, "Governance and Urban School Improvement: Lessons for New Jersey from Nine Cities," Institute on Education Law and Policy, Rutgers University at Newark, 2010, http://ielp.rutgers.edu/docs/MC%20Final.pdf.

58. Michelle Rhee, "In Budget Crises, an Opening for School Reform," *The Wall Street Journal Online*, Jan. 11, 2011, http://online.wsj.com/article/SB10001424052748704739504576068142896954626.html.

59. Isabel Mascarenas, "Student Teachers Speak Out on SB 736 on Teacher Merit Pay," *WTSP News website*, March 25, 2011, www.wtsp.com/news/article/183421/250/Student-teachers-speak-out-on-teacher-merit-pay; Michael C. Bender, "Rick Scott Names Michelle Rhee, Patricia Levesque to Education Transition Team," *Miami Herald blogs*, Dec. 2, 2010, http://miamiherald.typepad.com/nakedpolitics/2010/12/rick-scott-names-michelle-rhee-patricia-levesque-to-education-transition-team.html.

60. Laura Zuckerman, "Idaho Governor Signs Education Overhaul Into Law," Reuters, April 8, 2011, www.reuters.com/article/2011/04/09/us-idaho-education-idUSTRE7380GA20110409.

61. Amy Hetzner and Erin Richards, "Budget Cuts $834 Million from Schools," [Milwaukee] *Journal Sentinel online*, March 1, 2011, www.jsonline.com/news/statepolitics/117192683.html.

62. Rotella, *op. cit.*

63. "Nine States and the District of Columbia Win Second Round Race to the Top Grants," press release, U.S. Dept. of Education, Aug. 24, 2010, www.ed.gov/news/press-releases/nine-states-and-district-columbia-win-second-round-race-top-grants.

64. For background, see Michele McNeill, "Race to Top Winners Work to Balance Promises, Capacity," *Education Week*, March 30, 2011, www.edweek.org/ew/articles/2011/03/30/26rtt-states_ep-2.h30.html?tkn=RMOFJADRisIf48BKX1kxGbHNaOeVRca26WD1&print=1.

65. Andrew J. Rotheram, "Fenty's Loss in DC: A Blow to Education Reform?" *Time*, Sept. 16, 2010, www.time.com/time/nation/article/0,8599,2019395,00.html.

66. "Cathie Black," *Executive Profiles*, Bloomberg/*Business Week*, http://investing.businessweek.com/businessweek/research/stocks/private/person.asp?personId=79286149&privcapId=23675200&previousCapId=4160895&previousTitle=Bill%20&%20Melinda%20Gates%20Foundation.

67. Yoav Gonen, "Parents Fume Over Black's 'Birth Control' Quip About Overcrowding," *New York Post online*, Jan. 15, 2011, www.nypost.com/p/news/local/black_wisecrack_on_birth_control_a0EUsHTDjV-vWAMvA5qf6KI.

68. *Ibid.*

69. For background, see Kathy Koch, "National Education Standards," *CQ Researcher*, May 14, 1999, pp. 401-424.

BIBLIOGRAPHY

Books

Hess, Frederick M., *Education Unbound: The Promise and Practice of Greenfield Schooling,* **Association for Supervision and Curriculum Development, 2010.**
An analyst at the conservative American Enterprise Institute argues that today's schools shouldn't be reformed so much as scrapped so education entrepreneurs can devise specific solutions for different educational needs.

Merrow, John, *The Influence of Teachers: Reflections on Teaching and Leadership,* **LM Books, 2011.**
Based on his reporting throughout the country, a long-time PBS education reporter explores issues such as teaching quality, payment and evaluation of teachers.

Ravitch, Diane, *The Life and Death of the Great American School System: How Testing and Choice Are Undermining Education,* **Basic Books, 2010.**
A longtime education policymaker explains why she now rejects the market-oriented education-reform

theories she helped to develop for President George H. W. Bush.

Weber, Karl, ed., *Waiting for "Superman": How We Can Save America's Failing Public Schools*, PublicAffairs, 2010.
The companion book to the acclaimed 2010 school-reform documentary "Waiting for Superman" includes essays on how to improve U.S. education by charter-school leaders, education journalists and a teachers' union leader.

Articles

"Grading the Teachers: Value-Added Analysis," *Los Angeles Times* online, www.latimes.com/news/local/teachers-investigation.
An ongoing series of investigative articles from 2010 and 2011 explores the effectiveness of teacher evaluations based on students' standardized test scores. Includes a database with rankings of individual teachers and schools.

Banchero, Stephanie, "Bill Gates Seeks Formula for Better Teachers," *The Wall Street Journal* online, March 22, 2011, http://online.wsj.com/article/SB10001424052748703858404576214593545938506.html.
Microsoft cofounder and philanthropist Bill Gates explains how he's trying to develop better teacher evaluations and argues that cutting education budgets is probably unwise.

Barkan, Joanne, "Got Dough? How Billionaires Rule Our Schools," *Dissent*, winter 2011, www.dissentmagazine.org/article/?article=3781.
A writer for a left-leaning magazine argues that venture philanthropists like Bill Gates are gaining too much power.

Bryk, Anthony S., "Organizing Schools for Improvement," *Phi Delta Kappan*, April 2010, www.kappanmagazine.org/content/91/7/23.abstract, p. 23.
The president of the Carnegie Foundation for the Advancement of Teaching describes his research on Chicago's schools, showing that several critical aspects of a school's organization and leadership are major determinants of whether that school can improve.

Pellissier, Hank, "The Finnish Miracle," Great Schools website, www.greatschools.org/students/2453-finland-education.gs.
Finland's schools, which rose from mediocre to outstanding over the past quarter-century, have lessons for schools, teachers and parents. Notably, teaching is among Finland's most respected professions.

Rotella, Carlo, "Class Warrior: Arne Duncan's Bid to Shake Up Schools," *The New Yorker*, Feb. 1, 2010, p. 24.
President Obama's Secretary of Education is the former CEO of Chicago's public schools, with a reputation for closing low-achieving schools and reopening them with new staffs.

Reports and Studies

"Building a High-Quality Teaching Profession: Lessons from Around the World," Organisation for Economic Cooperation and Development, 2011, www.oecd.org/dataoecd/62/8/47506177.pdf.
Analysts for the international organization find that most countries with high-achieving schools recruit the best students as teachers, provide extensive on-the-job training and mentoring and involve teachers closely in efforts to improve schools.

Corcoran, Sean P., "Can Teachers be Evaluated by their Students' Test Scores? Should They Be? The Use of Value-Added Measures of Teacher Effectiveness in Policy and Practice," Annenberg Institute for School Reform, 2010, www.annenberginstitute.org/products/Corcoran.php.
A Columbia University assistant professor of economics explains how value-added evaluations of teacher quality work and examines the evidence on their reliability and implications for schools.

Suffren, Quentin, and Theodore J. Wallace, "Needles in a Haystack: Lessons from Ohio's High-performing, High-need Urban Schools," Thomas B. Fordham Institute, May 2010, www.scribd.com/doc/31987794/Needles-in-a-Haystack-Full-Report.
Analysts for a research organization supportive of school choice examine a group of public, magnet and charter schools in low-income urban areas in search of factors that help the schools improve student achievement.

For More Information

Albert Shanker Institute, 555 New Jersey Ave., N.W., Washington, DC 20001; (202) 879-4401; www.ashankerin st.org. An arm of the American Federation of Teachers that brings together experts to discuss education issues.

Annenberg Institute for School Reform, Brown University, Box 1985, Providence, RI 02912; (401) 863-7990; www .annenberginstitute.org. Analyzes school-system issues, works with community partners to improve school districts and publishes the quarterly journal *Voices in Urban Education.*

Economic Policy Institute, 1333 H St., N.W., Suite 300, East Tower, Washington, DC 20005-4707; (202) 775-8810; www.epi.org/issue/education. Examines school reform from a liberal viewpoint.

Education Next, Program on Education Policy and Governance, Harvard Kennedy School of Government, 79 JFK St., Cambridge, MA 02138; (877) 476-5354; http:// educationnext.org/sub/about. A reform-oriented online publication that examines all aspects of K-12 education.

The Hechinger Report, http://hechingerreport.org. A nonprofit online news organization based at the Teachers College of Columbia University that publishes in-depth reporting and commentary on education issues.

Hoover Institution, 434 Galvez Mall, Stanford University, Stanford, CA 94305-6010; (650) 723-1754; www.hoover .org. Studies and publishes reports on school reform and other topics from a conservative perspective.

National Center for Education Statistics, U.S. Department of Education, 1990 K St., N.W., Washington, DC 20006; (202) 502-7300; http://nces.ed.gov. Provides statistics on every aspect of American education.

Thomas B. Fordham Institute, 1016 16th St., N.W., 8th Floor, Washington, DC 20036; (202) 223-5452; www .edexcellence.net. A think tank dedicated to improving school performance through accountability and expanded options for parents.

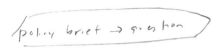

2

Fixing Urban Schools

Marcia Clemmitt and Charles S. Clark

Philadelphia police officers guard West Philadelphia High School on March 12, 2007, where a teacher was attacked by three students three days earlier. Experts suggest that a "behavior gap" between black and white students parallels the academic achievement gap between high- and low-performing students.

From *CQ Researcher*,
April 27, 2007 (updated June 5, 2012).

"I didn't go to school much in elementary, and they saw me as a bad girl" who skipped class, says Jeanette, a Houston high-school student who dropped out several times but is struggling to get a diploma. After her parents divorced when she was in grade school, she fell into a pattern typical of urban students, repeatedly "switching schools," sometimes living with her mother, sometimes her father and sometimes with an aunt who "didn't make us go to school" at all.[1]

In middle school, Jeanette began taking drugs but later got involved in sports, which motivated her to try, sometimes successfully, to keep up her grades and stay off drugs. Some teachers have tried hard to help her, but like many troubled urban kids, she pulls back. "If I need help . . . I don't say anything. . . . They have to ask me." Still, Jeanette is determined to avoid the fate of her parents, who dropped out of school when they had her. At the time, her mother was only 13. "I don't want to live like them. I want to have a better life," she says.

Jeanette typifies the daunting challenge that urban schools face in promoting academic achievement among children whose lives have been disordered and impoverished.

Most middle-class families with children have moved to the suburbs, leaving urban schools today overwhelmingly populated by low-income, African-American and Hispanic students. "Nationally, about 50 percent of all black and Latino students attend schools in which 75 percent or more of the students are low-income, as measured by eligibility for free and reduced-price lunch," according to the Center for Civil Rights at the University

Minority Districts Often Get Less Funding

In 28 states, school districts with high-minority enrollments received less per-pupil funding (shown as a negative number, top map) than districts with low-minority levels. For example, in Illinois, the highest-minority districts received an average of $1,223 less per student than the lowest-minority districts. In 21 states, the highest-minority districts received more per pupil (shown as a positive number, bottom map), than the districts with the lowest-minority enrollments. For example, in Georgia, the highest-poverty districts received $566 per student more than the lowest-poverty districts.

Minority Funding Gaps by State, 2004

States where high-minority districts received less funding than low-minority districts

Legend:
- -$2,000+
- -$1,001 to -$2,000
- -$500 to -$1,000
- -$1 to -$500

States where high-minority districts received more funding than low-minority districts

Legend:
- $0 to $500
- $500 to $1,000
- $1,001 to $2,000
- $2,000+

Note: Hawaii is not shown because data are not available.

Source: Funding Gaps 2006, The Education Trust, 2006

of North Carolina. Only 5 percent of white students attend such high-poverty schools.[2]

These schools, mostly urban, aren't making the grade, even in the context of lagging achievement in American schools overall.

Although states show significant variations, nationwide "71 percent of eighth-graders are not reading at grade level," and the percentage shoots up to between 80 and 90 percent for students of color, says former Gov. Bob Wise, D-W.Va., now president of the Alliance for Excellent Education, a broad-based coalition that advocates for academically stronger high schools.

Furthermore, of the approximately 15,000 U.S. high schools, 2,000 — mostly in cities — account for half of the nation's school dropouts, says Wise.

When President George W. Bush joined Massachusetts Sen. Edward M. Kennedy and other congressional Democrats to enact the No Child Left Behind Act (NCLB) in 2002, a key aim was requiring states to report achievement scores for all student groups. That ensured that lagging scores of low-income and minority students wouldn't be masked by having only state or district overall average scores reported.[3]

This year, Congress is expected to provide funding to keep the law in operation, but there's considerable disagreement about where federal education law should go next, and lawmakers may wait until next year to consider revisions.

NCLB's test-score reporting requirements "make it more possible to look at whether schools are doing well just for more affluent students or for poor students" as well, and that's valuable, says Jeffrey Henig, professor of political science and education at Columbia University's Teachers College.

But some supporters, including President Bush, say the NCLB has done more than just improve data-gathering, arguing that the law itself has pushed achievement upward. "Fourth-graders are reading better. They've made more progress in five years than in the previous 28 years combined," he said on March 2.[4]

Many education analysts disagree with that rosy assessment. The small improvement in fourth-grade reading and mathematics scores is part of a long-term trend, which began years before NCLB was even enacted, said Harvard University Professor of Education Daniel M. Koretz. "There's not any evidence that shows anything has changed" since NCLB, he said.[5]

And for urban schools, the post-NCLB picture is especially grim.

Of the non-achieving schools in New York state, for example, 90 percent are in cities and 80 percent in the state's five biggest cities, says David Hursh, an associate professor of teaching and curriculum at the University of Rochester's Margaret Warner Graduate School of Education.

The gap between average reading scores of black and white fourth-graders narrowed by only one point on the 500-point National Assessment of Educational Progress test (NAEP) between 2002 and 2005, and the narrowing appears to be part of a long-term trend, since it narrowed by three points between 1998 and 2005. Between 2002 and 2005, the reading-score gap between white and black eighth-graders actually widened, from 25 points to 28 points.[6]

The continuing severe achievement gap, newly highlighted by NCLB's data-reporting requirements, leaves lawmakers and educators scratching their heads about what to do next.

Some analysts say lagging achievement in urban schools demonstrates that poor families in poor communities require much more intense interventions than middle-class students, including better teachers and longer school days as well as improved health care, nutrition and parenting education.

A public school enrolling mainly middle-class white students has a one-in-four chance of producing good test scores, across years and in different subject matter, according to Douglas N. Harris, assistant professor of education policy at the University of Wisconsin, Madison. A school with a predominantly low-income minority population has a 1-in-300 chance of doing so.[7]

Experts blame the poor outcome on the fact that urban schools, like all schools, are staffed and organized to provide substantial extra help to only 15 percent of students and curriculum enrichment to another 15, while "the students in the middle are supposed to take care of themselves," says Robert Balfanz, associate research scientist at the Johns Hopkins University Center on the Social Organization of Schools and associate director of the Talent Development High School program, a reform initiative in 33 schools nationwide. The formula for extra help fits most suburban schools, "but in urban schools 50 to 60 percent, and sometimes up to

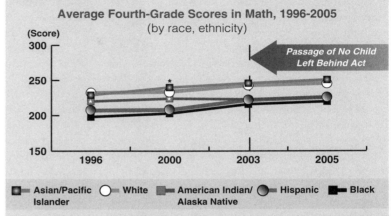

All Racial/Ethnic Groups Improved on Test

Fourth-graders in all racial and ethnic groups began modestly improving in math on the National Assessment for Educational Progress several years before passage of the No Child Left Behind Act.

Average Fourth-Grade Scores in Math, 1996-2005
(by race, ethnicity)

Passage of No Child Left Behind Act

Legend: Asian/Pacific Islander — White — American Indian/Alaska Native — Hispanic — Black

* Some data for 1996 and 2000 not available

Source: U.S. Department of Education, National Center for Education Statistics

80 percent, of the kids are 'high-needs,' defined as English-as-a-second-language students, special-education students or students below grade level or with severe attendance problems.

"We're not set up to respond when that many kids need one-on-one tutoring, monitoring of their attendance on a daily basis, [or] people calling up to say, 'Glad you came today,' " Balfanz says.

One of the biggest problems is the kind of "student mobility" experienced by Jeanette, the Houston dropout.

"Homelessness is much underreported," says James F. Lytle, a professor at the University of Pennsylvania and former school superintendent in Trenton, N.J. "Statistics are based on who's in shelters and on the streets. But 20 to 30 percent of our kids were living in 'serial households' on a day-to-day basis," or moving about from parents to grandparents to relatives to friends — not living in the same house all the time.

Inner-city schools have a 40 to 50 percent student-mobility rate, which means up to half the students change schools at least once a year because of parents losing or changing jobs, evictions and other factors, says Columbia University's Henig. That disrupts students' ability to keep up with work and build relationships with the adults in a school.

In addition, city students miss school for a wide range of reasons, including high asthma rates; lack of school buses, forcing kids to get to school on their own, often through unsafe neighborhoods; and family responsibilities, like caring for younger siblings.

"Imagine the teacher's dilemma in a classroom where the population is different every day," says Balfanz.

But some conservative analysts argue that a large proportion of high-needs students is still no reason for schools to fail.

"Schools frequently cite social problems like poverty . . . and bad parenting as excuses for their own poor performance," said Jay P. Greene, a senior fellow at the Manhattan Institute, a conservative think tank. "This argument that schools are helpless in the face of social problems is not supported by hard evidence. . . . The truth is that certain schools do a strikingly better job than others," including public, private and charter schools.[8]

Some educators say one solution for low-quality urban schools is establishing publicly funded "charter" schools and awarding vouchers for private-school tuition.[9] When choice is expanded, "urban public schools that once had a captive clientele must improve the education they provide or else students . . . will go elsewhere," said Greene.[10]

But others argue that lessons from successful urban schools, including charters, demonstrate that raising low-income students' achievement requires resources and staff commitment that may be tough for the nation to muster.

"Teachers in high-poverty urban schools are as much as 50 percent more likely to . . . leave than those in low-poverty schools," in part because of the intensity of the work, according to researchers at the University of California, Santa Cruz.[11]

A second-grade teacher fluent in Spanish who reported working 10 hours a day, six days a week said she'd probably stop teaching when she had children: "It's too time-consuming and energy-draining," she said.[12]

"None of the teachers in our sample could conceive of being a successful urban teacher without an extraordinary — perhaps unsustainable — commitment to the work," the researchers commented.[13]

Not just schools but communities must help in the effort to improve students' performance.

"There ought to be a parade through the heart of town" every time a student achieves an academic goal, says Hugh B. Price, a fellow at the Brookings Institution, a liberal think tank. "We need to wrap and cloak kids in this message of achievement." That's how the military successfully trains soldiers, Price says. "They will praise anything that's good."

Schools and communities also have a role in helping parents better equip their children for school, says Mayor Douglas H. Palmer of Trenton, N.J., president of the National Conference of Democratic Mayors. "You don't have to be rich to talk to your child, help her build vocabulary and learn to reason and negotiate," as psychologists recommend, he says. "We can help parents with these skills."

As educators and lawmakers debate the next steps to improving urban schools, here are some of the questions being asked:

Has the No Child Left Behind law helped urban students?

NCLB was intended to improve overall academic achievement and raise achievement for minority and low-income students, in particular, mainly by requiring more student testing, getting schools to report test data separately for student groups including minorities and the poor and requiring schools to employ better-qualified teachers.

The law, scheduled for reauthorization this year, gets praise for focusing attention on the so-called achievement gap between minority and low-income students and their middle-class counterparts. But critics say the legislation doesn't do enough to assure that low-performing urban schools get the excellent teachers they need.

Student achievement also has improved slightly under the law, some advocates point out. "Is NCLB really paying off? The answer is yes," U.S. Chamber of Commerce Senior Vice President Arthur J. Rothkopf told a joint House-Senate committee hearing on March 13. While current testing data is still "abysmal," it nevertheless "represents improvement from where this nation was" before the law.

The law has benefited urban schools by raising reading scores for African-American and Hispanic fourth- and eighth-graders and math scores for African-American and Hispanic fourth-graders to "all-time highs." Achievement gaps in reading and math between white fourth-graders and African-American and Hispanic fourth-graders also have diminished since NCLB, he noted.[14]

NCLB's data-reporting requirements have "lifted the carpet" to reveal two previously unrecognized facts about American education — "the continuing underperformance of the whole system and the achievement gap" for low-income and minority students, says Daniel A. Domenech, senior vice president and top urban-education adviser for publisher McGraw-Hill Education and former superintendent of Virginia's vast Fairfax County Public Schools.[15]

And while some critics complain that NCLB gave the federal government too much say over education — traditionally a state and local matter — "there needs to be a strong federal role for these kids" in low-income urban schools "because they have been left behind," says Gary Ratner, a public-interest lawyer who is founding executive director of the advocacy group Citizens for Effective Schools. "States and localities have not stepped up."

Now NCLB "has got the country's attention," and when Congress reauthorizes the law, "the federal role can

be redirected to focus on Title I schools" — those serving a large proportion of disadvantaged students — "and do more of the things that professional educators support," Ratner says.

NCLB's requirement that every school "have very qualified teachers is good," says Gary Orfield, a professor of social policy at the Harvard Graduate School of Education and director of The Civil Rights Project.

But critics argue that NCLB doesn't put muscle behind the high-quality teacher requirement and sets unrealistic goals and timetables for school progress.

NCLB actually "incentivizes teachers to leave failing schools," the last thing lawmakers intended, says Jennifer King-Rice, an economist who is associate professor of education policy at the University of Maryland, College Park. "Teachers say, 'I can't produce the AYP [average yearly progress] results' " the law calls for in low-performing schools with few resources and, frustrated, go elsewhere, she says. Nevertheless, it's still unclear whether and how the government can enforce the qualified-teacher rule.

The law provides no additional funding to help schools meet the teacher-quality goal, said Richard J. Murnane, professor of education and society at the Harvard Graduate School of Education. "Teaching in these schools is extremely difficult work," and "very few school districts provide extra pay or other inducements to attract talented teachers to these schools.[16]

"As a result, all too often these schools are left with the teachers other schools don't want," he continued. "And the teachers who do have options exercise seniority rights to leave . . . as soon as they can."[17]

The achievement targets set by NCLB are panned by many. The main goal schools must meet is moving kids over a standardized-testing threshold from "basic" or "below basic" understanding of reading and math to a "proficient" level or above. But focusing on that narrow goal as the key measure by which schools are judged created bad incentives to game the system, many analysts say.

Rather than concentrating on raising overall achievement or trying to give the most help to students who score lowest, many schools concentrate "on students who are on the bubble" — those who need to raise their scores by only a few points to move into the "proficient" range — and "forget the others," says Patrick McQuillan, an associate professor of education at Boston College's Lynch

Minority Enrollment and Teacher Quality

In Illinois, 88 percent of the schools that were virtually 100 percent minority ranked in the lowest quartile of the state's Teacher Quality Index (graph at left). By comparison, only 1 percent of the all-minority schools ranked in the highest quartile (right). High-quality teachers have more experience, better educations and stronger academic skills. Similar patterns are found in most other states.

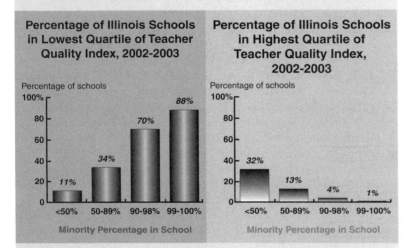

Percentage of Illinois Schools in Lowest Quartile of Teacher Quality Index, 2002-2003

Percentage of schools

	<50%	50-89%	90-98%	99-100%
	11%	34%	70%	88%

Minority Percentage in School

Percentage of Illinois Schools in Highest Quartile of Teacher Quality Index, 2002-2003

Percentage of schools

	<50%	50-89%	90-98%	99-100%
	32%	13%	4%	1%

Minority Percentage in School

Source: "Teaching Inequality: How Poor and Minority Students Are Shortchanged on Teacher Quality," The Education Trust, June 2006

School of Education. Schools that succeed at pushing the scores of "bubble" students up by a few points are deemed successful, according to current NCLB standards, even if they leave the neediest students even farther behind, he says.

The law's pronouncement that 100 percent of U.S. students will test at the "proficient" level is simply unrealistic, some critics say.

"We've never fully funded education in the United States," and achievement continues to lag far below the "proficient" level, especially for low-income students, says Domenech. So "let's not kid around and say that by 2014" all students will be academically proficient, he says. "That's like saying, 'I'm going to push you out the window, and I know you can fly.' "

Furthermore, NCLB's focus on a handful of standardized tests as the sole measures of children's progress puts teachers in an ethical bind that "definitely lowers their morale," says Marshalita Sims Peterson, an associate professor of education at Atlanta's Spelman College,

an historically black school for women.

Teachers in training are taught that students are individuals with a wide variety of learning styles, and that no single assessment can define a student, says Peterson. The NCLB's excessive focus on a single measurement of achievement "leaves the teacher in an awful position" she says. "You need to keep the job, but when you are actually completing that form" stating the single score "for a third-grader, you're asking, 'Is that all there is to this child?' "

Should governments make schools more racially and economically diverse?

Today, most African-American and Latino students attend urban schools with a high concentration of low-income students and very few white classmates.

Some advocates argue that the country has backtracked to an era of separate but unequal schools and say government programs aimed at creating more racially and socioeconomically diverse schools are good tools for narrowing the achievement gap. Opponents of government interference with children's attendance at neighborhood schools argue that with residential neighborhoods increasingly segregated by race and income, school integration is unrealistic, and that governments should focus instead on improving achievement in urban schools.[18]

"The effort to get the right racial balance is misguided" and represents a kind of "liberal racism — a belief that black children need to be in school with white children to learn," says Stephan Thernstrom, a history professor at Harvard University and a fellow at the conservative Manhattan Institute.

If integration "can be managed naturally, that's fine, but there is no clear correlation that can be drawn from data" showing it's important for closing the achievement gap, Thernstrom says. He rejects as incomplete and flawed studies that suggest integration does make a big difference. Furthermore, "if you need a white majority to learn," learning will soon be impossible in America, since Hispanic, Asian and African-American populations are growing faster than the current white majority, he notes.

Racial concentration is not the same as segregation and doesn't stand in the way of achievement, said his wife, Manhattan Institute Senior Fellow Abigail Thernstrom. School districts are powerless to change housing demographics, making it highly unlikely that racial concentration of students ever could be ended, she said.[19]

Some school districts are attempting to integrate lower-income and higher-income students, rather than integrating schools based on race. But Abigail Thernstrom argued that giving children a longer commute to schools outside their neighborhoods, for any reason, simply wastes time better spent in the classroom. "Busing doesn't raise the level of achievement," she told C-SPAN. "Now they're going to start busing on the basis of social class. And I have a very simple view of that. Stop moving the kids around and teach them."[20]

Meanwhile, some charter schools — such as the Knowledge Is Power Program (KIPP), begun in Houston — are making great strides in reducing the urban achievement gap, and for the most part those schools are not racially integrated, wrote *New York Times Magazine* features editor Paul Tough last year.

Most of the 70 schools that make up the three charter networks he observed have "only one or two white children enrolled, or none at all," he noted. Leaders of the networks, all of them white, actually intend to educate their students separately from middle-class students, according to Tough. However, unlike those who've argued that schools can be "separate but equal," the successful high-intensity charter schools aim for "separate but better." Their founders argue that

Blacks, Hispanics Attend High-Poverty Schools

Black and Hispanic students are more likely to be concentrated in high-poverty schools than white students. Forty-seven percent of black and 51 percent of Hispanic fourth-graders were in the highest-poverty schools in 2003 vs. 5 percent of white fourth-graders. By contrast, only 6 percent of black and Hispanic fourth-graders were in the lowest-poverty schools compared with 29 percent of whites.

Percentage of Fourth-Graders in High-Poverty Schools
(Based on proportion eligible for free or reduced-price lunch)

| Poverty Level: | ■ 10% or less | 11-25% | ■ 26-50% | 51-75% | □ More than 75% |

Source: "The Condition of Education 2004 in Brief" National Center for Education, June 2004

"students who enter middle school significantly behind grade level don't need the same good education that most American middle-class students receive; they need a better education," he said.[21]

But many advocates argue that data show a proven way to improve education for thousands of low-income students rather than for the handful that attend the highly successful charter schools is integration of minority and poor students with middle-class children.

School desegregation by race "has clear academic benefits," wrote R. Scott Baker, an associate professor of education at Wake Forest University. Data from Charlotte, N.C., show that the longer both black and white students spent in desegregated elementary schools, the higher their standardized test scores in middle and high school. Research also suggests that "where school desegregation plans are fully and completely implemented," local housing also becomes more integrated.[22]

In the 1960s and '70s some federal courts mandated programs to help urban minority families move to middle-class white suburbs. Long-term data from those cases show that children who moved did better than those who stayed behind, according to Howell S. Baum, a professor of urban studies and planning at the University of Maryland. In St. Louis, 50 percent of the black students who moved to the suburbs graduated from high school, compared to 26 percent of those who remained in the high-minority, low-income urban schools.[23]

Many policy analysts agree that segregating low-income children in some public schools "perpetuates failure," wrote the Century Foundation's Task Force on the Common School. Nevertheless, there is an "equally durable political consensus that nothing much can be done about it." The panel argued that this must change: "Eliminating the harmful effects of concentrated school poverty is the single most important step that can be taken for improving education in the United States."[24]

"Dozens of studies" dating back to the 1960s "find that low-income children have . . . larger achievement gains over time when they attend middle-class schools," said the panel.[25]

"The tragedy right now is that places that were once forced to [integrate their schools] now aren't allowed to," says Orfield of The Civil Rights Project. "That will be seen as a cosmic blunder" for white Americans as well, he said. "We're not preparing ourselves for the multiracial society and world" of the 21st century.

Are teachers prepared to teach successfully in urban classrooms?

Urban schools have high teacher turnover, low test scores and many reported discipline problems. Furthermore, most of America's teaching force still consists of white, middle-class women, while urban schoolchildren are low-income minorities, creating a culture gap that may be hard to bridge.

Consequently, some analysts argue that today's teachers aren't prepared to teach successfully in urban classrooms for a variety of reasons, from discipline to second-language issues. Others, however, point to sterling examples of teachers and schools that do succeed and argue that the real problem is teachers not following good examples.

Fifth-grade teacher Rafe Esquith, at the Hobart Elementary School in central Los Angeles, routinely coaches his urban Korean and Central American-immigrant students to top standardized-test scores. Furthermore, his classes produce Shakespearean plays so impressive they've been invited to perform with Britain's Royal Shakespeare Company, said Abigail Thernstrom.[26]

But despite Esquith's success, "nobody copies him," even in his own school, said Thernstrom. "I went to the fifth-grade [classroom] next door [to Esquith's] one day," and "it was perfectly clear nothing was going on." When Thernstrom suggested the teacher might copy Esquith's methods — which include beginning class as early as 6 a.m. and working with students at his home on weekends — he remarked that "it's an enormous amount of work."[27]

Today, around the country, "we do have shining examples" of schools that succeed at urban education, says Timothy Knowles, executive director of the University of Chicago's Center for Urban School Improvement and a former deputy school superintendent in Boston.

Ratner, of Citizens for Effective Schools, agrees. "I spent time in an elementary school in Chicago a few years ago where all the teachers were teaching reading," even at the upper grades, equipping students with the vocabulary and comprehension skills needed for future academic work, he says. "They had a good principal, and they were showing that it can be done."

But while successful urban schools and classrooms are out there, many education analysts say the know-how and resources needed to spread that success to millions of students are sorely lacking.

Some individual schools are closing the achievement gap for needy students, but "very few, if any" entire school districts have had equivalent success, says Knowles.

Charter schools also haven't seen their successes spread as widely as many hoped.

Out of Ohio's "300-plus charter schools," for example, "some . . . are indeed excellent, but too many are appalling," wrote analysts Terry Ryan and Quentin Suffran of the conservative Thomas B. Fordham Foundation in a recent report.[28]

There are reasons for that, said Mark Simon, director of the Center for Teacher Leadership at Johns Hopkins University, in Baltimore. "Teaching lower-class kids well is tougher than teaching middle-class kids." Furthermore, "it is surprising how little we know about teaching practices that cause students to succeed, particularly in high-poverty schools."[29]

"You have poverty in many districts, but in urban schools you have a concentration of it" that makes teaching successfully there much harder than in middle-class suburbs, says Timothy Shanahan, professor of urban education at the University of Illinois at Chicago and president of the International Reading Association. Schools are traditionally set up to deal with 15 to 20 percent of a student body having very high needs, says Shanahan. But urban schools usually have 50 percent or more of their students needing special attention of some kind, "and that's a huge burden on the teachers," he says.

"Literally, we have 5-year-olds who come into the Chicago school system not knowing their own names," he says. "I know local neighborhoods with gang problems, where the kids are up all night. Their mothers are hiding them under the bed to protect them from shootings in the street. Then teachers can't keep them awake in class."

The nation's rapidly growing Hispanic population is heavily concentrated in urban schools. That new phenomenon presents another tough obstacle for the urban teaching force, because "older teachers know nothing about working with non-native English speakers," says McQuillan of Boston College.

Not just language but race complicates urban-school teaching. As many as 81 percent of all teacher-education students are white women.[30]

"Those most often entering teaching continue to be white, monolingual, middle-class women," wrote Jocelyn A. Glazier, assistant professor of education at the University of North Carolina at Chapel Hill.[31]

Many teachers, especially white women, shy away from making tough demands on African-American students, according to a survey of urban community leaders by Wanda J. Blanchett, associate professor of urban special education at the University of Wisconsin, Milwaukee. "Especially with African-American males, you hear the teachers say, 'Oh, he is such a nice kid.' But . . . this irks me when teachers baby their students to death instead of pushing. . . . I get that a lot when you have white teachers who have never worked with black students from the urban environment."[32]

Many entering education students at Indiana University-Purdue University, in Indianapolis, balked at the school's fieldwork and student-teaching venues,

which were in urban schools, wrote Professor Christine H. Leland and Professor Emeritus Jerome C. Harste. "They saw our program's urban focus as an obstacle to their career goals" of teaching in schools like the suburban ones most had attended.[33]

Some viewed urban students as an alien race they didn't want to learn to know. "Students rarely felt the need to interrogate their underlying assumption that poor people deserve the problems they have" or "spent any time talking or thinking about issues such as poverty or racism," Leland and Harste wrote. After student teaching, however, some students changed their plans and applied to become urban teachers.[34]

Race is a taboo subject in America, which some analysts say compounds urban teachers' difficulties. Many teacher-preparation programs center on an effort not to see or at least not to acknowledge race differences, according to Glazier. But "by claiming not to notice [race], the teacher is saying that she is dismissing one of the most salient features of a child's identity."[35]

"Many teachers believe that if they recognize a student's race or discuss issues of ethnicity in their classroom, they might be labeled as insensitive and racist," wrote Central Michigan University graduate student in education Dreyon Wynn and Associate Dean Dianne L. H. Mark. But white teachers' deliberate color-blindness ignores students "unique culture, beliefs, perceptions, [and] values," blocking both learning and helpful student-teacher relationships, Mark and Wynn argue.[36]

BACKGROUND

Educating the Poor

American education has long struggled with providing equal education for the poor, racial minorities and non-English-speaking immigrants. Until recently, however, even people who never made it through high school could usually find a good job. A new, global, technical economy may be changing that.

In the earliest years in the United States, schooling wasn't widespread. A farm-based economy made extensive education unnecessary for most people. In 1805, more than 90 percent of Americans had completed a fifth-grade education or less, and education for richer people was often conducted by private tutors.[37]

1950s-1960s *Concerns grow over student achievement and racially segregated schools.*

1954 Supreme Court rules in *Brown v. Board of Education* that separate schools are inherently unequal.

1965 Title I of the new Elementary and Secondary Education Act (ESEA) targets the largest pool of federal education assistance to help schools serving disadvantaged students.

1966 Sociologist James S. Coleman's "Equality of Educational Opportunity" report concludes that disadvantaged African-American students do better in integrated classrooms.

1969 National Assessment of Educational Progress (NAEP) tests launched but report statewide average scores only, allowing states to mask lagging achievement among poor and minority students.

1970s-1980s *Latinos are becoming most segregated minority in U.S. schools. "Magnet schools" are established. School integration efforts gradually end.*

1973 Supreme Court rules in *San Antonio Independent School District v. Rodriguez* the Constitution does not guarantee equal education for all children. . . . In *Keyes v. School District No. 1*, the court bans city policies that segregate Denver schools.

1990s-2000s *Steady gains in African-American students' test scores over the past two decades begin to taper off by decade's end. . . . Poverty concentrates in cities. . . . Governors lead efforts to raise education standards.*

1990 New Jersey Supreme Court rules in *Abbott v. Burke* the state must provide more funding for poor schools than for richer ones.

1991 Minnesota enacts first charter-school law.

1994 In reauthorizing ESEA, Congress requires states receiving Title I funding for disadvantaged students to hold them to the same academic standards as all students.

1995 Knowledge Is Power Program charter schools launched in Houston and New York City. . . . Boston creates Pilot School program to research ideas for urban-school improvement.

1999 Florida establishes first statewide school-voucher program.

2000 Countywide, income-based school integration launched in Raleigh, N.C.

2002 Cambridge, Mass., schools begin integration based on income.

2002 No Child Left Behind Act (NCLB) requires states to report student test scores "disaggregated" by race, income and gender to avoid masking the failing scores of some groups. . . . U.S. Supreme Court rules in favor of Ohio's school-voucher program, which allows public funding for tuition at Cleveland parochial schools. . . . State takes over Philadelphia's bankrupt school system, allows private companies to run some schools.

2005 Hoping to halt isolation of the lowest-income students in inner-city schools, Omaha, Neb., tries but fails to annex neighboring suburban districts.

2006 Department of Education admits that few students in failing city schools receive the free tutoring NCLB promised and that no states have met the 2006 deadline for having qualified teachers in all classrooms. . . . Government Accountability Office finds that nearly one-third of public schools, most in low-income and minority communities, need major repairs.

2007 Gov. Deval L. Patrick, D-Mass., puts up $6.5 million to help schools lengthen their hours. . . . Democratic Mayor Adrian Fenty, of Washington, D.C., is the latest of several mayors to take control of schools. . . . New York City Schools Chancellor Joel Klein says he will fire principals of schools with lagging test scores. . . . Teachers' unions slam report calling for all high-school seniors to be proficient in reading and math by 2014. . . . Houston school district calls for state to replace NCLB-related standardized periodic testing on math and reading with traditional end-of-course subject-matter exams.

2007

June 2007 — U.S. Supreme Court invalidates school-attendance-zone plans used in Seattle and Louisville to achieve greater racial diversity. The 5-4 ruling in *Parents Involved in Community Schools v. Seattle Dist. No. 1* said the Seattle School District's plan to use race as a consideration in student assignments was unconstitutional.

2008

Nov. 26, 2008 — Washington, D.C., School Chancellor Michelle Rhee appears on the cover of Time.

2009-2010 *Educational reforms have been made by 28 states under the administration's $4 billion state grant education initiative, Race to the Top. The number of reforms is triple that of the previous two years.*

2009 — Education Secretary Arne Duncan rescinds pending scholarships under the D.C. Opportunity Scholarship Program, and Congress declines to reauthorize.

2010 — Obama administration unveils its blueprint to overhaul No Child Left Behind Act. . . . In the District of Columbia in June, school officials and the teachers' union finalize a contract that, in addition to granting a retroactive pay increase, requires all teachers in the system to be evaluated in part on whether their students' test scores improve, and offers sizable pay increases to teachers who opt for and succeed in a special new pay-for-performance arrangement. . . . Civil Rights Project at UCLA reviews school integration efforts and calls on the Obama administration to issue guidance on how race can be considered in public education. . . . Washington, D.C., School Chancellor Rhee dismisses 241 teachers.

2011 Thirty-seven states provide less funding to local schools than in the 2010-2011 school year.

January — Newly elected Republican governors and legislators in states including Wisconsin, Ohio, Indiana, Idaho, New Jersey and Florida propose bills to lower costs and improve education by ending teacher tenure, limiting teachers' collective bargaining rights, instituting merit pay and firing teachers based on student-achievement test results.

March — *USA Today* reports possible evidence of cheating on standardized tests at Washington, D.C., schools.

May — Georgia Bureau of Investigation reports that 178 teachers and principals in Atlanta conspired to change student-achievement test scores.

November — U.S. Department of Education data show that many districts don't provide high-poverty schools with resources equal to those provided to schools in wealthier neighborhoods.

2012

March — For the fourth consecutive year, many teachers in the Los Angeles and San Francisco school districts receive warnings that their jobs are at risk.

May — A committee of the Illinois legislature supports requiring school districts to provide more funding for charter schools; Chicago Teachers Union campaigns against the proposal. . . . Schools nationwide perform poorly on a science-achievement test, but black and Hispanic students slightly narrow the gap between their scores and those of white students. . . . Federal Communications Commission announces it will inform phone companies that they must follow a 15-year-old rule requiring them to give schools bargain prices so more can afford good Internet access.

2013

January 1 — Urban schools could face major cuts in federal Title I funds if Congress doesn't resolve a budget stalemate.

Dropouts' Problems Often Begin Early

Clear warning signs appear, such as skipping class

With the baby-boom generation on the verge of retirement, sustaining the American workforce and economy depends on having a cadre of new young workers to replace them, says former Gov. Bob Wise, D-W.Va., now president of the Alliance for Excellent Education. But with jobs in the fastest-growing economic sectors now requiring at least a high-school diploma and, often, two years or more of post-high-school training, coming up with an adequately trained new workforce won't be easy, Wise says.

The annual graduation rate has risen from a little over 50 percent per year in the late 1960s to 73.9 percent in 2003. If it's to rise higher, however, the improvement must come among poor and minority students, mostly in urban schools, who are far less likely than others to earn diplomas.[1]

For example, while about two-thirds of all students who enter ninth grade graduate four years later, on-time graduation rates for minority and low-income students, especially males, are much lower. In 2001, for example, only about 50 percent of African-American students and 51 percent of Latino students graduated on time, compared to 75 percent of white students and 77 percent of Asian and Pacific Islanders.[2]

Students with family incomes in the lowest 20 percent dropped out of school at six times the average rate of wealthier students.[3]

In about a sixth of American high schools, the freshman class routinely shrinks by 40 percent or more by the time students reach senior year. For the most part, those schools serve low-income and minority students. Nearly half of African-American students, 40 percent of Latino students and 11 percent of white students attend high schools where

graduation is not the norm. A high school with a majority of students who are racial or ethnic minorities is five times more likely to promote only 50 percent or fewer freshmen to senior status within four years than a school with a white majority.[4]

Meanwhile, the earning power of dropouts has been dropping for three decades. For example, the earnings of male dropouts fell by 35 percent between 1971 and 2002, measured in 2002 dollars. Three-quarters of state prison inmates and 59 percent of federal inmates are dropouts. In 2001, only 55 percent of young adult dropouts were employed. Even the death rate is 2.5 times higher for people without a high-school education than for people with 13 years or more of schooling.[5]

But if the consequences are known, the cures may be harder to pinpoint.

Many educators say dropping out starts early. "Disengagement doesn't start in the ninth grade. It starts in fifth," says James F. Lytle, a University of Pennsylvania professor and former superintendent of the Trenton, N.J., public schools. For on-track students in middle-class schools, "middle school has the most interesting, exciting stuff in class" — science experiments, readings about interesting people in history and studies "of how the world works" — he says.

But once students are judged to be reading behind grade level, as happens with many urban fifth-graders, middle schools turn to "dumbed-down remedial work" that's below students' real intellectual level and leaves them bored and dispirited, Lytle says. It doesn't have to be that way, he says. "But I wish that educational courseware was farther down the road" of providing ways to combine skills teaching with subject matter that is at students' actual age level.

State legislatures were just beginning to debate whether to establish free tax-funded schools for all children.[38] Nevertheless, even in those early days, some religious and other charitable groups considered it a moral duty to educate the poor. In New York City, for example, the Association of Women Friends for the Relief of the Poor opened a charity school in 1801. By 1823 the group was providing free elementary education for 750 children,

with some public assistance. Similar charity schools sprang up in most other major cities.

But as all states began establishing public education systems — between the late 18th and the mid-19th century — questions over equality in education arose, first for black students and later for immigrants. "When public schools opened in Boston in the late 18th century, black children were neither barred nor segregated,"

"Kids disengage early," says Lalitha Vasudevan, an assistant professor at Columbia University's Teachers College who works in an education program for young African-American males who've been diverted from jail and are mostly dropouts. "Often, early on, they've had teachers say things to them that they interpret as, 'You don't really care that I'm here,' " she says.

Dropping out "is not a decision that is made on a single morning," says a report from the Bill & Melinda Gates Foundation. In an extensive survey of dropouts, researchers found that "there are clear warning signs for at least one-to-three years" before students drop out, such as frequently missing school, skipping class, being held back a grade or frequently transferring among schools.[6]

Some key factors cited by the dropouts in the Gates study: Schools don't respond actively when students skip class and don't provide an orderly and safe environment. "In middle school, you have to go to your next class or they are going to get you," said a young male dropout from Philadelphia. "In high school, if you don't go to class, there isn't anybody who is going to get you. You just do your own thing."[7]

Lytle says cities could also establish post-dropout academies, like the Dropout Recovery High School he started in Trenton, which helped increase that city's graduation numbers.

"Rather than defining the whole problem as stopping dropouts, we can also reach out to those who already have," he says. "There are a slew of people around" who are out of school and would like to go back, from teenage mothers caring for their children to 60-year-olds, he says. "They need a school that is built around their lives. I simply don't understand why urban districts haven't been more imaginative" about this.

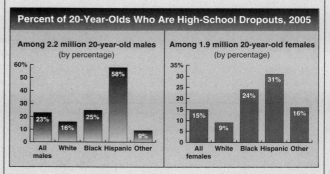

Majority of Dropouts Are Hispanic, Black

More than 50 percent of 20-year-old male high-school dropouts are Hispanic or African-American (graph at left). By comparison, 55 percent of the females are black or Hispanic (graph at right).

Percent of 20-Year-Olds Who Are High-School Dropouts, 2005

Among 2.2 million 20-year-old males (by percentage): All males 23%, White 16%, Black 25%, Hispanic 58%, Other 9%

Among 1.9 million 20-year-old females (by percentage): All females 15%, White 9%, Black 24%, Hispanic 31%, Other 16%

Source: "The Costs and Benefits of an Excellent Education for All of America's Children," Teachers College, Columbia University, January 2007

[1] Nancy Martin and Samuel Halperin, *Whatever It Takes: How Twelve Communities are Reconnecting Out-of-School Youth,* American Youth Policy Forum, www.aypf.org/publications/WhateverItTakes/WITfull.pdf.

[2] *Ibid.*

[3] *Ibid.*

[4] Robert Balfanz and Nettie Legters, "Locating the Dropout Crisis," Center for Social Organization of Schools, Johns Hopkins University, June 2004.

[5] Martin and Halperin, *op. cit.*

[6] John M. Bridgeland, John J. DiIulio, Jr. and Karen Burke Morison, *The Silent Epidemic: Perspectives of High School Dropouts*, Bill & Melinda Gates Foundation, March 2006.

[7] Quoted in *ibid.*

wrote Derrick Bell, a visiting professor at the New York University School of Law. "But by 1790, racial insults and mistreatment had driven out all but three or four black children."[39]

Later, some black families joined with white liberals to form black-only schools in Massachusetts and in other states. But complaints about poor conditions and poor teaching in those schools led others to sue for integrated education.

Even in the early 19th century, some courts were bothered by race-based inequities in education, said Bell. A federal court struck down a Kentucky law directing that school taxes collected from white people would maintain white schools, and taxes from blacks would operate black schools. "Given the great disparities in taxable resources" this would result in an inferior education for black children, the court said.[40]

The "Behavior Gap" Between Black and White Students

Many educators blame a system that's middle-class and white-centered

Data from around the country indicate that black students, especially males, are cited much more often for disciplinary infractions than whites. The resulting "behavior gap" parallels the much-talked-about academic achievement gap.

Many analysts blame the phenomenon in part on a "culture clash" between black students, many poor, and an education system that's white-centered and middle-class. But there's little agreement about exactly what the gap means and what to do about it.

"You find the gap in all schools," including wealthy ones, says Clara G. Muschkin, a researcher at the Duke University Center for Child and Family Policy. Nevertheless, some evidence suggests there may also be a behavior gap between richer and poorer students, which accounts for just under a third of the black-white gap, Muschkin says.

In North Carolina schools, the racial gap "is persistent at all the grades" but is widest in seventh grade, says Muschkin. About 30 percent of black seventh-graders and 14 percent of whites have at least one disciplinary infraction reported during the school year.

African-American male students have the highest rates of suspensions and expulsions in most metropolitan areas around the country, according to Denise L. Collier, a doctoral candidate in education at California State University, Los Angeles. In New York, for example, where African-American males are 18 percent of the student population, they account for 39 percent of school suspensions and 50 percent of expulsions. In Los Angeles, black males make up 6 percent of the population but account for 18 percent of suspensions and 15 percent of expulsions.[1]

Some educators say that many urban African-American students don't learn at home the kinds of communication behaviors that are the norm for the middle class, and that this lack of background accounts for much of the gap.

"Americans of a certain background learn . . . early on and employ . . . instinctively" techniques like sitting up straight, asking questions and tracking a speaker with their eyes in order to take in information, said David Levin, a founder of the Knowledge Is Power Program (KIPP) charter schools, which serve mainly black and Hispanic students in several cities.[2]

When students in one Levin class were asked to "give us the normal school look," they responded by staring off into space and slouching, recounted *New York Times Magazine* editor Paul Tough in an article last year on successful urban charter schools. "Middle-class Americans know intuitively that 'good behavior' is mostly a game with established rules; the KIPP students seemed to be experiencing the pleasure of being let in on a joke," Tough observed.[3]

Behavior like a proper in-school work ethic has to be taught "in the same way we have to teach adding fractions with unlike denominators," said Dacia Toll, founder of the Amistad Academy charter school in New Haven, Conn. "But once children have got the work ethic and the commitment to others and to education down, it's actually pretty easy to teach them."

The academic gap that puts many black students in remedial instruction as they move through school may worsen the problem, says Robert Balfanz, associate research scientist at the Johns Hopkins University Center on the Social Organization of Schools. "In traditional remedial

---

Around the 1820s, waves of non-English immigration began, raising new controversies over educating poor children of sometimes-despised ethnicities.

Before 1820, most U.S. immigrants were English, and a few were Dutch. But between 1820 and 1840 Irish immigrants became the first in a long parade of newcomers judged inferior by the predominantly English population. A rising tide of immigration in the late 19th and early 20th centuries included many non-English-speakers — Italians, Germans, Chinese, Russians, Poles and many others — who posed new challenges for schools and were looked down on by many citizens.

instruction, I assume you know nothing, so I teach the times table" and basic reading skills like letter sounds, he says. "But the majority of kids behind can actually read at a basic level. What they're missing is comprehension skill, vocabulary. So they get bored and frustrated."

Middle-class education majors student-teaching in urban schools found that using books about topics their students personally had encountered — including homelessness, racism and poverty — decreased discipline problems, even though the teachers initially resisted the books as inappropriate for children, according to Professor Christine H. Leland and Professor Emeritus Jerome C. Harste of Indiana University-Purdue University, Indianapolis. Once the student teachers broached the tough subject matter, they began reporting "fewer discipline problems . . . the children listened carefully and engaged in thoughtful discussions when they perceived that the issues being discussed were worth their attention."[4]

Many African-American student discipline problems involve "defiance" issues such as acting threatening or making excessive noise rather than activities like drug use or leaving the classroom without permission, according to University of Virginia Assistant Professor Anne Gregory.[5]

Seventy-five percent of African-American disciplinary referrals were for "defiance" behaviors in a study Gregory cites, many more than for other ethnic groups. That may suggest that teachers judge African-American students' behavior more "subjectively" than that of other students, Gregory says. Based on their past feelings of being restricted and excluded, some African-American students may be more likely to act out when they perceive that teachers are being unfair, Gregory suggests.

"If I was this little Caucasian boy or this preppy girl, she wouldn't talk with me that way. I am like the opposite. I am this little thug . . . I mean, she don't know," one student in Gregory's study said of a teacher perceived to be unfair.[6]

Avoiding excessive discipline battles in urban schools requires a seemingly contradictory set of characteristics that not everyone can muster, said Franita Ware, a professor of education at Spelman College, a historically black school for women in Atlanta. Teachers who succeed tend to be "warm demanders," those whom "students believed . . . did not lower their standards" but also "were willing to help them."[7]

"Sometimes I mean-talk them in varying degrees of severity," one teacher told Ware. But "sometimes you have to go back and say, 'What was really going on with you when I yelled at you? I'm just so sorry.' "[8]

Often the adult is the provocateur in the behavior situation, even if they don't realize it, such as when a student finds the nurse's office door locked at 3:02 and starts pounding on it, says James F. Lytle, a professor at the University of Pennsylvania and former school superintendent in Trenton, N.J.

"A lot of it is just the way you talk to people — respect," Lytle says. "Many are so accustomed to being denigrated. The kids have so little that the protection of one's ego is very important."

[1] Denise L. Collier, "Sally Can Skip But Jerome Can't Stomp: Perceptions, Practice, and School Punishment (Preliminary Results)," paper presented at the American Educational Research Association annual meeting, San Francisco, Calif., April 2006.

[2] Quoted in Paul Tough, "What It Takes To Make a Student," *New York Times Magazine*, Nov. 26, 2006, p. 51.

[3] *Ibid.*

[4] Christine H. Leland and Jerome C. Harste, "Doing What We Want to Become: Preparing New Urban Teachers," *Urban Education*, January 2005, p. 67.

[5] Anne Gregory, "Justice and Care: Teacher Practices To Narrow the Racial Discipline Gap," paper presented at the American Educational Research Association annual conference, San Francisco, Calif., April 2006.

[6] Quoted in *ibid.*

[7] Franita Ware, "Warm Demander Pedagogy: Culturally Responsive Teaching that Supports A Culture of Achievement for African-American Students," *Urban Education*, July 2006, p. 427.

[8] Quoted in *ibid.*

The new immigrants generally clustered in cities, the economic engines of the time, and overcrowded city schools were charged with integrating them into American life. Critics charged that the urban schools used rigid instruction and harsh discipline to control classrooms bursting with 60 or more children, many of whom spoke no English.

Two Tracks

In the economy of the early 20th century, however, there remained little need for most students to learn more than basic reading and writing, so the failure of poor urban schools to produce many graduates wasn't seen as a problem.

In current debates over U.S. education, "people aren't looking at education historically" and therefore expect American schools to do things they were never designed to do, says Ratner of Citizens for Effective Schools.

"We consciously decided to have a two-track system," he says. In the early 20th century, education experts generally agreed that "in the industrial age there are lots of immigrants and poor people, and most are going to work on the assembly line, so how about if we create an academic track and a general/vocational track" mostly for the poor?

The school system that we have "was never set up to educate all students to the levels of proficiency now being asked for," Ratner says.

"I graduated exactly 40 years ago, and then about half the kids — 52 percent — were graduating," says Wise of the Alliance for Excellent Education. "And the non-graduates could still get good jobs."

But today "the fastest-growing sectors of the economy require two years of post high-school training," says Daniel J. Cardinali, president of Communities In Schools, a dropout-prevention group that helps school districts bring services like tutoring and health care to needy students.

Calls in the 1990s for higher academic standards by groups like The Business Roundtable brought widespread attention to the problems of low student achievement, especially in low-income schools.

Today few question the premise that all students should attain higher levels of literacy, mathematical problem-solving and critical thinking. Many who work in schools argue that simply setting higher standards isn't nearly enough, however, especially for urban schools where most students already are behind grade level.

As standards rise, for example, "ninth-graders are increasingly placed in introductory algebra classes . . . despite skill gaps in fundamental arithmetic," wrote Balfanz and Ruth Curran Neild, research scientists at the Johns Hopkins University Center on the Social Organization of Schools.

But few resources exist to help kids catch up, "nor are there many curriculum materials that specifically target the spotty skills of urban ninth-graders," the Johns Hopkins researchers said. And when students reading behind grade level enter middle and high school, their "secondary-certified English teachers" — educated to teach high-school-level literature and composition — "are generally

unprepared" to diagnose reading problems or to teach the comprehension strategies and background vocabulary they need. Science and history teachers are even less prepared to help, Balfanz and Neild said.[41]

Retooling the school system to support higher standards may seem daunting, but "a quick walk through history" shows that it wouldn't be the first time the United States has made heroic efforts on education, says Wise. For example, "after World War II, you had soldiers coming home in need of better skills, and you had the GI Bill" to help them continue their educations.

Then "in the civil rights era we said, 'We believe that every child should be able to enter school,' and that happened," Wise says. "Now we're saying that every child should graduate."

For a time, the civil rights era seemed to be accelerating growing academic parity in learning, at least between black and white students. Following World War II, standardized test scores for black students began moving closer to white students' scores. The years from the 1960s to the '80s saw fully half of the black-white academic achievement gap eliminated, says The Civil Rights Project's Orfield.

In the late '80s, however, the progress of African-American students in closing the gap stalled, and between 1988 and 1994, average test scores for black students actually began falling.[42]

Minority Schools

U.S. schools briefly became more integrated after the civil rights battles of the 1950s and '60s, but shifting housing patterns have caused the concentration of poor, minority and non-English-speaking students in urban schools to rise for the past 25 years.

"One thing that's not fully understood is that, through a long historical process, we've concentrated our most needy students in a small subset of schools and districts" in rural and, mostly, urban areas, vastly increasing the burden those schools face in raising academic achievement, says Balfanz.

In its landmark 1954 *Brown v. Board of Education* ruling, the Supreme Court declared it illegal to intentionally segregate schools by race.[43] In 1964, Congress passed the Civil Rights Act, outlawing discrimination in any institution that received federal funds, including schools.[44] As a result, more schools accommodated lower-income students along with middle-class students, white students and students from other ethnic groups.

The civil rights era lasted a scant 20 years, however, and housing patterns and new waves of immigration soon led to concentrations of poor and minority students in many urban school districts again.

As early as 1974, the Supreme Court effectively set limits on how far racial integration of students could go. The court ruled in *Milliken v. Bradley* that the remedy to racial segregation in Detroit could not include moving children to schools in the surrounding suburbs.[45]

Then, in the 1980s, federal efforts to desegregate schools effectively ended. During the presidency of Ronald Reagan (1981-1988), the U.S. Justice Department backed off forcing states to comply with desegregation mandates. Two Supreme Court decisions in the early 1990s effectively declared the goal of black-white school integration had been addressed, as the court ruled that school districts could be excused from court-ordered busing if they had made good-faith efforts to integrate, even if they had not fully complied with court orders.[46]

At the same time, however, Hispanic students were becoming a new minority that concentrated in schools with bigger academic challenges than others, such as teaching English-language learners.

The segregation of Latino students soared during the civil rights era. In 1973, in *Keyes v. School District No. 1*, the Supreme Court outlawed policies in Denver that had the effect of segregating Hispanic and African-American children into separate schools. In ensuing years, however, this somewhat complex ruling was only spottily enforced, according to civil rights advocates.[47]

Today Latinos "are America's most segregated minority group," said Orfield. The average Latino student goes to a school that is less than 30 percent white, has a majority of poor children and an "increasing concentration" of students who don't speak English.[48]

Poor in School

Until around the 1970s, children of all races and classes attended urban schools, and their average achievement levels didn't draw the same alarmed attention as today. Urban sprawl and white flight from cities over the past three decades have not only increased the number of urban schools with high minority populations but also

Edwin Bradley listens to his fifth-grade daughter Antoinette read at the South Street School library in Newark, N.J. One of the poorest in the state, the school district has been encouraged under a new program to support parental involvement in an attempt to improve student performance.

increased the concentration of urban poverty as well, increasing the burden on urban schools.

"Sprawl is a product of suburban pulls and urban pushes," said the University of Maryland's Baum. "Families move to the suburbs for good housing, open space. They leave cities to avoid bad schools, threats to safety . . . contact with other races and poor public services."[49]

Furthermore, minority children are more concentrated in urban areas than the general population, largely because white families with children move to suburbs while childless whites are more likely to remain in the city, said Baum. Nationally, in nearly all school districts with more than 25,000 students, interracial contact has declined since 1986.[50]

Even more than ethnic minorities, poor people have concentrated in cities, says Balfanz. Over the past 20 years, even in periods when overall poverty has dropped, "the cities have gotten poorer and the concentration of poverty there deeper."

Between 1960 and 1987, the national poverty rate for people in central cities rose from 13.4 percent to 15.7 percent. At the same time, the poverty rate for rural residents fell by one-half and for suburban residents by one-third. By 1991, 43 percent of people with incomes below the federal poverty line lived in central cities.[51]

Would raising teacher pay help struggling schools?

YES
Patty Myers
Technology Coordinator,
Great Falls (Montana) Public Schools

From testimony on behalf of the National Education Association before U.S. Senate Committee on Finance, March 20, 2007

Ensuring a highly qualified teacher in every classroom is critical to closing achievement gaps and maximizing student learning. No single factor will make a bigger difference in helping students reach high academic standards. . . .

Unfortunately, difficulty in attracting quality teachers and high turnover rates severely hamper the ability to maintain a high-quality learning environment. Approximately one-third of the nation's new teachers leave the profession during their first three years, and almost one-half leave during their first five years. And turnover in low-income schools is almost one-third higher than the rate in all schools.

The teaching profession has an average national starting salary of $30,377. Meanwhile, computer programmers start at an average of $43,635, public accounting professionals at $44,668 and registered nurses at $45,570.

Annual pay for teachers has fallen sharply over the past 60 years in relation to the annual pay of other workers with college degrees. The average earnings of workers with at least four years of college are now over 50 percent higher than the average earnings of a teacher. Congress should reward states that set a reasonable minimum starting salary for teachers and a living wage for support professionals working in school districts. NEA recommends that all teachers in America enter the classroom earning at least $40,000 annually.

NEA also supports advancing teacher quality at the highest-poverty schools by providing $10,000 federal salary supplements to National Board Certified Teachers. Congress also should fund grants to help teachers in high-poverty schools pay the fees and access professional supports to become certified.

Often schools with the greatest needs and, consequently, the most challenging working conditions have the most difficulty retaining talented teachers. . . . Many hard-to-staff schools are high-poverty inner-city school or rural schools that, as a consequence of their location in economically depressed or isolated districts, offer comparatively low salaries and lack [the] amenities with which other districts attract teachers.

NEA strongly supports federal legislation with financial incentives for teaching in high-poverty schools, such as the Teacher Tax Credit Act introduced in the 109th Congress. The bill would provide a non-refundable tax credit to educators who work at schools that are fully eligible for federal Title I funds for disadvantaged students and would help hard-to-staff schools retain the quality teachers they need to succeed.

NO
Jay P. Greene
Senior Fellow, Manhattan Institute

Posted on the Web, 2006

The common assertion that teachers are severely underpaid is so omnipresent that many Americans simply accept it as gospel. But the facts tell a different story.

The average teacher's salary does seem modest at first glance: about $44,600 in 2002 for all teachers. But when we compare it to what workers of similar skill levels in similar professions are paid, we find that teachers are not shortchanged.

People often fail to account for the relatively low number of hours that teachers work. Teachers work only about nine months per year. During the summer they can either work at other jobs or use the time off however else they wish. Either way, it's as much a form of compensation as a paycheck.

The most recent data indicate that teachers average 7.3 working hours per day, and that they work 180 days per year, or about 1,314 hours. Americans in normal 9-to-5 professions who take two weeks of vacation and another 10 paid holidays put in 1,928 hours. This means the average teacher's base salary is equivalent to a full-time salary of $65,440.

In 2002, elementary-school teachers averaged $30.75 per hour and high-school teachers $31.01 — about the same as architects, civil engineers and computer-systems analysts. Even demanding, education-intensive professions like dentistry and nuclear engineering didn't make much more per hour.

Some argue that it's unfair to calculate teacher pay on an hourly basis because teachers perform a large amount of work at home — grading papers on the weekend, for instance. But people in other professions also do off-site work.

Many assume that teachers spend almost all of the school day teaching. But in reality, the average subject-matter teacher taught fewer than 3.9 hours per day in 2000. This leaves plenty of time for grading and planning lessons.

It is well documented that the people drawn into teaching these days tend to be those who have performed least well in college. If teachers are paid about as well as employees in many other good professions, why aren't more high performers taking it up?

One suspects that high-performing graduates tend to stay away because the rigid seniority-based structure doesn't allow them to rise faster and earn more money through better performance or by voluntarily putting in longer hours. In any case, it's clear that the primary obstacle to attracting better teachers isn't simply raising pay.

"The nation's student population is two-thirds middle class (not eligible for federally subsidized lunches), yet one-quarter of American schools have a majority of students from low-income households," according to The Century Foundation.[52]

Among the burdens urban schools bear are poverty-related learning deficiencies children bring to school with them, regulations and economic barriers that limit urban-school resources, and a historical role as job providers in inner cities.

A large body of research shows that many low-income parents interact with their children in ways that hinder them in school, wrote Tough last year in *The New York Times Magazine.* For example, professional parents speak to their young children about two-and-a-half more times in an hour than poor parents do and encourage them verbally about six times more often than they discourage them; low-income parents discourage their children about three times as often as they encourage them, he said.

Unlike poor parents, middle-class parents also encourage their children to question, challenge and negotiate. In short, "in countless ways, the manner in which [poor children] are raised puts them at a disadvantage" in a school culture, Tough noted.[53]

For a variety of reasons, urban schools also have a much harder time keeping good teachers. "Many thousands — perhaps millions — of urban students don't have permanent, highly qualified teachers, ones with the skill to communicate important stuff to kids," says Kitty Kelly-Epstein, a professor of education at the Fielding Graduate University in Santa Barbara, Calif. In California, at least, state rules force some urban school districts to rely on temporary teachers because not enough applicants have required certifications, she says. "There never has been a time when low-income schools were fully staffed," she says.

With joblessness high in cities, especially for minority applicants, it's also "not uncommon" for school districts to be the major job source in the area, according to Johns Hopkins University Associate Professor of Education Elaine M. Stotko and colleagues. In a tradition that dates back to patronage systems in the early 20th century, urban politicians often interfere with schools' hiring the best managerial and teaching candidates by pressuring them to hand out jobs "as political favors."[54]

The Supreme Court is due to rule by the end of June in two race-based integration cases. With a new conservative majority, the court is widely expected to rule in favor of the white parents who are seeking to end race-based school integration in Seattle and Louisville, Ky. Decisions against the school districts could end many similar programs around the country, many of which were court-ordered in the past.[55]

But some school districts still worry that schools with high concentrations of minority and poor students harm achievement. Over the past several years, a few districts, including Raleigh, N.C., and Cambridge, Mass., have experimented with integrating students by socioeconomic status. In 2000, for example, the school board in Wake County, N.C., which includes Raleigh and its suburbs, replaced its racial integration system with the goal that no school should have 40 percent of students eligible for free or reduced-price lunch.[56]

Raleigh's effort was simpler politically than most, because the school district contains both the area's low-poverty and high-poverty schools. If the higher-income suburbs had been outside the district, political push-back would have made the program a tougher sell.

Some early Raleigh results look promising. On the state's 2005 High School End of Course exams, 63.8 percent of the low-income students passed, as did 64.3 percent of its African-American seniors, compared to pass rates in the high-40 and low 50-percent range for the state's other urban districts.[57]

CURRENT SITUATION

Congress Divided

The No Child Left Behind Act (NCLB), enacted in 2002, is intended to push American schools to raise achievement for all students, including low-income and minority children. As such, it represents one more step down a road that Congress embarked on in its 1994 reauthorization of the Elementary and Secondary Education Act — exerting federal influence to ensure that all students meet higher academic standards.

With NCLB up for reauthorization, Congress is struggling to figure out its next steps, with little apparent agreement on the horizon. With the press of other business, and strong disagreements in Congress about the education law, it's not clear that it will be reauthorized this year. The new congressional Democratic majority has already begun to hold hearings, however.

Newsmakers/Getty Images/Chris Hondros

The Knowledge Is Power Program (KIPP) charter school in the Bronx, N.Y., boasts the highest test scores in the area. Although most KIPP schools are not racially integrated, they are reducing achievement gaps between black and white students.

U.S. businesses have become increasingly involved in education policy, and many business leaders are urging Congress to continue and strengthen federal efforts to raise academic standards and provide incentives for states and localities to extensively retool their school systems to improve student achievement.

"Unless we transform the American high school, we will limit economic opportunities for millions of Americans," declared Microsoft Chairman Bill Gates at a Senate Health, Education, Labor and Pensions Committee hearing on March 7.[58]

Meanwhile, a group of conservative congressional Republicans has introduced legislation that would replace most of the NCLB achievement and reporting requirements that determine funding with block-grant funding that states could get whether they met NCLB standards or not. The measure would restore states and localities to their traditional role as prime overseers of schools, said Rep. Peter Hoekstra, R-Mich., who sponsored the legislation. "President Bush and I just see education fundamentally differently," he said. "The president believes in empowering bureaucrats in Washington, and I don't."[59]

But many congressional Democrats argue that a strengthened federal hand in education is warranted, partly because NCLB data now clearly reveal that the state-run systems of old have left so many poor and minority children disastrously behind.

Rep. George Miller, D-Calif., and Sen. Kennedy, key supporters of NCLB and chairs of the House and Senate committees that govern it, have both held pre-authorization hearings this year. Both say they're committed to increasing resources for struggling schools in a new bill, especially by supporting the hiring and training of more and better teachers.

"We know the law has flaws, but we also know that with common-sense changes and adequate resources, we can improve it by building on what we've learned," said Kennedy in a statement.

Retooling NCLB?

Education analysts have no shortage of changes to suggest.

President Bush is looking at "tinkering" with NCLB in a reauthorization, but Democrats are "interested in something broader," says Cardinali of Communities in Schools. "The [current] law is too fixated on academics," he says. After 30 years of experience helping students get additional services they need like tutoring and health care, "we've learned that student services are a critical component," he says.

"The brutal truth is that there is only one institution in America where you can get to kids in a thoughtful way — the school," he says. "Let's make that the center" where parents and children can get needs met that are critical for learning readiness. "Are we trying to make public education something it's not? No. It's a holistic view" of what it takes to educate a child.

One gap the University of Chicago's Knowles would like to see rectified: In NCLB's reporting requirements "the unit of analysis is the kid, the school and the district, and there's a stunning absence there if we really believe that instruction is at the heart of learning." Research indicates, he says, that individual classroom teachers may be the strongest in-school influence on student achievement.

However, "Democrats' strong ties to labor" helped keep teacher accountability out of the bill, he says.

In addition, "higher ed has been given pretty much a free pass," Knowles says. A future bill should focus attention on which education schools are producing the best-quality teachers.

Low-achieving schools shouldn't be punished, but given the tools to do better, says Knowles. Supports like teacher development and well-integrated extra services like social workers, closely targeted on high-need schools, are a "precondition" for improvement, he says.

Another key: additional flexibility for leaders of low-achieving schools to hire and fire and set policy and schedules. Principals say, "Yeah, you give me the hiring and firing of teachers and I'll give you the better results," and they're correct, says Knowles.

Reporting data for accountability isn't the problem. It's the very narrowly focused reporting requirement, many analysts say.

"Replace the overreliance on standardized testing with multiple measures," such as attendance figures and accurate dropout rates, says the University of Rochester's Hursh.

The federal government should also support strong, unbiased research on what improves instruction, especially in the middle- and high-school years, which are federally funded at a tiny fraction of the level of elementary schools and colleges, says Wise of the Alliance for Excellent Education. "No state or local district has the money for this," he says.

OUTLOOK

Agreeing to Disagree

There's growing agreement that schools should be educating all students to a higher standard. However, there's still disagreement about how much and what kind of help schools would need to do it.

An ideal outcome would be for institutions that are the most lasting presence in cities, such as business groups like the Chamber of Commerce, local hospitals and colleges to take ownership of urban education to drive change, says Balfanz of Johns Hopkins. A movement in that direction may be beginning, he says. "For awhile, there were mainly rhetorical reports," but today groups like the Chamber of Commerce are producing more potentially useful policy work, he says.

"The climate is shifting" toward the conclusion that everyone needs a diploma, says Balfanz. "You can't even find an employer who says, 'I'll hire people who aren't high-school graduates.'" So when students drop out, "it just feeds the next generation of poverty," he says.

There's currently an opportunity to revise NCLB in a way that helps low-achieving schools, says the University of Chicago's Knowles. Nevertheless, "people have already formed hard opinions," and debate could turn solely partisan, he says.

Lawmakers must aim for a delicate balance on federal initiatives, says Columbia's Henig. Federal interventions must aim at "making local processes work," since local on-the-ground actions are ultimately what make or break schools, he says.

The University of Pennsylvania's Lytle fears that privatization may be on the verge of overwhelming education, with potentially disastrous consequences for low-income families.

"I think the K-12 education business is in the process of deconstructing," he says. "The middle class is looking outside the schools" to private tutoring companies and Internet learning for academics. "More and more, for them, schools are amounting to expensive child care." Some states are aggressively pioneering "virtual" online charter schools and charters granted to home-schoolers, he says.

"The cost side and the efficacy side of education are on a collision course, and I think Congress will end up endorsing fairly radical experimentation" with vouchers, for example, Lytle says. "They'll say, 'There's no evidence that reducing class size or other expensive measures helps, so let's let American ingenuity work. Where does that leave urban kids? Out of luck," Lytle says. "You've got to be pretty sophisticated to make market forces work for you."

But "there's been progress in the last decade with whole-school reform," says Balfanz. "The big question now is how we [change] whole school districts. "It's a big job but within human capacity," he says.

2010 UPDATE

An array of forces has slowed long-sought progress in narrowing the minority-student achievement gap among urban schools. Those forces include mixed results in nationwide test scores, three years of delay in reauthorizing the federal No Child Left Behind Act and a pivotal 2007 Supreme Court ruling on school desegregation that, combined with a severe recession, has steered the education debate toward favoring economic considerations over racial equity.

"As a nation we decided long ago against separate but equal, but the reality is we're moving fast to becoming a majority-minority population," former West Virginia Gov. Bob Wise, president of the Alliance for Excellent

Davis Guggenbeim, director of "Waiting Superma," a documentary about the public school in Amercia, and Michelle Rhee, D.C. Public Schools Chancellor, attend the Silverdocs Festival in Silver Spring, Md.

Education, said in a recent interview. "So we need to focus on each child having a quality school no matter where they live." Because the modern economy now requires success by poor children as well as by those bound for higher-paying jobs, Wise said, education reform must link both economic performance and social justice.

The economic pressure on schools continues. A recent study by labor economist Anthony Carnevale of Georgetown University found that two-thirds of the 47 million new jobs he expects the U.S. economy to create between 2008 and 2018 will require workers who have at least some college education.[60] That is a sea change from a half-century ago when nearly two-thirds of jobs were filled by those with only a high school diploma.

The latest student test scores from the nation's urban K-12 schools show some noteworthy but unspectacular improvements. According to a new experimental index of urban student performance in the reading portion of the National Assessment of Educational Progress (NAEP), average reading scores for students in large-city school districts in grades four and eight rose by several points on the proficiency scale between 2003 and 2009, a change that narrowed the achievement gap to 10 points when compared with the national sampling.[61]

Lagging in Math

In math, according to a March analysis of NAEP scores and state tests by the Council of the Great City Schools, 79 percent of districts increased the percentage of fourth-graders who scored at or above proficient between 2006 and 2009, with a fourth of the districts raising scores by more than 10 percent.[62] Yet "despite significant gains in performance and faster rates of improvement than their states," the assessment said, "the majority of urban school districts continue to score below state averages on fourth- and eighth-grade mathematics assessments."

The decades-old assumption that school districts should actively pursue racial integration was challenged by a June 2007 U.S. Supreme Court ruling that invalidated school-attendance-zone plans used in Seattle and metropolitan Louisville to achieve greater diversity. In a 5-4 ruling in *Parents Involved in Community Schools v. Seattle Dist. No. 1*, the majority, in an opinion written by Chief Justice John G. Roberts Jr., said, "The way to stop discrimination on the basis of race is to stop discriminating on the basis of race."[63] Roberts deplored what he saw as an "ends justify the means" approach to achieving integration. "[R]acial classifications," he argued, "are simply too pernicious to permit any but the most exact connection between justification and classification."

The dissent by the court's liberal justices argued that Roberts' opinion undermined the promise of integrated schools the court set down in its 1954 landmark decision in *Brown v. Board of Education*, a change that Justice John Paul Stevens called "a cruel irony." Justice Anthony Kennedy, in a concurring opinion, left open the possibility of a more modest consideration of race in drawing school boundaries.

The court's ruling was hardly the last word, however. In a June 2010 review of school integration efforts since the Supreme Court decision, the Civil Rights Project at UCLA said the "divided decision confused many educators and it was somewhat unclear what did remain legal."[64] It noted that "economic pressure is forcing school districts to make deep cuts in services, which is another potential constraint for integration efforts," and it called on the Obama administration to issue new guidance on how race can be considered.

One of the nation's most troubled urban districts, the District of Columbia, in spring 2010 became the scene for ratification of a highly innovative teachers' contract.

For nearly three years, national attention had focused on the controversial tenure of D.C. Public Schools Chancellor Michelle Rhee. Her efforts at reforming the system's bureaucracy and sweeping away incompetent teachers — she appeared on the Nov. 26, 2008, cover of *Time* holding a broom — had put her at odds with the local branch of the American Federation of Teachers. Her reputation for tough management has attracted private foundation money to help the D.C. schools, and her future in the job became an issue in the current mayoral race.

Further roiling the waters was Rhee's firing of 241 teachers this summer, including 165 who received poor appraisals under a new evaluation system based in part on students' standardized test scores.[65]

Paying for Success

But in June 2010, school officials and the teachers' union finalized a contract that, in addition to granting a retroactive pay increase, requires all teachers in the system to be evaluated in part on whether their students' test scores improve, and it offers sizable pay increases to teachers who opt for and succeed in a special new pay-for-performance arrangement.[66]

D.C.'s special constitutional status that gives Congress a major say in its education policies continued to play a role in the district's efforts to improve results. Since 2004, Congress has funded the D.C. Opportunity Scholarship Program, a unique, federally funded voucher option favored by many conservatives that has given some 3,700 students $7,500 per year to attend any accredited private school that will accept them.[67]

But the Democratic takeover of Congress and the election of President Obama brought a change in priorities. Education Secretary Arne Duncan in 2009 rescinded the pending scholarships, and Congress declined to reauthorize them. An Education Department report found that the voucher program had not demonstrated much impact on test scores, though graduation rates for students in the program topped those of other students in D.C. Public Schools.[68]

Virtually every tool in the school reform grab bag — from charter schools to new teacher-accountability rules to dropout-prevention efforts — will be affected by the long-delayed reauthorization of the Elementary and Secondary Education Act (ESEA), known since 2002 as

No Child Left Behind. The law has long been the center of disputes over reliance on student test scores. Its deadlines for improving student proficiency are seen by many as unrealistic, and critics have considered its funding levels inadequate. The bill has run into a new set of obstacles in the Obama era.

A Call for Flexibility

In a March 15, 2010, "blueprint" to overhaul No Child Left Behind, the Obama team argued that the law had "created incentives for states to lower their standards; emphasized punishing failure over rewarding success; focused on absolute scores, rather than recognizing growth and progress; and prescribed a pass-fail, one-size-fits-all series of interventions for schools that miss their goals." It called for greater flexibility in methodology to turn around some 5,000 schools labeled as underperforming.

But the reauthorization, though the subject of a dozen or more hearings this year in the House and Senate, has continued to divide Congress. One reason is the attention devoted to Obama's competitive $4 billion state grant education initiative, called Race to the Top. It is viewed by some as highly successful in providing incentives to states to enact reforms. Though only Delaware and Tennessee have won grants so far, 28 states have made reforms in 2009 and 2010, or triple the number during the previous two years, according to *Education Week*.[69] Yet in a surprise twist, the ravages to state and local budgets wrought by the current recession prompted the House to pass an emergency jobs bill that would shift funds from Race to the Top to preserve current teacher salaries.

In another division among education reformers, the teachers' unions want to make the rewrite of the law less "punitive" toward teachers and more cognizant of family income disparities. "Today, students' success in school depends in large part on the zip code where they live," National Education Association president Dennis Van Roekel told Congress. "Students who struggle the most in impoverished communities too often don't attend safe schools with reliable heat and air conditioning; too often do not have safe passage to and from school; and far too often do not have access to great teachers on a regular and consistent basis."[70]

Former Gov. Wise worries that if the reauthorization is not completed this year, the nation must continue with the existing No Child Left Behind, which he sees as inflexible and short on help for high schools. The law "focused on where the problems are, and a light has been shined on the fact that students of color or low economic status are not making it," Wise says. "But the law does not have adequate remedies. It's like a compact disc in an iPod world."

2012 UPDATE

As state and local governments continue to grapple with crippling funding shortages — and draconian cuts in federal spending loom — lawmakers and school districts look for economical ways to boost student achievement. Some argue for competition-based strategies such as closing schools and firing teachers based on test scores and allowing privately run charter schools to vie for public funding. Critics of such market-oriented reforms, however, argue that such measures won't solve the problems facing high-poverty urban schools.

Many states have cut their contribution to local school districts since the economic crisis began four years ago.

In the 2011-2012 school year, 37 states were providing less funding per student to local schools than they did in 2010-2011, according to the Center on Budget and Policy Priorities (CBPP), a liberal, nonprofit research group. Thirty states provide less local-school funding than they did four years ago, and 17 have cut per-student funding by more than 10 percent since the recession began in 2008. Four states — South Carolina, Arizona, California and Hawaii — cut per-student funding by more than 20 percent, according to the CBPP.[71]

Next year, the U.S. Department of Education (DOE) could suffer a 7.8 percent cut in its funding — most of which supports state and local education initiatives — unless Congress resolves a budget stalemate that began in 2011. Last fall, with congressional Republicans and Democrats unable to agree on a combination of spending cuts and tax increases to reduce the federal deficit, Congress agreed to allow the hefty DOE cut and other budget reductions to take effect on Jan. 1, 2013, if the legislative standoff continues. With House Republicans, in particular, continuing to declare that tax increases are

off the table for deficit reduction, a deal to avoid the mandatory cuts — including at least a $3.5 billion reduction in education funding — seems out of reach for now.[72]

More than a third of those cuts — about $1.3 billion — would come directly from federal funds for schools in low-income areas — known as Title I schools. Most Title I schools, which have large numbers of economically disadvantaged students and others at high risk of dropping out, are in urban areas.[73]

Funding Cuts

A DOE study concluded last year that Title I funds are being used to compensate for cuts in state and local education funding for high-poverty schools instead of merely supplementing those funds. As a result, the DOE concluded, poor school districts are spending substantially less per student than wealthier districts.[74]

For example, DOE found that in districts with both Title I and non-Title I schools, more than 40 percent of Title I schools spent less money per student on staffing than non-Title-I schools did.[75]

The "findings confirm an unfortunate reality in our nation's education system," said Education Secretary Arne Duncan. "Many schools serving low-income children aren't getting their fair share of funding," and "in far too many places Title I dollars are filling budget gaps rather than being extra."[76]

As a result of the financial crisis and related government budget struggles, severe financial troubles have plagued many urban schools.

In Ypsilanti, Mich., for example, schools face a debt expected to reach $9.4 million by the end of this school year, despite previous spending cuts. Reductions in school support staff, for example, have already gone "beyond a point where work can be completed effectively," according to a deficit-elimination plan prepared by district officials.[77]

While many states promised to restore the education funding once the financial crisis waned, some have decided instead to use the money for tax cuts.

Lawmakers in Kansas, for instance, slashed school funding by nearly $700 per student since 2008, resulting in — among other things — large-scale layoffs and school closures in Wichita and other urban schools. "We couldn't take another year like the last three," Wichita

Public Schools Superintendent John Allison said recently.[78]

So when he heard that the state would have a $300 million surplus this year, he said, "We thought, 'Finally, things are going to start getting back to normal.' " Instead, lawmakers last month used the surplus to reduce the top tax rate from 6.45 percent to 4.9 percent — the largest tax cut in state history. Critics said that by 2018 the tax cut would convert this year's surplus into long-term budget deficits totaling $2.5 billion. Education spending was increased by only $58 per student for next year.[79]

In some districts, staff and resource cuts are accompanied by a continuing atmosphere of worry and uncertainty that has eroded morale. In the San Francisco and Los Angeles school districts, for example, state law requires teachers who are at risk of being laid off within the next year to receive advance warning in March. By 2012, as budget woes continue, some teachers had received a warning for four years running.

Uncertainty saps energy needed to operate schools properly, teachers and administrators say. "I've seen teachers who have cried," said Phyllis Bradford, senior director of human resources for the Los Angeles Unified School District. "Others have moved out of state. . . . It's a very depressing time."[80]

Alternatives Sought

Looking for budget savings and an alternative to what they view as failing urban public schools, some lawmakers have embraced proposals to boost charter schools and other alternatives, such as vouchers to help families place their children in private schools, including religious schools. A wave of Republican governors and state legislators who swept into office in 2010 have been the principal, but not sole, backers of such plans.

In 2011, for example, newly elected Wisconsin Gov. Scott Walker, a Republican, shepherded a substantial expansion of Wisconsin's school-voucher program through the legislature. The program began as a low-income-only program for Milwaukee but was subsequently expanded to include Racine, the state's fifth-largest city. Among other changes, the expanded voucher program eliminated an enrollment cap; raised the income cap for eligible families to 300 percent of the federal poverty level while allowing families to continue receiving voucher support if their income rises after a student enrolls; and allows Milwaukee students to use vouchers at schools in the surrounding county.[81]

In Pennsylvania, newly elected Republican Gov. Tom Corbett tried but failed last year to form a statewide voucher program. Pennsylvania school-choice proponents, who have advocated for vouchers for the last two decades, expressed frustration after the state's Republican-controlled House of Representatives failed to approve Corbett's plan. "It's beyond disappointing," said Dawn Chavous, executive director of Students First PA, a nonpartisan group pushing to provide more alternatives to traditional schools. "We're going to keep fighting. I'm not going to go anywhere."[82]

In Philadelphia, school-system leaders announced this year that looming "severe, long-term deficits" estimated at $1.1 billion by 2017, plus slow progress in improving learning, make it imperative to close many neighborhood schools, restructure school-district administration and promote charter schools over the next five years.[83]

"In spite of progress" in academics," we are not improving nearly fast enough" compared to cities such as San Diego and Boston, school district leaders said in a report.[84] And while "efforts to reduce violence are paying off" — with violent incidents dropping from 3.7 per 100 students in 2007-08 to 2.6 in 2001-2011 — violence "continues to plague our schools."[85] One key to improving the schools while balancing the budget, the leaders said: "Promote equal access to quality choices for parents by expanding high-performing district and charter programs."[86]

But many local activists dub the proposal a stealth maneuver to privatize public schools and diminish the district's power under the guise of saving it. "No one would debate that there are financial problems in the district," said the Rev. Mark Kelly Tyler, pastor of Mother Bethel AME Church, in South Philadelphia. "But is it so bad that the only answer is to shutter 64 schools and remove the remaining 20 percent to charter schools?"[87]

In Illinois, a legislative committee backed a plan in May 2012 to require school districts to direct more money to charter schools. The measure, which has not yet been voted on by the full legislature, is intended to provide "equal funding for our charter schools, equal funding with the public schools," which is "an issue of fairness," said Rep. Daniel Burke, D-Chicago, the measure's sponsor.[88]

The Chicago Teachers Union has strongly opposed the legislation, however, arguing that traditional public schools, "funded almost entirely by taxes," may actually have fewer available resources than the many charter schools that "receive private money from corporate privatization proponents."[89]

Meanwhile, researchers continue to examine whether promoting measures such as charter schools and vouchers makes budgetary sense or improves learning. Findings are mixed. For example, statewide achievement scores in Illinois, released in December 2011, showed that one chain of nine charter schools in Chicago beat the district average, but scores at other charter chains fell well below district averages.[90]

By contrast, in one of the largest studies of its kind, the Center for Research on Education Outcomes (CREDO) at Stanford University found in 2009 that Chicago and Denver charter-school students outpaced their public-school counterparts on the National Assessment of Student Progress (NAEP), which is often called the "nation's report card." In Arizona, Ohio and Texas, charter-school students lagged public-school students' achievement, while in Washington, D.C., public- and charter-school students showed similar achievement levels, the study found.[91]

Groups such as the conservative Thomas B. Fordham Institute, an education-policy think tank in Washington, support charter schools partly because, theoretically, they are more likely to operate like businesses, facing bankruptcy and quick closure if they fail in their educational mission. However, a 2010 Fordham analysis found that 72 percent of the charter schools — and 80 percent of traditional public schools — that were low-achieving in 2004-2004 were still operating, and still performing poorly, five years later.[92]

Critics of urban public schools often charge that public school systems siphon money that could be used for student learning and that charter schools can reverse that pattern. However, Michigan State University Professor of Educational Administration David Arsen and University of Utah Assistant Professor of Educational Leadership and Policy Yongmei Ni, found that, at least in Michigan, charter schools spend twice as much per student on administration as traditional public schools and 20 percent less on instruction.[93]

Cheating Scandals

In the current wave of school reform plans that began about a decade ago — including the federal No Child Left Behind Act (NCLB), signed into law in 2002 — many seek to hold schools and, increasingly, individual teachers accountable for low student achievement by imposing sanctions if test scores or other measures don't improve.

Under NCLB, sanctions include expanded opportunities for parents to move their children to higher-performing schools. And if students' standardized-test scores continue to lag, schools could experience mass staff firings and reorganization.

How well such methods work is a matter of increasing debate, however, especially in the wake of several administrative scandals in which schools in several cities were suspected of altering students' test scores, presumably to avoid sanctions.

Throughout the 2000s, the Atlanta school system had gained nationwide attention for repeatedly raising test scores. But in 2008 and 2009, the *Atlanta Journal-Constitution* reported that, based on the paper's statistical analysis, many of the increases were so unlikely that they raised suspicions that the district had manipulated test results.

In July 2011, the Georgia Bureau of Investigation accused 178 Atlanta teachers and principals of engaging in a "conspiracy" to change students' test answers. In what has been called the biggest school-cheating scandal in U.S. history, 82 of the people named in the Bureau report confessed to the scheme, in which teachers and administrators erased students' wrong test answers and replaced them with correct responses.[94]

The Georgia Bureau of Investigation found that administrators rather than teachers were apparently the driving force behind most of the cheating. Several teachers who tried to blow the whistle on the scandal found themselves the subject of intimidation and, in one case, even an ethics investigation led by school administrators.[95]

Opponents of basing high-stakes decisions about schools and teachers primarily on standardized-test scores argue that the practice itself invites cheating. "When test scores are all that matter, some educators feel pressured to get the scores they need by hook or by crook," said Robert Shaeffer, a spokesman for National Center for Fair & Open Testing, which opposes heavy reliance on standardized tests for school decision making. "The higher the stakes, the greater the incentive to manipulate, to cheat."[96]

While Atlanta remains the most heavily substantiated case of widespread cheating, various analyses in the past two years have suggested that other districts also have cheated on the tests.

A March 2011 *USA Today* investigation, for example, concluded that patterns of erased-then-replaced test answers at some Washington, D.C., schools suggested that teachers and administrators may have changed students' answers to produce higher scores. At some D.C. schools that had been touted as nationwide models for learning improvement, students' tests had astonishingly high numbers of erasures in which wrong answers were changed to right answers — far more than would be likely to occur by chance, according to the paper.[97] Questions about the D.C. tests remain unresolved.

Investigations, mainly by newspapers, have turned up possible evidence of cheating in Baltimore, Dallas, Detroit, Houston and Los Angeles, as well as some non-urban districts.[98]

Adding Values

Meanwhile, efforts are expanding to hold individual teachers accountable for students' academic improvement, such as by offering merit pay based in whole or in part on standardized test scores.

In April 2011, for example, the Los Angeles Unified School District publicly released school-by-school results of its new so-called value-added measure of school and teacher performance and announced that it would soon take the more controversial step of telling individual teachers how they'd performed on the new measurement system. The value-added system compares progress of an individual student in a given year to the student's progress in previous school years, as measured by standardized tests. Teachers are then scored on how well their current students perform, compared to how those same students performed in

Thousands of teachers, school workers, students and parents participate in a "state of Emergency" rally in downtown Los Angeles on May 13, 2011, to protest proposed education budget cuts.

past years. By comparing each student only to his or her own past achievements, the method takes into account such factors as poverty or learning disabilities, which an individual teacher can't control, supporters of value-added rankings say.[99]

Many other analysts, as well as teachers' unions, argue that the test-based value-added measures are too narrow to use as a basis for evaluating teacher pay and promotions. In Los Angeles and New York City, for example, tense negotiations continue between the school districts and teachers and their unions over whether the measures should be used as a primary evaluation tool.[100]

Test Results

Recent test scores on student achievement show mixed results, both for the nation as a whole and for low-income and minority students, who make up a large part of the urban-school population.

On the most recent NAEP, only 32 percent of eighth-graders scored at a "proficient" level in science and only 2 percent at an "advanced" level, for example. However, a longstanding science achievement gap between white eighth-graders and black and Hispanic eighth-graders has slightly narrowed recently, as black and Hispanic students have raised their scores at a slightly faster rate than white students. Between 2009 and 2011, white students raised their average science score on the biannual test by 1 point, compared to three points for black students and five for Hispanics.[101]

Meanwhile, NAEP has undertaken an experimental, voluntary program that gathers detailed data from a group of urban districts as part of a project to determine whether NAEP can be used for district-to-district comparisons. In the experimental program, math scores in participating districts — all of them urban — improved somewhat in 2011 compared with 2009, but reading scores did not. Urban districts continue to lag far behind rural and suburban districts in NAEP scores, however, and most of the math-score increase in urban areas came from higher-income students. Still, most of the urban districts have improved in both math and reading since the early 2000s.[102]

"We've been able to close the gap between [large cities] and the nation by between 25 percent and 36 percent" since 2003, said Michael Casserly, executive director of the Council of the Great City Schools, a coalition of the city's largest urban school districts. "It says to us that many urban school districts in aggregate appear to be moving in the right direction."[103]

But progress is far too slow, said other analysts. "There's nobody who's performing at advanced levels," said Mark Schneider, a vice president of the American Institutes for Research, a Washington-based social-science research group that has been involved in NAEP and other federal education programs. "This is just really, really, really depressing."[104]

One surprise in the findings was Atlanta's results. While Atlanta cheated on the state tests, its performance on the national test — untainted by cheating — was well above average. On NAEP, Atlanta schools made significant continuing gains throughout the past decade, including in 2011, demonstrating that — despite the scandal —"what you saw by way of reform in the school district was real," said Casserly.[105]

NOTES

1. Quoted in Judy Radigan, "Reframing Dropouts: The Complexity of Urban Life Intersects with Current School Policy," paper presented at the Texas Dropout Conference, Houston, Oct. 6, 2006.

2. "The Socioeconomic Composition of the Public Schools: A Crucial Consideration in Student Assignment Policy," University of North Carolina Center for Civil Rights, Jan. 7, 2005, www.law.unc.edu/PDFs/charlottereport.pdf.

3. For background, see Barbara Mantel, "No Child Left Behind," *CQ Researcher*, May 7, 2005, pp. 469-492.

4. Quoted in David J. Hoff and Kathleen Kennedy Manzo, "Bush Claims About NCLB Questioned," *Education Week*, March 9, 2007, www.edweek.org.

5. Quoted in *ibid.*

6. "The Nation's Report Card: Reading 2005," U.S. Department of Education Institute of Education Sciences, www.nationsreportcard.gov.

7. Douglas N. Harris, "Ending the Blame Game on Educational Inequity: A Study of 'High-Flying' Schools and NCLB," Education Policy Studies Laboratory, Arizona State University, March 2006.

8. Jay P. Greene, "Education Myths," The American Enterprise Online, American Enterprise Institute, August 2006.

9. For background, see Charles S. Clark, "Charter Schools," *CQ Researcher*, Dec. 20, 2002, pp. 1033-1056; Kenneth Jost, "School Vouchers Showdown," *CQ Researcher*, Feb. 15, 2002, pp. 121-144.

10. Greene, *op. cit.*

11. Brad Olsen and Lauren Anderson, "Courses of Action: A Qualitative Investigation Into Urban Teacher Retention and Career Development," *Urban Education*, January 2007, p. 5.

12. Quoted in *ibid.*, p. 14.

13. *Ibid.*

14. Arthur J. Rothkopf, "Elementary and Secondary Education Act Reauthorization: Improving NCLB To Close the Achievement Gap," testimony before the Senate Committee on Health, Education, Labor, and Pensions and the House Committee on Education and Labor, March 13, 2007.

15. For background, see Kenneth Jost, "Testing in Schools," *CQ Researcher*, April 20, 2001, pp. 321-344.

16. Richard J. Murnane, "Improving the Education of Children Living in Poverty," unpublished paper, Jan. 25, 2007.

17. *Ibid.*

18. For background, see Kenneth Jost, "School Desegregation," *CQ Researcher*, April 23, 2004, pp. 345-372.

19. Quoted in "Center on Race and Social Problems Commemorates *Brown v. Board of Education*," University of Pittsburgh School of Social Work, May 7, 2004.

20. Quoted in Brian Lamb, "No Excuses: Closing the Racial Gap in Learning," transcript, "Booknotes," C-SPAN, Feb. 1, 2004.

21. Paul Tough, "What It Takes To Make a Student," *The New York Times Magazine*, Nov. 26, 2006, p. 70.

22. R. Scott Baker, "School Resegregation: Must the South Turn Back?" *Journal of Southern History*, November 2006, p. 993.

23. Howell S. Baum, "Smart Growth and School Reform: What If We Talked About Race and Took Community Seriously?" *Journal of the American Planning Association*, winter 2004, p. 14.

24. "Divided We Fail: Coming Together Through Public School Choice," Task Force on the Common School, The Century Foundation Press, 2002, p. 3.

25. *Ibid.*, p. 13.

26. Quoted in Lamb, *op. cit.*

27. *Ibid.*

28. Terry Ryan and Quentin Suffren, "Charter School Lessons from Ohio," *The Education Gadfly*, Thomas B. Fordham Foundation, March 15, 2007, www.edexcellence.net.

29. Mark Simon, "What Teachers Know," *Poverty & Race*, September/October 2004, www.prrac.org.

30. Dreyon Wynn and Dianne L. H. Mark, "Book Review: Educating Teachers for Diversity: Seeing With a Cultural Eye," *Urban Education*, May 2005, p. 350.

31. Jocelyn A. Glazier, "Moving Closer to Speaking the Unspeakable: White Teachers Talking About Race," *Teacher Education Quarterly*, winter 2003.

32. Wanda J. Blanchett, "Urban School Failure and Disproportionality in a Post-*Brown* Era," *Remedial and Special Education*, April 2005, p. 70.

33. Christine H. Leland and Jerome C. Harste, "Doing What We Want to Become: Preparing New Urban Teachers," *Urban Education*, January 2005, p. 60.

34. *Ibid.*, p. 62.

35. Glazier, *op. cit.*

36. Wynn and Mark, *op. cit.*

37. For background, see Wayne J. Urban and Jennings L. Wagoner, *American Education: A History* (2003); Stanley William Rothstein, *Schooling the Poor: A Social Inquiry Into the American Educational Experience* (1994).

38. For background, see Kathy Koch, "Reforming School Funding," *CQ Researcher*, Dec. 10, 1999, pp. 1041-1064.

39. Derrick Bell, *Silent Covenants:* Brown v. Board of Education *and the Unfulfilled Hopes for Racial Reform* (2004), p. 88.

40. *Ibid.*, p. 91.

41. Ruth Curran Neild and Robert Balfanz, "An Extreme Degree of Difficulty: The Educational Demographics of Urban Neighborhood High Schools," *Journal of Education for Students Placed at Risk*, spring 2006, p. 135.

42. V. W. Ipka, "At Risk Children in Resegregated Schools; An Analysis of the Achievement Gap," *Journal of Instructional Psychology*, December 2003, p. 294.

43. The case is *Brown v. Board of Education of Topeka*, 347 U.S. 483 (1954).

44. For background, see Jost, "School Desegregation," *op. cit.*; Gary Orfield and John T. Yun, "Resegregation in American Schools," The Civil Rights Project, Harvard University, June 1999, www.civilrightsproject.harvard.edu/research/deseg/reseg_schools99.php.

45. The case is *Milliken v. Bradley*, 418 U.S. 717 (1974).

46. Ipka, *op. cit.* The cases are *Board of Education of Oklahoma City v. Dowell*, 498 U.S. 237 (1991) and *Freeman v. Pitts*, 498 U.S. 1081 (1992).

47. Gary Orfield and Chungmei Lee, "Racial Transformation and the Changing Nature of Segregation," The Civil Rights Project, Harvard University, January 2006, www.civilrightsproject.harvard.edu; *Keyes v. School District No. 1*, Denver, Colorado, 413 U.S. 189 (1973).

48. Gary Orfield and Susan E. Eaton, "Back to Segregation," *The Nation*, March 3, 2003, p. 5.

49. Baum, *op. cit.*

50. *Ibid.*

51. Neild and Balfanz, *op. cit.*, p. 126.

52. "Divided We Fail," *op. cit.*, p. 17.

53. Tough, *op. cit.*

54. Elaine M. Stotko, Rochelle Ingram and Mary Ellen Beaty-O'Ferrall, "Promising Strategies for Attracting and Retaining Successful Urban Teachers," *Urban Education*, January 2007, p. 36.

55. Patrick Mattimore, "Will Court Put Integration on Hold?" *San Francisco Examiner*, Dec. 8, 2006, www.exaaminer.com. The cases — argued on Dec. 4, 2006 — are *Meredith v. Jefferson County Board of Education*, 05-915; and *Parents Involved in Community Schools v. Seattle School District No. 1*, 05-908.

56. Richard Kahlenberg, "Helping Children Move from Bad Schools to Good Ones," The Century Foundation, 2006, www.tcf.org/list.asp?type=PB&pubid=565.

57. *Ibid.*

58. Quoted in Michael Sandler, "Minding Their Business," *CQ Weekly*, April 2, 2007, p. 952.

59. Quoted in Jonathan Weisman and Amit R. Paley, "Dozens in GOP Turn Against Bush's Prized 'No Child' Act," *The Washington Post*, March 15, 2007, p. A1.

60. Written testimony of Anthony P. Carnevale, director, Georgetown University Center on Education and the Workforce, U.S. Senate Committee on Health, Education, Labor and Pensions, Feb. 24, 2010, http://help.senate.gov/imo/media/doc/Carnevale.pdf.

61. Council of the Great City Schools, press release, May 20, 2010, www.cgcs.org/pressrelease/TUDA_Reading2010.pdf.

62. "Beating the Odds: Analysis of Student Performance on State Assessments and NAEP," Council of the Great City Schools, March 2010.

63. Linda Greenhouse, "Justices Limit the Use of Race in School Plans for Integration," *The New York Times*, June 28, 2007, p. A1.

64. Civil Rights Project, University of California at Los Angeles, www.civilrightsproject.ucla.edu/research/deseg/school-integration-three-years-after-parents-involved.pdf.

65. Bill Turque, "Rhee dismisses 241 D.C. teachers; union vows to contest firing," *The Washington Post*, July 24, 2010, p. A1, www.washingtonpost.com/wp-dyn/content/article/2010/07/23/AR2010072303093.html.

66. Bill Turque, "D.C. Teachers' Contract Passes Its Final Hurdle; Council Unanimously Approves Pact that Bases Pay on Results," *The Washington Post*, June 30, 2010.

67. "Opportunity Denied," editorial, *The Washington Post*, June 23, 2010.

68. "Evaluation of the DC Opportunity Scholarship Program: Final Report," U.S. Department of Education, June 2010, http://ies.ed.gov/ncee/pubs/20104018/pdf/20104018.pdf.

69. Chad Adelman, "How Race to the Top Could Inform ESEA Reauthorization," *Education Week*, June 28, 2010.

70. Testimony before Senate Health, Education, Labor and Pensions Committee, March 9, 2010.

71. Phil Oliff and Michael Leachman, "New School Year Brings Steep Cuts in Funding for Schools," Center on Budget and Policy Priorities, Oct. 7, 2011, www.cbpp.org/files/9-1-11sfp.pdf.

72. Jamie Baxter, "We Must Avoid Sequestration: Savage Cuts in Education Funding Would Cripple Our Schools," *Post-Gazette.com* (Pittsburgh), May 3, 2012, www.post-gazette.com/stories/opinion/perspectives/we-must-avoid-sequestration-savage-cuts-in-education-funding-would-cripple-our-schools-634125.

73. *Ibid.*

74. Ruth Heuer and Stephanie Stullich, "Comparability of State and Local Expenditures Among Schools Within Districts: A Report from the Study of School-level Expenditures," U.S. Department of Education, 2011, www2.ed.gov/rschstat/eval/title-i/school-level-expenditures/school-level-expenditures.pdf; "The Potential Impact of Revising Title I Comparability Requirement to Focus on

School-level Expenditures," U.S. Department of Education, November 2011, www2.ed.gov/rschstat/eval/title-i/comparability-requirement/comparability-policy-brief.pdf.

75. "The Potential Impact of Revising Title I Comparability," *ibid.*, p. 3.

76. Quoted in Alyson Klein, "Poor Schools Shortchanges on Funding, Ed Dept. Says," *Education Week blogs*, Nov. 30, 2011, http://blogs.edweek.org/edweek/campaign-k-12/2011/11/for_years_advocates_for_poor.html.

77. "Narrative Section, Deficit Elimination Plan," School District of Ypsilanti, December 2011, www.ypsd.org/downloads/financial/2011-2012_deficit_elimination_plan_20111214_111811_7.pdf.

78. Mike Alberti, "States to residents, localities: forget promises to restore funding," Remapping Debate, www.remappingdebate.org/article/states-residents-localities-forget-promises-restore-funding.

79. *Ibid.*

80. Quoted in Christina Hoag, "California's Fourth Year of Teacher Layoffs Spurs Concerns," The Associated Press/ABC News, May 5, 2012, http://abcnews.go.com/US/wireStory/califs-4th-year-teacher-layoffs-spur-concerns-16285889#.T616a1JzaUk.

81. "2011-2013 Legislative Session," "Accurate Information About School Choice," School ChoiceWI.org, www.schoolchoicewi.org/stgov/detail.cfm?id=10; Patrick Marley and Jason Stein, "Senate OK'd Budget Goes to Walker," *Journal Sentinel online* (Milwaukee), June 16, 2011, www.jsonline.com/news/statepolitics/124004679.html, and Amy Hetzner and Erin Richards, "Budget Cuts $834 Million from Schools," *Journal Sentinel online* (Milwaukee), March 1, 2011, www.jsonline.com/news/statepolitics/117192683.html.

82. Quoted in Jan Murphy and Charles Thompson, "State House Rejects School-voucher Proposal," PennLive.com/*The Patriot-News* (Harrisburg), Dec. 14, 2011.

83. "A Blueprint for Transforming Philadelphia's Public Schools" (Draft), School District of Philadelphia, http://thenotebook.org/sites/default/files/BlueprintPublicPresentation_4_22_12.pdf.

84. *Ibid.*, p. 4.

85. *Ibid.*, p. 5.

86. *Ibid.*

87. Quoted in Julianne Hing, "The Remaking of Philadelphia Public Schools: Privatization or Bust," *Color Lines*, May 11, 2012, http://colorlines.com/archives/2012/05/the_remaking_of_philadelphia_public_schools_privatization_or_bust.html.

88. Jim Broadway, "Bill to Give More Cash to Charters Moves Forward," State School News Service/Catalyst Chicago, May 9, 2012, www.catalyst-chicago.org/notebook/2012/05/09/20105/bill-give-more-cash-charters-moves-forward.

89. Quoted in *ibid.*

90. Rosalyn Rossi and Art Golab, "Chicago Charter Schools Produce Wildly Uneven Results on State Tests," *Chicago Sun-Times*, Jan. 1, 2012, www.suntimes.com/news/education/9145306-418/story.html.

91. "Multiple Choice: Charter School Performance in 16 States," Center for Research on Education Outcomes, 2009, http://credo.stanford.edu/reports/MULTIPLE_CHOICE_CREDO.pdf.

92. David A. Stuit, "Are Bad Schools Immortal?" Thomas B. Fordham Institute, December 2010, www.edexcellencemedia.net/publications/2010/20101214_AreBadSchoolImmortal/Fordham_Immortal.pdf.

93. Emily Pfund, "Study Finds Michigan Charter Schools Spend Twice as Much as Public Schools," *Central Michigan Life*, Central Michigan University, April 26, 2012, www.cm-life.com/2012/04/26/study-focuses-on-michigan-charter-schools-finds-charter-schools-spend-twice-as-much-as-public-schools.

94. Patrik Jonsson, "America's Biggest Teacher and Principal Cheating Scandal Unfolds in Atlanta," *The Christian Science Monitor*, July 5, 2011, www.csmonitor.com/USA/Education/2011/0705/America-s-biggest-teacher-and-principal-cheating-scandal-unfolds-in-Atlanta; and "School Cheating Investigation: Atlanta Journal-Constitution Flags Improbable Test Scores in Analysis," Associated Press/*Huffington Post*, March 25, 2012, www.huffingtonpost.com/2012/03/24/schools-cheating-investig_n_1377767.html.

95. Jonsson, *ibid.*

96. Quoted in *ibid.*

97. Jack Gillum and Marisol Bello, "When Standardized Test Scores Soared in DC, Were the Gains Real?" *USA Today*, March 30, 2011, www.usatoday.com/news/education/2011-03-28-1Aschooltesting28_CV_N.htm.

98. "School Cheating Investigation: Atlanta Journal Constitution Flags Improbable Test Scores in Analysis," *op. cit.*

99. Jason Song and Jason Felch, "L.A. Unified Releases School Ratings Using 'Value-added' Method," *Los Angeles Times*, April 12, 2011, http://articles.latimes.com/2011/apr/12/local/la-me-0413-value-add-20110414; for background, see Marcia Clemmitt, "School Reform," *CQ Researcher*, April 29, 2011, pp. 385-408.

100. Fernanda Santos and Anna M. Phillips, "With Release of Teacher Data, Setback for Union Turns Into Rallying Cry," *The New York Times*, Feb. 26, 2012, www.nytimes.com/2012/02/27/nyregion/teacher-ratings-produce-a-rallying-cry-for-the-union.html.

101. Sarah D. Sparks, "Most 8th Graders Fall Short on NAEP Science Test," *Education Week*, May 10, 2012, www.edweek.org/ew/articles/2012/05/10/31naep_ep.h31.html?tkn=VPXFO3wzO2s%2Bbex2WwFqNNnCfYtzrpCNzSmA&cmp=ENL-EU-NEWS1,k, and "The Nation's Report Card: Science 2011," National Center for Education Statistics, May 2012, http://nces.ed.gov/nationsreportcard/pubs/main2011/2012465.asp.

102. Christina Samuels, "Urban NAEP Scores Show Math Scores Up, Reading Mostly Flat," *Education Week blogs*, Dec. 7, 2011, http://blogs.edweek.org/edweek/District_Dossier/2011/12/urban_naep_scores_show_math_up.html; and Joy Resmovits, "City-level National Tests Show Slight Math Growth, No Change in Reading," *Huffington Post*, Dec. 7, 2011, www.huffingtonpost.com/2011/12/07/urban-schools-test_n_1132775.html.

103. Quoted in Resmovits, *ibid.*

104. Quoted in *ibid.*

105. Quoted in *ibid.*

BIBLIOGRAPHY

Books

Kozol, Jonathan, *The Shame of the Nation: The Restoration of Apartheid Schooling in America*, Three Rivers Press, 2006.
A longtime education writer and activist reports on his five-year journey to closely observe 60 schools in 11 states. He describes almost entirely resegregated urban schools with dilapidated buildings, dirty classrooms and a dearth of up-to-date textbooks.

Rothstein, Richard, *Class and Schools: Using Social, Economic, and Education Reform to Close the Black-White Achievement Gap*, Economic Policy Institute, 2004.
A research associate at a think tank concerned with low- and middle-income workers and families argues that raising the achievement of urban students requires public policies that address students' multiple social and economic needs.

Thernstrom, Abigail, and Stephan Thernstrom, *No Excuses: Closing the Racial Gap in Learning*, Simon & Schuster, 2004.
A husband and wife who are senior fellows at the conservative Manhattan Institute for Public Policy Research argue that charter schools and the No Child Left Behind Act's focus on holding schools accountable for poor student achievement can close the achievement gap for urban students.

Articles

Boo, Katherine, "Expectations," *The New Yorker*, Jan. 15, 2007, p. 44.
A reform-minded superintendent closes Denver's lowest-achieving high school, hoping its students will accept the offer to enroll in any other city school, including some with mainly online classes. Mostly Latinos from the city's poorest families, the displaced students struggle with losing their old school, which has provided many with a sense of community, and with new choices that confront them, as well as the ever-present choice of dropping out.

Moore, Martha T., "More Mayors Are Moving To Take Over School System," *USA Today*, March 21, 2007, p. A1.

Albuquerque's mayor is among those who believe they could run schools better than their local school boards.

Saulny, Susan, "Few Students Seek Free Tutoring or Transfers From Failing Schools," *The New York Times*, April 6, 2006, p. 20.
The No Child Left Behind Act promises free tutoring for many students in low-achieving schools, but few of those students' families know about the option or have been able to enroll their children in good-quality tutoring programs.

Tough, Paul, "What It Takes To Make a Student," *The New York Times Magazine*, Nov. 26, 2006, p. 44.
A handful of charter schools are making strides against the achievement gap. But largely because low-income and minority students arrive at school with smaller vocabularies and far less knowledge about how to communicate with adults and behave in a learning situation, the work requires extra-long school hours and intense teacher commitment.

Reports and Studies

***Beating the Odds: An Analysis of Student Performance and Achievement Gaps on State Assessments: Results from the 2005-2006 School Year, Council of the Great City Schools*, April 2007.**
A group representing 67 of the country's largest urban school districts examines in detail the recent performance of urban students on state tests.

***Divided We Fail: Coming Together Through Public School Choice, Task Force on the Common School, The Century Foundation*, 2002.**
Basing its discussion on the idea that race- and class-segregated schools have proven a failure, a nonpartisan think tank explores the possibility of encouraging cross-district integration of low-income and middle-income students by methods like establishing high-quality magnet schools in cities.

***Engaging Schools: Fostering High School Students' Motivation to Learn, Committee on Increasing High School Students' Engagement and Motivation to Learn, National Research Council*, 2003.**
A national expert panel examines methods for re-engaging urban high-school students who have lost their motivation to learn, a problem they say is widespread but solvable.

Bridgeland, John M., John J. DiIulio, Jr., and Karen Burke Morison, *The Silent Epidemic: Perspectives of High School Dropouts, Bill & Melinda Gates Foundation*, March 2006.
Nearly half of high-school dropouts say they left school partly because they were bored. A third of the students left because they needed to work, and more than a fifth said they left to care for a family member.

Levin, Henry, Clive Belfield, Peter Muennig and Cecilia Rouse, "The Costs and Benefits of an Excellent Education for All of America's Children," *Teachers College, Columbia University*, January 2007; www.cbcse.org/media/download_gallery/Leeds_Report_Final_Jan2007.pdf.
A team of economists concludes that measures to cut the number of school dropouts would pay for themselves with higher tax revenues and lower government spending.

For More Information

Achieve, Inc., 1775 I St., N.W., Suite 410, Washington, DC 20006; (202) 419-1540; www.achieve.org. An independent bipartisan group formed by governors and business leaders to promote higher academic standards.

Alliance for Excellent Education, 1201 Connecticut Ave., N.W., Suite 901, Washington, DC 20036; (202) 828-0828; www.all4ed.org. A nonprofit research and advocacy group seeking policies to help at-risk high-school students.

The Center for Education Reform, 1001 Connecticut Ave., N.W., Suite 204, Washington, DC 20036; (202) 822-9000; www.edreform.com. A nonprofit advocacy group that promotes school choice in cities.

The Century Foundation, 41 E. 70th St., New York, NY 10021; (212) 535-4441; www.tcf.org. Supports research on income inequality and urban policy.

Citizens for Effective Schools, 8209 Hamilton Spring Ct., Bethesda, MD 20817; (301) 469-8000; www.citizenseffectiveschools.org. An advocacy group that seeks policy changes to minimize the achievement gap for low-income and minority students.

Council of the Great City Schools, 1301 Pennsylvania Ave., N.W., Suite 702, Washington, DC 20004; (202) 393-2427; www.cgcs.org. A coalition of 67 urban school systems dedicated to improving urban schools.

Education Next, Hoover Institution, Stanford University; www.educationnext.org. A quarterly journal on education reform published by a conservative think tank.

The Education Trust, 1250 H St., N.W., Suite 700, Washington, DC 20005; (202) 293-1217; www2.edtrust.org. Dedicated to closing the achievement gap in learning and college preparation for low-income and minority students.

National Center for Education Statistics, 1990 K St., N.W., Washington, DC 20006; (202) 502-7300; http://nces.ed.gov. A Department of Education agency that provides statistics and analysis on U.S. schools, student attendance and achievement.

3

Blighted Cities

Thomas J. Billitteri

Plans to revive Youngstown, Ohio — whose population of 75,000 is half what it was in 1950 — include razing abandoned houses and downsizing the city's developed footprint by providing incentives for residents to relocate to more viable neighborhoods.

From *CQ Researcher*, November 12, 2010.

When Dave Bing played professional basketball in the 1960s and '70s, he won praise as a tough competitor and inspiring leader. "If things go wrong," a teammate said, "Dave keeps you from putting your head down."[1]

But now, as mayor of Detroit, Bing faces the game of his life. Bing is leading a controversial effort to remake Detroit, which has been ravaged by massive job losses, mortgage foreclosure, crime and decay that have left vast stretches of the Motor City abandoned. The city's future, experts say, depends on its ability to integrate reforms of its educational, economic-development and transportation systems, reinvigorate Detroit's core and stem its physical decline.

A key challenge is to reconcile Detroit's sprawling 139-square-mile-footprint with a population that has shrunk from 1.8 million in 1950 to fewer than 900,000 today. The city's plunging fortunes have left its neighborhoods scarred by more than 33,000 vacant homes and 90,000 vacant lots, which together account for a third of the residential parcels.[2]

Reformers have pushed an array of proposals to clean up the blight, "shrink" the developed footprint of the city and, in the process, save it from having to provide trash pickup, road maintenance and other services in unsustainable neighborhoods. Among the ideas: Un-pave parts of Detroit and convert them to open space and urban farmland.

Bing says he wants to enlist the public's input before pushing forward with revival plans. Still, he has promised to bulldoze 10,000 dangerous and derelict structures by the end of his term in

Many Cities Have Lost Half Their Population

Cities across the United States, many in the Midwest Rust Belt, have experienced population declines of more than 50 percent since 1950; in Youngstown, Ohio, the decline exceeded 60 percent.

Population Trends in Major Shrinking Cities, 1950-2007

Source: Alan Mallach, "Facing the Urban Challenge: The Federal Government and America's Older Distressed Cities," Metropolitan Policy Program, Brookings Institution, May 2010

2013. He has backed away from suggesting Detroit might force people to relocate to more viable neighborhoods, although city officials say they may use incentives to induce residents to move.[3]

While some laud the demolitions, others fear gentrification and land-grabbing. One civil-rights leader likened Bing's plans to ethnic cleansing. "I call it poor cleansing," said the Rev. Horace Sheffield.[4]

But Bing is resolute. "I see things that are absolutely unbearable," he told NBC News. "I don't know how people live or are expected to live like some people are living right now. Our city is still living like we did 50 years ago. That doesn't work anymore. . . . We've got to build from the ground up again."[5]

Detroit's reasons for creative destruction aren't unique. Cities across the United States, many of them concentrated in the Midwest Rust Belt, face staggering population declines, ravaging blight and the unsustainable financial burden of providing municipal services to hollowed-out residential and industrial zones. Taking cues from "shrinking cities" strategies in Europe, some severely distressed American cities are demolishing vacant houses, experimenting with urban farming and looking for other ways to put vast stretches of vacant land to better use.

Yet efforts to fight blight and abandonment have sparked controversy. Critics say demolishing parts of cities is the wrong way to save them, and they point to failed urban-renewal efforts of the 1960s as evidence. But in many localities, advocates say their strategies are different from urban renewal and that bold steps are needed to move into the 21st century.

In Youngstown, Ohio, a former steelmaking titan whose population has plunged more than 50 percent since 1950, officials are five years into an aggressive program to tear down derelict structures, steer residents out of blighted areas and reduce infrastructure and service costs in depopulated areas of the city.

Youngstown has demolished more than 2,000 houses since 2005, but hundreds more are on the demo list, and a drive through town shows why: Clapboard houses with falling porches, peeling paint and plywood-covered windows, once the pride of middle-class steelworkers, hulk one beside each other, empty and abandoned.

Youngstown Mayor Jay Williams says the downsizing plan is necessary for the city to "survive, let alone thrive." He describes the strategy this way: "We're trying to tailor a suit for an individual who was a very portly, well-built size 48 who is now a size 36, much smaller and leaner — but still with a lot of assets."

Many localities are just now recognizing that their best years — measured, at least, by population — may be behind them. Conceding that reality has been difficult for elected officials and local civic boosters, policy experts say.

"Our economy is based on growth," says Frank Popper, who teaches land-use planning at Rutgers and Princeton universities. "The idea of smart shrinking or intelligently getting smaller is a very un-American idea, and it goes against the grain of the entire damn culture." And, he adds, "It's not just American civilization, it's all of Western civilization."

"There's a lot of rethinking about what it means to revitalize a city," adds Jennifer Vey, a Brookings Institution scholar who studies shrinking cities. "We've had a paradigm for a long, long time that revitalization requires population growth. The big shift here is that a lot of these cities are saying, look, we've lost a tremendous amount of our population, and it's not going to come back anytime soon. We've got to grapple with that reality and invest in the assets we have and build a stronger city."

No two strategies to deal with population loss and blight are the same, making the issue complex, evolving and, in many ways, difficult to generalize. In Youngstown, for example, whole sectors are all but devoid of residents, and officials are trying to shrink the developed footprint of the city.

Cleveland has about 20,000 vacant lots, but they tend to be dispersed in gap-tooth fashion throughout the city rather than concentrated in huge swaths, though some large patches of vacancy do exist on the city's east side, says Theresa Schwarz, director of the Cleveland Urban Design Collaborative at Kent State University.

In 2008-2009 alone, Cleveland demolished some 2,700 homes, and more have been torn down this year or are slated for demolition, she says.

But the city's main goal is not to downsize its footprint, halt services in certain neighborhoods or impose a blanket redevelopment plan to deal with population loss, says Schwarz.

Instead, she says, officials are trying to assess needs in individual neighborhoods and tailor strategies in ways that use vacant parcels to achieve long-term development goals for the city. That might mean designating some parcels for residential redevelopment near transit stops, while converting others into "green" uses such as storm-water management or urban farmland, Schwarz says.

In a controversial 2005 ruling on eminent domain, the U.S. Supreme Court ruled that New London, Conn., could condemn Susette Kelo's tidy house for private development, even though the house was not blighted, because the public would benefit.

By not redeveloping some parcels, the value of surrounding parcels can rise, helping to revitalize neighborhoods, she notes. "Value comes from scarcity, so we're actively trying to take some property out of the real estate market by repurposing it," Schwarz says.

Cleveland currently has 56 pilot projects under way, including an urban vineyard and an urban farm located in a decommissioned park in a depopulated area, Schwarz says. The farm is a joint effort between a private foundation and a nonprofit community development corporation, she says.

Schwarz emphasizes that Cleveland officials reject the "shrinking cities" label, partly because it implies permanence. "I'm not comfortable in saying a city will never re-grow," she says.

Whatever their differences, depopulated cities face big obstacles in their effort to realign themselves. Money is among the most daunting. Cities often depend on a crazy-quilt of government and philanthropic grants and tax revenue for planning, demolition and rehabilitation work, but officials complain that federal programs chronically favor big cities over smaller ones and development over demolition.

What's more, they grouse that cities that went on reckless building binges, such as Miami and Las Vegas, have tended to win out over smaller, old-line manufacturing towns in competition for grants from the Bush and Obama administration's stimulus programs. "They're

A Battered City Tries for a Comeback

Youngstown, Ohio, plans its revival around a smaller footprint.

On a chilly, damp Monday night in September, 700 citizen activists, elected officials and others packed Trinity United Methodist Church in downtown Youngstown, Ohio. The occasion was a revival, but it wasn't about saving souls. From the front, Pastor Michael Harrison chanted a litany of questions. "Are we tired of vacant properties?" he bellowed. "Yes!" came the booming response. "Do we need jobs in the valley?" Again, "Yes!" And "When do we need them?" "Now!"

"Now" is a lofty goal for any American city looking for economic resurrection these days, and especially so for old-line industrial areas like Youngstown. Its population, around 75,000, has shrunk by more than half since 1950 and more than 20 percent in just the past two decades.

The staggering contraction traces back to "Black Monday," Sept. 19, 1977, when Youngstown Sheet and Tube Co., centerpiece of the region's industrial economy, announced it would shut a big portion of its steelmaking operations in the area, foreshadowing a crash of the area's entire jobs base.

For years Youngstown reeled from the loss. But around 2002 the beleaguered community stirred to life. With considerable input from citizens and technical help from Youngstown State University, the city forged a revival plan called Youngstown 2010. Complex and far-reaching, it embraces, at its core, a vision of a smaller community rather than one trying to recapture its past glory days.

The plan, still a work in progress, calls for downsizing the developed footprint of the city by inducing residents of blighted areas to move to more viable ones.

To be sure, Youngstown has a lot going for it. It boasts acres of leafy parkland, an engaged citizenry and notable progress toward attracting a new generation of tech-oriented business.

Still, burned-out and boarded up houses, vacant factories and weed-choked lots scar the city. The whole east end of town, which planners optimistically slated in 1959 as the next boom sector, is a ghostly, rural no-man's-land traversed by ragged asphalt, with livestock and wild turkey in residence. Yet the city still provides trash pickup, road maintenance and other services across a 36-square-mile expanse that once accommodated 170,000 residents.

As part of Youngstown 2010, the city has razed more than 2,000 dilapidated and abandoned houses and focused tax incentives, government grants and philanthropic aid on several areas with the greatest potential of attracting new residents and investment. The transitional south-side Idora neighborhood, a pilot area where the city is focusing its full arsenal of revival strategies, is perhaps the most promising. Adjacent to a sprawling urban park, Idora includes stately Victorian-era homes on "millionaire's row" where the city's elite once lived, rental units and modest houses.

Since 2008 the city has torn down 48 of the most far-gone Idora structures and over the past year put 118 vacant parcels to new uses, including community gardens, says Ian Beniston, assistant director of the foundation-supported Youngstown Neighborhood Development Corp. The city also is working with a neighborhood association to spruce up landscaping and offering federally supported financial incentives to attract home restoration and new residents.

"We are seeing people moving back into Idora," Beniston says. He counts a suburban family and a California retiree among the newcomers. "The numbers are still small, but they're growing. Obviously we have to start somewhere."

Youngstown has promise on the business front, too. Downtown, the Youngstown Business Incubator has gained national attention as a nurturer of technology startups, and in 2009 *Entrepreneur* magazine named Youngstown among the top 10 U.S. cities to launch a business. General Motors' Lordstown assembly plant, maker of the highly promoted new Chevy Cruz, is 16 miles away. City-built infrastructure at three business and industrial parks, along with huge financial incentives that include 10-year tax abatements and nearly free land, have led to the creation of thousands of jobs, Youngstown officials say.

What's more, greater Youngstown is an export engine. Brookings Institution scholars say exports make up a "jaw-dropping" 18 percent of the Youngstown metropolitan area's "gross metropolitan product," or output, compared with a national metro average of 10.9 percent. And in 2008, about 30,000 export jobs existed in the Youngstown area. (The Akron area also had 30,000 export jobs, and the Cleveland metro area 110,000). [1]

One reason for Youngstown's export strength is Exal Corp., a maker of specialty-shaped aluminum cans and other products that has been contemplating its fourth Youngstown expansion. Another is V&M Star Steel, which this year announced a $650 million expansion that is expected to create 350 jobs. [2]

"We're not measuring our success solely by population," says Youngstown Mayor Jay Williams. "That's a trap a lot of cities fall into." Not that population is irrelevant, Williams adds, but it's not the only yardstick by which a city can appraise progress.

Still, five years into its regeneration plan, Youngstown remains a place of high ambition tempered by stark reality. Williams says "issues of blight continue to plague us," and officials worry that the decay is spreading faster in some neighborhoods than the city's ability to eliminate it.

Bill D'Avignon, Youngstown's director of community development and planning, gives mixed grades to Youngstown's progress. He assigns a grade of "B" for progress in remaking the downtown, a once-derelict area that now features new restaurants and nightclubs, a pleasing streetscape and a nearby $40 million sports and entertainment complex that was under way before Youngstown 2010 was adopted. "There's still a lot of work to be done," D'Avignon says, "but 10 years ago if someone would have imagined we'd be this far along, quite frankly they could have been put in a straitjacket."

D'Avignon gives a "D," however, to the part of the plan that aims to shrink the city's developed space and achieve what he says is the ultimate goal: "to bring every parcel back to productive use," whether that means turning abandoned lots into gardens, bringing older homes back to life or attracting new businesses to decaying storefronts.

While one block has been cleared of its last blighted home and the city was able to "vacate the street," D'Avignon says, "nothing large-scale" has occurred.

A major obstacle, D'Avignon says, has been "a lack of political will to do some of the harder-decision things," including withdrawing services from unsustainable areas and relocating residents to more viable neighborhoods. What's more, D'Avignon says that in a city with seven wards and seven council members, "there's a desire to have [resources] equally implemented" rather than focused on specific neighborhoods. "There are sustainable areas within each of those wards," he says. "It's a balancing act between implementation and politics that we face."

A community garden flourishes in Youngstown's Idora neighborhood where an abandoned apartment building once stood.

Joseph M. Schilling, associate director of the Metropolitan Institute at Virginia Tech, praises Youngstown for its political leadership and courage to face its problems. But he says that like many smaller cities, it lacks much of the technical expertise, money and administrative capacity to fully realize its ambition. What's more, he says, "you need a regional approach for these kinds of strategies to work." Schilling gives Youngstown "50-50" odds of achieving the vision laid out in its regeneration plan.

City officials remain optimistic that Youngstown is on a better path. But they also acknowledge steep obstacles, with blight among the biggest. "There is no neighborhood where we've said we've stopped it, home values have started to increase and it's a neighborhood of choice," says D'Avignon. "Until we get there, I don't think we can say Youngstown 2010 succeeded."

— *Thomas J. Billitteri*

[1] Bruce Katz and Jennifer Bradley, "Region has built the foundation for increased exports, new jobs," *Cleveland Plain Dealer*, Aug. 8, 2010, www.cleveland.com/opinion/index.ssf/2010/08/region_has_built_the_foundatio.html. Katz is vice president and director of the Brookings Institution's Metropolitan Policy Program, and Bradley is a fellow and co-director of the think tank's Great Lakes Economic Initiative.

[2] "V&M Start to Officially Expand, Create 350 Jobs," *WYTV.com*, Feb. 16, 2010, www.wytv.com/mostpopular/story/V-M-Star-to-Officially-Expand-Create-350-Jobs/jZTtmsTHLEmXAGqn1uvZtA.cspx.

Vacant Properties Are on the Rise

The percentage of vacant properties is increasing not only in older, distressed cities, such as Detroit and Flint, but also in Sun Belt cities such as Fort Myers and Las Vegas.*

Vacant Properties, 2006 and 2010

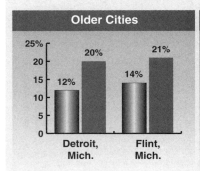

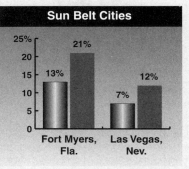

* Vacant properties include seasonal homes, houses under construction and houses where construction has been halted.

Source: Jennifer R. Leonard and Alan Mallach, "Restoring Properties, Rebuilding Communities," Center for Community Progress, October 2010

getting whopping sums to help address their issues, and we've been languishing in this for 30 years," says Bill D'Avignon, Youngstown's director of community development and planning.

Another impediment is the often torturous process of getting blighted and abandoned property out of the hands of irresponsible or destitute owners. But a growing number of states and localities are turning to new tools to speed the fight against blight. Among the most promising are so-called land banks — government or nonprofit entities that can acquire foreclosed or abandoned property and hold and manage it for future use or disposition. The severely depressed Flint area has pioneered a new generation of land banks that are aggressive at getting control of abandoned property and exerting strong redevelopment power.[6]

As cities struggle, here are some of the questions elected officials and community groups are asking:

Do property laws unfairly favor owners?

In Richmond, Va., city leaders have been looking into a promising tool to gain control of run-down or abandoned property that poses a public-nuisance threat.[7]

Known as vacant-property receivership, the approach allows cities to petition a court to appoint a receiver who can fix up the property, collect rent if it is occupied or sell it to a developer or nonprofit group that will rehabilitate it.

Joseph M. Schilling, associate director of the Metropolitan Institute at Virginia Tech University, likes the idea but says the Virginia Assembly is unlikely to approve it for Richmond because of resistance by property-rights advocates. "Conservative state legislators [erroneously] view receivership and similar remedies as efforts by local governments to take property," Schilling says.

Many urban-policy experts and elected officials say one of the biggest hurdles facing cities trying to improve vacant and abandoned property is a tradition of putting the interest of owners over those of the broader public.

"The real problem is that the laws don't recognize that there are different types of property owners," says Dan Kildee, president of the Center for Community Progress, a nonprofit group working on two fronts: urging a rethinking of state policies to broaden the use of land banks, and providing technical help to groups starting land banks. "Sometimes in the name of preserving property rights of a single irresponsible owner, we erode the property rights of dozens of property owners who live on that same street."

Owners don't always hold sway, of course. The U.S. Supreme Court demonstrated that in an explosively controversial 2005 decision on eminent domain. In *Kelo v. New London*, the court ruled 5-4 that local governments could take private property for economic development when they determine the taking will benefit the public, even if the property is transferred to a private company, isn't blighted and it's not known for sure whether the new project will succeed.[8]

But eminent domain, frequently used to clear land for new roads, convention centers or other public projects, may not be a weapon of choice for cities trying to downsize themselves. It can be an expensive, drawn-out process that can backfire, especially when used to force people to move from occupied dwellings.

Land banks, on the other hand, are intended to diminish reliance on that approach, Kildee says. He says 75 communities concentrated in about a dozen states now have land banks, and the number has been growing.

With a land bank, local authorities can acquire vacant and abandoned property and hold, manage, redevelop or sell it. Land banks can acquire property without an owner's consent when the owner has failed to pay property taxes after repeated warnings, Kildee says.

Proponents say land banks make it easier for localities to gain control of blighted property than if they use the traditional means of filing tax liens against delinquent owners and selling the property at public auction. That approach can take years, leave new buyers without clear title to the real estate and invite speculators who may buy the property at fire-sale prices and then sit on it or try to resell it for a profit without fixing it up.

In Flint, Mich., the Genesee County Land Bank has been in the forefront of the approach. Authorities in the beleaguered auto town have used it as an aggressive planning tool by acquiring and holding property and assembling it with other parcels for future development.

Since its formation in 2002, the Genesee County Land Bank Authority has acquired almost 10,000 empty houses, vacant buildings and abandoned lots, demolished more than 1,300 properties and redeveloped or "repurposed" more than 2,500 properties, according to an article by Kildee published by the Federal Reserve Bank of Philadelphia. "The land bank has used its land assembly and financing tools to attract over $60 million in new investment on previously forgotten land," he wrote.[9] It also has partnered with a private developer in the $30 million redevelopment of the historic Durant Hotel — which sat empty for 37 years — for apartments and commercial space.

Kildee, Genesee County's former treasurer, had a strong role in advocating changes to Michigan law to make the land bank a powerful planning tool. "We rewrote the tax-foreclosure system keeping in mind that we wanted to simultaneously protect the rights of property owners who might be behind [in their tax payments] but also go after abandoned-property owners much more aggressively," Kildee says.

The revised law, he says, gave homeowners facing financial difficulties two protections: It blunted the access of speculators to distressed property, and it expressly authorized county treasurers to postpone foreclosure proceedings against people behind in their property taxes because of hardship.

Kildee says that while the land bank has generated opposition among some real estate speculators, most developers have reacted favorably. "Very few honest-to-goodness developers go shopping for their next development opportunity at a public tax sale. Where we do get pushback is from the infomercial-watchers looking to flip property. They don't like this because we're basically taking the profit they would make and instead of converting it to wealth in their pocket, the [land bank] is creating public value."

New Jersey hasn't adopted land-bank legislation, but Alan Mallach, a senior fellow with the Center for Community Progress, says the state "has very strong laws that allow cities to crack the whip on property owners and, if need be, take the property if [the owner] is not willing to maintain it responsibly."

In 2004 New Jersey passed the Abandoned Properties Rehabilitation Act, which significantly accelerated the process for cities to take title to vacant properties through tax foreclosure. And in January New Jersey took more steps to help local governments get an upper hand on blighted properties in foreclosure. The state required lenders to notify municipalities when they initiate a foreclosure and also held lenders responsible for maintaining the property if the owner vacates it after the foreclosure filing but before the lender takes title to it at a sheriff's sale.

Still, Mallach, who also is a nonresident senior fellow at the Brookings Institution think tank, says much of the ability of a local government to control blight boils down to its "capacity" — whether it has a good database to accurately track vacant and abandoned property and enough professional staff to keep up with the avalanche of information coming in from banks and others required to file paperwork on the property and to act on that information.

Otherwise, a community will simply be sitting on "a pile of paper," Mallach says. Without a database, "you're not connecting the dots. You can pass a law, but if a city doesn't have capacity, the tool is not going to get used."

Is shrinkage a sound strategy for the most troubled cities?

For years Popper, the Rutgers land-use professor, and his wife Deborah, a geography professor at the College of Staten Island/City University of New York and Princeton, have studied the struggling Great Plains buffalo country, where often since the late-19th century communities have faced many of the problems afflicting Rust Belt cities: steep population loss, flagging local economies and the challenge of practicing what the Poppers call "smart decline" — embracing the reality of being smaller and reshaping everything from infrastructure and transportation systems to energy and food networks to reflect it.

Cities like Detroit, Flint and Youngstown are wise to engage in smart-decline strategies like tearing down abandoned houses, shutting sparsely used infrastructure and turning blighted neighborhoods into urban forests or parkland, Frank Popper says. He concedes that the proof such steps work "is off there in the distance," but says the "prudent gamble" is worth taking.

"If we let the situation go on as it does now, we will get more and more crime, poverty and racism, and all these things have harmed the country plenty," says Popper, who emphasizes that he does not favor forcing people to relocate. "By doing nothing, we guarantee it to go on."

But the smart-decline mantra isn't accepted universally. Some policy experts argue that tearing out parts of cities — even blighted ones — sucks the life out of urban areas and makes their poverty and economic decline worse.

"When you demolish, there is no momentum left," argues Roberta Brandes Gratz, a longtime urban-policy author, most recently of *The Battle for Gotham: New York in the Shadow of Robert Moses and Jane Jacobs*. "The only way you get a critical mass is by adding the positive, not trying to eliminate the negative. It doesn't work."

Gratz points out that some of today's most exclusive neighborhoods once were buried in blight: New York's Greenwich Village, Washington, D.C.'s Georgetown area, New Orleans' French Quarter, Philadelphia's Rittenhouse Square and Boston's Back Bay. "They were all slums maybe 30 or 40 years ago," Gratz says. "Can you imagine if shrinkage had eliminated what they have now?"

"Preservation is as vital to urban health as renovation," David Frum, a conservative journalist and former speechwriter for President George W. Bush, wrote last year in a column analyzing Detroit's decline. Noting that some will want to tear down the shuttered factories along the Detroit River, Frum counseled to "leave them be."

"Leave them for now as monuments and memorials of the achievements of the past; leave them for the future, when somebody will want them. Want them for what? Who can say? Who in 1950 could ever have imagined London's Docklands converted into condominiums? Who would have guessed that New York's emptied toolshops would provide some of the city's most coveted office space? . . . Cities can molder for a century or more, and then reawaken to a new era that rediscovers something of value in the detritus of an earlier time."[10]

But many urban-policy experts argue that decrepit neighborhoods in declining cities are too far gone — too dangerous, costly, unsightly and unusable — to be saved.

"People say it's the wrong approach, and I appreciate where they're coming from, but they basically don't get it," says Mallach. "These cities have an oversupply of houses, office buildings, factories and so on — not just for today but for five, 10, 20 years down the road. In Detroit, by some accounts, there are 40,000 to 50,000 vacant buildings, not counting those already demolished. It's not a choice between demolishing those and having them all occupied with manufacturing, silk screeners and coffee houses. Anybody who thinks it's a choice is kind of deficient in Economics 101."

Kildee says the first thing declining cities must do is to measure and accept "their true population trajectory and economic-growth prospects," then "act on the new reality." If they don't, he says, the consequences can be "dire," including the spread of "contagious blight" from defunct neighborhoods to weak but salvageable ones.

"Say a city has 100,000 people and it used to have 200,000," Kildee says. "If we can't figure out a way over time, through market forces, incentives and the voluntary movement of population, to configure neighborhoods in a fashion that's sustainable, you'll see more and more neighborhoods universally and simultaneously in decline."

That's a pattern that overwhelmed Kildee's hometown of Flint. General Motors was founded in the city in 1908, and for decades Flint crested on the rising tide of American auto production. But in the 1970s that tide began to ebb. In the last 50 years the city shed almost 80,000 GM jobs.[11] And for the year ending in July 2009 Flint lost the biggest percentage of residents of any other large U.S. city.[12]

Kildee says Flint is still using a master plan that was drafted in 1965, when planners expected the city to grow to 250,000 people. But Flint hit its peak in 1960, with a population of 197,000. Today's count is about 44 percent below that high-water mark, or roughly 111,000. The city recently received a $1.5 million federal grant to revise its master plan, Kildee says.

As residents have vanished, thousands of abandoned and vacant structures have been left in their wake.

Should people living in blighted and depopulated neighborhoods be forced to move?

Last February, Detroit Mayor Bing told a radio audience that relocating people from blighted neighborhoods was "absolutely" part of his plan for restoring the city. "There is just too much land and too many expenses for us to continue to manage the city as we have in the past," he said. "There are tough decisions that are going to have to be made. There will be winners and losers, but in the end we've got to do what's right for the city's future."[13]

Whatever Bing had in mind, he since has gone out of his way to assure nervous residents that his administration doesn't aim to use eminent domain to force people to leave blighted neighborhoods for healthier ones.

"I realize mistakes have been made in the past and residents have a long, long memory," he told the Detroit City Council in September. "This plan ultimately belongs to the people of Detroit. We won't succeed without their support and cooperation. We will not take the position of forcing people from their homes."[14]

Bing's attempts at reassurances speak to perhaps the most sensitive issue in any plan to remake a city ravaged by blight and abandonment: Whether and how residents should be steered from decaying and depopulated neighborhoods toward healthier ones. Using force to relocate people raises the specter of urban-renewal practices that displaced tens of thousands of families — often poor and minority ones — in the 1960s.

The Brookings Institution's Vey says cities have become "very conscious of the fact that they're not going to be using eminent domain" to force people to relocate. "It's much more [a strategy of] working with people.

City officials are saying, "We've got to get out there and talk to the community," Vey says. They're saying, "This isn't about forcing people to move, but [trying to get them] voluntarily on board and understanding what the community is doing," she says.

Still, as cities try to guide residents toward more viable neighborhoods using incentives and persuasion, they face huge obstacles, not the least of which is resistance from people who may choose to remain in familiar surroundings — even if those surroundings are blighted and city officials warn of municipal-service cuts.

In Youngstown, the city does not actively seek to relocate residents of blighted neighborhoods, says planning director D'Avignon. "There is no political will to force anybody to move," he says. But Youngstown does use a carrot-and-stick approach to try to induce residents to voluntarily relocate.

For example, if a low-income resident seeks a home-repair grant from the city — say to update his plumbing — and the house is in a blighted neighborhood, the city may deny the grant and instead offer up to $50,000 to help the resident relocate to a better neighborhood. The city explains that while the person can choose not to move, relocating makes sense because municipal services are shifting toward more viable neighborhoods and the blighted areas will be less safe and healthy in the future.

So far, though, Youngstown's strategy of waiting for such relocation opportunities to arise hasn't proved particularly successful. Only five people have been offered assistance — and only one has accepted — and that person subsequently had to enter an assisted-living facility, D'Avignon says. "It's a big issue," he says of resident resistance to moving and its effects on the city's efforts to shrink its footprint.

Many policy experts say the relocation issue is especially sensitive for cities because it often involves racial minorities living in low-income neighborhoods. D'Avignon acknowledges that race "certainly plays a part" in how Youngstown handles the relocation issue. "Some of the minority communities are in those areas that are less sustainable," he says. "Politically, that's why we don't do anything too heavy-handed or too aggressive."

Kildee says incentives have long been used to influence migration trends in the United States, and the same can be done on the local level.

"There are plenty of examples of ways to use incentives for development to draw population from one place to another," Kildee says. "There's a history of that in this country. We've built infrastructure, provided tax breaks to fund it and underwritten the cost of development to make it happen, It's equally possible within a city to provide tools and incentives to allow a population to re-center itself."

BACKGROUND

Decline of Roman Empire

Shrinking cities are not a new phenomenon, and neither have they been confined to the United States.

As far back, at least, as the Roman Empire, urban populations have waxed and waned according to political, economic and social changes.

"In Late Antiquity, the Middle Ages and the Early Modern periods[,] the collapse of the Roman Empire, diseases, war, fire and recurrent agricultural crises all left their mark on European and Asian cities that were never completely abandoned and usually resettled," a group of scholars, including Schwarz and Frank Popper, wrote.

They noted that in today's Europe the phenomenon is concentrated in formerly socialist countries, particularly Latvia, Bulgaria, Romania, Hungary, Slovakia and eastern Germany, as well as in Finland, Sweden, Italy and Spain.[15]

Worldwide, scholars have estimated that a fourth of cities with at least 100,000 people were shrinking even before the recent global recession and U.S. mortgage crisis.[16] And in the United States, post-World War II suburban growth sapped residents from many urban areas. Census estimates in 2006 show that 16 of the 20 cities that were the nation's largest in the 1950s have since shrunk in population.[17]

In many big cities, the population declines have been stark. For example, from 1950 to 2007, St. Louis lost 59 percent of its residents, Cincinnati 41 percent and Philadelphia 30 percent. Youngstown dropped more than

61 percent and Cleveland and Detroit more than 55 percent.[18] While the reasons for the declines are many and varied, the massive contraction of the auto and steel industries hastened the population drops in places like Detroit, Flint and Youngstown.

Yet, even as people fled central cities for sprawling suburbs or up-and-coming communities in the South and West, urban planners still tended to shape policies around the notion that growth was not only good but inevitable." [I]n the 1950s and 1960s American planning devices focused on 'growth control,' in the 1970s and 1980s on 'growth management,' and in the 1990s and 2000s on 'smart growth,'" wrote land-use experts Deborah and Frank Popper. "No zoning ordinance, still the most frequent tool of American local land-use planning, explicitly anticipates that the locality or its neighborhoods will lose population."[19]

Political Dilemma

Indeed, for decades politicians and business leaders avoided words like "downsizing," "shrinking" and "decline" for fear of being tagged as defeatists. "It's very difficult, having served in public office for 33 of my 52 years, to stand in front of your constituents and promise to become a smaller city," says Kildee, the former Genesee County treasurer.

Still, some planning experts are reluctant to say that even cities with the biggest population losses can't reverse course. "I don't think anybody can say today these cities will never grow" again, says Kent State's Schwarz. Detroit, she notes, has a deep base of technical know-how, vast infrastructure and lots of cultural amenities. "It's not like you're going to turn out the lights and people are going to leave southern Michigan forever," she says.

What's more, some argue that Sun Belt boom cities like Phoenix could well begin losing population as water becomes scarce and infrastructure becomes strained. "All cities have their own degree of obsolescence," Schwarz says.

And unexpected misfortune — a natural disaster or a recession, for instance — can befall cities and cause residents to flee. New Orleans' population plunged from about 485,000 in 2000 to an estimated 223,388 in 2006, the year after Hurricane Katrina ravaged the Gulf Coast (the Census Bureau's latest estimate put the city's population at 355,000 in 2009). Wide-scale destruction from

CHRONOLOGY

1940s-1950s *Postwar economic growth spurs massive flight to the suburbs, setting stage for urban decline.*

1947 Levittown, on Long Island, is model for suburban development.

1949 U.S. helps cities acquire blighted property for private redevelopment.

1954 U.S. Supreme Court in *Berman v. Parker* upholds use of eminent domain to take blighted properties for urban renewal.

1956 Interstate Highway System spurs suburban growth.

1960s-1970s *Urban blight, riots and economic decline shake American cities.*

1960 One-fifth of U.S. housing is dilapidated, Census of Housing says.

1961 Urban-policy critic Jane Jacobs' *The Death and Life of Great American Cities* blasts urban renewal.

1968 After riots in Los Angeles and Newark, Kerner Commission says racism is cities' biggest problem.

1971 Earliest major land-bank plan created in St. Louis.

1974 Congress approves Community Development Block Grants for cities.

1975 President Gerald R. Ford refuses federal aid to New York City, prompting *Daily News* headline, "Ford to City: Drop Dead."

1976 Ohio land-bank legislation allows creation of Cleveland Land Bank.

1977 Ohio's Youngstown Sheet and Tube announces closings, foreshadowing crash of regional industrial economy.

1980s-1990s *Cities suffer as federal aid declines, crime grows.*

1980 Federal aid for cities begins shrinking, affecting big revitalization projects.

1981 Michigan Supreme Court upholds use of eminent domain to take Detroit's Poletown neighborhood for auto-assembly plant.

1989 Louisville, Ky., creates land bank.

1991 Atlanta creates land-bank authority. . . . U.S. homicide rate surges amid crack-cocaine epidemic.

1992 U.S. Conference of Mayors leads March on Washington to seek "Marshall Plan for the Cities."

2000-Present *Shrinking cities prompt calls for revival efforts.*

2000 Eight of the nation's 15 largest cities have lost population for the fifth census in a row.

2002 Land bank in Flint, Mich., created. . . . Youngstown, Ohio, begins revival plan.

2004 Abandoned Properties Rehabilitation Act enables New Jersey cities to gain control of blighted property faster.

2005 U.S. Supreme Court rules 5-4 in *Kelo v. New London* that local governments can take private property for economic development. . . . Hurricane Katrina devastates New Orleans; population plunges; President George W. Bush proposes slashing Community Development Block Grants.

2009 Basketball star Dave Bing elected Detroit mayor, promises to demolish 10,000 derelict structures. . . . President Obama fulfills pledge to reverse attempts to cut block grants. . . . Cleveland-area land bank reaches agreement with mortgage giant Fannie Mae to acquire properties from Fannie's inventory of foreclosed homes.

2010 Senate Banking Committee passes Livable Communities Act but measure faces heavy criticism from conservatives. . . . Land-bank bills in Pennsylvania, New York legislatures move forward. . . . Survey finds Detroit has 33,000 abandoned homes, 90,000 vacant lots, totaling a third of the residential parcels. . . . Republicans take control of House, make major gains in Senate as unemployment hovers near 10 percent and voters display impatience with Obama administration's policies.

Shrinking East European Cities Serve as Models for U.S.

"In East Germany, there was an almost overnight collapse of industry after reunification."

As American policymakers try to revive cities saddled with plummeting population, unemployment and blight, many of them are looking to Europe — including the former East Germany — for ideas.

Cities in the once-communist nation were among the first to "openly recognize the phenomenon of shrinking cities and make it part of the political discourse," says Tamar Shapiro, director of comparative domestic policy for the German Marshall Fund, which promotes ties between the United States and Europe.

"A number of older industrial cities in the western part of Germany had a somewhat slower but dramatic industrial decline [over] the last couple of decades," she says. But "in East Germany, there was an almost overnight collapse of industry after [German] reunification" in 1990.

Compared to cities in Western Europe and the United States, Shapiro says, "cities in the former East Germany came more quickly to an acceptance of the fact they were not going to come back to their earlier size." That acceptance "allowed them to focus on how to become vibrant at a smaller size."

Many Eastern European cities in the post-Soviet era have shrunk in recent years, for reasons that are complicated. In Russia and much of Eastern Europe (including eastern Germany), economic upheaval spurred migration. People often moved to capitals or other large cities, depopulating smaller and more distant ones. In Germany, many people moved from East to West and to suburbs of big cities immediately after reunification. More recently several large cities have been growing again while smaller towns

have continued to struggle. What's more, birth rates are low in many European countries, magnifying the population decline.[1]

The loss of manufacturing jobs also helped spur shrinking in many European cities, especially in the former Soviet sphere.

But some European cities have begun to turn themselves around, offering lessons for urban planners in the United States. Of course, important differences exist between Europe and the United States, not the least of which is how quickly government has responded to the distress being felt by older cities.

"There's been huge support from [the equivalent of] the federal and state governments [in Europe] whereas until recently there was no interest by the [U.S. federal government], and the states are still trying to figure out what to do as well," says Joseph M. Schilling, associate director of the Metropolitan Institute at Virginia Tech University.

Still, experts say the European experience is instructive. One of the most closely watched cities is Leipzig, an hour's drive southwest of Berlin in the former East Germany.

A center of industry and commerce for centuries, Leipzig was among Germany's five biggest cities in the 1930s, with more than 700,000 residents. Still, even before World War II, when the city was heavily bombed, Leipzig was losing residents. The losses continued after the war and rose sharply after the Berlin Wall fell.

Reunification led to currency reforms and privatization of industry that quickly made it hard for companies in Leipzig and other cities in the former East Germany to

the storm and ensuing flooding sparked bitter debates over whether to demolish parts of the city or rebuild them.

Florida, traditionally one of the nation's most powerful magnets for newcomers, saw its population decline between 2008 and 2009 for the first time since the end of World War II as recession, mortgage foreclosures and

job losses took their toll. (Florida returned to a modest growth mode last year.)[20]

The Orlando area, which drew tens of thousands of new arrivals annually before the current recession, lost an estimated 9,700 residents between April 2008 and April 2009. "We've gone from feast to famine in a pretty fast time, and these population numbers are a symptom of compete on global markets. Manufacturing jobs vanished, and vacancy and abandonment worsened.

A 2008 London School of Economics and Political Science study of seven European cities found that from 1990 to 2000, Leipzig lost more than 12 percent of its population. Manufacturing employment plunged by 87,000 jobs from 1989 to 1996. In fact, from 1970 to 2005 Leipzig lost nearly 90 percent of its manufacturing employment, leaving only about 10 percent of the workforce in that field, down from more than 25 percent in 1970.[2]

As the city's fortunes declined, so did its physical infrastructure and housing stock, which already were in poor shape before reunification. In 1990, 25,000 apartments were uninhabitable, and many buildings, some dating to the 1870s, were in decay.[3]

Yet over the past decade Leipzig has begun to recover. That's not to say it doesn't still face significant problems. Unemployment has been in double digits, in large part because of the loss of so many industrial jobs, and some neighborhoods remain hobbled by high vacancy rates and significant poverty.

But new employers, including BMW and Amazon, have moved in, technology and service employment has been rising and the city's population, now about 500,000, has been edging back up.

Leipzig has taken a variety of steps to deal with its shrinkage. It has demolished thousands of derelict housing units, created new green spaces where buildings were torn down or vacant parcels sat, instituted programs to refurbish run-down buildings and put them to use, enlisted public input in shaping neighborhood plans and made downtown revitalization a priority.

The downtown projects have included renovation of the city's central train station and addition of a retail center, done with significant private investment.

Shapiro says that in recognizing that its population had shrunk, Leipzig adopted new planning tools and focused them on key neighborhoods with significant needs.

Getty Images/Sean Gallop

New industries in Leipzig, Germany, including a BMW assembly plant, above, and Amazon, have given a boost to the city of 500,000. To cope with population shrinkage, it is demolishing hundreds of derelict structures.

Planning for roads, public transit and other infrastructure was integrated into plans for educational facilities, medical institutions, parks and so on.

The "integration across disciplines" and targeting of neighborhoods were "strongly encouraged" by the German federal government, she says. And that government funding, she adds, has been "critical" to Leipzig's recovery.

— *Thomas J. Billitteri*

[1] Hilda Blanco, Marina Alberti, *et al.*, "Shaken, Shrinking, Hot, Impoverished and Informal: Emerging Research Agenda in Planning," Progress in Planning 72, 2009.

[2] Anne Power, Jörg Plöger and Astrid Winkler, "Transforming Cities Across Europe: An interim report on problems and progress," London School of Economics and Political Science, Centre for Analysis of Social Exclusion, Report 49, March 2008, http://sticerd.lse.ac.uk/dps/case/cr/CASEreport49.pdf.

[3] Stadt Leipzig, www.leipzig.de/int/en/stadt_leipzig.

that," Orange County Mayor Rich Crotty said. "In the future, it's how do we adapt to declining growth."[21]

Urban Renewal's Shadow

While many localities are prone to population loss, at least in the short term, it is the steep, protracted and perhaps permanent declines plaguing many old-line industrial cities that are of most concern. As policy makers attempt to address the declines, they are haunted by the legacy of urban renewal programs of the 1950s and '60s, when cities struggled to compete with suburbs that drew affluent residents, jobs and commerce in droves.

A hallmark of that effort was the vast demolition of slums and other areas deemed blighted and the dislocation of poor residents — often minorities — to make way for new commercial and residential development and highways.

The 1960 Census of Housing found that about a fifth of the nation's dwelling units were dilapidated or deteriorating, most of them in slums or blighted areas.[22] Wolf Von Eckardt, a prominent architecture critic, wrote in 1963 that "[u]rban blight is proving more contagious than poliomyelitis ever was, and far more difficult to cure and prevent."[23]

Yet strategies to heal the blight proved highly controversial. Preservationists and other critics complained that viable buildings or whole blocks — many of historic or architectural significance — were needlessly bulldozed, sometimes replaced by upscale apartments and shops that dislocated the poor; that small businesses were seized through eminent domain; and that families were relocated to public housing projects or otherwise forced to leave established neighborhoods.

"Urban renewal means Negro removal," celebrated African-American author James Baldwin declared in a 1963 television interview.[24]

Between passage of the Housing Act of 1949, which spurred the urban-renewal movement by providing federal aid to cities for slum clearance and redevelopment, and Sept. 30, 1962, more than 146,000 families were displaced by federally assisted urban renewal projects. About 80 percent of the displaced families moved to homes the families bought, private rental housing or public housing. A little more than 7 percent moved into substandard housing.[25]

"By the late 1950s urban renewal and Interstate highways were converging on neighborhoods near the center of cities, uprooting families by the thousands," Bernard J. Frieden and Lynne B. Sagalyn wrote in their 1989 book, *Downtown, Inc.: How America Rebuilds Cities.* They added: "Of all the families displaced by urban renewal from 1949 through 1963, 63 percent of those whose race was known were nonwhite, and of these families 56 percent of nonwhites and 38 percent of whites had incomes low enough to qualify for public housing, which, however, was seldom available to them."[26]

In her best-selling 1961 book, *The Death and Life of Great American Cities*, urban activist Jane Jacobs lashed out against urban renewal and "the sacking of cities" by planners pursuing expensive, ill-conceived projects.[27]

"[P]eople who get marked with the planners' hex signs are pushed about, expropriated and uprooted much as if they were the subjects of a conquering power," she wrote. "Thousands upon thousands of small businesses are destroyed, and their proprietors ruined, with hardly a gesture at compensation. Whole communities are torn apart and sown to the winds, with a reaping of cynicism, resentment and despair that must be heard and seen to be believed."[28]

Urban-renewal practices evolved over the years, with growing emphasis on preservation and rehabilitation of aging structures and neighborhoods and less on wholesale demolition.

Budget Squeeze

Still, cities continued to face both criticism and obstacles in their urban revitalization efforts.

A big stumbling block was, and still is, money. Beginning in the 1980s, federal aid for cities shrank, leaving them with fewer resources to pursue large-scale revitalization projects. During the Republican administrations of Presidents Ronald Reagan (1981-1989) and George H. W. Bush (1989-1993), for example, Community Development Block Grants for Philadelphia dropped by more than half, according to John Kromer, senior consultant at the University of Pennsylvania's Fels Institute of Government.[29]

At the same time, many city officials became more selective in the use of eminent domain to seize property and force residents and businesses to relocate.

Among the dissenters in the Supreme Court's *Kelo* decision was Justice Clarence Thomas, who argued that urban renewal has long been associated with the displacement of minorities, poor and elderly. Among the incidents he cited was the uprooting of Detroit's predominantly low-income and elderly Poletown neighborhood in the early 1980s to benefit General Motors.

Many experts balk at comparisons between the circumstances surrounding urban renewal in the mid-20th century and those facing cities like Detroit and Youngstown today. Cities like New York and Boston, deeply troubled in the 1960s, have since revived, and they are benefiting from a "megatrend" in which younger, affluent families are leaving the suburbs and returning to the cities in search of cultural amenities, public transit, historic charm and other benefits. But shrinking cities are a category apart, experts such as Mallach of the Center for Community Progress argue.

"If you look at the broad trend of urban history, there's no question it was downhill in the 1950s into the '80s," he says. "That meant New York was losing population, as was Boston, and housing was being abandoned. But it was not because those regions didn't have economic fundamentals. It was because everybody was getting the hell out of cities and disinvesting. In the last 25 years that's turned around dramatically. Cities are no longer no-man's lands. As a broad category, they're very attractive to investors, young couples, all kinds of people. Overall, many cities have held up better in the current recession in terms of their housing market than outer-suburban areas. It's no longer an issue of cities generically losing jobs and being abandoned."

So-called shrinking cities, however, are "a different animal," Mallach adds. "People who say, 'Oh, you're just trying to go back to urban renewal' " are wrong, he continues. "There've been fundamental changes. What's going on in these cities [today] is very different than what went on back in the '70s."

Still, if the circumstances surrounding cities have changed, the legacy of the old urban-renewal era continues to shape the way officials in shrinking cities are dealing with depopulation and blight.

Schilling of Virginia Tech says many politicians are reluctant to acknowledge that their cities are shrinking and to take steps to deal with the problem because they fear the perception that they are using the heavy hand of government to push people around. And because abandoned neighborhoods are chiefly home to minorities, the potential for sparking racial tensions makes the issue all the more challenging.

To overcome those problems, "there's got to be some kind of outreach or engagement" with citizens by city leaders, Schilling says. "Part of the pushback as to why political leaders haven't embraced these concepts is because of our historic fear of big government, the whole phobia over urban renewal and the *Kelo* decision" on eminent domain. "To be able to do this kind of planning intelligently, it has to be driven by residents and neighbors who live there. It's not like you can just announce a plan."

Mallach argues for a federal policy shaped specifically for older distressed cities. In a recent study, he wrote that although "the federal government is already heavily

Banishing Blight

Despite staggering job loss, mortgage foreclosures, crime and decay, many older manufacturing cities are fighting to make a comeback. In downtown Detroit, rejuvenated Campus Martius Park has become a popular gathering spot, with two stages, sculptures, public spaces and a seasonal ice-skating rink (top). In Buffalo, Dewey Avenue is a well-kept street in the Central Park neighborhood on the city's East Side (bottom).

invested in these cities, its investment has been piecemeal and sporadic. Remaking America's distressed older cities as smaller and stronger should be central to the future federal engagement with those cities. . . . Federal initiatives have lacked a coherent strategy, have lacked coordination and have failed to make a sustained commitment to any project, neighborhood or community."[30]

Washington, under Republican and Democratic administrations, has poured billions of dollars into education, housing, anti-poverty programs and other urban activities, Mallach noted. Yet, "for all the programs launched and dollars spent . . . it is hard to show much connection between the American urban condition today — either the revival of cities like Atlanta and Boston or the continued distress of Detroit and Buffalo — and the federal initiatives of the past sixty years."[31]

Indeed, many urban-policy experts are calling for new federal policies aimed specifically at helping distressed cities "right-size" themselves and reshape their economies, social-welfare systems and infrastructure for the 21st century.

"I do think absolutely there needs to be a federal policy to specifically address this," says Williams, the Youngstown mayor. "Under the previous administration, we had to fight just to maintain block grants."

CURRENT SITUATION

Action in Congress

As depopulation, property abandonment and other woes continue to plague cities, Congress has been taking steps — albeit incomplete ones so far — to ease the distress.

In August the Senate Banking Committee passed the Livable Communities Act (S. 1619), a top priority of committee Chairman Christopher J. Dodd, D-Conn., who announced last summer he wouldn't seek a sixth term. The measure aims largely to provide planning and project grants to help growing communities coordinate their transportation, housing and community-development policies.

The Dodd bill has faced heavy criticism from conservatives. The Internet publication *American Thinker* characterized it as "top-down central planning aimed at changing where we live and work and how we travel."[32] Still, some observers believe the Dodd bill has a chance, however slim, for passage in a post-election lame-duck session this fall.

Folded into the bill is a separate measure called the Community Regeneration, Sustainability and Innovation Act (CRSI), which aims to create competitive HUD grants to help older industrial cities confront decline and integrate those efforts with programs promoting sustainability and "green" policies.

U.S. Rep. Tim Ryan, D-Ohio, a sponsor of CRSI, told a gathering of Youngstown residents in September that "it's very difficult, and has been for a long time, for cities the size of Youngstown to try to compete with an L.A. or New York" for federal urban-development grants. The aim of his bill, he said, is to have a "separate pot of money" for cities fighting population loss and decay.

Urban-policy experts see the Dodd bill as complementary to HUD's Sustainable Communities Regional Planning Grant program, which seeks to improve regional planning efforts that combine housing and transportation decisions and increase communities' capacity for land-use improvement.[33]

Congress appropriated $150 million in fiscal 2010 for the sustainable-communities program, according to Mara D'Angelo, a program manager at Smart Growth America, a coalition of roughly 70 national, state and local organizations. An initial round of grants totaling nearly $140 million was disbursed to localities and regions around the nation in October, D'Angelo says.

Northeast Ohio received one of the biggest, at $4.25 million.

Congress has not permanently enshrined the program in law, and while lawmakers have considered appropriating another $150 million in fiscal 2011, no decision has been made, D'Angelo says.

Lavea Brachman, executive director of the Greater Ohio Policy Center, a think tank and grassroots organization in Columbus, believes the HUD grants and potentially the Dodd bill could help spur planning officials to work more effectively across entire metropolitan regions rather than simply within city or county boundaries.

Meanwhile, many urban-policy experts are of two minds on whether the Obama administration has pushed hard enough to help distressed cities. On the plus side they cite the formation of the White House Office of Urban Affairs, its Neighborhood Revitalization Initiative and the White House Council on Automotive Communities and Workers. But they also want more concrete action.

"There hasn't been as much as we would have liked, but it's certainly a good start" and "significantly more" than occurred during the George W. Bush administration,

Is shrinkage a sound strategy for the most troubled cities?

YES

Deborah E. Popper
Professor of Geography, City University of New York/College of Staten Island

Frank J. Popper
Professor of Land-Use Planning, Rutgers University

Written for *CQ Researcher*, November 2010

America's most troubled cities have no choice but to cope with shrinkage. Today's shrinkage strategies are not the 1950s' assertive-government urban renewal that bulldozed functioning communities and moved residents to make way for new buildings. Instead, today's depopulating big cities have reacted too slowly to their losses and suffered from too little policy to deal with them.

Detroit, Youngstown, Memphis, Oakland and their many counterparts with half or less of their former populations see empty structures and vacant lots scattered throughout. Remaining residents live with decaying or boarded-up houses, garbage-strewn plots and empty factories.

City governments must provide roughly the same services as when the tax base was larger and richer. Housing prices are low, demand even lower. Shrinking cities take these conditions as givens. They ask: Now what?

The emerging redevelopment policies sensibly target seedy downtowns, which tend to be pre-automobile, walkable spaces that long ago lost out to suburban malls. Shrinking cities try to revitalize their old, often architecturally attractive buildings. They take the open spaces and use them for cultural events, street and food fairs and community gardens and parks. They can attract suburbanites or tourists, but even if they don't, their success comes in betterment for the local residents.

The new focus on clearing vacant lots addresses the most overt symptom — desertion — with achievable goals like useful, safe open spaces. Such places enrich residents' living landscape while they boost civic engagement, improve the food supply and increase fitness choices.

A shrinking city's hardest task is always job creation. Its economy has lost out to forces beyond local control. But shrinkage policies can improve residents' skill sets, widen the neighborhoods' choices and supply the labor to make them happen. Shrinking cities should support K-12 and adult-education efforts to train for environmental awareness and assessment. They can build skills in salvage and restoration, as well as soil-, air- and water-quality management. They can work closely with local colleges on the ecological assessment of cleared spaces to promote sensible reuses.

Shrinking cities must accept that large patches will not grow in the foreseeable future. But they can still be good places to live.

NO

Roberta Brandes Gratz
Author, The Battle For Gotham: New York in the Shadow of Robert Moses and Jane Jacobs

Written for *CQ Researcher*, November 2010

Theories abound as to what to do about shrinking cities. But little thought has entered the conversation that focuses on how to add density instead of losing more of it, how to foster the new economy instead of just acknowledging that the old one is not renewing itself.

Cities need density. Without it, they become car-dependent suburbs. The challenge is how to add to the shrinking fabric, not to shrink it further, to nurture a new economy, not bemoan the lost old one. Urban rebirth, wherever it exists, occurs only when something positive is added and transforms the negative.

I keep asking where has the theory worked in practice that shrinking infrastructure, consolidating neighborhoods, tearing down often-renewable structures actually benefits a city? Observation tells us that what gets built on cleared neighborhood land (often years after clearance) is suburban in density. Anyone who understands the DNA of a city understands that suburban density undermines urbanism.

Consolidating neighborhoods often means removing by eminent domain homeowners who could instead be the building blocks of a renewed neighborhood. Removing city services like fire and police often leads to new, expensive crime, refuse and gang problems. Removing blighted but salvageable structures destroys an environmental and economic resource never to be replaced.

The crux of the matter is that funding is more available for shrinkage than for repurposing or preservation. Where is the advocacy to change this? If one looks at regeneration stories from Pittsburgh to New Orleans to New York and many places in between, it worked only with the cobbling together of funding sources, the overcoming of anti-density, antiquated government regulations and the energy of local change-makers.

Where is the conversation about how to make this the new paradigm versus the easier route of clearance and acquiescence to defeat? Why do the redevelopment resources have to favor the corporate suburban-style new-home builders instead of giving equal treatment to small renovating developers?

Pockets of rebirth and new economic energy are occurring in shrinking cities from Detroit to Buffalo. Who is asking how to learn from this, how to nourish more of it and how to create the next Apple in a garage, Facebook in a dormitory room or Starbucks in a farmers' market?

Big corporations and thriving urban neighborhoods don't emerge in full bloom from nowhere. All big change starts small and grows slowly. How to find the seedlings and cultivate them is the real challenge.

General Motors headquarters rises behind an abandoned factory in Detroit. Mayor Dave Bing has promised to bulldoze 10,000 dangerous and derelict structures by the end of his term in 2013, but he has backed away from suggesting the city might force people to relocate to more viable neighborhoods.

says Brachman, also a nonresident senior fellow at the Brookings Institution. "We'd like to see more action items coming out of the [Obama] administration, but the rhetoric is right, and they talk a lot about capacity-building" to help cities tackle entrenched problems, she adds.

State Land Banks

Some states are moving forward with plans to form land banks to acquire and manage vacant and abandoned property. In Ohio, lawmakers this year expanded an existing state law applying only to Cuyahoga County (Cleveland area), giving other counties the ability to set up land banks.[34]

Meanwhile, the Pennsylvania House this year passed a comprehensive land-bank bill, but the measure remains in the appropriations committee.[35] In New York state, the Senate also passed a comprehensive land-bank measure, but it has not yet cleared the Assembly.[36]

"It's hard to get [land-bank legislation] through" state legislatures, the Center for Community Progress's Kildee says. Land banks "are not seen as a central part of urban policy — they're seen more related to the tax system," which is a "boring, sleepy" subject for many state lawmakers, he says. Kildee says part of his job is to "educate policy makers."

In the Cleveland area, the Cuyahoga County Land Reutilization Corp. acquired more than 200 properties in its first year, and the organization's president said last summer that he expected the number to exceed 700 by year's end.[37]

Under a landmark agreement, Fannie Mae, the federal mortgage giant, has been selling low-value foreclosed homes to the Cuyahoga land bank for $1 and paying $3,500 of demolition costs for those that are unsalvageable. The land bank also has an agreement with HUD to acquire some of that agency's lowest-value foreclosed properties for as little as $100 apiece. In addition, the land bank was part of a consortium that received nearly $41 million in federal Neighborhood Stabilization Program funds for demolition and renovation work in the Cleveland area.[38]

Philanthropic Aid

Foundations, long involved in urban-regeneration efforts, also are mounting new initiatives aimed at helping distressed cities restructure themselves.

In May the Ford Foundation, the nation's second-largest private philanthropy, announced plans to spend $200 million over the next five years to help metropolitan areas, including shrinking ones like Detroit, work in a more coordinated, collaborative fashion that melds housing, transportation, land-use policy and economic development efforts.

"The notion that suburbs can thrive while city centers atrophy has proved damaging to our nation," said foundation President Luis A. Ubiñas. "We now know that metropolitan areas share a common economic destiny. Metropolitan areas that manage to interweave urban and suburban development, everything from transportation to arts and culture, attract more people, and more investment."[39]

The Ford Foundation said it planned to support several transportation projects that link people and jobs, including Detroit's Woodward, or "M1," Light Rail project linking the city's entertainment district, commercial areas, cultural and medical facilities and other spots. The roughly $450-$500 million project, whose first $125 million phase is a 3.4-mile stretch expected to open in 2012 or 2013, has drawn a wide variety of corporate and foundation backers as well as federal funding and state support.[40]

Ford's plans also include support for creation of regional land-bank authorities to help urban areas restore blighted areas and improve housing opportunities. The funding includes support for the Center for Community Progress.

Ford is also a supporter of Living Cities, a 19-year-old collaborative of major foundations and financial institutions that focuses on improving conditions for low-income residents and urban areas.[41]

Neil Kleiman, the organization's director of policy and research, says three years ago the collaborative began a new effort to work directly with city and state elected officials on forging an integrated set of policy issues on such matters as housing, transportation, education and poverty reduction. The first effort has been in Cleveland, where Living Cities has spent two-and-a-half years, and $2.5 million in grants, loans and other support, working with local officials and the governor's office on forging a collaborative strategy for dealing with Cleveland's myriad challenges.

And this fall Living Cities was set to divide a total of $80 million in competitive grants and loans among five more cities — Cleveland, Minneapolis-St. Paul, Detroit, Newark and Baltimore.

Among the foundations active in Living Cities is the Detroit-based Kresge Foundation, which is working to attack problems in its own back yard.

With an endowment of about $2.9 billion, Kresge is taking a leading role in remaking Detroit. It commissioned a prominent urban planner to help the city with its restructuring plan and is working with Detroit officials and civic leaders on issues ranging from education reform to development of Detroit's "green" economy.

"What we really want to do is develop a model of a resilient city so that when population fluctuations happen, it's not the end of the line," says Laura Trudeau, senior program director at Kresge and head of its Detroit program. "Whether that's possible or not, we're going to give it a really good try."

The overall goal, she says, is "to bring back an older industrial city and reorient the region more to the core." Studies have shown that the Detroit region has consumed land at a rate more than five times the rate of its population growth in recent decades, she says. "We don't think we can maintain that."

Trudeau says the city's population loss and blight are symptoms of deeper problems that need critical attention, such as education quality and the lack of jobs.

Kresge has provided support for Detroit since 1924, including more than $250 million in grants over the past decade, Trudeau says. The foundation plans to continue making grants totaling $25 million to $30 million in Detroit annually, she says.

One of Kresge's signature grants has been $35 million for the light-rail project. Trudeau says the foundation hopes Kresge's money, along with that of other private and government supporters, will help leverage enough federal funds for the region to complete the line's entire nine-mile run.

"We want Detroit to compete well with other cities in attracting residents," Trudeau says.

In nearby Flint, the Charles Stewart Mott Foundation has granted $5.9 million since 1997 to help get the Genesee County Land Bank Authority off the ground, assist it in advising a dozen other Michigan counties to start similar land banks and start the Center for Community Progress, according to Neal Hegarty, director of the foundation's Flint-area program.

"We know the land bank itself can't turn around the problematic housing markets or rebuild the manufacturing economy" in Flint, Hegarty says. But, he adds, Mott looks for "metrics of success" that show the city and its residents are making progress. "Are they able to deal with the flood of vacant land in a better way, spur redevelopment efforts . . . , stop the contagion of blight and find suitable use for the land?"

OUTLOOK

Coordinated Action

As Brachman of the Greater Ohio Policy Center points out, the roots of the decline eating away at cities are decades old. No strategy or policy is going to solve the problem overnight. Part of what is needed, she says, is coordinated action at the local, state and federal levels. "It's really about comprehensive solutions," she says. "It can't be incremental."

> "What we really want to do is develop a model of a resilient city so that when population fluctuations happen, it's not the end of the line."
>
> — *Laura Trudeau,*
> *Senior Program Director,*
> *Kresge Foundation*

Virginia Tech's Schilling suggests a three-pronged approach for distressed cities to follow in their vacant-property reclamation efforts: creation of a land bank or similar mechanism; establishment of a "green infrastructure plan" that includes not just parks and gardens but renewable-energy facilities, wetlands and other systems; and most crucially, outreach to residents. "You've got to engage the community," Schilling says.

Yet as old-line manufacturing cities struggle to remake themselves, government aid will also be crucial — and likely harder to get, especially with tax-cutting Republicans gaining new power in Congress.

Mallach sees three big challenges ahead for blighted cities:

• Reusing surplus land and buildings. "How do you deal with huge amounts of land that no longer has an economic use in the traditional sense?" Mallach asks.

• Figuring out how to preserve viable neighborhoods. Tax law doesn't always help. Mallach is critical of situations in which builders use low-income housing tax credits to build new rental units in cities already oversupplied with affordable housing.

In Dayton, Ohio, Mallach found a 14 percent vacancy rate in rental units for low-income residents there, yet more affordable-housing projects being built. "You pretty much guarantee that for every unit you add, another is going to be abandoned in the same neighborhood or the same city," Mallach says.

• Rebuilding and stabilizing the economies of blighted cities, which may be the most daunting challenge of all. "Ultimately, if you don't have the economy," Mallach says, "you're not going to have much else. If these cities are not going to be manufacturing powerhouses, which they're not, what do they rebuild around?"

NOTES

1. Quoted in *NBA Encyclopedia*, Dave Bing Bio, www.nba.com/history/players/bing_bio.html. The quote is attributed to Otto Moore.

2. Figures on number of abandoned homes and vacant lots are from a survey by the Detroit Data Collaborative. See, "Survey: A third of all Detroit lots are vacant or abandoned," The Associated Press, Feb. 20, 2010, www.mlive.com/news/detroit/index.ssf/2010/02/survey_a_third_of_all_detroit.html.

3. Christine MacDonald, "Bing presents reshaping plan to Council, shows doubts with urban farming," *Detroit News*, Sept. 8, 2010, http://detnews.com/article/20100908/METRO01/9080403/Bing-presents-reshaping-plan-to-Council--shows-doubts-with-urban-farming.

4. CNN, "American Morning," Transcript, April 29, 2010, http://transcripts.cnn.com/TRANSCRIPTS/1004/29/ltm.01.html.

5. "Debating fears and hopes for a 'new' Detroit," NBC News, Sept. 17, 2010, accessed at www.bing.com/videos/watch/video/debating-fears-and-hopes-for-a-new-detroit/61bie3e.

6. See, for example, "Revitalizing Foreclosed Properties with Land Banks," U.S. Department of Housing and Urban Development, Office of Policy Development and Research, August 2009, www.huduser.org/Publications/PDF/landbanks.pdf.

7. Ryan Nobles, "Richmond Explores New Tool to Fight Property Blight," WWBT NBC12, Aug. 20, 2010, www.nbc12.com/Global/story.asp?S=13020631. See also Lavea Brachman, "Vacant and Abandoned Property: Remedies for Acquisition and Redevelopment," Lincoln Institute of Land Policy,

October 2005, www.lincolninst.edu/pubs/1057_
Vacant-and-Abandoned-Property.

8. *Kelo v. City of New London*, 545 U.S. 469 (2005).
See Kenneth Jost, *Kelo v. City of New London*, *CQ
Supreme Court Collection* (2005); and Charles Lane,
"Justices Affirm Property Seizures," *The Washington
Post*, June 24, 2005, www.washingtonpost.com/wp-
dyn/content/article/2005/06/23/AR2005062
300783.html.

9. Dan Kildee, "Land Banks as a Redevelopment Tool,"
Cascade, No. 75, Fall 2010, Federal Reserve Bank of
Philadelphia, www.philadelphiafed.org/community-
development/publications/cascade/75/04_land-
banks-as-redevelopment-tool.cfm.

10. David Frum, "What killed Detroit?," *National Post*,
Aug. 4, 2009, http://network.nationalpost.com/np/
blogs/fullcomment/archive/2009/08/04/david-
frum-what-killed-detroit.aspx.

11. Gordon Young, "What Dan Kildee wants America
to learn from the sorry tale of Flint, Mich.," *Slate*,
July 16, 2010, http://network.nationalpost.com/np/
blogs/fullcomment/archive/2009/08/04/david-
frum-what-killed-detroit.aspx.

12. Kristin Longley, "Flint tops large U.S. cities in population decline," *Flint Journal*, June 22, 2010, www
.mlive.com/news/flint/index.ssf/2010/06/flint_
tops_large_cities_in_nat.html.

13. Jonathan Oosting, "Detroit Mayor Dave Bing:
Relocation 'absolutely' part of plan to downsize
city," *MLive.com*, Feb. 25, 2010, www.mlive.com/
news/detroit/index.ssf/2010/02/detroit_mayor_
dave_bing_reloca.html. Bing made his comments
on WJR AM-760.

14. MacDonald, *op. cit.*

15. Justin B. Hollander, Karina M. Pallagst, Terry
Schwarz and Frank J. Popper, "Chapter 4: Planning
shrinking cities," Hilda Blanco, Marina Alberti,
et al., "Shaken, shrinking, hot, impoverished and
informal: Emerging research agenda in planning,"
Progress in Planning 72 (2009), pp. 195-250.

16. *Ibid.* The authors cite Philipp Oswalt and Tim
Rieniets, *Atlas of Shrinking Cities* (2006).

17. *Ibid.*

18. Alan Mallach, "Facing the Urban Challenge: the
Federal Government and America's Older Cities,"
Brookings Institution, May 2010, www.urban.org/
uploadedpdf/1001392-urban-challenge.pdf. The
sources of the data are U.S. Census Bureau Census
of Population and American Community Survey.

19. Deborah Popper and Frank Popper, "Smart Decline
in Post-Carbon Cities: The Buffalo Commons Meets
Buffalo, New York," from Richard Heinberg and
Daniel Lerch, eds., *The Post Carbon Reader: Managing
the 21st Century's Sustainability Crises* (2010).

20. "Florida's population grows again after first decline
since mid-1940s," *University of Florida News*, Sept.
2, 2010, http://news.ufl.edu/2010/09/02/florida-
pop-2010. The article cites data from the University
of Florida Bureau of Economic and Business
Research.

21. Jeff Kunerth and Linda Shrieves, "Central Florida is
shrinking. Orlando, Orange County and the state
saw populations dip for the first time in decades,"
Orlando Sentinel, Aug. 20, 2009, http://articles
.orlandosentinel.com/2009-08-20/news/pop
drop_1_population-growth-central-florida-orl
.ando-area.

22. W. B. Dickinson Jr., "Urban Renewal Under Fire,"
Editorial Research Reports (now *CQ Researcher*), Aug.
21, 1963.

23. Quoted in *ibid.* Von Eckardt's comment appeared in
The New Republic, June 1, 1963.

24. Quoted in *ibid.* Baldwin made his comment on
WNDT-TV in New York City on May 28, 1963.

25. *Ibid.*

26. Bernard J. Frieden and Lynne B. Sagalyn, *Downtown,
Inc.: How America Rebuilds Cities* (1989), p. 28.

27. Jane Jacobs, *The Death and Life of Great American
Cities* (1961), p. 4.

28. *Ibid.*, p. 5.

29. John Kromer, *Fixing Broken Cities* (2010), p. 292.

30. Mallach, *op. cit.*, p. 2.

31. *Ibid.*, p. 16.

32. Ed Braddy, "The Livable Communities Act,"
American Thinker, Aug. 11, 2010, www.american

thinker.com/2010/08/the_livable_communities_act_1.html.

33. "Sustainable Communities Planning Grant Program," U.S. Department of Housing and Urban Development, http://portal.hud.gov/portal/page/portal/HUD/program_offices/sustainable_housing_communities/grant_program.

34. See Ken McCall, "Land banks can acquire, manage abandoned properties under new law," *Dayton Daily News*, July 9, 2010, www.daytondailynews.com/news/dayton-news/land-banks-can-acquire-manage-abandoned-properties-under-new-law-803596.html.

35. Pennsylvania House Bill 712.

36. New York Assembly Bill 700.

37. Sandra Livingston, "Cuyahoga County land bank marks first year with series of accomplishments," *Plain Dealer*, July 4, 2010, www.cleveland.com/open/index.ssf/2010/07/cuyahoga_county_land_bank_mark.html.

38. *Ibid.*

39. "Helping America's Metropolitan Regions Build Prosperity and Expand Opportunity," press release, Ford Foundation, May 18, 2010, www.fordfoundation.org/newsroom/news-from-ford/375.

40. See Mike Scott, "Mass transit for Motor City," CNNMoney.com, Feb. 15, 2010, http://money.cnn.com/2010/02/15/smallbusiness/detroit_m1_light_rail/index.htm.

41. Living Cities, www.livingcities.org.

BIBLIOGRAPHY

Books

Frieden, Bernard J., and Lynne B. Sagalyn, *Downtown, Inc.: How America Rebuilds Cities*, MIT Press, 1989.
This dated but useful examination traces the progression of city centers from the "bulldozer days" of urban renewal in the 1950s and '60s to efforts to revitalize the nation's downtowns.

Gallagher, John, *Reimagining Detroit*, Wayne State University Press, 2010.
A veteran *Detroit Free Press* journalist analyzes emerging ideas to reverse Detroit's decline and argues that the possibility of reform lies "mostly in an unqualified acceptance of Detroit as a smaller but potentially better city."

Jacobs, Jane, *The Death and Life of Great American Cities*, Random House, 1961.
In this classic of city-planning literature, Jacobs blasts the urban renewal practices of the 1950s and early '60s, arguing that "there is nothing economically or socially inevitable about either the decay of old cities or the fresh-minted decadence of the new unurban urbanization."

Kromer, John, *Fixing Broken Cities*, Routledge, 2010.
An urban-policy expert and former director of housing in Philadelphia examines strategies for turning around distressed urban areas and in doing so focuses on a central issue: Who should benefit from such efforts?

Articles

Bennett, Drake, "How to Shrink a City," *The Boston Globe*, Sept. 5, 2010, www.boston.com/bostonglobe/ideas/articles/2010/09/05/how_to_shrink_a_city/.
"A few planners and politicians are starting to try something new: embracing shrinking," notes this useful overview of strategies being considered in cities such as Detroit, Youngstown and Cleveland.

Chozick, Amy, "Motown Becomes Movietown," *The Wall Street Journal*, Sept. 17, 2010, p. W1, http://online.wsj.com/article/SB10001424052748703743504575493773596572154.html?KEYWORDS=motown.
Detroit may be marred by blight and population decline, but the city, benefiting from Michigan's generous tax incentive for filmmaking, is looking to the entertainment sector to be "a lifeboat as the auto industry adapts and restructures," Wayne County Executive Robert A. Ficano says.

Kotlowitz, Alex, "All Boarded Up," *The New York Times*, March 8, 2009, www.nytimes.com/2009/03/08/magazine/08Foreclosure-t.html.
Cleveland experienced 10,000 home foreclosures in two years, and its population has dropped by half since 1960,

notes this profile of a city where "hope comes in small morsels."

Young, Gordon, "The Incredible Shrinking American City," *Slate*, **July 16, 2010, www.slate.com/ id/2260473/.**
A freelance journalist and Flint, Mich., native profiles land-bank advocate Dan Kildee and his work in the beleaguered auto town.

Reports and Studies

Mallach, Alan, "Facing the Urban Challenge," Brookings Institution, May 10, 2010, www.brook ings.edu/papers/2010/0518_shrinking_cities_ mallach.aspx.
A community-development expert argues that "an explicit federal policy focus on distressed older cities" is needed.

Pallagst, Karina, *et al.,* **"The Future of Shrinking Cities: Problems, Patterns and Strategies of Urban Transformation in a Global Context," Institute of Urban and Regional Development, University of California, Berkeley, May 2009, http://iurd.berkeley .edu/sites/default/files/pubs/MG-2009-01.pdf.**
Scholars provide an international perspective on the problem of shrinking cities and examine the phenomenon in the United States.

Popper, Deborah, and Frank Popper, "Smart Decline in Post-Carbon Cities: The Buffalo Commons Meets Buffalo, New York," Post Carbon Institute, July 20, 2010, www.postcarbon.org/Reader/PCReader-Popper-Decline.pdf.
A husband-and-wife team draws on their scholarly research on the buffalo country of the Great Plains to argue for "smart-decline" policies in shrinking cities.

"Revitalizing Foreclosed Properties with Land Banks," U.S. Department of Housing and Urban Development, Office of Policy Development and Research, August 2009, www.huduser.org/ Publications/PDF/landbanks.pdf.
This is a useful overview of the history of land banks, obstacles to communities trying to set up such mechanisms and emerging trends as financially strapped local governments try to manage a growing inventory of foreclosed and abandoned property.

Power, Anne, Jörg Plöger and Astrid Winkler, "Transforming Cities Across Europe," London School of Economics and Political Science, Centre for Analysis of Social Exclusion, March 2008, http:// sticerd.lse.ac.uk/dps/case/cr/CASEreport49.pdf.
Scholars cover, with detailed graphs and data, the progress of seven European cities that are trying to recover from a decline in their industrial bases.

For More Information

Brookings Institution, 1775 Massachusetts Ave., N.W., Washington, DC 20036; (202) 797-6000; www.brookings.edu. Think tank that studies urban policy.

Charles Stewart Mott Foundation, 503 S. Saginaw St., Suite 1200, Flint, MI 48502-1851; (810) 238-5651. Private grant maker that has aided in land-bank formation.

Cleveland Urban Design Collaborative, Kent State University, 1309 Euclid Ave., Suite 200, Cleveland, OH 44115; (216) 357-3434; www.cudc.kent.edu. Houses Kent State's graduate program in urban design and provides technical help and research to urban communities.

Center for Community Progress, (877) 542-4842; www.communityprogress.net. Nonprofit group that advocates broader use of land banks.

Ford Foundation, 320 E. 43rd St., New York, NY 10017; (212) 573-5000; www.fordfoundation.org. Private grant maker aiding Detroit and other shrinking cities.

Genesee County Land Bank, 452 S. Saginaw St., 2nd Floor, Flint, MI 48502; (810) 257-3088; www.thelandbank.org. Acquires foreclosed or abandoned property and manages it for future use or disposition.

Greater Ohio Policy Center, 399 East Main St., Suite 140, Columbus, OH 43215; (614) 224-0187; www.greaterohio.org. Think tank and grassroots organization advocating policies that encourage regional cooperation in the state.

Kresge Foundation, 3215 West Big Beaver Road, Troy, MI 48084; (248) 643-9630; www.kresge.org. Private grant maker aiding Detroit.

Youngstown Neighborhood Development Corp., 201 E. Commerce St., Suite 140, Youngstown, OH 44503; (330) 480-0423; www.yndc.org. A partnership between the City of Youngstown and the Raymond John Wean Foundation.

Lunchtime crowds pack Atlanta's Fairlie-Poplar Historic District for weekly concerts. Across the country, once moribund downtown areas have become clean, chic and expensive, thanks in part to new convention centers, stadiums and performing-arts complexes. But some critics say downtowns' newfound popularity will fade as affluent city dwellers start families and move to the suburbs. Meanwhile, they say, low-income residents are being forced out of gentrifying neighborhoods.

From *CQ Researcher*,
June 23, 2006 (updated June 13, 2012).

4

Downtown Renaissance

Alan Greenblatt, Charles S. Clark, and Bill Wanlund

One fine May afternoon, Sam Kleckley was sitting in downtown Greenville, S.C., enjoying watching people meandering across the new pedestrian bridge overlooking the waterfalls cascading down the Reedy River. Nodding toward a wedding party posing for pictures, he said, "It's amazing the number of people who came here for prom pictures, too."

The chance for photo ops is new in downtown Greenville. A few years ago, a large vehicular bridge blocked the view of the falls. Today it's gone, and the 18-month-old pedestrian bridge and the park surrounding it are the city's leading tourist attraction.

But they're not the only draw in a downtown that suddenly finds itself crowded with shoppers and folks hunting for places to eat. Main Street, which had only four restaurants 20 years ago, now boasts more than 75. There's a busy performing-arts center, and the new minor league ballpark just up the street has largely silenced local complaints about the home team's quirky name, The Drive. And the number of downtown residential units has jumped 50 percent in the last five years.

"It is phenomenal," says Kleckley, owner of a restaurant with an impressive river view. "Ten years ago, this area was like a slum."

Greenville's revitalization *is* phenomenal, but it's far from unique. After decades of decline, America's downtowns are making a comeback. From Phoenix to Philadelphia, from Memphis to Minneapolis, once derelict areas have become clean, chic and expensive.

"If you look at the numbers, there's no question that downtowns are coming back and are healthy in ways that we never expected," says David Feehan, president of the International Downtown Association.

Suburbs Outpacing Central Cities

Suburbs throughout the United States are growing rapidly, especially in the South and West. In contrast, central cities are growing more slowly. In the Midwest, however, they are declining.

Population Change in Central Cities and Suburbs of Large Metropolitan Areas, 2000-2004
(By percent change)

[Bar chart showing Central Cities (light) and Suburbs (dark) by region:
- Northeast: Central Cities 0.1%, Suburbs 2.5%
- Midwest: Central Cities -0.9%, Suburbs 4.3%
- South: Central Cities 2.8%, Suburbs 9.9%
- West: Central Cities 4.4%, Suburbs 8.6%
Y-axis from -2 to 10%]

Source: The Brookings Institution, "Living Cities Census Series," September 2005

Greenville suffered many of the same woes that befell other American cities after World War II, when an explosion of cars and road building lured city dwellers to the suburbs. Even today, Greenville accounts for only 56,000 residents in a sprawling county of 400,000.

But central business districts were never meant as places to live. They were where people went to work and shop. And they were famous for their huge department stores, women's-wear shops and, improbable as it may seem, car dealers. But the retail outlets and car dealerships soon followed their customers to the suburbs, where giant malls began rising in the 1940s. By 2000, downtown retail sales accounted for less than 5 percent of the nation's total, says Feehan.

Office workers still came downtown to shop, since many jobs remained in the cities, even through the worst of times. But casual visitors stayed away: Parking was scarce and expensive, many retail outlets had closed and crime became a major concern, particularly after a crack epidemic left drug addicts, homelessness and panhandlers in its wake. Cities in the 1970s and '80s were "places of crime and danger," says Paul Levy, president of the Philadelphia Center City District.

Downtowns had become the empty center of the metropolitan donut. But while suburban population and job growth continue to outpace downtowns, central cities are experiencing an undeniable, if perhaps fragile, renaissance. A strong economy and better policing techniques, as pioneered in New York City, have helped bring crime way down. Violent crimes dropped by 32 percent between 1995 and 2004, according to the FBI.[1]

Moreover, says Feehan, between 1995 and 2005 major crimes declined 58 percent in U.S. cities. Business-improvement districts (BIDs) such as Levy's, invested heavily in sprucing up appearances, which helped downtowns look cleaner and safer. Many BIDs imposed levies or even helped pass tax increases that paid for new convention centers, stadiums and performing-arts complexes.

Movies and television shows like "Ally McBeal" and "Sex and the City" began depicting urban living as the lifestyle choice of hip, single, young adults. "The cultural change reflected demographic change," says Levy, "and these things are reinforcing each other."

Today, many young people aspire to live in cities because that's where the action is. For a generation that grew up knowing only the vast, anonymous spaces of shopping malls and suburban sprawl, downtowns feel richer in history and a sense of place. "People are looking for denser social experiences, a greater sense of civic life," says Alison Isenberg, a Rutgers University historian and author of the 2004 book *Downtown America.* "That's something that's very hard to find in suburbs."

Fifteen or 20 years ago, feasibility studies suggested no one would want to live downtown. But after a few developers took a risk and began converting abandoned old buildings into condos, the "loft" spaces became an important new trend.

"In the studies, no one could get it in their minds what it was like to live downtown," says Richard T. Reinhard, managing director of urban development and public infrastructure at the Urban Land Institute. "Yet when the product was put on the market, people discovered it was something that they really liked."

The lofts, coffee shops and hookah bars that now are common in many contemporary downtowns are catnip to young people. Older folks whose children are grown — so-called empty nesters — also find themselves drawn back to city living. Many baby boomers, it seems, find they no longer need 5,000-square-foot homes in suburban cul-de-sacs and instead prefer to walk to work or to downtown attractions.

Some worry that the influx of middle- and upper-income residents is driving out long-term, low-income residents. But others say that busier downtowns, which were never primarily residential areas, are a boon. Downtowns that once were barren after 6 o'clock are now bustling at night with tourists or residents with more disposable income than children. In Greenville, ballgames, outdoor concerts and other events draw people downtown and encourage them to loiter at restaurants and cafes. "There's something going on every night from Wednesday on," says Kleckley, the restaurant owner.

Many cities now rely on a similar formula of attractions and leisure spending, leading some critics to warn that downtowns are becoming Disneyfied versions of themselves — all with the same chain restaurants and not enough sustainable business activity of substance, such as legal and professional services. Downtowns certainly don't command the same dominant share of either jobs or

Downtown Revival Lagging in Some Cities

Only five downtown areas are fully developed in the United States, including Boston and Chicago, according to a Brookings Institution study. Another five are on the verge of taking off, and a baker's dozen are emerging. However, St. Louis and Detroit are among a dozen cities experiencing population declines.

Status of Downtowns in Major Cities

Fully Developed — Large, densely settled, sustained positive household growth in past three decades; highly educated, relatively affluent populace has highest rates of homeownership.

Boston	Lower Manhattan	Philadelphia
Chicago	Midtown Manhattan	

Emerging — Located primarily in the South and West, smaller and far less dense than fully developed downtowns; only experienced growth in the 1990s and are much less affluent; show promise of becoming fully developed if high household growth rates continue.

Atlanta	Cleveland	Memphis	Portland, Ore.
Baltimore	Denver	New Orleans	San Diego
Charlotte	Los Angeles	Norfolk	San Francisco
			Seattle

About to Take Off — Larger than emerging downtowns but slightly less dense; experienced greater losses in households between 1970-1990 than emerging downtowns but made a comeback in the '90s with higher rates of homeownership and educational attainment; relatively more affluent than emerging downtowns.

Chattanooga	Miami	Washington, D.C.
Dallas	Milwaukee	

Slow-Growing — Majority are in the South and West; the smallest and least dense of all the downtown categories. Experienced growth in the 1990s after significant losses in the previous two decades; generally lower average education attainment rates and less affluence than cities above.

Albuquerque	Boise	Indianapolis	Pittsburgh
Austin	Colorado Springs	Lafayette	Salt Lake City
	Columbus, Ohio	Phoenix	

Declining — Primarily in the Midwest and South, these downtowns are smaller and have less density; all lost households in each of the last three decades and by 2000 had just 65 percent of the households they had in 1970; small percentage of downtown residents have bachelor's degrees.

Cincinnati	Detroit	Mesa, Ariz.	San Antonio
Columbus, Ga.	Jackson, Miss.	Minneapolis	Shreveport
Des Moines	Lexington, Ky.	Orlando	St. Louis

Source: The Brookings Institution, "Living Cities Census Series," September 2005

City Shoppers Find Plenty of Merlot, But No Diapers

The Park Slope section of Brooklyn is now stroller infested, a prime place for parents wanting to raise their children in a leafy, upscale neighborhood. It is still adjusting, however, to its new demographics, with well-publicized disputes between parents and the childless as more and more places become child-friendly — even taverns.[1]

But the neighborhood hasn't fully given itself over to the prerogatives of parents. For one thing, there aren't enough disposable diapers. Eager shoppers are known to form long lines at the few places that carry the products whenever a delivery is expected.

Even in cities that have thriving downtown office and entertainment districts filled with crowded restaurants and condo and loft dwellers, retail has been slow to follow. Downtowns and their big department stores dominated retail during the first half of the 20th century, but only a paltry amount of goods are sold downtown today. "Even the office worker" — once the most loyal group of downtown shoppers — "has to be competed for against the suburban mall," says Alison Isenberg, author of *Downtown America.*

Shopping in urban areas is a lot different than in the suburbs, where well-stocked big-box and warehouse stores come equipped with lifetime supplies of groceries, household goods and other sundry items that are either hard to find in the inner city or are sold after a high markup in small convenience stores.

But that may be changing, at least in some places. Wal-Mart, the world's largest retailer, announced in April that it would open 50 stores in blighted urban areas over the next couple of years.[2] Its rival, Target, has already opened stores in several urban malls, including a two-story location in its hometown of Minneapolis. Even supermarkets, which have been fleeing urban settings since the 1970s, are returning.[3]

People may not want to drive very far to buy the goods and services that they need on a daily basis, such as groceries and dry cleaning. But, as with live entertainment or sports, suburbanites have become willing to come downtown for "destination shopping" — unique boutiques that have items that can't be found anywhere else, or stores that make shopping into an event.

"You don't go to Williams-Sonoma just to buy a frying pan," says David Feehan, president of the International Downtown Association. "It's all about the experience. They can teach you how to prepare French meals."

But author Joel Kotkin, a skeptic about the extent of downtown revivals, is dubious that downtown retail is going to make a dent in suburban sales. "It's very difficult in American cities now to find a unique anything," he says. "Why go to a Gap in Harvard Square when there's a Gap in every shopping mall?"

Although downtowns have found it tough to attract retail outlets, that is only natural, says Christopher B. Leinberger, a visiting fellow at the Brookings Institution. Retailers are followers of real estate, he says, reluctant to enter downtown markets until there is enough population in place to support them.

"The housing must be in place before a grocery can build a store," he says. "As a downtown redevelops, there are not enough households initially to justify the conventional grocery store."

Limitations on land present special challenges for big stores, especially for parking. But there are enough people moving into some downtowns to more than justify the headaches. In Manhattan, for example, more than 40 cash registers at the 59,000-square-foot Whole Foods store at Columbus Circle, on the Upper West Side, barely keep up with the crowds at lunch time and during the evening rush hour.[4]

"Grocery stores in particular are finding urban locations exceedingly profitable due to less shelf space devoted to low-profit paper goods, like diapers, and more space for more profitable take-out food for busy professional households," Leinberger concluded in a Brookings research brief.[5]

---

[1] Chris Erikson, "Lowering the Bar," *The New York Post*, Dec. 20, 2005, p. 42.

[2] Abigail Goldman, "Wal-Mart Plans Stores in Ailing Urban Areas," *Los Angeles Times*, April 5, 2006, p. C3.

[3] Alan Ehrenhalt, "The Grocery Gap," *Governing*, April 2006, p. 9.

[4] Teri Karush Rogers, "Turning Supermarkets Into Restaurants, Too," *The New York Times*, Aug. 28, 2005, p. 3:24.

[5] Christopher B. Leinberger, "Turning Around Downtown: Twelve Steps to Revitalization," Brookings Institution, March 2005, p. 19.

retail sales they once did. Indeed, the Census Bureau stopped tracking downtown retail sales in 1977 because the number had become such a small percentage of overall metropolitan sales — just 4 percent compared with 50 percent in 1920. Thus, rather than being revitalized, downtowns are being reinvented, Isenberg suggests.

Despite the naysaying, there's no question that dozens of American downtowns are livelier places than they were just a few years ago. "If we're filling up the buildings and we're attracting middle- and upper-income people and we're having lively streets and restaurants, where's the problem?" wonders Feehan. "I don't see it."

As people contemplate the changing nature of downtowns and their future, here are some of the questions they're debating:

Are downtowns making a sustainable comeback?

Greenville has drawn people back downtown using several methods that have become popular with city governments: It helped build a large hotel for business meetings, a pair of large performing-arts venues and the new ballpark. Those attractions provided anchors for downtown development along Main Street, encouraging both people and retailers to return to the area.

Although many downtowns today clearly are healthier than they were a few years ago, many experts fear their success is not built on solid foundations. Because many reviving downtowns rely heavily on entertainment, skeptics wonder how long such "urban theme parks" will remain popular. And downtown growth — in terms of business, retail and residential — still represents only a fraction of the continued oceanic swelling of American suburbs.

"The numbers are pretty overwhelming that what is happening in downtowns is real but very, very small compared to suburbs," says Joel Kotkin, a senior fellow at the New America Foundation and author of several books and studies about cities. "Perhaps most troubling, there is not a huge amount of job growth in most of the traditional downtowns, even though we have a strong [nationwide] expansion. My sense is that many cities are becoming more residential, in part, because the office demands are not there."

Pittsburgh Cultural Trust (both)

Transformation in Pittsburgh

In the 1980s, the Harris Theater was one of many X-rated attractions in downtown Pittsburgh. Today the dramatically revitalized central city features a dozen theaters and performance spaces and numerous art galleries.

Downtowns might be able to survive as "Disneylands for adults," as Kotkin calls them, but some analysts worry they'll lose their shine over time. New downtown residents are overwhelmingly young professionals who may very well move back to the suburbs soon after starting families because, while public schools in many large cities have shown measurable

Top Cities Are Fun, Hip and Affordable

The cities that Americans most want to live in feature good values in home prices, reasonable costs of living, high quality of life, access to quality health care and a strong economy, according to a survey by *Kiplinger's Personal Finance*. Here are the top 10 cities on the magazine's list of the 50 most desirable cities:

1. *Nashville, Tenn.* — Affordable homes, mild climate, lively entertainment scene.

2. *Minneapolis-St. Paul, Minn.* — Hip and progressive atmosphere with a Midwestern sensibility, multiple cultural outlets, professional teams in all four major sports, a dozen universities and colleges and a diverse economy.

3. *Albuquerque, N.M.* — Resort-town ambience, boomtown economy but reasonable prices.

4. *Atlanta, Ga.* — Vibrant city with a rich history, good health care, hip cultural scene and genteel neighborhoods shaded by magnificent dogwood and magnolia trees.

5. *Austin, Texas* — State capital features a medley of culture, history and politics, including the University of Texas, the Zachary Scott Theater and the Umlauf Sculpture Garden and Museum.

6. *Kansas City* — Straddling the Kansas and Missouri state line, offers stately houses, downtown suburbs, world-class museums and barbecue.

7. *Asheville, N.C.* — A virtually franchise-free downtown with fine cuisine, unique crafts, live-music venues, fine arts and beautiful mountain views.

8. *Ithaca, N.Y.* — In the scenic Finger Lakes region, liberal home of Cornell University; farms provide rich assortment of organic products.

9. *Pittsburgh, Pa.* — Undergoing an ongoing renaissance; distinctive neighborhoods, tree-lined streets, glittering skyscrapers, upscale shops and a diversified economy.

10. *Iowa City, Iowa* — Oasis on the prairie bursting with creative and intellectual energy, including an annual jazz festival, a Shakespeare festival and the home of the University of Iowa.

Source: "50 Smart Places to Live," *Kiplinger's Personal Finance*, June 2006

and planning at MIT. "That's the big litmus test even for people who are big city lovers — the quality of the public schools, outdoor space, the ability to pick up the things you need without having to take a large chunk out of your day."

Indeed, says Meg Boyco, a loft dweller in downtown St. Louis, having to drive miles to buy groceries or rent videos gets old fast. "It seems nice, but are people going to grow old here?" she asked. "Is it going to be people moving in and out for three years at a time, while they get established and then bump into the suburbs?"[2]

However, downtown boosters note that even in their heyday, downtowns weren't home to very many people. And they don't think downtowns will ever return as singularly important economic centers. But that doesn't mean urban centers can't become healthier.

"Some people are saying that downtown revitalization is a myth because the numbers aren't growing like in the suburbs," says Feehan, of the International Downtown Association. "Of course not — it's a built area."

And even if they only appeal to a limited subset of people — young professionals and empty nesters — that's still a sizable, growing market as baby boomers retire and the 25-to-35-year-old cohort expands. After all, points out Christopher B. Leinberger, a visiting fellow at the Brookings Institution's Metropolitan Policy Program, three-quarters of U.S. households do not have school-age children.

"Clearly, downtowns play a central role in the identity of a region," says Lee Munnich, director of the state and local policy program at the University of Minnesota's

improvement of late, they remain poor performers compared to suburban schools.

"Clearly, cities can maintain a certain amount of vitality with empty nesters and young professionals, but to sustain their health there has to be more infrastructure," says Lorlene Hoyt, a professor of urban studies

Hubert H. Humphrey Institute of Public Affairs. "They're still major employment centers, and they're increasingly a place where people are choosing to live and spend their leisure time."

Cities long sought magic bullets — such as sports arenas or free parking — to solve their downtown woes. "The history of downtowns contains a lot of false optimism," says Otis White, an Atlanta-based consultant to cities. "There was always a search for an easy solution to fixing downtowns, but they were in the grip of bigger forces than beautification can deal with."

Since then, says Rutgers historian Isenberg, cities have realized that no one thing — whether retail, residential or entertainment — is going to restore downtowns. Rather, the mix of attractions will need regular updating and maintenance, just as shopping centers and industrial parks do, and downtowns will have to be adaptable. And unlike the urban-renewal movement of the 1950s and '60s — when entire neighborhoods were destroyed, hundreds of acres at a time, to make way for new developments — planners today "envision more incremental progress," she argues.

"There is no, one, stable set of ideas, no one stable set of needs that can be met downtown," Isenberg says. "What we see as aesthetically pleasing today, or what we want to see downtown, will be different in 30 years."

Does gentrification hurt longtime residents?

Much of the recent downtown revitalization has been fostered by tax breaks. Cities often agree to forego a percentage of property taxes to get more attractive properties built. In Houston's rapidly gentrifying Third Ward, however, Texas state Rep. Garnet Coleman is using the same tax-financing arrangements to put limits on growth.

A board he partially controls has been buying up land in order to keep it away from developers who want to tear down low-cost housing and replace it with high-priced condominiums. He's also trying to impose restrictive deeds and covenants on existing properties to ensure that they are used only for rental housing in perpetuity.

"We can give tax abatements out the wazoo for lofts and condominiums," Coleman told *Governing* magazine. "The question is . . . whether we are willing to

Milwaukee's popular River Walk blossomed from the city's once-undeveloped waterfront in the late 1990s. It now features condominiums, restaurants and entertainment.

Milwaukee Dept. of City Development

spend the same money on people who need a nice, affordable, clean place to live."[3]

While Coleman's tactics are unusual, his motivation is not. As middle- and upper-income people move into downtowns, there has been widespread concern that lower-income residents will be priced out of their long-time neighborhoods.

In May the Los Angeles City Council approved a one-year moratorium on conversions of 14,000 single-room occupancy (SRO) hotel rooms, which generally serve the poor, into high-end condos. It is also considering a broader slowdown on residential redevelopment.

"Landlords were evicting tenants so they could flip those properties," says Eva Kandarpa, an aide to Councilwoman Jan Perry, who sponsored the ordinance. "We wanted to stop that until we could come up with a comprehensive plan for more affordable housing."

Columbia University urban-planning professor Lance Freeman lauds the goal of trying to get more affordable housing built but says trying to halt gentrification won't achieve that aim. In a 2005 study, Freeman concluded that residents of gentrifying neighborhoods were no more likely to move than residents of non-gentrifying neighborhoods. Older neighborhoods tend to have a high turnover in any event, he found, but improvements in gentrifying areas — such as increased jobs and falling

A critic of the Supreme Court's controversial *Kelo v. New London* decision makes his position clear at a Senate Judiciary Committee hearing last year. The court ruled that New London, Conn., could force homeowners to sell their land to make way for a $350 million pharmaceutical factory.

crime rates — were likely to be a boon to long-term residents, who then are more inclined to stay.[4]

Freeman concedes, however, that lower-income residents may feel the wealthier newcomers change the fabric of the community, and renters may be forced out if the affordable housing stock is limited. Even so, cities that do not gentrify will be no better off, he says.

"It's hard to argue that cities are better off if housing is affordable because no one wants to live there," he says.

Similarly, Duke University economist Jacob Vigdor, who has studied gentrification in Boston, says gentrification is a symptom, not the cause of housing-affordability problems. In other words, residents are often displaced because land values throughout a regional market are going up — not just in their neighborhood — which encourages new development that in turn attracts new people.

No one is going to go to the expense of renovating an old warehouse, Vigdor says, until property values have already climbed enough to justify the investment.

"People assume that the arrival of yuppies [young urban professionals] causes price escalation," he says. "But when the prices start to go up, that's what gets developers' juices flowing."

In addition, since unused, old warehouses — along with schools, jails, office buildings and even grain elevators — often are converted into urban housing, that means no one is being displaced, say some downtown boosters. If no one was living there previously, how can they be forced out?

"A lot of downtowns historically have not had much in the way of housing," Freeman says. "If you add housing to the downtown, and no one was living there previously or it was predominantly manufacturing, then you wouldn't expect much displacement."

But such analyses don't sit well with longtime residents of New York's Harlem or San Francisco's Mission District, who feel their neighborhoods are being overrun by latte-sippers who are driving up property costs and forcing them out. To prevent that, many cities require developers of high-end projects to create a certain number of affordable-housing units.

"Lower-class housing and work-force housing are diminishing," says Donald J. Borut, executive director of the National League of Cities. "Where cops and teachers can afford to live — it's not a small issue."

"Atlanta is gentrifying at a very substantial rate," says Larry Keating, a professor of city and regional planning at Georgia Institute of Technology, who recently chaired a gentrification task force for the City Council. "The displacement [of low-income renters] is substantial."

While urban improvements enhance a city's overall tax base, he says, they reduce the amount of affordable housing, forcing poor residents to the city's fringes or the suburbs, tearing apart their social networks.

"Absolutely, people are being displaced," says Brookings' Leinberger. He recommends policies to help transfer some of cities' growing wealth into programs to subsidize affordable housing.

He mordantly recalls a multi-panel cartoon that illustrates some of the negative social dynamics associated with gentrification. The first panel shows a white couple moving out to the suburbs during the 1950s and extolling their good fortune. The second shows an African-American couple moving to the suburbs during the 1990s and feeling equally lucky to be leaving the city.

C H R O N O L O G Y

1940s-1960s *Downtowns lose business and cities lose population to suburbs.*

1948 Downtown's share of retail trade — nearly one-third before the Great Depression — falls to 11 percent.

1949 Housing Act provides federal funds to help cities acquire and clear slum and blighted property for private redevelopment.

1961 Jane Jacobs publishes *The Death and Life of Great American Cities*, arguing that small, dense mixed-use neighborhoods are more vital and safer than huge developments.

1965 Congress creates Department of Housing and Urban Development (HUD), the first Cabinet-level agency devoted to urban problems.

1968 Assassination of civil rights leader the Rev. Martin Luther King Jr. sparks rioting in 125 cities, killing 39 and damaging 2,600 buildings.

1970s-1980s *Federal government scales back its commitment to urban programs; cities begin attracting specialty shops and new customers.*

1973 President Richard M. Nixon freezes most HUD programs to control costs and address allegations of mishandled funds.

1974 Congress approves Community Development block grants for city infrastructure improvements.

1975 President Gerald R. Ford refuses federal aid to financially ailing New York City, prompting *Daily News* headline, "Ford to City: Drop Dead."

1976 Developer James Rouse opens Faneuil Hall Marketplace in historic Boston building, beginning string of urban "festival" markets.

1977 Community Development Reinvestment Act requires lenders to invest in their areas of service.

1984 *Newsweek* declares "The Year of the Yuppie" in response to the growing number of affluent white-collar workers in some cities.

1987 President Ronald Reagan abolishes revenue sharing, which distributed federal funds to states and cities.

1990s-2000s *The nation's improving economy helps revive cities that provide professional or technological services; cities succeed in developing a mix of attractions that lure some downtown inhabitants.*

1991 Driven partly by the crack cocaine epidemic of the late 1980s, the U.S. homicide rate peaks at 9.8 per 100,000 population, largely affecting urban areas.

1992 U.S. Conference of Mayors leads thousands in March on Washington, proposes "Marshall Plan for the Cities" to be paid for with $35 billion in new federal funds. . . . Baltimore opens Camden Yards stadium, a much-imitated home for baseball's Orioles that is integrated with its downtown, its bustling harbor and the city's mass-transit system.

1993 Congress rejects President Bill Clinton's $16 billion economic-stimulus package for cities.

1995 Clinton creates urban-empowerment and enterprise zones in cities receiving federal funds and tax incentives for development and social services.

2000 Eight of the 15 cities that had been among the nation's 15 largest in 1950 have lost population for the fifth census in a row.

2004 Chicago opens its downtown Millennium Park, a $475 million, 24-acre sculpture garden.

2005 President George W. Bush's budget would slash Community Development Block Grants. . . . U.S. Supreme Court upholds cities' ability to take control of private property through eminent domain in *Kelo v. New London* case. . . . Hurricane Katrina devastates New Orleans.

2006 During the first five months of the year, 23 state legislatures pass bills to restrict cities' use of eminent domain. . . . Federal housing officials announce that more than 5,000 public housing units in New Orleans will be razed in favor of mixed-income developments.

2009

January — President Obama takes office during a severe economic downturn but with a solid base of urban voters

(Continued)

(Continued)

and a willingness to use federal power to steer resources to cities.

May 5 — Former NBA basketball star Dave Bing is elected mayor of Detroit.

Sept. 14 — Bing launches strategic plan to remake Detroit's downtown, including projects to convert abandoned residential property to farmland.

Dec. 16 — Cleveland-area Cuyahoga County Land Reutilization Corporation (CCLRC) reaches agreement with mortgage giant Fannie Mae allowing CCLRC to acquire properties from Fannie's inventory of foreclosed homes.

2010

Jan. 13 — CCLRC transforms its first property into a community garden.

Jan. 15 — CCLRC receives $40 million from U.S. Department of Housing and Urban Development (HUD) to rehabilitate homes for resale to low- and middle-income families.

April 10 — The 2010 decennial U.S. census concludes. As its findings are made public in the coming years, the data will show continued population growth in urban areas, but a shift in concentration away from central cities and into expanding suburbs. Cities in the South and West are generally experiencing the greatest growth rates.

April 22 — CCLRC receives $400,000 from U.S. Environmental Protection Agency to help assess environmental contamination in industrial, residential and commercial sites.

July 2 — CCLRC reaches agreement with HUD in which HUD's foreclosed properties in Cuyahoga County appraised for $20,000 or less can be transferred to the land bank for $100.

Oct. 13-15 — Cleveland scheduled to host CCLRC conference on the reclamation of vacant properties.

2011

January-December — For the first time since 1960, Washington, D.C.'s black population drops below 50 percent. It stands at 49.2 percent; whites comprise 35.3 percent.

Sept. 11 — President Obama submits legislation dubbed The Jobs Act (S.1549). Among its provisions is Project Rebuild, which would allocate $15 billion for "rehabilitating homes, businesses and communities, leveraging private capital and scaling land banks and other public-private collaborations," according to the White House.

2012

January — Conservative Manhattan Institute think tank releases a study indicating that America's 70,000 neighborhoods are now virtually desegregated, with only one-half of 1 percent of communities showing no African-American residents — generally in sparsely populated rural areas.

April 5 — In a consent agreement with the State of Michigan, Detroit agrees to cede most economic decision-making to a nine-member advisory board. The move is deeply unpopular with public-employee unions and many civic activists, but a bare majority of the City Council says the city's dire financial condition leaves them no option.

May 17 — U.S. Census Bureau estimates that as of July 1, 2011, just over half of U.S. babies — 50.4 percent — were being born to minority parents. It marked the first time minorities comprised more than half of American newborns.

May 24 — Census Bureau releases 2006-2010 American Community Survey Selected Population Tables, providing estimates of detailed social, economic and housing characteristics for many racial, tribal, Hispanic and ancestry population groups in urban areas.

The last panel shows the white couple returning happily to the city, saying, "It worked."

Should greater restrictions be placed on government use of eminent domain to acquire land?

Some recent downtown development, especially major projects covering many acres, has been fostered by cities using their power of eminent domain — the process of condemning private land for public use.

The Constitution forbids governments from "seizing" private property without compensating its owners, but cities have long used eminent domain — or condemnation — to force owners to sell when it is determined that the land is needed for the public's

"Walkable Urbanity" Livens Up the Burbs

The population of Sugar Hill, Ga., about 40 miles north of Atlanta, has tripled over the last decade, leading local officials to try to think of new ways to improve things. When they polled townspeople about the changes they would most like to see, the answer was overwhelming: They wanted a lively, pedestrian-friendly downtown.

Sugar Hill is now building itself a downtown — from scratch — along a road that will be lined with 15-foot-wide sidewalks. Developers are eager to start filling in the area with stores and restaurants.

"They wanted that hometown, downtown walking area, and that's what the mayor and council have said they'll have," says City Manager Bob Hail. "We are not renovating. We are doing the 'build it and they will come.' "

Sugar Hill is not the first place in the area to try to create instant urbanism. Many communities within the sprawling 17-county metro Atlanta region have decided they need town centers, both to provide a distinct identity for their communities and to afford residents the pleasures of a walkable downtown shopping and entertainment district without having to drive into the big city.

"Deprived by the difficulty of driving to social and cultural activities, people are bringing those activities to the suburbs," says Michael M. Sizemore, whose firm designed a downtown for Smyrna, 35 miles west of Sugar Hill. "When they do, it starts to provide the anchor or catalyst for revitalizing their downtowns."

The suburbs are associated with strip malls and other signs of sprawl, but some observers predict they will increasingly become convenient, urban-style gathering places. "There is so much pent-up demand for walkable urbanity that it cannot all be satisfied in the traditional downtown," says Christopher B. Leinberger, an urban strategist and developer.

Even more common than the creation of new downtowns is the phenomenon of older suburbs attempting to revitalize central business and shopping districts — often located near mass-transit lines — that had long been neglected. In Decatur, which sits along Atlanta's eastern border, the shopping district is undergoing extensive renovation, and the first new downtown residential units are being built since the Great Depression, all within easy walking distance of a stop on Atlanta's citywide rail system.

"The 1950s and 60s suburban ideal was you don't want to live anywhere near a storefront, you want to get as far away as possible from commercial development," said Brian J. Nickerson, director of the Michaelian Institute for Public Policy and Management at Pace University in New York City. "Now, you want to live above the storefront."[1]

In many suburbs, old-fashioned shopping malls are giving way to "town centers" or "lifestyle centers" — shopping complexes that mimic some of the qualities of the walkable downtowns. In some cases, this amounts to a direct swap. In Centennial, Colo., the 1974-vintage Southglenn Mall will be replaced with a development called The Streets at Southglenn that will feature — in addition to about 100 stores — sidewalk cafes, shaded walkways and little nooks for relaxing.

More than 60 lifestyle centers will open around the country this year and next, compared with just one traditional covered mall, according to the International Council of Shopping Centers.[2] "In both suburban downtowns and new town developments, you've got civic leaders and developers trying to replicate the success of urban downtowns," says Brad Segal, president of Progressive Urban Management Associates, a development-consulting firm in Denver.

Segal questions the staying power of the new shopping developments, warning they offer too many of the same chain stores and have a homogeneous, cookie-cutter feel as a result. Urban "downtowns have a competitive advantage in terms of organic qualities that have evolved over time — they have 100 or 200 years of history, and you can see it," he says. "These new lifestyle centers are really a product of 2006."

For now, though, it is clear that many suburbs covet sophisticated little shopping areas of their own. Perhaps the new downtown designers in Sugar Hill will be able to pull a page from Smyrna's successful urban playbook. Retail sales and property values there have increased so much that the city has been able to lower its property tax rates every year since construction of the downtown began in the late 1980s.

"For about a half-mile all around it, there are all kinds of development," Sizemore says. "If you create a place that's great for everybody, starting with the kids, everybody wants to be there, and they're willing to pay for it."

---

[1] Debra West, "Adding More Urban to Suburbia," *The New York Times*, May 14, 2006, Section 14WC, p. 1.

[2] Thaddeus Herrick, "Fake Towns Rise, Offering Urban Life Without the Grit," *The Wall Street Journal*, May 31, 2006, p. A1.

San Diego Convention and Visitors Bureau

San Diego's PETCO Park, a new open-air stadium built in the East Village area near the historic Gaslamp Quarter, is part of a comprehensive plan to revitalize the city's aging downtown.

benefit. Although governments usually buy property through normal real estate transactions, they sometimes use eminent domain to take control of large parcels of land rather than having to deal with scattered holdouts reluctant to sell.

In the past, local governments used eminent domain to acquire land for public infrastructure, such as roads, bridges, railroads or schools. But during the urban-renewal movement that flourished from the 1940s to the 1960s, they began using eminent domain for economic purposes, taking over blighted sections of towns — often occupied primarily by African-Americans or poor residents — that were ripe for redevelopment.

Recently, cash-strapped cities have begun using their powers of eminent domain again to promote economic development by condemning commercially viable properties or middle-income homes to make way for pricier hotels, retail shops or condominiums. The higher-end

use of the land will bring in greater tax revenues, the cities argue, thus benefiting the common good. For example, Greenville employed eminent domain to acquire rundown riverfront warehouses for a large hotel, office, condo and artists' studio complex.

CBS' "60 Minutes" highlighted a city that went so far as to redefine "blighted" to include park-side homes with only a single-car garage so middle-class homes could be condemned to make way for upscale condos with a park view. In Minnesota, a car dealership was forced to sell out five years ago to make way for Best Buy's $160 million corporate headquarters in suburban Richfield.

"We cannot understand how giving our property to a multibillion-dollar company like Best Buy serves a 'public purpose' as the law mandates," said Barbara Jerich, general counsel for Walser Automotive Group.[5]

Cities and developers, however, point out that a big electronics headquarters, for example, generates more income and jobs than a car dealer and a few dozen homes, benefiting the entire community. Losing such a moneymaker due to the intransigence of a single property owner would have been a big blow to the area, said the project's supporters.

Nevertheless, the practice has stirred up stiff resistance among affected landowners, who claim cities are "stealing" private land to sell it to rich developers at reduced rates. When a city condemns land, it normally only pays the appraised value for the land — usually lower than the price developers would have to pay on the open market. If a redevelopment project is such a wise investment, argue affected landowners, developers should just buy the land on the open market.

The simmering controversy burst into the open in 2005, when the U.S. Supreme Court ruled in *Kelo v. New London* that New London, Conn., could legally force landowners in the "distressed municipality" to sell their land to make way for a $350 million pharmaceutical factory. Fifteen homeowners didn't want to sell, but in a 5 to 4 decision the Supreme Court ruled that the increased potential economic activity generated by the plant justified the city's taking of the land. Swelling the tax base amounted to a "public purpose," the court ruled.[6]

"Promoting economic development is a traditional and long accepted function of government," Justice John Paul Stevens wrote. "Clearly, there is no basis for exempting economic development from our traditionally broad understanding of public purpose."[7]

But in her dissenting opinion Justice Sandra Day O'Connor wrote: "Under the banner of economic development, all private property is now vulnerable to being taken and transferred to another private owner, so long as it might be upgraded. The specter of condemnation hangs over all property. Nothing is to prevent the state from replacing any Motel 6 with a Ritz-Carlton, any home with a shopping mall or any farm with a factory."

If eminent domain was not a sexy topic before, *Kelo* turned it into one, stirring up a hornet's nest of opposition in cities across the country. "I was down about the decision for about 20 minutes," recalls Scott Bullock, a senior attorney with the libertarian Institute for Justice in Arlington, Va., who argued New London landowner Susette Kelo's case before the court. Then he saw O'Connor's passionate dissent and realized she had handed him a gift. "I read the dissenting opinions and realized that there's a real opportunity here to take what was a terrible decision and turn it into something that was very positive for property owners."

Indeed, both conservatives and liberals opposed the decision. Conservatives disliked the apparent expansion of governmental power over private property. Liberals — recalling the massive displacement of poor communities during the urban-renewal movement — feared the practice could be used to once again force low-income citizens from their homes to make way for the wealthy.

Before the decision, nine state supreme courts had already forbidden the use of eminent domain to build revenues or employment.[8] In fact, Justice Stevens explicitly pointed out that states have the power to curb the use of eminent domain — and many have quickly done so. In the past year, two-dozen states have passed new restrictions on the use of eminent domain, and bills to restrict the practice have been introduced in Congress and nearly every state legislature. Initiatives are on the ballot in four states, and petitions are circulating in California and eight other states to put it before voters in November, according to the American Planning Association.

"What I don't like is where somebody has a higher and better use in their minds, and they give the land to a private developer," says Indiana state Rep. David

Wolkins, who sponsored a bill that would discourage the practice by narrowing the state's definition of blight and forcing redevelopment agencies to pay ousted owners 150 percent of the appraised value of a property.

Similar arguments were made in Iowa, where the legislature this year voted to restrict the use of eminent domain to areas that are 75 percent blighted. But developers and local officials say that's a bad idea, because areas targeted for redevelopment will have to decline further before a city can step in to improve them. They cite the example of downtown Des Moines, which was legally declared a slum 30 years ago — dominated by dilapidated buildings, abandoned stores and seedy hotels. The city has since helped foster an impressive renaissance, using eminent domain to make way for several office and retail complexes and other projects that have increased the taxable value of the area by more than $1 billion.

"We would not have the development activity we have within the downtown core right now if we didn't have eminent domain," says Councilwoman Christine Hensley, who represents the area. The legislature went overboard in reaction to anti-*Kelo* emotions, she says. Sounding emotional herself, she adds, "It pisses me off." Perhaps responding to such reasoning — if not the emotion — Gov. Tom Vilsack vetoed the eminent-domain bill.

Indianapolis Mayor Bart Peterson says eminent domain should be left intact because it is self-regulating — taking private property is usually so controversial public officials don't do it unless it's absolutely necessary. "Elected officials rightly know they cannot go around taking property at will," he says.

If they didn't know it before, they've certainly gotten the message since *Kelo*. Ironically, the decision didn't expand local governments' powers; it merely affirmed them. But in so doing, the court set the stage for a political backlash that has left many cities with more limited tools for promoting economic development.

In that regard, says the National League of Cities' Borut, "It was like winning the Super Bowl and then not having a team."

BACKGROUND

Industrial Age

America's cities grew rapidly as the country industrialized in the late 19th century, and millions left their farms or

Blossoming Cities

(Top): Architect Santiago Calatrava designed a recent addition to the Milwaukee Art Museum, right. New condos are rising nearby. (Middle): Several big projects in Phoenix, including expansion of the Convention Center, are pumping new life into the city. (Bottom): New York's Harlem has undergone a dramatic revival that has seen the arrival of new businesses and residents and restoration of the world-famous Apollo Theater.

their home countries and poured into American downtowns. Between 1790 and 1890, the total U.S. population grew 16-fold — but the nation's urban population grew to 139 times its 1790 size.[9]

Downtowns were often referred to as the cities' heart, with streetcars bringing workers in each morning and carrying them home each night. Not every town had a skyscraper or an opera house, but they all had commercial Main Streets, points out author Isenberg in *Downtown America*.[10] Downtowns also served as a melting pot for the cities — the one area where people from all over came and felt welcome.

"The central business district was the one bit of turf common to all," writes historian Jon C. Teaford. "Along the downtown thoroughfares, wealthy financiers passed by grubby beggars, rubbed shoulders with horny-handed porters and draymen and jostled for space with clerks and stenographers."[11]

Downtowns were also home to railroad and ferry terminals, department stores and often the cities' sole business and financial districts. As late as 1890, downtowns were often the only part of town with electricity.[12] They were compact, crowded places for industry and shopping, often occupying less than a square mile but generating more trade than the rest of the city combined. And they generated a huge percentage of urban property-tax valuations — more than 20 percent in St. Louis, for example, and almost half in Cincinnati.[13]

Downtowns in the early 20th century also became great manufacturing centers, and it was convenient to have lawyers, accountants and other professional services nearby. Convenience also drew women shoppers downtown, where they could find everything they wanted in one of the mammoth department stores that dominated retail sales. Novelist William Kennedy recalls "booming, bustling" downtown Albany, where "crowds were six abreast on the sidewalks at high noon and all day Saturday, when all the trolley cars were crowded, and you had to stand in line to get into the movies."[14]

By 1925, the 18 cities with populations of more than 400,000 had grown by an average of 71 percent since the dawn of the century. Los Angeles had ballooned by 609 percent; Detroit had more than tripled.[15] As cities grew more crowded, many families became willing to ride an hour to distant neighborhoods or out to the country to avoid living under or over another family. As a result, cities desperately needed rapid transit, especially as automobile traffic began to clog downtown streets.

Many cities talked of building subways to deliver every resident to within a half-mile of his job, but few invested the large sums required. By the late 1920s, New York and Boston boasted more than 90 percent of the nation's subway traffic.[16]

Moving on Out

Faced with congestion and high downtown land values, industry began to move out of the central cities by the late 1920s, first to peripheral neighborhoods and then to suburbs. In suburban Dearborn, Mich., Ford's River Rouge facility — the largest factory in the world when it opened in 1928 — was more than double the size of downtown Detroit. Secondary business districts also began to spring up, with some professional firms moving their administrative offices out and banks beginning to set up branch offices.

Retailers soon followed suit. Because a central-city location no longer guaranteed proximity to shoppers, a proliferation of chain stores moved into the suburbs. Joseph Appel, president of Wanamaker's department store, wrote in 1928 that it was time for the store to go to its customers rather than try "to force them to come to us."[17]

The Great Depression of the 1930s, which hit inner cities disproportionately hard, accelerated the trend outward. Hotels and other downtown properties fell widely into receivership, and more office buildings were being torn down during the decade than were going up. Desperate owners tore down tall buildings, replacing them with one- or two-story parking lots, in order to decrease their tax burdens and generate some income. Chicago's land value dropped by as much as 78.5 percent from 1930 to 1935, while New York City's assessed values by 1939 had dropped below 1889 levels.[18] *Business Week* declared in 1940: "Every American city of 6,000,000 or 6,000 population shows symptoms of identical dry rot at its core."[19]

By the end of World War II, central-business-district organizations had sprung up in most cities to lobby for tax and zoning policies that would promote downtowns as places worth visiting. They studied how to improve transportation and even the idea of banning downtown traffic, but the forces favoring the decentralization of commerce were ultimately much stronger.

After the war, even though the nation's economy boomed, downtowns stagnated. The newly built parking lots didn't generate jobs, and new freeways meant that more and more downtown land was devoted to traffic

City of Greenville

Newly revitalized Greenville, S.C., turned the Reedy River and its scenic falls into the city's most popular attraction. Main Street, which had only four restaurants 20 years ago, now boasts more than 75. There's also a performing-arts center and a new minor league ballpark just up the street.

and parking and less to trade. Congestion remained a problem, prompting many big businesses to follow heavy industry to the suburbs.[20] Several insurance companies moved from New York to leafy Westchester County, just north of Manhattan, as did General Foods, Standard Oil and other large corporations. Cargill, the country's largest grain trader, left Minneapolis for Lake Minnetonka.[21] In 1948, 80 percent of the new manufacturing, retail and wholesale jobs were being created in the suburbs.[22]

That year, in fact, downtowns' share of the nation's retail trade, which had been nearly one-third in 1929, plummeted to just 11 percent.[23] (The first regional shopping center had been built in Los Angeles a year earlier.) Over the next six years, retail sales downtown climbed by just 1.6 percent while increasing 32.3 percent in suburbs.[24]

As the president of the TG&Y variety store chain declared, "We do not think the housewives (who are our main customers) will drive miles and miles to get downtown when they can obtain the same merchandise in better facilities in the suburbs."[25]

Urban "Jungles"

During the early 1950s, 84 percent of the nation's population growth occurred in the 168 metropolitan areas, but less than 2 percent was in central cities.

"The upper and middle classes were moving to the periphery and the suburbs," writes MIT urban historian Robert M. Fogelson in his 2001 book *Downtown.* "But the lower class, many of whose members belonged to one or another of the nation's ethnic and racial minorities, were staying put — some because they did not want to move, others because they could not afford to."[26]

As downtown retailers lost their best customers, private interests sought to raze the slums in the inner city to make way for large-scale development. Local governments hoping for increased property assessments were eager to help them. A 1955 *Life* magazine article, headlined "An Encroaching Menace," captured the tone of their plea: "The slums of Chicago each year have pushed closer to the heart of the city. Some of the worst came only six blocks from the glittering skyscrapers. There a newly aroused and desperate city stopped them."[27]

States such as New York and New Jersey gave private companies the power of eminent domain, authorizing them to acquire land for redevelopment. Congress got involved, passing the Housing Act of 1949, which further spurred urban clearance and redevelopment. In theory, private initiatives were supposed to improve and rebuild low-income housing, but that rarely happened. By 1961, 126,000 residential units had been demolished but only 28,000 built to replace them.[28] A study that year found that in 60 cities that had undertaken urban-renewal projects, 60 percent of the dispossessed simply relocated to other substandard housing.[29]

During the 1960s, Presidents John F. Kennedy and Lyndon B. Johnson dramatically expanded the scope of federal urban policy. In 1965, Johnson created the Department of Housing and Urban Development (HUD), the first Cabinet-level position to address the problems of urban America. Its first major initiative — Model Cities — sought to include community wishes in comprehensive rebuilding plans.

But inner cities continued to become islands of ethnicity due to "white flight" to the suburbs. Between 1960 and 1970, the white population of the 20 largest Northeastern and Midwestern cities fell by more than 2.5 million, or 13 percent. The decline was even more precipitous in the 1970s, dropping by another 4 million, or 24.3 percent.[30] Meanwhile, the black share of central city populations shot up 725 percent from 1960 to 1968.[31]

The urban riots of the late 1960s and early '70s made matters worse. Anecdotal and newspaper accounts suggested that rioters in Los Angeles, Harlem, Washington and elsewhere targeted white merchants they felt had long cheated them economically. Whatever the rationale, riots certainly did not help urban America's fortunes.

As Rutgers University's Isenberg writes, "certainly people were less likely to make shopping excursions with riot threats hanging in the air."[32] Suburbanites began to think of downtown as a dangerous no-man's land. In 1969, a *Newsweek* cover report looked at "The Sick, Sick Cities."

With the central cities continuing to lose jobs, many local leaders despaired. St. Louis Mayor A. J. Cervantes declared in 1968: "We just can't make it anymore."

New Orleans Mayor Moon Landrieu echoed the sentiment: "The cities are going down the pipe."

HUD Secretary George Romney said in 1972, "The whole social web that makes living possible [in the cities] is breaking down into a veritable jungle."[33]

A year later, President Richard M. Nixon froze most HUD programs following allegations the funds were being mishandled. He folded Model Cities and other urban-renewal programs into Community Development Block Grants, which gave localities wide discretion over the types of programs that could be funded. Cities foundered financially, as exemplified by New York City's $726 million budget deficit in 1975. President Gerald R. Ford's refusal to aid the city led to the memorable New York *Daily News* headline, "Ford to City: Drop Dead," which Ford believed cost him the 1976 election.

Hitting Bottom

Ford's opponent, Jimmy Carter, created new grant programs to send money directly to neighborhoods, rather than passing it through lower levels of government. During his first year in office, Congress approved the Community Development Reinvestment Act, which required banks to invest funds in the communities they served.

Many of Carter's programs for cities, though, were dismantled by his successor, Ronald Reagan. In fact, Reagan was following a Carter administration advisory panel that recommended helping city residents move to the suburbs. The federal government's role should be "to assist communities to adjust to redistributional trends, rather than attempt to reverse them," the commission concluded."[34]

AT ISSUE

Are downtowns undergoing a real renaissance?

YES
David Feehan
President, International Downtown Association

Written for *CQ Researcher*, June 2006

The evidence is irrefutable: Downtowns in the United States have made a remarkable, perhaps historic, comeback. After decades of decline, disinvestment and near abandonment, American downtowns are experiencing what can only be called a renaissance.

This remarkable phenomenon is not without its critics and cynics. The most prominent of these, however, blithely ignore the overwhelming body of evidence and instead engage in sensationalistic arguments based on highly selective data and flawed reasoning. Often they compare downtown growth with suburban growth, which is a bit like comparing a minivan and a sports car — they both are gasoline-powered vehicles with four wheels, but with decidedly different purposes and ancestries.

Let's look at the facts: In the early 1990s, an economist studying downtown's economic importance found that it contributed more than $19 in tax revenues to various taxing bodies for every dollar in services it consumed. City managers, finance directors and other city officials have confirmed that these numbers are reasonably representative of most downtowns and central cities in the United States. Clearly, downtown is the economic engine that pulls the city's train. Strong downtowns make stronger core cities possible, which in turn helps to support regional economic health.

The downtown office market is showing strength and resiliency. Occupancy rates nationally since 1990 have favored downtowns over suburbs. The downtown housing market is strong and has grown explosively in many cities, including cities of every size and region — from New York, Philadelphia and Washington to Miami, Los Angeles and Seattle; and from Memphis to Des Moines to Fort Worth to Albuquerque. People want to live downtown and will pay a premium to do so.

Dining, entertainment, sports, meetings and conventions and tourist attractions have all expanded in downtowns. Crime is at historic lows. Downtown public spaces not only look better but also are managed better than ever through a plethora of public-private partnerships and business-improvement districts.

Downtowns are stronger than at any time in the past 50 years, and as downtowns continue to improve they provide the resources cities need to improve neighborhoods, schools and services. The downtown renaissance is little more than a decade old, and it may take another decade or two for urban neighborhoods to catch up. But now, with revitalized downtowns, they may have the resources and opportunity to do so. Few would argue that this is a very important goal.

NO
Joel Kotkin
Irvine Senior Fellow, New America Foundation

Written for *CQ Researcher*, June 2006

Even amidst a strong economic expansion, the most recent census data reveal a renewed migration out of our urban centers. This gives considerable lie to the notion, popularized over a decade — particularly among the media — that cities are enjoying a historic rebound.

In 1999 *The Economist* suggested "Americans [are] abandoning their love affair with far-flung suburbs and shopping malls." The recovery in some downtowns, suggested Jonathan Fanton, president of the MacArthur Foundation, heralded a new "urban renaissance."

But this may be more wishful thinking than reality. Since 1950 more than 90 percent of all growth in U.S. metropolitan areas has been in the suburbs. Nor is this trend showing any sign of turning around. Census data show that since 2000 even healthy urban centers like New York, Boston, Portland, Ore., and San Francisco have experienced slowing or declining population growth. Meanwhile, suburbs in those regions and elsewhere have been capturing an ever-expanding percentage of both people and jobs.

The simple fact is that most Americans — including 86 percent of all Californians, according to a recent survey — express a great preference for single-family homes, which for most means choosing suburbia. Unless there is some radical and unexpected change, most new population growth and expansion of the built environment (which is estimated to grow 50 percent by 2030) will occurr in the suburbs, particularly in the South and West — places dominated by low-density, automobile-dependent growth.

The tapering housing bubble has created a false notion of an urban renaissance driven by, among other things, empty nesters returning to the city. In many urban cores, from New York to San Diego, large numbers of condo units — in some cases upwards of a third — have been bought not by new urbanites but by speculators. So we have the odd phenomenon of more housing units, at higher costs, but fewer full-time residents.

Instead of luring the "hip and cool" with high-end amenities, cities should address issues that concern businesses as well as middle-class families. These include such basic needs as public safety, maintenance of parks, improving public schools and cutting taxes — in other words, all those unsexy things that contribute to maintaining a job base and upward mobility.

Cities can't thrive merely as amusement parks for the rich, the nomadic young and tourists. To remain both vital and economically relevant, they must remain anchored by a large middle class, and by families and businesses that feel safe and committed to the urban place.

Reagan eliminated Carter's Office of Neighborhoods and cut programs for cities by nearly a quarter during his first two years in office. He ended federal revenue sharing, by which Washington sent funds to other levels of government to spend as they saw fit.

Without the federal government to help them out, city and business leaders decided they were responsible for improving the lot of the cities. Many businesses were willing to pay additional assessments in order to clean up downtowns and make them safer. The first business-improvement district (BID) was created in New Orleans in 1975, and BIDs became widespread in the 1980s.

Cities also welcomed their first good retail news in decades with the creation of "festival marketplaces" — shopping areas built in historic districts or among the ruins of old industrial sites, including Ghirardelli Square in San Francisco, the Inner Harbor in Baltimore and Faneuil Hall in Boston. Although often criticized as Potemkin villages — pockets of prosperity that did little for the wider city surrounding them — they were successful and widely imitated. They appealed to the nostalgia many people felt for the downtowns of yore — before crime, congestion and despair overran the cities. The American city, as Isenberg points out, had become a commodity to be marketed rather than a place in decline to be ignored.

At the same time, the National Trust for Historic Preservation's Main Street program began encouraging downtown business owners in small communities to properly restore their storefronts as a way to use the charm of a community's historic ambience to revive struggling local economies. Scores of communities across the country have benefited from the downtown face-lifts under Trust guidance, helping them battle the often overpowering competition from regional malls and discounters.[35]

Some cities, such as New York, Denver and Houston, even enjoyed job growth during the 1980s with the rise of the service sector, but older industrial cities such as Detroit, Philadelphia and Baltimore were left behind. Jobs continued their exodus to the suburbs. During a three-year period, Atlanta's suburbs gained twice as many jobs as the city; the suburbs of St. Louis, Chicago and San Francisco gained five times as many jobs as those cities, and Detroit's suburbs outstripped the city by nearly 700 percent.[36]

The cities, meanwhile, continued to struggle, having fallen into a downward spiral. Whites who fled the cities during the 1960s grew increasingly reluctant to come to downtowns

that had become scenes of poverty, crime and drug abuse — particularly given the crack epidemic of the 1980s.

Likewise, homelessness became a headline issue, as the share of the nation's poor who lived in central cities had increased by a third since 1960.[37] In 1992, *Business Week* declared, "The breeding ground for economic misery is the American city."[38]

The sense of urban uncertainty continued into the booming 1990s despite falling crime rates, a growing economy and a set of exceptionally gifted mayors, including Rudolph Giuliani of New York, Ed Rendell of Philadelphia and Richard M. Daley of Chicago.

Even Rendell, after a highly praised tenure during which he pulled Philadelphia back from the brink of bankruptcy, said as he left office in 1998, "Forget all the good things I've done. Philadelphia is dying."[39]

CURRENT SITUATION

Success Stories

Rendell's pessimism aside, his city has thrived in recent years. Or, at least its center city has. The downtown is now home to a thriving arts district anchored by the massive Kimmel Center. Condos around Rittenhouse Square are in great demand, and a city that once had no outdoor cafes now has 167. The prosperity that surrounds the downtown area is starting, slowly, to spread to blighted areas around it.

Levy, of the Philadelphia Center City District, argues that rather than being caught in a vicious downward cycle, as they were for decades, cities are starting to recover.

Levy and some other urban observers say that cities, ironically, have the federal government to thank, because when the government turned its back on the cities, local officials realized they could only depend on themselves. "The withdrawal of federal agencies has done more for the cities than all previous federal activities combined," says MIT's Hoyt. "Now you have business-improvement districts, universities and hospitals partnering with cities and raising resources in creative ways."

The federal government today is only minimally interested in helping cities. For the past two years the Bush administration has tried to slash funding for Community Development Block Grants — the last major source of federal grants for local governments — and to merge it with other economic-development programs within the Commerce Department. Although the program still exists, city and county lobbyists aren't optimistic that it will remain robust. The administration also wants to eliminate the Section 8 rental-assistance program and Hope VI grants to cities to rebuild housing.

"The federal doctor doesn't make house calls anymore," says Levy. Cities have relatively few champions in GOP-dominated Washington. Urbanites historically do not vote for Republicans.

"It's hard to think of urban constituencies to whom the Republicans owe anything," says Michael S. Greve, director of the American Enterprise Institute's Federalism Project.

So cities are pulling up their bootstraps and doing for themselves. Using BIDs, downtown employers collect taxes to pay for the services they once sought from government. "They allowed people to tax themselves extra to get signage, plantings, additional police services," says urban consultant White. "The rise in property values has more than covered whatever people have paid in taxes."

In the 1990s, cities tried various schemes to draw people back downtown, spending billions on new sports stadiums and convention centers. With his 1997 book, *The Rise of the Creative Class*, Richard Florida convinced many civic leaders that the path to prosperity lies not in granting tax breaks to businesses but in presenting the right blend of social and cultural amenities to attract well-educated workers.

However, none of the ideas proved to be a magic bullet.[40] Sports stadium promoters' promises of thousands of new jobs and millions in additional city revenues rarely panned out, but the improvement ideas did begin to rouse central cities from their long slumber and pessimism.[41]

Cities entered into partnerships with the private sector to construct multi-million-dollar projects. Government used its eminent-domain power to amass land, secured tax-exempt financing and provided fast-track approvals. Private partners determined what the market wanted, and together they built convention centers, performing-arts facilities, hotels and other ambitious projects that began to attract people back downtown, albeit in fits and starts.

Cities eventually learned how to attract people with money. Consider the sprawling desert city of Phoenix.

Suburban houses rise next to a dairy farm east of Los Angeles. Despite odors, flies and pollution from hundreds of dairy farms in the surrounding Chino Basin, the quest for affordable, new homes draws a steady stream of immigrants from the city.

Having grown from 100,000 people in 1950 to more than 1 million today, it is a classic Sun Belt town, better known for ranch-resort tourism than for downtown vitality. It has no distinguishing topography and little historical cachet.

"Phoenix had sprawled out to the suburbs and pretty much abandoned the central city," says City Councilman Claude Mattox. Left behind were "the homeless, vagrants and prostitutes."

But today, with new baseball, basketball and hockey facilities, two major new museums and two concert halls, an upscale retail complex and a $600 million expansion of the convention center, Phoenix draws tens of thousands of people downtown every night. Convinced that sports and tourism weren't enough to make downtown healthy, city leaders have also promoted residential construction and gave the planned site of a new football stadium to a big biomedical campus.

"Over the last two or three years, the residential part is starting to kick in, creating quite a vibrant area," says Maricopa County Administrator David R. Smith.

In March, city voters approved an $878 million bond package to help fund a wide variety of projects, most aimed at revitalizing downtown. Eventually, a chunk of Arizona State University will move into the city from suburban Tempe, drawing 15,000 students, faculty and administrators downtown.

Phoenix's success story has been replicated in many other cities. Although the specific details may differ, downtowns have become chic places for young professionals and empty nesters to buy low-maintenance lofts and condos, surrounded by a mix of outdoor cafes, entertainment options and plenty of people-watching. For instance, Washington, D.C.'s Seventh Street corridor — next door to Chinatown — had historically been an important shopping district. But a decade ago it was rundown and lined with vacant buildings. In 1997, a new basketball arena was opened up nearby, followed by a popular museum and dozens of restaurants — including one with an $18 million interior.

On a recent Friday night, patrons browsed in a bookstore before curtain time at the neighboring Shakespeare Theater. Teenagers watched a "bucket drummer" banging on seven upside-down plastic tubs. Small kids won tee shirts and balloon hats from a radio station's street festival. Inside a new retail alley designed to look like old cast-iron storefronts, a line snaked round and doubled back on itself at a cineplex showing thrillers, cartoons, hip-hop comedies and independent films.

Buffalo's BID sponsors a downtown concert series that now draws 8,000 to 12,000 people a week. Detroit has had more housing starts than any other jurisdiction in Michigan in the last two years. A developer in Nashville is building a 65-story, luxury condo tower.[42]

Cities and their private partners have learned to integrate stadiums and ballparks into neighborhoods in ways that encourage people to walk around and see other things. As a result, downtowns are animated after the 9 to 5 workday, and retailers have added five or six hours to their business day.

However, downtowns are still relatively small potatoes in the broader economic scheme of things. Few central cities have attracted more than a few thousand new residents, while suburbs — including new towns sprouting up on the far metropolitan fringe — continue to draw millions. Attracting just 2 percent of the city's population to live downtown remains an elusive goal almost everywhere.

But downtowns have always been primarily places for commerce, and the fact that so many people with high disposable incomes are either living downtown or visiting regularly represents an impressive turnaround.

Cities still have a long way to go in some fundamental areas, such as lowering the disparities in wealth between loft-dwellers and the poor and providing higher-quality education. But Levy argues that rather than being caught in a vicious downward cycle, as they were for decades, cities are starting to build on their increasing strengths and attractiveness.

"I don't think we're going to have downtowns dominating regions like they did in 1900," he says, "but we're long past the point where downtowns are embarrassments to their regions."

OUTLOOK
Multicentered Regions

Levy of the Philadelphia Center City District and many others speak of "multicentered regions," in which commerce is spread among many business districts. Brookings fellow Leinberger says while sprawling cities like Los Angeles and Atlanta were once the model of urban development, Washington now represents the future.

Washington's Metro system, he says, has fostered a series of thriving downtown commercial districts scattered along the subway lines — not just around the downtown Seventh Street area but in suburbs such as Bethesda and Silver Spring in Maryland and Arlington and Alexandria in Virginia. Most building permits now being issued in the region, Leinberger says, are for attached properties rather than the stand-alone projects that define sprawl.

Kotkin, the New America Foundation fellow who is perhaps the leading debunker of downtown cheerleading, argues that America's future lies in the suburbs, just as it has for decades. Downtowns may be attracting a few more people, but they represent a paltry share of the nation's population growth, he says.

"I'm not saying it's not real, but it's not significant," Kotkin says. "Most real-estate bankers and analysts — not, of course, developers and their PR people — will tell you the condo market is overbuilt."

Even downtown boosters are concerned that center cities won't attract a stable, long-term population until the public schools improve. Test scores are up even in some tough districts, such as Chicago, Boston and Philadelphia, but inner-city schools as a rule cannot compete with private or suburban schools. Until they can, only small numbers of affluent parents will raise their families in or around downtowns.

"The quality of school systems is actually an economic-development tool," says Steve Moore, president of the

Washington DC Economic Partnership. "You want people to stay for years and raise their kids here."

Moore points out, however, that cities have become "cool for a particular kind of person," if not for parents of school-age children. Brad Segal, a development consultant in Denver, thinks downtowns will benefit from demographic trends that will lead to increased numbers of those particular kinds of persons — both young workers without children and older adults with grown children — who have been repopulating center cities.

Segal also believes that more people will be drawn to downtowns and inner suburbs because of the same factors that kicked off the gentrification trend of the 1970s — they're fed up with long commutes, congestion and the rising cost of gasoline. "Urban living is a far more resource-efficient way of life," Segal says. "The ability to recapture time is a huge factor that will move people more toward urban living. The long-term economics of resource depletion are going to push us back into cities whether we like it or not."

Despite recent spikes, however, gas prices eat up a smaller portion of personal spending than they did back in 1981. And most cities, despite their glitzy, new downtown neighborhoods, are still losing population, or at least population share, to the suburbs.

"When they talk about 5,000 units in downtown L.A., does anyone understand what that means in a region of 15 million people?" asks Kotkin. "Some of these downtowns are going to have a lot of nomadic people."

2010 UPDATE

Since taking over as mayor of Detroit in May 2009, former pro basketball star Dave Bing has been captaining an aggressive zone defense of the Motor City's crumpled image. The blighted picture includes a once-proud auto industry in federal receivership, a crime rate seared in the national consciousness in photos of abandoned homes burning on Halloween, a formerly gleaming football stadium sold for a paltry $583,000 [43] and a Detroit suburb named in a recent study as the nation's worst city for job seekers. [44]

This September, Bing launched as his administration's top priority a long-term urban land-use initiative aimed at stabilizing neighborhoods, boosting development and attracting new residents. The focus of his Detroit Strategic Framework Plan will be to "right-size" the decaying city through the unusual strategy of clearing abandoned inner-city properties and turning the land into urban "farms."

Classic Tools

Beginning with a series of community meetings to enlist citizen support over the next year, the multi-faceted plan would proceed over five to 10 years with a combination of classic downtown revitalization tools such as exploiting historical and cultural resources, encouraging public transit and embracing environmental sustainability. [45] The envisioned new green spaces and agricultural enterprises would do double duty by shrinking the area that must be covered, for example, by law enforcement and garbage pickup services.

There is, however, a key obstacle: No money is available for the effort — unless philanthropists step in. "When I look at the focus of this," Bing said, "we've still got to talk about how we create jobs . . . how it's going to impact public safety, how it's going to impact education and finally, financial stability. It's not an overnight plan." [46]

Bright Spot

Still, at least one bright spot shimmers on Detroit's horizon. Last April, conservationists who created the city's Campus Martius Park, a 2.5-acre green space shaped from a previously desolate downtown parcel, received a prestigious national award and $10,000 from the Urban Land Institute for an "outstanding example of a public open space that has catalyzed the transformation of the surrounding community." [47]

Other cities also are trying to grapple with blight and economic decline. In the Cleveland area, for example, the Cuyahoga County Land Reutilization Corporation (CCLRC) has formed a partnership with such agencies as the Department of Housing and Urban Development (HUD), the Environmental Protection Agency and mortgage giant Fannie Mae to make it easier for people to buy foreclosed homes and to protect the surrounding community. [48]

Established in December 2008 in response to mounting foreclosures and a residential exodus, the CCLRC — or County Land Bank — works closely with area cities to determine how demolished properties can be

Officials in Cleveland are grappling with high levels of blight and economic decliine, made worse by the recession and home-foreclosure crisis. The Cuyahoga County Land Reutilization Corporation has formed a partnership with the federal government and Fannie Mae to make it easier for people to buy foreclosed homes.

turned into small parks and other public resources. In January, CCLRC acquired its first property, which is set to become a neighborhood garden. The land bank currently has 60 properties set for demolition.

Stabilizing Neighborhoods

In December 2009, CCLRC reached an agreement with Fannie Mae to halt the sale of low-price properties to speculators. Now, properties valued at $25,000 or less can be acquired from Fannie and resold to low- and middle-income families or redeveloped. Pilot projects are under way in Minneapolis/St. Paul, Phoenix and other cities.

CCLRC also secured $40 million from HUD to help stabilize neighborhoods suffering from high rates of foreclosure and home abandonment. In addition, CCLRC is working with the Cleveland Housing Network to provide first-mortgage financing to people trying to buy homes through lease-purchase agreements. [49]

While Cleveland, Detroit and other blighted cities are taking steps to redevelop themselves over the long term, the recession has upset even short-term downtown-revitalization plans. Since the fall of 2008, the economic downturn has cost millions of Americans jobs and

houses while depriving local governments of funds for planning and development.

The city centers that have survived — or fared the least poorly — during the economic earthquake are those with "clearly diversified land use that includes office, retail and residential [components] as well as a good pedestrian fabric," says Paul Levy, president and CEO of the Central City District, a business-improvement area in Philadelphia. Downtowns in places such as Philadelphia, New York City, San Francisco and Portland, Ore., for the most part "hold up better than suburban office districts further out from the center." Levy says that harder-hit cities such as Phoenix, Atlanta and Miami have higher office vacancy rates, and he notes that the home vacancy rate, just 7 percent in Philadelphia, is as high as 40 percent in Phoenix, Atlanta and Las Vegas.

Diversified Downtowns

The downtowns that have held up usually have a three-legged economic approach, Levy adds: They have diversified to attract tourism, conventions and business travelers. Detroit and Las Vegas, by contrast, "are single-industry towns."

An inevitable rise in fuel prices in coming years favors inner-city growth that is less auto-dependent, Levy says. Another urban-friendly trend is cultural and demographic. Americans who were young in the 1990s experienced a largely positive view of cities — one in which single women walk alone at night — from romanticized renderings in TV shows such as "Seinfeld," "Friends" and "Ally McBeal," as well as from movies such as "You've Got Mail," Levy says. "Those images have predisposed those in their 20s to early 40s to think urban. That's in contrast to the influence of the scary portrait of New York City that spread in the 1970s via the film 'The French Connection,' " about heroin smuggling. On top of that, he adds an "overlay of interest in sustainability" among today's 20- and 30-somethings.

Many urban planners' visions for downtowns have stressed an orchestrated effort to lure residents from a dependency on the automobile in favor of public transit and walkable space. But those values do not apply in many localities around the country, asserts Joel Kotkin, an author and scholar on social trends who is a

Distinguished Presidential Fellow in Urban Futures at Chapman University in Orange, Calif.

"We've been putting lots of money into transit for a long time, and there's not much evidence that it helps downtowns," he says. "Yes, light rail helps with some real estate investment, but look at the [glutted] condo market in Los Angeles, Phoenix or Miami. It would be a bleeding sore for many cities," he adds, noting that in cities such as Dallas, fewer than 2 percent of employees work downtown.

Revitalizing downtowns cannot work "if there are no jobs," Kotkin continues. And the growth and investment in jobs is still occurring more in the middle-class suburbs than in the burned-out inner cities, where the work force tends to possess fewer skills and education.

Fate of the Suburbs?

Not all analysts are so optimistic about the suburbs. William H. Lucy, an urban planning professor at the University of Virginia, argues that the spate of home foreclosures in suburban America has combined with demographic trends to give new impetus to downtown growth. In "Foreclosing the Dream: How America's Housing Crisis Is Reshaping Our Cities and Suburbs," published in February 2010 by the American Planning Association, he cites higher rates of foreclosures in new suburbs and exurbs than in cities. And he reports that the number of households in the 30-to-45 age group has declined by 3.4 million since 2000, reducing demand for large suburban houses.

The stereotypical "white flight" exodus from central cities, he writes, has been reversed in most large metropolitan areas. "Changing demographics and consumer attitudes coupled with political support for compact development, transit investments and awareness about climate change all point to a dramatic shift in development patterns." [50]

The recession's impact on the balance between suburbia and the inner cities was laid out in an Urban Land Institute study released in January 2010. Scholar John K. McIlwain noted that middle-aged and older members of the baby-boom generation, many of whom are trapped in houses that lost value in the mortgage crisis, are more likely than younger people to stick to suburbia, while members of the more mobile Generation Y are more likely to gravitate toward walkable, close-in communities.

"All of these groups have some characteristics that reflect a desire to live in more pedestrian-friendly, transit-oriented, mixed-use environments that de-emphasize auto dependency, whether the location is urban or suburban," he writes. "Economic and land constraints make it impossible for urban infill development to accommodate all the housing demand represented by all the demographic groups." As a result, suburban development "must adapt or it will be obsolete." [51]

Obama Administration

The Obama administration, soon after taking office in 2009, was greeted by a Brookings Institution study recommending that it retool federal agencies to confront changing demographics affecting the nation's suburban-urban mix. The study documented a slowdown in domestic migration because of the recession; a trend among recent immigrants to pick suburban locations over urban ones; an aging baby-boomer population that will stick to suburbs; and widening gaps in income and education levels among ethnic groups.

The study's authors noted that "even as the nation enters an extended period of economic uncertainty, the continued demographic dynamism of our metropolitan areas raises key policy and program issues" for the Obama administration. "Steps to implement the administration's economic-recovery package wisely, pursue immigrant integration alongside immigration reform, close educational achievement and attainment gaps, combine the planning of transportation and housing, and provide needed support to low-income workers and families should take account of our constantly evolving and changing metropolitan populations," they wrote. [52]

Kotkin, however, says any high priority that Obama might give to urban revitalization will be short-lived.

For the most part, the administration has focused stimulus-package aid on job creation, aid to homeowners facing foreclosure and long-term infrastructure funding for transit projects such as high-speed rail.

"Since the 2008 election, everything has been stacked for Obama and the urban vote, but this will be over in November," Kotkin says, adding that the vast majority of Congress comes from low-density, non-urban districts. "Only 3 to 5 percent of the population takes transit," he says. "Why would someone in suburban Kansas City want to subsidize high-speed rail to take people from

Milwaukee to Madison or from Tampa to Orlando? It's an attempt to engineer history that won't work."

Cities need to "heal themselves," he says, "and become more economically competitive" without help from the suburbs and the federal government.

2012 UPDATE

American cities are undergoing remarkable demographic and socioeconomic transformations, according to preliminary analysis of data from the 2010 decennial U.S. census. The changes stem from the economic slowdown, decades-old policy decisions and evolving attitudes about race and ethnicity.

America is steadily urbanizing, though population is still more likely to be concentrated in suburbs and the metropolitan areas of the Sun Belt, which are increasingly attracting moderate-income minorities. The Census Bureau reports that 46 of the 50 fastest-growing metro areas in the United States from 2010 to 2011 were in the South or West. Meanwhile, relatively affluent whites are moving into gentrifying downtown areas of older, larger cities. This increasingly urban America is on track to become a "minority-majority" country sometime in the 2040s, when non-Hispanic whites would no longer comprise at least half the population, the Census Bureau predicts.

Immigration Nation

The Census Bureau announced May 17 that, for the first time, most American babies were being born into minority groups. Minorities comprised 50.4 percent of the U.S. population younger than age 1 as of July 1, 2011, up from the 49.5 percent recorded in the 2010 census.

Hispanics are the largest and fastest-growing U.S. minority. They number 52 million — up 3.1 percent from last year — and make up 16.7 percent of the population. (The increase in Hispanics is due more to a younger population and higher fertility rates than to immigration, according to Jeffrey Passel, senior demographer at the Washington-based Pew Hispanic Center.

Blacks are the second-largest minority, at 12.3 percent of the U.S. population, followed by Asian-Americans, at 4.8 percent.

Nonwhites and Hispanics accounted for 98 percent of population growth in large metro areas from 2000 to 2010. Forty-two of the 100 largest metro areas lost white population, and non-Hispanic whites are a minority in 22 of the country's 100 largest metropolitan areas. [53]

An End to the Segregated City?

A January 2012 report by the conservative Manhattan Institute concluded that American cities today are virtually desegregated: Only one-half of 1 percent of American neighborhoods have no African-American residents, and these are mostly in sparsely populated rural areas, it said. "All-white neighborhoods are effectively extinct," the report declared, due to government policies outlawing housing discrimination, changing racial attitudes that both direct and reflect those policy changes and the easing of credit standards that opened many neighborhoods to moderate-income African-American families.

"The integration of some ghetto neighborhoods — by immigrants or gentrifying whites — plays only a small role in the overall decline in segregation," the report concludes. "Instead, the dominant trend in predominantly black neighborhoods nationwide has been population loss. Particularly in the formerly hyper-segregated cities of the Northeast and Midwest, ghetto neighborhoods have witnessed profound population declines, as former residents decamp for the suburbs or for the rapidly growing cities of the Sun Belt — where segregation is generally very low." [54]

While desegregation is generally viewed as a good thing, some experts interpret the data cautiously and aren't so quick to minimize the importance of immigration. "Although all-white neighborhoods have largely disappeared, this is more due to the entry of Latinos and Asians into formerly all-white neighborhoods," said Princeton University sociologist Douglas Massey. And, said Reynolds Farley, research professor emeritus at the University of Michigan's Population Studies Center: "There is now very much more black-white neighborhood integration than 40 years ago. Those of us who worked on segregation in the 1960s never anticipated such declines. Nevertheless, blacks remain considerably more segregated from whites than do Hispanics or Asians." [55]

Washington provides an example of outmigration of blacks from an urban center. Sometime early in 2011, the city lost its majority African-American status, a distinction it had held since the 1960 census. The black population today stands at about 49 percent, down from its peak of 71 percent in 1970. Observers generally agree that higher housing costs, which drove many of the city's lower-income blacks to more affordable suburbs, is a major factor in the population shift. In large part, younger, more affluent whites filled the vacuum; whites now comprise about 35 percent of D.C.'s population.

In addition to the shift of minorities to the suburbs, as in Washington, a reversal of the "Great Migration" of blacks from the rural South to the urban North — a major transfer of population that occurred largely in the first half of the 20th century — may be occurring. "Economic progress, cultural ties and an emerging black middle class have driven greater numbers of blacks to prosperous Southern metropolitan areas like Atlanta, Dallas, Houston and Raleigh [N.C., while] Illinois and Michigan showed for the first time absolute losses in black population," said demographer William H. Frey, a senior fellow in the Brookings Institution's Metropolitan Policy Program. "About three-quarters of the country's black population growth last decade took place in the South, compared with 65 percent in the 1990s." [56]

Detroit's Cautionary Tale

Recent history has been rough on Detroit, which is often seen as the unhappy model of American urban decline. The 2010 census pegged Detroit's population at 713,000, down 25 percent from 2000 and the lowest in nearly a century. In 1960 Detroit boasted the highest per capita income among U.S. cities. But today, more than a third of the population is below the poverty line, and per capita income, at $15,062, is less than half the national average. Meanwhile, Detroit is running a budget deficit of about $265 million, and long-term debt is estimated at $13.2 billion. [57]

Some blame inept and corrupt city management, greedy public-sector unions and poor planning for Detroit's woes. "Detroit has brought this completely upon itself," said L. Brooks Patterson, county executive of neighboring Oakland County. "Here is a city that is infamous for mismanagement and kicking the can down the road." Others blame external forces — regional, state and federal policies that siphoned away the city's resources, plus a nationwide economic slump that hit Detroit's automobile industry particularly hard.

Raleigh, N.C., above is among several properous Southern metropoliotan areas, such as Atlanta, Dallas and Houston, that have seen influxes of middle-class African-Americans.

And many spread the blame. "It's impossible to deny that there has been mismanagement in Detroit and that it has contributed to the city's problems," said Betty Buss, a senior research associate at the Citizens Research Council of Michigan, a think tank in Livonia, Mich. "But policies coming from the suburban governments and the state also contributed, and it's impossible to deny that racism and segregation [have] played a big role." [58]

Eighty-three percent of Detroit's population is African-American, according to the 2010 census.

Contentious "Consent"

Whatever the causes of Detroit's crisis, city leaders have found their backs to the wall. In April, after months of intense political and legal wrangling, a bitterly divided City Council approved a consent agreement with the state that takes financial decision-making from the mayor and council and puts it in the hands of a nine-member advisory board. In return, the state will support the city's economic-recovery efforts, though details remain unclear.

Some Detroiters resent what they see as erosion of their city's sovereignty. JoAnn Watson, a City Council member who opposed the agreement, called state officials "forces of evil." Activist minister Malik Shabazz told pro-agreement council members, "It's going to be hard for the people to forgive you." City-employee unions criticized restrictions on collective-bargaining rights called for in the consent agreement. The agreement could face a long string of legal challenges before its impact on Detroit's future is known. [59]

While state and city authorities hash out the details and consequences of the consent agreement, one Detroiter is hoping to bring urban agriculture and aquaculture to three square miles of a largely abandoned neighborhood. With a four-year, $1 million grant from the Fred A. and Barbara M. Erb Family Foundation of Bloomfield Hills, Mich., the Recovery Park redevelopment agency is working to establish small farm plots on abandoned and unused property. The aim is to grow soybeans, lettuce and other suitable crops — with recovering drug addicts as the farmers. Part of the plan would turn an abandoned municipal garage into a fish farm that eventually could produce 5 million pounds of tilapia each year for sale in the Detroit region.

The plan still needs approval from city authorities, who are approaching the unusual concept with caution. Recovery Park President Gary Wozniak knows it will be a struggle — he joked that, when he first made his proposal to the Erb Family Foundation board, "they wanted me to take a urine test." But perhaps because of Detroit's straitened circumstances, and because there has been so little success with more conventional redevelopment strategies, the foundation agreed to the plan. Businessman John M. Erb, the foundation's president, said, "We don't see urban agriculture as curing all the needs Detroit has, but it's an added benefit to Detroit . . . It's ridiculous that lettuce is grown in California and shipped cross-country. You can grow lettuce here 10 months out of the year and don't have to have such a carbon footprint." [60]

Pittsburgh Revival

Across the country, other communities and cities are struggling to rebuild themselves. Some choose gentrification. In the 1950s, Pittsburgh's East Liberty neighborhood was a thriving commercial area with more than 500 businesses. By the 1980s, however, suburban migration and failed urban-renewal efforts had caused most of the area's businesses — and half of its residents — to flee.

But East Liberty Development Inc., a nonprofit community organization formed by the East Liberty Chamber of Commerce, developed a revitalization plan in partnership with Pittsburgh's Urban Redevelopment Authority, developers and other for-profit companies and local universities to attract major retailers back to the area. The effort has paid off. Home Depot, Whole Foods, Trader Joe's and Target have put outlets in East Liberty. The American Automobile Association has moved a regional office there, and an abandoned Nabisco bakery is now home to a Google engineering office and the technology-development center of the University of Pittsburgh Medical Center. And the area abounds with cafes, restaurants and bars.

East Liberty chose to court big companies to facilitate its road to recovery. However, this meant upheaval and resettlement for many of its lower-income, African-American residents. Now the city is building a 75,000-square foot, mixed-use housing and retail entity estimated to cost about $13 million. It will include 54 apartments, 38 of them reserved for low-income households. Residents displaced by the neighborhood's redevelopment will have first crack at the apartments. "Urban renewal has been a recurring theme in East Liberty for the past 50 years," said Sabina Deitrick, a co-director of the Urban and Regional Analysis Program at the University of Pittsburgh. "Pittsburgh grows so slowly that gentrification means something different here. The recent stages of development could be a way to reunite neighborhoods that were separated by urban renewal." [61]

Meanwhile, Vallejo, Calif., is recovering from a barrage of blows that culminated in the city's bankruptcy in 2008: the national housing crisis, the loss of jobs when a large local shipyard closed and bloated salaries and pensions for city employees. At one time, more than 80 percent of the city's budget was going for compensation. The crime rate soared as police were laid off and budgets for the fire department and other city services were slashed. As part of the bankruptcy settlement, the city paid its creditors only 5 cents on the dollar.

But the painful reality of bankruptcy also was a wake-up call. Citizens volunteered for neighborhood crime-watch groups, city maintenance and other services. And, they agreed to a city sales tax increase in return for the ability to vote on how the revenue would be spent. Vallejo hasn't fully recovered — crime is still high, and the housing market hasn't bounced back — but it's doing well enough that the courts released it from bankruptcy in November 2011. Assistant City Manager Craig Whittom said the bankruptcy may have been a blessing: "It was effective at helping us re-create ourselves and change the culture so that we could restart from a stronger financial footing." [62]

Despite the different environments in which these redevelopment efforts are unfolding, each features a combination of citizen involvement, private capital and government cooperation. Tom Murphy, senior resident fellow at the Urban Land Institute, believes cities that ultimately are successful will be:

- well managed and safe, offer excellent education opportunities and have reasonable tax rates;
- committed to economic innovation and the availability of capital and embrace entrepreneurial public/private/institutional partnerships;
- vibrant places to live, providing a high quality of life, reasonably priced housing and a regional vision.

"Unlike many places in the world where land use and education and industrial policies are centrally planned, in the United States these policies are overwhelmingly decided by local governments," Murphy said. "There are 74,019 local governments and 13,506 school districts in the United States that control many land use and education policies. The country's ability to compete globally is very much dependent on the willingness of thousands of locally elected officials to invest in the future and build the public/private partnerships essential to harnessing the strengths of the community." [63]

NOTES

1. Terry Frieden, "FBI: Violent crime rate drops again," CNN.com, Oct. 17, 2005, www.cnn.com/2005/LAW/10/17/crime.rate/. For recent coverage, see Rick Lyman, "Surge in Population in the Exurbs Continues," *The New York Times*, June 21, 2006, p. A10.

2. Quoted in Matt Sepic, "St. Louis Escapes Its Rust-Belt Past," National Public Radio, May 17, 2006.

3. John Buntin, "Land Rush," *Governing*, March 2006, p. 26.

4. Lance Freeman, "Displacement or Succession?: Residential Mobility in Gentrifying Neighborhoods," *Urban Affairs Review*, 2005, p. 463.

5. Scott Carlson, "Richfield Wins Court Battle to Condemn Car Dealership Site," *St. Paul Pioneer Press*, Jan. 20, 2001, p. 1C.

6. For background see Kenneth Jost, "Property Rights," *CQ Researcher*, March 4, 2005, pp. 197-220.

7. Linda Greenhouse, "Justices Uphold Taking Private Property for Development," *The New York Times*, June 24, 2005, p. A1.

8. Avi Salzman and Laura Masnerus, "For Homeowners, Anger and Frustration at Court Ruling," *The New York Times*, June 24, 2005, p. A20.

9. Arthur M. Schlesinger Jr., "The City in American Civilization," in *American Urban History* (1969), p. 35.

10. Alison Isenberg, *Downtown America: A History of the Place and the People Who Made It* (2004), p. 7.

11. Jon C. Teaford, *The Twentieth Century American City*, 2nd ed. (1993), p. 17.

12. Robert M. Fogelson, *Downtown: Its Rise and Fall, 1880-1950* (2001), p. 13.

13. *Ibid.*, p. 193.

14. William Kennedy, *O Albany!* (1983), p. 8.

15. Robert A. Beauregard, *Visions of Decline: The Postwar Fate of U.S. Cities* (1993), p. 75.

16. Fogelson, *op. cit.*, p. 109.

17. *Ibid.*, p. 199.

18. Isenberg, *op. cit.*, p. 129.

19. *Ibid.*, p. 142.

20. For background, see "Business Migrates to the Suburbs," *CQ Researcher*, Nov. 14, 1986.

21. Fogelson, *op. cit.*, p. 387.

22. Michael A. Burayidi, ed., *Downtowns: Revitalizing the Centers of Small Urban Communities* (2001), p. 1.

23. Fogelson, *op. cit.*, p. 223.

24. Isenberg, *op. cit.*, p. 174.

25. *Ibid.*, p. 178.

26. Fogelson, *op. cit.*, p. 318.

27. Isenberg, *op. cit.*, p. 188.

28. Herbert J. Gans, "The Failure of Urban Renewal," in *American Urban History, op. cit.*, p. 568.

29. *Ibid.*, p. 569.

30. W. Dennis Keating *et al.*, eds., *Revitalizing Urban Neighborhoods* (1996), p. 207.

31. Beauregard, *op. cit.*, p. 171.

32. Isenberg, *op. cit.*, p. 239.

33. Beauregard, *op. cit.*, p. 201.

34. For background, see Charles S. Clark, "Revitalizing the Cities," *CQ Researcher*, Oct. 13, 1995, pp. 897-920.

35. For background see Richard L. Worsnop, "Historic Preservation," *CQ Researcher*, Oct. 7, 1994, pp. 865-888.

36. Beauregard, *op. cit.*, p. 231.

37. *Ibid.*, p. 259.

38. Christopher Farrell and Michael Mandel, "The Economic Crisis of Urban America," *Business Week*, May 18, 1992, p. 38.

39. Quoted in William H. Hudnut, *Cities on the Rebound* (1998), p. 1.

40. William Fulton, "The Panacea Patrol," *Governing*, October 2004, p. 62.

41. Alan Ehrenhalt, "Ballpark Dreaming," *Governing*, November 2004, p. 6.

42. Lisa Chamberlain, "Creating Demand for City Living in Nashville," *The New York Times*, June 21, 2006, p. C10.

43. Mark Guarino, "New Tale of Detroit's Woe: Pontiac Silverdome Sold for $583,000," *The Christian Science Monitor,* Nov. 18, 2009, www.csmonitor .com/Business/2009/1118/new-tale-of-detroits-woe-silverdome-sold-for-583000

44. Joel Kotkin, "The Worst Cities for Jobs: No. 1: Warren-Troy-Farmington Hills, Michigan," Forbes. com, cited on ABC News, May 2, 2010, http://abc news.go.com/print?id=10510368.

45. Suzette Hackney and Naomi R. Patton, "Bing: City Needs Detroiters' Help," *Detroit Free Press,* Aug. 18, 2010, www.freep.com/article/20100817/NEWS 01/100817031/Bing-s-land-use-plan-to-reshape-Detroit.

46. *Ibid.*

47. Urban Land Institute press release, April 16, 2010.

48. Cuyahoga County Ohio Land Bank, www.cuyaho galandbank.org.

49. Jim Rokakis, "Cuyahoga County Land Bank Is Fighting Back Against the Foreclosure Crisis," *Plain Dealer* (Ohio), July 13, 2010, www.cleveland.com/ opinion/index.ssf/2010/07/cuyahoga_county_land_ bank_is_f.html.

50. American Planning Association press release.

51. Urban Land Institute press release, "Housing in America: The Next Decade," Jan. 27, 2010.

52. William H. Frey, Alan Berube, Audrey Singer and Jill H. Wilson, "Getting Current: Recent Demographic Trends in Metropolitan America," Brookings Institution, March 2009, www.brookings.edu/ reports/2009/03_metro_demographic_trends.aspx.

43. Mark Guarino, "New tale of Detroit's woe: Pontiac Silverdome sold for $583,000," *The Christian Science Monitor*, Nov. 18, 2009, www.csmonitor .com/Business/2009/1118/new-tale-of-detroits-woe-silverdome-sold-for-583000.

44. Joel Kotkin, "The Worst Cities for Jobs: No. 1: Warren-Troy-Farmington Hills, Michigan," *Forbes.com*, cited on ABC News, May 2, 2010, http://abcnews .go.com/print?id=10510368.

45. Suzette Hackney and Naomi R. Patton, "Bing: City Needs Detroiters' Help," *Detroit Free Press*, Aug. 18, 2010, www.freep.com/article/20100817/NEWS 01/100817031/Bing-s-land-use-plan-to-reshape-Detroit.

46. *Ibid.*

47. Urban Land Institute press release, April 16, 2010.

48. Cuyahoga County Ohio Land Bank, www.cuya hogalandbank.org.

49. Jim Rokakis, "Cuyahoga County Land Bank Is Fighting Back Against the Foreclosure Crisis," *Plain Dealer* (Ohio), July 13, 2010, www.cleve land.com/opinion/index.ssf/2010/07/cuyahoga_ county_land_bank_is_f.html.

50. American Planning Association press release.

51. Urban Land Institute press release for "Housing in America: The Next Decade," Jan. 27, 2010.

52. William H. Frey, Alan Berube, Audrey Singer and Jill H. Wilson, "Getting Current: Recent Demographic Trends in Metropolitan America," Brookings Institution, March 2009, www.brookings.edu/ reports/2009/03_metro_demographic_trends.aspx.

53. "Most Children Younger Than Age 1 are Minorities, Census Bureau Reports," press release, U.S. Census Bureau, May 17, 2012, www.census.gov/newsroom/releases/archives/population/cb12-90.html.

54. Edward Glaeser and Jacob Vigdor, "The End of the Segregated Century: Racial Separation in America's Neighborhoods, 1890-2010," The Manhattan Institute, January 2012, www.manhattan-institute .org/html/cr_66.htm.

55. Massey and Farley quoted in Sam Roberts, "Segregation Curtailed in U.S. Cities, Study Finds," *The New York Times*, Jan. 30, 2012, www.nytimes .com/2012/01/31/us/Segregation-Curtailed-in-US-Cities-Study-Finds.html?_r=1&pagewanted=all.

56. William H. Frey, "A Pivotal Decade for America's White and Minority Populations," The Brookings Institution, March 25, 2011, www.brookings.edu/research/opinions/2011/03/25-census-demographics-frey.

57. Matt Helms, "Bing administration says 2,500 job cuts, privatization will save Detroit $250M," *Detroit Free Press*, April 23, 2012, www.freep.com/article/20120423/NEWS01/120423019/Bing-administration-says-2-500-layoffs-privatization-will-save-Detroit-250M-?odyssey=tab|mostpopular|text|FRONTPAGE.

58. Michael Alberti, "Detroit's woes can be eased, but region's officials avert their eyes," *Remapping Debate*, May 21, 2012, www.remappingdebate.org/article/detroit%E2%80%99s-woes-can-be-eased-regions-officials-avert-their-eyes?page=0,0.

59. For reporting on Detroit's consent agreement with the State of Michigan, see coverage by Leonard N. Fleming, Darren A. Nichols and Christine MacDonald in the *Detroit News*, April 5, 2012, www.detroitnews.com/article/20120405/METRO01/204050398#ixzz1uxmifF5k; Sarah Cwiek, "Detroit City Council approves consent agreement — what's next?," Michigan Radio, April 5, 2012, http://michiganradio.org/post/detroit-city-council-approves-consent-agreement-whats-next; and Dawson Bell and Paul Egan, "Consent agreement: How the state will help save Detroit," *Detroit Free Press*, April 8, 2012, www.freep.com/apps/pbcs.dll/article?AID=2012304080003.

60. Nancy Derringer, "Urban farm plan reels in cash, tilapia," *Bridge*, May 15, 2012, http://bridgemi .com/2012/05/urban-farm-plan-reels-in-cash-tilapia/.

61. Christine H. O'Toole, "Slumbering Pittsburgh Neighborhood Reawakens," *The New York Times*, March 2, 2010, www.nytimes.com/2010/03/03/realestate/03pittsburgh.html; Diana Nelson Jones, "Ground broken for East Liberty housing, retail building," *Pittsburgh Post-Gazette*, March 15, 2012, www.post-gazette.com/stories/local/breaking/ground-broken-for-east-liberty-housing-retail-building-340100/.

62. Ariana Eunjung Cha, "Vallejo, Calif., once bankrupt, is now a model for cities in an age of austerity," *The Washington Post*, May 24, 2012, www.washingtonpost.com/business/economy/vallejo-calif-once-bankrupt-is-now-a-model-for-cities-in-an-age-of-austerity/2012/05/23/gJQAjLKglU_print.html.

63. Tom Murphy, "Adapting Cities for the Future," Urban Land Institute, July 13, 2011, http://urbanland.uli.org/Articles/2011/July/MurphyCities.

BIBLIOGRAPHY

Books

Fogelson, Robert M., *Downtown: Its Rise and Fall, 1880-1950*, Yale University Press, 2001.
An MIT professor of urban studies and history examines how downtowns lost their retail dominance.

Isenberg, Alison, *Downtown America: A History of the Place and the People Who Made It*, University of Chicago Press, 2004.
A Rutgers University historian examines downtowns during the 20th century, with particular attention to how retail trends reflected broader racial and economic issues.

Articles

Boddy, Trevor, "Vancouverism vs. Lower Manhattanism," Archnewsnow.com, Sept. 20, 2005.
The architecture critic for the *Vancouver Sun* explains how the downtown population of the British Columbia city doubled over the past 15 years, making it the highest residential density urban area in North America.

Buntin, John, "Land Rush," *Governing*, March 2006, p. 26.
Residential development is taking off around downtown Houston and other cities, but some feel that the government should intervene to preserve old neighborhoods.

Chan, Sewell, "Standard & Poor's Upgrades City's Credit Rating to Best Ever," *The New York Times*, May 23, 2006, p. B1.
A major bond-rating agency upgraded New York City's debt rating, citing surging tax revenues, new money for school construction and a new retiree health-insurance trust fund.

DiMassa, Cara Mia, and Roger Vincent, "Retailers Not Sold on Grand Avenue," *Los Angeles Times*, April 25, 2006, p. A1.
A leading architect and influential civic boosters are promoting new office and condo towers along Grand Avenue in Los Angeles but failing to lure high-end retailers back.

Hampson, Rick, "Studies: Gentrification a Boost for Everyone," *USA Today*, April 19, 2005, p. 1A.
Studies suggest gentrification drives comparatively few low-income residents from their homes, but anecdotal testimony indicates the poor are being priced out of their homes.

Leroux, Charles, and Ron Grossman, "Putting the 'Chic' Back in Chicago," *Chicago Tribune Magazine*, Feb. 5, 2006, p. 10.
Areas such as North Kenwood/Oakland, which had long struggled, have suddenly become fashionable.

MacGilless, Alec, "Region's Job Growth a Centrifugal Force," *The Washington Post*, June 18, 2006, p. A1.
Job and population growth in the National Capital Area continue to be much stronger in suburbs far from Washington, to the dismay of planners who wished for more density and better integration with transit.

Maler, Kevin, "Suburbs Want Downtowns of Their Own," *The New York Times*, April 30, 2006, Sec. 11, p. 10.
An increasing number of suburbs around Minneapolis-St. Paul are building their own downtowns.

Mehren, Elizabeth, "States Acting to Protect Private Property," *Los Angeles Times*, April 16, 2006, p. A1.
In response to a Supreme Court decision allowing cities to take control of properties for private development, all but three states have considered legislation to curb the practice.

Montgomery, Lori, "Education Becoming Top Issue for D.C.," *The Washington Post*, May 24, 2006, p. A1.
Business leaders with a stake in Washington's economic revival argue that healthy public schools are vital.

Mui, Ylan Q., "Wal-Mart to Enter Urban Markets," *The Washington Post*, April 5, 2006, p. D1.
The leading retailer announces it will build stores in more than 50 blighted urban areas.

Reports and Studies

Birch, Eugenie L., "Who Lives Downtown," *Living Cities Census Series,* Brookings Institution, November 2005.
An analysis of 44 cities finds that downtown populations are growing after decades of decline.

Freeman, Lance, "Displacement or Succession?: Residential Mobility in Gentrifying Neighborhoods," *Urban Affairs Review*, 2005, p. 463.
A Columbia University urban-planning professor finds that gentrification plays a minor role, if any, in displacing poor city dwellers.

Kotkin, Joel, "The New Suburbanism: A Realist's Guide to the American Future," The Planning Center, November 2005.
Despite urban planners' love for central cities, suburbs will continue as the stage for America's future growth.

Leinberger, Christopher B., "Turning Around Downtown: Twelve Steps to Revitalization," The Brookings Institution, March 2005.
A consultant lays out the template for revitalizing downtowns, from initial planning through housing strategy to attracting retail.

For More Information

International Downtown Association, 1250 H st, 10th Floor, Washington, DC 20005; (202) 393-6801; www.ida-down town.org. The association provides information and support to business-improvement districts.

Metropolitan Policy Program, Brookings Institution, 1775 Massachusetts Ave., N.W., Washington, DC 20036; (202) 797-6139; www.brookings.edu/metro. The think tank's urban program issues studies and supports scholars whose work can help communities grow in sustainable ways.

National League of Cities, 1301 Pennsylvania Ave., N.W., Suite 550, Washington, DC 20004; (202) 626-3000; www.nlc.org. The nation's oldest and largest association representing municipal governments.

National Trust for Historic Preservation, 1785 Massachusetts Ave., N.W., Washington, DC 20036; (202) 588-6000; www.mainstreet.org. Sponsors educational activity and advocates for neighborhood conservation, preservation law and downtown Main Street initiatives.

Urban Land Institute, 1025 Thomas Jefferson St., N.W., Suite 500 West; Washington, DC 20007; (202) 624-7000; www.uli.org. Initiates research into trends in land use and property development.

5

Attracting Jobs

Marcia Clemmitt

Boeing's 2,160-worker plant in Wichita, Kan. — centerpiece of the local economy — is closing. Just two years after the state spent $43 million to build a training center for aerospace workers, Boeing announced the plant would shut down by year's end because of high operational costs. States and localities spend up to $70 billion annually on business subsidies. Proponents say they generate prosperity. Critics say they often fail to deliver promised jobs and end up losing money.

From *CQ Researcher*, March 2, 2012.

Shocking news greeted the 2,160 employees at Boeing's military aircraft plant in Wichita, Kan., in early January. After 80-plus years as a centerpiece of the city's economy — and two years after Kansas spent $43 million to build a training center for aerospace workers — Boeing announced it was shutting down the plant.

Republican Gov. Sam Brownback, a former U.S. senator, called Boeing's decision "very disappointing," noting that, "no one worked harder for the success of the Boeing Company than Team Kansas."[1]

But according to a company executive, "Business costs in Wichita are not competitive" for Boeing's operations.[2]

Kansas is far from alone in offering millions of dollars in tax breaks, plus millions more for training centers, roads and other incentives aimed at enticing companies to relocate to an area or keep jobs from moving elsewhere. Such tax-funded perks have proliferated over the past decade as the economy has cratered and unemployment has soared.

But serious questions are being raised about the effectiveness of incentives, which can put a big dent in state and local revenues. Economists say many companies that receive perks fail to deliver promised jobs. And many also question whether the intense rivalry for jobs among states leads to little more than an economic shell game, with jobs moving from one place to another without a significant net national gain in employment.

In the case of Boeing, it eliminated most of its jobs in Wichita and moved the rest to company operations in Oklahoma and Texas.

117

"Right-to-Work" Laws Enacted in 23 States

Twenty-three states, mostly in the South and Midwest, have enacted laws that bar companies and unions from signing contracts requiring employees to join or pay fees to a union. Some industries, such as federally regulated airlines, are exempt. Proponents say the laws give states a business-friendly advantage in competing for jobs, but critics say they reduce wages and don't promote job growth.

Source: "Right to Work States," National Right to Work Legal Defense Foundation, 2012, www.nrtw.org/rtws.htm

"In a given year, it is estimated that, on average, some 15,000 communities vie for roughly 1,500 major industrial projects available nationally," wrote Jonathan Q. Morgan and David M. Lawrence at the University of North Carolina, Chapel Hill.[3] "This creates an intensely competitive and often costly situation in which the odds of success are low for many communities."[4]

Estimates of how much states and localities spend on location incentives annually range between $40 billion and $70 billion.[5] The amounts have skyrocketed nationwide. In Arizona, for example, businesses in 1994 claimed just $5 million in state tax credits, which reduce companies' state tax bill. By 2008 the credits had grown 17-fold, to $86 million.[6]

Proponents of business subsidies insist, however, that they generate jobs and help localities prosper.

Kentucky is seeing large effects from new tax breaks enacted in 2009, said Larry Hayes, who heads the Kentucky Cabinet for Economic Development, the state's main economic-development agency. Those breaks

include a tax credit for filmmakers that shoot in the state and job-creation incentives for companies both existing and new to Kentucky. The more than 200 companies working their way through the new programs' approval process could potentially generate more than 13,500 jobs and help retain 4,800 existing ones in Kentucky, he said.[7]

But Kentucky isn't the only state attracted by Hollywood's glitter. About 45 states offer tax credits to filmmakers. Rhode Island's filmmaker credits, which totaled $56.7 million between 2005 and 2009, created 4,184 full-time jobs in that period — including jobs directly connected to movie production and in other industries such as food and lodging that saw increased business while the movies were made, wrote Edward M. Mazze, a business professor at the University of Rhode Island.[8]

Although tax incentives can give an area an economic boost, focusing on a quick local hit misses some big-picture questions, says Joseph J. Seneca, a professor of economics at the Edward J. Bloustein School of Planning and Public Policy at Rutgers University in New Jersey. What's seldom asked — but probably should be — is "whether those jobs are taken away from, say, Brooklyn, or whether they're jobs the company would have created anyway," even if it hadn't received an incentive, he says.

Many communities, especially rural ones, have offered incentives to lure so-called "big box" retail stores such as Walmart and Home Depot. Those transactions can be as pricey — and as uncertain in their effects — as incentives to lure manufacturing companies.

Last year, towns that had provided significant incentives to lure Borders book stores were left high and dry when the retailer went bankrupt. Pico Rivera, an eastern suburb of Los Angeles, for example, had spent $1.6 million in federal grant money to get a Borders outlet, including helping to pay the store's rent for eight years. When the chain went bust, the town lost more than just jobs and a bookstore that was a center of economic activity. It also will be on the hook for rent until a new tenant is found for the vacated 18,100-square-foot site, plus for other costs, the *Whittier Daily News* reported.[9]

In 2009 alone, Walmart stores got $1.8 million in tax credits to build five stores in Louisiana. Bridgeton, Mo., approved a $7.2 million deal in 2010 to bring a single Walmart outlet to town.[10]

Businesses are growing accustomed to incentives and often tell states and localities to "fight amongst yourselves" to win our favor, says Katherine Chalmers, an assistant professor of economics at California State University, Sacramento.

Yet, the ammunition communities often use to outgun their rivals, including so-called business-climate rankings, can be suspect. Many such rankings give top billing to states that offer generous business tax breaks and go easy on environmental or workplace regulations. But some economists say a high ranking on such lists doesn't necessarily equate with a strong or competitive economy.

South Dakota, for example, ranks second in a 2012 index from the Tax Foundation, a business-oriented think tank in Washington, and 17th — comfortably in the top half of states — in a *Forbes* ranking.[11] The state's unemployment rate was 4.2 percent in December, compared to 8.2 percent nationally.[12]

But South Dakota contains four of the nation's 15 poorest counties, including the three poorest, according to the latest census data.[13] Moreover, South Dakota's economy rests largely on only two legs: agriculture and public employment at Ellsworth Air Force Base, the state's second-largest employer, near Rapid City.[14]

Development Subsidies Take Many Forms

States and local governments offer a variety of subsidies to attract businesses ranging from tax cuts to cash grants.

Common Types of Economic Development Subsidies

Tax abatements — Reduce or eliminate taxes paid to state and local governments. Often apply to property, inventory or sales taxes.

Tax credits — Reduce or eliminate corporate income taxes by allowing companies to deduct a percentage of certain expenses, such as research-and-development or new-equipment costs.

Industrial revenue bonds — Bonds with tax-free interest, giving companies what amounts to low-interest loans.

Infrastructure assistance — Reduces construction costs by giving local governments the responsibility for improving roads, sewers, water lines and other utilities.

Grants — Cash subsidies that companies may use for general or specific purposes.

Land-price write-downs — Reduce land-purchasing costs typically through third-party transfers. Local governments may also pay for such expenses as eminent domain or environmental cleanup.

Tax-increment financing — Uses property tax collected on the appreciation value of a new development to pay for infrastructure, land acquisition or other related costs.

Enterprise zones — Economically depressed areas in which companies are eligible for multiple subsidies.

Source: "Beginner's Guide," Good Jobs First, 2010, www.goodjobsfirst.org/accountable-development/beginners-guide

Robert W. Wassmer, a professor of economics also at Cal State, Sacramento, points to South Dakota as typical of many states that may rank high in some economic-climate measures but "don't have other things" that businesses need to thrive, such as access to markets and raw materials, good infrastructure and a skilled workforce. Rank, Wassmer says, doesn't necessarily translate to overall economic strength.

The disjoint exists because breaks on taxes and regulation have less influence on business-location decisions than many think, Wassmer argues. California, with relatively high business taxes and tough regulations, has a good record of retaining companies and jobs, he says. "Not that many businesses are being driven out," Wassmer asserts. Meanwhile, low-tax, lightly regulated Reno in neighboring

Rural Areas Find Barriers to Job Creation

"Before incentives can matter, fundamentals have to be strong."

Hard as it is to generate jobs in cities, it's even tougher in rural areas. An aging workforce and less easy access to markets and suppliers are among the barriers to expanding employment in rural counties. Even so, economic-development experts say some strategies show promise.

In North Carolina, for example, "metro areas are doing well income-wise, but the other 90 counties aren't," says Jason Jolley, senior research director of the Carolina Center for Competitive Economies at the University of North Carolina, Chapel Hill. North Carolina's core economy has shifted from tobacco, textiles and furniture to high-tech industries such as pharmaceuticals, but many jobs in new industries have gone to people moving into the state, Jolley says, while native rural residents lack access to similar opportunities.

In economists' perfect world, people would simply move where jobs are. "But people aren't as mobile as economic theory would argue" — especially since the housing crash left many with houses they can't sell, says Robert Greenbaum, professor of public policy at Ohio State University. That makes finding ways to develop rural jobs crucial, he and others say.

Rural areas lose young, educated workers at a high rate, another factor making those areas less attractive to employers, wrote Jonathan Q. Morgan, associate professor of public administration at the University of North Carolina (UNC), Chapel Hill, and colleagues. Nationwide, the median age in rural counties was 40.1 years in 2007, compared to 36.1 in metropolitan areas. Moreover, 16.3 percent of rural residents were 65 or older, compared to 11.9 percent in metro areas. [1]

Like most states that provide incentives to businesses, North Carolina gives larger ones to companies that put jobs in high-need areas, says Morgan. But if fundamentals such as adequate sewers and transportation infrastructure are lacking — often the case in rural areas — most businesses aren't interested, he says. "Before incentives can matter, fundamentals have to be strong."

"For the longest time, rural areas did what everybody else did — try to recruit big industry," says Morgan. "Some had success, but even they are realizing that they need a more diversified base so they are not dependent on one big company that might move offshore."

Options exist, though none is close to foolproof, and different areas need different approaches, economists say.

Localities shouldn't necessarily disdain retail and service jobs, despite their low wages and a prevailing view that only exporting industries can sustain an economy, says Katherine Chalmers, an assistant professor of economics at California State University, Sacramento. "With computer manufacturing, for example, you worry that it'll be outsourced, but it's hard to outsource your hairdresser."

In West Texas, where Chalmers grew up, retailing essentially is an export industry for towns where it's clustered, "because people drive long distances to shop there," she says.

Policymakers waste effort using strategies suited only for urban areas in rural places, says Thomas G. Johnson, a professor of development economics at the University of Missouri's Harry S Truman School of Public Affairs in Columbia. "Urban areas exist because there is value in clustering; rural areas exist because there's a value in space," he says.

Nevada "should be booming right now. Everybody should be flooding there, but they're not," Wassmer says.

"There's a consensus among economists that smokestack chasing is not effective," says Laura Kalambokidis, an associate professor of applied economics at the University of Minnesota, St. Paul. For one thing, "using tax incentives to chase employers is pretty much universal now, so they're not going to be effective" because businesses can get similar breaks from virtually any state, she says.

Policymakers who promote location incentives intend to boost job prospects for local residents, but the measures can fail on that score even when they bring jobs, says Robert Greenbaum, a professor of public policy at Ohio State University. If the targeted companies are suitable to a different — that is, a mobile or more educated — workforce than the local one, for instance, "people coming in from out of state take the jobs."

For rural jobs, "you should look at sparsity-based businesses" such as forestry and tourism as well as manufacturing that doesn't depend on having complementary industries nearby.

In North Carolina, some coastal and mountain towns are trying to start clusters of heritage-based enterprises by helping artisans such as potters and woodworkers strengthen their businesses and enticing more artisans to the area. Morgan says those efforts often begin with "revitalizing Main Streets," which "are the heart and soul of towns," then using "quality of life to attract entrepreneurs who are located elsewhere," as well as tourists and, possibly, retirees looking for an interesting place to settle.

How well this approach works "is not fully documented," but there is evidence that it has encouraged some communities to pull together with a "can-do attitude" to try to revitalize themselves, says Morgan. "At issue is whether such approaches "can make a dent, when you realize how many jobs aren't coming back."

Nevertheless, "there's a lot of literature showing that small businesses are job creators if they can stay alive," says Karen Chapple, associate director of the Institute of Urban and Regional Development at the University of California, Berkeley. So providing help to local small businesses, such as assistance with tax analysis and preparation, might help sustain entrepreneurs, she says.

One oft-heralded economic-development tool is the cluster — a geographical concentration of companies that are interconnected by being in the same industry, being part of the same supply chain or using the same set of job skills, for example. But while clusters can work for rural areas, they're no silver bullet, economists say.

"If there is a misperception" about clusters "it's that these programs have the potential to be adopted almost everywhere," says David L. Barkley, professor emeritus of applied economics at South Carolina's Clemson University.

Existing businesses with solid growth potential to form the seed of the cluster are essential, Barkley says. Sometimes creativity is required to discover growth potential. For example, while American textile manufacturing has moved offshore, in South Carolina the industry has "spotted growth in the 'miracle fiber' sector," such as athletic apparel that wicks away moisture and extra-warm lightweight hikers' clothing, he says.

Even then, Barkley says, "you still have to be introspective and ask, 'Do we have the resources needed' " to compete with other places to attract companies, including areas that have a head start. In the current economy, especially, "many communities aren't likely to be able to do it."

Despite difficulties, however, "there are lots of interesting" small-scale clusters sustaining local economies, including rural ones, Barkley says. Montana sports a high-end custom log cabin industry, Kentucky has houseboat builders and an area in Mississippi manufactures custom upholstered furniture.

In North Carolina, a group of four distressed rural counties hopes to piggyback on an existing cluster in a nearby metropolitan area — the high-tech Research Triangle Park area, near Durham, just to their south, says Morgan. "They are trying to get economies of scale by collaborating on a large industrial park" that might attract complementary businesses "interested in the lower-cost" living of the rural counties.

— *Marcia Clemmitt*

[1] Jonathan Q. Morgan, William Lambe and Allan Freyer, "Homegrown Responses to Economic Uncertainty in Rural America," *Rural Realities*, Mid-year [Issue 2] 2009, http://ruralsociology.org/StaticContent/Publications/Ruralrealities/pubs/RuralRealities3-2.pdf.

Nevertheless, lawmakers are very reluctant to give up the incentives because they "are good politics," wrote Terry F. Buss, a professor of public policy at Carnegie Mellon University's Heinz School of Business campus in Adelaide, Australia. "There is little risk to politicians when incentives fail because failure can be blamed on . . . market forces" or other hard-to-control factors. Then, when economic times are good, "policymakers can claim credit" — but only if they've enacted incentives, said Buss.[15]

Economists see things very differently. "I think the academic consensus would be, 'It would be best if we didn't have interstate competition' " to offer incentives, says Seneca, at the Bloustein School of Planning and Public Policy. "The real things that incentivize [business] investment" are states' long-term commitment to providing good "infrastructure, effective and efficient regulation and taxation, research and development spending, education and quality of life" that

More Companies Receiving Tax Breaks

Forty-two states offered companies multiyear property tax breaks known as abatements in 2007, a nearly threefold increase from four decades earlier. The incentives reduce or eliminate property taxes paid to state and local governments in exchange for doing business in the area.

States Offering Companies Multiyear Property Tax Abatements, 1964-2007

(No. of states)

Year	No. of states
1964	15
1979	31
1991	33
2004	35
2007	42

Source: Robert W. Wassmer, "The Increasing Use of Property Tax Abatement as a Means of Promoting Sub-National Economic Activity in the United States," Social Science Research Network, December 2007, papers.ssrn.com/sol3/papers.cfm?abstract_id=1088482

thanks to its proximity to Boeing's Seattle headquarters. Instead, the plant went to South Carolina, which will pay Boeing approximately $3,100 in incentives per job created, said Labeau.[16]

The Charleston, S.C., *Post and Courier* reported that the total incentive package, which the state government did not officially announce, totaled more than $900 million, twice as much as state officials announced.[17] By contrast, Idaho, with its small population, offers companies that create jobs only a small tax credit, worth thousands, not millions, of dollars, a harsh economic reality that may have doomed Boise in this case, according to the *Idaho Statesman.*[18]

apply to all residents and businesses, not specially targeted efforts.

"In a sense, you do want states to compete with one another — but to be able to say that 'we are the best-run state,'" says Kalambokidis, at the University of Minnesota.

As policymakers and taxpayers consider how best to bring jobs to their towns and cities, here are some of the questions being asked:

Do state and local tax incentives for businesses create jobs?

Over the past few decades, states and metropolitan areas have offered an increasing number of special tax breaks for businesses that pledge to bring new jobs to their areas. Economic-development officials say the incentives are effective in leading businesses to create local jobs. Most economists, however, argue that often the tax breaks don't create jobs but merely induce companies to move them from one place to another, often rewarding companies for location decisions that they would have made anyway.

"Incentives do work," said Alex Labeau, president of the Idaho Association of Commerce and Industry, a business lobby. Idaho recently learned a hard lesson when Boeing bypassed its capital, Boise, as the site for a new $750 million plant the state had hoped to snag

"When it comes down to two or more equally satisfactory sites, a superior incentive package and 'red carpet treatment' can clinch a deal," wrote Bill Schweke, who recently retired as a senior fellow at the Corporation for Enterprise Development, a group in Washington that focuses on low-income communities.[19]

Alabama, Louisiana and Texas, widely considered to be "leading in the economic recovery" from the recession, "excel in their incentive offerings" to business, according to *Area Development*, a magazine for corporate site-selection professionals. The Texas Development Fund, for example, offers cash grants and tax breaks to companies making a final location decision between Texas and another state.[20] (Many large and medium-sized Texas cities, along with some in Alabama and Louisiana, have repeatedly topped lists of cities showing strong recession recovery.)[21]

Timothy J. Bartik, senior economist at the W.E. Upjohn Institute for Employment Research, an independent group in Kalamazoo, Mich., acknowledged that some critics of incentives argue that they are "too small" compared to a company's total costs "to affect business location." But, he wrote, that argument is "unpersuasive." "Many states and metropolitan areas will be close substitutes" as sites, "offering similar access to markets and suppliers," so that "even small . . . cost differentials" such as what might come from a tax credit "could prove decisive for a particular . . . decision," he said.[22]

Many economists who criticize location-based tax and cash incentives for businesses, however, argue that such incentives don't create jobs but simply cause them to shift from one place to another — and generally don't do that as efficiently as economic-development officials claim.

One of the oldest forms of tax incentive are so-called enterprise-zone programs, in which businesses get tax breaks for locating in distressed areas. "There is really no evidence that these zones boost employment," says David Neumark, a professor of economics at the University of California, Irvine. Research findings on enterprise zones are clear enough, he says, that policymakers have only two realistic choices — "either kill them, or scale them way back to test" whether some specific tweaks and applications may make them work better.

Shawn M. Rohlin, a University of Akron assistant professor of economics, says his research shows enterprise zones do attract some businesses, especially retail and service operations. "However," he adds in an email interview, "the overall effect is smaller than one would anticipate, making the program quite expensive per new firm/employee." Furthermore, areas neighboring enterprise zones "seem to have lost almost as many firms as the zone gained, indicating that the zones improved at the expense of the neighboring areas."

In a study of North Carolina's tax credits, "We found that slightly more than half of companies had more jobs" after receiving a credit, but "45 percent had fewer," says Jason Jolley, senior research director of the Carolina Center for Competitive Economies at the University of North Carolina, Chapel Hill. "Many companies told us that they didn't even know they were getting" some of the state credits, which seriously undercuts the argument that they are a vital factor in attracting and retaining companies, says Jolley.

"Firms that relocate are typically in declining industries" that must keep cutting costs to stay afloat, and this can mean successful job-luring efforts are short-lived victories, wrote Scott Loveridge, a professor of agricultural economics at Michigan State University.[23]

"For example, North Carolina gave away $240 million in tax credits to Dell in 2004 to lure them . . . while the closest competitor offered only $30 million,"

Jennifer Lawrence waits for her cue during filming of "The Hunger Games" in North Carolina, one of more than 40 states offering tax subsidies and other inducements to filmmakers. Critics call for more transparency for incentives. Since they often come in the form of tax credits or other tax breaks that are not included in state budgets, they don't face the annual legislative reviews given to other government programs.

according to the Institute on Taxation and Economic Policy (ITEP) a Washington think tank that studies tax fairness. But six years later, as the market for personal computers became increasingly cost-focused, a struggling Dell announced that it would shut the North Carolina plant, "leaving at least 400 people without jobs," according to ITEP.[24]

"Several good studies . . . suggest that well-run, customized job training and manufacturing extension services" — government- or university-run initiatives that provide expertise to help local businesses improve their practices — "are far more cost-effective in creating jobs than is true of general business tax cuts or business tax incentives," wrote Bartik at the Upjohn Institute.[25]

Are location-based business incentives good for communities?

Critics of incentives offered to attract businesses to new locations say that many of the tax breaks actually have a reverse effect, siphoning public funds needed to provide roads, airports and other infrastructure and services that businesses need to thrive. The effect, critics say, is that the incentives may actually discourage job growth in the long run.

Supporters of incentives argue, however, that even when companies don't quite meet job goals, bringing businesses to an area and helping them stay profitable improves communities in many ways.

After the Sears Holdings Corp., in Hoffman Estates, Ill., announced in December that it would close more than a 100 Sears and Kmart stores, officials in Jackson, Miss., and other towns said that tax breaks to keep their stores would be worth the cost. Should its Sears store close, Jackson stands to lose $129,000 annually in property taxes plus one of only two large "anchor" stores that bring in enough customers to a Jackson shopping mall to keep it alive for other businesses.[26]

Many businesses argue that a valid purpose for incentives is helping local companies stay competitive by lowering their costs, says UNC's Jolley.

In Tulsa, Okla., some taxpayers cried foul when McLean, Va.-based media giant Gannett Co. moved a 500-worker call center out of state last year after receiving $260,000 in tax breaks from the city. But the fact that Gannett had supplied 500 jobs at the center for four years means that "the state gave Gannett nothing" and has no spilt milk to cry over, said Mike Neal, president of the Tulsa Chamber of Commerce. Gannett supplied jobs, "paid taxes, and they, in return, have got a little bit of that tax returned to them," making the situation a win for Tulsa, despite the move, he said.[27]

Many economists call the relocation of jobs from state to state or city to city a "zero-sum" game with no net benefits for the national economy. But Upjohn's Bartik argues that "such reshuffling may benefit the nation," at least in some cases. If jobs move to a high-unemployment area — as they may under enterprise-zone programs, for example — those areas "will benefit more" from the jobs than the business' previous location would have, since "the social benefits from hiring the average unemployed person are higher" than the benefits derived from hiring a less needy person, Bartik wrote.[28]

Critics of incentive programs argue that the economic improvements they spur are often short-lived and benefit the wrong people while the tax breaks drain needed public funds.

Incentives such as the tax credits that states often give to moviemakers filming on location are intended to produce only temporary jobs. Critics of the program say that this and other common features of incentives raise questions about their value.

Massachusetts' filmmaker credits allow moviemakers to take the credits in cash or sell them to others if their state tax bills aren't high enough to need the full credit as an offset, even though the movie jobs won't "even be there next year," said Peter Enrich, a professor at Northeastern University School of Law, in Boston. In 2008, the state issued $100 million in film credits, but only $100,000 was used to reduce filmmakers' own tax liabilities, while "the rest was paid out in cash or to reduce the taxes of insurance companies and banks" that bought the credits.[29] It's not clear that taxpayers would see that result as much of a boon to the community, Enrich says.

But taxpayers, and even lawmakers, often don't know the details of incentives that have been in place for years, says UNC's Jolley. Many incentives come in the form of tax credits or other tax breaks that are not included in state budgets, so they don't face annual legislative review as other government programs do, he says.

Some of North Carolina's filmmaker subsidy will go to the company that's filming the action movie "Iron Man 3" in Wilmington this year, says Jolley. And because the state basically hands over the credit, with no say in how it's used, "for all we know we could be subsidizing [lead actor] Robert Downey Jr.'s salary for up to $1 million," he says. "This makes you say, 'Wait a minute. Shouldn't we consider whether this is what we really want to do?' "

Even when monetary caps and so-called "sunset" provisions — which require lawmakers to reauthorize credits periodically — are written into credit programs most lawmakers uncritically extend the credits and raise the caps when businesses ask them to, said Missouri state Sen. Jason Crowell, a Republican. "History has shown" that "we will just raise those caps in exchange for campaign contributions."[30]

Some analysts argue that incentives ostensibly designed to bring jobs to high-need areas can actually end up increasing inequality of opportunity.

A study of Ohio's enterprise zones, for example, found that "higher-income districts reap most of the jobs and investment," even though the program aims to improve economies in low-income areas.[31]

Another Ohio study, by Good Jobs First, a Washington, D.C.-based national policy resource center that seeks accountability in subsidies, found that many taxpayer-funded relocations in the Cleveland and Cincinnati areas moved jobs away from public-transit-accessible neighborhoods, potentially putting the jobs out of reach of residents who cannot afford cars.[32]

Some praise tax credits as a valuable counterbalance to high business tax rates, which they argue inhibit economic growth, but many economists disagree. "People say, 'Taxes distort markets,' and I agree. But then they say, 'Tax credits will offset that distortion,' and I say, 'No, it just gives you two distortions,'" says Thomas G. Johnson, a professor of development economics at the University of Missouri's Harry S Truman School of Public Affairs, in Columbia. "Unless tax credits are really well designed, they get people to do things they don't want to do," which promotes economic inefficiency, not improvement, he says.

Should states and localities compete for business locations?

Some analysts say interstate business-incentive competition has become a "race to the bottom" in which governments undermine their neighbors and even themselves by giving away more than they can afford. Others argue, however, that interstate competition has always been a valuable spur to improvement.

"Competition for economic growth is undeniably, irrevocably American — and therefore unavoidable. In some ways, the whole history of the United States is the history of communities competing with each other," wrote William Fulton, an economic-development expert and a former mayor of Ventura, Calif.[33]

Tax competition "is an effective restraint on state and local taxes," keeping them at business-friendly levels, says a 2012 study by the conservative The Tax Foundation.[34]

"There is a role for competition" when each state strives to create the best "general tax-and-spend policy," said Arthur J. Rolnick, a former research director of the Federal Reserve Bank of Minneapolis and now a senior fellow at the University of Minnesota's Humphrey School of Public Affairs. "Such competition leads states to provide a more efficient allocation of public and private goods."[35]

"I do believe that states and localities should compete but not in superficial ways," says the University of Missouri's Johnson. "They should compete to be better

Borders stores in cities around the country, including this one in Washington, D.C., closed after the retailer declared bankruptcy last year. Many of the communities had provided incentives to lure the stores. Pico Rivera, a suburb of Los Angeles, for example, had spent $1.6 million, including helping to pay the store's rent for eight years.

AFP/Getty Images/Mandel Ngan

hosts to jobs," mainly using longer-term strategies such as beefing up transportation and other infrastructure and workforce training, and creating an efficient tax system.

Competition on infrastructure and education can constitute a race to the top, rather than to the bottom, says Ohio State's Greenbaum. "If a business you brought in leaves, tax breaks may be wasted, but human and infrastructure investments" remain.

But much interstate competition takes the form of location-based incentives and has grown so intense that "politicians aren't acting rationally, and they're giving away too much," says Wassmer at California State University.

Competition on giveaways — unlike competition to improve state systems and services — quickly becomes an inescapable trap, even for states that believe it may not be in their best interest, said Rolnick. "As long as a single state engages in this practice, others will feel compelled to compete."[36]

When state competition "takes the form of preferential treatment for specific businesses," it undercuts the goal of having a strong national economy by causing some businesses to locate in places that might not be the best sites for them in the long run and also may decrease tax revenues so that money can't go to transportation projects or schools, for example, said Rolnick.[37]

"Ideally, you would expect a firm to locate where things are most efficient for it," not in the place that fought hardest to attract it, says Tonya Hansen, an assistant professor of economics at Minnesota State University Moorhead. "If a firm is only local because of an incentive," then it may not be operating in the most efficient business mode, she says.

Federal-level programs generally are more efficient than state competition because "they bring in more money, the money is more stable, and it blankets the 50 states" with similar incentives "so it's not pitting state against state," says Chalmers, at Cal State. In addition, the most blighted, neediest areas may have a better chance of capturing federal dollars because when decisions are made on the state level "the self-interest of politicians to get reelected" sometimes shifts dollars toward communities with more votes rather than high needs.

BACKGROUND

Early Competition

The first property-tax break for a North American business was awarded in 1640 — more than 125 years before the United States was founded. Given in the region that later became Connecticut, it started a persistent tradition. Along the way, doubts arose about whether interstate competition for business was an effective strategy. But local self-interest has won the day, and competitive use of business incentives has steadily increased.[38]

In 1791, Treasury Secretary Alexander Hamilton and other investors persuaded the New Jersey Assembly to exempt from state and county taxes a group called the Society for Useful Manufactures. They argued that the tax break would provide, "by moderate calculation," jobs for "20,000 persons" in the state.[39]

Nearby states reacted with horror. The "powers, rights and privileges, given to this company would be . . . very injurious to this state as well as other states," complained a member of the Pennsylvania House of Representatives.[40]

As the country grew, competition for businesses spread. After the Civil War, Southern states excused some companies from property taxes in an attempt to get Eastern and Midwestern industries to relocate.

In the 1920s, a wealthy industrial real estate executive, Felix Fantus, founded the Fantus Corp., the first consultancy to specialize in helping companies find the most advantageous locations for facilities — a service that

included analysis of tax breaks and other incentives. By the 1950s, the company advised businesses to encourage state competition for lucrative incentive packages.[41]

Beginning in 1975, Fantus published the first state "business climate" rankings, which helped drive interstate competition on incentives.[42]

In the 1980s, worries began about American industrial jobs "getting slashed" by automation and foreign, low-wage competition, says Ohio State's Greenbaum. In hopes of bringing jobs back to the United States and placing them in struggling neighborhoods, the states and later the federal government established enterprise-zone programs. The zones "had appeal in a time when government budgets were limited, since they targeted" high-need areas with the incentives, he says.

Economics vs. Politics

The University of North Carolina's Jolley says that while studies show that location-based tax incentives don't work well, researchers "have failed to convince policymakers" of that.

"Our political and government structure is not set up for the most efficient economic policies," says Kalambokidis, of the University of Minnesota. Business supply chains and markets relate to geographic and demographic features that span regions rather than stop at city or state borders.

Most tax breaks decrease government revenues in later years — leaving "the cost to fall on future officeholders" — but demonstrate to voters that today's politicians are working to bring in jobs, says Greenbaum. As a result, he says, many lawmakers are reluctant to end them.

"One legislator told us, 'This is the best study we've ever ignored,' " says Jolley, whose legislature-requested 2008 study showed that North Carolina's incentives aren't effective.[43] "There was excitement" in the legislature when Jolley and colleagues said that scaling back the tax breaks would allow the state to lower corporate tax rates. But lawmakers so far have opted to keep the incentives. "They wouldn't be able to demonstrate" immediate budget savings if they traded the incentives for lower corporate tax breaks, and economic-development officials insist that "there's value in staying in the game," Jolley says.

Lawmakers and courts have long been ambivalent about location-based incentives.

CHRONOLOGY

1960s-1970s *As the nation's hot economy slows, policymakers look for ways to create jobs.*

1967 Sen. Robert F. Kennedy, D-Mass., introduces a bill to award tax credits to businesses for bringing jobs to low-income urban "enterprise zones," but Congress doesn't act.

1975 Fantus Corp. publishes first rankings of advantageous locations for facilities, including analysis of tax breaks and other incentives.

1980s-1990s *As manufacturing jobs dwindle, lawmakers hope tax-advantaged "enterprise zones" in low-income areas can create jobs.*

1980 Prime Minister Margaret Thatcher's conservative government introduces enterprise zones in the United Kingdom. Presidential candidate Ronald Reagan and two New York representatives, Republican Jack Kemp and Democrat Robert Garcia, propose enterprise-zone bills, but they are not enacted. . . . Connecticut and Louisiana adopt enterprise-zone legislation in 1981.

1985 Early evidence that enterprise zones attract business to depressed areas — although sometimes only through relocation from nearby neighborhoods — spurs at least 40 states to enact enterprise-zone laws.

1993 First federal enterprise zones created in cities including Atlanta and Baltimore and rural areas including Mississippi's Delta region and Texas's Rio Grande Valley.

1997 Spurred by research showing that fierce state job competition doesn't create jobs but merely moves them, progressive lawmaker Rep. David Minge, D-Minn., proposes legislation to impose a heavy federal tax on states' location-based tax credits to business; Congress doesn't act on the measure.

2000s *State competition for business relocations heats up, but studies find most programs are ineffective.*

2005 Sen. George Voinovich, R-Ohio, and bipartisan list of cosponsors introduce a bill to guarantee states the right to compete for business sites using tax incentives. Congress doesn't act on the measure.

2007 U.S. cities have built 28 major-league stadiums and arenas since 2000, as teams encourage cities to compete for them using taxpayer-funded incentives.

2008 As recession begins, some states require businesses to forgo incentive funds if job-creation goals aren't met.

2009 Walmart gets $1.8 million in tax credits to build five stores in Louisiana. . . . South Carolina attracts new Boeing plant by offering financial incentives and a lower-wage workforce because the state's right-to-work law makes unionization less likely. . . . In fierce competition to attract conventioneers, American cities have spent $23 billion since 1993 to build convention centers; 320 cities now have them.

2010 Reflecting the growing trend of transparency for subsidies, 37 states post some information online about business-subsidy recipients, up from 23 states in 2007.

2011 Jackson, Miss., officials propose tax breaks to keep a Sears store open after Sears Holdings Corp. announces closures of about 100 Sears and Kmart stores. . . . Newspaper publisher Gannett moves a 4-year-old call center out of Oklahoma despite receiving $260,000 in tax credits. . . . North Carolina lures Chiquita Brands International's headquarters from Cincinnati to Charlotte with $22 million in incentives.

2012 Boeing closes Wichita military aircraft plant, moves jobs to Texas and Oklahoma, two years after Kansas built a $43 million aerospace training center. . . . Proposal for a new Minnesota Vikings football stadium, with about $700 million in taxpayer funding, may reach state lawmakers this spring. . . . Indiana becomes first Rust Belt state and 23rd nationwide to enact business-friendly "right-to-work" legislation banning contracts requiring workers to join or pay dues to a union. . . . Louisiana Republican Gov. Bobby Jindal proposes allowing localities to offer 10-year tax abatements for facilities such as corporate headquarters and data centers.

Subsidies Spark Debate — and New Ideas

"At least give them to companies that reflect your values."

Public officials aren't likely to stop using tax incentives and other benefits to lure businesses and jobs to their communities. But experts see ways to make such subsidies more effective.

"It's hard to end the incentives, but you can try to mend them," says economist Robert W. Wassmer, a professor at California State University, Sacramento.

Step one might be for policymakers to expand their vision of where jobs come from, says Jonathan Q. Morgan, associate professor of public administration at the University of North Carolina, Chapel Hill. Recruiting businesses to a location by offering subsidies and other inducements has been at the top of most states' agendas, he says.

But "business retention and expansion and figuring out how to help" businesses grow that are already in a community is "an important and under-appreciated tool of job creation." Finding ways to help residents who want to "create new businesses from scratch" is another, Morgan says.

Public officials should consider offering tax breaks to lure business relocations only under very specific circumstances, Wassmer says. "Do a benefit-cost assessment" for any incentive under consideration, he says: "Am I just being played by this plant?" Only a company known to face a real choice between very suitable, profit-making locations should be offered an incentive package, Wassmer wrote. Otherwise, he argued, taxpayer dollars will go to companies that would have moved in anyway.

Furthermore, Wassmer advised sober analysis to make sure businesses receiving incentives will generate enough tax revenues, jobs and other benefits to more than compensate for the cost of the inducements. [1]

But it's not always easy to persuade local politicians to cast a skeptical eye on business incentives, Wassmer says.

"Asking those questions goes against the whole political movement" that's driven increased state competition on subsidies for decades, he says. "If more politicians would do it, though, we'd see the end of those bidding wars" between states and cities that consume public money.

Some researchers note that emotions can get in the way of making realistic decisions about which job-building strategies to use.

It's "enormously difficult to do economic development" with analysis done just by local policymakers and officials, says David L. Barkley, professor emeritus of applied economics at South Carolina's Clemson University. A person has a tendency to "exaggerate both the good and the bad of one's own area, saying, 'We have great schools' or 'Woe is me, we have no possibilities here,'" he says. Bringing in outside analysts who can be objective and know what competing regions are doing is necessary, he says.

"A public-private partnership" that includes scholars who study the regional economy could "figure out what kinds of business could thrive in a region, and that, I think, could be beneficial," says Laura Kalambokidis, associate professor of applied economics at the University of Minnesota, St. Paul. "Pitfalls include the fact that every state wants to be the next 'green revolution' state or the next Silicon Valley, but that simply won't work everywhere."

"If you're going to use incentives, at least give them to companies that reflect your values," such as paying workers well and having environmentally sustainable practices, says Jason Jolley, senior research director of the Carolina Center for Competitive Economies at the University of North Carolina, Chapel Hill. To accomplish that, states are better off requiring the legislature or another official body to choose each incentive recipient, rather than automatically offering incentives to any company that meets statutory requirements, Jolley says.

Research shows that some types of incentives are simply more effective at expanding employment and strengthening economies, scholars say.

Tax credits that simply reward companies for hiring the unemployed are relatively efficient and effective, partly because they have relatively low administrative costs, says David Neumark, professor of economics at the University of California, Irvine.

Tax credits that go only to new companies or companies with definite plans to expand also have promise, says Jolley.

Building in accountability provisions also matters. A periodic vetting process involving both the legislature and a state bureaucracy should be part of all incentive programs, to ensure "that they're worth doing long term," Jolley says.

A strong requirement for firms to report their employment numbers is also vital, says Tonya Hansen, assistant professor of economics at Minnesota State University Moorhead. Accurate performance data can be a basis for awarding further incentives and studying program effectiveness, she says.

States are getting smarter, says the University of North Carolina's Morgan. Incentive agreements that impose performance standards and force companies to return incentive money to the government if they don't meet agreed-upon goals will grow more common, "slowly but surely," he says.

— *Marcia Clemmitt*

---

[1] For background, see Robert W. Wassmer, "The Increasing Use of Property Tax Abatement as a Means of Promoting State and Local Economic Activity in the United States," in *Erosion of the Property Tax Base: Trends, Causes, and Consequences*, Nancy Augustine, Michael Bell, David Brunori and Joan Youngman, eds., 2009, pp. 221-259.

Prior to 1789, when the Articles of Confederation governed the United States, "the states were very autonomous, and the standard was to impose tariffs" on out-of-state business to protect in-state companies, says Enrich, of Northeastern Law School. Part of the impetus to adopt the Constitution's stronger central government was to keep "interstate commerce" flowing, since "the Framers recognized that tariff competition between the states didn't make sense" for a country that needed to establish a strong national economy, he argues.

Under the Commerce Clause of the Constitution, Congress alone has the power to "regulate commerce . . . among the several states." The clause has been interpreted as banning states from regulating — including imposing taxes — in ways that interfere with interstate business dealings.[44]

The Supreme Court has repeatedly upheld states' right to discriminate between in-state and out-of-state businesses by actions such as buying services from local rather than out-of-state businesses, since those aren't regulatory acts, just market activity, Enrich says. Rulings in regulation- and tax-related cases have been mixed.

In a case that reached the Supreme Court in 2006, Enrich and attorney Terry Lodge, working on behalf of some Michigan and Ohio residents, challenged tax incentives the city had offered to keep a DaimlerChrysler Jeep plant in town. They argued, among other things, that a property-tax exemption in the package interfered with interstate commerce because it favored the Ohio plant over other businesses, including out-of-state companies. The court didn't rule on the merits of the case, however, but dismissed the challenge on the grounds that the citizens who brought it had not suffered actual harm and therefore had no standing to sue.[45]

Congress should enact legislation clarifying which incentives are allowable and which are not, many say — and have said for decades.

"Congress alone can provide for a full and thorough canvassing of the multitudinous and intricate factors which compose the problem of the taxing freedom of the states and the needed limits on such state taxing power," Supreme Court Associate Justice Felix Frankfurter wrote in 1959.[46]

During the 1990s, Rep. David Minge, D-Minn., tried several times to blunt the effect of state incentives. His

Many communities, especially rural ones, offer substantial incentives to lure "big box" retail stores such as Walmart. In 2009, Walmart got $1.8 million in tax credits to build five stores in Louisiana. Bridgeton, Mo., approved a $7.2 million deal in 2010 to bring a single Walmart outlet to town. Above, a Walmart store in Valley Stream, N.Y.

bills would have levied high federal taxes on any "preferential" state subsidies, thus making them worthless to businesses.[47]

Conversely, in 2005, two Ohio Republicans — U.S. Sen. George Voinovich and Rep. Patrick Tiberi — introduced legislation, with bipartisan support, to allow most subsidies. Their bill would have barred commerce clause-based legal challenges of "all state and local tax incentives," with seven narrow exceptions.[48]

No bill on incentives has made it out of committee.

Regional Cooperation and Accountability

Regional cooperation on economic development is still rare, but some states seek greater accountability for subsidies.

Some multistate economic-development programs do exist, says Rutgers' Seneca. For example, the New York/New Jersey Port Authority opened in 1921, with congressional authorization, to develop the harbor region the states share.[49] Since economic regions don't stop at state boundaries, "that's the kind of thing that gives a positive return on investment," Seneca said.

Two jurisdictions in the Columbus, Ohio, area recently "agreed to disarm from competition" after the headquarters of the Bob Evans restaurant chain "got a lot of state incentives to move from a depressed area" in the

If Cities Build Stadiums, Will Fans Come?

Critics view sports subsidies as waste of tax dollars.

The Minnesota Vikings ended the 2011 football season with three wins and 13 losses, but they could end the year victorious anyway. The Vikings may finally come out on top of a years-long battle to score a new, mostly public-funded stadium if state lawmakers approve a plan this spring supported by Democratic Gov. Mark Dayton.[1]

Minnesotans have wrangled for years over which jurisdiction should house the facility and how to cover two-thirds of the stadium's estimated $1 billion cost using public funds. Last fall, for example, Minneapolis and nearby Ramsey County both tried to sweeten their bids by proposing to levy new sales taxes without first getting voters' approval. But the legislature upheld a Minnesota law requiring a vote, and those plans, like earlier ones, went back to the drawing board.[2]

The push for tax-subsidized stadiums is happening not only in Minnesota. Professional sports teams and their supporters, who include some lawmakers, repeatedly argue that new arenas create jobs and spur economic activity. Regions from Los Angeles to Tampa Bay are locked in struggles over proposed facilities for both major- and minor-league teams.[3]

Between 2000 and 2007, 28 new arenas for Major League Baseball, basketball, football and hockey teams were built around the country at a total cost of about $9 billion, with at least $5 billion paid by taxpayers.[4]

"There is likely no major metropolitan area in this country that has not been held hostage at some point by the owner of a sports franchise" who threatened to move the team if taxpayers didn't ante up, Arthur J. Rolnick, former research director of the Federal Reserve Bank of Minneapolis, told Congress in 2007, when the Vikings battle was already under way.

At the time, construction had just begun for a new Minnesota Twins baseball stadium after a 10-year fight in which the team finally secured "about $400 million in public financing" from "a previously reluctant state legislature," said Rolnick, now a senior fellow at the University of Minnesota's Humphrey School of Public Affairs.[5]

Proponents say the public funding has value for communities.

When jurisdictions in the Washington area vied for a Major League Baseball team that was set to come in 2005, supporters of a Northern Virginia site predicted their plan would give the state more than a $287 million annual boost. The National Football League urges cities to build large, updated stadiums partly to snag the annual Super Bowl, which the league claims brings about $400 million in business to the host city.[6]

Skeptics of taxpayer-funded business subsidies, along with many academic economists, disagree about the benefits, however.

The New York Yankees' stadium that opened in the Bronx in 2009 with substantial public funding created jobs, but most "are part time and low wage" and of little help to the neighborhood, argued Bettina Damiani, project director of Good Jobs New York, an advocacy group that seeks accountability in business subsidies.

"Few fields of empirical economic research offer virtual unanimity of findings. Yet independent work on the economic impact of stadiums and arenas has uniformly found there is no statistically positive correlation between sports facility construction and economic development," wrote Andrew Zimbalist, a professor of economics at Smith College, in Northampton, Mass.[7]

region "to a higher-income area nearby," says Ohio State's Greenbaum. To avoid an escalating economic arms race — and to limit the harm to the lower-income area that lost the facility — the towns agreed to share tax revenues from the project, he says.

Regional agreements are tough to enforce, however, says Enrich. In the 1990s, Illinois, Indiana and Wisconsin agreed not to discriminate against employers based in any of the states, but after one state was suspected of doing so, the compact broke down, he says.

Some advocacy groups, such as Good Jobs First, are pushing for greater accountability for subsidies, such as requiring public disclosure and periodic legislative scrutiny of tax credits or other incentives.[50]

The controversy extends beyond sports. Many cities use public funds to build convention centers, museums and similar venues in hopes of attracting paying visitors to town.

U.S. cities have poured more than $23 billion into convention centers from 1993 to 2009, when there were 320 throughout the country, reported *Next American City* magazine.[8]

As with sports arenas, hopes that a business boom will follow can be misplaced. As the number of convention centers rose between 1996 and 2003, attendance at many declined, the magazine reported. In response, many cities actually undertook major facility expansions, competing to snag the very biggest conventions, which previously found only a few cities with facilities large enough to host them, such as Las Vegas.

But that strategy has proved disappointing in many cities. A 420,000-square-foot expansion of Houston's George R. Brown Center, for example, was expected to bring 600,000 single-night visits to Houston in 2005. But it yielded only 220,000 — just over a third of expectations.[9]

— *Marcia Clemmitt*

Getty Images/Hannah Foslien

The Minnesota Vikings and Denver Broncos play at the Hubert H. Humphrey Metrodome in Minneapolis on Dec. 4, 2011. Minnesota lawmakers are considering long-debated plans to build a new $1 billion stadium, mostly with public funds.

[1] Mike Kaszuba, "Vikings Stadium Plan East of Dome Now on Fast Track," *Star Tribune* [Minneapolis], Feb. 5, 2012, www.startribune.com/politics/statelocal/138721284.html.

[2] Tom Scheck, "Dayton and Legislative Leaders Say Sales Tax Increase Won't Work for Stadium," MPR News, Minnesota Public Radio, Nov. 1, 2011, http://minnesota.publicradio.org/collections/special/columns/polinaut/archive/2011/11/dayton_and_legi.shtml.

[3] For background, see Michael Hunt, "NFL Teams Are Bold Because They Can Be," *Journal Sentinel* [Milwaukee], Feb. 9, 2012, www.jsonline.com/sports/nfl-teams-are-bold-because-they-can-be-iv44veu-139067354.html; Barry Wilner, "Goodell: 34 Teams Likely if LA Included," Associated Press/Globe [Boston], Feb. 3, 2012, http://articles.boston.com/2012-02-03/sports/31022006_1_concussion-research-la-stadium-brain-trauma.

[4] Sarah Wilhelm, "Public Funding of Sports Stadiums," Policy Perspectives, Center for Public Policy and Administration, University of Utah, April 30, 2008, www.imakenews.com/cppa/e_article001083889.cfm?x=b11,0,w.

[5] Arthur J. Rolnick, "Congress Should End the Economic War Among the States Testimony," The Federal Reserve Bank of Minneapolis website, Oct. 10, 2007, www.minneapolisfed.org/publications_papers/studies/econwar/rolnick_testimony_2007.cfm.

[6] Robert A. Baade, Robert Baumann, and Victor A. Matheson, "Selling the Game: Estimating the Economic Impact of Professional Sports Through Taxable Sales," *Southern Economic Journal*, January 2008, pp. 794-810, www.allbusiness.com/government/public-finance-taxes-taxation/7068215-1.html.

[7] Quoted in "Build It and They Will Come: Do Taxpayer-Financed Sports Stadiums, Convention Centers and Hotels Deliver as Promised For America's Cities?" Hearing transcript, House Oversight and Government Reform Domestic Policy Subcommittee, March 29, 2007, www.gpo.gov/fdsys/pkg/CHRG-110hhrg38037/html/CHRG-110hhrg38037.htm.

[8] Josh Stevens, "Unconventional Thinking," *Next American City*, Summer 2009, http://americancity.org/magazine/article/unconventional-thinking.

[9] *Ibid.*

Some state programs have accountability features. New Jersey's Business Employment Incentive Program "has some very attractive elements that other states have emulated" such as paying companies only if they create a net number of new jobs, based on verifiable tax records, says Seneca.[51]

As of December 2010, 37 states posted online information about what companies received at least one major state subsidy, up from only 23 states that did so in 2007, according to Good Jobs First.[52]

Yet, many politicians continue to resist transparency. In 2010, for example, Gov. Arnold Schwarzenegger, R-Calif., vetoed a bill that would have disclosed tax-credit recipients.[53]

"This is public money and there is a big accountability issue, but you can't make the negotiation public; your

An opponent of the proposed "right-to-work" law in Indiana demonstrates outside the State House on Jan. 23, 2012. On Feb. 1 Indiana became the 23rd state to enact such legislation, which bans workplace contracts requiring people to join or pay dues to a union. Republican governors and state legislators have pushed the laws, which they say give states a business-friendly edge in jobs competition.

prospects" — businesses considering a move to one's state —"will walk away and just laugh at you," said Graham Toft, president of the Indiana Economic Development Council.[54]

CURRENT SITUATION

Tight Times

With jobs on voters' minds, many policymakers are pushing new incentive competition in 2012.

In February, Louisiana's Republican governor, Bobby Jindal, proposed allowing localities to offer up to 10 years of tax breaks to facilities such as corporate headquarters, data centers and research-and-development operations.

The move would ultimately bring 10,000 jobs, Jindal said.[55]

Last December, the Illinois legislature and Democratic Gov. Pat Quinn approved at least $100 million in tax breaks to keep Sears Holdings Co. and the Chicago Mercantile Exchange, a financial and commodities trading market, in the state.[56] "If Ohio is offering $400 million to Sears . . . we will defend ourselves," said Quinn.[57]

States are adopting many kinds of tax incentives. "Tax stabilization agreements" — which guarantee a business's tax rates won't rise — are used in 12 states, says Hansen, of Minnesota State University. "Nearly everything else" in the way of tax incentives is used by at least 40 states today, she says.

Some states are courting not just employers but the site-location consultants who advise corporations about where to locate. Last spring, New Jersey economic-development officials entertained executives from the top 12 site-location firms. From the comfort of a hotel suite, they watched the NCAA basketball tournament and met with New Jersey's governor.[58]

Concerns are building about whether incentives deliver.

A group of local governments in the St. Louis area recently determined that more than $5.8 billion in public funds had gone to business incentives over the past 20 years, more than 80 percent of it to develop big-box stores and shopping centers. Despite the huge outlay, the number of retail jobs ticked up only slightly, "retail sales or per capita spending have not increased in years" and more than 600 small businesses closed, eliminating nearly as many jobs as the new stores brought in, said the group.[59]

Right to Work

Republican governors and state legislators have pushed to enact "right-to-work" laws that ban workplace contracts requiring people to join or pay dues to a union. Proponents argue that the laws give states a business-friendly edge in the jobs competition.

On Feb. 1, Indiana became the 23rd state to enact right-to-work legislation and the first in the once-vibrant Midwest and Northeastern industrial heartland to do so.[60] New Hampshire, Michigan, Wisconsin and Ohio also are considering such measures.[61]

Opponents see no relationship between right-to-work laws and job creation. "Both the highest and the lowest unemployment rates in the country are found in states"

Do "right-to-work" laws help states attract businesses?

YES Paul Kersey
Director of Labor Policy,
Mackinac Center for Public Policy

Written for CQ Researcher, March 2012

Under a state right-to-work law, an employee cannot be forced to pay union dues or fees as a condition of employment; individual workers can support a union or withhold their support. The law does not change the process for recognizing a union or lessen the obligation to bargain with a union once it has proved it has majority support in the workforce. Since the evidence indicates that most workers join the union in their workplace voluntarily in right-to-work states, right-to-work is actually a fairly modest change.

Yet unions treat right-to-work with alarm, while employers respond very positively to the provision of worker choice.

The attraction of right-to-work for employers is hard to deny. Between 2002 and 2010, employment was up 3 percent on average in right-to-work states and down 3 percent in non-right-to-work states. Union apologists have argued that the job gains in right-to-work states have been due to weather or other factors, but research into economic growth along the borders between right-to-work and non-right-to-work states shows that job growth is one-third higher in counties that have right-to-work than in neighboring counties that don't.

In a right-to-work state, employers know that unions will have the resources workers want them to have, no more and no less. Union officials must pay close attention to the desires of workers who can leave the union and keep their dues money if they are not happy.

Without that protection, unions are tempted to substitute their own ideological agenda for workers' real-world interests. Most employers accept the need for bargaining with employees and understand that over the long term they are better off if employees are happy with their wages and working conditions. If workers prefer to bargain collectively, so be it, but employers want to know that the union they bargain with will pursue the best interests of their employees, not the preferences of union officials.

But the real reason why states should pass right-to-work laws is because they respect the First Amendment right of workers to associate as they see fit, to join a union or not, to give or withhold support from an institution that they may or may not support. If political leaders really value workers, in terms of both recognizing their rights and respecting their judgment, they won't hesitate to give workers that choice. There is every reason to have confidence that workers will use that choice responsibly, to the benefit of both businesses and workers themselves.

NO Gordon Lafer
Associate Professor, Labor Education and
Research Center University of Oregon

Written for CQ Researcher, March 2012

In 2011-12, statehouses across the country saw renewed battles over so-called "right-to-work" (RTW) laws. Contrary to what the public might assume, right-to-work does not guarantee anyone a job. Rather, it makes it illegal for unions to require each employee who benefits from the terms of a contract to pay his or her fair share of the costs of administering it.

The aim of RTW — according to its backers — is to cut wages and benefits on the gamble that this will bring more jobs into a state. As the Indiana Chamber of Commerce explains, "unionization increases labor costs," and therefore "makes a given location a less attractive place to invest new capital." By giving up unions and lowering wages, workers are supposed to increase their desirability in the eyes of manufacturers.

Research shows that RTW cuts wages and benefits — but fails to promote job growth. According to multiple studies, RTW laws lower average income by about $1,500 a year and decrease the odds of getting health insurance or a pension through your job — for union and nonunion workers. But RTW does not boost job growth.

It may be that companies in the 1980s moved to RTW states in search of lower wages. But in the globalized economy, companies looking for cheap labor overwhelmingly look to China or Mexico.

In this sense, the most important case study for any state considering RTW in 2012 is that of Oklahoma, which adopted RTW in the post-NAFTA era.

When Oklahoma debated RTW in 2001, corporate location consultants told legislators that if the state adopted RTW, it would see "eight to 10 times as many prospects." What happened? The number of new companies coming into the state has fallen by one-third in the 10 years since RTW was adopted. Manufacturing employment has decreased 30 percent.

Surveys of manufacturers confirm that RTW is not a significant draw; in 2010 manufacturers ranked it 16th among factors affecting location decisions. For higher-tech, higher-wage employers, nine of the 10 most-favored states are non-RTW.

RTW is promoted as providing a competitive advantage to a state. But to the extent more states go RTW — or a national bill passes — wages will be lowered in all states, no one will have an advantage and the number of jobs in the country will be exactly the same as before. This is how RTW undermines the American middle class.

> Even as some proponents of location-based incentives question their value, fierce struggles among states to lure employers are likely to continue. "It's like a nuclear-arms standstill. No one is willing to blink first."
>
> — *Jon Shure Director, State Fiscal Strategies, Center on Budget and Policy Priorities*

with right-to-work laws, wrote Gordon Lafer, an associate professor of political economics at the University of Oregon's Labor Education and Research Center. The auto industry's continued commitment to Michigan — traditionally a union bastion — shows that workforce skills and state technology-development projects are more important to at least some companies, he wrote.[62]

But James Hohman, assistant director of fiscal policy at the Mackinac Center for Public Policy, a free market-oriented think tank in Midland, Mich., argued that because Michigan has no right-to-work law, the state was forced to offer millions of dollars in incentives to retain the car companies. That would not have been necessary had the state had "an attractive business environment," with a right-to-work law, Hohman said.[63]

Tax incentives have made an appearance in the 2012 presidential race. In January, former House Speaker Newt Gingrich, R-Ga., blasted former Sen. Rick Santorum, R-Pa., for endorsing 1997 Pennsylvania legislation that gave the Pittsburgh Steelers football team and Pittsburgh Pirates baseball team taxpayer dollars for stadiums — often touted as job creators — without requiring repayment.[64]

Meanwhile, another contender for the Republican presidential nomination, former Massachusetts Gov. Mitt Romney, approved at least one location-based tax break for job creation as governor: a tax rebate for biotechnology companies.[65]

President Obama is proposing a new federal "growth zone" plan to replace the longstanding enterprise zone program. Under the new plan, which Congress so far has not approved, 20 rural and urban areas with economic-growth potential would get federal funds for business tax credits and other incentives for job creation.[66]

Some economists say such federally administered programs work better than state incentives in part because they're less politicized. However, any locality offering incentives, no matter how they're administered and paid for, feeds the fevered competition, says Hansen at Minnesota State. "No state or locality will unilaterally disarm" unless federal policy simply eliminates the use of incentives altogether, she says.

OUTLOOK
Beyond Incentives

Even some incentive proponents now question whether interstate competition for jobs is the best strategy. Hanging over the whole enterprise, meanwhile, is the question of whether the United States can actually expand the number of good jobs.

Fierce struggles among states to lure employers are likely to remain the norm for some time, many say.

"It's like a nuclear-arms standstill. No one is willing to blink first," said Jon Shure, director of state fiscal strategies at the Center on Budget and Policy Priorities, a liberal think tank in Washington.[67]

Among state officials, "a few more are skeptical than 10 years ago, but an awful lot still say, 'We need this tool,'" says Enrich, of Northeastern University Law School.

Still, says the University of North Carolina's Morgan, incentive agreements that impose performance standards and force companies to return incentive money to the government if they don't meet agreed-upon goals will grow more common "slowly but surely," he says.

Congress has the constitutional right to either ban or authorize incentive competition, but while legislation giving a green light to it seemed a strong possibility several years ago, the current Senate's Democratic leadership reportedly wouldn't support such a move, says Enrich.

Even without location-based incentives, localities engaged in fierce competition for jobs can still spur employment in their areas, says Karen Chapple, associate director of the Institute of Urban and Regional Development at the University of California, Berkeley. For example, governments might offer various kinds of targeted assistance to businesses that try to create entirely new labor-intensive industries, she says.

Meanwhile, with the environment a growing concern, localities might offer expert assistance and even cash to business startups interested in "green retrofitting" of buildings or in recycling throwaway materials into new products such as carpets, she says. Recycling-based manufacture could be a net job creator because it would require more workers than the old throwaway economy, and "states and local economies can do something to help develop these new capacities and help develop markets" for new products, she says.

Offshore competition has made it more and more difficult to create jobs in America, "but energy and climate change could someday change that," bringing manufacturing and agriculture back to America so that states no longer have to engage in such bitter rivalries for a dwindling number of good jobs, adds California State's Wassmer. "Shipping all these containers from China" may become too costly and environmentally damaging, "and you might end up with more domestic goods production" — and the jobs that go with it.

NOTES

1. For background, see Aubrey Cohen, "Boeing Closing Wichita Plant," *Seattle Post-Intelligencer*, Jan. 4, 2012, www.seattlepi.com/business/boeing/article/Boeing-closing-Wichita-plant-2440784.php; and Emily Knapp, "Governments Rob Taxpayers of Billions to Fund Ill-advised Incentive Programs," *Wall St. Cheat Sheet*, Jan. 19, 2012, http://wallstcheatsheet.com/stocks/governments-rob-tax-payers-of-billions-to-fund-ill-advised-incentive-programs.html.

2. Cohen, *ibid.*

3. Jonathan Q. Morgan and David M. Lawrence, "Economic Development," County and Municipal Government in North Carolina, Chapel Hill School of Government, 2007, p. 2, http://sogpubs.unc.edu/cmg/cmg26.pdf. Morgan is an associate professor of public administration; Lawrence is now retired as a professor of government.

4. *Ibid.*

5. For background, see "Boeing Tax Grab Shows Peril of Offering Tax Dollars for Growth," Bloomberg, Jan. 19, 2012, www.bloomberg.com/news/2012-01-19/boeing-job-grab-shows-peril-of-offering-tax-dollars-for-growth.html, and "Money-Back Guarantees for Taxpayers," Good Jobs First, January 2012, www.goodjobsfirst.org/moneyback. Alan Peters and Peter Fisher, "The Failures of Economic Development Incentives," *Journal of the American Planning Association*, Issue 1, 2004, pp. 27-37.

6. Ronald J. Hansen, "Arizona Tax Credits Rising for Business," *The Arizona Republic*, Nov. 22, 2011, www.azcentral.com/news/articles/2011/11/21/20111121arizona-tax-credits-rising-for-business.html.

7. "Kentucky Business Climate Boosted by State Incentives," *BusinessClimate.com*, http://businessclimate.com/kentucky-economic-development/kentucky-business-climate-boosted-state-incentives.

8. Edward M. Mazze, "The Economic Impact of the Motion Picture Production Tax Credit on the Rhode island Economy for the Years 2005-2009," www.film.ri.gov/MazzeStudy.pdf.

9. Ruby Gonzales, "Pico Rivera Faces Paying Rent Even With Borders Leaving," *Whittier Daily News* [Calif.], March 19, 2011, www.whittierdailynews.com/news/ci_17652157.

10. Stacy Mitchell, "Don't Subsidize Big Boxes at Local Shops' Expense," *Bloomberg BusinessWeek*, Sept. 9, 2011, www.businessweek.com/small-business/dont-subsidize-big-boxes-at-local-shops-expense-09092011.html.

11. Mark Robyn, "2012 State Business Tax Climate Index," Jan. 25, 2012, www.taxfoundation.org/news/show/22658.html; "The Best States for Business," *Forbes*, www.forbes.com/pictures/mli45ggdd/17-south-dakota/#content.

12. "Unemployment Rates — Most Current Available," South Dakota Department of Labor and Regulation, http://dlr.sd.gov/unemploymentrate.aspx; "Employment Situation Summary," U.S. Bureau of Labor

Statistics news release, Feb. 3, 2012, www.bls.gov/news.release/empsit.nr0.htm.

13. "The Poorest Counties in the America," MSN Money, http://money.msn.com/family-money/the-poorest-counties-in-america.

14. Vincent Fernando and Betty Jin, "10 States With Ridiculously Low Unemployment," MSNBC/Business Insider, www.msnbc.msn.com/id/38838429/ns/business-us_business/t/states-ridiculously-low-unemployment/#.TzLAcoH0izV.

15. Terry F. Buss, "The Effect of State Tax Incentives on Economic Growth and Firm Location Decisions: An Overview of the Literature," *Economic Development Quarterly*, February 2001, http://edq.sagepub.com/content/15/1/90.abstract.

16. Quoted in Kiersten Valle Pittman and Tim Funk, "In Scramble for New Jobs, Incentives Play a Key Role," *Idaho Statesman*/McClatchy Newspapers, Dec. 13, 2011, www.idahostatesman.com/2011/12/13/1914317/in-scramble-for-new-jobs-incentives.html.

17. David Stade and Katy Stech, "Boeing's Whopping Incentives," *The Post and Courier* [Charleston], Jan. 17, 2010, www.postandcourier.com/news/2010/jan/17/boeings-whopping-incentives.

18. Pittman and Funk, *op. cit.*

19. Bill Schweke, "Major Questions About Economic Development, Part V," CFED website, Dec. 2, 2009, http://cfed.org/blog/inclusiveeconomy/major_questions_about_economic_development_part_v.

20. Mali R. Schantz-Feld, "Top Site Selection Factors: Tax Rates, Exemptions, and Incentives — Keeping an Eye on the Competition," *Area Development*, November 2011, www.areadevelopment.com/laborEducation/November2011/site-selection-factors-skilled-labor-220743.shtml.

21. For background, see "2011 Best-performing Cities," Milken Institute, http://bestcities.milkeninstitute.org.

22. Timothy J. Bartik, "Boon or Boondoggle? The Debate Over State and Local Economic Development Policies," in *Who Benefits from State and Local Economic Development Policies?* W.E.

Upjohn Institute for Employment Research, pp. 1-16, http://research.upjohn.org/up_book chapters/88.

23. Scott Loveridge, "Local Industrial Recruitment: Boondoggle or Boon?" May 1995, www.rri.wvu.edu/pdffiles/wp9510.pdf.

24. "Taxes and Economic Development 101," Institute on Taxation and Economic Policy, September 2011, www.itepnet.org/pdf/pb42.pdf.

25. Timothy J. Bartik, "State Economic Development Policies: What Works," presentation at the Center on Budget and Policy Priorities Annual State Fiscal Policy Conference, Washington, D.C., Nov. 30, 2011, http://research.upjohn.org/presentations/27.

26. Alice Hines, "As Sears Plans Closings, Cities Fight to Keep Stores," *Huffington Post*, Jan. 26, 2012, www.huffingtonpost.com/2012/01/26/sears-closes-cities_n_1231326.html?ref=mostpopular.

27. Quoted in Ashli Sims, "Tulsa Taxpayers Upset After Company Receiving State Rebate Shuts Down," NewsOn6 website, April 11, 2011, www.newson6.com/story/14426304/quality-jobs-program.

28. Bartik, "Boon or Boondoggle?" *op. cit.*

29. Quoted in Penelope Lemov, "Is the Hollywood Tax Credit Under Attack?" *Governing*, March 16, 2011, www.governing.com/columns/public-finance/hollywood-tax-credit-under-attack.html; for background, see "Tax Credits for Filmmakers — By U.S. State and Canadian Province," Making the Movie website, http://makingthemovie.info/2006/07/tax-credits-for-filmmakers-state-by-state.html.

30. Quoted in Brian R. Hook, "Critics Blast Tax Credit Proposals by Missouri Review Panel," Missouri Watchdog website, Dec. 2, 2010, http://missouri.watchdog.org/7972/critics-blast-tax-credit-proposals-by-missouri-review-panel.

31. Mark Cassell, "Zoned Out; Distribution and Benefits in Ohio's Enterprise Zone Program," Policy Matters Ohio, October 2003, www.kent.edu/cpapp/research/upload/eco-enterprise-zones.pdf.

32. Greg LeRoy and Leigh McIlvaine, "Paid to Sprawl: Subsidized Job Flight for Cleveland and Cincinnati," Good Jobs First, www.goodjobsfirst.org/paidtosprawl, July 2011.

33. William Fulton, *Romancing the Smokestack: How Cities and States Pursue Prosperity* (2010), p. 4.

34. Robyn, *op. cit.*

35. Arthur J. Rolnick, "Congress Should End the Economic War Among the States," The Federal Reserve Bank of Minneapolis website, Oct. 10, 2007, www.minneapolisfed.org/publications_papers/studies/econwar/rolnick_testimony_2007.cfm.

36. Quoted in "Professional Sports Stadiums: Do They Divert Public Funds From Critical Public Infrastructure?" Hearing transcript, House Oversight and Government Reform Domestic Policy Subcommittee, Oct. 10, 2007.

37. *Ibid.*

38. For background, see Robert W. Wassmer, "The Increasing Use of Property Tax Abatement as a Means of Promoting State and Local Economic Activity in the United States," in Nancy Augustine, Michael Bell, David Brunori and Joan Youngman, eds., *Erosion of the Property Tax Base: Trends, Causes and Consequences* (2009), pp. 221-259, and P.G. Marshall, "Do Enterprise Zones Work?" *Editorial Research Reports*, 1989 (Vol. 1).

39. Joseph J. Seneca, James W. Hughes and George R. Nagle, "An Assessment of the New Jersey Business Employment Incentive Program," July 27, 2004, www.policy.rutgers.edu/reports/beip/beip_report.pdf.

40. Quoted in *ibid.*

41. Ann R. Magnusen and Katherine Nesse, "Institutional and Political Determinants of Incentive Competition," in *Reining in the Competition for Capital*, W.E. Upjohn Institute for Employment Research, 2007, pp. 1-42, http://research.upjohn.org/up_bookchapters/237.

42. *Ibid.*

43. Brent Lane and G. Jason Jolley, "An Evaluation of North Carolina's Economic Development Incentive Programs: Summary of Analysis, Findings and Recommendations," University of North Carolina Center for Competitive Economies, Jan. 21, 2009, www.kenan-flagler.unc.edu/kenan-institute/about/organization/competitive-economies/~/media/Files/kenaninstitute/UNC_KenanInstitute_NCIncentivesStudy.ashx.

44. For background, see David G. Savage, *Guide to the U.S. Supreme Court* (5th ed.) (2010), Vol. 1, p. 142.

45. The decision is *DaimlerChrysler v. Cuno*, 547 U.S. 332 (2006). For background, see Russell Mokhiber and Robert Weissman, "Corporate Shakedown in Toledo," *Common Dreams*, Feb. 8, 2000, www.commondreams.org/views/021000-105.htm, and Chris Atkins, *Cuno v. DaimlerChrysler: A Pyrrhic Victory for Economic Neutrality*, Fiscal Facts, Tax Foundation, April 18, 2005, www.taxfoundation.org/publications/show/344.html.

46. *Northwestern States Portland Cement Co. v. Minnesota*, 358 U.S. 450 (1959) (Frankfurter, J. dissenting). "Dissent of Justice Felix Frankfurter," http://caselaw.lp.findlaw.com/scripts/getcase.pl?court=us&vol=358&invol=450.

47. Quoted in "Professional Sports Stadiums: Do They Divert Public Funds From Critical Public Infrastructure?" Hearing transcript, House Oversight and Government Reform Domestic Policy Subcommittee, Oct. 10, 2007, Government Printing Office, www.gpo.gov/fdsys/pkg/CHRG-110hhrg51756/html/CHRG-110hhrg51756.htm; for background, see H.R. 3044.IH, Thomas, Library of Congress, http://thomas.loc.gov/cgi-bin/query/z?c105:H.R.3044.IH:.

48. For background, see "S. 1066: Economic Development Act of 2005," govtrack.us, www.govtrack.us/congress/bill.xpd?bill=s109-1066&tab=summary; Michael Mazerov, "Should Congress Authorize States to Continue Giving Tax Breaks to Businesses?" Center on Budget and Policy Priorities, June 30, 2005, www.cbpp.org/files/2-18-05sfp.pdf; "Voinovich, Tiberi, Stabenow and Chandler Propose Bill to Protect Key Economic Development Tools," press release, website of Rep. Pat Tiberi, May 19, 2005, http://tiberi.house.gov/News/DocumentSingle.aspx?DocumentID=32632.

49. For background, see "History of the Port Authority," The Port Authority of New York & New Jersey, www.panynj.gov/about/history-port-authority.html.

50. For background, see "Key Reforms: Overview," Good Jobs First website, www.goodjobsfirst.org/accountable-development/key-reforms-overview.

51. For background, Seneca, Hughes and Nagle, *op. cit.*

52. "Show Us the Subsidies," Good Jobs First, December 2010, www.goodjobsfirst.org/sites/default/files/docs/pdf/showusthesubsidiesrpt.pdf.

53. Ronald J. Hansen, "Ariz. Tax Credits Rising for Business," *Arizona Republic*, Nov. 22, 2011, www.azcentral.com/arizonarepublic/news/articles/2011/11/21/20111121arizona-tax-credits-rising-for-business.html.

54. Quoted in David Fettig, "A Report from the Battlefield," *The Region*, Minneapolis Federal Reserve Bank, June 1, 1996, www.minneapolisfed.org/publications_papers/pub_display.cfm?id=3660.

55. Ed Anderson, "Proposed Business Tax Breaks Could Produce 10,000 Jobs, Gov. Bobby Jindal Says," *The Times Picayune* [New Orleans], Feb. 2, 2012, www.nola.com/business/index.ssf/2012/02/proposed_business_tax_breaks_c.html.

56. Christopher Wills and David Mercer, "In the Game of Tax Breaks, States Play at Their Own Risk," Associated Press/*Salt Lake Tribune*, Dec. 17, 2011, www.sltrib.com/sltrib/money/53126758-79/tax-illinois-state-companies.html.csp.

57. Quoted in Kathy Bergen, "Tax Breaks for Sears, CME Head to Governor," *Chicago Tribune*, Dec. 14, 2011, http://articles.chicagotribune.com/2011-12-14/business/ct-biz-1214-cme-sears-20111214_1_corporate-income-tax-tax-rate-business-tax.

58. Alejandra Cancino and Julia Wernau, "States Go All Out With Tax Incentives, Deals to Hook Firms," *The Chicago Tribune*, May 15, 2011, http://articles.chicagotribune.com/2011-05-15/business/ct-biz-0515-incentives-20110515_1_tax-incentives-state-incentives-illinois-companies.

59. "An Assessment of the Effectiveness and Fiscal Impacts of the Use of Development Incentives in the St. Louis Region," East-West Gateway Council of Governments, January 2011, www.ewgateway.org/pdffiles/library/dirr/TIFFinalRpt.pdf, and Stacy Mitchell, "Don't Subsidize Big Boxes at Local Shops'

Expense," *Bloomberg Businessweek*, Sept. 9, 2011, www.businessweek.com/small-business/dont-subsidize-big-boxes-at-local-shops-expense-09092011.html.

60. For background, see Mary Beth Schneider and Chris Sikich, "Indiana Becomes Rust Belt's First Right-to-Work State," *The Indianapolis Star/USA Today*, Feb. 2, 2012, www.usatoday.com/news/nation/story/2012-02-01/indiana-right-to-work-bill/52916356/1.

61. For background, see Steven Greenhouse, "Strained States Turning to Laws to Curb Labor Unions," *The New York Times*, Jan. 3, 2011, www.nytimes.com/2011/01/04/business/04labor.html?pagewanted=all; Kyle Maichle, "Midwest States Are Focus of a New Push for Right-to-Work in 2011," Dec. 10, 2010, http://ballotpedia.org/wiki/index.php/Midwest_states_are_focus_of_a_new_push_for_Right-To-Work_in_2011.

62. Gordon Lafer, 'Right to Work': The Wrong Answer for Michigan's Economy, *EPI Briefing Paper*, Economic Policy Institute, Sept. 15, 2011, www.epi.org/publication/right-to-work-michigan-economy. Garry Rayno, "Hundreds Gather to Fight Right-to-work Bill," *UnionLeader.com*, Feb. 10, 2012, www.unionleader.com/article/20120210/NEWS06/702109989.

63. Quoted in Tom Gantert, "Debate: Could Union Costs Be Pricing Michigan Out of Auto Jobs?" CAPCON: Michigan Capitol Confidential, Mackinac Center for Public Policy, Oct. 13, 2011, www.michigancapitolconfidential.com/15873.

64. Pema Levy, "Newt Goes Ballistic on Pretty Much Everyone," *Talking Points Memo*, Jan. 9, 2012, http://2012.talkingpointsmemo.com/2012/01/newt-is-not-here-to-make-friends.php; for background, see Kevin Clark Forsythe, "The Stadium Game Pittsburgh Style: Observations on the Latest Round of Publicly Financed Stadia in Steel Town, USA, and Comparisons With 28 Other Major League Teams," *Marquette Sports Law Review*, Spring 2000, http://scholarship.law.marquette.edu/cgi/viewcontent.cgi?article=1470&context=sports law.

65. Jeanne Sahadi, "Mitt Romney's Tax Record: Tax Cutter or Tax Hiker?" *CNNMoney*, Jan. 23, 2012, http://money.cnn.com/2012/01/23/news/economy/Romney_tax_record/index.htm.

66. For background, see "2012 Federal Budget Proposals," CCH Group, Feb. 17, 2011, http://tax.cchgroup.com/downloads/files/pdfs/legislation/treasury-greenbook.pdf.

67. Quoted in Cancino and Wernau, *op. cit.*

BIBLIOGRAPHY

Books

Fulton, William, *Romancing the Smokestack: How Cities and States Pursue Prosperity*, Solimar Books, 2010.
In a collection of articles, a longtime economic-development analyst describes the many methods cities use to attract and retain jobs and businesses.

LeRoy, Greg, *The Great American Jobs Scam: Corporate Tax Dodging and the Myth of Job Creation*, Berrett-Koehler Publishers, 2005.
The head of the advocacy group Good Jobs First, which promotes accountability for tax subsidies, argues that case studies demonstrate community harm from interstate and inter-local subsidy competition, including deteriorating infrastructure and sprawl.

Articles

Johnston, David Cay, "On the Dole, Corporate Style," Tax.com, Jan. 4, 2011.
Tax breaks for business are increasing worldwide, but Canada and the European Union are trying to curb the trend. Some sought-after businesses, such as companies that store data for Internet giants Yahoo! and Google, produce few jobs and therefore may be particularly questionable recipients of subsidies.

Pittman, Kirsten Valle, and Tim Funk, "In Scramble for New Jobs, Incentives Play a Key Role," *Idaho Statesman*/McClatchy Newspapers, Dec. 13, 2011, www.idahostatesman.com/2011/12/13/1914317/in-scramble-for-new-jobs-incentives.html.
Some Idaho economic-development officials say they lost a Boeing aircraft plant to South Carolina because their state wouldn't give the company a big enough financial incentive, but other analysts argue that states should be cautious about such interstate competition.

Schantz-Feld, Mali R., "Top Site Selection Factors: Tax Rates, Exemptions and Incentives — Keeping an Eye on the Competition," *Area Development Online*, November 2011, www.areadevelopment.com/taxesIncentives/November2011/site-selection-factors-taxes-incentives-224443.shtml.
Some states that offer location incentives to meet specific companies' wish lists are emerging from the recession with stronger job growth than average, according to a magazine for business site-selection professionals.

Spathelf, Christof, "First Person: The Site Selection Process Behind VW's First U.S. Manufacturing Facility," *Area Development Online*, November 2011, www.areadevelopment.com/Automotive/November2011/VW-Christof-Spathelf-Overseas-manufacturing-77780192.shtml.
A training partnership with a local university and community college played a role in bringing a Volkswagen plant to Chattanooga, Tenn.

Reports and Studies

"Money-Back Guarantees for Taxpayers," Good Jobs First, January 2012, www.goodjobsfirst.org/sites/default/files/docs/pdf/moneyback.pdf.
With states and cities spending an estimated $70 billion annually on economic-development subsidies, governments are monitoring the outcomes of subsidy programs more closely but are far from requiring real accountability, says a subsidy watchdog group.

"Report of the Missouri Tax Credit Review Commission," Missouri Tax Credit Review Commission, Nov. 30, 2010, http://tcrc.mo.gov/pdf/TCRCFinalReport113010.pdf.
A panel of Missouri lawmakers and business and community representatives concludes that "there currently exists a problem in interstate competition where states manipulate the marketplace with incentives and cannibalize each other's industries."

"Show Us the Subsidies," Good Jobs First, December 2010, www.goodjobsfirst.org/showusthesubsidies. Analysts for a nonprofit group that advocates for subsidy accountability finds that states are disclosing more information about who gets business incentives but that complete transparency is a long way off.

Bartik, Timothy J., "State Economic Development Policies: What Works?" Upjohn Institute, Nov. 30, 2011, http://research.upjohn.org/presentations/27. Research shows that well-administered customized job-training programs are much better than tax cuts and tax incentives at creating good-paying jobs in a state.

Coates, Dennis, and Brad R. Humphreys, "The Stadium Gambit and Local Economic Development,"

Regulation, Cato Institute, Summer 2000, www.cato .org/pubs/regulation/regv23n2/coates.pdf. In a report for a libertarian magazine, two University of Maryland economists say that evidence over the years demonstrates that bringing a professional sports team to a city doesn't increase residents' per capita income and isn't worth the taxpayer dollars spent.

Fisher, Peter S., "Corporate Taxes and State Economic Growth, Iowa Fiscal Partnership," February 2011, www .iowafiscal.org/2011docs/110209-IFP-corptaxes.pdf. A University of Iowa professor emeritus of urban and regional planning argues that because taxes make up a relatively small portion of business costs, tax breaks have much less effect than policymakers believe in influencing companies' location decisions.

For More Information

Area Development, www.areadevelopment.com. Advertising-supported magazine for the site-location industry.

Good Jobs First, 1616 P St., N.W., Suite 210, Washington, DC 20036; 202-232-1616; www.goodjobsfirst.org. Research and advocacy group that tracks accountability in economic-development subsidies.

HandMade in America, P.O. Box 2089, Asheville, NC 28802; 828-252-0121; www.handmadeinamerica.org. Group that works to revitalize small towns in North Carolina through small-scale economic development.

International Economic Development Council, 734 15th St., N.W., Suite 900, Washington, DC 20005; 202-223-7800; www.iedconline.org. Membership group for the economic-development profession.

New Carolina, 1411 Gervais St., Suite 315, Columbia, SC 29201; 803-760-1400; www.newcarolina.org. Group that works on public and private projects to strengthen industry clusters in South Carolina.

Site Selection, 6625 The Corners Parkway, Suite 200, Norcross, GA 30092-2901; 770-446-6996; www.siteselection. com. Magazine of the Industrial Asset Management Council; covers corporate real estate and economic development.

The Tax Foundation, National Press Building, 529 14th St., N.W., Suite 420, Washington, DC 20045-1000; 202-464-6200; http://taxfoundation.org. Research group that publishes state business-climate rankings.

W.E. Upjohn Institute for Employment Research, 300 S. Westnedge Ave., Kalamazoo, MI 49007-4686; 269-343-5541; www.upjohninst.org. Research group that studies ways to prevent unemployment.

6

Rapid Urbanization

Jennifer Weeks and Reed Karaim

AFP/Getty Images/Rob Elliott

Children scavenge for recyclables amid rubbish in the Dharavi slum in Mumbai, India. About a billion people worldwide live in slums — where sewer, water and garbage-collection services are often nonexistent. If impoverished rural residents continue streaming into cities at current rates, the world's slum population is expected to double to 2 billion within the next two decades, according to the United Nations.

From *CQ Researcher*,
April 2009 (updated June 14, 2012).

India's most infamous slum lives up to its reputation. Located in the middle of vast Mumbai, Dharavi is home to as many as 1 million people densely packed into thousands of tiny shacks fashioned from scrap metal, plastic sheeting and other scrounged materials. Narrow, muddy alleys crisscross the 600-acre site, open sewers carry human waste and vacant lots serve as garbage dumps. There is electricity, but running water is available for only an hour or so a day. Amid the squalor, barefoot children sing for money, beg from drivers in nearby traffic or work in garment and leather shops, recycling operations and other lightly regulated businesses.

Moviegoers around the globe got a glimpse of life inside Dharavi in last year's phenomenally popular Oscar-winning film "Slumdog Millionaire," about plucky Jamal Malik, a fictional Dharavi teenager who improbably wins a TV quiz-show jackpot. The no-holds-barred portrayal of slum life may have been shocking to affluent Westerners, but Dharavi is only one of Asia's innumerable slums. In fact, about a billion people worldwide live in urban slums — the ugly underbelly of the rapid and haphazard urbanization that has occurred in many parts of the world in recent decades. And if soaring urban growth rates continue unabated, the world's slum population is expected to double to 2 billion by 2030, according to the U.N.[1]

But all city dwellers don't live in slums. Indeed, other fast-growing cities presented cheerier faces to the world last year, from Dubai's glittering luxury skyscrapers to Beijing's breathtaking, high-tech pre-Olympic cultural spectacle.

World Will Have 26 Megacities by 2025

The number of megacities — urban areas with at least 10 million residents — will increase from 19 to 26 worldwide by the year 2025, according to the United Nations. The seven new megacities will be in Asia and sub-Saharan Africa. Most megacities are in coastal areas, making them highly vulnerable to massive loss of life and property damage caused by rising sea levels that experts predict will result from climate change in the 21st century.

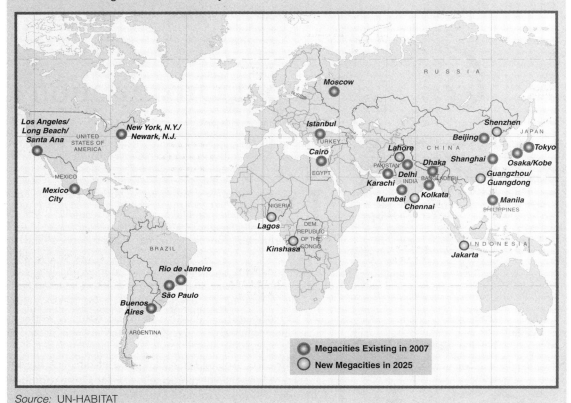

Source: UN-HABITAT

Today, 3.3 billion people live in cities — half the world's population — and urbanites are projected to total nearly 5 billion (out of 8.1 billion) worldwide by 2030.[2] About 95 percent of that growth is occurring in the developing world, especially in Africa and Asia.[3]

These regions are going through the same threefold evolution that transformed Europe and North America over a 200-year period between 1750 and 1950: the industrialization of agriculture, followed by rural migration to cities and declining population growth as life expectancy improves. But today's developing countries are modernizing much faster — typically in less than 100 years — and their cities are expanding at dizzying rates: On average, 5 million people in developing countries move to cities every month. As urban areas struggle to absorb this growth, the new residents often end up crowded into already teeming slums. For instance, 62 percent of city dwellers in sub-Saharan Africa live in slums, 43 percent in southern Asia, 37 percent in East Asia and 27 percent in Latin America and the Caribbean, according to UN-HABITAT, the United Nations agency for human settlements.[4]

UN-HABITAT defines a slum as an urban area without at least one of the following features:

- Durable housing,
- Adequate living space (no more than three people per room),
- Access to clean drinking water,
- Access to improved sanitation (toilets or latrines that separate human waste from contact with water sources), or
- Secure property rights.[5]

But all slums are not the same. Some lack only one basic necessity, while others lack several. And conditions can be harsh in non-slum neighborhoods as well. Thus, experts say, policies should focus on specific local problems in order to make a difference in the lives of poor city dwellers.[6]

Cities "are potent instruments for national economic and social development. They attract investment and create wealth," said HABITAT Executive Director Anna Tibaijuka last April. But, she warned, cities also concentrate poverty and deprivation, especially in developing countries. "Rapid and chaotic urbanization is being accompanied by increasing inequalities, which pose enormous challenges to human security and safety."[7]

Today, improving urban life is an important international development priority.[8] One of the eight U.N. Millennium Development Goals (MDGs) — broad objectives intended to end poverty worldwide by 2015 — endorsed by world leaders in 2000 was environmental sustainability. Among other things, it aims to cut in half the portion of the world's people without

Tokyo Is by Far the World's Biggest City

With more than 35 million residents, Tokyo is nearly twice as big as the next-biggest metropolises. Tokyo is projected to remain the world's largest city in 2025, when there will be seven new megacities — urban areas with at least 10 million residents. Two Indian cities, Mumbai and Delhi, will overtake Mexico City and New York as the world's second- and third-largest cities. The two largest newcomers in 2025 will be in Africa: Kinshasa and Lagos.

Population of Megacities, 2007 and 2025
(in millions)

2007		2025 (projected)	
Tokyo, Japan	35.68	Tokyo, Japan	36.40
New York, NY/Newark, NJ	19.04	Mumbai, India	26.39
Mexico City, Mexico	19.03	Delhi, India	22.50
Mumbai, India	18.98	Dhaka, Bangladesh	22.02
São Paulo, Brazil	18.85	São Paulo, Brazil	21.43
Delhi, India	15.93	Mexico City, Mexico	21.01
Shanghai, China	14.99	New York, NY/Newark, NJ	20.63
Kolkata, India	14.79	Kolkata, India	20.56
Dhaka, Bangladesh	13.49	Shanghai, China	19.41
Buenos Aires, Argentina	12.80	Karachi, Pakistan	19.10
Los Angeles/Long Beach/ Santa Ana (CA)	12.50	Kinshasa, Dem. Rep. Congo	16.76
Karachi, Pakistan	12.13	Lagos, Nigeria	15.80
Cairo, Egypt	11.89	Cairo, Egypt	15.56
Rio de Janeiro, Brazil	11.75	Manila, Philippines	14.81
Osaka/Kobe, Japan	11.29	Beijing, China	14.55
Beijing, China	11.11	Buenos Aires, Argentina	13.77
Manila, Philippines	11.10	Los Angeles/Long Beach/ Santa Ana (CA)	13.67
Moscow, Russia	10.45	Rio de Janeiro, Brazil	13.41
Istanbul, Turkey	10.06	Jakarta, Indonesia	12.36
		Istanbul, Turkey	12.10
		Guangzhou/Guangdong, China	11.84
		Osaka/Kobe, Japan	11.37
		Moscow, Russia	10.53
		Lahore, Pakistan	10.51
		Shenzhen, China	10.20
		Chennai, India	10.13

New megacities in 2025

Source: UN-HABITAT

access to safe drinking water and achieve "significant improvement" in the lives of at least 100 million slum dwellers.[9]

Global Population Is Shifting to Cities

Half a century ago, less than a third of the world's population lived in cities. By 2005, nearly half inhabited urban areas, and in 2030, at least 60 percent of the world's population will be living in cities, reflecting an unprecedented scale of urban growth in the developing world. This will be particularly notable in Africa and Asia, where the urban population will double between 2000 and 2030.

Worldwide Urban and Rural Populations

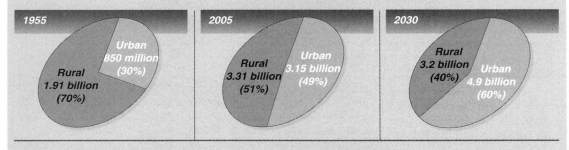

Source: U.N. Department of Economic and Social Affairs; U.N. Population Fund

Delivering even the most basic city services is an enormous challenge in many of the world's 19 megacities — metropolises with more than 10 million residents. And smaller cities with fewer than 1 million inhabitants are growing even faster in both size and number than larger ones.[10]

Many fast-growing cities struggle with choking air pollution, congested traffic, polluted water supplies and inadequate sanitation services. The lack of services can contribute to larger social and economic problems. For example, slum dwellers without permanent housing or access to mass transit have trouble finding and holding jobs. And when poverty becomes entrenched it reinforces the gulf between rich and poor, which can promote crime and social unrest.

"A city is a system of systems. It has biological, social and technical parts, and they all interact," says George Bugliarello, president emeritus of Polytechnic University in New York and foreign secretary of the National Academy of Engineering. "It's what engineers call a complex system because it has features that are more than the sum of its parts. You have to understand how all of the components interact to guide them."

Improving life for the urban poor begins with providing shelter, sanitation and basic social services like health care and education. But more is needed to make cities truly inclusive, such as guaranteeing slum dwellers' property rights so they cannot be ejected from their homes.[11]

Access to information and communications technology (ICT) is also crucial. In some developing countries, ICT has been adopted widely, particularly cell phones, but high-speed Internet access and computer use still lag behind levels in rich nations. Technology advocates say this "digital divide" slows economic growth in developing nations and increases income inequality both within and between countries. Others say the problem has been exaggerated and that there is no critical link between ICTs and poverty reduction.

Managing urban growth and preventing the creation of new slums are keys to both improving the quality of life and better protecting cities from natural disasters. Many large cities are in areas at risk from earthquakes, wildfires or floods. Squatter neighborhoods are often built on flood plains, steep slopes or other vulnerable areas, and poor people usually have fewer resources to escape or relocate.

For example, heavy rains in northern Venezuela in 1999 caused mudslides and debris flows that demolished many hillside shantytowns around the capital city of Caracas, killing some 30,000 people. In 2005 Hurricane Katrina killed more people in New Orleans' lower-income neighborhoods, which were located in a flood plain, than in wealthier neighborhoods of the Louisiana port city that were built on higher ground. As global warming raises sea levels, many of the world's largest cities are expected to be increasingly at risk from flooding.

Paradoxically, economic growth also can pose a risk for some cities. Large cities can be attractive targets for terrorist attacks, especially if they are symbols of national prosperity and modernity, such as New York City, site of the Sept. 11, 2001, attack on the World Trade Center. Last November's coordinated Islamic terrorist attacks in Mumbai followed a similar strategy: Landmark properties frequented by foreigners were targeted in order to draw worldwide media coverage, damage India's economy and send a message that nowhere in India was safe.[12]

Today the global economic recession is creating a new problem for city dwellers: Entry-level jobs are disappearing as trade contracts evaporate and factories shut down. Unable to find other jobs, many recent migrants to cities are returning to rural areas that are ill-prepared to receive them, and laborers who remain in cities have less money to send to families back home.[13]

As national leaders, development experts and city officials debate how to manage urban growth, here are some issues they are considering:

Does urbanization make people better off?

With a billion city dwellers worldwide trapped in slums, why do people keep moving to cities? Demographic experts say that newcomers hope to earn higher incomes and find more opportunities than rural areas can offer.

"Often people are fleeing desperate economic conditions," says David Bloom, a professor of economics and demography at Harvard University's School of Public Health. "And the social attractions of a city — opportunities to meet more people, escape from isolation or in some cases to be anonymous — trump fears about

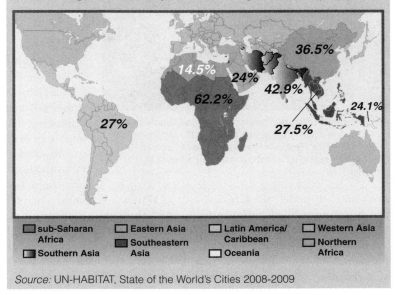

Most African City Dwellers Live in Slums

Most of the world's slum dwellers are in developing countries, with nearly two-thirds of sub-Saharan Africa's city dwellers living in slums.

Percentage of Urban Populations Living in Slums, by Region

36.5%
14.5%
24%
42.9%
62.2%
24.1%
27%
27.5%

sub-Saharan Africa
Southern Asia
Eastern Asia
Southeastern Asia
Latin America/ Caribbean
Oceania
Western Asia
Northern Africa

Source: UN-HABITAT, State of the World's Cities 2008-2009

difficult urban conditions. If they have relatives or friends living in cities already, that reduces some of the risk."

When nations attract foreign investment, it creates new jobs. In the 1990s both China and India instituted broad economic reforms designed to encourage foreign investment, paving the way for rapid economic growth. That growth accelerated as information technology advances like the Internet, fiber-optic networks and e-mail made it faster and cheaper to communicate worldwide in real time.[14] As a result, thousands of manufacturing and white-collar jobs were "outsourced" from the United States to India, China and other low-wage countries over the past decade.[15]

These jobs spurred major growth in some cities, especially in areas with educated, English-speaking work forces. The large southern Indian city of Bangalore became a center for information technology — dubbed "India's Silicon Valley." Other cities in India, Singapore and the Philippines now host English-language call centers that manage everything from computer technical support to lost-baggage complaints for airlines. In a

Packed buses in Dhaka take residents in the Bangladeshi capital to their homes in outlying villages on the eve of the Muslim holiday Eid al-Adha — the "Festival of Sacrifice." Rapidly growing cities have trouble keeping up with the transportation needs of residents.

twist on this model, the Chinese city of Dalian — which was controlled by Japan from 1895 through World War II and still has many Japanese speakers — has become a major outsourcing center for Japanese companies.[16]

Some observers say an increasingly networked world allows people to compete for global "knowledge work" from anywhere in the world instead of having to emigrate to developed countries. In his best-seller *The World Is Flat*, author and *New York Times* columnist Thomas Friedman cites Asian call centers as an example of this shift, since educated Indians can work at the centers and prosper at home rather than seeking opportunity abroad. While he acknowledges that millions of people in developing countries are poor, sick and disempowered, Friedman argues that things improve when people move from rural to urban areas.

"[E]xcess labor gets trained and educated, it begins working in services and industry; that leads to innovation and better education and universities, freer markets, economic growth and development, better infrastructure, fewer diseases and slower population growth," Friedman writes. "It is that dynamic that is going on in parts of urban India and urban China today, enabling people to compete on a level playing field and attracting investment dollars by the billions."[17]

But others say it's not always so simple. Educated newcomers may be able to find good jobs, but migrants without skills or training often end up working in the "informal economy" — activities that are not taxed, regulated or monitored by the government, such as selling goods on the street or collecting garbage for recycling. These jobs are easy to get but come without minimum wages or labor standards, and few workers can get credit to grow their businesses. Members of ethnic minorities and other underprivileged groups, such as lower castes in India, often are stuck with the dirtiest and most dangerous and difficult tasks.[18]

And some countries have experienced urban growth without job growth. Through the late 1980s, many Latin American countries tried to grow their economies by producing manufactured goods at home instead of importing them from abroad.

"Years of government protection insulated these industries from outside competition, so they did not feel pressure to become more productive. Then they went under when economies opened up to trade," says Steven Poelhekke, a researcher with DNB, the national bank of the Netherlands. "In Africa, industrialization has never really taken off. And without job creation governments cannot deliver benefits for new urbanites."[19]

Meanwhile, when cities grow too quickly, competition for land, space, light and services increases faster than government can respond. Real estate prices rise, driving poor residents into squatter neighborhoods, where crowding and pollution spread disease. "When cities get too big, the downsides to city life are bigger than the benefits for vulnerable inhabitants," says Poelhekke.

Broadly, however, urbanization has reduced the total number of people in poverty in recent years. According to a 2007 World Bank study, about three-quarters of the world's poor still live in rural areas. Poor people are urbanizing faster than the population as a whole, so some poverty is shifting to cities. Yet, clearly, many of those new urbanites are finding higher incomes — even if they end up living in city slums — because overall poverty rates (urban plus rural) fall as countries urbanize. While the persistence of urban poverty is a serious concern, the authors concluded, if people moved to the cities faster, overall poverty rates would decline sooner.[20]

Many development advocates say policy makers must accept urbanization as inevitable and strive to make it more beneficial. "We need to stop seeing migration to cities as a problem," says Priya Deshingkar, a researcher at the Overseas Development Institute in Hyderabad, India. "These people were already vulnerable because they can't make a living in rural areas. Countries need to rethink their development strategies. The world is urbanizing, and we have to make more provisions for people moving to urban areas. They can't depend on agriculture alone."

Should governments limit migration to cities?

Many governments have tried to limit urban problems by discouraging migration to cities or regulating the pace of urban growth. Some countries use household registration policies, while others direct aid and economic development funds to rural areas. Political leaders say limiting migration reduces strains on city systems, slows the growth of slums and keeps villages from languishing as their most enterprising residents leave.

China's *hukou* system, for example, requires households to register with the government and classifies individuals as rural or urban residents. Children inherit their *hukou* status from their parents. Established in the 1950s, the system was tightly controlled to limit migration from agricultural areas to cities and to monitor criminals, government critics and other suspect citizens and groups.[21]

In the late 1970s China began privatizing farming and opened its economy to international trade, creating a rural labor surplus and greater demand for city workers. The government offered rural workers temporary residence permits in cities and allowed wealthy, educated citizens to buy urban *hukou* designations. Many rural Chinese also moved to cities without changing their registration. According to recent government estimates, at least 120 million migrant workers have moved to Chinese cities since the early 1980s.[22] Today *hukou* rules are enforced inconsistently in different Chinese cities, where many rural migrants cannot get access to health care, education, affordable housing or other urban services because they are there illegally.

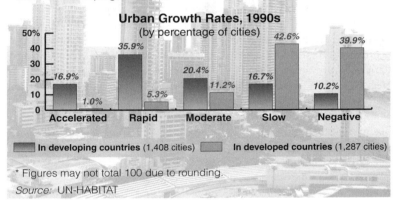

Cities in Developing World Growing Rapidly

More than half the developing world's cities experienced fast annual growth in the 1990s, compared to just 6.3 percent of those in wealthier countries. Conversely, more than 80 percent of cities in the wealthier countries had slow or negative growth, compared to about a quarter of those in developing countries.

Urban Growth Rates, 1990s
(by percentage of cities)

	Accelerated	Rapid	Moderate	Slow	Negative
In developing countries (1,408 cities)	16.9%	35.9%	20.4%	16.7%	10.2%
In developed countries (1,287 cities)	1.0%	5.3%	11.2%	42.6%	39.9%

■ **In developing countries** (1,408 cities)   ■ **In developed countries** (1,287 cities)

* Figures may not total 100 due to rounding.
Source: UN-HABITAT

Chinese officials say they must manage growth so all areas of the country will benefit. In a 2007 report to the 17th Communist Party Congress, President Hu Jintao promised to promote "a path of urbanization with Chinese characteristics" that emphasized "balanced development of large, medium-sized and small cities and towns."[23]

But critics say the *hukou* system has created an urban underclass and should be scrapped. When the municipality of Chongqing (which omits an estimated 4.5 million migrant workers from its official population figures) established November 4 as Migrant Workers' Day in 2007, the *Asia Times* commented, "By not changing the [*hukou*] system and instead giving the migrant workers a special holiday, it's a bit like showing starving people menus instead of feeding them."[24]

India and Vietnam also control migration to urban areas by requiring people to register or show local identity cards to access social services. "They're both trying to promote rural development and keep from overburdening urban areas," says Deshingkar at the Overseas Development Institute. "But it doesn't work. People move despite these regulations. It just makes it harder for them, and if they can access services it's at a price."

Many experts say governments should not try to halt rural-to-city migration because when migrant workers send large shares of their wages home to their families in the country it helps reduce rural poverty and inequality. In Dhaka, Bangladesh, for example, remittances from city workers provide up to 80 percent of rural households' budgets, according to the Coalition for the Urban Poor.[25]

Urban growth also helps rural economies by creating larger markets for agricultural products — including high-value products like meat, chicken and fish that people tend to add to their diets as their incomes rise. Cities can promote economic growth in surrounding areas by creating a demand for local farmers' products. For instance, South Africa's Johannesburg Fresh Produce Market offers vendors stalls, overnight storage space, business-skills training and financing; it also requires market agents to buy at least 10 percent of their produce from small, low-income farms.[26]

However, the rootless lifestyle adopted by so-called circular migrants — those who move back and forth between the city and the country — makes people vulnerable, Deshingkar points out. "There are roughly 100 million circular migrants in India now, and they're completely missed by official statistics because the government only counts permanent migrants," she says. "They can't get any insurance or social services, so they carry all the risk themselves."

Beyond the fact that anti-migration policies usually fail, experts say the biggest factor driving population increase in many fast-growing cities is not new residents moving in but "natural increase" — the rate at which people already living there have children. Natural increase accounts for about 60 percent of urban growth worldwide, while 20 percent comes from domestic and international migration and 20 percent results from reclassification of rural areas as urban.[27]

Family-planning programs helped reduce poverty rates in several developing Asian countries — including South Korea, Taiwan, Thailand, Singapore, Indonesia and Malaysia — where having smaller families increased household savings and reduced national education costs.[28] In contrast, artificial birth control is difficult to obtain in the Philippines, where the population is 80 percent Catholic and the government supports only "natural" family planning. Several professors at the University of the Philippines have calculated that if Filipinos had followed Thailand's example on family planning in the 1970s, the Philippines would have at least 4 million fewer people in poverty and would be exporting rice rather than importing it. Instead, the Philippine government's opposition to family planning "contributed to the country's degeneration into Southeast Asia's basket case," said economist Arsenio Balisacan.[29]

Can we make large cities greener?

Many fast-growing cities are unhealthy places to live because of dirty air, polluted water supplies and sprawling waste dumps. City governments worldwide are increasingly interested in making their cities greener and more sustainable.

Greening cities has many up-front costs but can provide big payoffs. For example, energy-efficient buildings cost less to operate and give cities cachet as centers for advanced technology and design.

Green policies also may help cities achieve broader social goals. When Enrique Peñalosa was elected mayor of Bogotá, Colombia, in 1998, the city was overrun with traffic and crime. Wealthy residents lived in walled-off neighborhoods, while workers were squeezed into shanties on the city's outskirts. Under Peñalosa's rule, the city built hundreds of new parks and a rapid-transit bus system, limited automobile use, banned sidewalk parking and constructed a 14-mile-long street for bicyclists and pedestrians that runs through some of the city's poorest neighborhoods. The underlying goal of the programs: Make Bogotá more people-friendly for poor residents as well as the rich.

"[A]nything that you do in order to increase pedestrian space constructs equality" said Peñalosa, who now consults with city officials in other developing countries. "It's a powerful symbol showing that citizens who walk are equally important to those who have a car."[30] His administration also invested funds that might otherwise have been spent building highways in social services like schools and libraries. Air pollution decreased as more residents shifted to mass transit. Crime rates also fell, partly because more people were out on the streets.[31]

"Mobility and land use may be the most important issues that a mayor can address, because to unlock the economic potential of cities people have to be able to move from one area to another," says Polytechnic University's Bugliarello. "You also have to take care of water supplies and sanitation, because cities concentrate people and pathologies. Appropriate technologies aren't always the most expensive options, especially if cities get together and form markets for them."

For example, bus rapid transit (BRT) systems, which create networks of dedicated lanes for high-speed buses, are much cheaper than subways but faster than conventional buses that move in city traffic. By 2007 some 40 cities worldwide had developed BRT systems, including Bogotá; Jakarta, Indonesia; and Guayaquil, Ecuador. Many others are planned or under construction.[32]

Some developing countries are planning entire green cities with walkable neighborhoods, efficient mass transit and renewable-energy systems. Abu Dhabi, part of the United Arab Emirates on the Persian Gulf, is designing a $20 billion project called Masdar City, which it bills as the world's first carbon-neutral, zero-waste city. Located on the coast next to Abu Dhabi's airport, Masdar City will be a mixed-use community with about 40,000 residents and 50,000 commuters traveling in to work at high-tech companies. Plans call for the city to be car-free and powered mainly by solar energy.[33]

Abu Dhabi wants to become a global hub for clean technologies, according to Khaled Awad, property development director for the Masdar initiative. "It lets us leverage our energy knowledge [from oil and gas production] and our research and development skills and adapt them to new energy markets," he said.

"If we can do it there, we can do it anywhere," said Matthias Schuler, an engineer with the German climate-engineering firm Transsolar and a member of the international Masdar City design and planning team.[34] He points out that average daytime summer temperatures in Abu Dhabi are well over 100 degrees Fahrenheit, and coastal zones are very humid. "You can't find a harsher climate."

In China, meanwhile, green urban design is gaining support as a way to attract foreign investment and demonstrate environmental awareness. But some showpiece projects are falling short of expectations.

Huangbaiyu was supposed to be a sustainable "green village" that would provide new homes for a farming town of more than 1,400 in rural northeast China. But the master plan, produced by a high-profile U.S. green architecture firm, called for 400 densely clustered bungalows without enough yard space for livestock. This meant that villagers would lose their existing income from

backyard gardens, sheep flocks and trout ponds. The plan also proposed to use corncobs and stalks to fuel a biogas plant for heat, but villagers needed these crop wastes as winter feed for their goats.

By December 2008 the Chinese builder had constructed 42 houses, but only a few were occupied. The designer blamed the builder for putting up low-quality houses, but others said the plan did not reflect what villagers wanted or needed.[35] Planners "inadvertently designed an ecologically sound plan — from the perspectives of both birds and the green movement — that would devastate the local economy and bankrupt the households whose lives were to be improved," wrote Shannon May, an American graduate student who lived in the old village of Huangbaiyu for two years and wrote her dissertation on the project.[36]

Dongtan, a larger Chinese city designed as a green project with zero-carbon-emission buildings and transit systems, has also been sidetracked. Groundbreaking on the model city of 500,000 on a Manhattan-sized island near Shanghai is more than a year behind schedule. Highrise towers are sprouting up around the site, leading some observers to call the project expensive "greenwashing" — attempting to make lavish development acceptable by tacking on environmentally friendly features.

" 'Zero-emission' city is pure commercial hype," said Dai Xingyi, a professor at Fudan University in Shanghai. "You can't expect some technology to both offer you a luxurious and comfortable life and save energy at the same time. That's just a dream."[37]

Construction is also under way on a new green city southeast of Beijing for 350,000 residents, co-developed by China and Singapore. Tianjin's features include renewable-energy sources, efficient water use and green building standards. Premier Wen Jiabao attended the 2008 groundbreaking.[38]

Although China's green development projects have a mixed record so far, "The government is starting to recognize that it has responsibility for environmental impacts beyond its borders, mainly by promoting renewable energy," says Alastair MacGregor, associate vice president of AECOM, an international design firm with large building projects in China. "Chinese culture is playing catch-up on sustainability."

More than 130 buildings designed to LEED (Leadership in Energy and Environmental Design)

China Aggressively Tackles Air Pollution

"No country in developing Asia takes those challenges more seriously"

China's large cities have some of the world's worst air pollution, thanks to rapid industrial growth, heavy use of coal and growing demand for cars.

The capital, Beijing, lost its 1993 bid to host the 2000 Summer Olympic Games partly because the city was so polluted. A chronic grey haze not only sullied Beijing's international image but also threatened to cause health problems for athletes and impair their performances.

When Beijing was chosen in 2001 to host the 2008 Summer Games, it pledged to put on a "green Olympics," which was widely understood to include clearing the air.

Between 2001 and 2007, however, China's economy grew beyond all predictions, with its gross domestic product expanding by up to 13 percent a year.[1] Beijing's air pollution worsened as new factories, power plants and cars crowded into the city. Winds carried in more pollutants from other burgeoning cities, including nitrogen oxides and sulfur dioxide — which contribute to acid rain and smog — and fine particulates, which can cause or worsen heart and lung problems.

With the Olympic deadline looming, many observers predicted Beijing would not meet its targets even if it relied heavily on authoritarian measures like shutting down factories and limiting auto use.[2] International Olympic Committee President Jacques Rogge said some outdoor endurance sports might have to be postponed if they occurred on high-pollution days — an embarrassing prospect for Chinese leaders.[3]

But China met its promised target, keeping Beijing's daily air pollution index — based on combined measurements of sulfur dioxide, nitrogen dioxide and fine particulates — below 100 during the month the Olympics took place. A 100 index score means air quality will not affect daily activities, compared to a maximum score of 500, when officials warn residents to stay indoors. In fact, during the Olympics in August 2008 Beijing's daily air pollution reached the lowest August measurements since 2000, sometimes even dropping into the 20s.[4]

"No country in Asia has bigger air quality challenges than China, but no country in developing Asia takes those challenges more seriously," says Cornie Huizenga, executive director of the Clean Air Initiative for Asian Cities (CAI-Asia), an international network based in the Philippines and founded by the Asian Development Bank, the World Bank and the U.S. Agency for International Development. "China has taken a whole series of long-term structural measures to address air pollution. The Olympics put a

standards — which measure energy efficiency and healthy indoor working conditions — are planned or under construction in Beijing, Shanghai, Chongqing, Wuhan and other Chinese cities.[39] Chinese investors see LEED buildings as premium products, not as an everyday model, said MacGregor.

Some Chinese cities are developing their own green standards. About half of worldwide new construction between 2008 through 2015 is projected to occur in China, so even greening a modest share of that development would be significant.

"China could end up being a sustainability leader just by virtue of its size," MacGregor predicted.[40]

BACKGROUND
From Farm to Factory

At the beginning of the 19th century only 3 percent of the world's population lived in cities, and only Beijing had more than a million inhabitants.[41] Then new technologies like the steam engine and railroads began to transform society. As the Industrial Revolution unfolded, people streamed from rural areas to manufacturing centers in Europe and the United States seeking a better income and life. This first great wave of urbanization established cities like London, Paris and New York as centers of global commerce.

magnifying glass on Beijing and made them focus there, but its programs are much bigger."

For instance, China continuously monitors air quality in more than 100 cities, requires high-polluting provinces and companies to close small, inefficient emission sources and install pollution-control equipment and has new-car emissions standards roughly equivalent to U.S. and Western European laws.

"For the Olympics China took temporary measures on top of those policies, like closing down large facilities and keeping cars off the roads. All of this plus good weather let Beijing deliver what it promised for the Games," says Huizenga.

Now China is further expanding air pollution regulations. During the Olympics, the Ministry of Environment announced that in 2009 it would start monitoring ultra-fine particle and ozone pollution — persistent problems in many developed countries. And Beijing officials plan to increase spending on public transportation.

Local pollution sources, weather patterns and geography influence air pollution, so China's policies for cleaning up Beijing's air might not work in other large cities. Mexico City, for instance, also has tried to reduce its severe air pollution but is hampered by the city's high altitude (7,200 feet). Car engines burn fuel inefficiently at high altitudes, so they pollute more than at sea level. And while automobiles are the biggest emission sources, scientists also found that leaking liquefied petroleum gas (LPG) — which most Mexican households burn for

cooking and heating — also contributes to Mexico City's air pollution.[5]

"We need better-harmonized air quality monitoring in developing countries before we can compare them," says Huizenga. "But other cities should be able to make progress on a large scale like Beijing. There's a lot of low-hanging fruit, such as switching to cleaner transportation fuels, getting rid of vehicles with [high-polluting] two-stroke engines, managing dust at construction sites and cutting pollution from coal-fired power plants. But to make them work, you also need effective agencies with enough people and money to carry [out] policies."

---

[1] Michael Yang, "China's GDP (2003-2007)," forum.china.org.cn, Nov. 10, 2008; "China Revises 2007 GDP Growth Rate to 13%," Jan. 15, 2009, http://english.dbw.cn.

[2] Edward Russell, "Beijing's 'Green Olympics' Test Run Fizzles," *Asia Times*, Aug. 10, 2007; Jim Yardley, "Beijing's Olympic Quest: Turn Smoggy Sky Blue," *The New York Times*, Dec. 29, 2007; David G. Streets, *et al.*, "Air Quality during the 2008 Beijing Olympic Games," *Atmospheric Environment*, vol. 41 (2007).

[3] "IOC President: Beijing Air Pollution Could Cause Events to Be Delayed During 2008 Olympics," The Associated Press, Aug. 7, 2007.

[4] "Summary: AQ in Beijing During the 2008 Summer Olympics," Clean Air Initiative for Asian Cities, www.cleanairnet.org/caiasia/1412/article-72991.html. Weather conditions are important factors in air pollution levels — for example, summer heat and humidity promote the formation of ground-level ozone, a major ingredient of smog — so to put conditions during the Olympics in context, scientists compared them to readings taken in August of previous years.

[5] Tim Weiner, "Terrific News in Mexico City: Air Is Sometimes Breathable," *The New York Times*, Jan. 5, 2001.

It also spawned horrific slums in factory towns and large cities. Tenement houses became a feature of working-class neighborhoods, with little access to fresh air or clean drinking water. Often whole neighborhoods shared a single water pump or toilet, and trash was usually thrown into the streets.[42]

German social scientist and a co-founder of communist theory Friedrich Engels graphically described urban workers' living conditions in cities like London and Manchester in 1844: "[T]hey are penned in dozens into single rooms. . . . They are given damp dwellings, cellar dens that are not waterproof from below or garrets that leak from above. . . . They are supplied bad, tattered or

rotten clothing, adulterated or indigestible food. . . . Thus are the workers cast out and ignored by the class in power, morally as well as physically and mentally."[43]

Engels and his collaborator Karl Marx later predicted in *The Communist Manifesto* that oppression of the working class would lead to revolution in industrialized countries. Instead, public health movements began to develop in Europe and the United States in mid-century. Seeking to curb repeated cholera and typhoid epidemics, cities began collecting garbage and improving water-supply systems. A new medical specialty, epidemiology (the study of how infections are spread) developed as scientists worked to track and contain illnesses. Cities built

CHRONOLOGY

1700s-1800s *Industrial Revolution spurs rapid urban growth in Europe and the U.S. Expanding slums trigger reforms and public health laws.*

1804 World population reaches 1 billion.

1854 British doctor John Snow discovers the connection between contaminated drinking water and a cholera outbreak in London.

1897 Brazil's first *favela* (shanty town), is established outside Rio de Janeiro.

1900-1960s *Europe and the United States are the most urbanized. Africa and Asia begin gaining independence and struggle to develop healthy economies.*

1906 An earthquake and subsequent fire destroy much of San Francisco, killing more than 3,000 people.

1927 World population reaches 2 billion.

1949 Chinese communists defeat nationalists, establishing the People's Republic of China, which aggressively promotes industrial development.

1960 World population hits 3 billion.

1964 Tokyo becomes first Asian city to host the Olympic Games and soon after that displaces New York as the world's largest city.

1970s-1990s *Urbanization accelerates in Asia and Africa. Many U.S. and European cities shrink as residents move to suburbs.*

1971 East Pakistan secedes from West Pakistan and becomes the independent nation of Bangladesh; populations in Dhaka and other cities grow rapidly.

1974 World population reaches 4 billion.

1979 China initiates broad economic reforms, opens diplomatic and trade relations with the United States and starts to ease limits on migration to cities.

1985 An earthquake in Mexico City kills some 10,000 people and damages water-supply and transit systems.

1987 World population reaches 5 billion.

1991 India institutes sweeping market reforms to attract foreign investors and spur rapid economic growth.

1999 World population reaches 6 billion.

2000s *Most industrialized countries stabilize at 70-80 percent urban. Cities continue to grow in Asia and Africa.*

2000 International community endorses the U.N. Millennium Development Goals designed to end poverty by 2015, including improving the lives of slum dwellers.

2001 Many international companies shift production to China after it joins the World Trade Organization; migration from rural areas accelerates. . . . Terrorists destroy World Trade Center towers in New York City, killing thousands. . . . Taiwan completes Taipei 101, the world's tallest skyscraper (1,671 feet), superseding the Petronas Towers in Kuala Lumpur, Malaysia (1,483 feet).

2005 United Nations condemns Zimbabwe for slum-clearance operations that leave 700,000 people homeless.

2007 The nonprofit group One Laptop Per Child unveils a prototype $100 laptop computer designed for children in developing countries to help close the "digital divide" between cities and rural areas.

2008 More than half of the world's population lives in cities. . . . Beijing hosts Summer Olympic Games. . . . Coordinated terrorist attacks in Mumbai kill nearly 170 people and injure more than 300.

2009 A global recession leaves millions of urban workers jobless, forcing many to return to their home villages.

2030 World's urban population is expected to reach 5 billion, and its slum population could top 2 billion.

2070 About 150 million city dwellers — primarily in India, Bangladesh, China, Vietnam, Thailand, Myanmar and Florida — could be in danger due to climate change, according to a 2008 study.

2010

January — The number of "megacities," with more than 10 million inhabitants, reaches 21, up from 16 a decade earlier. Another seven cities are projected to top the 10 million mark by 2020.

July-August — Record heat wave through Russia and much of Europe kills an estimated 11,000 people in Moscow alone. Experts say many cities are particularly susceptible to extreme weather events, expected to be exacerbated by climate change.

2011

January — China announces plans to create the world's largest megacity by merging nine cities in the Pearl River Delta manufacturing region. The city would have

42 million residents and cover a space 26 times the size of greater London.

October — United Nations Population Fund estimates that the world population has exceeded 7 billion. Roughly half live in cities, a proportion expected to reach 70 percent by 2070.

2012

March — More than 3,000 experts gather in London for Planet Under Pressure 2012, an international conference to examine how best to minimize the environmental impacts and other problems associated with rapid urbanization.

April — About 1,000 families protest outside an Indian official's home in New Delhi over plans by the Delhi Development Authority to raze slum dwellings in Gayatri Colony, one of several protests by slum dwellers in recent years to protect their communities.

green spaces like New York's Central Park to provide fresh air and access to nature. To help residents navigate around town, electric streetcars and subway trains were built in underground tunnels or on elevated tracks above the streets.

Many problems persisted, however. Homes and factories burned coal for heat and power, blanketing many large cities in smoky haze. Horse-drawn vehicles remained in wide use until the early-20th century, so urban streets were choked with animal waste. Wealthy city dwellers, seeking havens from the noise, dirt and crowding of inner cities, moved out to cleaner suburban neighborhoods.

Despite harsh conditions, people continued to pour into cities. Economic growth in industrialized countries had ripple effects in developing countries. As wealthier countries imported more and more raw materials, commercial "gateway cities" in developing countries grew as well, including Buenos Aires, Rio de Janeiro and Calcutta (now Kolkata). By 1900, nearly 14 percent of the world's population lived in cities.[44]

End of Empires

Worldwide migration from country to city accelerated in the early-20th century as automation spread and fewer

people were needed to grow food. But growth was not uniform. Wars devastated some of Europe's major cities while industrial production swelled others. And when colonial empires dissolved after World War II, many people were displaced in newly independent nations.

Much of the fighting during World War I occurred in fields and trenches, so few of Europe's great cities were seriously damaged. By the late 1930s, however, long-range bombers could attack cities hundreds of miles away. Madrid and Barcelona were bombed during the Spanish Civil War, a prelude to intensive air attacks on London, Vienna, Berlin, Tokyo and elsewhere during World War II. In 1945 the United States dropped atomic bombs on the Japanese cities of Hiroshima and Nagasaki, destroying each. For centuries cities had walled themselves off against outside threats, but now they were vulnerable to air attacks from thousands of miles away.

After 1945, even victorious nations like Britain and France were greatly weakened and unable to manage overseas colonies, where independence movements were underway. As European countries withdrew from their holdings in the Middle East, Asia and Africa over the next 25 years, a wave of countries gained independence, including Indonesia, India, Pakistan, the Philippines, Syria, Vietnam and most of colonial Africa. Wealthy countries

Cities Need to Plan for Disasters and Attacks

Concentrated populations and wealth magnify impact

Flash floods in 1999 caused landslides in the hills around Caracas, Venezuela, that washed away hundreds of hillside shanties and killed an estimated 30,000 people — more than 10 times the number of victims of the Sept. 11, 2001, terrorist attacks in the United States.

Because cities concentrate populations and wealth, natural disasters in urban areas can kill or displace thousands of people and cause massive damage to property and infrastructure. Many cities are located on earthquake faults, flood plains, fire-prone areas and other locations that make them vulnerable. The impacts are magnified when high-density slums and squatter neighborhoods are built in marginal areas. Political instability or terrorism can also cause widespread destruction.

Protecting cities requires both "hard" investments, such as flood-control systems or earthquake-resistant buildings, and "soft" approaches, such as emergency warning systems and special training for police and emergency-response forces. Cities also can improve their forecasting capacity and train officials to assess different types of risk.[1] Although preventive strategies are expensive, time-consuming and often politically controversial, failing to prepare for outside threats can be far more costly and dangerous.

Global climate change is exacerbating flooding and heat waves, which are special concerns for cities because they absorb more heat than surrounding rural areas and have higher average temperatures — a phenomenon known as the urban heat island effect. According to a study by the Organization for Economic Cooperation and Development (OECD), about 40 million people living in coastal areas around the world in 2005 were exposed to so-called 100-year floods — or major floods likely to occur only once every 100 years. By the 2070s, the OECD said, the population at risk from such flooding could rise to 150 million as more people move to cities, and climate change causes more frequent and ferocious storms and rising sea levels.

Cities with the greatest population exposure in the 2070 forecast include Kolkata and Mumbai in India, Dhaka (Bangladesh), Guangzhou and Shanghai in China, Ho Chi Minh City and Hai Phong in Vietnam, Bangkok (Thailand), Rangoon (Myanmar) and Miami, Florida. Cities in developed countries tend to be better protected, but there are exceptions. For example, London has about the same amount of flooding protection as Shanghai, according to the OECD.[2]

"All cities need to look at their critical infrastructure systems and try to understand where they're exposed to natural hazards," says Jim Hall, leader of urban research at England's Tyndall Centre for Climate Change Research. For example, he says, London's Underground subway system is vulnerable to flooding and overheating. Fast-growing cities planning for climate change, he adds, might want to control growth in flood-prone areas, improve water systems to ensure supply during droughts or build new parks to help cool urban neighborhoods. "Risks now and in the future depend on what we do to protect cities," says Hall.

In some cities, residents can literally see the ocean rising. Coastal erosion has destroyed 47 homes and more than 400 fields in recent years in Cotonou, the capital city of the West African nation of Benin, according to a local nonprofit called Front United Against Coastal Erosion. "The sea was far from us two years ago. But now, here it is. We are scared," said Kofi Ayao, a local fisherman. "If we do not find a solution soon, we may simply drown in our sleep one day."[3]

began providing aid to the new developing countries, especially in Asia and Latin America. But some nations, especially in Africa, received little focused support.

By mid-century most industrialized countries were heavily urbanized, and their populations were no longer growing rapidly. By 1950 three of the world's largest cities — Shanghai, Buenos Aires and Calcutta — were in developing countries. Populations in developing countries continued to rise through the late 1960s even as those nations struggled to industrialize. Many rural residents moved to cities, seeking work and educational opportunities.

In the 1950s and '60s U.S. urban planners heatedly debated competing approaches to city planning. The top-down, centralized philosophy was espoused by Robert

Social violence can arise from within a city or come as an attack from outside. For example, in 2007 up to 600 people were killed when urban riots erupted in Kenya after a disputed national election.[4]

Urban leaders often justify slum-clearance programs by claiming that poor neighborhoods are breeding grounds for unrest. Others say slums are fertile recruiting grounds for terrorist groups. Slums certainly contain many who feel ill-treated, and extreme conditions may spur them into action. Overall, however, experts say most slum dwellers are too busy trying to eke out a living to riot or join terrorist campaigns.

"Poverty alone isn't a sufficient cause [for unrest]," says John Parachini, director of the Intelligence Policy Center at the RAND Corp., a U.S. think tank. "You need a combination of things — people with a profound sense of grievance, impoverishment and leaders who offer the prospect of change. Often the presence of an enemy nearby, such as an occupying foreign power or a rival tribal group or religious sect, helps galvanize people."

Last November's terrorist attacks in Mumbai, in which 10 gunmen took dozens of Indian and foreign hostages and killed at least 164 people, showed an ironic downside of globalization: Wealth, clout and international ties can make cities terrorist targets.

"Mumbai is India's commercial and entertainment center — India's Wall Street, its Hollywood, its Milan. It is a prosperous symbol of modern India," a RAND analysis noted. Mumbai also was accessible from the sea, offered prominent landmark targets (historic hotels frequented by

A Bangladeshi boy helps slum residents cross floodwaters in Dhaka. Rising waters caused by global warming pose a significant potential threat to Dhaka and other low-lying cities worldwide.

foreigners and local elites) and had a heavy media presence that guaranteed international coverage.[5]

But serendipity can also make one city a target over another, says Parachini. "Attackers may know one city better or have family links or contacts there. Those local ties matter for small groups planning a one-time attack," he says.

Developing strong core services, such as police forces and public health systems, can be the first step in strengthening most cities against terrorism, he says, rather than creating specialized units to handle terrorist strikes.

"Basic governance functions like policing maintain order, build confidence in government and can pick up a lot of information about what's going on in neighborhoods," he says. "They make it harder to do bad things."

[1] George Bugliarello, "The Engineering Challenges of Urban Sustainability," *Journal of Urban Technology*, vol. 15, no. 1 (2008), pp. 64-65.

[2] R. J. Nicholls, *et al.*, "Ranking Port Cities with High Exposure and Vulnerability to Climate Extremes: Exposure Estimates," *Environment Working Papers No. 1*, Organization for Economic Cooperation and Development, Nov. 19, 2008, pp. 7-8, www.olis.oecd.org/olis/2007doc .nsf/LinkTo/NT0000588E/$FILE/JT03255617.PDF.

[3] "Rising Tides Threaten to Engulf Parts of Cotonou," U.N. Integrated Regional Information Network, Sept. 2, 2008.

[4] "Chronology: Kenya in Crisis After Elections," Reuters, Dec. 31, 2007; "The Ten Deadliest World Catastrophes 2007," Insurance Information Institute, www.iii.org.

[5] Angel Rabasa, *et al.*, "The Lessons of Mumbai," *RAND Occasional Paper*, January 2009.

Moses, the hard-charging parks commissioner and head of New York City's highway agency from 1934 to 1968. Moses pushed through numerous bridge, highway, park and slum-clearance projects that remade New York but earned him an image as arrogant and uncaring.[45] His most famous critic, writer and activist Jane Jacobs, advocated preserving dense, mixed-use neighborhoods, like

New York's Greenwich Village, and consulting with residents to build support for development plans.[46] Similar controversies would arise later in developing countries.

By the 1960s car-centered growth characterized many of the world's large cities. "Circle over London, Buenos Aires, Chicago, Sydney, in an airplane," wrote American historian Lewis Mumford in 1961. "The original container has completely disappeared: the sharp division between city and country no longer exists." City officials, Mumford argued, only measured improvements in quantities, such as wider streets and bigger parking lots.

"[T]hey would multiply bridges, highways [and] tunnels, making it ever easier to get in and out of the city but constricting the amount of space available within the city for any other purpose than transportation itself," Mumford charged.[47]

Population Boom

In the 1970s and '80s, as populations in developing countries continued to grow and improved agricultural methods made farmers more productive, people moved to the cities in ever-increasing numbers. Some national economies boomed, notably the so-called Asian tigers — Hong Kong, Singapore, Taiwan and South Korea — by focusing on manufacturing exports for industrialized markets and improving their education systems to create productive work forces. Indonesia, Malaysia, the Philippines and Thailand — the "tiger cubs" — went through a similar growth phase in the late 1980s and early '90s.

After China and India opened up their economies in the 1980s and '90s, both countries became magnets for foreign investment and created free-trade areas and special economic zones to attract business activity. Cities in those areas expanded, particularly along China's southeast coast where such zones were clustered.

As incomes rose, many Asian cities aspired to global roles: Seoul hosted the 1988 Summer Olympics, and Malaysia built the world's tallest skyscrapers — the Petronas Twin Towers, completed in 1998, only to be superseded by the Taipei 101 building in Taiwan a few years later.

Some Asian countries — including Malaysia, Sri Lanka and Indonesia — implemented programs to improve living standards for the urban poor and helped reduce poverty. However, poverty remained high in Thailand and the Philippines and increased in China and Vietnam.[48]

Cities in South America and Africa also expanded rapidly between 1970 and 2000, although South America was farther ahead. By 1965 Latin America was already 50 percent urbanized and had three cities with populations over 5 million (Buenos Aires, São Paulo and Rio de Janeiro) — a marker sub-Saharan Africa would not achieve

for several decades.[49] Urban growth on both continents followed the "primacy" pattern, in which one city is far more populous and economically and politically powerful than all the others in the nation. The presence of so-called primate cities like Lima (Peru), Caracas (Venezuela) or Lagos (Nigeria) can distort development if the dominant city consumes most public investments and grows to a size that is difficult to govern.

Latin America's growth gradually leveled out in the 1980s: Population increases slowed in major urban centers, and more people moved to small and medium-sized cities.[50] On average the region's economy grew more slowly and unevenly than Asia's, often in boom-and-bust cycles.[51] Benefits accrued mostly to small ruling classes who were hostile to new migrants, and income inequality became deeply entrenched in many Latin American cities.

Africa urbanized quickly after independence in the 1950s and '60s. But from the mid-1970s forward most countries' incomes stagnated or contracted. Such "urbanization without growth" in sub-Saharan Africa created the world's highest rates of urban poverty and income inequality. Corruption and poor management reinforced wealth gaps that dated back to colonial times. Natural disasters, wars and the spread of HIV/AIDS further undercut poverty-reduction efforts in both rural and urban areas.[52]

New Solutions

As the 21st century began, calls for new antipoverty efforts led to an international conference at which 189 nations endorsed the Millennium Development Goals, designed to end poverty by 2015. Experts also focused on bottom-up strategies that gave poor people resources to help themselves.

An influential proponent of the bottom-up approach, Peruvian economist Hernando de Soto, stirred debate in 2000 with his book *The Mystery of Capital: Why Capitalism Triumphs in the West and Fails Everywhere Else.* Capitalist economies did not fail in developing nations because those countries lacked skills or enterprising spirit, de Soto argued. Rather, the poor in those countries had plenty of assets but no legal rights, so they could not prove ownership or use their assets as capital.

"They have houses but not titles; crops but not deeds; businesses but not statutes of incorporation," de Soto wrote. "It is the unavailability of these essential representations that explains why people who have adapted every other Western invention, from the paper clip to the nuclear reactor, have not been able to produce sufficient capital to make their domestic capitalism work." But, he asserted, urbanization in the developing world had spawned "a huge industrial-commercial revolution" which clearly showed that poor people could contribute to economic development if their countries developed fair and inclusive legal systems.[53]

Not all experts agreed with de Soto, but his argument coincided with growing interest in approaches like microfinance (small-scale loans and credit programs for traditionally neglected customers) that helped poor people build businesses and transition from the "extra-legal" economy into the formal economy. Early microcredit programs in the 1980s and '90s had targeted mainly the rural poor, but donors began expanding into cities around 2000.[54]

The "digital divide" — the gap between rich and poor people's access to information and communications technologies (ICTs) — also began to attract the attention of development experts. During his second term (1997-2001), U.S. President Bill Clinton highlighted the issue as an obstacle to reducing poverty both domestically and at the global level. "To maximize potential, we must turn the digital divide among and within our nations into digital opportunities," Clinton said at the Asia Pacific Economic Cooperation Forum in 2000, urging Asian nations to expand Internet access and train citizens to use computers.[55] The Millennium Development Goals called for making ICTs more widely available in poor countries.

Some ICTs, such as mobile phones, were rapidly adopted in developing countries, which had small or unreliable landline networks. By 2008, industry observers predicted, more than half of the world's population would own a mobile phone, with Africa and the Middle East leading the way.[56]

Internet penetration moved much more slowly. In 2006 some 58 percent of the population in industrial countries used the Internet, compared to 11 percent in developing countries and only 1 percent in the least developed countries. Access to high-speed Internet service was unavailable in many developing regions or was too expensive for most users.[57] Some antipoverty advocates questioned whether ICTs should be a high priority for poor countries, but others said the issue was not whether but when and how to get more of the world's poor wired.

Security officers forcibly remove a woman from her home during land confiscations in Changchun, a city of 7.5 million residents in northeast China, so buildings can be demolished to make way for new construction. Some rapidly urbanizing governments use heavy-handed methods — such as land confiscation, eviction or slum clearance — so redevelopment projects can proceed.

"The more the better, especially broadband," says Polytechnic University's Bugliarello.

While development experts worked to empower the urban poor, building lives in fast-growing cities remained difficult and dangerous in many places. Some governments still pushed approaches like slum clearance, especially when it served other purposes.

Notoriously, in 2005 President Robert Mugabe of Zimbabwe launched a slum-clearance initiative called Operation Murambatsvina, a Shona phrase translated by some as "restore order" and others as "drive out the trash." Thousands of shacks in Zimbabwe's capital, Harare, and other cities across the nation were destroyed, allegedly to crack down on illegal settlements and businesses.

"The current chaotic state of affairs, where small-to-medium enterprises operated outside of the regulatory framework and in undesignated and crime-ridden areas, could not be countenanced much longer," said Mugabe.[58]

But critics said Mugabe was using slum clearance as an excuse to intimidate and displace neighborhoods that supported his opponents. In the end, some 700,000 people were left homeless or jobless by the action, which the United Nations later said violated international law.[59] Over the next several years Mugabe's government failed to carry out its pledges to build new houses for the displaced families.[60]

Slum Redevelopment Plan Stirs Controversy

Conditions for the 60,000 families living in Mumbai's Dharavi neighborhood (top) — one of Asia's largest slums — are typical for a billion slum dwellers around the globe. Slums often lack paved roads, water-distribution systems, sanitation and garbage collection — spawning cholera, diarrhea and other illnesses. Electric power and telephone service are usually poached from available lines. Mumbai's plans to redevelop Dharavi, located on 600 prime acres in the heart of the city, triggered strong protests from residents, who demanded that their needs be considered before the redevelopment proceeds (bottom). The project has stalled recently due to the global economic crisis.

CURRENT SITUATION

Economic Shadow

The current global economic recession is casting a dark cloud over worldwide economic development prospects. Capital flows to developing countries have declined sharply, and falling export demand is triggering layoffs and factory shutdowns in countries that produce for Western markets. But experts say even though the overall picture is sobering, many factors will determine how severely the recession affects cities.

In March the World Bank projected that developing countries would face budget shortfalls of $270 billion to $700 billion in 2009 and the world economy would shrink for the first time since World War II. According to the bank, 94 out of 116 developing countries were already experiencing an economic slowdown, and about half of them already had high poverty levels. Urban-based exporters and manufacturers were among the sectors hit hardest by the recession.[61]

These trends, along with an international shortage of investment capital, will make many developing countries increasingly dependent on foreign aid at a time when donor countries are experiencing their own budget crises. As workers shift out of export-oriented sectors in the cities and return to rural areas, poverty may increase, the bank projected.

The recession could mean failure to meet the Millennium Development Goals, especially if donor countries pull back on development aid. The bank urged nations to increase their foreign aid commitments and recommended that national governments:

- Increase government spending where possible to stimulate economies;
- Protect core programs to create social safety nets for the poor;
- Invest in infrastructure such as roads, sewage systems and slum upgrades; and
- Help small- and medium-size businesses get financing to create opportunities for growth and employment.[62]

President Barack Obama's economic stimulus package, signed into law on Feb. 17, takes some of these steps and contains at least $51 billion for programs to help U.S. cities. (Other funds are allocated by states and may provide more aid to cities depending on each state's priority list.) Stimulus programs that benefit cities include $2.8 billion for energy conservation and energy efficiency, $8.4 billion for public transportation investments, $8 billion for high-speed rail and intercity passenger rail service, $1.5 billion for emergency shelter grants, $4 billion for job training and $8.8 billion for modernizing schools.[63]

Governments in developing countries with enough capital may follow suit. At the World Economic Forum in Davos, Switzerland, in January, Chinese Premier Wen Jibao announced a 4 trillion yuan stimulus package (equivalent to about 16 percent of China's GDP over two years), including money for housing, railways and infrastructure and environmental protection. " 'The harsh winter will be gone, and spring is around the corner,' " he said, predicting that China's economy would rebound this year.[64]

But according to government figures released just a few days later, more than 20 million rural migrant workers had already lost their jobs in coastal manufacturing areas and moved back to their home towns.[65] In March the World Bank cut its forecast for China's 2009 economic growth from 7.5 percent to 6.5 percent, although it said China was still doing well compared to many other countries.[66]

In India "circular migration" is becoming more prevalent, according to the Overseas Development Institute's Deshingkar. "Employment is becoming more temporary — employers like to hire temporary workers whom they can hire and fire at will, so the proportion of temporary workers and circular migrants is going up," she says. "In some Indian villages 95 percent of migrants are circular. Permanent migration is too expensive and risky — rents are high, [people are] harassed by the police, slums are razed and they're evicted. Keeping one foot in the village is their social insurance."

Meanwhile, international development aid is likely to decline as donor countries cut spending and focus on their own domestic needs. "By rights the financial crisis shouldn't undercut development funding, because the total amounts given now are tiny compared to the national economic bailouts that are under way or being debated in developed countries," says Harvard economist Bloom. "Politically, however, it may be hard to maintain aid budgets."

At the World Economic Forum billionaire philanthropist Bill Gates urged world leaders and organizations to keep up their commitments to foreign aid despite the global financial crisis. "If we lose sight of our long-term priority to expand opportunity for the world's poor and abandon our commitments and partnerships to reduce inequality, we run the risk of emerging from the current economic downturn in a world with even greater disparities in health and education and fewer

Reflecting China's stunningly rapid urbanization, Shanghai's dramatic skyline rises beside the Huangpu River. Shanghai is the world's seventh-largest city today but will drop to ninth-place by 2025, as two south Asian megacities, Dhaka and Kolkata, surpass Shanghai in population.

opportunities for people to improve their lives," said Gates, whose Bill and Melinda Gates Foundation supports efforts to address both rural and urban poverty in developing nations.[67]

In fact, at a summit meeting in London in early April, leaders of the world's 20 largest economies pledged $1.1 trillion in new aid to help developing countries weather the global recession. Most of the money will be channeled through the International Monetary Fund.

"This is the day the world came together to fight against the global recession," said British Prime Minister Gordon Brown.[68]

Slum Solutions

As slums expand in many cities, debate continues over the best way to alleviate poverty. Large-scale slum-clearance operations have long been controversial in both developed and developing countries: Officials typically call the slums eyesores and public health hazards, but often new homes turn out to be unaffordable for the displaced residents. Today development institutions like the World Bank speak of "urban upgrading" — improving services in slums instead of bulldozing them.[69]

This approach focuses on improving basic infrastructure systems like water distribution, sanitation and electric power; cleaning up environmental hazards and building schools and clinics. The strategy is cheaper than massive demolition and construction projects and

Reuters/George Esiri

Two-thirds of sub-Saharan Africa's city dwellers live in slums, like this one in Lagos, Nigeria, which has open sewers and no clean water, electric power or garbage collection. About 95 percent of today's rapid urbanization is occurring in the developing world, primarily in sub-Saharan Africa and Asia.

provides incentives for residents to invest in improving their own homes, advocates say.[70]

To do so, however, slum dwellers need money. Many do not have the basic prerequisites even to open bank accounts, such as fixed addresses and minimum balances, let alone access to credit. Over the past 10 to 15 years, however, banks have come to recognize slum dwellers as potential customers and have begun creating microcredit programs to help them obtain small loans and credit cards that often start with very low limits. A related concept, micro-insurance, offers low-cost protection in case of illness, accidents and property damage.

Now advocates for the urban poor are working to give slum dwellers more financial power. The advocacy group, Shack/Slum Dwellers International (SDI), for example, has created Urban Poor Funds that help attract direct investments from banks, government agencies and international donor groups.[71] In 2007 SDI received a $10 million grant from the Gates foundation to create a Global Finance Facility for Federations of the Urban Poor.

The funds will give SDI leverage in negotiating with governments for land, housing and infrastructure, according to Joel Bolnick, an SDI director in Cape Town, South Africa. If a government agency resists, said Bolnick, SDI can reply, " 'If you can't help us here, we'll take the money and put it on the table for a deal in Zambia instead.' "[72]

And UN-HABITAT is working with lenders to promote more mortgage lending to low-income borrowers in developing countries. "Slum dwellers have access to resources and are resources in themselves. To maximize the value of slums for those who live in them and for a city, slums must be upgraded and improved," UN-HABITAT Executive Director Tibaijuka said in mid-2008.[73]

Nevertheless, some governments still push slum clearance. Beijing demolished hundreds of blocks of old city neighborhoods and culturally significant buildings in its preparations to host the 2008 Olympic Games. Some of these "urban corners" (a negative term for high-density neighborhoods with narrow streets) had also been designated for protection as historic areas.[74] Developers posted messages urging residents to take government resettlement fees and move, saying, "Living in the Front Gate's courtyards is ancient history; moving to an apartment makes you a good neighbor," and "Cherish the chance; grab the good fortune; say farewell to dangerous housing."[75]

Beijing's actions were not unique. Other cities hosting international "mega-events" have demolished slums. Like Beijing, Seoul, South Korea, and Santo Domingo in the Dominican Republic were already urbanizing and had slum-clearance programs under way, but as their moments in the spotlight grew nearer, eviction operations accelerated, according to a Yale study. Ultimately, the study concluded, the benefits from hosting big events did not trickle down to poor residents and squatter communities who were "systematically removed or concealed from high-profile areas in order to construct the appearance of development."[76]

Now the debate over slum clearance has arrived in Dharavi. Developers are circling the site, which sits on a square mile of prime real estate near Mumbai's downtown and airport. The local government has accepted a $3 billion redevelopment proposal from Mukesh Mehta, a wealthy architect who made his fortune in Long Island, N.Y., to raze Dharavi's shanties and replace them with high-rise condominiums, shops, parks and offices. Slum dwellers who can prove they have lived in Dharavi since 1995 would receive free 300-square-foot apartments, equivalent to two small rooms, in the new buildings. Other units would be sold at market rates that could reach several thousand dollars per square foot.[77]

Mehta contends his plan will benefit slum residents because they will receive new homes on the same site.

"Give me a better solution. Until then you might want to accept this one," he said last summer.[78] But many Dharavi residents say they will not be able to keep small businesses like tanneries, potteries and tailoring shops if they move into modern high-rises, and would rather stay put.

"I've never been inside a tall building. I prefer a place like this where I can work and live," said Usman Ghani, a potter born and raised in Dharavi who has demonstrated against the redevelopment proposals. He is not optimistic about the future. "The poor and the working class won't be able to stay in Mumbai," he said. "Many years ago, corrupt leaders sold this country to the East India Company. Now they're selling it to multinationals."[79]

OUTLOOK

Going Global

In an urbanizing world, cities will become increasingly important as centers of government, commerce and culture, but some will be more influential than others. Although it doesn't have a precise definition, the term "global city" is used by city-watchers to describe metropolises like New York and London that have a disproportionate impact on world affairs. Many urban leaders around the world aspire to take their cities to that level.

The 2008 *Global Cities Index* — compiled by *Foreign Policy* magazine, the Chicago Council on Global Affairs and the A. T. Kearney management consulting firm — ranks 60 cities on five broad criteria that measure their international influence, including:

- Business activity,
- Human capital (attracting diverse groups of people and talent),
- Information exchange,
- Cultural attractions and experiences, and
- Political engagement (influence on world policy making and dialogue).[80]

The scorecard is topped by Western cities like New York, London and Paris but also includes developing-country cities such as Beijing, Shanghai, Bangkok, Mexico City and São Paulo. Many of these cities, the authors noted, are taking a different route to global stature than

their predecessors followed — a shorter, often state-led path with less public input than citizens of Western democracies expect to have.

"Rulers in closed or formerly closed societies have the power to decide that their capitol is going to be a world-class city, put up private funds and spell out what the city should look like," says Simon O'Rourke, executive director of the Global Chicago Center at the Chicago Council on Global Affairs. "That's not necessarily a bad path, but it's a different path than the routes that New York or London have taken. New global cities can get things done quickly — if the money is there."

Abu Dhabi's Masdar Initiative, for example, remains on track despite the global recession, directors said this spring. The project is part of a strategic plan to make Abu Dhabi a world leader in clean-energy technology. "There is no question of any rollback or slowing down of any of our projects in the renewable-energy sector," said Sultan Ahmed Al Jaber, chief executive officer of the initiative, on March 16.[81] Last year the crown prince of Abu Dhabi created a $15 billion fund for clean-energy investments, which included funds for Masdar City.

Money is the front-burner issue during today's global recession. "Unless a country's overall economic progress is solid, it is very unlikely that a high proportion of city dwellers will see big improvements in their standard of living," says Harvard's Bloom. In the next several years, cities that ride out the global economic slowdown successfully will be best positioned to prosper when world markets recover.

In the longer term, however, creating wealth is not enough, as evidenced by conditions in Abu Dhabi's neighboring emirate, Dubai. Until recently Dubai was a booming city-state with an economy built on real estate, tourism and trade — part of the government's plan to make the city a world-class business and tourism hub. It quickly became a showcase for wealth and rapid urbanization: Dozens of high-rise, luxury apartment buildings and office towers sprouted up seemingly overnight, and man-made islands shaped like palm trees rose from the sea, crowded with multi-million-dollar second homes for jetsetters.

But the global recession has brought development to a halt. The real estate collapse was so sudden that jobless expatriate employees have been fleeing the

Will redevelopment of the Dharavi slum improve residents' lives?

YES
Mukesh Mehta
Chairman, MM Project Consultants

Written for *CQ Global Researcher,* April 2009

Slum rehabilitation is a challenge that has moved beyond the realm of charity or meager governmental budgets. It requires a pragmatic and robust financial model and a holistic approach to achieve sustainability.

Dharavi — the largest slum pocket in Mumbai, India, and one of the largest in the world — houses 57,000 families, businesses and industries on 600 acres. Alarmingly, this accounts for only 4 percent of Mumbai's slums, which house about 7.5 million people, or 55 percent of the city's population.

Mumbai's Slum Rehabilitation Authority (SRA) has undertaken the rehabilitation of all the eligible residents and commercial and industrial enterprises in a sustainable manner through the Dharavi Redevelopment Project (DRP), following an extensive consultative process that included Dharavi's slum dwellers. The quality of life for those residents is expected to dramatically improve, and they could integrate into mainstream Mumbai over a period of time. Each family would receive a 300-square-foot home plus adequate workspace, along with excellent infrastructure, such as water supply and roads. A public-private partnership between the real estate developers and the SRA also would provide amenities for improving health, income, knowledge, the environment and socio-cultural activities. The land encroached by the slum dwellers would be used as equity in the partnership.

The primary focus — besides housing and infrastructure — would be on income generation. Dharavi has a vibrant economy of $600 million per annum, despite an appalling working environment. But the redevelopment project would boost the local gross domestic product to more than $3 billion, with the average family income estimated to increase to at least $3,000 per year from the current average of $1,200. To achieve this, a hierarchy of workspaces will be provided, including community spaces equivalent to 6 percent of the built-up area, plus individual workspaces in specialized commercial and industrial complexes for leather goods, earthenware, food products, recycling and other enterprises.

The greatest failure in slum redevelopment has been to treat it purely as a housing problem. Improving the infrastructure to enable the local economy to grow is absolutely essential for sustainable development. We believe this project will treat Dharavi residents as vital human resources and allow them to act as engines for economic growth. Thus, the DRP will act as a torchbearer for the slums of Mumbai as well as the rest of the developing world.

NO
Kalpana Sharma
Author, Rediscovering Dharavi:
Stories from Asia's Largest Slum

Written for *CQ Global Researcher,* April 2009

The controversy over the redevelopment of Dharavi, a slum in India's largest city of Mumbai, centers on the future of the estimated 60,000 families who live and work there.

Dharavi is a slum because its residents do not own the land on which they live. But it is much more than that. The settlement — more than 100 years old — grew up around one of the six fishing villages that coalesced over time to become Bombay, as Mumbai originally was called. People from all parts of India live and work here making terra-cotta pots, leather goods, garments, food items and jewelry and recycling everything from plastic to metal. The annual turnover from this vast spread of informal enterprises, much of it conducted inside people's tiny houses, is an estimated $700 million a year.

The Dharavi Redevelopment Plan — conceived by consultant Mukesh Mehta and being implemented by the Government of Maharashtra state — envisages leveling this energetic and productive part of Mumbai and converting it into a collection of high-rise buildings, where some of the current residents will be given free apartments. The remaining land will be used for high-end commercial and residential buildings.

On paper, the plan looks beautiful. But people in Dharavi are not convinced. They believe the plan has not understood the nature and real value of Dharavi and its residents. It has only considered the value of the land and decided it is too valuable to be wasted on poor people.

Dharavi residents have been left with no choice but to adapt to an unfamiliar lifestyle. If this meant a small adjustment, one could justify it. But the new form of living in a 20-story high-rise will force them to pay more each month, since the maintenance costs of high-rises exceed what residents currently spend on housing. These costs become unbearable when people earn just enough to survive in a big city.

Even worse, this new, imposed lifestyle will kill all the enterprises that flourish today in Dharavi. Currently, people live and work in the same space. In the new housing, this will not be possible.

The alternatives envisaged are spaces appropriate for formal, organized industry. But enterprises in Dharavi are informal and small, working on tiny margins. Such enterprises cannot survive formalization.

The real alternative is to give residents security of tenure and let them redevelop Dharavi. They have ideas. It can happen only if people are valued more than real estate.

country, literally abandoning their cars in the Dubai airport parking lot.[82]

Truly global cities are excellent in a variety of ways, says O'Rourke. "To be great, cities have to be places where people want to live and work." They need intellectual and cultural attractions as well as conventional features like parks and efficient mass transit, he says, and, ultimately, they must give residents at least some role in decisionmaking.

"It will be very interesting to see over the next 20 years which cities can increase their global power without opening up locally to more participation," says O'Rourke. "If people don't have a say in how systems are built, they won't use them."

Finally, great cities need creative leaders who can adapt to changing circumstances. Mumbai's recovery after last November's terrorist attacks showed such resilience. Within a week stores and restaurants were open again in neighborhoods that had been raked by gunfire, and international travelers were returning to the city.[83]

The Taj Mahal Palace & Tower was one of the main attack targets. Afterwards, Ratan Tata, grand-nephew of the Indian industrialist who built the five-star hotel, said, "We can be hurt, but we can't be knocked down."[84]

UPDATE

The rapid urbanization of the world population continues unabated, despite a global economic downturn that some analysts thought might slow or reverse the trend.

By 2030 more people will live in cities than in rural areas in all the world's regions — including Asia and Africa, according to the United Nations.[85] About half the world's population already lives in cities, and virtually all the population growth through 2050 is expected to be in urban areas.

"Urbanization . . . is unstoppable now," says Shobhakar Dhakal, executive director of the Global Carbon Project, based in Tsubuka, Japan, which studies urbanization as part of a larger focus on climate change. "An additional 2.8 billion people will be living in urban areas by 2050."

Migration from rural areas to cities is a long-standing trend, but the shift challenges the developing world the most because that is where the population is growing the

In addition to Dubai's glittering, new downtown area filled with towering skyscrapers, the city's manmade, palm-tree-shaped islands of Jumeirah sport hundreds of multi-million-dollar second homes for international jetsetters. Development has skidded to a temporary halt in the Arab city-state, much as it has in some other rapidly urbanizing cities around the globe, due to the global economic downturn.

fastest. By 2020, according to the United Nations Human Settlements Programme (U.N.-HABITAT), up to 1.4 billion city dwellers will be living in urban slums.[86] To keep up with that burgeoning population, governments struggle to find ways to reduce slums, build adequate infrastructure and protect the environment.

Reducing Slums

Reducing the number of people living in urban slums is perhaps the biggest concern for governments in developing countries. The U.N.'s Millennium Development Goals, adopted by all 193 member nations, set a target of "achieving a significant improvement in the lives of at least 100 million slum dwellers" by 2020.[87]

Progress toward that goal is ahead of schedule, according to a 2010/2011 U.N. report. Between 2000 and 2010 more than 200 million people in poor countries were lifted out of slum conditions, the report said. "In other words, governments have collectively exceeded the Millennium Target by at least a multiple of two," concluded Anna K. Tibaijuka, under-secretary general and executive director of U.N.-HABITAT.[88]

And China and India have improved the lives of more slum dwellers than any other country during that time, lifting a total of about 125 million people out of slums.

AFP/Getty Images/Torsten Blackwood

The seaside town of Sydney, Australia, is expanding in geographic size as its population tops 4.6 million. Researchers have predicated that between 2000 and 2030, the world's cities will triple the amount of land they cover, growing by an additional 580,000 square miles — roughly the size of Germany, France and Spain combined.

Globally, the proportion of urban dwellers who live in slums has declined, but because of the rapid growth in urban populations, the number of people remaining in slums is still rising by about 6 million a year.[89]

Meanwhile, slum dwellers are fighting efforts to move them. For example, residents of Vila Autódromo, a decades-old slum in Rio de Janeiro, have taken to the streets and courts to halt plans to tear down their neighborhood to clear space for the 2016 Olympics. [90] The most recent attempt to redevelop Dharavi, in Mumbai, India — made famous in the movie "Slumdog Millionaire" — also has stalled in the face of local political opposition.[91]

Building Infrastructure

In 2011, nearly 450 cities had more than 1 million inhabitants; by 2020 at least 527 cities are expected to be that large. Last year the world's 100 largest cities averaged about 7.6 million people, but by 2020, the average will be 8.5 million.[92] Thus, in less than eight years 100 cities will be slightly larger than present-day New York City.

Cities still reeling from the economic downturn that began in 2007 are struggling to maintain an adequate infrastructure to support those populations. Maintaining city streets and roads has been a particular problem in the United States, as both local and state governments have trimmed budgets. A 2010 study by the U.S. Public

Interest Research Group (PIRG), a nonprofit consumer organization, found that about 63 percent of American urban roads were not in good condition.[93] And aging water and sewer systems in several major U.S. cities, such as Washington, D.C., need upgrades, according to expert analysis.[94]

Urban infrastructure needs are greatest in the developing world. Globally, according to the U.N., the number of city dwellers without access to safe drinking water and other basic services grew by 20 percent from 2000 to 2008.[95] For instance, more than 55 million people in Africa's cities lack access to safe drinking water, up from about 30 million in 1990, according to a U.N. report. During the same period, the number of African city dwellers without sanitation services doubled, to around 175 million.[96]

And while emerging nations such as China and India have made significant infrastructure investments in recent decades, urban growth has outstripped the improvements.

Protecting the Environment

Climate change worries officials in rapidly growing cities, in part because of the role of large cities in causing global warming as well as their vulnerability to the consequences of a warming planet.

Although about half the world's population lives in cities, they account for about 80 percent of the world's energy use and roughly the same percentage of greenhouse gas emissions, according to the World Bank.[97] Meanwhile, urban populations are particularly susceptible to the effects of climate change.

By 2025, the U.N. estimates, 74 percent of world's urban dwellers will live in coastal areas.[98] That will make them susceptible to rising sea levels and ocean storms. In addition, large expanses of heat reflecting off concrete and steel raises urban temperatures, exacerbating heat waves.

But the sheer size of the world's rapidly growing cities is also attracting attention. Michail Fragkias, executive officer of the Urbanization and Global Environmental Change project at Arizona State University, Tempe, says recent research indicates that from 2000 to 2030 cities around the globe could grow by an additional 1.5 million kilometers (580,000 square miles), an area roughly equal to Germany, France and Spain combined.

"If you start thinking about tripling the amount of urban land, which is what this would represent, it's quite significant," Fragkias says. "If it's going to happen in coastal areas [where many cities are located] or fragile ecosystems, you're talking about something that could have a very serious impact."

The combination of climate change and urban sprawl led the U.N. to warn in 2011 that "the effects of urbanization and climate change are converging in dangerous ways, which threaten to have unprecedented negative impacts upon quality of life, and economic and social stability."[99]

However, many experts say cities can help solve the challenge of global warming if they are built and run properly. In March 2012, more than 3,000 urban experts met in London to discuss building sustainable urban communities. Analysis has found that, with the exception of Chinese cities, where public transportation has lagged behind rapid growth, densely populated cities generally have lower greenhouse gas emissions per capita.[100]

Fragkias says new research indicates that having population growth concentrated in cities can be more energy efficient. "Some arguments have started to come out for the benefits of the larger cities, that [having] people aggregated together can make sense for energy systems and climate change," he says.

If U.S.-style urban sprawl prevails globally, however, analysts believe it could have serious consequences for the environment. "If we follow what we did in the past, it will result in more congestion, environmental pollution, CO_2 emissions and consumption of scarce natural resources, including energy," says Dhakal. "The environmental consequence of the unfolding rapid urbanization will depend on how urbanization is managed."

NOTES

1. Ben Sutherland, "Slum Dwellers 'to top 2 billion,'" *BBC News*, June 20, 2006, http://news.bbc.co.uk/2/hi/in_depth/5099038.stm.

2. United Nations Population Fund, *State of World Population 2007: Unleashing the Potential of Urban Growth* (2007), p. 6.

3. UN-HABITAT, *State of the World's Cities 2008/2009* (2008), p. xi.

4. UN-HABITAT, *op cit.*, p. 90.

5. *Ibid.*, p. 92.

6. *Ibid.*, pp. 90-105.

7. Anna Tibaijuka, "The Challenge of Urbanisation and the Role of UN-HABITAT," lecture at the Warsaw School of Economics, April 18, 2008, p. 2, www.unhabitat.org/downloads/docs/5683_16536_ed_warsaw_version12_1804.pdf.

8. For background see Peter Katel, "Ending Poverty," *CQ Researcher*, Sept. 9, 2005, p. 733-760.

9. For details, see www.endpoverty2015.org. For background, see Peter Behr, "Looming Water Crisis," *CQ Global Researcher*, February 2008, pp. 27-56.

10. Tobias Just, "Megacities: Boundless Growth?" Deutsche Bank Research, March 12, 2008, pp. 4-5.

11. Commission on Legal Empowerment of the Poor, *Making the Law Work for Everyone* (2008), pp. 5-9, www.undp.org/legalempowerment/report/Making_the_Law_Work_for_Everyone.pdf.

12. Angel Rabasa, *et al.*, "The Lessons of Mumbai," *RAND Occasional Paper*, 2009, pp. 1-2, www.rand.org/pubs/occasional_papers/2009/RAND_OP249.pdf.

13. Wieland Wagner, "As Orders Dry Up, Factory Workers Head Home," *Der Spiegel*, Jan. 8, 2009, www.spiegel.de/international/world/0,1 518,600188,00.html; Malcolm Beith, "Reverse Migration Rocks Mexico," *Foreign Policy.com*, February 2009, www.foreignpolicy.com/story/cms.php?story_id=4731; Anthony Faiola, "A Global Retreat As Economies Dry Up," *The Washington Post*, March 5, 2009, www.washingtonpost.com/wp-dyn/content/story/2009/03/04/ST2009030404264.html.

14. For background, see David Masci, "Emerging India, *CQ Researcher*, April 19, 2002, pp. 329-360; and Peter Katel, "Emerging China," *CQ Researcher*, Nov. 11, 2005, pp. 957-980.

15. For background, see Mary H. Cooper, "Exporting Jobs," *CQ Researcher*, Feb. 20, 2004, pp. 149-172.

16. Ji Yongqing, "Dalian Becomes the New Outsourcing Destination," *China Business Feature*, Sept. 17, 2008, www.cbfeature.com/industry_spotlight/news/dalian_becomes_the_new_outsourcing_destination.

17. Thomas L. Friedman, *The World Is Flat: A Brief History of the Twenty-First Century*, updated edition (2006), pp. 24-28, 463-464.

18. Priya Deshingkar and Claudia Natali, "Internal Migration," in *World Migration 2008* (2008), p. 183.

19. Views expressed here are the speaker's own and do not represent those of his employer.

20. Martin Ravallion, Shaohua Chen and Prem Sangraula, "New Evidence on the Urbanization of Global Poverty," World Bank Policy Research Working Paper 4199, April 2007, http://siteresources.worldbank .org/INTWDR2008/Resources/2795087-1191427 986785/RavallionMEtAl_UrbanizationOfGlobal Poverty.pdf.

21. For background on the *hukou* system, see Congressional-Executive Commission on China, "China's Household Registration System: Sustained Reform Needed to Protect China's Rural Migrants," Oct. 7, 2005, www .cecc.gov/pages/news/hukou.pdf; and Hayden Windrow and Anik Guha, "The Hukou System, Migrant Workers, and State Power in the People's Republic of China," *Northwestern University Journal of International Human Rights*, spring 2005, pp. 1-18.

22. Wu Zhong, "How the Hukou System Distorts Reality," *Asia Times*, April 11, 2007, www.atimes .com/atimes/China/ID11Ad01.html; Rong Jiaojiao, "Hukou 'An Obstacle to Market Economy,' " *China Daily*, May 21, 2007, www.chinadaily.com.cn/ china/2007-05/21/content_876699.htm.

23. "Scientific Outlook on Development," "Full text of Hu Jintao's report at 17th Party Congress," section V.5, Oct. 24, 2007, http://news.xinhuanet.com/ english/2007-10/24/content_6938749.htm.

24. Wu Zhong, "Working-Class Heroes Get Their Day," *Asia Times*, Oct. 24, 2007, www.atimes.com/atimes/ China_Business/IJ24Cb01.html.

25. "Internal Migration, Poverty and Development in Asia," *Briefing Paper no. 11*, Overseas Development Council, October 2006, p. 3.

26. Clare T. Romanik, "An Urban-Rural Focus on Food Markets in Africa," The Urban Institute, Nov. 15, 2007, p. 30, www.urban.org/publications/411604.html.

27. UN-HABITAT, *op. cit.*, pp. 24-26.

28. "How Shifts to Smaller Family Sizes Contributed to the Asian Miracle," *Population Action International*, July 2006, www.popact.org/Publications/Fact_ Sheets/FS4/Asian_Miracle.pdf.

29. Edson C. Tandoc, Jr., "Says UP Economist: Lack of Family Planning Worsens Poverty," *Philippine Daily Inquirer*, Nov. 11, 2008, http://newsinfo.inquirer .net/breakingnews/nation/view/20081111- 171604/Lack-of-family-planning-worsens-poverty; Blaine Harden, "Birthrates Help Keep Filipinos in Poverty," *The Washington Post*, April 21, 2008, www .washingtonpost.com/wp-dyn/content/story/ 2008/04/21/ST2008042100778.html.

30. Kenneth Fletcher, "Colombia Dispatch 11: Former Bogotá Mayor Enrique Peñalosa," Smithsonian.com, Oct. 29, 2008, www.smithsonianmag.com/travel/ Colombia-Dispatch-11-Former-Bogota-mayor-Enrique-Penalosa.html.

31. Charles Montgomery, "Bogota's Urban Happiness Movement," *Globe and Mail*, June 25, 2007, www .theglobeandmail.com/servlet/story/RTGAM .20070622.whappyurbanmain0623/BNStory/ lifeMain/home.

32. Bus Rapid Transit Planning Guide, 3rd edition, Institute for Transportation & Development Policy, June 2007, p. 1, www.itdp.org/documents/Bus%20 Rapid%20Transit%20Guide%20%20complete%20 guide.pdf.

33. Project details at www.masdaruae.com/en/home/ index.aspx.

34. Awad and Schuler remarks at Greenbuild 2008 conference, Boston, Mass., Nov. 20, 2008.

35. "Green Dreams," Frontline/World, www.pbs.org/ frontlineworld/fellows/green_dreams/; Danielle Sacks, "Green Guru Gone Wrong: William McDonough," *Fast Company*, Oct. 13, 2008, www .fastcompany.com/magazine/130/the-mortal-messiah.html; Timothy Lesle, "Cradle and All," *California Magazine*, September/October 2008, www .alumni.berkeley.edu/California/200809/lesle.asp.

36. Shannon May, "Ecological Crisis and Eco-Villages in China," *Counterpunch*, Nov. 21-23, 2008, www .counterpunch.org/may11212008.html.

37. Rujun Shen, "Eco-city seen as Expensive 'Green-Wash,' " *The Standard* (Hong Kong), June 24, 2008, www.thestandard.com.hk/news_detail.asp?we_ cat=9&art_id=67641&sid=19488136&con_ type=1&d_str=20080624&fc=8; see also Douglas

McGray, "Pop-Up Cities: China Builds a Bright Green Metropolis," *Wired*, April 24, 2007, www.wired.com/wired/archive/15.05/feat_popup.html; Malcolm Moore, "China's Pioneering Eco-City of Dongtan Stalls," *Telegraph*, Oct. 19, 2008, www.telegraph.co.uk/news/worldnews/asia/china/3223969/Chinas-pioneering-eco-city-of-Dongtan-stalls.html; "City of Dreams," *Economist*, March 19, 2009, www.economist.com/world/asia/displaystory.cfm?story_id=13330904.

38. Details at www.tianjinecocity.gov.sg/.

39. "LEED Projects and Case Studies Directory," U.S. Green Building Council, www.usgbc.org/LEED/Project/RegisteredProjectList.aspx.

40. Remarks at Greenbuild 2008 conference, Boston, Mass., Nov. 20, 2008.

41. Population Reference Bureau, "Urbanization," www.prb.org; Tertius Chandler, *Four Thousand Years of Urban Growth: An Historical Census* (1987).

42. Lewis Mumford, *The City In History: Its Origins, Its Transformations, and Its Prospects* (1961), pp. 417-418.

43. Frederick Engels, *The Condition of the Working Class in England* (1854), Chapter 7 ("Results"), online at Marx/Engels Internet Archive, www.marxists.org/archive/marx/works/1845/condition-working-class/ch07.htm.

44. Population Reference Bureau, *op. cit.*

45. Robert A. Caro, *The Power Broker: Robert Moses and the Fall of New York* (1975).

46. Jane Jacobs, *The Death and Life of Great American Cities* (1961).

47. Mumford, *op. cit.*, pp. 454-455.

48. Joshua Kurlantzick, "The Big Mango Bounces Back," *World Policy Journal*, spring 2000, www.worldpolicy.org/journal/articles/kurlant.html; UN-HABITAT, *op. cit.*, pp. 74-76.

49. BBC News, "Interactive Map: Urban Growth," http://news.bbc.co.uk/2/shared/spl/hi/world/06/urbanisation/html/urbanisation.stm.

50. Licia Valladares and Magda Prates Coelho, "Urban Research in Latin America: Towards a Research Agenda," MOST Discussion Paper Series No. 4 (undated), www.unesco.org/most/valleng.htm#trends.

51. Jose de Gregorie, "Sustained Growth in Latin America," Economic Policy Papers, Central Bank of Chile, May 2005, www.bcentral.cl/eng/studies/economic-policy-papers/pdf/dpe13eng.pdf.

52. UN-HABITAT, *op cit.*, pp. 70-74.

53. Hernando de Soto, *The Mystery of Capital: Why Capitalism Triumphs in the West and Fails Everywhere Else* (2000), excerpted at http://ild.org.pe/en/mystery/english?page=0%2C0.

54. Deepak Kindo, "Microfinance Services to the Urban Poor," *Microfinance Insights*, March 2007; World Bank, "10 Years of World Bank Support for Microcredit in Bangladesh," Nov. 5, 2007; "Micro Finance Gaining in Popularity," *The Hindu*, Aug. 25, 2008, www.hindu.com/biz/2008/08/25/stories/2008082550121600.htm.

55. Michael Richardson, "Clinton Warns APEC of 'Digital Divide,' " *International Herald Tribune*, Nov. 16, 2000, www.iht.com/articles/2000/11/16/apec.2.t_2.php.

56. Abigail Keene-Babcock, "Study Shows Half the World's Population With Mobile Phones by 2008," Dec. 4, 2007, www.nextbillion.net/news/study-shows-half-the-worlds-population-with-mobile-phones-by-200.

57. "Millennium Development Goals Report 2008," United Nations, p. 48, www.un.org/millenniumgoals/pdf/The%20Millennium%20Development%20Goals%20Report%202008.pdf.

58. Robyn Dixon, "Zimbabwe Slum Dwellers Are Left With Only Dust," *Los Angeles Times*, June 21, 2005, http://articles.latimes.com/2005/jun/21/world/fg-nohomes21.

59. Ewen MacAskill, "UN Report Damns Mugabe Slum Clearance as Catastrophic," *Guardian*, July 23, 2005, www.guardian.co.uk/world/2005/jul/23/zimbabwe.ewenmacaskill.

60. Freedom House, "Freedom in the World 2008: Zimbabwe," www.freedomhouse.org/uploads/press_release/Zimbabwe_FIW_08.pdf.

61. "Crisis Reveals Growing Finance Gaps for Developing Countries," World Bank, March 8, 2009, http://web.worldbank.org/WBSITE/EXTERNAL/NEWS/

0,,contentMDK:22093316~menuPK:34463~pageP K:34370~piPK:34424~theSitePK:4607,00.html.

62. "Swimming Against the Tide: How Developing Countries Are Coping with the Global Crisis," World Bank, background paper prepared for the G20 finance Ministers meeting, March 13-14, 2009, http:// siteresources.worldbank.org/NEWS/Resources/ swimmingagainstthetide-march2009.pdf.

63. "Major Victories for City Priorities in American Recovery and Reinvestment Act," U.S. Conference of Mayors, Feb. 23, 2009, www.usmayors.org/usmayor newspaper/documents/02_23_09/pg1_major_ victories.asp.

64. Carter Dougherty, "Chinese Premier Injects Note of Optimism at Davos," *The New York Times*, Jan. 29, 2009, www.nytimes.com/2009/01/29/business/ 29econ.html?partner=rss.

65. Jamil Anderlini and Geoff Dyer, "Downturn Causes 20m Job Losses in China," *Financial Times*, Feb. 2, 2009, www.ft.com/cms/s/0/19c25aea-f0f5-11dd-8790-0000779fd2ac.html.

66. Joe McDonald, "World Bank Cuts China's 2009 Growth Forecast," The Associated Press, March 18, 2009.

67. "Bill and Melinda Gates Urge Global Leaders to Maintain Foreign Aid," Bill and Melinda Gates Foundation, Jan. 30, 2009, www.gatesfoundation.org/ press-releases/Pages/2009-world-economic-forum-090130.aspx.

68. Mark Landler and David E. Sanger, "World Leaders Pledge $1.1 Trillion to Tackle Crisis," *The New York Times*, April 4, 2009, www.nytimes.com/2009/ 04/03/world/europe/03summit.html?_r=1&hp.

69. "Is Demolition the Way to Go?" World Bank, www .worldbank.org/urban/upgrading/demolition.html.

70. "What Is Urban Upgrading?" World Bank, www .worldbank.org/urban/upgrading/what.html.

71. For more information, see "Urban Poor Fund," *Shack/Slum Dwellers International*, www.sdinet .co.za/ritual/urban_poor_fund/.

72. Neal R. Peirce, "Gates Millions, Slum-Dwellers: Thanksgiving Miracle?" *Houston Chronicle*, Nov. 22, 2007, www.sdinet.co.za/static/pdf/sdi_gates_ iupf_neal_peirce.pdf.

73. "Statement at the African Ministerial Conference on Housing and Urban Development," UN-HABITAT, Abuja, Nigeria, July 28, 2008, www.unhabitat.org/ content.asp?cid=5830&catid=14&typeid=8&subM enuId=0.

74. Michael Meyer, *The Last Days of Old Beijing* (2008), pp. 54-55; Richard Spencer, "History is Erased as Beijing Makes Way for Olympics," *Telegraph* (London), June 19, 2006, www.telegraph.co.uk/news/ worldnews/asia/china/1521709/History-is-erased-as-Beijing-makes-way-for-Olympics.html; Michael Sheridan, "Old Beijing Falls to Olympics Bulldozer," *Sunday Times* (London), April 29, 2007, www.time sonline.co.uk/tol/news/world/asia/china/article1 719945.ece.

75. Meyer, *op. cit.*, pp. 45, 52.

76. Solomon J. Greene, "Staged Cities: Mega-Events, Slum Clearance, and Global Capital," *Yale Human Rights & Development Law Journal*, vol. 6, 2003, http://islandia.law.yale.edu/yhrdlj/PDF/Vol%206/ greene.pdf.

77. Slum Rehabilitation Authority, "Dharavi Development Project," www.sra.gov.in/htmlpages/Dharavi.htm; Porus P. Cooper, "In India, Slum May Get Housing," *Philadelphia Inquirer*, Sept. 22, 2008.

78. Mukul Devichand, "Mumbai's Slum Solution?" BBC News, Aug. 14, 2008, http://news.bbc.co .uk/2/hi/south_asia/7558102.stm.

79. Henry Chu, "Dharavi, India's Largest Slum, Eyed By Mumbai Developers," *Los Angeles Times*, Sept. 8, 2008, www.latimes.com/news/nationworld/world/ la-fg-dharavi8-2008sep08,0,1830588.story; see also Dominic Whiting, "Dharavi Dwellers Face Ruin in Development Blitz," Reuters, June 6, 2008, http:// in.reuters.com/article/topNews/idINIndia-33958520080608; and Mark Tutton, "Real Life 'Slumdog' Slum To Be Demolished," CNN.com, Feb. 23, 2009, www.cnn.com/2009/TRAVEL /02/23/dharavi.mumbai.slums/.

80. Unless otherwise cited, this section is based on "The 2008 Global Cities Index," *Foreign Policy*, November/December 2008, www.foreignpolicy .com/story/cms.php?story_id=4509.

81. T. Ramavarman, "Masdar To Proceed with $15 Billion Investment Plan," *Khaleej Times Online*, March 16, 2009, www.khaleejtimes.com/biz/inside .asp?xfile=/data/business/2009/March/business_ March638.xml&section=business&col=; Stefan Nicola, "Green Oasis Rises From Desert Sands," *Washington Times*, Feb. 2, 2009, www.washington-times.com/themes/places/abu-dhabi/; Elisabeth Rosenthal, "Gulf Oil States Seeking a Lead in Clean Energy," *The New York Times*, Jan. 13, 2009, www .nytimes.com/2009/01/13/world/middleeast/ 13greengulf.html.

82. David Teather and Richard Wachman, "The Emirate That Used to Spend It Like Beckham," *The Guardian*, Jan. 31, 2009, www.guardian.co.uk/world/2009/ jan/31/dubai-global-recession; Robert F. Worth, "Laid-Off Foreigners Flee as Dubai Spirals Down," *The New York Times*, Feb. 12, 2009, www.nytimes .com/2009/02/12/world/middleeast/12dubai.html; Elizabeth Farrelly, "Dubai's Darkening Sky: The Crane Gods are Still," *Brisbane Times*, Feb. 26, 2009, www.brisbanetimes.com.au/news/opinion/dubais-darkening-sky-the-crane-gods-are-still/2009/02/ 25/1235237781806.html.

83. Raja Murthy, "Taj Mahal Leads India's Recovery," *Asia Times*, Dec. 3, 2008, www.atimes.com/atimes/ South_Asia/JL03Df01.html.

84. Joe Nocera, "Mumbai Finds Its Resiliency," *The New York Times*, Jan. 4, 2009, http://travel.nytimes .com/2009/01/04/travel/04journeys.html.

85. "State of the World's Cities 2010/2011: Bridging the Urban Divide," United Nations Human Settlement Programme, p. viii, www.unhabitat.org/pmss/list ItemDetails.aspx?publicationID=2917.

86. *Ibid.*, p. 30.

87. "The UN Millennium Declaration and its Goals," U.N.-HABITAT, ww2.unhabitat.org/mdg/.

88. Anna K. Tibaijuka, "Introduction," "State of the World's Cities 2010/2011," *op. cit.*

89. *Ibid.*

90. Simon Romero, "Slum Dwellers Are Defying Brazil's Grand Design for Olympics," *The New York Times*, March 4, 2012, www.nytimes.com/2012/03/05/

world/americas/brazil-faces-obstacles-in-prepara tions-for-rio-olympics.html?pagewanted=all.

91. Jason Burke, "Money, power and politics collide in the battle for Mumbai's slums," *The Guardian*, March 5, 2011, www.guardian.co.uk/world/2011/ mar/05/money-power-politics-battle-mumbai-slums.

92. "Global Report on Human Settlements 2011: Cities and Climate Change," U.N.-HABITAT, 2011, www .unhabitat.org/content.asp?typeid=19&catid=555 &cid=9272.

93. Travis Madsen, Benjamin Davis and Phineas Baxandall, "Road Work Ahead: Holding Government Accountable for Fixing America's Crumbling Roads and Bridges," U.S. PIRG Education Fund, April 2010, p. 9, www.uspirg.org/sites/pirg/files/reports/ Road-Work-Ahead.pdf.

94. "Failure to Act: The economic impact of current investment trends in water and wastewater treatment infrastructure," American Society of Civil Engineers, 2011, www.asce.org/uploadedFiles/Infrastructure/ Failure_to_Act/Water%20Report%20Executive %20Summary.pdf. Also see Ashley Halsey III, "Billions needed to upgrade America's leaky water infrastructure," *The Washington Post*, Jan. 2, 2012, www.washingtonpost.com/local/billions-needed-to-upgrade-americas-leaky-water-infrastructure/2011/ 12/22/gIQAdsE0WP_story.html.

95. "Water and Sanitation in an Urbanizing World," U.N.-HABITAT's Water and Sanitation Trust Fund, 2011, www.unhabitat.org/pmss/listItemDetails .aspx?publicationID=3191.

96. "Fast pace of African urbanization affecting water supplies and sanitation," United Nations Environment Programme, March 21, 2011, http://hqweb.unep .org/Documents.Multilingual/Default.asp?Documen tID=664&ArticleID=8666&l=en&t=long.

97. "Cities and Climate Change: An Urgent Agenda," The International Bank for Reconstruction and Development/The World Bank, December 2010, p. 15, http://siteresources.worldbank.org/INTUWM/ Resources/340232-1205330656272/Citiesand ClimateChange.pdf.

98. "Global Report on Human Settlements 2011: Cities and Climate Change," *op. cit.*, p. 4.

99. *Ibid.*, p. 1.

100. *Ibid.*, p. 40.

BIBLIOGRAPHY

Books

Meyer, Michael, *The Last Days of Old Beijing: Life in the Vanishing Backstreets of a City Transformed, Walker & Co.*, 2008.
An English teacher and travel writer traces Beijing's history and describes life in one of its oldest neighborhoods as the city prepared to host the 2008 Olympic Games.

Silver, Christopher, *Planning the Megacity: Jakarta in the Twentieth Century, Routledge*, 2007.
An urban scholar describes how Indonesia's largest city grew from a colonial capital of 150,000 in 1900 into a megacity of 12-13 million in 2000, and concludes that overall the process was well-planned.

2007. State of the World: Our Urban Future, Worldwatch Institute, Norton, 2007.
Published by an environmental think tank, a collection of articles on issues such as sanitation, urban farming and strengthening local economies examines how cities can be healthier and greener.

Articles

"The 2008 Global Cities Index," *Foreign Policy*, November/December 2008, www.foreignpolicy.com/story/cms.php?story_id=4509.
Foreign Policy magazine, the Chicago Council on World Affairs and the A.T. Kearney management consulting firm rank the world's most "global" cities in both industrialized and developing countries, based on economic activity, human capital, information exchange, cultural experience and political engagement.

"Mexico City Bikers Preach Pedal Power in Megacity," *The Associated Press*, Dec. 28, 2008.
Bicycle activists are campaigning for respect in a city with more than 6 million cars, taxis and buses.

Albright, Madeleine, and Hernando De Soto, "Out From the Underground," *Time*, July 16, 2007.
A former U.S. Secretary of State and a prominent Peruvian economist contend that giving poor people basic legal rights can help them move from squatter communities and the shadow economy to more secure lives.

Bloom, David E., and Tarun Khanna, "The Urban Revolution," *Finance & Development*, September 2007, pp. 9-14.
Rapid urbanization is inevitable and could be beneficial if leaders plan for it and develop innovative ways to make cities livable.

Chamberlain, Gethin, "The Beating Heart of Mumbai," *The Observer*, Dec. 21, 2008, www.guardian.co.uk/world/2008/dec/21/dharavi-india-slums-slumdog-millionaire-poverty.
Eight boys growing up in Dharavi, Asia's largest slum, talk about life in their neighborhood.

Osnos, Evan, "Letter From China: The Promised Land," *The New Yorker*, Feb. 9, 2009, www.newyorker.com/reporting/2009/02/09/090209fa_fact_osnos.
Traders from at least 19 countries have set up shop in the Chinese coastal city of Guangzhou to make money in the export-import business.

Packer, George, "The Megacity," *The New Yorker*, Nov. 13, 2006, www.newyorker.com/archive/2006/11/13/061113fa_fact_packer.
Lagos, Nigeria, offers a grim picture of urban life.

Schwartz, Michael, "For Russia's Migrants, Economic Despair Douses Flickers of Hope," *The New York Times*, Feb. 9, 2009, www.nytimes.com/2009/02/10/world/europe/10migrants.html?n=Top/Reference/Times%20Topics/People/P/Putin,%20Vladimir%20V.
Russia has an estimated 10 million migrant workers, mainly from former Soviet republics in Central Asia — some living in shanty towns.

Reports and Studies

"Ranking of the World's Cities Most Exposed to Coastal Flooding Today and in the Future," *Organization for*

Economic Cooperation and Development, 2007, www
.rms.com/Publications/OECD_Cities_Coastal_
Flooding.pdf.
As a result of urbanization and global climate change, up
to 150 million people in major cities around the world
could be threatened by flooding by 2070.

"State of World Population 2007," *U.N. Population
Fund*, **2007, www.unfpa.org/upload/lib_pub_file/
695_filename_sowp2007_eng.pdf.**

A U.N. agency outlines the challenges and opportunities
presented by urbanization and calls on policy makers to
help cities improve residents' lives.

**"State of the World's Cities 2008/2009: Harmonious
Cities," UN-HABITAT, 2008.**
The biennial report from the U.N. Human Settlements
Programme surveys urban growth patterns and social,
economic and environmental conditions in cities
worldwide.

For More Information

Chicago Council on Global Affairs, 332 South Michigan
Ave., Suite 1100, Chicago, IL 60604; (312) 726-3860; www
.thechicagocouncil.org. A nonprofit research and public
education group; runs the Global Chicago Center, an initiative to strengthen Chicago's international connections, and
co-authors the Global Cities Index.

Clean Air Initiative for Asian Cities, CAI-Asia Center,
3510 Robinsons Equitable Tower, ADB Avenue, Ortigas
Center, Pasig City, Philippines 1605; (632) 395-2843; www
.cleanairnet.org/caiasia. A nonprofit network that promotes
and demonstrates innovative ways to improve air quality in
Asian cities.

Institute for Liberty and Democracy, Las Begonias 441,
Oficina 901, San Isidro, Lima 27, Peru; (51-1) 616-6100;
http://ild.org.pe. Think tank headed by economist Hernando
de Soto that promotes legal tools to help the world's poor move
from the extralegal economy into an inclusive market economy.

Overseas Development Institute, 111 Westminster Bridge
Road, London SE1 7JD, United Kingdom; (44) (0)20 7922

0300; www.odi.org.uk. An independent British think tank
focusing on international development and humanitarian
issues.

Shack/Slum Dwellers International; (+27) 21 689 9408;
www.sdinet.co.za. The Web site for the South Africa-based
secretariat of an international network of organizations of
the urban poor in 23 developing countries.

UN-HABITAT, P.O. Box 30030 GPO, Nairobi, 00100,
Kenya; (254-20) 7621234; www.unhabitat.org. The
United Nations Human Settlements Programme; works
to promote socially and environmentally sustainable cities
and towns.

World Bank, 1818 H Street, N.W., Washington, DC 20433,
USA; (202) 473-1000; http://web.worldbank.org. Two
development institutions with 185 member countries, which
provide loans, credits and grants to middle-income developing countries (International Bank for Reconstruction and
Development) and the poorest developing countries (International Development Association).

Voices From Abroad:

DAVID DODMAN

Researcher, International Institute for Environment and Development, England

Cities aren't to blame for climate change.
"Blaming cities for climate change is far too simplistic. There are a lot of economies of scale associated with energy use in cities. If you're an urban dweller, particularly in an affluent country like Canada or the U.K., you're likely to be more efficient in your use of heating fuel and in your use of energy for transportation."

Toronto Star, March 2009

BABATUNDE FASHOLA

State Governor Lagos, Nigeria

Megacities create many challenges.
"Because of human activities there will be conflict and there will be the issue of security, everybody fighting for control, and these are some of the challenges that come with the status of a megacity. It is really a status that creates certain challenges that the government must respond to."

This Day (Nigeria), November 2007

JONATHAN WOETZEL

Director, McKinsey & Company, Shanghai

Migration to China could cause problems.
"The fact that 40 to 50 per cent of [Chinese] cities [by 2025] could be made up of migrant workers is a real wake-up call. Smaller cities in particular are going to face a growing challenge if they are to provide equal access to social services."

Irish Times, March 2008

Cagle Cartoons, La Prensa, Panama/Arcadio Esquivel

THE WORLD BANK

Singapore does it right.
"Improving institutions and infrastructure and intervening at the same time is a tall order for any government, but

Singapore shows how it can be done. . . . Multi-year plans were produced, implemented and updated. For a city-state in a poor region, it is also not an exaggeration to assert that effective urbanization was responsible for delivering growth rates that averaged 8 per cent a year throughout 1970s and 1980s."

World Development Report 2009

THORAYA AHMED OBAID

Executive Director, U.N. Population Fund

Informal work has value.
"Many of tomorrow's city dwellers will be poor, swelling the ranks of the billion who already live in slums, but however bad their predicament, experience shows that newcomers do not leave the city once they have moved. . . . They are also remarkably productive. Economists agree that informal work makes a vital contribution to the urban economy and is a key growth factor in developing countries."

The Guardian (England), July 2007

ZHU TONG

Environmental Scientist, Peking University

Different air standards cause confusion.
"Different countries vary in their air quality standards, and the WHO does not have a binding set of standards. China's national standards are not as high as those in developed countries, which has led to disagreements, confusion or even misunderstandings."

South China Morning Post, July 2008

SUDIRMAN NASIR

Lecturer, University of Hasanuddin, Indonesia

Opportunities lead to migration.
"The lack of job and economic opportunities in rural areas justifies migration to the cities as a survival strategy. It is a rational choice made by villagers because cities generally have more jobs to offer. It's impossible to reduce urbanization through the repressive approach."

Jakarta Post (Indonesia),
October 2008

7

Aging Infrastructure

Marcia Clemmitt and Reed Karaim

Steam explodes from a burst pipe near Manhattan's Grand Central Station on July 18, 2007. One person was killed and several injured. Throughout the country, many facilities and systems are 50-100 years old, and engineers say they have been woefully neglected. Now lawmakers are debating whether aging infrastructure merits higher taxes or other measures, such as turning more highways into privately managed toll roads.

From *CQ Researcher*,
September 28, 2007 (updated June 14, 2012).

O n Aug. 1, 24-year-old Gary Babineau was driving across the I-35 West bridge in Minneapolis when it collapsed, plunging more than 100 vehicles into the Mississippi River and killing 13 people.

After falling about 30 feet, Babineau's pickup truck dangled over the edge of a bridge section as cars hurtled past him into the water. "The whole bridge from one side of the Mississippi to the other just completely gave way," Babineau told CNN. "I stayed in my car until the cars quit falling for a second, then I got out real quick." He and other survivors then helped children in a school bus scramble off the bridge.[1]

The fatal collapse brought to mind other recent infrastructure failures — including the aging underground steam pipe that burst in New York City two weeks earlier, killing a pedestrian and injuring several others. More important, the collapse raised concern about the condition of the nation's dams, water and sewer lines, electric power networks and other vital systems. Many were constructed decades ago, during a 75-year building boom, and are nearing the end of their intended lifespan, engineering groups say.

"The steam pipe that blew up in New York was over 80 years old," says David G. Mongan, president-elect of the American Society of Civil Engineers (ASCE).[2]

Indeed, because of increasing user demand and years of neglected maintenance, the U.S. infrastructure overall rates a near-failing grade of "D" from the ASCE. The group says a $1.6-trillion, five-year investment is needed to bring facilities up to snuff.[3]

Many Bridges Are "Structurally Deficient"

Twelve percent of all bridges in the United States — nearly 75,000 structures — are structurally deficient, according to the Department of Transportation. In four states — Oklahoma, Iowa, Pennsylvania and Rhode Island — more than 20 percent of the bridges are deficient.

Percentage of Structurally Deficient Bridges by State, 2006

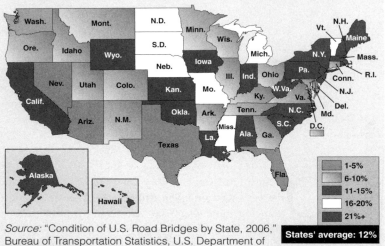

1-5%
6-10%
11-15%
16-20%
21%+

States' average: 12%

Source: "Condition of U.S. Road Bridges by State, 2006," Bureau of Transportation Statistics, U.S. Department of Transportation

Much of the existing U.S infrastructure was built in the 1930s, '40s and '50s and today carries loads that "are magnitudes beyond" what its builders anticipated, he says.

As the Water Environment Foundation (WEF) puts it: "A hundred years ago, Teddy Roosevelt was president, crossword puzzles hadn't been invented, Las Vegas had a population of 39 people and your sewer system was brand new." The nonprofit advocacy group seeks to focus attention on infrastructure that's mainly out of sight and out of mind until a catastrophic event like a bridge collapse.

Infrastructure consists of the structures and systems that "we can't do without," says Paula R. Worthington, a lecturer in economics at the University of Chicago's Harris School of Public Policy.

While vital, infrastructure is also easy to ignore. In fact, a good definition of infrastructure could be "all the things that we take for granted somebody is taking care of," says Linda Kelly, the WEF's managing director of

public communications and the former deputy director of the Portland, Ore., water system.

But Americans have not been taking good care of their infrastructure, many analysts say. For one thing, politicians generally believe they gain more political capital from new projects than from maintaining and upgrading old systems, even heavily used ones.

Washington "is a classic case," says Heywood Sanders, a professor of public administration at the University of Texas, San Antonio. "There are a great number of older highways" in the nation's capital that need fixing, disastrously deteriorating school buildings and more, Sanders says. "But what you've got is a new convention center and a brand-new ballpark. In a city that needs a great many things, those are the things that happen."

Focusing public attention on the need for maintenance funds "unfortunately takes some kind of major problem," says Rob Villee, executive director of the Plainfield Area Regional Sewerage Authority in Middlesex, N.J. The result is that few infrastructure agencies "do proactive maintenance." In every town, many interests fight for a piece of the public budget, "and until [a sewer] backs up into the house of somebody important," sewer maintenance seldom commands attention and dollars, he says.

Ownership issues also work against proper maintenance and improvements to privately owned infrastructure, such as the electric system, says Richard Little, director of the Keston Institute for Public Finance and Infrastructure Policy at the University of Southern California (USC).

Since government-imposed ownership rules were removed for electrical utilities during the 1990s, "the new owners of transmission capacity" — power lines — "aren't in the electricity-generation business," says Little. Such owners may have little financial incentive to upgrade their systems, he says. "When the system was vertically integrated" — with the same companies owning both power-generation facilities and transmission lines — "there was a stronger business reason for keeping it up." Today, however, "the great national transmission grid is not as integrated as we think" — and potentially more vulnerable to failures such as blackouts.

As the Minneapolis bridge collapse starkly showed, neglect comes with a price.

After the accident, a construction-industry official told the *Minneapolis Star-Tribune* that some workers at the Minnesota Department of Transportation had been "deathly afraid that this kind of tragedy was going to be visited on us." Some "were screaming" to have "fracture-critical" bridges like I-35 West "replaced" sooner than the state had budgeted for.[4]

Bridges aren't the only infrastructure sector that is collapsing. The increasing frequency of sinkholes that swallow people and property is evidence of deteriorating wastewater infrastructure, says Kelly. When an underground sewer pipe springs a leak, soil seeps into the crack and is carried away, and eventually "the soil can't support heavy cars or a building," she explains.

Last December, a 64-year-old Brooklyn, N.Y., woman carrying groceries home was injured when she fell into a five-foot-deep sinkhole that opened under the sidewalk. The same month, a 30-foot-deep sinkhole shut down a stretch of California's famed Pacific Coast Highway near Malibu, while in Portland, Ore., a sinkhole swallowed a 40-foot-long sewer-repair truck. A few months earlier, a 2-year-old boy in Irving, Texas, may have disappeared into a sinkhole while playing in a park; the child was never recovered.[5]

Dams are another growing concern. At least 23 have failed in the past four years, including Ka Loko Dam in Kauai, Hawaii, which collapsed in March 2006 killing seven people and causing at least $50 million in property and environmental damage.[6]

And the spate of air-traffic delays that stranded thousands of vacation travelers just this summer is directly due to a lack of important upgrades to the air-traffic control system, says the ASCE's Mongan. Airports can't land as many planes as they could because outdated radar tracking systems make it unsafe to space planes as closely as modern GPS tracking systems would allow, he says.

Virtually all infrastructure analysts say upgrades and maintenance require more funding, but increasing taxes to raise the money is sparking hot debate in Washington. As early as the 1930s, states introduced fuel taxes to pay for road construction, and the main federal source of highway funds today is an 18.4-cents-per-gallon gasoline tax, last increased in 1993.[7]

"I consider it ludicrous that the United States has the lowest gas taxes in the world," says Lt. Gen. Hank Hatch, a former chief of the U.S. Army Corps of Engineers who chairs the Board on Infrastructure and Environment at the National Research Council. "If we had a higher one, we could do amazing things."

But the Bush administration and some conservatives oppose any tax increases.

"Increasing federal taxes and spending would likely do little, if anything, to address either the quality or performance of our roads," Secretary of Transportation Mary E. Peters told the House Transportation Committee on Sept. 5. The occasion was a hearing on legislation sponsored by Committee Chairman James Oberstar, D-Minn., to raise the federal gas tax to 23.3 cents to create a bridge-maintenance trust fund.[8]

Later, President George W. Bush told Democratic and Republican backers of the increase that the real problem with highway upkeep is funding that lawmakers divert to low-priority pet projects. Bush opposes increasing the gas tax, he said, because it "could affect economic growth" negatively.[9]

With tax funds hard to come by, some highway and water agencies are opting for long-term lease agreements allowing private companies to operate and perhaps build facilities and collect tolls for their upkeep. Such "public-private partnerships" also are hotly debated.

Proponents praise the private sector's ingenuity and efficiency. "We need flexible solutions and, quite often, the most flexible minds are in the private sector," says Eli Lehrer, a senior fellow at the libertarian Competitive Enterprise Institute.

But most citizens feel more confident that their interests will be protected if local government manages infrastructure, said Wenonah Hauter, executive director of the advocacy group Food and Water Watch, which challenges private takeover of water systems. "They don't want a really important public service like water to be privatized," Hauter said. "They don't want the customer call center to be 1,000 miles away. They don't want their water rates going up."[10]

When it comes down to a choice between taxes and user fees like tolls, the public's first choice is "neither,"

Federal Spending Cuts Shift Burden to States

The percentage of federal spending on transportation and water infrastructure has been decreasing since 1981, forcing cash-strapped states to pick up more of the expenses.

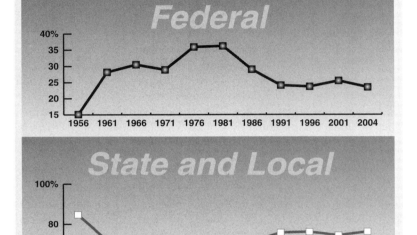

Percentage of Public Spending Spent on Infrastructure, 1956-2004

Source: "Trends in Public Spending on Transportation and Water Infrastructure, 1956 to 2004," Congressional Budget Office, August 2007

says Little. "People would rather ride on a nice road for free than pay $6."

As voters, legislators and engineers contemplate solutions to crumbling highways and sewer lines, here are some questions being asked:

Does aging infrastructure endanger Americans?

No one argues the U.S. infrastructure is not deteriorating. But opinions vary about the amount of danger the deterioration poses.

"All materials deteriorate, and fatigue will hit every bridge eventually," says Thomas Baber, an associate professor of engineering at the University of Virginia. "If you put a bridge out there long enough," exposed to traffic stress, water, sulfurous chemicals in the air in industrial areas and road salts, "it will get corrosion," he says. Water

alone "is a very effective solvent, eating through paints and through steel," Baber says.

But even engineers are sometimes surprised by structural deterioration, says Ziyad Duron, a professor of engineering at Harvey Mudd College in Claremont, Calif. A few years ago, Duron was "leaning on a bridge in Massachusetts, and all of a sudden I found myself with one of the bolts in my hand."

Life-threatening events like dangerous sinkholes are on the rise, while the risk of other catastrophic events like dam and bridge failures is also increasing, some experts say.

The condition of many U.S. bridges is "quite scary" because many "are approaching the end of their useful life, which is typically 50 to 75 years," and "due to less than adequate maintenance over the years on some of these structures, anything could happen without warning," says Abi Aghayere, a professor of civil engineering at New York's Rochester Institute of Technology.

Dams are likely in worse condition than bridges, some engineers say.

Since 1998, the number of unsafe dams in the United States has increased by 33 percent, according to the American Society of Civil Engineers. The total number of dams whose failure could cause loss of life has risen from 9,281 to 10,094 over that period, largely because of population growth immediately downstream from dams and underfunding of government dam-safety agencies, according to the advocacy group Dam Safety Coalition.[11]

"Every moment of every day, unsafe dams form a vast reservoir of danger throughout America," warned journalist Gaylord Shaw, who won a 1978 Pulitzer Prize for a *Los Angeles Times* series investigating the nation's dams. "When a dam fails . . . the events usually are viewed as local, transitory incidents rather than a symbol of a national problem," but "the cumulative hazard posed by unsafe dams is huge."[12]

And it's not just dams and bridges. The past year has seen a near-epidemic of sinkholes in most states, and the trend is likely to continue.

When underground sewer pipes break, the soil above falls into the crack and the "broken pipes whisk dirt away like a vacuum cleaner," said Thomas Rooney, CEO of Insituform Technologies, a pipe-repair company in Chesterfield, Mo. "When enough soil disappears above the pipe, but below a road or park or home, a sinkhole forms."

"All over America, engineers are telling city councils, water boards, sewer districts and other public agencies and officials about the dismal conditions of their water and sewer pipes," said Rooney. But "they would rather wait until the next catastrophe."[13]

Nevertheless, most of the infrastructure is basically safe, say many experts.

So-called "truss" bridges, like Minneapolis' I-35 West bridge, aren't dangerous in and of themselves, for example, says the University of Virginia's Baber. "We have been building truss structures for about 150 years, and by and large, they're very safe."

Furthermore, "We're much better today at monitoring" structures to catch problems before catastrophic failures, says Donald Vannoy, professor emeritus of civil engineering at the University of Maryland. "This failure in Minnesota is very strange and unusual."

"I don't think we're moving into an era of regular catastrophic failure, like a Minneapolis bridge every three months," says Little at the University of Southern California. In Minneapolis, "a certain bridge didn't get what it needed, and there was a failure."

The main effects of infrastructure aging are low-level, chronic problems, not catastrophes, many analysts say.

For example, if water quality deteriorates because of aging pipes in a region's water-supply system, "there's no explosion, or 100,000 people" suddenly inundated, as in a dam collapse, says Charles N. Haas, a professor of environmental engineering at Philadelphia's Drexel University. Nevertheless, what does result is "a low-level but continuous exposure" to chemical and biological hazards for hundreds of thousands of people, which may seriously harm the health of some, Haas says.

Some undue alarm about aging infrastructure comes from the way infrastructure deficiencies are categorized and

Water from the Ka Loko Reservoir rushes over an earthen dam that gave way on March 14, 2006, killing several people in Lilhue, Hawaii. It is one of 23 U.S. dams that have collapsed in the last four years.

AP Photo/Bruce Asato

sold to the public and policy makers both by federal agencies and private groups, says Sanders at the University of Texas.

When engineers calculate totals of obsolete structures, the number usually includes both "functionally obsolete" facilities — those that aren't big enough to accommodate today's needs — and "structurally deficient" structures — those that are falling into disrepair, Sanders explains. Furthermore, a "structurally deficient" bridge "may have a bad roadway," which can be fixed by resurfacing and doesn't pose any danger of the bridge falling down, he says. It's important to sort out those categories and not simply assume that all "deficient" structures are actually dangerous, he says.

Should taxes be increased to overhaul the infrastructure?

As both publicly and privately owned infrastructure age, maintenance and replacement costs are inevitable, as are costs for monitoring their safety and reliability. Some analysts argue that current decision-making processes are so flawed that money raised by tax increases would be squandered.

Maintaining aging infrastructure undoubtedly costs more money than we have been spending, most analysts say.

As in many other areas of life, with infrastructure age comes increasing responsibility, says Bernard Wasow, an

Report Card Shows No Improvement

The nation's transportation infrastructure has not significantly improved since 2001, according to the American Society of Civil Engineers (ASCE). Much of the infrastructure has remained either structurally deficient or functionally obsolete, according to the ASCE. Moreover, in most instances, spending for maintenance, repairs and replacements has not met the group's requirements.

Infrastructure Grades, 2001 and 2005

Subject	2001 grade	2005 grade
Bridges	C	C
The percentage of the nation's structurally deficient or functionally obsolete bridges decreased from 28.5 to 27.1 percent from 2000 to 2003. However, it will cost $9.4 billion a year for the next 20 years to eliminate all deficiencies.		
Dams	D	D
Since 1998, the number of unsafe dams has risen by 33 percent to over 3,000. Federally owned dams are in good condition. It will cost $10.1 billion over the next 12 years to address all non-federal dams in critical condition.		
Drinking Water	D	D-
The United States faces an $11 billion annual shortfall to replace aging water facilities and comply with safe-drinking-water regulations. In 2005, federal funding for drinking water totaled $850 billion, 10 percent less than the total national requirement.		
National Power Grid	D+	D
Continual growth in electricity demand and investment in new power plants have not been matched by investments in new transmission facilities. Existing transmission capability leaves consumers vulnerable to blackouts. Maintenance spending has decreased by 1 percent annually since 1992.		
Roads	D+	D
Poor road conditions cost motorists $54 billion a year in operating costs and repairs. Americans spend 3.5 billion hours a year stuck in traffic, costing the economy $63.2 billion. Spending on transportation infrastructure currently totals $59.4 billion, well below the necessary $94 billion.		
Wastewater	D	D-
Aging wastewater systems discharge billions of gallons of untreated sewage into surface waters each year. The EPA estimates that $390 billion over the next 20 years will be required to replace existing systems, but in 2005 Congress cut funding for wastewater management for the first time in eight years.		

Source: American Society of Civil Engineers, www.asce.org/reportcard/2005/page.cfm? id=103

economist and senior fellow at the liberal Century Foundation. "It's just like when your kids get older and need a college education. With time, come things you've got to pay for."

Furthermore, "compared to other nations like Japan, we do spend a smaller amount of [the gross domestic product]" on infrastructure, says Texas' Sanders.

In fact, it's the dauntingly high cost of properly maintaining the nation's vast infrastructure that has partly prevented the job from being done, says Little at the University of Southern California (USC). "We need to spend a couple of hundred billion dollars a year forever," and that prospect is too daunting for most policy makers to face, he says.

Many analysts say fuel taxes and other infrastructure-supporting taxes are too low, as are fees for infrastructure use, such as household water fees and highway tolls.

As an anti-tax movement has flourished over the past few decades, distrust of government and the belief that any tax is too high a tax have spread, says Jeffrey Buxbaum, a transportation consultant with Massachusetts-based Cambridge Systematics. Infrastructure maintenance has been stinted by "the legacy of 'No taxes' and 'The government isn't to be trusted,'" he says.

Furthermore, "there's a lack of understanding of how much people actually pay in the form of gas taxes," a common funding source for transportation infrastructure, says Buxbaum. In Massachusetts, for instance, the average person pays about "$150 a year" in state fuel taxes, "and if you wanted to raise it by a few cents" to pay for maintenance, "that would amount to less than $100 a year" per household, he says.

Anti-tax protests over the past couple of decades have all but paralyzed politicians on infrastructure, says Little. "Even if they want to do the progressive thing, they worry because the anti-tax groups are going to get them."

"We've been spoiled in this country. We don't pay market rates for much of anything, and we have allowed the tax rebels to drive the agenda," says Little. "We have people in California in $100-million homes paying only hundreds of dollars in taxes. How silly is that?"

Many infrastructure-related fees also are too low, many analysts say.

"We aren't charging enough" for water to either residential or business users, for example, says Drexel University's Haas.

The federal gasoline tax and many state gasoline taxes are flat, cents-per-gallon taxes that have remained the same for years. Many economists argue that fuel taxes should be "indexed" to inflation or some other economic marker, simply to prevent them from losing value as all other costs in the nation rise — including the cost of maintaining roads and bridges.

Not only does a non-indexed tax lose its value over time, but the "unit-tax" structure of the current federal gas tax can actually cause tax revenues to drop when the price of gas rises, says Joel B. Slemrod, a professor of business economics and public policy at the University of Michigan. If a higher price leads people to buy less gas, then revenue drops from a cents-on-the-gallon tax, he explains.

Gas taxes "absolutely" should be indexed to rise with other prices, says Robert W. Poole Jr., director of transportation studies at the libertarian Reason Foundation in Los Angeles. "But I've talked myself blue in the face trying to convince" conservative colleagues of that, he says. "Indexing of the fuel tax is not a tax increase; it's just a way of keeping the value of the tax from completely deteriorating over time," says Poole.

New, highly targeted — but relatively painless — taxes also could meet some non-highway infrastructure

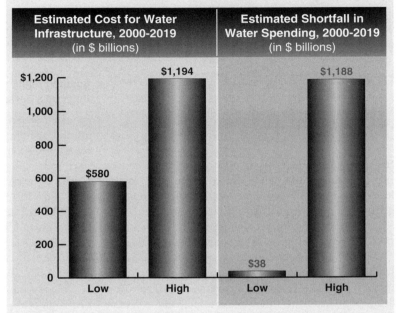

Shortfall Projected in Water Spending

The United States will need up to $1.1 trillion to meet future U.S. water infrastructure needs (left). However, Environmental Protection Agency analysts say if present funding trends continue, the U.S. could end up as much as $1.1 trillion short of that goal (right).

Estimated Cost for Water Infrastructure, 2000-2019 (in $ billions)		Estimated Shortfall in Water Spending, 2000-2019 (in $ billions)	
Low: $580	High: $1,194	Low: $38	High: $1,188

Sources: "Water Infrastructure: Comprehensive Asset Management Has Potential to Help Utilities Better Identify Needs and Plan Future Investments," General Accounting Office, March 2004; Claudia Copeland and Mary Tiemann, "Water Infrastructure Needs and Investment: Review and Analysis of Key Issues," Congressional Research Service, June 13, 2007

needs, says Little. To pay for water infrastructure, "you could put a very small 1-cent-per-roll tax on toilet tissue or on soap. That would create a tremendous amount of money," he says. "We would need a responsible agency to dispense it well, however."

Nevertheless, the Bush administration strongly opposes any tax increases, including the gas-tax hike some members of Congress propose to finance a repair fund for aging bridges.

And one federal lawmaker goes so far as to argue that even cutting gas taxes to decrease the cost of driving in this era of high fuel prices would not harm infrastructure maintenance.

Rep. John "Randy" Kuhl, R-N.Y., has introduced legislation to cut the gas tax by 10 cents a gallon if the price

AP Photo/*St. Cloud Times*/Kimm Anderson

A sinkhole blocks a road in St. Cloud, Minn., on July 19, 2007. Sinkholes are often caused by deteriorating underground sewer pipes. When they spring a leak, soil seeps into the crack and is carried away, undermining roads and other sites above the pipes.

of gas rises above $3. The tax cut wouldn't "hurt money that is directed to the Highway Trust Fund . . . as the lower gas prices will send more people to the pumps and generate similar revenue," said Kuhl in a statement.[14]

Even many who support higher taxes say new revenues might accomplish little without better priority-setting.

Maintenance of current infrastructure often loses out in the political process to flashy, perhaps unnecessary, new projects like ballparks or oversized bridges, says Texas' Sanders. "If you pour more money into a system that favors certain kinds of outcomes, you'll just continue to get the same outcomes."

Even when citizens vote for higher taxes to shore up infrastructure, lawmakers often reserve the option to shift the funding to other purposes, says Little.

In 2002, nearly 70 percent of California voters approved legislative Proposition 42 to allocate a portion of the state sales tax to transportation infrastructure. "But there was a kick-out clause," says USC's Little. "The governor could take the money and spend it for a non-transportation budget emergency" if he chose. "So even when you've had a designated [infrastructure] fund, it still gets robbed," he says.

About $2.5 billion of supposedly dedicated transportation funds has been diverted to other purposes under the state's Proposition 42 escape clause since 2002, according to Transportation California, an advocacy group seeking stronger protection for the funds.[15]

But even if infrastructure agencies can hold onto their funds, they should be required to make more thoughtful use

of the money, said Robert Puentes, a fellow in the Metropolitan Policy Program at the centrist Brookings Institution.

"Billions of dollars of additional federal investments, without significant reform, will do precious little to fix our rusting bridges, expand our overcrowded transit systems, or unclog our ports," Puentes said. As a condition of approving any new funding, such as a gas-tax hike, "agencies should set annual performance objectives, and consequences should be established for . . . poor implementation," Puentes said.[16]

Should private companies run more of America's infrastructure?

In search of better financing and efficiency, governments around the United States and worldwide are turning roads, bridges and water systems over to private companies under long-term leases and other arrangements. Critics argue that social equity may be threatened, however, when for-profit operators aggressively raise fees to levels that threaten people's access to public facilities.

"Roads run by private companies tend to be kept up a little better because the companies are under contract and have to do certain things or they don't get paid," says Little, at USC's infrastructure institute.

Private groups "really do look at a road as a business," says Poole of the Reason Foundation. For example, while public agencies will immediately build all the on and off ramps they believe a highway will ever need, "a private company is more likely to "just build some, and leave the option of adding more later," speeding the building process and saving upfront dollars, he says.

A major reason for turning over infrastructure operation to a private enterprise that will collect fees for the service is governments' need to find new sources of funding, say privatization supporters.

"Cities, counties and states are maxing out their debt limits," and many can't pay for new infrastructure, says Richard Norment, executive director of the National Council for Public-Private Partnerships, a membership group. That's where the private sector can step in to help, he says.

"Public-private partnerships tap into a much broader and deeper range of funding sources" than are available to governments alone, says the Reason Foundation's Poole. Governments borrow in the municipal bond market, which has inflexible rules and requires money to be repaid on a fixed schedule, says Poole. Guaranteeing such fixed investor returns on an infrastructure project can become impossible "if a project misses its traffic target for five years," for example, he says.

Private companies, on the other hand, can "tap brand-new equity investment funds" whose investors are paid "only when the project is in the black," Poole explains.

But privatized infrastructure projects also have their downsides. In many cases, "governments may lose more than they gain," said Brookings' Puentes. "All that upfront cash looks sweet, but the long-term revenue stream is lost since all the toll receipts flow directly to the private operators. Governments also lose the option to borrow against those future revenues."[17]

Wasow of the Century Foundation questions whether the private sector will maintain its interest in infrastructure over the long haul. "Will private companies necessarily want to keep running infrastructure projects" as roads and structures age and require greater upkeep? he asks. "The first 10 years after something's constructed you've got low maintenance costs. But over time they'll rise," he says.

Furthermore, "what happens to fairness?" Wasow asks. "Everybody — left, right and center — basically believes that maintaining infrastructure is ultimately the province of government," since infrastructure like roads is, by definition, something that all residents need to go about their daily business, he says. "This means that a reasonable question to ask is, If government is not providing these goods that we all agree are public, what happens to fairness? Should everyone be required to pay private tolls" to use public facilities like water and bridges, even those who make very little money?

Experts on all sides of the issue generally agree that the details of a private-management contract can make or break it.

"The key thing" is making sure that private companies "actually take the risk," and not just rake in profits "while the public sector gets screwed" if the private managers fail or bail, says Lehrer of the Competitive Enterprise Institute. There should be "no explicit or implicit guarantee" that the government will bail out a private entity that gets into trouble managing an infrastructure asset, he says. "I believe the profit system is very good for society, but the flip side is that private entities must be exposed to the loss" if they don't manage projects well.

The key to a project that succeeds is "picking your partners carefully," says Norment. In some high-profile private-management failures, contracts have been awarded for political reasons or through cronyism, he says. A Mexican city whose privatized water system collapsed had awarded the contract to a company owned "by a guy who'd never built a water project before, the brother-in-law of the governor," he says.

But while good contracts are crucial, good infrastructure-contracting practices are "probably hard for local governments to understand" today, says Shama Gamkhar, an associate professor of public affairs at the University of Texas, Austin. While the United States did have private toll roads in the 18th and 19th centuries, in recent memory U.S. toll roads have been operated by governments, as are most water systems. Today, however, privatization of toll-based infrastructure like roads and water is a new trend, and "people just learn [about contract design and management] on the job," she says. "There's not much experience to fall back on."

BACKGROUND
Meeting Needs

The late-19th through the mid-20th century was a time of massive infrastructure building in the United States, from interstate highways to sewer lines and water-treatment plants. And in the days when narrow, unpaved roads made travel a nightmare and untreated sewage contaminated rivers and other drinking-water sources, Americans weren't all that reluctant to ante up dollars for improvements.[18]

So vital was municipal infrastructure that water-treatment and power plants often were conceived as "objects of immense civic pride and sometimes monumental beauty," according to the advocacy group Environmental Defense. Buildings like the Boston Water Works were designed by top architects and became models of design for their communities, their styles copied by residential and commercial builders alike. The facilities "served as potent symbols of common purpose and progress in a young and rapidly growing nation," says the group.[19]

The need for clean drinking water to prevent disease spurred heroic infrastructure-building efforts around the country. At the turn of the 20th century, deadly waterborne diseases like cholera and typhoid killed many Americans,

CHRONOLOGY

1900s-1960s *Federal government helps states build national transportation and water infrastructure.*

1908 Jersey City is first water district to chlorinate drinking water.

1916 Congress enacts Federal-Aid Highway Program, giving federal matching funds to states for road building.

1927 New York City and Jersey City are linked beneath the Hudson River by the Holland Tunnel, named for Clifford Holland, who invented the tunnel's fan system — including an 80-foot-diameter fan — that vents deadly car exhaust.

1940 First section opens on Pennsylvania Turnpike, the first U. S. highway with no cross streets, railroad crossings or traffic lights.

1956 President Dwight D. Eisenhower commits $25 billion to the national highway system, raising the federal funding share from 50 percent to 90 percent.

1965 Major power blackout in the Northeast spurs establishment of North American Electric Reliability Council (NAERC), a public-private consortium of power producers to set voluntary infrastructure standards for the electricity industry.

1970s *Federal role in infrastructure building peaks.*

1972 Clean Water Act spurs localities to enlarge water-treatment plants.

1977 President Jimmy Carter becomes an advocate for dam safety after a 78-year-old dam in his home state of Georgia collapses, killing 39 people.

1980s *Concern grows about aging infrastructure.*

1988 "Fragile Foundations" report by the National Council on Public Works Improvement recommends doubling infrastructure spending.

1990s-2000s *Federal funding is cut for highways and wastewater cleanup as engineers complain about neglected maintenance.*

1993 Sewage in Milwaukee's drinking water kills 100 residents.

2000 Milwaukee's Hoan Bridge partially collapses; no one is injured.

2001 Environmental Protection Agency (EPA) says $151 billion is needed over the next 20 years to upgrade drinking-water systems.

2003 Failure of Michigan's Silver Lake Dam causes $100 million in damage. . . . Electrical-transmission grid fails, blacking out 50 million customers in the Eastern U.S. and Canada for up to 24 hours and shutting down air traffic, mass transit and sewer and water systems. . . . EPA says $390 billion is needed to upgrade wastewater systems over 20 years.

2004 Failure of Mississippi's Big Bay Lake Dam destroys 100 homes. . . . NAERC declares "urgent need" for Congress to replace voluntary reliability standards for electric companies with mandates.

2005 Businesses in Taunton, Mass., close for a week after the 173-year-old, 12-foot-tall wooden Whitenton Mills Dam begins to buckle. . . . New Orleans floods when Hurricane Katrina overwhelms the inadequate levee system. . . . Chicago's Skyway toll bridge comes under private management. . . . More than 10 billion gallons of untreated sewage spill into Lake Erie because of broken pipes and overflows from overburdened local sewage systems in northern Ohio.

2006 Ka Loko Dam in Kauai, Hawaii, fails, killing seven people. . . . Three-hour power failure at a Washington, D.C., sewage-treatment plant spills 17 million gallons of raw sewage into Potomac River.

2007 An 80-year-old underground steam pipe bursts in Manhattan, killing one person. . . . A 95-year-old water pipe breaks in Seattle, cutting off residential water service and creating a sinkhole that swallows two cars. . . . I-35 West bridge over the Mississippi River collapses in Minneapolis at rush hour, sending dozens of cars into the water and killing 13 people. In public opinion poll a week later, two-thirds of the respondents oppose raising gas taxes to fix the nation's bridges.

2008

January — A steep economic downturn takes hold, reducing state and local revenues for infrastructure projects and maintenance.

2009

January — Gallup poll finds Americans rank near bottom among citizens of developed nations in satisfaction with public transportation.

March — The American Society of Civil Engineers gives U.S. infrastructure a grade of D and estimates it would take $2.2 trillion over five years to update it to "good" condition.

February — President signs the American Recovery and Reinvestment Act of 2009, commonly known as the Stimulus Act, which includes $64 billion — or 8 percent of the total — for roads, public transport, rail, bridges, aviation and wastewater systems.

2010

Summer — Stimulus spending for infrastructure reaches its peak, but fails to meet most expectations. Republican

Govs. Scott Walker of Wisconsin and John Kasich of Ohio reject stimulus funds for high-speed rail as unwise federal spending; Florida Gov. Rick Scott follows suit in 2011.

2011

January — In his State of the Union address, President Obama renews his call to improve nation's crumbling infrastructure.

March — Sens. John Kerry, D-Mass., and Kay Bailey Hutchinson, R-Texas, cosponsor bill to create federal infrastructure bank to fund projects though loans and loan guarantees. Obama backs proposal, but it fails to gain congressional support.

September — Obama proposes American Jobs Act, which includes $75 billion in new infrastructure spending. Republicans object to paying for the measure through higher taxes on the wealthy and corporations.

2012

June — Congress struggles to pass new two-year transportation spending bill amid warnings that the Highway Trust Fund, which pays for highways and mass transit, will run out of money in 2014.

as untreated sewage contaminated drinking-water sources. In 1891, for example, 178 out of every 100,000 Chicago residents died of typhoid.[20]

In Chicago, Rudolph Hering, chief engineer for the water-supply system, carried out the massive project of digging a new channel to reroute the Chicago River away from its natural outlet, Lake Michigan, the source of the city's drinking water. Redirecting the Chicago — the dumping ground for the city's raw sewage and industrial waste — into rivers that drain to the Mississippi River immediately gave the city much cleaner drinking water.[21]

In the nation's drier regions, like Southern California, scarce water also led to massive infrastructure efforts. In 1905, Los Angeles voters approved a $1.5-billion bond issue to erect aqueducts to bring drinking water to the city from the Owens River, more than 230 miles north of the city.[22]

Even financially conservative leaders supported such infrastructure efforts. In 1956, for example, Republican

President Dwight D. Eisenhower signed the Federal-Aid Highway Act, calling for states and the federal government to build a vast Interstate Highway System — 41,000 miles of high-quality roads to link the nation.[23] Spurred by his memory of a 1919 cross-country trip that took U.S. Army vehicles 62 days to travel from Washington, D.C., to San Francisco, hindered by rutted roads and sagging bridges, Eisenhower committed the federal government to assume 90 percent of the cost.[24]

Infrastructure-building programs such as the Works Progress Administration and Civilian Conservation Corps, created as part of President Franklin D. Roosevelt's New Deal initiative in the 1930s and '40s, played key roles in "creating fixed assets for the nation," in the form of dams, bridges, post offices, parks and much more, says Michael Pagano, a professor of public administration at the University of Illinois, Chicago.

Not often considered in the budgets and agendas of such programs, however, was the inescapable fact that

Should America Take the Toll Road?

With roads aging, economists say tolls make sense.

The nation's first private toll road opened in 1794, spanning the 62 miles between Philadelphia and Lancaster. Private toll roads flourished in America's early days, as cash-strapped states turned to private investors to fund roads for farmers, merchants and manufacturers to carry goods to market. [1] Today, privately run toll roads may be making a comeback, as states look for ways to expand and maintain aging, overcrowded highway systems.

Over the past decade, states including California, Indiana, South Carolina, Texas and Virginia have entered agreements with private companies to build and/or operate toll roads, with varying degrees of success, and many more are contemplating such arrangements. In 2006, Chicago signed a 99-year lease with private operators to run the existing Chicago Skyway toll road.

In most agreements, the state retains ownership of the road, bridge or other structure, while a company leases it for a specified period — such as 50 years — agreeing to maintain it while collecting toll revenue. [2]

The draw for states is getting upfront cash — typically paid when the lease is signed — without tapping into the government treasury or borrowing on their own.

When private investors built the Southern Connector toll road around Greenville, S.C., "the state was able to get a $200-million federal interstate built without using precious state resources or using the state bond limit," said Pete Poore, communication director for the South Carolina Transportation Department. [3]

While private toll roads exist in many countries, most Americans are familiar only with some publicly run turnpikes and bridges erected during the interstate-highway building boom that began in the 1950s. Most of the tolls were eliminated once the roads were paid for. But with aging highway infrastructure needing critical maintenance as well as expansion, this is a new day, some transportation analysts say.

"In the past, tolling has been there to build a project, and theoretically you take it off when you've paid off the capital debt," says Jeffrey Buxbaum, a transportation consultant with Massachusetts-based Cambridge Systematics. "But the cost of a highway continues when the debt is paid off," and today's tolls would be permanent, not temporary, funding sources.

Economists have long thought a precisely calibrated, distance-based toll would have been the best means of paying for and maintaining interstate highways, "but it was just too difficult to collect," says Michael Pagano, a professor of public administration at the University of Illinois, Chicago. New technologies are making precise toll-collection feasible, however.

Future tolls also will likely feature "congestion pricing," says Pagano. Sensors in the pavement will "fine tune traffic on a highway" by triggering a rise in tolls — which will be posted

time brings more costs, Pagano says. "For the first 20 years, upkeep doesn't cost much," but after that the price of maintenance and replacement inevitably rises, often steeply, "and we just haven't ever incorporated those true costs into our thinking," he says.

Additional factors complicate today's infrastructure-upkeep problem. For one thing, infrastructure is owned and operated by many different entities, including the federal government, states, localities and private companies.

Perhaps surprisingly, about 85 percent of U.S. infrastructure is "owned and operated by the private sector,"

says Daniel Ostergaard, CEO of a homeland-security consultancy, Pelorus Enterprises, and a senior policy fellow at Western Carolina University's Institute for Economy and Future. About 68 percent of U.S. dams are privately owned, for example, according to the U.S. Army Corps of Engineers. [25]

Private ownership of so many public conveniences "poses a unique challenge for the federal government," which has no direct control over infrastructure like the electrical grid and telecommunications networks but nevertheless is ultimately held responsible for keeping Americans safe and productive, Ostergaard says.

on overhead signs — when traffic gets heavy, thus discouraging some drivers from entering the road, Pagano says.

California highways developed under public-private franchise agreements in San Diego and Orange County employ such technology today, according to Robert W. Poole Jr., director of transportation studies at the libertarian Reason Foundation in Los Angeles. "At any time during the day when traffic has built to a maximum, they'll up the rate by 25 cents per mile." The high-tech approach permits toll lanes in one congested California freeway to move at 65 mph even at rush hour, Poole says.

Many economists praise tolling as a way of ensuring that those who benefit from a highway are the same people who pay for it. Toll roads are a way to ensure that "people get what they pay for and pay for what they get," says Thomas A. Firey, managing editor of *Regulation* magazine, published by the libertarian Cato Institute. "Americans deep down really do appreciate fair pricing," so if highway tolls are clearly used to maintain a highway, "then they can probably accept that," he says.

Good lease agreements with private road managers can ensure that acceptance, says Poole. Private companies are "more aggressive in toll revenue — increasing the rates annually," for example, he says. "All the recent, highly publicized public-private partnerships like Chicago's Skyway have an annual index for raising tolls" by linking toll hikes to some measure of general economic change, such as the Consumer Price Index, he says.

Such indexing "wouldn't raise tolls much each year, but over 20 or 30 years the increases make a big difference" in the amount of revenue that could be applied to highway upkeep, Poole says. By contrast, the Indiana public toll roads that were handed over to private management in 2006 "had not had an increase in 19 years," even as the roads deteriorated and the cost of maintenance rose, he says.

But critics of private toll roads argue there's too much room in leasing agreements for money to be shifted away from highway needs and that private companies have no reason to care about the general public that uses their roads.

In the past, "public toll roads built in the United States were designed to provide a high-quality ride for the lowest possible toll" to best serve the public, Gregory M. Cohen, president of the American Highway Users Alliance, told the House Highways and Transit Subcommittee in May.

Under private ownership, however, investors would most likely seek "the highest possible returns," shifting the purpose of toll roads from "maximizing the public good to maximizing profits for investors," Cohen said. "Under such a scenario, tolls are raised regularly, and the process is not subject to public or political review." [4]

---

[1] For background, see Daniel B. Klein and John Majewski, "Turnpikes and Toll Roads in Nineteenth-Century America," *Encyclopedia*, History of Economics Society, http://eh.net/encyclopedia/article/Klein.Majewski.Turnpikes.

[2] For background, see Robert W. Poole, Jr., "For Whom the Road Tolls," Reason Foundation Web site, February 2006, www.reason.org; Sylvia Smith, "U.S. Public-Private Agreements Have Mixed Record," *The Times of Northwest Indiana*, Jan. 23, 2006, www.thetimesonline.com/articles/2006/01/23/news/top_news/73a0efca3665c38b862570fe001a1bee.txt.

[3] Quoted in Smith, *op. cit.*

[4] Gregory M. Cohen, "Highway Users' Perspectives on Public-Private Partnerships," testimony before House Subcommittee on Highways and Transit, May 24, 2007.

Increasingly, though owned and operated separately, aspects of the national infrastructure rely on each other to function, Ostergaard points out. "We can't just look at the water supply on its own but have to look at the electrical grid," too, for example, since water systems need power to function. "You need a great deal of dialogue" to meet such challenges, and cooperative decision-making isn't easy to promote, he says. "If you look from a purely economic viewpoint, each system looks out for its own best interest."

Another threat to proper maintenance grows out of the fact that infrastructure benefits often cross geographic boundaries, and those who pay most to update or maintain infrastructure aren't necessarily those who benefit most. For example, there is a national benefit to having a well-maintained Interstate Highway System, even in sparsely populated areas, but must local residents shoulder costs for big roads that they themselves don't much need?

Water infrastructure is especially prone to such dilemmas. So-called watershed districts in some states — areas that drain into a specific bay, lake or river system — are government-established entities that have responsibility for water quality and flooding throughout the system. But is it fair to make upstream landowners pay for improvements that will only benefit those downriver? Bitter disagreements over this question have stalled many water projects since water-infrastructure efforts began flourishing in the 19th century, and they continue today.

"There's a responsibility for all residents in the watershed . . . to manage the watershed as a whole," even though some will pay for improvements from which they won't directly benefit, said John Hoopingarner, executive director of the Muskingum watershed district in northeastern Ohio, where debate rages over money for dam and reservoir repairs.[26]

But upstream residents often vigorously disagree. "It's unfair. It's unreasonable," said Tony Zadra, who owns a satellite-dish business in New Philadelphia, an upriver town. "People in the upper highlands aren't responsible for [flood] damage downstream."[27]

"You have a property-tax assessment that doesn't increase property value," said Scott Levengood, a farmer in another upriver town, Mineral City.[28]

Rust Never Sleeps

While funding for upkeep is seldom figured into construction budgets, civil engineers think a lot about the future in trying to design infrastructure to last, although the task is ultimately futile.

"All bridges are going to deteriorate," says the University of Virginia's Baber. But "you use the best materials, the best design and the best maintenance you can afford, such as regular painting. And you use as little road salt as you can to make [the structure] last as long as possible."

In the heyday of American highway building — the 1950s through the 1970s — state-of-the-art bridges were expected to last for around 50 years. But even "state of the art" is only as good as the times.

For example, "in the 1960s, [metal] fatigue wasn't as well understood as it is today," a factor that likely played a role in the I-35 West bridge collapse, says the University of Maryland's Vannoy.

The bridge "probably wouldn't have been built in the exact same way today," says Baber. The design was fine, based on "what we knew in 1967 but not quite right given what we know in 2007. Right now, we aim to design for 75 years," and more structural redundancy is incorporated, he adds. "You don't see many bridges now with only two load-carrying members. You're more likely to see five or six."

Part of improving upkeep involves learning how to build better in the first place, but research funds aren't always adequate for some important but overlooked infrastructure, such as water systems, some engineers say.

The federal Environmental Protection Agency (EPA) devotes under $10 million a year to drinking-water research, and even taking all private and public research funders together, "I'd be surprised if you get close to $100 million" annually, says Drexel University's Haas. By contrast, hundreds of millions of dollars is probably spent every year to research technology related to the nation's electrical grid, he says.

One of the toughest infrastructure-design problems is predicting future usage. For bridges, "it's very difficult to predict traffic trends more than five or six years in advance," says Baber. "Plus, sometimes the bridge attracts traffic," a particularly difficult thing for planners to foresee, he says. "This has happened to a lot of interstate bridges."

"People in the early 1950s did not envision the 21st century," says USC's Little. For example, the inability of planners to accurately see into the future led designers to focus highway and public-transit systems mainly on accommodating transportation between suburbs and central cities, he says. Today, however, the growing prevalence of suburb-to-suburb travel is helping make the transportation system obsolete.

"We also never anticipated the huge growth in imports," which requires not only expanded ports but highway and rail systems to carry a huge proportion of the country's goods inland, Little says.

Also unanticipated in highway design was the new model for stocking large retail stores that freight-hauling companies and retailers like Wal-Mart and Dell Computer have developed over the past few decades, Little says.

Instead of building large warehouses to store goods awaiting shipment, industry now keep much of the nation's freight cargo on trucks traveling the highways at all times. The resulting huge increase in truck traffic wears down roads that were never built for such constant, heavy loads.[29]

"Trucks are responsible for virtually 100 percent of the damage to the roads" because of their high weight per axle, says transportation consultant Buxbaum.

The trucking problem isn't complex to fix, theoretically, but it would involve a major — expensive — overhaul, says the Reason Foundation's Poole. "One idea that has a lot of promise is a truck-only toll lane" equipped with special "high-strength pavement," he says.

Paying It Forward

Between the mid-1950s and today, overall infrastructure spending has risen annually. But funding hasn't kept up with aging and the rapid development of new demands and technologies. Faulty priority-setting processes also cause problems.

So-called pork-barrel spending — inserted into congressional bills as "earmarks" — is a big problem, says the Reason Foundation's Poole. Ostensibly, members of Congress direct funding to specific local projects to please constituents. But "when I talk to [state transportation] directors, they say the projects they get in the federal bills are . . . way, way down the list," Poole says.[30]

The water pipes and roadways we use most are local, giving Congress little obvious role in those major infrastructure sectors. A federal role comes in when "externalities" — benefits and burdens connected to infrastructure — extend to people outside the region, explains Ghamkar of the University of Texas.

The federal role has applied mostly to new construction, she says. Cars and trucks drive across all states, including the less populous ones in the middle of the country, but sparsely populated areas could not be expected to build national-scale highways on their own, so Congress stepped in.

In a similar way, the Clean Water Act of 1972 acknowledged the federal role in assuring that both upstream and downstream communities get clean drinking water. Because upstream communities dump wastewater into rivers that supply drinking water to people downstream, Congress offered federal grants to improve water-treatment plants everywhere to improve water quality regionally.

Some other infrastructure, such as ports, and air-traffic control, for example, is primarily a national responsibility.

Between 1956 and the mid-1970s, federal spending on infrastructure increased by about 7 percent annually, compared to around 1 percent growth in state and local spending, according to the nonpartisan Congressional Budget Office. The federal share of infrastructure spending peaked in 1977, at 38 percent.[31]

Since then, primary responsibility for most government-funded infrastructure has shifted to states and localities. In 2004, the latest year for which complete data are

Pedestrians crowd New York City's Queensboro Bridge to Queens on Aug. 14, 2003, after a power blackout crippled the city and much of the Northeastern United States and Canada.

available, the federal government spent $73.5 billion, or about 24 percent, of the total $312 billion in infrastructure spending in the United States. States and localities spent $238.7 billion. Of the total, $143.6 billion went to project construction, while the remaining $168.7 billion funded operation and maintenance, a proportion that's remained relatively stable for the past two decades, despite infrastructure aging.

About 45 percent of federal funds for maintenance and operation go to run the nation's air-traffic control system, and 60 percent of federal construction funds pay for highway projects. Total spending to build capital projects has grown by about 2 percent per year since 1981, while spending on maintenance and operation has risen 2.1 percent.[32]

While states and localities do the bulk of infrastructure funding and planning, Congress periodically modifies federal law to shore up vital systems. For example, the National Dam Safety Act of 2006 offered grants to improve states' dam-safety programs in response to reports that the number of deteriorating dams is increasing, along with the proportion of the population living in the flood path of a shaky dam.[33]

The bill stopped short of offering federal funding for repairs. Dam safety remains primarily a state and private-sector responsibility. The federal government owns only about 4 percent of the nation's dams, and states have primary oversight responsibility for dams, 68 percent of which are privately owned.[34]

Other infrastructure — such as water and sewage systems and the electrical and telecommunications systems, which are privately owned — is funded by user fees. But charging fees high enough to support upgrades is difficult in those sectors as well.

Utilities constantly face the question — Should we patch or replace infrastructure? says New Jersey sewerage Director Villee. "Logically," that decision would be based "on some cost ratio, like, 'If patching exceeds 50 percent we will replace it,' " Villee says "Unfortunately, factors other than logic often take precedence. Money and politics are two of the major players."

It's like having a 10-year-old car with a transmission problem, Villee says. "Logic says get a new car," but "money says we can't afford that. So you roll the dice, fix the transmission and gamble that you can extend the life of the car until you can pay for a new one. That is the game most utilities play. We defer maintenance and capital improvements to keep rates at a politically acceptable level."

CURRENT SITUATION

Bridge Tax?

Since the Minnesota bridge collapse, Congress has been mulling a tax increase for bridge repair, but President Bush opposes it.

House Transportation and Infrastructure Committee Chairman Oberstar is circulating a plan to hike the federal gas tax by five cents per gallon to repair some 6,000 "structurally deficient" bridges, and Congress is expected to discuss the proposal this fall.

But more taxes won't help, said Transportation Secretary Peters at a Sept. 5 hearing. "It is not that we don't have the money," she said, "it's where we're spending" it.[35]

Democratic and some Republican lawmakers say more money is needed and that congressional "earmarking" of funds to specific projects — criticized by many, including the White House — has increased bridge safety.

Ohio Rep. Steven C. LaTourette, a Republican moderate, said that two structurally deficient bridges in his district are being repaired thanks to congressional earmarks. "To say that all things are not on the table," including a tax hike, "cheats the American motoring public, and I

would hope that the administration would rethink its position," LaTourette said.[36]

Academic analysts say a more stable long-term funding source and a means to ensure that money is dedicated to the highest-priority problems are also needed.

The gas-tax boost would be "a nice little stopgap solution," says the University of Illinois' Pagano. But as cars' fuel efficiency increases "revenue collections would still fall" under the plan, he points out.

On Aug. 6, President Bush signed a bill sponsored by the Minnesota congressional delegation to waive the $100-million-per-state limit on federal funding for emergency highway reconstruction and allow up to $250 million in funds for the Minnesota bridge.

How the measure will play out is in doubt, however, since actual funds would only be approved as part of highway appropriations legislation, and Bush has already said he'll veto the "irresponsible and excessive" $104.4 billion appropriations measure that's moving through Congress.[37]

Other Proposals

Debate also rages over the Water Resources Development Act of 2007, a bill that in its current form authorizes — but does not actually appropriate — about $21 billion in funding for projects to be undertaken by the U.S. Army Corps of Engineers.[38]

President Bush has threatened to veto the bill, which he and other critics call an expensive mishmash of pork projects.[39]

Some of the bill's earmarks authorize "a series of costly projects that benefit the rich and influential," said Ronald D. Utt, a senior research fellow at the conservative Heritage Foundation. "Notwithstanding continuing concern" over flood protection for cities like New Orleans, "this Congress appears intent on diverting taxpayer dollars . . . to water-sports and other low-priority schemes."[40]

Some congressional Republicans, including self-described fiscal conservatives like Sen. James M. Inhofe of Oklahoma, top-ranking Republican on the Senate Environment and Public Works Committee, strongly oppose Bush's veto threat.[41]

Congress has also held hearings this year on the idea of turning more infrastructure over to private companies for management. "The battle has been joined" over the value of privately operated toll roads, with the Bush

Funding Programs Discouraged Smart Planning

Upkeep was often ignored.

Local economies and home values depend on infrastructure maintenance, but even programs like federal grants for infrastructure building often have ignored the need for continued upkeep.

"We depend vitally on infrastructure services, and ignoring them can cause trouble for communities" down the line, says Richard Little, director of the Keston Institute for Public Finance and Infrastructure Policy at the University of Southern California.

If a community lets its infrastructure — water, sewer and transportation — languish while neighboring communities don't, "pretty soon businesses will say, 'Let's go somewhere else,'" as potholed roads and sewer overflows mount up, says Little. "People will go to a newer place where there don't seem to be the same problems. Housing values drop, so we all have a real vested interest in maintenance," he says.

Federal grants have helped communities build big projects, such as massive water-treatment plants and 10- or 12-lane roads and bridges, for example. But building big may mean ignoring equally important priorities.

The federal Clean Water Act of 1972 offered grants to encourage communities to improve water-treatment plants, says Linda Kelly, managing director of public communications for the Water Environment Foundation (WEF), a nonprofit advocacy group. The law worked, up to a point, she says.

"People got very excited about putting big water plants in. My own utility had 15 little, bitty wastewater plants and consolidated them into four," says Kelly, former deputy general manager of wastewater treatment in Portland, Ore. Meanwhile, localities were left on their own to oversee — and often ignore — thousands of miles of underground pipes, which are the main source of water-system troubles today, she says. "The big plants were new in the 1970s, but the infrastructure in the ground is upwards of 100 years old."

With federal grants available for big projects — and sometimes not available for smaller projects to cover the same needs — many communities over the years have opted to build the biggest ones they could, whether that was the smartest choice or not.

In one classic care of "overbuilding," in 1976 in Pittsburgh, the large Birmingham Bridge replaced the Brady Street Bridge, which, though only a third the size, was nevertheless "adequate" for the site, says Joel A. Tarr, professor of history and policy at Carnegie-Mellon University's Heinz School of Public Policy and Management.

Planned as part of a larger highway system that never materialized, the bridge was reconfigured for local use.

The bridge remains too large for the neighborhood traffic it carries and its redesigned on and off ramps twist and turn to link the bridge with local streets it was originally meant to bypass.

"Why is it so big? Because that's the only way they could get funding," says Tarr.

Similar structures abound nationwide, says Michael Pagano, professor of public administration at the University of Illinois, Chicago. Cities and states should have asked, "Do we need 12-lane roads?" Pagano says. Instead, many localities draw up the grandest plans they can to snag federal grants that often favor the biggest projects. Under the Clean Water Act, the federal government would pay 75 percent of the cost, Pagano says. "So the obvious response was, 'Hell, I'll build the biggest plant I can get.'"

Federal grants also sometimes encourage infrastructure neglect, says Heywood Sanders, a professor of public administration at the University of Texas, San Antonio. If a city can get federal funds for a major overhaul, it's easy for local officials to neglect routine maintenance for which they'd have to spend their own money, he says.

"The other big problem with federal funding is the transfer of money among the states," says Robert W. Poole Jr., director of transportation studies at the libertarian Reason Foundation in Los Angeles. The grant formula "was created to get interstate highways built" through sparsely populated regions like Montana that didn't need the highways for their own use. That meant that low-population, low-growth areas get considerably more money than they would if grants were based on population numbers, he says.

But as infrastructure ages, current highway needs run in exactly the opposite direction, Poole says. Today's top transportation need is for upgrades and expansion in the top 25 urban areas, all located in states that get less than the average per-capita share of federal grants, he says.

Within states, a similar problem makes it hard to direct funds to the high-population areas with roads most in need of expansion and heavy-duty maintenance, says Poole. For political reasons, "you have to share the money among all the legislative districts," no matter how little some may need the funds.

Over the years, Congress has made a few attempts to shift more grant money to high-population states but the Senate — where low-density states have equal representation with high-density states — has successfully fought such efforts, Poole says. "There's not much chance" formulas will change in the foreseeable future, he says.

Are toll roads the best way to maintain highways and bridges?

YES — Robert W. Poole Jr.
Director of Transportation Studies,
The Reason Foundation

From testimony before House Subcommittee on Highways and Transit,
Feb. 13, 2007

To properly maintain of our highways and bridges, we should be spending $6 billion more every year. And to improve the system, to cope with increases in auto and truck travel, we should be spending $51 billion more every year.

The existing state and federal fuel tax and highway trust-fund system seems to be unable to meet these investment needs. Neither the Congress nor most state legislatures have increased fuel taxes to levels that would even offset increases in fuel efficiency and the ravages of inflation, let alone cope with increased travel demand. So increasingly, states are turning to toll finance and public-private partnerships (PPPs). . . .

The newest trend is the long-term concession model, in which an investor-owned company will finance, design, build, operate, modernize and maintain a highway project, financing its expenditures from toll revenues. What this model is all about is extending the investor-owned utility concept from network industries like electricity and telecommunications to the network industry of limited-access highways. This model is what built most of the postwar toll motorway systems in France, Italy, Portugal and Spain, and the trend has more recently spread to Australia, Latin America, Canada, Britain, Germany and other countries.

PPPs offer access to large, new sources of capital; the ability to raise larger sums for toll projects and shift risk from taxpayers to investors.

Long-term concessions are a good vehicle for organizing multi-state projects such as truck-only toll lanes to serve major shipping routes. These projects need to be developed in a unified manner, but individual states are not well-positioned to develop such unified projects; concession companies are.

Comparing the typical U.S. state-run toll agency with the typical European or Australian toll road company, it's clear that the latter are far more customer-oriented, more innovative and generally more commercial. Many state-operated toll agencies are run by short-term political appointees rather than by career toll-road professionals. . . .

One of the most important advantages of investor-owned toll-road companies is their motivation to innovate to solve difficult problems or improve their service, such as by varying tolls to discourage traffic congestion.

None of the transactions that have occurred or are being planned — either for existing toll roads or for new ones — involves the sale of any roads. The government remains the owner at all times, with the private partner carrying out only the tasks spelled out for it.

NO — Bill Graves
President, American Trucking
Associations (ATA)

From testimony before House Subcommittee on Highways and Transit,
May 24, 2007

We strongly believe that while private financing of highway infrastructure may play a limited role in addressing future transportation needs, certain practices may generate unintended consequences whose costs will vastly exceed their short-term economic benefits. We are very concerned about attempts by some states to carve up the most important segments of the highway system for long-term lease. . . .

Highway user fees should be reasonably uniform in application among classes of highway users and be based chiefly on readily verifiable measures of highway and vehicle use. ATA believes that fuel taxes meet the above criteria, while tolls fail on certain critical points.

Fuel-tax evasion is relatively low compared to other highway user fees. Tolls, on the other hand, are often easily evaded, usually by motorists using alternative, less safe routes that were not built to handle high levels of traffic. There are significant capital and operating costs associated with collecting tolls, while fuel taxes are relatively inexpensive to administer.

Private toll-road operators need not be concerned about the social impacts of toll rates on low-income workers or on the costs to businesses that depend on the highway. Nor do private operators care about the extent of traffic diversion to lesser quality, usually less safe, roads. Their sole concern is to maximize the toll road's profitability. . . .

Privatization boosters point to caps on toll-rate increases that have been a standard part of privatization agreements. However, the two major lease agreements that have been completed in the United States — the Indiana Toll Road and Chicago Skyway — have been accompanied by very large initial rate increases combined with caps on future increases. . . .

It has been suggested that these massive toll-rate escalations are unrealistic because, as has been demonstrated on other facilities, including the Ohio Turnpike, raising the toll rate too high forces significant traffic off the highway. However, the lessee will set a toll rate to a level that maximizes profitability, not traffic.

Indeed, a recent financial report by [Australia-based toll-road developer Macquarie Infrastructure Group] revealed that while traffic on the Indiana Toll Road's barrier system — jointly operated by Macquarie and Spain-based Cintra Concesiones de Infraestructuras de Transport — actually declined by 1.6 percent between July 2006 and March 2007, and increased by just 0.2 percent on the ticket system, revenues shot up by a whopping 46.2 percent due to large toll-rate increases.

administration a strong proponent, says the Reason Foundation's Poole.

Some key Democrats have been highly skeptical, however. In a May 10 letter to state officials, Transportation Committee Chairman Oberstar and Rep. Peter DeFazio, D-Ore., warned against "rushing" into public-private partnerships (PPPs) and said their committee would undo any such agreements "that do not fully protect the public interest." In June, however, the lawmakers softened their stance, saying that "under the right circumstances and conditions," PPPs can be efficient and effective.[42]

Also in the legislative mix, though receiving little attention, is a proposal by Sens. Christopher J. Dodd, D-Conn., and Chuck Hagel, R-Neb., for an independent federal entity, the National Infrastructure Bank. It would analyze infrastructure projects costing $75 million or more and report to Congress on how to prioritize and pay for them.[43]

The Minnesota bridge collapse spurred quick action by many state and local governments to step up monitoring and repair of aging bridges. On Aug. 29, the Missouri Legislature approved a plan to repair 802 bridges in the next five years, about four times as many as previously contemplated. Tennessee will inspect bridges annually, up from the two-year inspection cycle federal law requires. Wisconsin will install stress sensors to monitor the state of 14 bridges that are more than 50 years old.[44]

In general, states are making better progress than the federal government on improving decision-making processes, says Poole. In California, a state Transportation Commission with members appointed by government bodies with various missions sets priorities. "There is some politics still, but they do a reasonably good job," says the Reason Foundation's Poole.

Some state and local leaders are spotlighting infrastructure needs. Atlanta Mayor Shirley Franklin conducted an aggressive public-awareness campaign on the city's long-neglected water system, "and now the community is funding it," says the Water Environment Foundation's Kelly.

But public support may not be as tough a sell as many believe, says transportation consultant Buxbaum. "Washington state has passed two gas tax increases" in just the past few years, after the state "built more accountability and transparency" into the highway-construction process, he says.

Buxbaum acknowledges that funding may be easier to get in the West, where infrastructure is still being built.

A helicopter prepares to drop a sandbag in an attempt to plug the breached London Avenue Canal levee in New Orleans in the wake of flooding caused by Hurricane Katrina in September 2005.

Eastern states must mainly fund repairs, and "that's not as sexy," he says.

OUTLOOK
Threats Increase

Infrastructure problems won't get easier to resolve as systems age, population grows and developments like global warming change the very nature of the challenge.

But while problems continue to simmer, most analysts believe the public interest sparked by the Minnesota bridge collapse will be fleeting. "I've learned that the half-life of the public attitude on this issue is very short," says former Corps of Engineers chief Hatch.

Nevertheless, technological developments may make prioritizing maintenance tasks easier, says Harvey Mudd's

A car rests against a tree near Purvis, Miss., after a dam holding back Big Bay Lake collapsed, flooding more than 50 homes on March 13, 2004. There are 10,094 dams in the United States whose failure could cause loss of life, according to the American Society of Civil Engineers.

Duron, who has developed sensors to measure internal threats to a structure's stability that inspectors can't pick up visually.

Such sensors could be attached to structures at all times, at regularly scheduled times throughout the year, or during stressful times — such as during repairs, when the I-35 West bridge collapsed — Duron says. Technology is making it possible to get "a real-time assessment of changing conditions" that can trigger structural failure, and the cost is dropping, he says. Armed with that information, engineers will be better able to explain to policy makers which projects are highest priority, Duron says.

But while technology may help, other changes will increase infrastructure strains.

Climate change will likely trigger more extreme storms and floods, including massive floods in mountainous regions caused by the melting of natural "ice dams" that form glacial lakes today, according to the International Rivers Network. "The world's more than 45,000 existing large dams have not been built to allow for a rapidly intensifying hydrological cycle," says a 2005 article in the group's journal, *World Rivers Review*.[45]

More regions may face drought as climate changes, and that will require attention to water-system deficiencies, says Nancy Connery, an infrastructure consultant in Woolwich, Maine, who chaired the congressionally created National Council on Public Works Improvement in the 1980s. "So much water is lost today, so many leaks and so much flushed down the toilet," she says. "This is a very expensive problem, and one we'll have to face sooner than we imagine."

The future will demand "dramatically new ideas" about infrastructure, perhaps even a new version of the early 20th-century era when infrastructure building was seen as heroic, says Connery.

For example, the myriad small drinking-water systems around the country might be re-envisioned as "regional, networked operations" that share an expert staff, Connery says. But attaining such efficiencies of scale would require new incentives for agencies to inform the public about their operations and to cooperate with each other, she says.

As an example of the innovative thinking she hopes to see more of, Connery cites a small company that tried to run fiber-optic cable carrying broadband Internet house to house alongside existing sewer lines. The plan ultimately stalled after Hurricane Katrina hit their planned roll-out city, New Orleans, in 2005. Nevertheless, the scheme represents "the kind of imaginative idea that could build excitement," she says. "There's so much more that's possible."

Infrastructure "is not about engineering, and it's not about financing," says Little at USC's infrastructure institute. "It's about what we want to leave to our grandchildren, and that's more than blue sky and green trees. It's the infrastructure that allows us to live," he says. "Neglecting it is a failure of imagination."

UPDATE

Since 2007, the United States has avoided catastrophic infrastructure failures such as the 2005 collapse of the dikes in New Orleans after Hurricane Katrina or the I-35 West bridge collapse in Minneapolis two years later. But analysts say smaller failures continue and significant safety hazards exist. Meanwhile, the price tag for bringing America's infrastructure up to acceptable levels has risen by at least another $600 billion since 2007, according to the most comprehensive study.[46]

The United States also continues to lag significantly behind most of the developed world in its annual investment in physical infrastructure, which includes highways, bridges, water systems and the power grid. The United States spends 2.4 percent of its gross domestic product on infrastructure, less than half Europe's 5 percent.[47] The World Economic Forum rates the United States 24th globally in the quality of its infrastructure, roughly tied with Malaysia.[48]

Yet, many infrastructure experts and political observers doubt the nation's ability to address the problem anytime soon. The economic downturn has hobbled the financial resources of many state and local governments. And a fierce partisan divide in Congress has made passing major federal infrastructure-spending legislation extremely difficult.

"We've become even more politically fragmented" since 2007, says Richard Little, director of the Keston Institute for Public Finance and Infrastructure Policy at the University of Southern California in Los Angeles. "The ability to get things done that used to be considered pretty bipartisan, like transportation bills or infrastructure improvements, just isn't there."

But allowing the infrastructure to continue to deteriorate will only accelerate the cost, warns Gregory DiLoreto, president-elect of the American Society of Civil Engineers (ASCE) and CEO of the Tualatin Valley Water District in Oregon. "It's like neglecting repairs on your house," he says. "You don't want to let it fall down so that you have to rebuild it again."

While Congress has been deadlocked, the U.S. infrastructure continues to deteriorate. According to a 2009 ASCE "report card" on the state of the nation's infrastructure, the most recent available:

- The nation's systems earned an overall grade of D, the same as in 2005, but the cost — for all levels of government — to upgrade the system to "good" rose

A car sits in a sinkhole caused by a broken water main that collapsed in Chevy Chase, Md., on Dec. 3, 2010. The World Economic Forum recently ranked the quality of the U.S. infrastructure as 24th globally, roughly tied with Malaysia.

from $1.6 trillion in 2005 to $2.2 trillion.[49] Current spending is only about half that.

- The nation's roads, drinking water, wastewater-treatment facilities, levees and inland waterways received a D-minus. Crumbling roads and highways cost Americans $67 million a year in vehicle repairs and higher operating costs. Plus, increasing traffic congestion costs drivers 4.2 billion hours a year, a $78.2 billion ($710 per driver) drain on the economy.[50]

- More than one in four American bridges, which received a C grade overall, are either "structurally deficient or functionally obsolete."[51]

- More than 4,000 dams are deficient, including 1,819 deemed "high hazard." The average age of the nation's 85,000 dams is just over 51 years, and maintenance is being neglected. "Over the past six years, for every deficient, high-hazard-potential dam repaired, nearly two more were declared deficient," the ASCE concluded.[52]

The $787 billion economic stimulus package signed into law by President Obama in 2009 boosted infrastructure spending in real terms for the first time since 2002, according to the Congressional Budget Office (CBO).[53] However, the package largely failed to meet the expectations of infrastructure-improvement advocates. While the administration publicized investment in high-speed rail and other high-profile projects, only a fifth of overall stimulus spending went to infrastructure under the broadest definition.[54] And roads, bridges, public transportation including rail, aviation and wastewater treatment received only $64 billion — or 8 percent of the total.[55]

"The stimulus money didn't really do what those of us in the infrastructure business hoped it would do," says DiLoreto. "Spread over 50 states, it just wasn't that much. The projects were mostly small. They didn't last that long, and now the money's all gone."

Last September, Obama proposed an additional $75 billion in infrastructure spending as part of the $447 billion "American Jobs Act." The plan would invest $25 billion to upgrade public schools and $50 billion for highways, transit, rail and aviation projects.[56] The president also called on Congress to pass legislation creating a National Infrastructure Bank, originally introduced by Sens. John Kerry, D-Mass., and Kay Bailey Hutchinson, R-Texas. The bank would be capitalized with $10 billion in federal money, which would be earmarked for loans and loan guarantees to help pay for infrastructure projects.

However, Republicans have blocked the two measures in the Senate, objecting to tax increases on wealthier Americans and corporations that would have paid for the new spending. They also said further stimulus spending won't help the struggling economy.

"Democrats' sole proposal is to keep doing what hasn't worked," Senate Minority Leader Mitch McConnell, R-Ky., said.[57]

Some parts of the legislation eventually passed, but not the infrastructure spending. In June Obama renewed his call for Congress to pass the infrastructure portion of the bill, but action remains highly unlikely.

Republicans and Democrats continue to disagree on a transportation-spending bill, which finances road construction and mass transit. Congress has passed nine stopgap measures since the last multi-year transportation act expired in 2009. The Senate passed a bill that would fund the program through 2014, but House Republicans have been unable to agree on legislation.

"I think the best way to get a highway bill passed would be for Obama to come out against it, and then the House would be compelled to support it," says Little. "That's being facetious, but it's almost where we are at now."

The Highway Trust Fund, which finances road construction and mass transit, will run out of money in 2014 without additional revenue, according to the CBO.[58] Money for the fund comes from an 18.4-cents-per-gallon federal gasoline tax, which hasn't been raised since 1993.

In early June, House Speaker John Boehner, R-Ohio, said he might favor another stop-gap extension of transportation funding if agreement on new legislation can't be reached by June 30.[59]

Despite Washington's gridlock, infrastructure spending may enjoy more public support than politicians realize. The Center for Transportation Excellence, a nonpartisan policy research center, found that between 2008 and 2011 — despite economic hard times — voters approved more than 76 percent of state transportation ballot measures. [60]

NOTES

1. For background, see "Driver Who Survived Bridge Collapse: 'I Can't Believe I'm Alive, ' " CNN.com, Aug. 3, 2007, www.cnn.com/2007/US/08/02/bridge.survivors/index.html.

2. For background, see James Barron, "Steam Blast Jolts Midtown, Killing One," *The New York Times*, July 19, 2007, p. B4.

3. For background, see "Report Card for America's Infrastructure," American Society of Civil Engineers, www.asce.org/reportcard.

4. Quoted in Laurie Blake, *et al.*, "MnDOT Feared Cracking in Bridge but Opted Against Making Repairs," [Minneapolis] *Star Tribune*, Aug. 3, 2007, p. 1A, www.startribune.com.

5. For background, see William Yardley, "U.S. Faces a Sinkhole Epidemic As Its Century-Old Water and Sewer Infrastructure Leaks and Erodes," *The New York Times*, Feb. 8, 2007, p. A19; Chris Mayer, The Sinkhole Syndrome, *The Daily Wealth blog*, May 8. 2007, www.dailywealth.com; Thomas Rooney, "The

Looming Sinkhole Crisis," March 28, 2007, *Los Angeles Times*, p. A21.

6. "The Need for a National Dam Rehabilitation Program," Dam Safety Coalition, www.damsafety coalition.org.

7. For background, see Robert Puentes and Ryan Prince, "Fueling Transportation Finance: A Primer on the Gas Tax," Brookings Institution Center on Urban and Metropolitan Policy, March 2003, www .brookings.org.

8. Quoted in Frederic J. Frommer, "Push to Raise Gas Tax for Bridget Repairs," The Associated Press, Sept. 6, 2007, http://ap.google.com.

9. "President Bush Discusses American Competitiveness Initiative During Press Conference," transcript, White House press conference, Aug. 9, 2007, www .whitehouse.gov/news/releases/2007/08/200708 09-1.html.

10. Quoted in Megan Tady, "A Win in the Water War," *In These Times* Web site, Aug. 1, 2007, www.inthese times.com.

11. Dam Safety Coalition, *op. cit.*

12. Gaylord Shaw, "The Enormous U.S. Dam Problem No One Is Talking About," *The Christian Science Monitor*, Jan. 3, 2006, p. 9.

13. Thomas Rooney, "Fixing Failing Pipes Is a Public Health Issue," *The Chief Engineer* Web site, www .chiefengineer.org.

14. "Kuhl Reintroduces Gas Price Relief Bill," press release, http://kuhl.house.gov/News/Document Print.aspx?DocumentID_65980.

15. For background, see "Transportation California Is Working to Close the Proposition 42 Loophole," Transportation California, www.transportationca.com/ displaycommon.cfm?an=1&subarticlenbr=156.

16. Robert Puentes, "Don't Raise that Gas Tax . . . Yet!" position statement, Aug. 22, 2007, www .brookings.edu.

17. Robert Puentes, "Cashing in on the BP Beltway," op-ed originally published in the *Hartford Courant*, March 1, 2007, www.brookings.edu/views/op-ed/ puentes/20070301_beltway.htm.

18. For background, see "Trends in Public Spending on Transportation and Water Infrastructure, 1956 to 2004," Congressional Budget Office, August 2007, www.cbo.gov; Kate Asher, *The Works: Anatomy of a City* (2005); Joel A. Tarr, ed., *Devastation and Renewal: An Environmental History of Pittsburgh and its Region* (2005).

19. Michael Singer, Ramon J. Cruz and Jason Bregman, "Infrastructure and Community," Environmental Defense, 2007.

20. "Reversal of the Chicago River," Of Time and the River Web site, Illinois Department of Natural Resources, www.oftimeandtheriver.org. For background, see Richard L. Worsnop, "Water Resources and National Water Needs," *Editorial Research Reports*, 1965, Vol. II, *CQ Researcher Plus Archives*, www.cqpress.com.

21. "Water Supply and Distribution History II — Early Years," Greatest Engineering Achievements of the 20th Century, National Academy of Engineering, www.greatestachievements.org.

22. "Water Supply and Distribution III — Thirsty Cities," Greatest Engineering Achievements of the 20th Century, National Academy of Engineering, www.greatestachievements.org.

23. For background, see David Hosansky, "Traffic Congestion," *CQ Researcher*, Aug. 27, 1999, pp. 729-752; W. Street, "Interstate Highway System at 25," *Editorial Research Reports 1981*, Vol. II; M. Packman, "New Highways," *Editorial Research Reports 1954*, Vol. II; and B. W. Patch, "Federal Highway Aid and the Depression," *Editorial Research Reports 1932*, Vol. II, all available at *CQ Researcher Plus Archives*, www.cqpress.com.

24. Daniel Schulman and James Ridgeway, "The Highwaymen," *Mother Jones*, January/February 2007, www.motherjones.com.

25. Dam Safety Coalition, *op. cit.*

26. Quoted in Robert Wang, "District Raises Taxes Without a Vote," *The Canton* [Ohio] *Repository*, Aug. 26, 2007, p. 1A.

27. Quoted in *ibid.*

28. *Ibid.*

29. For background, see Kathy Koch, "Truck Safety," *CQ Researcher*, March 12, 1999, pp. 209-232.

30. For background, see Marcia Clemmitt, "Pork-Barrel Politics," *CQ Researcher*, June 16, 2006, pp. 529-552.

31. "Trends in Public Spending on Transportation and Water Infrastructure, 1956 to 2004," Congressional Budget Office, August 2007, www.cbo.gov.

32. *Ibid.*

33. Dam Safety Coalition, *op. cit.*

34. *Ibid.*

35. Quoted in Kathryn A. Wolfe, "Funding to Repair Bridges Caught in Ideological Gap," *CQ Today*, Sept. 5, 2007.

36. Quoted in *ibid.*

37. *Ibid.*

38. For background, see David Hosansky, "Reforming the Corps," *CQ Researcher*, May 30, 2003, pp. 497-520.

39. For background, see Avery Palmer, "No Conflict Seen in Water Resources Bill, Earmarks and Ethics Measure," *CQ Today*, Sept. 4, 2007.

40. Ronald D. Utt, *The Water Resources Development Act of 2007: A Pork Fest for Wealthy Beach-Front Property Owners*, Heritage Foundation, May 15, 2007, www .heritage.org/Research/Budget/wm1458.cfm.

41. Palmer, *op. cit.*

42. Quoted in Ken Orski, "Committee Chairs Soften Stance Against Public-Private Transportation Deals," *Budget and Tax News*, The Heartland Institute, August 2007, www.heartland.org.

43. "Bill Proposes National Infrastructure Bank," *WaterWeek*, American Water Works Association, Aug. 3, 2007, www.awwa.org.

44. Judy Keen, "States Act Swiftly on Bridge Repairs," *USA Today*, Sept. 3, 2007, p. 1A.

45. Patrick McCully, "And the Walls Came Tumbling Down: Dam Safety Concerns Grow in Wake of Failures, Changing Climate," *World Rivers Review*, June 2005, www.irn.org.

46. "2009 Report Card for America's Infrastructure," The American Society of Civil Engineers, March 25, 2009, p. 8, www.infrastructurereportcard.org.

47. "America's Transport Infrastructure: Life in the slow lane," *The Economist*, April 28, 2011, www.econo mist.com/node/18620944.

48. "The Global Competitiveness Report 2011-2012," 2011, World Economic Forum, p. 412, www3.wefo rum.org/docs/WEF_GCR_Report_2011-12.pdf.

49. "2009 Report Card for America's Infrastructure," *op. cit.*, p. 8.

50. *Ibid.*, p. 4.

51. *Ibid.*, p. 3.

52. *Ibid.*, p. 1.

53. "Public Spending on Transportation and Water Infrastructure," Congressional Budget Office, November 2010, p. 5, www.cbo.gov/sites/default/files/ cbofiles/ftpdocs/119xx/doc11940/11-17-infrastruc ture.pdf. Also see, Marcia Clemmitt, "Public-Works Projects," *CQ Researcher*, Feb. 20, 2009, pp. 153-176.

54. The rest of the money was spent on, among other things, tax rebates, education, state budget assistance and home weatherization grants.

55. "False Expectations: the historic infrastructure investment that wasn't," *The Economist*, Oct. 21, 2010, www.economist.com/node/17311851.

56. American Jobs Act website, www.americanjobsact .com/putting-workers-back-on-the-job.html.

57. Stephanie Condon, "Senate Republicans block Obama's jobs package," CBS News Political Hotsheet, Oct. 11, 2011, www.cbsnews.com/8301- 503544_162-20118915-503544.html.

58. Brad Plumer, "In two years, Congress won't have any money for transportation," *The Washington Post*, March 15, 2012, www.washingtonpost.com/blogs/ ezra-klein/post/in-two-years-congress-wont-have- any-money-left-for-transportation/2012/03/15/ gIQAw2SKES_blog.html.

59. Keith Hill, "Speaker Boehner says he prefers six-month highway bill extension," *The Hill*, June 7, 2012, http://thehill.com/blogs/transportation- report/highways-bridges-and-roads/231537-boeh ner-i-am-not-interested-in-some-30-day-extension- if-highway-conference-fails.

60. Past Elections webpage, Center for Transportation Excellence, www.cfte.org/success/pastelections.asp.

BIBLIOGRAPHY

Books

Ascher, Kate, *The Works: Anatomy of a City*, Penguin Press, 2005.

The executive director of the New York City Economic Development Corporation explains how the city's complex infrastructure works and what maintenance engineers and planners do to keep it running.

Tarr, Joel A., ed., *Devastation and Renewal: An Environmental History of Pittsburgh and Its Region*, University of Pittsburgh Press, 2005.

Essays assembled by a Carnegie Mellon University professor of history and policy detail the conflicting roles of money, politics, industry and the environment in shaping the infrastructure of Pittsburgh and the surrounding region.

Articles

Duke, Kenny, "If the Feds Can't Fix the Bridge, Should We?" *The Cincinnati Post*, Aug. 29, 2007, http://news.cincypost.com/apps/pbcs.dll/article?AID=/20070829/NEWS01/708290365.

A Kentucky state senator proposes a new state finance authority with the power to sell bonds and impose tolls to fund the huge rebuilding projects required by the aging national highway system, such as bridges over the Ohio River.

Hughes, John, and Angela Greiling Keane, "Bridge Disaster Fuels Push to Raise Tax for Repairs," *Bloomberg.com*, Aug. 20, 2007, www.bloomberg.com/apps/news?pid=20601103&sid=aUfj43QPplT8&refer=us.

The recent bridge collapse in Minneapolis puts new pressure on federal lawmakers and 2008 presidential candidates to offer plans for future infrastructure funding and priority setting.

Shaw, Gaylord, "The Enormous U.S. Dam Problem No One Is Talking About," *The Christian Science Monitor*, Jan. 3, 2006.

A long-time reporter on dam safety argues that state and federal neglect has led to catastrophic dam failures in the past and threatens to allow more in the future.

Reports and Studies

Hargen, David T., and Ravi K. Karanam, *16th Annual Report on the Performance of State Highway Systems*, The Reason Foundation, June 2007.

A libertarian think tank specializing in transportation issues state-by-state rankings of road performance, capacity and funding.

Drinking Water Distribution Systems: Assessing and Reducing Risks, Committee on Public Water Supply Distribution Systems, National Research Council, 2006.

A national expert panel pinpoints the top priorities in maintaining and upgrading drinking-water systems and describes how new technologies may increase safety.

The Fuel Tax and Alternatives for Transportation Funding, Transportation Research Board, 2006.

A national expert panel examines the history and potential of fuel taxes as the primary funding source for transportation infrastructure and concludes that direct user fees are a better option for the future.

2006 Long-Term Reliability Assessment: The Reliability of the Bulk Power Systems in North America, North American Electric Reliability Council, October 2006.

The industry council that sets voluntary standards for electrical-power delivery finds that in the next decade electricity demands will far outstrip planned maintenance and capacity-building by power-generation and transmission companies.

Privatization of Water Services in the United States: An Assessment of Issues and Experience, Committee on Privatization of Water Services in the United States, National Research Council, 2002.

A national expert panel summarizes the history of U.S. water and wastewater utilities and dissects pros and cons of various privatization schemes.

Report Card for America's Infrastructure 2005, American Society of Civil Engineers, March 2005, www.asce.org/reportcard/2005/page.cfm?id=203.

The most recent in a series of periodic infrastructure assessments by a public-works engineers' group analyzes infrastructure health sector by sector and state by state and references local media coverage of infrastructure issues. The ASCE gives the overall U.S. infrastructure a grade of "D."

Surface Transportation: Strategies Are Available for Making Existing Road Infrastructure Perform Better, Government Accountability Office, July 2007.
Congress' nonpartisan auditing office concludes that greater private-sector involvement, expansion of user tolls and management reforms including the setting of performance measures would improve America's roads.

Trends in Public Spending on Transportation and Water Infrastructure, 1956 to 2004, Congressional Budget Office, August 2007.
Congress' nonpartisan financial-analysis office describes historical patterns in federal and state infrastructure spending for dams, mass transit, railways, air-traffic control and other systems.

For More Information

American Association of State Highway and Transportation Officials, 444 N Capitol St., N.W., Suite 249, Washington, DC 20001; (202) 624-5800; www.transportation.org/. Represents state highway departments.

American Public Works Association, 1401 K St., N.W., 11th Floor, Washington, DC 20005; (202) 408-9541; www.apwa.net. Provides information and analysis on infrastructure-related public policy.

American Society of Civil Engineers, 1801 Alexander Bell Dr., Reston, VA 20191-4400; (703) 295-6300; www.asce.org/. Issues a periodic report card on U.S. infrastructure needs and updates a list of infrastructure-related news stories.

American Water Works Association, 6666 W. Quincy Ave., Denver, CO 80235; (303) 794-7711; www.awwa.org. Provides information and public-policy analysis.

Federal Highway Administration, U.S. Department of Transportation, 1200 New Jersey Ave., S.E., Washington, DC 20590; (202) 366-065-; www.fhwa.dot.gov/. Monitors bridge and highway safety and transportation funding needs.

Greatest Engineering Achievements of the Twentieth Century, National Academy of Engineering; www.greatachievements.org. Web site that details the modern history of infrastructure systems including roads and water systems.

Keston Institute for Public Finance and Infrastructure Policy, School of Policy, Planning, and Development, Marshall School of Business, University of Southern California, Ralph and Goldy Lewis Hall 232, Los Angeles, CA 90089-0626; (213) 740-4120; www.usc.edu/schools/sppd/keston/index.php. Provides research and analysis on California and national infrastructure issues.

National Council for Public-Private Partnerships, 1660 L St., N.W., Suite 510, Washington, DC 20036; (202) 467-6800; http://ncppp.org/. Organization of businesses and public officials interested in joint initiatives to provide public services.

Reason Foundation, 3415 S. Sepulveda Blvd. Suite 400, Los Angeles, CA 90034; (310) 391-2245; www.reason.org/index.shtml. Libertarian think tank that analyzes transportation-infrastructure problems and issues reports on highways.

Water Environment Foundation, 601 Wythe St., Alexandria, VA 22314-1994; (800) 666-0206; www.wef.org/Home. Provides information and public-policy advocacy on water-quality issues.

8

High-Speed Trains

Thomas J. Billitteri and Roland Flamini

AFP/Getty Images/Josep Lago

Spain's sleek, new bullet train, the AVE, completes the 410-mile Barcelona to Madrid run in two-and-a-half hours at an average speed of 164 mph. Seven European and four Asian countries have high-speed rail. In the United States, however, the only high-speed train is Amtrak's Acela, which hits 150 mph for short stretches along the Northeast Corridor. Several more U.S. systems are under consideration.

From *CQ Researcher*, May 1, 2009 (updated January 5, 2012).

It's the dream of grounded airline passengers and aggravated drivers everywhere: Hop a sleek, futuristic train that whisks you in living-room comfort to your destination hundreds of miles away at speeds two, three or even four times that of an auto.

Outside the United States, the idea is hardly new. "Bullet trains" first appeared in Japan 45 years ago, and countries as diverse as France, Germany, Spain, Italy, China, Taiwan and South Korea have high-speed systems running or under construction.[1]

In America, supertrain development has long been stalled — but maybe not for long. President Barack Obama, seeking to make 21st-century train travel a signature issue of his administration, added $8 billion to this year's economic stimulus package for high-speed and other rail projects — the most ever allotted for rail at once.[2] In addition, Obama's 2010 budget proposes state grants for high-speed rail totaling $5 billion over five years.[3]

The money is aimed at two very different versions of what in the United States is defined as high-speed rail: conventional electric- or diesel-powered trains that can move at 110 miles an hour, or about 40 percent faster than most Amtrak trains travel today; and European-style high-speed trains that require special tracks and sophisticated locomotives to speed passengers at hundreds of miles an hour toward their destinations.

Right now, Amtrak's Washington-New York-Boston Acela Express counts as the closest thing to high-speed rail in the United States. It is capable of reaching 150 mph but averages roughly 80 mph on its Washington-New York route over tracks shared with freight and commuter trains.[4]

High-Speed Rail Corridors Designated

The Federal Railroad Administration has designated 10 high-speed rail corridors as potential recipients of federal money, plus the Northeast Corridor. The 1,920-mile Midwest corridor based in Chicago is the longest, followed by the 1,022-mile Gulf Coast corridor.

Proposed High-speed Rail Corridors

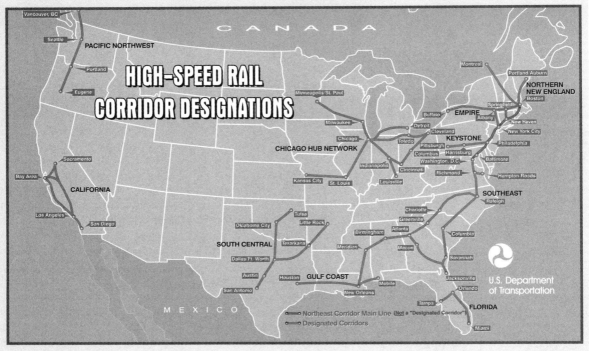

Source: Federal Railroad Administration

Experts say the $8 billion in stimulus money isn't enough to pay for even one high-speed system. Much of the money, they say, will be used to improve existing tracks shared by passenger and freight trains, to help traditional passenger trains run faster in key corridors, such as one linking Chicago with other Midwest cities. But some of the money will likely be used for real bullet trains proposed in California, Florida, Texas and elsewhere. The government has identified 10 intercity corridors, plus the Northeast Corridor linking Washington and Boston, as potential recipients of federal money.

Obama said the nation requires "a smart transportation system equal to the needs of the 21st century."[5] Transportation Secretary Ray LaHood calls high-speed rail a "transformational initiative" for the economy.[6] In April the president issued a strategic plan for high-speed rail, and by June the Transportation Department must explain how groups can seek grants.[7] The competition for money "is going to be pretty severe," said Democratic Gov. Jim Doyle of Wisconsin, which is part of the Midwest high-speed rail effort.[8]

However the stimulus money is used, rail advocates say it marks an historic shift in federal transportation policy, which for decades has favored highways and airports over trains.

"It is laying the groundwork for a high-speed rail system, and it's setting the tone that we're going to have one," says James P. RePass, founder and CEO of the National

Corridors Initiative, a group that advocates transportation-infrastructure development, with an emphasis on rail. While both government and private money will be required to develop high-speed trains, RePass says, the federal stimulus money signals "a sea change in the attitude of the national administration about rail."

Ross B. Capon, president of the National Association of Railroad Passengers, calls the stimulus money "a serious beginning."

"Eight billion dollars is not going to fulfill the dreams of people who see a [French-style 200 mph] TGV going everywhere," he says, "but it can lay the groundwork for that if it's the first installment on a serious commitment."

But high-speed trains face huge obstacles in the United States. Beyond massive infrastructure outlays, experts say they require a distinct set of geographic and demographic circumstances to make them worthwhile. They must serve cities within a few hundred miles of each other — otherwise it's faster for passengers to fly. Population densities along the route must be high — otherwise trains can't generate adequate revenue. Passengers must have an easy, cheap way to get from a train station to their final destination — requiring integrated public-transit systems in urban areas. And with gasoline far cheaper in the United States than in Europe, consumers must have an incentive to ditch their cars in favor of trains.

"Unlike Europe, we've been wedded to the auto in so many ways," says Carlos Schwantes, a professor of transportation studies at the University of Missouri-St. Louis. "Our cities are very diffuse, very spread out. Urban sprawl goes on for hundreds of miles. If we put in high-speed trains, where would we site the stations that would benefit many Americans? People don't live downtown, and they would have to secure space to park their autos. We don't have a support network of trolleys, trams and so on."

Efforts to build true high-speed systems have faltered in the past. In Florida, where a Tampa-Orlando-Miami route has long been contemplated, voters passed a constitutional amendment in 2000 directing the

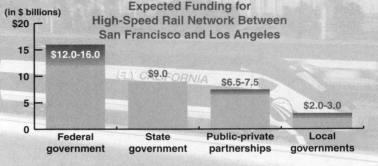

California System Would Cost $45 Billion

Three-fourths of the $45 billion cost of a statewide, 800-mile high-speed rail network in California would be spent on building the San Francisco-Los Angeles/Anaheim leg, with the estimated $33.6 billion cost mostly provided by government, according to the California High-Speed Rail Authority.

Expected Funding for High-Speed Rail Network Between San Francisco and Los Angeles

(in $ billions)

Federal government	State government	Public-private partnerships	Local governments
$12.0-16.0	$9.0	$6.5-7.5	$2.0-3.0

Source: California High-Speed Rail Authority

legislature to develop a system capable of going faster than 120 mph. But Republican Gov. Jeb Bush helped quash the project. Efforts to build systems in Texas and California also failed in the past.

Today a renewed effort in California has come closest to achieving a true high-speed system. In November voters approved the sale of $9.95 billion in bonds to help pay for a 220-mph system between San Francisco and Los Angeles/Anaheim and eventually Sacramento and San Diego. However, the state — mired in a fiscal crisis — faces a challenge in raising the money.

The California High-Speed Rail Authority says the 800-mile system will cost $45 billion in government and private funds to build. Once in operation, the system will generate more than $1 billion in annual profits and need no operating subsidies, the authority claims.[9] It also says the system will create thousands of jobs, have huge environmental benefits and draw as many as 117 million riders a year by 2030.

"By building this system, California will retain its rightful place as America's premier economic, transportation and environmental leader," declared Quentin Kopp, chairman of the state rail authority.[10]

But critics say California's claims are grossly exaggerated. A study by the Reason Foundation, a free-market-oriented think tank, and two other groups — Citizens

President Barack Obama signs legislation creating the $787 billion economic stimulus package, in Denver on Feb. 17, 2009. The president added $8 billion for high-speed and other rail projects, making high-speed rail a signature project of his administration. Vice President Joseph Biden looks on.

Against Government Waste and the Howard Jarvis Taxpayers Association — concluded that the system would cost tens of billions more than the authority's estimate and that ridership and greenhouse-gas reductions would be much lower.[11]

"My bottom line: It is a terrible financial loser," says Wendell Cox, a transportation consultant and coauthor of the study.

As rail backers begin vying for federal stimulus money, a fundamental question remains: How much funding should be allocated for true high-speed systems and how much for incremental improvements in existing rail systems to make traditional trains run faster.

Joseph Vranich, coauthor of the Reason Foundation study and former president of the High Speed Rail Association, said he would "focus all this money where

it's needed": on a true high-speed rail system in the New York-Washington corridor, "by far the No. 1 market" for high-speed rail.

"Population density in the corridor is high, distances are short enough to make trains a viable alternative to airplanes, rights-of-way for new track already exist and construction of a new airport in the New York area to accommodate future travel demand would be difficult," he says. "Once the country — public agencies and private companies — are smarter about how to build a high-speed system, then we can evaluate some other lines."

But Capon of the rail passengers group argues that concentrating stimulus money in a single rail market would simply discourage others from moving ahead with projects that he contends are vitally needed. "If we say to 49 states, this is not your money, states may just give up."

As government officials, private companies, taxpayers and rail experts ponder the future of high-speed rail, here are some of the questions they are debating:

Do high-speed trains make economic sense?

Rick Harnish, executive director of the Midwest High Speed Rail Association — a Chicago-based advocacy group representing 1,500 individuals, cities and corporations — sees huge economic benefits to high-speed rail. It would cut travel costs, induce more people to go places and foster commercial ties between cities, he says.

The group's immediate goal is upgrading tracks, signals and crossings between Chicago and other Midwest cities so conventional diesel-powered trains could travel up to 110 mph. On the 289-mile St. Louis route, that would cut the travel time to less than four hours, from the current 5.5 hours.

The association's ultimate goal is a 220-mph system linking Chicago with metropolitan areas throughout the Midwest.

"Our current system doesn't make sense economically," Harnish says. "Our airline industry is dying. The auto industry is dying. The Highway Trust Fund required an $8 billion subsidy last year. Households are hurting because they're spending too much on transportation. The only way to make a significant difference in getting transportation costs down is by expanding the railroad network."

Howard A. Learner, executive director of the Chicago-based Environmental Law and Policy Center, an advocacy group that backs high-speed rail in the Midwest, says rail projects not only create jobs but also "pull together the regional economy," making it easier for people to move between cities "in a way that makes business work better."

But critics remain unconvinced that expensive high-speed and supertrain systems can ever pay off.

"Close scrutiny of these plans reveals that they do not live up to the hype," argues Randal O'Toole, a senior fellow at the Cato Institute, a conservative think tank in Washington. "As attractive as 110-to-220-mile-per-hour trains might sound, even the most optimistic forecasts predict they will take few cars off the road. At best, they will replace for-profit private commuter airlines with heavily subsidized public rail systems. Taxpayers and politicians should be wary of any transportation projects that cannot be paid for out of user fees."[12]

O'Toole says the average Japanese rides that country's *Shinkansen* bullet train only 400 miles a year. "If we're going to move the average American 400 miles a year, it's not worth it" to build high-speed rail systems, he says.

The debate over the economic impact of high-speed rail is bound to heat up as competition grows over the federal stimulus money, especially for multi-state corridors. "Economists like to say, let's allocate the costs and the benefits among the states by population, distance, density and so on," says Steven R. Ditmeyer, former director of research and development at the Federal Railroad Administration. "It's like the theological debates over angels on the heads of pins. There are no right answers, and the debates can go on endlessly."

A 2000 report prepared for Amtrak and state transportation agencies concluded that an improved and expanded passenger rail system in the Midwest would produce $1.70 in benefits for every dollar spent to build, finance, operate and maintain the system.[13] In Florida, a 2002 report said a 150-mph route between Tampa and Orlando would generate $1.27 in benefits for every dollar in costs.[14]

And in California, boosters say the high-speed train project will create nearly 160,000 construction-related jobs plus another 450,000 permanent jobs by 2035 resulting from economic growth spurred by the rail system. They also claim the system will generate more than $1 billion in surplus revenue annually and increase productivity by easing congestion.[15]

Likewise, a 2008 study by the Bay Area Council Economic Institute, a public-private partnership of business, labor, government and higher education, concluded that in the San Francisco Bay Area high-speed rail would generate a sustained 1.1 percent increase in employment by 2030 — 48,000 new jobs — and spur tourism, construction spending and business productivity, the latter by reducing commuting time.[16]

In addition, the study said an expandable statewide rail system offers "the potential to meet a significant part" of California's needs for new airport and freeway construction in coming decades.[17]

But critics say the California plan is all but a pipe dream. The Reason Foundation study concluded it was unlikely that enough private money and public subsidies could be found to finance the complete plan and that "claims of profitability could not conceivably be credible under even the most optimistic assumptions, unless some or all capital and debt costs are ignored." The San Francisco-Los Angeles portion alone would lose up to $4.17 billion annually by 2030, "with a small profit possible under only the most optimistic and improbable conditions."[18]

California officials defend their projections. "This has been extensively studied," says Dan Levitt, deputy director of the state's high-speed rail authority. The state's assumptions "are based on an analysis of other systems that have been operating for decades in other parts of the world and [that have been] extensively proved," Levitt says.

Moreover, rail advocates point out that for more than half a century the federal government has poured billions of dollars into the Interstate Highway System and other roadways, subsidized car travel by keeping gasoline taxes low, funded airport expansion and, after the 2001 terrorist attacks, bailed out the airline industry.[19]

"There are people who, when someone buys cars or gas, they say that is the free market at work — hurrah!" says Capon of the National Association of Railroad Passengers. "And when the government puts on a tax to build a railroad, they say that's socialism, that's bad. They usually don't talk about all the government taxes, direct and indirect, that support highways and aviation

Nations From Spain to China Boast Bullet Trains
Japan set the trend in high-speed rail in 1964.

Ever since the introduction of Japan's bullet train system — the Shinkansen — in 1964, 10 other nations overseas have offered high-speed train service to passengers. Seven Western European countries currently have such trains, with several countries working to link up their systems. The introduction of high-speed rail trains in Asian countries such as China, Taiwan and South Korea has been credited with helping to boost their economic growth.

High-speed Rail in Operation, Planned or Under Construction

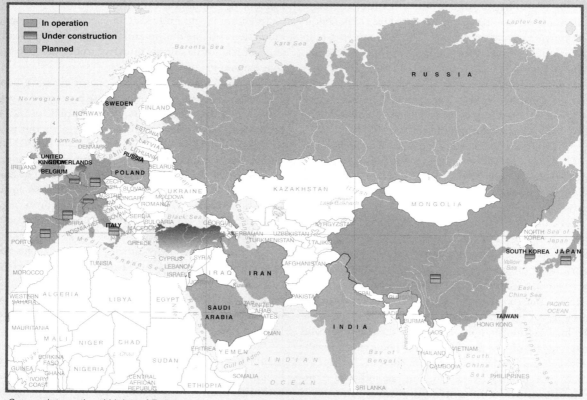

Source: International Union of Railways

because those systems have been constructed to give the false sense of minimal public subsidy."

Skeptics of high-speed rail don't buy such arguments, though. In a 2001 report, the fiscally conservative National Taxpayers Union pointed out that airline passengers and auto users pay a broad range of federal taxes designated for such things as air traffic control and roads.

On the other hand, it said, Amtrak is funded through an annual congressional appropriation from the general fund and has received billions of dollars in state and federal subsidies since its formation in 1971.

"Amtrak's dismal track record and constant need for subsidies suggests that rail, high-speed or not, may not be viable in the United States," the group said.[20]

Would high-speed trains relieve highway and airport congestion?

When Ditmeyer, the former Federal Railroad Administration official, thinks about places where high-speed rail systems might make the most sense, he refers to a Census Bureau map featuring the U.S. land area in black, with groupings of white dots indicating lights in populated areas. The so-called "Nighttime Map" shows a pattern of brightness that Ditmeyer calls "the string of pearls." The Northeast Corridor looks ablaze. So, too, do corridors in Florida, North Carolina and ones radiating from Chicago. Out West, bright dots gleam along corridors in California and Colorado.

"Looking at that map tells you where high-speed rail fits," Ditmeyer says. The key requirements, he says: population density, reasonable proximity — 250 miles or so — between cities, and economic ties between the cities that will generate passenger volume. And, Ditmeyer adds, "it also helps if other modes of transportation are congested. Otherwise, people won't have much of a reason for diverting" from cars and planes to the train.

Congestion relief is indeed a key selling point among high-speed rail advocates. Drivers "will switch because [a fast train] is a good option," argues Learner of the Environmental Law and Policy Center. He also points to Chicago's O'Hare International Airport and its legendary congestion and says rail "will enable people to have a third option for intercity travel around the Midwest."

"The primary modes of intercity passenger travel now are highway or air, and both our roads and our airspace are challenged by costly congestion," Transportation secretary LaHood noted. "And driving a car doesn't allow a driver to use the time for work or recreation the way train travel does. With train stations largely within cities, access is simpler. That direct access to our intercities is very much consistent with our focus on creating livable communities."[21]

But skeptics question whether trains can lure enough people away from highways and airports to make much of a dent in congestion. Because California is furthest along among the states in planning for high-speed rail, some of the most vigorous debates so far have occurred there.

The California High-Speed Rail Authority said super-trains would alleviate the need for some 3,000 miles of new freeway lanes, five airport runways and 90 departure gates over the next two decades, at a total cost of almost $100 billion. Intercity and local travelers would save more than $42 billion by 2050 in congestion relief and another $14 billion in accident and pollution reduction. Airline passengers would realize another $2 billion in delay-reduction benefits, and airlines would see $1.8 billion in such benefits.[22]

Philip J. Romero, dean of the College of Business and Economics at California State University, Los Angeles, found that high-speed rail service not only would cut travel time between Los Angeles and San Francisco by at least 50 percent compared with auto travel but also ease auto congestion within Los Angeles County.[23] At least 41 percent of high-speed train trips in California would be for business travel, with the largest number — more than 18 million — within the county, according to Romero. "While the system has been designed with intercity travel in mind, the most common passengers will be Los Angeles-area commuters."[24]

Romero also argued that high-speed rail would encourage denser development near stations, further reducing car traffic. "Nearly 35,000 fewer undeveloped acres will be consumed by development in L.A. County by 2035" if high-speed rail is built, he wrote.[25]

Others are similarly optimistic. Dan Tempelis, project manager of the Los Angeles-to-Palmdale segment of California's proposed system, argued in the *Los Angeles Times* that freeway and airport congestion costs the state's economy about $20 billion a year in lost time and wasted fuel.[26] And Kopp, chairman of the California effort, warned that airports in Los Angeles, San Diego and San Francisco will reach capacity in 20 years. "Building the 220-mph train system to solve this need for expanded capacity will require only one-third of the cost of pouring new concrete to add freeways and runways."[27]

But critics are highly skeptical of much of the data produced by the California planners. For one thing, they say, no matter how fast the train goes, local commuters heading to and from jobs are unlikely to abandon their cars in large numbers, especially if they don't have easy access to a rapid, convenient transit system that will whisk them from doorstep to train station.

Rail expert Vranich, coauthor of the Reason Foundation study, rejects the claim that high-speed rail

High-Speed Rail on Fast Track in Europe, Asia

Eleven nations have networks, with many more on the way.

Forty-five years after the first bullet train began operating in Japan, 10 other countries also have high-speed rail networks, and the United States just barely.*

High-speed rail has become one of the most practical solutions for land travel across Japan, where more than 70 percent of the land is unsuited for road travel due to mountainous and uninhabitable terrain. Construction of the world's first high-speed line — the *Shinkansen* ("Bullet Train") — was completed in 1964 from Tokyo to Osaka in the south, with a then-top speed of 130 mph; today it is 186 mph. In 1973 the transport minister, recognizing the interrelationship between land development and the high-speed rail network, approved construction plans to expand the *Shinkansen* nationwide with five additional lines.

Spurred by Japan's success, France in 1981 launched its *Train à Grande Vitesse* ("High-Speed Train") — better known as the TGV (pronounced tay jay vay) — between Paris and Lyon. Unlike Japan's *Shinkansen*, however, the TGV uses existing track in urban areas as well as high-speed rail infrastructure. The dual-route capability facilitated the creation of new lines in France in the 1980s and '90s.

---

* High-speed rail is usually defined as capable of 125 mph or more; the Amtrak Acela in the Northeast Corridor can hit 150 mph on short segments of the route.

Cross-border service into Germany eventually led to the construction of Germany's own ICE ("Inter City Express") lines in the late 1980s, also fitted for operation over older tracks and compatible with existing signaling systems.

Today seven European countries have high-speed rail services, with Spain becoming the latest newcomer. Launched in 2008, the sleek AVE (*Alta Velocidad Española*, or "Spanish High Speed") train completes the 410-mile journey from Barcelona to Madrid — a popular business route — in two-and-a-half hours at an average speed of 164 mph. Construction plans anticipate that all provincial cities will be no more than four hours from Madrid, the capital and largest city. And as in Japan, all routes are being assembled from scratch.

Ridership statistics indicate growing acceptance for the AVE. In early 2008 airlines accounted for 72 percent of the 4.8 million long-distance passengers in Spain who traveled by air or rail. Today that figure is down to 60 percent. High-speed rail travel in the country grew by 28 percent during the same period.

"The numbers will be equal within two years," says Josep Valls, a professor at the ESADE Business School in Barcelona.[1]

Moreover, high-speed rail tickets tend to be more affordable than air or road travel thanks largely to government subsidies, with one-way fares for the Madrid-Barcelona line

will reduce auto traffic. "Most congestion occurs with commuters going to work" — not on long stretches of highways linking cities that might be served by rail.

"[F]ew people live or work in downtowns anymore," wrote the Cato Institute's O'Toole. "As a result, even a 200-mph train won't take more than 3 or 4 percent of cars off the highways it parallels. Instead, the main effect of this heavily subsidized train will be to put struggling (and relatively unsubsidized) short-haul airlines out of business."[28]

Many also argue that U.S. policies that keep gas prices and road tolls low dampen demand for passenger rail — and its potential to reduce auto congestion. Without a change in U.S. oil policy, high-speed rail "is

certainly less viable" here than in Europe or Asia, says Louis Thompson, who served as rail-policy adviser at the World Bank and associate administrator of the Federal Railroad Administration.

"In Europe and Japan, gas is $5 or $6 a gallon. That's what restricts auto travel. In the United States, we're pursuing what amounts to a conflicting policy."

Is high-speed rail good for the environment?

Besides high-speed rail's impact on infrastructure costs and congestion, a primary benefit of rail, proponents say, is its ability to reduce environmental damage. But skeptics say the environmental benefits of supertrains are often exaggerated.

as low as $50. Renfe, the state-owned company that operates the trains, claims a 99 percent on-time departure rate.

Doubts linger, however, over the profitability of such endeavors. Government-subsidized expansions to Japan's *Shinkansen*, along with the growth of air travel, had put the state-owned Japanese National Railways in the red by $200 billion by 1987, eventually leading to the privatization of high-speed rail in Japan. Further expansions, though, continue to receive government subsidies. A growing auto industry has also contributed to a steady decline in high-speed ridership, even during periods of rising fuel prices.

Similar subsidies abound in Europe, where motor fuel taxes of between 300 and 400 percent provide annual rail subsidies of about $100 billion. Furthermore, as in Japan, many countries are experiencing declining passenger levels at the expense of expanding automobile traffic.

The declining ridership has led TGV construction planners to reconsider the placement of intermediate stations in certain French localities, according to a report by the UK rail-research organization Greengauge21.[2]

But amid doubts over their viability, and even some questions over their usefulness, more and more high-speed lines are cropping up worldwide. Even China is getting on board. In April 2007 the country began operating several high-speed lines between major cities. Indeed, China's 3,800-mile network is longer than all European lines combined. China also boasts the Shanghai Maglev Train — the fastest commercial train in the world at 267 mph — although there have been criticisms over high ticket prices, limited operating hours and remote terminal locations.

A high-speed rail network also has emerged in nearby South Korea, with more planned in the Middle East and South Asia, in countries such as Iran, Saudi Arabia and India.

Despite the popularity of such trains, a lack of synergy between systems has historically complicated connections across national borders. Passengers on the TGV, for example, cannot easily make connecting reservations for high-speed trains on Germany's ICE system or take a train from southern France to Barcelona.

Last July seven European transportation representatives banded together to form Railteam, an alliance to create a seamless, high-speed network across Western Europe. Functioning much like an airline alliance, Railteam is coordinating a common reservation system that's scheduled to begin later this year.

"The idea of a European network of high-speed rail is at last being realized," said Guillaume Pépy, chairman of the high-speed London-Brussels-Paris Eurostar train service. "It will be a real alternative to air travel."[3]

— *Darrell Dela Rosa*

[1] See Giles Tremlett, "Spain's High-Speed Trains Win Over Fed-Up Flyers," *The Guardian*, Jan. 13, 2009, www.guardian.co.uk/world/2009/jan/13/spain-trains.

[2] See "High Speed Trains and the Development and Regeneration of Cities," *Greengauge21*, June 2006.

[3] See Carol Matlack, "High-Speed Trains Erode Europe's Borders," *Spiegel Online*, Jan. 10, 2008, www.spiegel.de/international/business/0,1518,druck-527794,00.html.

Capon of the National Association of Railroad Passengers calls rail "green" transportation. "It is environmentally friendly, more energy efficient, supports energy-efficient real estate development as opposed to sprawl and it addresses quality-of-life issues and room-for-growth issues. In many cases the space doesn't exist to build the highways or airports that would be needed if you try to continue to be the only major industrialized nation that did it without a modern train system."

In California, the proposed train system would cut the state's carbon dioxide (CO_2) emissions — the main component of climate-warming greenhouse gases — by 12 billion pounds each year and reduce foreign-oil dependence by nearly 13 million barrels a year by 2030,

the rail authority said. "Since it will use electric power, high-speed trains can be a key element in helping California meet . . . greenhouse-gas reduction goals" under a 2006 state act requiring emissions to drop to 1990 levels by 2020, "and will have far less environmental impact than expanding highways and airports."[29]

High-speed trains would reduce intercity car travel and provide Californians with more than $13.8 billion in highway-related benefits stemming from reduced traffic accidents and air pollution, the state rail authority says. That estimate likely understates environmental benefits, it says, because it includes only reductions in primary pollutants such as carbon monoxide and hydrocarbons.

C H R O N O L O G Y

1869-1960 *Train travel booms, but jet travel and interstate highways lead to a decline.*

1869 Transcontinental Railroad completed.

1893 Train reaches record 112.5 mph in western New York.

1920 Passenger volumes on U.S. railroads peak, but then plunge during the Great Depression.

1941-1945 *Wartime restrictions on autos spur ridership, but growing car ownership, the Interstate Highway System and jet travel soon lure people away from railroads.*

1960 Trains carry about 327 million Americans, less than a third of the peak volumes of the 1920s.

1960s-1970s *Japan launches bullet train, but supertrains remain stalled in U.S.*

1964 Japanese Shinkansen bullet-train links Tokyo and Osaka.

1965 High Speed Ground Transportation Act starts federal effort to develop high-speed rail technologies.

1968 Gordon T. Danby and James R. Powell of Brookhaven National Laboratory patent a magnetic levitation train.

1969 Metroliner begins service between Washington and New York.

1970 Rail Passenger Service Act leads to creation of Amtrak.

1974 Vehicle on rails sets speed record of 255.4 mph in Pueblo, Colo.

1978 U.S. airline industry is deregulated, helping to introduce low-cost fares and further suppress rail travel.

1980s-1990s *France and Germany make huge strides in high-speed rail, but plans stall in U.S.*

1981 French TGV high-speed passenger rail line links Paris and Lyon.

1990 Department of Transportation commits $10 million for study of magnetic levitation rail technology; TGV hits record 320 mph.

1991 Germany introduces InterCity Express (ICE) high-speed rail service.

1992 Federal officials designate high-speed rail corridors in Midwest, Florida, California, Southeast and Pacific Northwest.

1998 German ICE train derails, killing 101 and injuring 88 in worst high-speed rail disaster. . . . Transportation Equity Act for the 21st Century authorizes six additional high-speed corridors.

2000-Present *High-speed rail gets financial boost from Washington.*

2000 Amtrak's Acela Express begins service between Washington and Boston; Florida voters pass constitutional amendment requiring that a bullet train be built in the state, but the project is opposed by then-Gov. Jeb Bush; the amendment is repealed in 2004.

2001 Terrorist attacks in New York, Washington and Pennsylvania lead to shutdown of commercial airline system and surge in Amtrak ridership, notably in Northeast Corridor.

2007 Japan announces plan for privately financed magnetic levitation train in 2025.

2008 Gas prices surge to more than $4 a gallon before falling back, helping to revive support for passenger rail. . . . California voters approve $9.95 billion bond issue to help pay for proposed high-speed rail line between San Francisco and Los Angeles. . . . Plans for a German maglev train linking central Munich to city's airport are halted.

2009 Obama administration includes $8 billion for high-speed and other rail projects in $787 billion economic stimulus bill and seeks $5 billion over five years in 2010 budget; stimulus money boosts hopes of rail supporters but leads to Republican charges of wasteful spending; Obama administration issues strategic plan for high-speed rail, with grants to come as soon as late summer.

2010

Jan. 28 — Government announces states chosen to receive segments of the $8 billion in federal funds for high-speed rail (HSR) development. At a town hall meeting in Tampa, President Obama observes, "There's no reason why other countries can build high-speed rail lines and we can't."

Sept. 16 — A somewhat skeptical white paper on HSR prepared for the National Conference of State Legislators concludes, "The sustainability of high-speed rail in the U.S., then, will finally be determined by state and federal policy makers, who find themselves in the familiar position of having to make difficult choices in light of competing priorities, scarce resources and political and economic uncertainty."

2011

Feb. 14 — President Obama sends Congress his federal budget proposals for fiscal 2012, including $8 billion for HSR.

Feb. 16 — Gov. Rick Scott, R-Fla., announces he is returning $2 billion in federal funds already earmarked to construct HSR between Tampa and Orlando. Scott says he is abandoning the project because cost overruns would put too big a financial burden on the state. Scott was following the lead of Republican governors in Wisconsin and Ohio who returned HSR development money to Washington late last year.

June 28 — Spain closes HSR service from Toledo to Albacete, opened in December, because it was serving an average of just nine passengers daily.

July 23 — Deadly crash of two high-speed trains in Wenzhou, in China's eastern Zhejiang Province, leaves at least 35 passengers dead and over 200 injured. Beijing orders an inquiry into the crash and lowers the speed limit for its high-speed train network.

Sept. 22 — House slashes funds for President Obama's signature HSR initiative in the 2012 budget to zero, and the Senate follows suit. But the full Appropriations Committee puts back $100 million, which will be used to improve tracks.

In the Midwest, 110-mph trains running between Chicago and St. Louis would spew lower amounts of harmful gases, such as volatile organic compounds (VOCs) and carbon monoxide (CO), than cars and airplanes, and less nitrous oxides than cars per passenger mile, the Midwest High Speed Rail Association says.[30]

"High-speed trains draw power from the electrical grid, which is fueled primarily by domestically produced energy sources, such as coal," wrote Paul Weinstein Jr., chief operating officer of the Progressive Policy Institute, a liberal think tank in Washington. "Plus, trains require about one-third as much energy per passenger mile as automobiles and airplanes. Although nothing powered through the grid is entirely carbon-neutral, high-speed trains produce no direct emissions."

What's more, Weinstein said, high-speed rail produces half the carbon-dioxide emissions as airplanes and one-sixth that of cars.[31]

But critics are highly skeptical of the environmental benefits claimed by supporters.

"People trying to pass this off as green are almost bordering on the scary," says Alan E. Pisarski, author of a series of statistical reports on commuting trends published by the Transportation Research Board, part of the National Academy of Sciences. He points to the "embedded costs" and greenhouse-gas emissions inherent in building tracks and tunnels, leveling ground and doing other construction work for high-speed rail.

What's more, he says, the energy-saving potential of a rail system depends significantly on how electricity is generated to power the trains. If a train uses hydropower generated by the Hoover Dam, that's one thing, Pisarski says, "but if there are railcars bringing coal from Chicago" to run a bullet train, "it doesn't make a whole lot of sense."

Others are similarly skeptical. "[T]he environmental benefits will be minuscule," the Cato Institute's O'Toole argued. He labeled as "flawed," for example, an estimate that high-speed rail in California would save the amount of energy used to build the system in just five years.

"Maglev" Proponents Push Projects in U.S.

But critics cite high cost and limited passenger demand.

The world's most advanced method of ground transport is attracting renewed attention in the United States. Magnetic levitation is as controversial as it is remarkable.

"Maglev" uses industrial-strength magnets to lift train cars a small distance above a special guideway and propel them at airplane speeds — 260 mph or even faster.

The theories behind magnetic levitation technology have been around for decades, but obstacles ranging from financing and logistics to questionable passenger demand and worries about the effects of electromagnetism on health have slowed maglev development, especially in the United States.

Now, however, proponents in Nevada, Pennsylvania and elsewhere are moving ahead with plans they hope will result someday in full-fledged maglev systems.

Critics say maglev systems are costly to build, require special infrastructure that regular trains can't utilize and consume such vast amounts of energy that they are harmful to the environment.

"You talk about an electricity hog," charges transportation consultant Wendell Cox, a former member of the Los Angeles County Transportation Commission, who is critical of high-speed rail projects generally. "Maglev is an environmental outlaw."

Moreover, some argue that maglev systems won't draw enough riders to justify their cost. While they can be super swift, such systems are not much faster than some less expensive high-speed trains that use conventional steel

tracks. On the other hand, maglev systems don't move as rapidly as jet aircraft, making it hard for them to compete with planes on longer routes.

Proponents, however, have a far different view of maglev. They argue that the technology is more efficient than traditional steel-rail systems and less costly to maintain.

Magnetic levitation systems "represent a transportation revolution because several inherently undesirable characteristics of wheeled transport are eliminated or dramatically reduced, namely vibration, noise and wear and tear on parts from friction," according to Kevin C. Coates, a founder of the International Maglev Board. "Higher speeds are achievable without the penalty of increased maintenance costs. This translates into higher system reliability and increased sustainability due to the resulting longer service life and lower life-cycle costs."[1]

While maglev technology has been in development for decades in Japan and elsewhere, few systems are running or planned so far worldwide.

China, as one example, operates a system linking the Pudong commercial district in Shanghai to the city's airport. Speeds reach 268 miles per hour on the 19-mile route, cutting a 45-minute car trip to eight minutes.[2] But protests have arisen over extending the system, and residents have expressed concern over noise and potential effects of electromagnetic radiation. [3] In addition, 80 percent of the seats often are empty, and travelers have complained that the terminus station "is in the middle of nowhere, requiring a

"If autos and airplanes become, over the life of the high-speed rail project, an average of 20 percent more fuel efficient than they are today, then the payback period for high-speed rail rises to 25 years," he wrote. And that payback period "crucially depends" on the train system attracting the "high" ridership forecast by the rail authority.

"If ridership is lower, the payback period will be longer. And since rail lines require expensive and energy-intensive reconstruction and rehabilitation about every 30 years, it is quite possible that high-speed rail will save no energy at all."[32]

Levitt, the California rail authority deputy director, defends the environmental benefits of a supertrain system in his state, however.

"Not only would it cost more" to expand highways and airports to meet future travel demand, he says, "but the environmental impacts would be considerably greater. It's not only in the fact that high-speed rail brings benefits for reduced CO_2 emissions and reduced energy consumption and dependence on fossil fuels. High-speed rail also is more compatible with California's goals for sustainable development. So it's not just the cost of building the roads, it's the environmental cost and transfer to taxi or subway," according to *Wired*'s *Autopia* blog last year.[4]

In Japan, where maglev demonstrations have gone on for years, the country's central railway company announced plans in 2007 to build a maglev train linking Tokyo and Nagoya. The 180-mile route is supposed to open in 2025 and be financed entirely by the private sector.[5]

But in Germany, which also has had successful maglev demonstrations, plans for a maglev link from central Munich to the city's airport were halted last year. Construction costs had nearly doubled from $2.9 billion to $5.33 billion.[6]

No maglev systems operate in the United States, but proponents have been hoping that money set aside for high-speed rail in this year's $787 billion federal stimulus package will include maglev funding.

The federal government separately has made $45 million available to help finance preliminary work related to a proposed maglev link between Las Vegas and Anaheim, Calif., and it will soon make another $45 million available for projects east of the Mississippi River, according to Federal Railroad Administration (FRA) spokesman Warren Flatau. From fiscal 1999 to fiscal 2005, another $60 million was provided to maglev projects around the country, he said.

The East Coast region includes a proposed maglev system linking the Pittsburgh airport with the city and its eastern suburbs. The FRA is close to issuing an environmental impact statement for the project, Flatau said. That could bring it a step closer to reality. Other projects that have been proposed in the eastern United States would link Baltimore and Washington, and Atlanta with Chattanooga.

The Las Vegas-Anaheim system has been in the planning stages for two decades. But funding and other obstacles so

A maglev train links Shanghai's financial district with the city's airport. Speeds reach 268 miles per hour on the 19-mile route.

AFP/Getty Images/Mark Ralston

far have kept it from being built, and now it faces competition from a proposed, privately financed electric or diesel/electric wheel-on-steel train.[7]

[1] Kevin C. Coates, "Finally, Maglev Leadership," *Engineering News-Record*, March 2, 2009, http://enr.construction.com/opinions/viewPoint/2009/0225-MaglevLeadership.asp.

[2] "Maglev — the Great Debate," railway-technology.com, Feb. 11, 2008, www.railway-technology.com/features/feature1606/.

[3] *Ibid.*

[4] Alexander Lew, "Maglev Project in Munich: Cancelled," *Autopia* blog, March 28, 2008, http://blog.wired.com/cars/2008/03/maglev-project.html.

[5] "Maglev — The Great Debate," *op. cit.*

[6] Lew, *op. cit.*

[7] Abby Sewell, "City Council Votes to Support Anaheim to Vegas Train," *Desert Dispatch*, April 2, 2009.

the future-growth-of-the-state costs that need to be considered."

BACKGROUND

The Golden Spike

Railroads have operated in the United States since the early 19th century, but it was a golden spike, driven into the barren soil of northern Utah in 1869, that trumpeted rail's promise to move people long distances at relatively fast speeds. There, at Promontory Summit, the Union Pacific and Central Pacific railroads were joined in the nation's first transcontinental system, spanning more than 1,500 miles from Omaha to Sacramento.

The project was marred by the Credit Mobilier scandal, in which Union Pacific officials enriched themselves in building the rail line. Nonetheless, the six-year endeavor stands as a watershed of technological achievement and personal mobility and a model of what high-speed rail enthusiasts hope to see repeated today.[33]

The transcontinental railroad was an example of "bold action and big ideas" accomplished during a time of "economic upheaval and transformation," President Obama reminded a joint session of Congress in February. "In the midst of civil war, we laid railroad tracks from one coast to another that spurred commerce and industry."[34]

As technology advanced in the late 19th and early 20th centuries, so too did train speeds. In 1893, the steam locomotive Empire State Express No. 999 reached a record 112.5 mph in western New York, becoming the first object on wheels to exceed 100 mph.[35] In the 1930s, the diesel-powered Zephyr matched that speed on a Denver-to-Chicago run.[36]

Still, ridership waxed and waned during the last century. The number of passengers carried by trains doubled between 1900 and the end of World War I but then dropped more than 60 percent during the Great Depression. Ridership regained some ground during World War II as government restricted the use of private autos. But after the war, rising car ownership, construction of the Interstate Highway System and the advent of jet travel all helped to throw train travel into reverse. By 1960, passenger counts were only about half what they were in the opening years of the century.[37]

Meanwhile, the heavily regulated railroad industry was losing freight business to trucking, crimping the ability of the railroads to subsidize money-losing passenger routes.

In a review of high-speed rail issues in the mid-1990s, Thompson, the former World Bank adviser, wrote that "misguided government regulation of the railways — politically distorted rates and inability to adjust services — was one of the primary reasons for the rail dilemma," along with government support of the highway and airline systems.[38]

Financial problems among the railroads led to a number of mergers and attempts by rail executives to close money-draining passenger routes. The federal government resisted many of those efforts, but as the 1960s came to a close passenger service in the United States was losing steam fast.

"The number of trains, which had reached 20,000 in 1920, was down to 500, and over 100 of these were the subject of discontinuance proceedings," economics professor George W. Hilton wrote in a 1980 study for the American Enterprise Institute.[39]

High-Speed Rail

Meanwhile, new high-speed rail technology was emerging on the global scene. In 1964 Japan began *Shinkansen* bullet-train service between Tokyo and Osaka, initially running at up to 125 mph.[40] In France, test runs of the electrified TGV (*Train à Grande Vitesse*) had begun in the early 1970s.

In the United States, bullet trains gained no traction. Still, federal officials remained interested in fast-rail travel. In 1965 Congress passed the High-Speed Ground Transportation Act, marking the start of an effort by the federal government to improve travel speeds.[41]

"In recent decades we have achieved technological miracles in our transportation," President Lyndon B. Johnson said in signing the act, "but there is one great exception. . . . We have the same tired and inadequate mass transportation between our towns and cities that we had 30 years ago."[42]

The Office of High-Speed Ground Transportation, then in the Department of Transportation, financed the development of new technology for use in the busy Northeast Corridor: electrically powered Metroliners for the Washington-New York segment, and gas-turbine-powered trains for the New York-Boston segment that would tilt around curves to help them travel faster. Metroliners and the jet-engine Turbotrains were capable of 160 and 170 mph, respectively, though track conditions and other problems forced considerably lower speeds.[43]

At the heart of the Metroliner's development was the late Robert Nelson, a professor of transportation economics who became head of the new Office of High-Speed Ground Transportation in 1965.

Nelson commissioned a study by Massachusetts Institute of Technology engineers to forecast transportation innovations over the next 15 years, according to a *Washington Post* obituary on Nelson, who died last month. "In their report, the engineers envisioned jet-propelled, rail-less trains whisking through enclosed tubes on a cushion of air, [but] Dr. Nelson wanted more immediate results," the newspaper said.

"He prodded the Pennsylvania Railroad into signing a contract to demonstrate the viability of high-speed trains in the Washington-New York corridor" and won White House support and congressional and media attention. "To the surprise of almost everyone, the first Metroliner demonstration trains began running in 1968" — just a year after the Department of Transportation and the Federal Railroad Administration were created.[44]

While the Metroliner was a promising development, the American railroad industry was all but bankrupt by the early 1970s, and passenger rail needed rescuing if it was to survive at any speed.

Creation of Amtrak

In 1970 Congress passed legislation that led to the formation of Amtrak, which began operating the following year. It assumed from freight railroads the costly job of operating intercity rail service in most of the nation, including the busy Northeast Corridor.[45]

Today, the Congressional Research Service noted in a recent report, Amtrak operates some 44 routes over 22,000 miles of track, nearly all of it owned by freight-rail companies. (Exceptions are the 440-mile Northeast Corridor and a small section of track in Michigan.)

Although Amtrak was created as a for-profit enterprise, it has not made money — something it has in common with intercity passenger rail services in other nations, the report said. "During the last 35 years, federal assistance to Amtrak has amounted to approximately $30 billion."[46]

Under the $787 billion stimulus bill passed this year by Congress, Amtrak will get $1.3 billion for bridge and passenger-car repairs and other needs. "For too long," said Vice President Joseph Biden, a regular rider and strong supporter of the railway, "we haven't made the investments we needed to make Amtrak as safe, as reliable, as secure as it can be. That ends now."[47]

Over the years, though, some have been highly critical of Amtrak. "[T]he organization spends its capital subsidies on fruitless programs and remains insensitive to the travel marketplace," former High Speed Rail Association president Vranich wrote in a 2004 book, *End of the Line: The Failure of Amtrak Reform and the Future of America's Passenger Trains*. "[W]hile the United States needs passenger trains in selected heavily populated corridors, it does not need Amtrak's antiquated, far-flung route system, high operating costs, poor management practices that deflect innovation and capital program with abysmal rates of return."[48]

But supporters of Amtrak say government officials have stacked the deck against passenger rail, in part by subsidizing highways and air travel while withholding adequate money for infrastructure improvements to the rail network. Advocates such as National Corridors Initiative CEO RePass want to change that.

"Passenger trains do not pay for themselves anywhere in the world," he says. "They're too capital-intensive. But

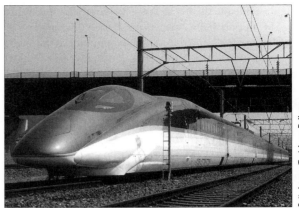

High-Speed, into the Future

The East Japan Railway's next-generation bullet train (top) is slated to hit 223 mph. Taiwan's bullet train (bottom) went into service in January 2007, linking the island's north and south at speeds up to 190 mph. Japan launched the high-speed era in 1964 with its Shinkansen bullet train between Tokyo and Osaka. France, another high-speed pioneer, began test runs of the TGV in the early 1970s.

if you have a system to reinvest some revenue, then they can pay for themselves." RePass favors a system of Transportation Infrastructure Investment Zones, in which a portion of tax revenue collected within an area bordering a rail corridor is dedicated to infrastructure improvements along the rail line.

In Search of Supertrains

In the early 1980s, partly in hopes of expanding Amtrak's political and funding support in Congress, Amtrak and the Department of Transportation began studying regions outside the Northeast Corridor that conceivably could support higher-speed systems. Grants totaling $4 million were allocated in 1984 for state studies on high-speed rail, and by 1986 at least a half-dozen states, including California, Florida and Texas, had created high-speed rail entities.[49]

Still, no supertrains emerged on the American landscape, but several states tried to move forward with private ventures, as Thompson noted in his mid-1990s review.[50]

• In California, Amtrak and Japanese investors proposed a Japanese bullet train-style system. The effort failed because of local opposition, doubts about ridership forecasts, questions about the ability of the private sector to bring the project to reality and the refusal of the federal and state governments to help finance the project.

• In Texas, a private consortium sought to link Dallas/Fort Worth, Houston and San Antonio using French TGV technology, but "the private sector alone simply was not capable of bringing the project to fruition," Thompson wrote.[51] In addition, it ran into opposition from Southwest Airlines, which saw the train as potential competition.[52]

• In Florida, a state commission offered a concession to private investors who would build and operate a system linking Tampa, Orlando and Miami, and a group headed by a real-estate development firm was named the winner. But projected profits were deemed insufficient, and state and federal officials declined to provide money.

Florida continued to try to develop a high-speed rail system, and in 2000 voters approved a constitutional amendment requiring that a bullet train be constructed in the state. But the project met heavy opposition from former Republican Gov. Jeb Bush, and voters subsequently repealed the amendment.

Ultimately, it was Amtrak that developed what has come to stand as the nation's most visible effort at high-speed train service: the Acela Express. Amtrak CEO Joe Boardman said the Acela has demonstrated that "we can do high-speed rail and reduce the trip time enough to make rail competitive with air."[53]

But the Acela also has drawn sharp criticism. In *End of the Line*, Vranich, a former public-affairs spokesman for Amtrak, offers a highly critical rendering of Acela's development, pointing to design flaws, neglected infrastructure and on-time performance problems. "The bottom line is that no other country in the world took so long to create a train as Amtrak did with Acela only to wind up with so technologically deficient a product," Vranich says.

While some rail proponents express disappointment that Amtrak hasn't done more to foster European-style high-speed rail in the United States, Thompson, in his mid-1990s review of the issue, noted the challenges Amtrak faces.

Amtrak's role is fragmented among providing high-density service in the Northeast Corridor, short intercity routes such as Los Angeles-San Diego and long-haul routes, he pointed out. Its "support comes from a political coalition requiring the agreement of supporters of all three types of service. Anything leading Amtrak too much in one direction comes at the potential cost of one of the others, and Amtrak's annual struggle for funding is usually too serious to permit offending any of its supporters."[54]

As individual states contemplate regional high-speed rail lines, some rail proponents advocate a nationwide web of supertrains — a 21st-century version of the transcontinental railroad that transformed the nation in the 19th century.

But others are deeply skeptical that a supertrain network spanning the entire continental United States makes sense. Schwantes, the University of Missouri transportation-studies professor, points out that distances from one end of the United States to another are far greater than in a country like France. "Chicago to Los Angeles would take, full bore, probably 10 hours" at the speed of a French TGV. "That," he says, "is still six hours longer than aviation."

Even without a nation-spanning system, the question remains why no true bullet trains have been built here, even on a regional or intercity basis, either by private investors or Amtrak, when they have been in existence elsewhere for more than 40 years.

"The key reasons are geography and demographics," says Thompson. "With some exceptions, we don't have the relatively short-haul, high-density markets that the Europeans have. That doesn't mean we won't develop them in the future, or that high-speed rail won't cause them to develop."

Low gas prices and massive investments in the Interstate Highway System also give Americans an incentive to drive rather than ride the rails, Thompson says.

And, he says, deregulation of the U.S. airline industry since 1978 also has lured travelers away from rail.

In Europe and Japan, airlines were for many years run as state monopolies that kept air fares high, spurring rail travel, Thompson says. But, he says, passenger volume on some European trains has fallen as discount airlines have arisen to serve short routes such as Amsterdam-Paris.[55]

CURRENT SITUATION

Obama's Efforts

Before passage of the $787 billion stimulus bill — and its $8 billion for high-speed rail — White House Chief of Staff Rahm Emanuel asked House and Senate negotiators for an even bigger rail allocation: $10 billion, according to the online publication *Politico*.

"I put it in there for the president," Emanuel said. "The president wanted to have a signature issue in the bill, his commitment for the future."[56]

"This is not some fanciful, pie-in-the-sky vision of the future," Obama insisted in April as he announced the administration's strategic rail plan. "It's happening now. The problem is, it's happening elsewhere," the president said, citing countries that already have high-speed rail, such as Japan and France.[57]

But as the Obama administration presses ahead with spending on high-speed rail, Republican opponents are pushing back, underscoring the steep political terrain that proponents must climb if they are to see their dreams become reality.

Gov. Bobby Jindal of Louisiana, in the Republican response to Obama's address to Congress in February, said the stimulus package was "larded with wasteful spending," and he pointed to the $8 billion rail allocation as an example.[58]

Earlier, some Republicans tried to attribute the rail allocation in the federal stimulus bill to Senate Majority Leader Harry Reid, claiming he'd wanted it for a proposed high-speed line between Las Vegas in his home state of Nevada and Anaheim, Calif. But Reid told *Politico* he "didn't have much to do with" getting the rail outlay into the stimulus bill, and indeed the publication said, "there's little evidence that Reid had a decisive role."[59]

As the Department of Transportation figures out how to divide up the stimulus money among competing rail projects, fiscal reality is tempering the enthusiasm of those

who hope to see European-style supertrains speeding through the American landscape.

For one thing, says former Federal Railroad Administration official Thompson, "$8 billion will not build very much. It may be good seed money, but if anybody thinks it's going to lead to a shiny, new high-speed rail system in a few years, no it isn't."

What's more, the Transportation Department can use the $8 billion in any of three ways: to improve existing intercity passenger service, upgrade conventional trains to 110-mph service or help pay for high-speed rail development. It is not clear how the money will be divided among those options.

Nor is it clear whether outlays for high-speed rail will be concentrated in a few regions, such as California, the Northeast Corridor and the Midwest, or allocated more broadly among the federally designated high-speed corridors.

GOP Response

Beyond the stimulus money, Obama proposed an additional $5 billion in his budget for high-speed rail over five years. It is not clear how the proposal will fare in congressional budget battles. An alternate budget plan released by House Republicans in March makes no mention of rail projects and says the administration's budget "spends too much, taxes too much and borrows too much."[60]

Still, some Republicans have voiced strong support for high-speed rail projects. In addition to Transportation Secretary LaHood, they include Florida Rep. John L. Mica, the ranking Republican on the House Transportation and Infrastructure Committee. Mica has praised the $8 billion allocation for high-speed rail despite having voted against the overall $787 billion stimulus measure.

"If we could put a man on the moon, we should be able to move people from city to city quickly instead of wasting time on a congested highway," said Mica, whose home state is a prime high-speed rail contender. "I applaud President Obama's recognition that high-speed rail should be part of America's future."[61]

Mica has promoted the idea of a line between New York and Washington that would cut travel time to less than two hours, compared with the Acela's current 2 hours, 42 minutes, with stops.[62] "We think the United States shouldn't become a Third World country when it comes to high-speed service," Mica said.[63]

Is high-speed rail a good investment?

YES

William W. Millar
*President, American Public
Transportation Association*

Written for *CQ Researcher*, April 2009

Investment in high-speed rail now is essential for our country's future. It will not only provide greater mobility but also create economic prosperity, combat climate change and help to reduce our dependence on foreign oil. The vision of a connected America will not be complete without world-class high-speed rail.

It is time for an integrated transportation strategy that will increase mobility by maximizing the capacity and the efficiency of the nation's rail, road and aviation network. Congestion on our country's highways needs to be alleviated. The latest data from the Texas Transportation Institute state that highway congestion costs the United States more than $78 billion each year, and the average traveler is delayed in traffic almost 40 hours a year.

Intercity rail and high-speed rail that connect with airports and city core areas can also do a lot to mitigate air-traffic congestion. In much of Europe and in the Northeast Corridor of the United States, train travel is faster than airline travel, door-to-door. While air travel is the logical alternative for longer-distance trips, high-speed rail can efficiently accommodate many of the shorter-distance corridor services, connecting regional economic centers and providing a feeder service to airlines.

Beyond improving mobility and helping reduce congestion, the use of high-speed rail travel — instead of short-distance air travel and longer-distance highway trips — will significantly reduce energy consumption and greenhouse-gas emissions. Currently the use of public transportation in the United States saves 4.2 billion gallons of gasoline and reduces carbon emissions by 37 million metric tons. Imagine how much greater our energy savings and carbon reduction could be with the addition of high-speed rail service in corridors across the country.

The economic stimulus funds provided by the American Recovery and Reinvestment Act represent a down payment on what will become an ongoing high-speed and intercity rail program. This program will be the foundation of a new vision for American communities, while providing green jobs and helping create a sustainable future.

The bottom line is that a high-speed rail network can help America meet its national goals of economic growth, sustainability, energy independence and mobility. As a worthwhile investment for our future, high-speed rail is an idea that is right for the times and right for a new America.

NO

Randal O'Toole
Senior Fellow, Cato Institute

Written for *CQ Researcher*, April 2009

I love trains, so at first the idea of high-speed rail sounded great. But when I examined it in detail, I found high-speed trains are an expensive form of travel that few people will use.

Throughout history, passenger trains served mainly a wealthy elite and have never given the average people of any nation even half as much mobility as our interstate highways. Moreover, the interstates paid for themselves out of gas taxes and other user fees, while high-speed rail requires huge subsidies from general taxpayers.

Adjusting for inflation, Japan has spent as much per capita, and France at least half as much, on high-speed rail as we spent on our Interstate Highway System. The average American travels 4,000 miles each year, and ships 2,000 ton-miles of freight, on the interstates. Meanwhile, the average residents of Japan and France ride only 400 miles per year on their bullet trains and TGVs, which carry no freight.

In developed nations, people of all income levels regularly travel by car, while only a small number regularly ride high-speed trains. For example, the average American drives for 85 percent of travel; the average resident of France 79 percent — not much difference.

Travelers pay at least $99 to ride Amtrak's subsidized Acela from New York to Washington. When unsubsidized bus fares start at $20, regular Acela riders are mainly bankers, bureaucrats and lobbyists whose expenses are covered by their employers.

High-speed rail's environmental benefits are also questionable. Autos and airplanes get more energy efficient every year. By the time high-speed trains are running, they are likely to use as much energy and emit as much greenhouse gas, per passenger mile, as the average car or jet plane. The moderate-speed, 110-mile-per-hour diesel trains that President Obama proposes in most regions will be especially polluting.

True high-speed trains are electrically powered, but electricity that comes from fossil fuels will produce as much greenhouse gas, per passenger mile, as autos or planes. As we develop more renewable electricity, we would do better to dedicate that power to plug-in hybrids or electric cars than to expensive but little-used trains.

We have a choice between a transportation system that everyone uses and that pays for itself, or one that everyone pays for through their taxes but is regularly used by only a small elite. Which is the better symbol for the America President Obama wants to build?

On the Drawing Board

As federal officials prepare to begin allocating the rail-related stimulus money, a number of projects are likely contenders. Among them:

- **The Midwest network** — Covering some 3,000 miles in nine states — Illinois, Indiana, Iowa, Michigan, Minnesota, Missouri, Nebraska, Ohio and Wisconsin — it would use trains reaching 110 mph. A trip between Chicago and St. Paul, now eight hours, could be reduced to five hours, 30 minutes.[64]

"A network of states produces much better results than each individual state going its own way," said Randy Wade, passenger rail manager at the Wisconsin Department of Transportation, which is coordinating the Midwest effort. "We now have a political network, too, comprised of at least 18 U.S. senators."[65]

Learner, of the Environmental Law and Policy Center, points out that not only are Obama and chief of staff Emanuel from Illinois but so too are other key administration figures, including LaHood, Federal Railroad Administration chief Joseph Szabo and Amtrak board chairman Thomas Carper. Agriculture Secretary Tom Vilsack is a former governor of Iowa, another state in the Midwest network.

Learner also noted that Democratic Illinois Sen. Dick Durbin has been doggedly pushing for rail funding in his home state and has played a role in getting expanded funding for Amtrak.

"I don't want to pretend it's a done deal," Learner says of federal support for the Midwest rail network. "It's not right just to look at Illinois. On the other hand, the stars are very well-aligned for substantial federal support on the merits and because its advocates are well-positioned in the current administration and Congress."

- **North Carolina** — A goal is 85-mph service linking Charlotte and Raleigh as part of building faster rail service along the 450-mile Southeast corridor between Washington and Charlotte. Officials say the passengers could go from Charlotte to Raleigh in two hours and 15 minutes, or about an hour less than is possible today.[66]

"You're not building a high-end, sexy bullet train, but you're building network capacity and reliability," Patrick

AFP/Getty Images/John MacDougall

Germany's high-speed ICE ("Inter City Express") trains were launched in the late 1980s. Last July seven European nations formed an alliance to create a seamless, high-speed network across Western Europe. Railteam will operate a coordinated reservation system that's scheduled to begin in late 2009.

Simmons, director of the North Carolina Department of Transportation rail division, told the *Charlotte Observer.*[67]

- **Florida** — Advocates are trying to revive plans for a high-speed route linking Tampa, Orlando and Miami after its derailment by former Gov. Bush. But the project depends on the support of current Republican Gov. Charlie Crist, who only recently endorsed the high-speed rail project.[68]

The Florida High Speed Rail Authority, which met in February for the first time in four years, wants to seek $2.5 billion in rail funds, according to the *Orlando Sentinel.* The newspaper said a 25-mile segment linking the Orange County Convention Center, Orlando International Airport and Celebration, a residential community developed by Walt Disney World, would run $1 billion. A line between the Orlando airport and Tampa would cost $2.5 billion, the *Sentinel* said.[69]

- **Texas** — Supporters want a train averaging 200 mph between Houston, San Antonio and Dallas by 2020, and after the state's failed attempt at high-speed rail 15 years ago, they are taking a new approach.[70]

"In the past, high-speed rail was not completed in Texas primarily because it was a top-down model driven by lobbyists out of Austin," the state capital, Robert Eckels, chairman of the nonprofit Texas High Speed Rail and Transportation Corp., told a state transportation briefing.[71]

But Eckels said a consortium that includes elected leaders, cities and counties and two airlines has now sought to address concerns of past opponents, according to the *Houston Chronicle.* A spokesman for Southwest Airlines told the *Chronicle* the company was neutral on the current proposal.[72]

Still, some landowners along the proposed route are troubled. "From a rural, agricultural standpoint, we're very concerned," Central Texas farmer Richard Cortese, a county commissioner and a leader in the Texas Farm Bureau, told the *San Antonio Express News.* "It just seems like every time we turn around, someone's got us in their crosshairs."[73]

• **Las Vegas-Anaheim** — The proposed route would feature revolutionary magnetic levitation technology, which uses powerful magnets to suspend trains on a cushion of air and propel them at rapid speeds along a special guideway. The Nevada project has been in the works for years but has struggled over money and other obstacles. It was unclear this spring whether the project will qualify for federal stimulus funds.[74]

OUTLOOK

California Dreaming

Efforts to improve passenger rail in the United States face daunting twists and turns in the years ahead, whether the plan involves boosting the speed of conventional trains to 110 mph or building a true supertrain system like the one planned in California.

Because it would be the nation's most ambitious rail corridor and most like the bullet-train systems found overseas, the California project is generating some of the most attention.

Some are optimistic that it can attract sufficient money from private sources, in addition to government funds, to become reality. Development around stations will help make the project financially feasible, they contend.

But others are highly skeptical. "Unless they come up with a massive dose of federal money, I can't conceive of

them going through with it," says Pisarski, the transportation consultant and author on commuting trends.

Less elaborate projects, such as raising the speed of conventional passenger trains in the Midwest, may not stir the same degree of excitement as do true bullet trains, but that doesn't bother supporters.

"Let's not let perfection get in the way of good," says Learner of the Environmental Law and Policy Center. Speeds of 110 mph "can be a huge jump-start. We ought to get that up and running."

Noting Obama's commitment to trains, Learner says, "We have a once-in-a-lifetime political and economic opportunity to achieve a breakthrough in higher-speed rail. At the same time, we ought to be thinking longer-term and planning for a future in which we can upgrade to European- or Japanese-style 200-mph high-speed rail. But one does not preclude the other."

Others, too, point to the Obama influence as a harbinger of growing government support for passenger rail.

"The fact that Mr. Obama seems to have stepped forward and said trains [are a priority] is important," says Ditmeyer, the former Federal Railroad Administration research and development director. "Some of us have waited our entire career for someone to say something like that."

But critics of high-speed rail worry that Washington's efforts to pour money into passenger rail will become something akin to adding steam to a runaway locomotive.

"We've got a little momentum, they're going to spend a bunch of money, it's not going to do much good, agencies are going to claim great success and the few people who ride [high-speed rail] are going to join coalitions to get more," says the Cato Institute's O'Toole.

Pisarski compares the push to finance new high-speed rail networks — especially expensive ones like the California supertrain — to "going to the moon" during the Kennedy administration.

"It suggests you're taking a new direction," he says. "But I would hope they do a rational analysis. I can't think of a situation where they could possibly justify it, other than on the grounds of greater glory."

UPDATE

France's much-vaunted high-speed train, the TGV, covers the 489 miles between Paris and Marseilles in about three hours, averaging an impressive 163 m.p.h. And in China, the Beijing-Shanghai Express rockets at 190 m.p.h., completing the 819-mile trip in just five hours.

But in the United States, the country's fastest high-speed train, the Acela Express, takes seven hours to complete the 442-mile Washington-Boston run, mostly lumbering along at 70 m.p.h. That pretty much tells the story of U.S. high-speed rail today — and very likely for the immediate future. Indeed, the United States took one step forward and two back in 2011 in the latest chapter of its long history of intermittent efforts to develop high-speed rail (HSR) service nationwide.

President Barack Obama took the step forward in February when he proposed a $53 billion, six-year inter-city passenger rail development program utilizing high-speed rail. Obama has said he wants to give 80 percent of Americans access to HSR within 25 years. But by year's end, backward steps by the Republican-dominated Congress and some governors had — as *The New York Times* put it — dealt "a major blow to one of Mr. Obama's signature transportation goals."[75]

The first step back came in April when newly elected Republican governors in Florida, Wisconsin and Ohio rejected billions of federal dollars already earmarked for high-speed trains in key states in the 2009 stimulus package (The American Recovery and Reinvestment Act). The funds had already been accepted by their mainly Democratic predecessors, but the Republican governors said that the states' anticipated share of the cost would not be sustainable.

Risk vs. Benefits

For example, Florida Republican Gov. Rick Scott returned $2.4 billion to Washington, saying, "The project would be far too costly to taxpayers, and I believe the risk far outweighs the benefits."[76] Yet experts said the money virtually would have paid for the planned 84-mile Tampa-Orlando line, which could have served as a model for other HSR projects.

The second backwards step came in November, when Congress, seeking cuts in the fiscal 2012 budget, slashed $8 billion in HSR funding. Lawmakers further agreed to eliminate any funding earmarked for high-speed trains. The cuts meant "the end of HSR development for this

The deadly crash of two high-speed trains in Zhejiang Province in eastern China on July 23, 2011, killed at least 35 people and left the future of China's HSR system — with some 5,000 miles of track — uncertain.

spending cycle," says Robert Puentes, a transportation expert at the Brookings Institution, a centrist think tank in Washington.

The 11 HSR projects that ultimately had received stimulus funding were winnowed down from an initial 45 applications from 24 states requesting HSR money.[77] Now, only three or four, depending on how you count, remain in the pipeline.

Most important of the surviving projects is the San Francisco to Fresno route, to be served by a 220 m.p.h. "bullet" train. HSR in California eventually will extend through Southern California to San Diego, with a branch line to Anaheim (home of Disneyland).

To date, California has spent $3.6 billion in stimulus money on the project, with construction scheduled to start in 2012. But even some Californians have been getting nervous about reports of cost overruns and construction delays. The initial estimated total expenditure of $33 billion has tripled, and the 2020 completion date has slid back to 2033.[78]

Litany of Arguments

Still, in an editorial, the *Los Angeles Times* conceded that while the HSR project was "a gamble, and not one to be taken lightly . . . gasoline isn't going to be any cheaper in the future, and the freeways aren't going to get less clogged. We think California can find a way to get the train built."[79]

Meanwhile, the litany of arguments pro and con continues unabated. Supporters claim HSR would create jobs, boost the economy and ease congestion on overcrowded highways and airline routes; opponents challenge these claims, noting, especially, that the projects would be budget-busters. High-speed trains were said to be environmentally friendly and to reduce both dependence on foreign oil and reduce greenhouse gas emissions. But some environmentalists also complained that the trains would kill animals that strayed onto the tracks.[80]

Nora Friend, Washington representative of Talgo, the Spanish high-speed train company, says that because there are no U.S. manufacturers of high-speed, hi-tech train equipment, major European train manufacturers — "with the expectation that HSR was finally going to take off" — had come to the United States last year, planning to set up stateside manufacturing operations.

Talgo, which has operated trains at moderate speeds in the Pacific Northwest since 1998, has won some new contracts for surviving projects and is opening a small factory in Milwaukee; but French and German companies have for the moment lost interest in the U.S. market. More employment would have resulted from improving miles of track to allow trains to travel at marginally higher speeds — or laying new, dedicated tracks to take speeds of up to 200 m.p.h.

At the heart of the opposition — say HSR supporters — was the Republicans' determination to prevent Obama from claiming credit for developing HSR. But it's also arguable, say some experts, that the idea was not in sync with the current economic climate. Puentes points out that the governors cut their respective HSR projects "as part of a larger austerity approach."

Politics and Mindset

Anyone trying to assess the prospects of HSR becoming a reality knows that the problem is not just politics, observes Friend. "It's politics, but it's also mindset, it's lack of public policy, it's lack of a national policy on transport at all." Puentes adds, "The heart of the matter is that the Federal Transit Administration lacks a unified program, leaving the states in the driver's seat. The future prospects for HSR are strong, but we need to be more realistic and more judicious about where we place the investment."

What that means in practice is more attention to initiating projects in areas with high population density and therefore high ridership potential. San Francisco to Los Angeles is a good choice, Puentes says, because it's the right distance to establish competitiveness with air transportation and has a lot of business travel. But the first phase of construction for California HSR is planned through the less densely populated, mainly agricultural Central Valley — which hardly shows the bullet train at its true value.

"There's a lot of skepticism for high-speed rail, and the program needs a total re-think," says Ken Button, director of the Center for Transportation Policy at George Mason University, in Fairfax, Va., near Washington. In the process, he says, "you need to take into account that public transport usually underestimates cost and over-rates ridership."

In addition, Button says, terrain can be a huge factor in an HSR project, especially in laying track. The quickest return on investment, Button says, is "300 to 400 miles of dead-straight track with no mountains in the way, but that's not what you've got in the United States."

European, Asian Service

Petra Todorovich, director of the America 2050 program, an independent effort to help the nation meet future development, environment and infrastructure needs, argues that "every other major industrialized nation has recognized that high-speed rail is key to economic growth and mobility."

But how relevant is the HSR situation in Europe or Asia to the U.S. situation? Amtrak, the main U.S. rail service operator, is privately owned. Similarly, America's burgeoning rail freight is in the hands of seven private corporations. In Europe, on the other hand, most rail services are state-run — the U.K. being the most notable exception. The same is true of Asia. Moreover, "No HSR links anywhere in the world have earned enough to cover both construction and operating costs," the nonpartisan Congressional Research Service reported. "Typically, governments have paid the construction costs, and in many cases have subsidized the operating costs as well."[81]

Further complicating the issue, safety concerns about HSR increased after a deadly collision of two bullet trains in Wenzhou, China, leaving 40 passengers dead.

The Chinese authorities ordered speeds reduced on all high-speed trains, even as the accident raised questions about the future of China's ambitious rail program.[82]

For Obama, the issue is as much a matter of national prestige as of economic development. "There is no reason why other countries can build high-speed rail lines and we can't," he declared in 2010.[83]

But Republicans and other critics see, at best, a long, slow and expensive journey to reach that goal.

NOTES

1. For background see Richard L. Worsnop, "High-Speed Rail," *CQ Researcher*, April 16, 1993, pp. 313-336 and Peter Katel, "Emerging China," *CQ Researcher*, Nov. 11, 2005, pp. 957-980.

2. Brian Naylor, "Stimulus Puts High-Speed Rail On The Fast Track," National Public Radio, Feb. 24, 2009, www.npr.org/templates/story/story.php?storyId=101073906. For background see Marcia Clemmitt, "Public-Works Projects," *CQ Researcher*, Feb. 20, 2009, pp. 153-176.

3. For background see Kenneth Jost, *et al.*, "The Obama Presidency," *CQ Researcher*, Jan. 30, 2009, pp. 73-104.

4. See Brian Hansen, "Future of Amtrak," *CQ Researcher*, Oct. 18, 2002, pp. 841-864.

5. Brian Knowlton, "Obama Seeks High-Speed Rail System Across U.S.," *The New York Times*, April 16, 2009, www.nytimes.com/2009/04/17/us/politics/17train.html?ref=politics.

6. "Is High-Speed Rail Worth It?" *National Journal Expert Blogs*, March 23, 2009, response of Ray LaHood, Secretary of Transportation, http://transportation.nationaljournal.com/2009/03/is-highspeed-rail-worth-it.php.

7. Marilyn Adams, "$8 billion could help revive travel by train," *USA Today*, March 16, 2009.

8. Quoted in *Ibid.*

9. California High-Speed Rail Authority, "Questions & Answers: Financing/Costs," accessed March 18, 2009, www.cahighspeedrail.ca.gov/faqs/financing.htm.

10. Quentin Kopp, "High-speed trains will power California forward," *Capitol Weekly*, April 17, 2008, www.capitolweekly.net/article.php?issueId=x1uh8zbb6q8afq&xid=x1uzt54ux6stf4&_adctlid=v%7Cjq2q43wvsl855o%7Cx1wzkesety80ym.

11. Wendell Cox, Joseph Vranich and Adrian T. Moore, "The California High Speed Rail Proposal: A Due Diligence Report," Reason Foundation, Citizens Against Government Waste and Howard Jarvis Taxpayers Foundation, September 2008.

12. Randal O'Toole, "High-Speed Rail: The Wrong Road for America," Cato Institute, "Policy Analysis No. 625," Oct. 31, 2008, www.cato.org/pubs/pas/pa-625.pdf.

13. "Midwest Regional Rail System," Transportation Economics & Management Systems Inc., February 2000, p. 21, www.midwesthsr.org/pdfs/railmidwest.pdf.

14. "Florida High Speed Rail Authority 2002 Report to the Legislature," HNTB Corp., January 2002, pp. 4-7 to 4-9, www.floridahighspeedrail.org/uploaddocuments/p25/January_2002_Report_to_the_Legislature.pdf.

15. California High-Speed Rail Authority, "California's High-Speed Train System Will Boost California's Economy," www.cahighspeedrail.ca.gov/news/JOBS_lr.pdf.

16. Sean Randolph, "California High-Speed Rail: Economic Benefits and Impacts in the San Francisco Bay Area," Bay Area Council Economic Institute, October 2008, p. 1, www.bayeconfor.org/media/files/pdf/CaliforniaHigh-SpeedRailOct2008Web.pdf.

17. *Ibid.*, p. 5.

18. Cox *et al.*, *op. cit.*

19. Peter Katel, "Future of the Airlines," *CQ Researcher*, March 7, 2008, pp. 217-240.

20. Paul Gessing, "High-Speed Rail: Making Tracks at Taxpayer Expense," National Taxpayers Union, *NTU Issue Brief 130*, Oct. 18, 2001, p. 3, www.ntu.org/main/press_issuebriefs.php?PressID=199&org_name=NTU.

21. "Is High-Speed Rail Worth It?" *op. cit.*

22. "California High-Speed Train Business Plan," November 2008, California High-Speed Rail Authority, pp. 6, 12, www.cahighspeedrail.ca.gov/images/chsr/20081107134320_CHSRABusinessPlan2008.pdf. Amounts are for 2010-2050 and are present value in 2008 dollars, discounted 4 percent through 2050.

23. Philip J. Romero, "Unlocking the Gridlock in Los Angeles County's Transportation System: The Local Economic Benefits of High-Speed Rail," California High-Speed Rail Authority, www.cahighspeedrail.ca.gov/news/ReleaseLA.pdf, Oct. 8, 2008.

24. *Ibid.*

25. *Ibid.*

26. Dan Tempelis, "A boost for our economy, infrastructure and environment," *Los Angeles Times*, Oct. 20, 2008.

27. Kopp, *op. cit.*

28. O'Toole, *op. cit.*, p. 2.

29. "California High-Speed Train Business Plan," *op. cit.*, p. 13.

30. Midwest High Speed Rail Association, "Why Railroads: A Cleaner Environment," www.midwesthsr.org/whyRail_cleaner.htm.

31. Paul Weinstein Jr., "Putting America's Transportation System on Track," Progressive Policy Institute, September 2008, p. 4, www.ppionline.org/documents/High-Speed-Rail-0908.pdf.

32. *Ibid.*, pp. 2, 8.

33. Stephen E. Ambrose, *Nothing Like It In the World: The Men Who Built the Transcontinental Railroad 1863-1869* (2000).

34. "Obama's Speech to Congress," transcript, CBS News, Feb. 24, 2009, www.cbsnews.com/stories/2009/02/24/politics/main4826494.shtml.

35. "Historian's Note: Empire State Express No. 999," Genesee County, N.Y., www.co.genesee.ny.us/dpt/historian/ese999.html.

36. PBS American Experience, "People & Events: The Burlington Zephyr's Dawn-to-Dusk Run," www.pbs.org/wgbh/amex/streamliners/peopleevents/e_dawn.html.

37. "Seventy-Fourth Annual Report on Transport Statistics in the United States for the Year ended Dec. 31, 1960," Bureau of Transport Economics and Statistics, Table 155, p. 106.

38. Louis S. Thompson, "High-Speed Rail (HSR) in the United States — Why Isn't There More?" *Japan Railway & Transport Review*, October 1994, p. 33.

39. Hilton is quoted in Joseph Vranich, "End of the Line: The Failure of Amtrak Reform and the Future of America's Passenger Trains," p. 9. Hilton's study is *Amtrak, The National Railroad Passenger Corporation* (1980). The quote is from p. 13 of the study.

40. "Shinkansen High-Speed 'Bullet Train', Japan," railway-technology.com, www.railway-technology.com/projects/shinkansen/.

41. U.S. Department of Transportation, Federal Railroad Administration, "High-Speed Ground Transportation for America," September 1997, p. 1-1, www.fra.dot.gov/Downloads/RRDev/cfs0997all2.pdf.

42. Lyndon B. Johnson, "Remarks at the Signing of the High-Speed Ground Transportation Act," Sept. 30, 1965, American Presidency Project, University of California, Santa Barbara, www.presidency.ucsb.edu/ws/index.php?pid=27281.

43. "Late Arrival of the Fast Trains," *Time*, Jan. 3, 1969.

44. Joe Holley, "Transport Expert Called 'Father of the Metroliner," *The Washington Post*, March 20, 2009, p. 6B, www.washingtonpost.com/wp-dyn/content/article/2009/03/19/AR2009031903864.html.

45. U.S. Department of Transportation, *op. cit.*

46. John Frittelli and David Randall Peterman, "Amtrak: Budget and Reauthorization," Congressional Research Service, Feb. 6, 2009.

47. "Vice President Biden, Railroad Administrator, Members of Congress Announce Funding for Amtrak in Recovery Act," news release, White House, March 13, 2009.

48. Vranich, *End of the Line, op. cit.*, p. 11.

49. U.S. Department of Transportation, *op. cit.*, pp. 1-2.

50. Thompson, *op. cit.*, p. 34.

51. *Ibid.*

52. Peggy Fikac, "High-speed rail idea re-embarking," *Houston Chronicle*, Jan. 29, 2009, p. 1A.

53. Quoted in Marilyn Adams, "$8 billion could help revive travel by train," *USA Today*, March 16, 2009.

54. Thompson, *op. cit.*, p. 36.

55. See "Modern Rail, Modern Europe: Towards an Integrated European Railway Area," Directorate-General for Energy and Transport, European Commission, 2008, http://ec.europa.eu/transport/publications/doc/modern_rail_en.pdf.

56. David Rogers, "Obama plots huge railroad expansion," *Politico*, Feb. 17, 2009, www.politico.com/news/stories/0209/18924.html.

57. "Obama: Better Trains Foster Energy Independence," The Associated Press, April 16, 2009, www.nytimnes.com.

58. "The Republican Response by Gov. Bobby Jindal," transcript, *The New York Times*, Feb. 24, 2009.

59. Rogers, *op. cit.*

60. "The Republican Road to Recovery," March 2009, www.gop.gov/solutions/budget/road-to-recovery-final.

61. Quoted in Michael Falcone, "Republicans Hail Parts of Bill That Few of Them Supported," *The New York Times*, Feb. 20, 2009, p. 18.

62. Michael Dresser, "Bringing the Country Up to Speed With 21st Century Transportation," *Baltimore Sun*, Dec. 29, 2008, p. 3A.

63. Quoted in *Ibid.*

64. Jon Hilkevitch, "On the fast track — finally," *Chicago Tribune*, Oct. 6, 2008, p. 13.

65. Quoted in *Ibid.*

66. Steve Harrison and Bruce Siceloff, "Hoping for Fast Rail to Raleigh," *Charlotte Observer*, March 1, 2009, p. 1A.

67. Quoted in *Ibid.*

68. Dan Tracy, "Board: Bullet train rides on Crist's blessing," *Orlando Sentinel*, Feb. 27, 2009, p. 1B. See also, "Crist: Go For High Speed Rail Money," *Lakeland Ledger Blogs*, April 15, 2009, http://politics.theledger.com/default.asp?item=2364360.

69. *Ibid.*

70. Fikac, *op. cit.*

71. *Ibid.*

72. *Ibid.*

73. Peggy Fikac, "Landowners question high-speed rail," *San Antonio Express-News*, Feb. 8, 2009, p. 1B.

74. Abby Sewell, "City Council Votes to Support Anaheim to Vegas Train," *Desert Dispatch*, April 2, 2009.

75. Michael Cooper, "Budget Deal Deeply Cuts High-Speed Rail Program," *The New York Times*, April 12, 2011, www.nytimes.com/2011/04/13/us/politics/13rail.html.

76. "Florida Gov. Rick Scott Rejects Federal High Speed Rail," Office of the 45th Governor of Florida, Feb. 16, 2011, www.flgov.com/2011/02/16/florida-governor-rick-scott-rejects-federal-high-speed-rail/.

77. David Randall Peterman, *et al.*, "High Speed Rail (HSR) in the United States," Congressional Research Service, Dec. 8, 2009, www.fas.org/sgp/crs/misc/R40973.pdf.

78. Juliet Williams, "Calif. Rail Project to Cost $98B," *San Jose Mercury News*, Oct. 31, 2011.

79. "Still on board the bullet train," editorial, *Los Angeles Times*, Nov. 4, 2011, www.latimes.com/news/opinion/opinionla/la-ed-train-20111104,0,7045793.story.

80. "Debate about California High Speed Rail Continues," Rose Institute of State and of State and Local Government, Claremont McKenna College, http://rosereport.org/home/entry/debate-about-california-high-speed-rail-continues-1.

81. *Ibid.*: see report summary.

82. Aaron Colter, "Chinese High-Speed Rail Stumbles After Crash," *EarthTechling*, Aug. 23, 2011, www.earthtechling.com/2011/08/china-high-speed-rail-stumbles-after-crash/.

83. Bryan Walsh, "Can High Speed Rail Succeed in America?" *Time online*, Jan. 29, 2010, www.time.com/time/health/article/0,8599,1957575,00.html.

BIBLIOGRAPHY

Books

Ambrose, Stephen E., *Nothing Like It In the World: The Men Who Built the Transcontinental Railroad 1863-1869*, Simon & Schuster, 2000.
A prominent historian provides a sweeping look at "the greatest achievement of the American people in the 19th century."

Lynch, Thomas, ed., *High Speed Rail in the U.S.: Super Trains for the Millennium*, Gordon and Breach Science Publishers, 1998.
A collection of technically oriented articles covers land-use planning issues, financing of high-speed rail in Europe and noise abatement related to fast trains, among other topics.

Vranich, Joseph, *End of the Line: The Failure of Amtrak Reform and the Future of America's Passenger Trains*, American Enterprise Institute, 2004.
A former president of the High Speed Rail Association argues that "while fast rail can help on some short routes, "there is no justification whatsoever for a national high-speed rail network."

Articles

Cooper, Michael, "Slice of Stimulus Package Will Go to Faster Trains," *The New York Times*, Feb. 20, 2009, www.nytimes.com/2009/02/20/us/20rail.html?scp=1&sq=%22slice%20of%20stimulus%20package%20will%20go%22&st=cse.
The $8 billion added to the economic stimulus package for high-speed rail won't likely do much, Cooper says.

Kopp, Quentin, "High-speed trains will power California forward," *Capitol Weekly*, April 17, 2008, www.capitolweekly.net/article.php?xid=x1uzt54ux6stf4.
The chairman of the California High-Speed Rail Authority argues that high-speed rail will combat global warming, create good jobs and alleviate freeway congestion.

Rogers, David, "Obama plots huge railroad expansion," *Politico*, Feb. 17, 2009, www.politico.com/news/stories/0209/18924.html.
White House chief of staff Rahm Emanuel says President Obama sees high-speed rail as a "signature issue" of his administration.

Thompson, Louis S., "High-Speed Rail (HSR) in the United States — Why Isn't There More?" *Japan Railway & Transport Review*, October 1994.
A former rail-policy adviser at the World Bank examines the myriad reasons — still pertinent 15 years after the article's publication — why the United States has lagged far behind Europe and Japan in rapid-train development.

Reports and Studies

"High-Speed Ground Transportation for America," U.S. Department of Transportation, Federal Railroad Administration, September 1997, www.fra.dot.gov/Downloads/RRDev/cfs0997all2.pdf.
Still highly useful more than a decade after its publication, the report delves into the historical background, financial assumptions, trends and other subjects related to high-speed rail.

"High Speed Rail and Greenhouse Gas Emissions in the U.S.," Center for Clean Air Policy and Center for Neighborhood Technology, January 2006, www.cnt.org/repository/HighSpeedRailEmissions.pdf.
The groups' analysis concludes that high-speed rail can bring about "substantial" greenhouse-gas emission savings.

"Vision for High-Speed Rail in America," U.S. Department of Transportation, Federal Railroad Administration, April 2009, www.fra.dot.gov/Downloads/RRdev/hsrstrategicplan.pdf.
The Obama administration offers its strategic plan for high-speed passenger rail service in intercity corridors.

Cox, Wendell, Joseph Vranich and Adrian T. Moore, "The California High Speed Rail Proposal: A Due Diligence Report," Reason Foundation, Citizens Against Government Waste and Howard Jarvis Taxpayers Foundation, www.reason.org/ps370.pdf.
The report questions a proposal for high-speed rail linking San Francisco, Sacramento, Los Angeles and San Diego.

Frittelli, John, and David Randall Peterman, "Amtrak: Budget and Reauthorization," Congressional Research Service, Feb. 6, 2009.
Last fall Congress passed an Amtrak reauthorization bill that included $1.5 billion in grants for 11 high-speed rail corridors.

O'Toole, Randal, "High-Speed Rail the Wrong Road for America," Cato Institute, *Policy Analysis No. 625*, Oct. 31, 2008, www.cato.org/pubs/pas/pa-625.pdf. Proposals for high-speed rail are "high-cost, high-risk" projects that offer "little or no congestion relief, energy savings, or other environmental benefits," says a conservative analyst.

Weinstein, Paul Jr., "Putting America's Transportation System on Track," Progressive Policy Institute, September 2008, www.ppionline.org/documents/High-Speed-Rail-0908.pdf. The chief operating officer of the liberal think tank and a visiting fellow at The Johns Hopkins University says that if the United States is serious about repairing the "mess" in air travel and alleviating congestion on highways, "there is a real, long-term solution: high-speed rail."

For More Information

American Public Transportation Association, 1666 K St., N.W., Suite 1100, Washington, DC 20006; (202) 496-4800; www.apta.com. Represents public bus and commuter rail systems and others involved in transit.

California High-Speed Rail Authority, 925 L St., Suite 1425, Sacramento, CA 95814; (916) 324-1541; www.cahighspeedrail.ca.gov. State agency promoting high-speed rail system linking major California cities.

Cato Institute, 1000 Massachusetts Ave., N.W., Washington, DC 20001-5403; (202) 842-0200; www.freetrade.org. Libertarian think tank that advocates global free markets and limited government.

Federal Railroad Administration, 1200 New Jersey Ave., S.E., Washington, DC 20590; www.fra.dot.gov. Enforces railroad safety and supports national railroad policy.

Midwest High Speed Rail Association, P.O. Box 805877, Chicago, IL 60680; (773) 334-6758; www.midwesthsr.org.

Advocacy group promoting high-speed rail system linking Chicago hub with cities in the Midwest.

National Association of Railroad Passengers, 900 Second St., N.E., Suite 308, Washington, DC 20002; (202) 408-8362; www.narprail.org. Advocacy group for train and rail-transit passengers.

National Corridors Initiative, 59 Gates St., Boston, MA 02127; (617) 269-5478; www.nationalcorridors.org. Advocates transportation infrastructure development, with emphasis on rail.

Reason Foundation, 3415 S. Sepulveda Blvd., Suite 400, Los Angeles, CA 90034; (310) 391-2245; www.reason.org. Free-market public-policy research group that studies transportation and other issues.

Transportation Research Board, 500 Fifth St., N.W., Washington, DC 20001; www.trb.org. A division of the National Academies that studies innovation in transportation.

9

Police Misconduct

Kenneth Jost

Natalie Gomez holds a picture of her brother, 22-year-old Alan Gomez, who was killed last year by Albuquerque, N.M., police. Ms. Gomez participated in a rally on June 14, 2011, protesting the police department's use of lethal force. The department's police union was found to have been giving officers involved in fatal shootings $500 to help them recover from stress. Critics have called the payments a bounty system for killing suspects.

From *CQ Researcher*,
April 6, 2012.

AP Photo/The Albuquerque Journal/Greg Sorber

Wendell Allen was wearing only pajama bottoms when New Orleans police officers on a marijuana raid broke into his house in the city's middle-class Gentilly neighborhood on the evening of March 7. Armed with a search warrant, six officers, clad in plain clothes covered by jackets identifying them as police, announced their presence and, after receiving no response, barged in.

Allen, a 20-year-old former high school basketball star with a previous marijuana-related conviction, was in the stairwell, unarmed, when Officer Joshua Colclough fired a single gunshot that hit Allen in the chest. The bullet penetrated Allen's heart, aorta and lungs. He died "almost instantly," New Orleans Parish Coroner Frank Minyard said later.[1]

Allen's death, the second fatal shooting of an African-American youth by New Orleans police within a week, remains under what Superintendent Ronal Serpas promises will be "a complete and thorough" investigation. Colclough, in his fifth year with the force, gave a voluntary statement to investigators a week after the shooting. His attorney, Claude Kelly, says an "honest" investigation will show the shooting was justified.

Allen's family and leaders of the city's African-American community, however, have no doubt that the shooting was unwarranted. "There have been egregious wrongs done to the black community of New Orleans," W. C. Johnson, leader of the United New Orleans Front, declared as protesters massed outside police headquarters two days after the shooting. Helen Shorty, Allen's grandmother, called for Colclough to be booked for murder.[2]

Justice Department Targets Police Misconduct

U.S. Department of Justice investigators have examined the policies and practices of more than two dozen law enforcement agencies over the past decade and found a range of illegal or otherwise improper practices, ranging from harsh treatment of suspects and racial profiling to failure to probe allegations of sexual assault. Here are highlights from five recent Justice Department reports.

New Orleans

(March 17, 2011) Use of excessive force; unconstitutional stops, searches and arrests; biased policing; racial, ethnic and sexual-orientation discrimination; failure to provide effective policing services to persons with limited English proficiency; systemic failure to investigate sexual assaults and domestic violence.

Puerto Rico

(Sept. 7, 2011) Excessive force; unreasonable force, other misconduct designed to suppress exercise of First Amendment rights; unlawful searches and seizures; evidence of frequent failure to police sex crimes and incidents of domestic violence; evidence of discriminatory practices targeting individuals of Dominican descent; "staggering level" of crime and corruption.

Maricopa County, Ariz. (includes Phoenix)

(Dec. 15, 2011) Racial profiling of Latinos; unlawful stops, detentions and arrests of Latinos; unlawful retaliation against individuals who complain about or criticize the office's policies or practices; reasonable cause to believe the office operates its jails in a manner that punishes Latino inmates with limited English proficiency for failing to understand commands given in English and denying critical services provided to other inmates.

Seattle

(Dec. 16, 2011) Use of unnecessary or excessive force; lack of adequate training on use of force; failure of supervisors to provide oversight on use of force; serious concerns about possible discriminatory policing, particularly relating to pedestrian encounters.

East Haven, Conn.

(Dec. 19, 2011) Systematic discrimination against Latinos, including targeting Latinos for discriminatory traffic enforcement, treating Latino drivers more harshly than non-Latino drivers after a traffic stop and intentionally and woefully failing to design and implement internal systems of control that would identify, track and prevent such misconduct.

Source: U.S. Department of Justice, www.justice.gov/crt/about/spl/findsettle.php.

The shootings come as the long-troubled department is negotiating with the U.S. Department of Justice (DOJ) the terms of a possible agreement on wide-ranging reforms to be supervised by a federal court. The negotiations follow a scathing report by the Justice Department's civil rights division in March 2011 that accused the New Orleans police of routine constitutional violations, including use of excessive force, improper searches and racial and ethnic discrimination.[3]

The 158-page report is one of nine published so far by the civil rights division's so-called "special litigation section" under President Obama that have held police departments around the country up to highly critical scrutiny. In three reports published within five days in mid-December, Justice Department investigators upbraided Seattle police for use of excessive force and the Maricopa County, Ariz., sheriff's office and East Haven, Conn., police department for ethnic profiling of Latinos.

Racial profiling is also at the heart of the nationwide controversy over the Feb. 26 fatal shooting of a black Florida teenager by a white neighborhood watch volunteer. Trayvon Martin, 17, was shot as he was returning from a convenience store to the house of his father's girlfriend in Sanford, an Orlando suburb. George Zimmerman, whose mother is Hispanic, claims he shot the unarmed Martin in self-defense after following the youth because of what he regarded as suspicious behavior. The incident has touched off nationwide debate not only over racial profiling but also over Florida's so-called Stand Your Ground law, which allows someone to use deadly force when feeling threatened, with no duty to attempt to retreat.

The most recent reports by the Justice Department's police accountability unit exemplify its more aggressive stance after an eight-year period of dormancy under President George W. Bush. "They've been very assertive," says Samuel Walker, a professor of criminal justice, emeritus, at the University of Nebraska-Omaha and the nation's senior academic expert on police-accountability issues. In all, the unit is conducting 20 investigations of state or local law enforcement agencies.

Local police officials sometimes challenge the Justice Department's findings. "The department is not broken," a defiant Seattle Police Chief John Diaz declared as the DOJ's report was being released on Dec. 16. The city's mayor, Mike McGinn, backed him up.

Over time, however, local officials generally yield to federal authorities. In East Haven, Police Chief Leonard Gallo retired on Jan. 30 in the wake of DOJ criticism. In Seattle, McGinn rethought his initial skepticism about the report in the face of public criticism and directed Diaz to begin carrying out some of the Justice Department's proposed changes.

In Arizona, however, the outspoken Maricopa County Sheriff Joe Arpaio is refusing the Justice Department's insistence for court supervision of changes in police and jail policies. "None of us agreed to allow a federal monitor to come remove my authority as the elected sheriff of Maricopa County," Arpaio declared on April 3. The government now has the option of going to federal court on its own to force changes.[4]

Holding police departments accountable to the law has been an intractable problem since the era of urban police departments began in the 1830s.[5] The 20th century saw a succession of efforts to reduce or eliminate police misconduct, starting with a movement to professionalize policing and continuing through the mid-century criminal-law revolution under Chief Justice Earl Warren.

In the decades since, civilian review boards or other independent auditing mechanisms have advanced from

Killings of Arrestees by Police on Rise

From 2003 through 2009, law-enforcement officials committed 2,931 arrest-related killings, whether criminal or justifiable, of people in their custody. Some experts caution that the upward trend over the seven-year period may reflect improvements in data reporting.

Arrest-Related Killings by Law Enforcement Personnel, 2003-2009

Year	Killings
2003	376
2004	375
2005	377
2006	447
2007	455
2008	404
2009	497

Source: Andrea M. Burch, "Arrest-Related Deaths, 2003-2009 — Statistical Tables," Bureau of Justice Statistics, U.S. Department of Justice, November 2011, p. 4, bjs.ojp.usdoj.gov/content/pub/pdf/ard0309st.pdf

objects of fierce debate to structures viewed by police organizations themselves as "best practices." Congress in 1994 also gave the Justice Department a direct role in police reform by passing a law authorizing the federal government to sue state or local law enforcement agencies if it found a "pattern or practice" of violations of constitutional or federally protected rights.

The reforms have borne fruit in a general strengthening of policies and improved conduct by police officers in the nation's nearly 18,000 state or local law enforcement agencies nationwide. "We've seen a progressive improvement in the professionalism of law enforcement over the last 30 years," says Andrew Scott, a police consultant since his retirement as Boca Raton, Fla., police chief in 2006, after 30 years in law enforcement.

"Police departments have come a long way, both in terms of the officers and the leadership in policing," says Hubert Williams, president of the Police Foundation, a Washington-based research organization, and a former Newark, N.J., police chief.

Walker, a civil liberties-minded researcher on police practices and policies since the 1970s, agrees that police behavior has generally improved over the past few decades. But he says there is a continuing gap between the country's best and worst departments. "Some departments are taking up what I call the new accountability measures, moving forward, doing the right thing, and

Getty Images/Mario Tama

An opponent of a controversial New York City Police Department "stop and frisk" policy marches in the Bronx borough on Jan. 27, 2012. The NYPD says the policy helps to prevent crime, but critics accuse the police of racial profiling and civil rights abuses. Out of 684,330 persons stopped by NYPD officers in 2011, the vast majority — 87 percent — were black or Hispanic.

reducing misconduct," Walker says. "And there are some that slip back."

The New Orleans department, by common agreement, ranks low on those measures. "The New Orleans Police Department has never been a model of good behavior so to speak," says Marjorie Esman, executive director of the American Civil Liberties Union of Louisiana (ACLU-La.).

Walker is even blunter: New Orleans is "everybody's candidate for the worst police department."

Far from fighting the Justice Department's findings, New Orleans superintendent Serpas joined the DOJ's civil rights chief Thomas Perez in the March 17, 2011,

news conference to release the report. Serpas said it contained few surprises and went on to pledge improvement. "I am convinced we will be a world-class police department," he said. A week later, Serpas said many of the reforms were already being put into effect.[6]

The Justice Department launched its investigation in May 2010 at the request of the city's newly inaugurated mayor, Mitch Landrieu. The investigation came on top of ongoing federal prosecutions of officers implicated in the attempted cover-up of the shooting of six unarmed black civilians on the Danziger Bridge six days after Hurricane Katrina devastated the city in September 2005.

By May 2010, four officers had already pleaded guilty to obstruction-type charges in connection with the shooting. In addition to one other guilty plea, five officers were convicted in August 2011 on federal civil rights charges after a seven-week trial. U.S. District Court Judge Kurt Engelhardt imposed sentences ranging from 38 to 65 years on four of the five defendants after an emotional sentencing hearing on April 4; a fifth defendant drew a six-year term. One other defendant is awaiting a retrial, set to begin in May, after a mistrial in January.[7]

As in previous investigations, Justice Department lawyers are negotiating with New Orleans officials on possible reforms. The changes would be included in a consent decree to be overseen by a federal court for a specified period. The department has followed the same procedure since the mid-1990s in such major cities as Pittsburgh, Cincinnati, Detroit and Los Angeles.

A one-day roundtable with police officials, experts and others convened by the Justice Department in June 2010 concluded the procedure has been effective in reforming police department practices. Experts generally agree. "Departments have come out of this much better than they went in," says David Harris, a professor at the University of Pittsburgh School of Law.

Some of the officials at the roundtable, however, complained that the process creates a "negative stigma" that takes time for a department to overcome.[8]

As assistant attorney general for civil rights, Perez has pushed the "pattern or practice" process more vigorously than any of his predecessors. In addition to New Orleans, Perez personally attended news conferences to announce the reports in Seattle and Maricopa County. "When police officers cross the line, they need to be held accountable," Perez told *The Washington Post.* "Criminal prosecutions alone will not change the culture of a department."[9]

One of the supposed deterrents to police misconduct, however, is being weakened by the Supreme Court under Chief Justice John G. Roberts Jr., according to civil liberties advocates. The Roberts Court has issued three decisions in the past six years that somewhat narrow the exclusionary rule — the court-created doctrine that prohibits the use of evidence police find during illegal searches.

Meanwhile, the New York City Police Department, the nation's largest, is under a national spotlight after news reports, particularly by The Associated Press, detailing the department's secret infiltration and surveillance of Muslim and some liberal groups as part of counterterrorism investigations. The AP stories, dating from summer 2011 and continuing, show that the department investigated hundreds of mosques and Muslim student groups and infiltrated dozens. City officials are defending the practice, but some Muslim leaders are calling for the resignation of Police Commissioner Raymond Kelly.[10]

The Justice Department investigations, coupled with the recurrent local controversies over police behavior, focus increased national attention on such issues as use of force, racial profiling and police accountability. Here are some of the arguments being heard as those issues are debated:

Should police do more to control excessive force?

John Williams was carrying a board and an open wood-carving knife at an

Police Handle Tense Situations in Steps

Most law enforcement agencies have policies that guide their use of force. Such policies describe an escalating series of actions an officer may take to resolve a situation. Officers are instructed to respond with a level of force appropriate to the situation. An officer may move from one part of the continuum to another in a matter of seconds.

A typical use-of-force continuum:

Officer Presence — No force is used. Considered the best way to resolve a situation.
- The mere presence of a law-enforcement officer works to deter crime or defuse a situation.
- Officers' attitudes are professional and nonthreatening.

Verbalization — Force is not physical.
- Officers issue calm, nonthreatening commands, such as "Let me see your identification and registration."
- Officers may increase their volume and shorten commands in an attempt to gain compliance. Short commands might include "Stop" or "Don't move."

Empty-Hand Control — Officers use bodily force to gain control of a situation.
- *Soft technique.* Officers use grabs, holds and joint locks to restrain an individual.
- *Hard technique.* Officers use punches and kicks to restrain an individual.

Less-Lethal Methods — Officers use less-lethal technologies to gain control of a situation.
- *Blunt impact.* Officers may use a baton or projectile to immobilize a combative person.
- *Chemical.* Officers may use chemical sprays or projectiles embedded with chemicals to restrain an individual. Pepper spray is an example.
- *Conducted Energy Devices (CEDs).* Officers may use a device such as a Taser to immobilize an individual. Such devices discharge a high-voltage, low-amperage jolt of electricity at a distance.

Lethal Force — Officers use lethal weapons to gain control of a situation. These should be used if a suspect poses a serious threat to an officer or other individual.
- Officers use deadly weapons such as firearms to stop an individual's actions.

Source: www.nij.gov/nij/topics/law-enforcement/officer-safety/use-of-force/continuum.htm

Half of Arrest-Related Killings Are of Minorities

More than half of the 2,958* people who were killed while under arrest from 2003 through 2009 were black or Hispanic. Whites comprised 42 percent of the total. All but 27 of the deaths were at the hands of law enforcement officers.

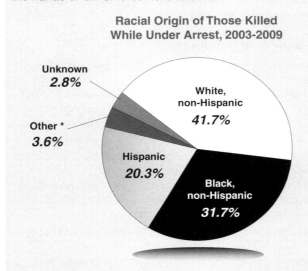

Racial Origin of Those Killed While Under Arrest, 2003-2009

Unknown 2.8%

Other * 3.6%

White, non-Hispanic 41.7%

Hispanic 20.3%

Black, non-Hispanic 31.7%

* Includes American Indians, Alaska Natives, Asians, Native Hawaiians, other Pacific Islanders and persons of two or more races.

Figures do not total 100 because of rounding.

Source: Andrea M. Burch, "Arrest-Related Deaths, 2003-2009 — Statistical Tables," Bureau of Justice Statistics, U.S. Department of Justice, November 2011, p. 6, bjs.ojp.usdoj.gov/content/pub/pdf/ard0309st.pdf

intersection near Seattle's Pioneer Square on Aug. 30, 2010, when Police Sgt. Ian Birk spotted him, got out of his patrol car and ordered him to drop the knife. When the hearing-impaired Williams failed to respond, Birk fired four shots from about nine feet away. Williams, a fixture at the nearby social service center for Native Americans, died at the scene.

Williams' death added to long simmering concerns about use of force by Seattle police forces. Led by the ACLU of Washington State, a coalition of 34 community groups asked the Justice Department to investigate. The department's devastating report, released on Dec. 16, found routine violations of constitutional rights when force was used, with a small number of officers responsible for a disproportionate number of instances and with scant internal review of the incidents. "Seattle

cannot control its own officers," says Jennifer Shaw, deputy director of the ACLU affiliate.[11]

Statistics are hard to come by, but experts appear to agree that police use force less frequently today than in the past. "Overall, it is less frequent than it was in the 1960s," says the Police Foundation's Williams. A study by the International Association of Chiefs of Police (IACP), published in 2001, found that police used force 3.6 times per 10,000 service calls during the 1990s. Citing the IACP's and a more recent study, the National Institute of Justice, the Justice Department's research arm, concluded in 2011 that use of excessive force is "rare," even while conceding the difficulty of defining "excessive."[12]

As in Seattle, a small number of officers are typically found most likely to resort to force or to use excessive force in encounters with civilians. "The vast majority of officers do not engage in excessive use of force," says former chief Scott. "It is the small minority of officers who abuse their power."

The U.S. Supreme Court has given only limited guidance on use of force by police. The court ruled in 1985 that police can use deadly force when pursuing a fleeing suspect only if the suspect poses a significant threat of death or serious physical injury to the officer or others. In a broader ruling, the court held in 1989 that any use of force by an officer must be objectively reasonable. Factors to be considered include the severity of the crime, whether the suspect poses "an immediate safety threat" and whether the suspect is "actively resisting arrest" or attempting to escape. The court added that the "calculus of reasonableness" should take into account an officer's need to make "split-second judgments."[13]

"The legal standards are pretty loose," says Robert Kane, an associate professor at the University of Baltimore's School of Criminal Justice and co-author of a forthcoming book on police accountability issues. "There's a lot of gray in terms of trying to judge the appropriateness of force."

City governments are occasionally hit with five-, six- or even seven-figure damage awards in suits by victims of police beatings or shootings. As one dramatic example, Rodney King was awarded $3.8 million for the beating he suffered from Los Angeles police officers in 1991 after a high-speed car chase. Criminal prosecutions are more difficult. The King case ended in state court acquittals of four officers and a federal civil rights trial that ended with two convictions and two acquittals.

Internally, police departments appear to reject most citizen complaints of excessive force. In a recent study of eight local police departments, researchers at Michigan State University and Central Florida University found that six took no action on at least 90 percent of the complaints during the two-year period studied. Only three officers were suspended and one terminated because of use-of-force complaints during the period.[14]

The IACP's model policy on use of force largely restates the general guidelines from the Supreme Court, with added advisories against firing warning shots or shooting at a moving vehicle. Many departments provide more detailed guidance, including a so-called use of force continuum that correlates the level of force to be used with the suspect's level of resistance or threat to safety.

Walker says policies and training are the keys to reducing excessive force by police. "If you have a bad use-of-force incident, it's a mistake to focus on the officer because the underlying cause is some failure by the department: lack of proper training or lack of proper supervision," he says.

Should police do more to prevent racial and ethnic profiling?

Many studies over the past two decades have shown that African-American and Hispanic drivers are more likely to be stopped for traffic enforcement than white motorists. In a mammoth journalistic project, the *Hartford Courant* took the issue one step further earlier this year by analyzing what happened in Connecticut to drivers after they were stopped by local police.

The newspaper's analysis of more than 100,000 traffic stops found that blacks and Hispanics were far more likely to get a citation than whites stopped for the same

offense. As one example, blacks were twice as likely and Hispanics four times as likely to be ticketed for improper taillights as whites stopped for the same reason. "This is beyond profiling," Glenn A. Cassis, executive director of the state's African-American Affairs Commission, told the newspaper. "This goes to actually a level of discrimination, and who gets the wink and who doesn't get the wink."[15]

The Justice Department's recent reports found similar evidence of racial or ethnic profiling in New Orleans, Maricopa County and East Haven. In New Orleans, investigators found that police shot 27 civilians during a 16-month period, all of them African-Americans. In Maricopa County, Latino drivers were four to nine times more likely to be subjected to traffic stops than similarly situated non-Latino drivers. In East Haven, Latinos make up about 10 percent of the population, but accounted for nearly 20 percent of traffic stops.[16]

The tensions between police departments, historically predominantly white, and African-American and Hispanic communities are of long standing. The U.S. Supreme Court's initial decision, in 1936, limiting police conduct during interrogations came in the case of three black tenant farmers who confessed to murder only after being tortured. Los Angeles police tacitly abetted white servicemen attacking Latinos in the "Zoot Suit" riots in 1943. The Kerner Commission report on urban riots of the 1960s listed the "deep hostility between police and ghetto communities as a primary cause of the disorders."

Racial profiling advanced to the top of the national agenda in the mid- and late-1990s — as seen in the popularizing of the grimly ironic phrase "driving while black." In litigation that documented the experiences of many African-Americans, ACLU affiliates in several states filed suits contesting the practice. Some states, including Connecticut, responded by passing laws requiring demographic statistics-gathering on traffic stops to try to spot signs of racial profiling.

Racial and ethnic profiling appears to be continuing despite increasing diversity on local police forces. The New Orleans police force is now majority black. In New York City, a majority of the police officers are black, Latino or Asian; whites comprise only 47 percent. Out of 684,330 persons stopped by NYPD officers in 2011, however, the vast majority — 87 percent — were either black or Hispanic.[17]

Harris, the Pittsburgh law professor and author of a book on racial profiling, says the practice "is a police issue, not a race issue." Profiling, he says, "is a product of the training, culture and customs within that department. Black officers are going to be trained like all others. They're going to want to fit in just like all officers."

Other experts say profiling results naturally from the demographics of crime. "This is a social issue," says the University of Baltimore's Kane. "We know that race and class are strongly tied up with crime, perceptions of crime and urban disorder. Crime and race are not randomly distributed across America."

"It is a problem, and it will continue to be a problem," says police consultant Scott. "But it may not be extending from a police officer's bigotry. If you have a particular segment of the community that is particularly involved in a particular crime, part of the profiling has to be the ethnicity of the offender."

Identifying impermissible profiling can also be difficult, Scott adds. "It may be insidiously nontransparent as to why an officer has stopped a particular individual," he says. In its report on East Haven, the Justice Department accused the force of "intentionally and woefully failing to design and implement internal systems of control that would identify, track, and prevent such misconduct." The report on Maricopa County faulted Sheriff Arpaio by name for using "unverified tips or complaints" that were "infected with bias against Latino persons."

Police Foundation president Williams says the responsibility for stopping the practice rests with police officials. "Are chiefs dealing with the problem?" he asks rhetorically. "I think they have policies that prohibit it, and from that perspective they're dealing with it. It's the enforcement of those policies that's the big question mark. In that area, there's more of a question mark."

Should police adopt stronger disciplinary measures for misconduct?

Jason Mucha has had a checkered career with the Milwaukee Police Department since being hired as an aide in 1996 while still a teenager. He was promoted to sergeant in 2005, but over the next few years was accused by 10 different suspects of either beating them or planting drugs or both. Although he was never disciplined, a state appeals court explicitly questioned Mucha's credibility as a witness, and the U.S. attorney's office dropped one case rather than put him on the stand.

The department's disciplinary procedure has now caught up with Mucha, however, after he and fellow squad members were accused of invasive body searches in drug investigations. Mucha and seven officers in his unit were stripped of police powers and reassigned to desk duties in March because of the accusations, according to the *Journal Sentinel.* Without confirming the report, Chief Edward Flynn told a news conference on March 22 that if the allegations were true, the searches would have violated state law.[18]

The *Journal Sentinel* has been on the department's case over discipline for years. A three-part series in October 2011 criticized the department for allowing "at least" 93 officers to remain on the force despite offenses such as drunken driving and domestic violence. A similar, nine-part series by the *Sarasota Herald Tribune* in December found that "thousands" of officers remain on the job in Florida police departments despite "arrests or evidence" implicating them in crimes punishable by prison sentences.[19]

Despite such newspaper investigations, some experts give police departments generally good marks for disciplining rogue cops. "Internal discipline is taken seriously by most if not all American police departments," the University of Baltimore's Kane says. "Police commanders and departments can often determine that a police officer is not good for the department and not good for the public."

Police Foundation president Williams gives a mixed review. "Some police departments are very good at discipline — a lot, not just a few," he says. "But I wouldn't want to say that all police departments are like that."

ACLU officials are more critical. "We have found problems with internal disciplinary procedures around the country," says Vanita Gupta, deputy legal director for the national ACLU. "To say that they are an adequate remedy for these violations is a real problem. It's just not how it plays out."

The disciplinary procedures that exist today are the culmination of decades of pressure from outside groups — in particular, groups such as the ACLU and other civil rights organizations — for more effective oversight of police practices in general and in specific cases. "Some form of citizen oversight exists in almost every city," according to the University of Nebraska's Walker.

In contrast to civilian review boards — perhaps the most common oversight mechanism — Walker says he prefers the appointment of an independent auditor for a department. "They have authority to review the operations of an agency and to make public reports," Walker explains. "That's the best solution for improving the department, not just finding guilt or innocence in a particular incident."

Roger Goldman, a professor at St. Louis University School of Law who has specialized in police accountability issues, notes that even when an officer has been removed from a force, he or she often looks for — and sometimes finds — a job with another law enforcement agency. To remedy the problem, Goldman favors a system of "decertifying" an officer for any police work after a finding of misconduct — akin to disbarment for lawyers, for example. "The problem can't be left up to local municipalities and police departments to handle," he says.

Police consultant Scott says police unions represent a big obstacle to strengthened discipline. "The unions can protect the incompetent, and the malicious, and allow them to get back on the streets," Scott says. "The unions have lost their way as to who they're supposed to represent in the bigger picture of law enforcement."

Other experts, however, stress the role of leadership at the top in improving discipline. "What you've got to have," says Williams, "is commitment at the highest levels of the department." The ACLU's Gupta agrees. "We know and police experts know how to implement best practices in this area," she says. "There are best practices out there, but there still remains a lot of work to be done."

BACKGROUND

Police Problems

Police misconduct has been a persistent problem since full-time police forces were first organized in the United States in the mid-19th century. Political patronage and financial corruption were dominant concerns in the 1800s; use of force and other coercive tactics and racial and ethnic discrimination became major issues in the 1900s. A reform movement to professionalize policing dates from the early 20th century. The Supreme Court began to exercise oversight by the 1930s and then brought about significant changes in police practices with decisions in the 1960s establishing new limits on interrogations and searches.[20]

The constables and night watches of the colonial and early post-independence years proved inadequate for law enforcement by the mid-19th century. The emergence of urban centers brought with it the breakdown of law and order due to interethnic clashes, economic discontent and conflict over political issues, including slavery. Philadelphia and Boston created police forces in the 1830s — not long after Sir Robert Peel in 1829 had created the first urban police force in London, England. New York City followed in 1845.

The 19th century officer was typically unarmed and untrained, inefficient and largely ineffective in preventing crime. He was likely chosen on the basis of political patronage and afforded no job security.* Corruption was "epidemic," according to a textbook by the University of Nebraska's Walker and Arizona State University professor of criminology Charles Katz, but reform efforts typically consisted merely of replacing supporters of one political faction with those of another. And "no attention" was given to the two issues that would dominate the 20th century: excessive force and racial discrimination.[21]

More serious reform efforts began in the early 20th century as part of Progressive Era movements to replace spoils-system, moneyed-interest politics with popular democracy and professional government services. Walker and Katz credit August Vollmer, chief of the Berkeley, Calif., police force from 1905 to 1932, as the father of the movement to define policing as a profession. He created college-level courses in police work and, along with other reformers, favored raising standards for hiring officers, eliminating political influence and placing control in the hands of qualified administrators.

But police reform "progressed very slowly," Walker and Katz write. And in 1931 Vollmer co-authored a critical report by the presidentially appointed National Commission on Law Observance and Enforcement, commonly called the Wickersham Commission. Among its findings: Physical brutality was "extensively practiced" by police departments around the country.

---

*Chicago is now believed to have hired the first female officer in 1891; Portland, Ore., followed in 1905, Los Angeles in 1910.

CHRONOLOGY

1960s *Supreme Court lays down rules for police searches, interrogation.*

1961 Supreme Court says states must adopt exclusionary rule to bar use of evidence found by police during unconstitutional searches (*Mapp v. Ohio*).

1966 Supreme Court requires police to advise suspects of rights before in-custody interrogation (*Miranda v. Arizona*).

1968 National Advisory Commission on Civil Disorders (Kerner Commission) report says distrust between police and "ghetto communities" was major cause of urban riots. . . . Law Enforcement Assistance Administration is established to provide federal grants to state, local law enforcement agencies; in 14-year lifetime, agency promotes accreditation standards, provides funds for officer training.

1990s *Justice Department gains power to investigate state, local law enforcement agencies.*

1991, 1992 Videotaped beating of Rodney King by Los Angeles police officers provokes debate over use of force, leads to riots in African-American neighborhoods after officers are prosecuted but acquitted.

1994 Congress authorizes Justice Department (DOJ) to investigate state, local law enforcement agencies for "pattern or practice" of violations of constitutional or statutory rights (42 U.S.C. § 14141).

Mid- to late '90s *Justice Department uses new law to get Pittsburgh and Steubenville, Ohio, police departments to agree to reforms; launches investigations in other cities, including Washington, D.C.*

1999, 2000 Los Angeles Police Department is rocked by disclosures of corruption, excessive force by antigang unit in predominantly Latino Rampart neighborhood; Justice Department, city agree in 2000 on reforms, court supervision.

2001-Present *Bush administration pulls back on police department investigations; Obama administration takes aggressive stance.*

2003 Detroit agrees to institute police reforms after investigation initiated in December 2000.

2005 Two African-American civilians killed, four others wounded by New Orleans police officers while crossing Danziger Bridge to flee post-Katrina flooding.

2006 Supreme Court allows use of evidence found in Detroit drug raid despite officers' failure to follow knock-and-announce rule (*Hudson v. Michigan*); first of Roberts Court rulings weakening enforcement of exclusionary rule.

2009 Eric Holder is named first African-American attorney general; chooses Thomas Perez to head Justice Department's civil rights division.

2010 Roundtable convened by Justice Department finds police investigations "effective" in promoting reform; some police officials complain of "negative stigma."

2011 Justice Department report sharply criticizes New Orleans Police Department for excessive force, discriminatory policing; police chief promises reforms (March 17). . . . Five New Orleans officers are convicted in federal civil rights trial in Danziger Bridge case (Aug. 5); five others had pleaded guilty earlier. . . . DOJ report lambasts Puerto Rico Police Department for excessive force, other issues (Sept. 7). . . . Three more DOJ reports fault police in Maricopa County (Phoenix), Ariz.; Seattle; East Haven, Conn. (Dec. 15, 16, 19).

2012 East Haven Police Chief Leonard Gallo retires (Jan. 30). . . . African-American teenager Trayvon Martin is shot and killed by neighborhood watch coordinator George Zimmerman in Sanford, Fla. (Feb. 26); death touches off debate over authorities' failure to arrest Zimmerman, Florida law easing rule on self defense. . . . Seattle mayor, police chief adopt plan to revise use-of-force policies, review racial profiling (March 29). . . . Puerto Rico Police Chief Emilio Díaz Cólon resigns to avoid hurting reforms (March 29). . . . Maricopa County Sheriff Joe Arpaio rejects Justice Department demand for court-supervised consent decree (April 3). . . . Justice Department weighs requests for formal investigations of police in Albuquerque, Omaha, elsewhere.

Supreme Court Eases Rules on Police Searches

Evidence gleaned illegally allowed in criminal trials.

Detroit police officers thought they were raiding a big crack-cocaine house when they converged, seven strong, on Booker Hudson's home on the afternoon of Aug. 27, 1998. Wary of being shot, Officer Jamal Good shouted, "Police. Search warrant," and then paused only a moment before barging in.

Good's nearly instantaneous entry violated a Supreme Court decision issued three years earlier, in *Wilson v. Arkansas*, that imposed a so-called knock-and-announce rule requiring police to wait a reasonable period after the initial knock before entering a private home.

When Hudson was tried on cocaine charges, he sought to exclude the evidence that police found in their search: five individually wrapped "rocks" of crack cocaine that he had in his pants pockets. Michigan courts refused, and so did the U.S. Supreme Court — in the first of three decisions under Chief Justice John G. Roberts Jr. that critics say have seriously weakened the so-called exclusionary rule against using evidence found during an illegal police search.

Writing for the majority in *Hudson v. Michigan* (2006), Justice Antonin Scalia said the costs of applying the exclusionary rule to knock-and-announce violations in terms of releasing criminals would outweigh any benefits in terms of protecting privacy or deterring improper police behavior. As one reason, Scalia pointed to what he called the "substantial" existing deterrents to police violations of search rules.

David Moran, then a Wayne State University law professor who represented Hudson before the Supreme Court, sharply disagreed. "It's a joke to say that the police will comply with the knock-and-announce rule without the exclusionary rule as a sanction," he said. [1]

The exclusionary rule, a distinctively U.S. legal doctrine, dates from a 1914 Supreme Court ruling applying it to federal court cases. The Supreme Court forced the same rule on state courts in 1961 in one of the first decisions under Chief Justice Earl Warren that expanded the rights of suspects and criminal defendants. The court trimmed but did not eliminate the rule under the next two chief justices, Warren E. Burger and William H. Rehnquist.

Supporters of the exclusionary rule, criminal defense attorneys and civil liberties advocates among others, echo Moran's view that the only effective deterrent to police misconduct in conducting searches is to exclude the evidence from trial. Critics say there are other deterrents, including police disciplinary procedures and civil damage suits.

As a White House lawyer under President Ronald Reagan, Roberts helped lay the basis for a series of attacks aimed at either amending or abolishing the exclusionary rule. Now, as chief justice, Roberts leads a five-vote conservative majority that critics say is transforming those broadsides into legal precedent. [2]

The *Hudson* case came in Roberts' first full term as chief justice. Three years later, Roberts wrote for the same 5-4 majority in a second decision cutting back on the exclusionary rule. The decision in *Herring v. United States* (2009) allowed the use of evidence that an Alabama man was carrying when he was arrested in 2004 on the basis of what was later found to be an outdated arrest warrant. Roberts said the exclusionary rule applies only to police conduct that is "sufficiently deliberate that exclusion can meaningfully deter it, and sufficiently culpable that such deterrence is worth the price paid by the justice system." [3]

In a third decision, the court in June 2011 held that the exclusionary rule does not require suppression of evidence obtained by police if they relied in good faith on an established court precedent, even if it was later overruled as violating the Fourth Amendment's protections against unreasonable searches and seizures (*Davis v. United States*). In January, however, the court gave defense lawyers and civil liberties advocates a significant victory by limiting the authority of police to attach a GPS tracking device to a vehicle for surveillance purposes. The unanimous ruling in *United States v. Jones* apparently requires police to get a search warrant unless they can show a reason for an exception. [4]

— Kenneth Jost

---

[1] Account taken from Kenneth Jost, *The Supreme Court Yearbook 2005-2006*.

[2] See Adam Liptak, "Justices Step Closer to Repeal of Evidence Ruling," *The New York Times*, Jan. 31, 2009, p. A1.

[3] See Kenneth Jost, *The Supreme Court Yearbook 2008-2009*.

[4] For coverage, see Adam Liptak, "Justices Reject GPS Tracking in a Drug Case," *The New York Times*, Jan. 24, 2012, p. A1.

The Supreme Court first entered the field in 1936 with a unanimous decision, *Brown v. Mississippi*, declaring the use of confessions obtained by torture-like interrogation to be a violation of the Due Process Clause. Over the next three decades, the court adopted a case-by-case approach that barred confessions if induced by either physical or psychological coercion.

By the 1960s, the court saw the need to adopt a stronger, preventive safeguard. The result was the controversial but now largely accepted decision, *Miranda v. Arizona* (1966), which required police to advise a suspect of his or her rights, including the right to remain silent, before any custodial interrogation — that is, any interrogation during which the suspect is not free to leave. Five years earlier, in *Mapp v. Ohio* (1961), the court had established another landmark limitation on police conduct by requiring states to enforce the exclusionary rule, which bars the use of evidence obtained by police during an unconstitutional search or arrest.[22]

The 1960s also saw agreement between Congress and the president to increase the federal role in professionalizing state and local police agencies. Since the 1930s, the FBI had been allowing local police officers to enroll in what was originally called the FBI Training School, now the FBI National Academy, in Quantico, Va. In 1968, Congress created, as part of the Omnibus Crime Control and Safe Streets Act, a new agency to support state and local law enforcement: the Law Enforcement Assistance Administration (LEAA).

In its 14 years of existence, LEAA funneled about $8 billion in grants to state and local police agencies. It was abolished in 1982, unpopular in Congress and among some experts, in part because of a penchant for funding expensive gadgetry. But it also is credited with helping establish standards for police and corrections agencies and with providing funds for training state and local police officers.

"LEAA was the catalyst that promoted the education of police officers by creating a significant amount of money for police officers to get educated," Police Foundation president Williams says today.[23]

Police Accountability

Despite widely acknowledged improvements in professionalism and accountability, major police departments around the country were beset by high-profile scandals during the final decades of the 20th century. Major controversies in New York City and Los Angeles resulted in the formation of blue-ribbon commissions that recommended significant changes, some eventually adopted. In Washington, Congress laid the foundation for increased police accountability with two legislative enactments: the 1994 provision authorizing Justice Department suits against rights-violating police departments and a 2000 provision requiring data collection on arrest-related deaths.

Financial corruption of the sort widespread in earlier eras continued as a recurrent issue. In the most dramatic episode, New York City police detective Frank Serpico blew the whistle on widespread bribery and extortion in the NYPD in a newspaper expose in 1970 and a year later as a witness before the blue-ribbon Knapp Commission.[24] The city's response to the commission's recommendations for internal reforms was criticized as timid. Two decades later, however, Mayor Rudy Giuliani established a standing independent commission to combat police corruption. Today, critics in New York continue to highlight allegations of misconduct, but the commission credits the department's Internal Affairs Bureau generally with "thorough and diligent investigations" of accusations.[25]

In the 1990s, the Los Angeles Police Department experienced two major scandals, each of which made national headlines. In the first, an onlooker captured on videotape the seemingly unjustified beating of an African-American suspect, Rodney King, by LAPD officers on the night of March 3, 1991, after a high-speed automobile chase. The blue-ribbon Christopher Commission created in the wake of the incident found that "a significant number" of officers repetitively used excessive force against suspects. The acquittals of the officers charged in the King beating in 1992 touched off riots in the city's largely African-American neighborhoods and helped force the resignation of Police Chief Daryl Gates. He was succeeded by Willie Williams, the LAPD's first African-American chief.

The King beating also led to the federal law authorizing the Justice Department to sue local police departments for rights violations. Members of Congress from California pushed the proposal unsuccessfully in 1991 and 1992; it was enacted in 1994 as a provision in the omnibus Violent Crime Control and Law Enforcement

Act, thanks in part to a push from then-Senate Judiciary Committee Chairman Joseph Biden. Despite its later importance, the provision attracted little attention. A detailed Justice Department fact sheet on the law failed to mention the provision.

By 1996, however, the department's civil rights division was beginning to use the new powers with investigations initiated in response to citizen complaints of police departments in Pittsburgh and Steubenville, Ohio. By the end of the decade, those cases had resulted in consent decrees requiring organizational changes. Nine other investigations were pending as the decade ended, including one in Washington, D.C., requested in 1999 by a new chief of police.

The department had already investigated the Los Angeles Police Department for three years when a new scandal erupted in 1999, featuring wide-ranging excessive force, corruption and obstruction of justice accusations against members of an antigang unit assigned to one of Los Angeles' predominantly Latino communities. The wide-ranging allegations of misconduct by Rampart Division officers included unprovoked shootings and beatings, planting of evidence, stealing and dealing in narcotics and covering up of the offenses. The scandal led to disciplinary actions against 58 officers, but an independent commission later criticized the department's response as inadequate.

The Justice Department intensified its investigation of the LAPD after the scandal. By mid-2000, government lawyers were threatening to sue the city in federal court unless it agreed to wide-ranging internal reforms. Mayor Richard Riordan resisted any agreement, but painstaking negotiations eventually resulted in the city's agreement to an enforceable consent decree that the city council approved by a vote of 11-2 on Nov. 2, 2000. Among other provisions, the agreement required creation of a new division to investigate all uses of force. The decree, formally entered in June 2001, was terminated in 2009.[26]

Meanwhile, Congress gave the federal government an additional tool for police accountability by passing the Death in Custody Reporting Act to collect data on deaths of inmates in prisons and jails and of suspects in police custody. The bill was approved by voice vote in the House of Representatives in June 2000 and by the Senate in September; President Bill Clinton signed it into law on Oct. 13. After setting up procedures, the Bureau of Justice Statistics began collecting reports on police-custody deaths in fiscal 2003.

Changing Priorities

The Justice Department's oversight of local law enforcement agencies lagged under President George W. Bush. Investigations and cases already initiated were continued, but reports on newly opened investigations took a deferential tone toward police policies. Obama's selection of civil rights-minded officials for key posts at the Justice Department signaled a likely change in priorities. Even before Perez's confirmation to head the civil rights division, the special litigation section's report on one local department took a sharper tone than those in the Bush years. By the end of 2011, the section's activist stance was evident with a record number of investigations open and stinging reports issued on five law enforcement bodies within four months.

As a presidential candidate in 2000, Bush said he believed police matters should be handled locally. Under Bush, the civil rights division became highly politicized, morale declined sharply and career lawyers left in droves. A later report by the Government Accountability Office found that the special litigation section suffered an attrition rate of 31 percent in 2005, 24 percent in 2006 and 18 percent in 2007.[27]

The special litigation section had achieved important victories early in the Bush years in investigations begun by the Clinton administration of police forces in Washington, D.C.; Detroit; and Prince George's County, Md. The investigation in Washington found "a pattern . . . of excessive force" by officers in the 1990s and applauded new efforts to reduce the problem. Police officials agreed to the appointment of a monitor to oversee the department for five years. In Detroit, a consent decree agreed to in June 2003 similarly provided for an outside monitor to check compliance with changes that included new steps to track officers named in excessive-force complaints. In Prince George's County in suburban Washington, D.C., the police agreed in January 2004 to curb excessive force by officers and restrict the use of police dogs, with compliance to be tracked by an outside monitor.[28]

In later years, however, reports on police departments appeared to steer clear of pointed criticism or threats of litigation. Instead, reports, such as one in August 2008 suggesting the Orange County (Fla.) Sheriff's Office

Florida Police Under Scrutiny in Trayvon Martin Case

Critics question handling of shooting by armed civilian.

The fatal shooting of an African-American teenager by a volunteer neighborhood watch coordinator in a gated suburban community in Florida has ignited a racially charged debate over the police department's handling of the case. The episode also puts a national spotlight on Florida's controversial Stand Your Ground law, which allows a civilian to use potentially lethal force in self-defense in public places without first trying to retreat to safety. [1]

Some six weeks after the Feb. 26 death of Trayvon Martin, a special state prosecutor is set to present evidence in the case on April 10 to a Seminole County grand jury. [*Update*: Special prosecutor Angela Corey announced on April 9 that the case would not be presented to the grand jury on April 10, but specified that the investigation was continuing.] The U.S. Justice Department is also reviewing the case. The moves have come, however, only after local and national protests over the authorities' decision that night not to file charges against George Zimmerman, a neighborhood watch volunteer since August 2011.

Martin, 17, was returning from a convenience store to the home of his father's girlfriend in the Retreat at Twin Lakes community in Sanford, Fla., shortly after 7 p.m. when he drew Zimmerman's suspicions. Martin was unarmed; he was carrying a bag of candy and a can of iced tea and wearing a gray hoodie to protect himself from the rain. Zimmerman, 28, a resident of white and Hispanic ancestry, was carrying a 9 mm handgun — despite earlier instructions from the Sanford police department's neighborhood watch liaison that volunteers should not be armed.

Zimmerman had volunteered for the neighborhood watch in August 2011 because of several burglaries in the gated community of some 260 homes. Suspicious of Martin, he placed a 911 call to the Sanford Police Department. Zimmerman said Martin was "just walking around" and appeared to be "up to no good." The police dispatcher advised Zimmerman not to follow Martin and to wait to meet a patrol officer. Later in the recorded four-minute call, Zimmerman is heard saying something listed on the police transcription as "unintelligible" and interpreted by others in the subsequent debate as a racial epithet.

An altercation of some sort ensued after Zimmerman — 5-foot-10, 170 pounds — got out of his vehicle and Martin — 6-foot-1, 150 pounds — realized he was being surveilled. An unidentified girlfriend of Martin's says Martin called her to complain about being followed. Zimmerman's father says his son told police that Martin challenged him, used a racial epithet, forced him to the ground and pummeled him with his fists.

Whatever the exact course of the dispute, Zimmerman fired a single shot that hit Martin in the chest. Martin died at the scene. The police officers who arrived handcuffed Zimmerman and took him to the police station, where he was questioned and released without having been tested for drugs or alcohol. A video appears to show a gash on the back of Zimmerman's head but no serious injury to his face despite Zimmerman's claim to have suffered a broken nose during the altercation. A funeral director who examined Martin's body said it showed no scrapes, bruises or other signs of a fight other than the single gunshot wound to his chest.

Martin's death drew no news coverage for almost two weeks until his father, Tracy Martin, held a news conference on March 8 to call for Zimmerman's arrest and demand the release of the tapes of Zimmerman's 911 call. The tapes, released over the next weekend, turned the episode from an overlooked local story into a round-the-clock nationwide controversy.

adopt new policies on the use of Tasers, generally included language specifying that the "technical assistance" being provided was viewed "as recommendations and not mandates."[29]

Obama's appointment of Eric Holder as the first African-American to serve as attorney general signaled a likely reinvigoration of the Justice Department's role in civil rights enforcement, including police-accountability

In the weeks since, Martin has been described as a typical teenage boy, with good manners and good attitude, but a record of three suspensions from his high school in north Miami-Dade County, where he lived with his mother. In February, he was staying with his father in Sanford after having been hit with a 10-day suspension because of marijuana residue found in his backpack.

Zimmerman is described as a former altar boy with unrealized ambitions of becoming a police officer, capable of kindness but also with a volatile temper. He was arrested in summer 2005 after pushing a Florida state alcohol agent during a raid at a college-area bar; the charge was dropped after Zimmerman agreed to a pretrial diversion program. A month later, he and his ex-fiancée obtained reciprocal domestic violence injunctions based on mutual accusations of physical violence.

From the outset, authorities in Sanford and Seminole County explained that Zimmerman had not been charged in the shooting in part because of a law Florida enacted in 2005 making it harder to prosecute individuals in the face of a claim of self-defense. The Stand Your Ground law extends the long-established "castle doctrine" — allowing the use of deadly force in self defense inside one's home — to any setting, private or public.

In its central provision, the 1,000-word statute provides that someone in a place where he or she has a right to be "has no duty to retreat and has the right to stand his or her ground and meet force with force, including deadly force if he or she reasonably believes it is necessary to do so to prevent death or great bodily harm to himself or herself or another or to prevent the commission of a forcible felony." The law specifically provides immunity from criminal or civil liability if the use of force is justified. [2]

Similar laws are on the books in about half the states. Coverage of the Florida episode has led to a national debate over the laws. Prosecutors in Florida said the law had made it harder to bring charges in homicides where the suspect claimed self-defense. Police organizations have criticized the laws, but gun-rights groups have defended them.

Only after a full month had passed since the shooting was it reported that Sanford Detective Chris Serino, the lead investigator in the case, had initially recommended

Protesters in downtown Los Angeles mark the one-month anniversary of the Feb. 26, 2012, killing of unarmed black teenager Trayvon Martin by a neighborhood watch volunteer in Florida.

charging Zimmerman with manslaughter only to be overruled by his chief and by state's attorney Norman Wolfinger, who has declined to comment on the report. Wolfinger was removed from the case after Gov. Rick Scott and Attorney General Pamela Bondi appointed Angela Corey, the state's attorney from the Jacksonville area, as special prosecutor.

— Kenneth Jost

[1] For a comprehensive overview, see Dan Barry, Serge F. Kovaleski, Campbell Robertson and Lizette Alvarez, "In the Eye of a Firestorm: In Florida, an Intersection of Tragedy, Race and Outrage," *The New York Times*, April 2, 2012, p. A1, www.nytimes.com/2012/04/02/us/trayvon-martin-shooting-prompts-a-review-of-ideals.html?_r=1&hp. The rapidly changing, heavily annotated Wikipedia entry on the case includes links to the 911 call made on the night of Trayvon Martin's shooting, to other police documents and to collections of news and commentary in *The New York Times* and *Wall Street Journal*, http://en.wikipedia.org/wiki/Shooting_of_Trayvon_Martin. Background details drawn from both accounts.

[2] See Title XLVI, Chap. 0776, www.flsenate.gov/Laws/Statutes/2011/Chapter0776/All.

investigations. As deputy attorney general in the Clinton administration, Holder had helped oversee police department investigations, including the filing of the suit against the Los Angeles Police Department in 2000. To head the

civil rights division, Obama and Holder picked Perez, a former criminal prosecutor in the division from 1988 to 1995 who had gone on to hold political posts as deputy to the head of the division (1998-1999) and head of the

Office of Civil Rights in the Department of Health and Human Services (1999-2001). Perez drew Republican opposition because of his work with the immigrant rights group CASA de Maryland, but eventually won Senate confirmation on Oct. 6, 2009, by a vote of 72-22.[30]

Even before Perez took office, a slight change of tone was seen in the section's report on the Yonkers, N.Y., police department. The June 2009 report included the same "not a mandate" language used in earlier reports, but followed with a sentence "strongly" urging the department to adopt the recommendations listed. A report on the Inglewood, Calif., department issued in December "strongly" urged adoption of the recommended changes.

Stronger reports came in quick succession in 2011, beginning with the one on New Orleans in March. A report on Puerto Rico, issued on Sept. 7, found a pattern of "unreasonable force" along with "other misconduct" aimed at limiting free speech rights as well as "troubling evidence" of "discriminatory policing practices" targeting persons of Dominican descent. In releasing the report, Perez told reporters that the section had 17 investigations under way. The investigations are "really a cornerstone of our work," Perez said. Three months later, he elevated the issue further by personally attending December news conferences releasing the Seattle and Maricopa County reports.[31]

CURRENT SITUATION

Investigations Urged

With 20 investigations already under way, the Justice Department is being urged by citizen groups in several other cities to look into police departments with troubling records of fatal shootings and other uses of force against arrestees and suspects.

In the most recent request, the Omahans for Justice Alliance asked the Justice Department and U.S. Attorney Deborah Gilg on March 13 to investigate the Omaha Police Department. The 10-page letter cited an alleged pattern of excessive force, illegal arrests, disregard of state law and department polices and other misconduct.

"The kind of incidents that we've had are very, very serious and appear to get worse," University of Nebraska professor Walker, one of three co-signers of the letter, said at a news conference to announce the request. Supporting organizations include the ACLU of Nebraska, Nebraskans for Peace, Black Men United of Omaha, the NAACP's Omaha Branch and the Progressive Research Institute of Nebraska.[32]

In a prepared statement, Lt. Darci Tierney, a police spokeswoman, noted that the Justice Department had previously reviewed use-of-force incidents as part of "normal business practices." She voiced no objection to scrutiny of the additional incidents noted in the letter. "We strive to be a transparent agency, and if a citizen group feels the need for the Department of Justice to review these events, we welcome the review," Tierney said.[33]

Also in March, an Albuquerque citizens' group stepped up its calls for a federal investigation of the city's police department after two fatal shootings in mid-March brought the total to 18 over the past two years. Most of those killed have been young Hispanic men, according to Jewell Hall, executive director of the Martin Luther King Jr. Memorial Center. "I hope that they will do an investigation to get deep inside the Albuquerque Police Department," says Hall, a retired teacher.

The Albuquerque department drew national attention with the disclosure that the police union has had a practice for several years of giving officers involved in fatal shootings $500 to help them take time off to recover from stress related to the incidents. Critics said the payments appeared to be a bounty for killing a suspect. Police Chief Ray Schultz said he was unaware of the practice. With the controversy raging, two top officers of the Albuquerque Peace Officers Association resigned on March 27; their successors joined Schultz and Mayor Richard Berry on March 30 in announcing an end to the practice.[34]

Walker, who co-authored a study of the Albuquerque police department in 1997, says the number of deaths at the hands of police appeared to warrant a Justice Department investigation. "That's a lot of shootings," he told The Associated Press.[35]

The Justice Department has acknowledged the preliminary inquiry into the Albuquerque department but says it has made no decision on whether to open a formal investigation. The Justice Department had no response to the Omaha request in news coverage immediately afterward. Investigations are being sought in other cities, including Las Vegas, The Associated Press reported. Justice Department officials did not respond to a request from *CQ Researcher* for a complete list of current investigations.

Is the exclusionary rule needed to deter illegal police searches?

YES
Norman L Reimer
Executive Director, National Association of Criminal Defense Lawyers

Written for *CQ Researcher*, April 2012

While it is true that the Supreme Court has at times over the past decade treated the exclusionary rule with disdain, fortunately the court has not yet completely disavowed it. It is perhaps the only tool the courts have to circumscribe police behavior that violates the Fourth Amendment. Let me give you an example.

The Supreme Court in January decided a case — *U.S. v. Jones* — that is sure to be the first of many that will test the limits of government's ability to use modern technology to invade individual privacy. The court unanimously upheld the suppression of GPS tracking data, rejecting the government's sweeping claim that it can track a person's movements without spatial or temporal limitation, and without a warrant or any judicial oversight.

The idea that such surveillance could occur solely at the government's discretion prompted Chief Justice John G. Roberts Jr. to ask in astonishment whether, in the government's view, the FBI could put GPS monitors on the cars of every member of the court. The government's position was a resounding "yes." Fortunately for the future of privacy in a world in which technology now permits once unfathomable invasions of privacy, the court's decision was an equally resounding "no."

How massively was this taking place before the court's decision? During the oral argument, the deputy solicitor general acknowledged that the federal government alone has been using GPS devices "in the low thousands annually." Separate from that, state and local law enforcement authorities frequently employ GPS tracking devices — subjecting untold thousands to surveillance.

Was the court's invocation of the exclusionary rule, a venerable remedy that will soon celebrate its 100th anniversary in American jurisprudence, an effective tool to vindicate fundamental rights guaranteed by the Fourth Amendment? You bet it was. Within weeks, the FBI's general counsel, Andrew Weissmann, said the ruling in *U.S. v. Jones* caused a "sea change" in law enforcement. Following the oral argument and in anticipation of the ruling, the FBI scrambled to ensure that the government had warrants for 3,000 active GPS tracking devices.

After the decision, 250 of those tracking devices remained shut down. Many may eventually be reactivated where there is legal cause — as they should be. No doubt, states and localities are responding similarly to ensure compliance with the dictates of the Fourth Amendment. Thus, once again, the power of the exclusionary rule to rein in governmental abuse is vindicated.

NO
William J. Fitzpatrick
District Attorney, Onondaga County, N.Y.

Written for *CQ Researcher*, April 2012

As a prosecutor for 35 years, I have never met a cop who was deterred by a judicial opinion written five years after he or she made a split-second decision. The Supreme Court-crafted exclusionary rule has morphed from its intended restraint on police misconduct into a judicially sanctioned version of roulette.

Antoine Jones, a Washington, D.C., nightclub owner, was making money the old-fashioned way, entertaining his customers with hip-hop music and running the District's largest cocaine distribution ring. Rather than spend countless hours legally following Jones, police in 2005 decided to place a GPS tracking device on his wife's car, and even though not required, they actually got a search warrant to track the location of this vehicle.

This innovative tactic resulted in Jones' arrest and conviction as well as the seizure of five kilos of cocaine and $850,000 in ill-gotten drug proceeds.

Inexplicably, when the U.S. Attorney's office authorized the installation of the tracking device, the police did so one day beyond the sanctioned 10-day window.

In *United States v. Jones*, the Supreme Court ruled — for the first time — that the installation of a GPS device by the authorities on a suspect's car constituted a search under the Fourth Amendment. Thus the evidence obtained in the case was suppressed, despite the fact that, prior to the decision, the prevailing law was murky at best. Pardon me if I'm confused as to how this deters police misconduct. Would it not make more sense to punish the appropriate grammar school teachers who failed to properly train the future attorneys on how to read a calendar?

My colleagues have no problem with the GPS warrant requirement. What concerns us is the uncertainty and Draconian response to what may be charitably called a technical error. If we track EZ-Pass holders to locate an abducted child or trace a terrorist by using cell-tower records, do the criminals go free? While technology is changing rapidly, police who make life-and-death decisions do not have the luxury of waiting for the courts to delineate these constitutional boundaries before they take action.

Even the learned justices in *Jones* had little consensus on the grounds for the decision. Prosecutors merely want a rational approach to evidence suppression where concepts such as proportionality and good faith have some standing. You do not "deter" cops with a system that is, as Justice Lewis Powell said, "intolerably confusing." You only confuse cops and make the public less secure.

In both Omaha and Albuquerque, the groups pressing for federal investigations complained that civilians involved in police shootings or use-of-force incidents were predominantly people of color. The Omaha group also cited figures from a state commission showing that black drivers are stopped almost as often by the Omaha Police Department as white drivers are.

Both forces are predominantly white. In 2000, about 80 percent of the Omaha officers were white, and the Albuquerque department was 60 percent Anglo and 36 percent Hispanic, according to federal Bureau of Justice Statistics data.[36]

In Omaha, the citizens' group also is urging the city to re-establish the office of Public Safety Auditor. The office was created in 2001, but Mayor Mike Fahey fired Tristan Bonn from the post in October 2006, barely a week after she delivered a report sharply critical of the department. The city fought Bonn's lawsuit to regain the position and has failed to refill the position, according to the citizens' group.[37]

The current mayor, Jim Suttle, says there is no need for an auditor. "We have a lot of faith in our police chief," he told an Omaha television station in September 2011 in the midst of a controversy over the videotaped beating and kicking of a suspect in police custody.[38]

In Albuquerque, an officer involved in a November 2009 shooting was fired the next year after the department's internal affairs unit and the Independent Review Officer found the shooting unjustified. Schultz said he fired Brandon Carr because the officer lied to investigators about the events.

The city paid the victim's family $950,000 to settle a civil suit, but on March 30 the district attorney's office announced no criminal charges would be brought against Carr. Out of 29 police shootings since 2009, eight are awaiting grand jury action, but no criminal charges have been brought in the other 21, according to the *Albuquerque Journal*.[39]

Reforms Outlined

The Seattle Police Department is preparing to adopt a 20-point reform plan aimed at answering criticisms from citizens' groups and the Justice Department and perhaps avoiding federal court supervision for several years.

The plan, released by Mayor McGinn on March 29, includes steps to revamp use-of-force policies, strengthen the role of a newly established Force Review Board, collect data on possible racial profiling and improve diversity training. In one specific change, the plan responds to criticism of how police dealt with Occupy Seattle protesters in November by prohibiting the use of pepper spray except in self-defense or as "a last resort."

Seattle and Justice Department officials met behind closed doors the next day to discuss the plan. Seattle officials appeared to hope the department would back away from insisting that the city agree to a court order giving a federal judge supervisory authority over the plan's implementation for a specified number of years.[40]

Progress on a reform plan in Seattle came after negotiations between the Justice Department and New Orleans officials had stalled because of a bizarre incident involving the federal government's point person in the talks. Sal Perricone withdrew from the talks and then resigned from the U.S. Attorney's office in New Orleans in March after he acknowledged having used a pseudonym to post hundreds of online comments about law enforcement-related stories on the *Times-Picayune*'s website, nola.com.[41]

Two of the major groups involved in requesting the Justice Department investigation of the Seattle Police Department reacted approvingly to what McGinn called the 20/20 plan — 20 steps to be put into effect over 20 months. Estela Ortega, executive director of the Hispanic advocacy group El Centro de la Raza, appeared at the news conference with McGinn and Chief John Diaz and praised their willingness to work with community leaders on the plan.

In a brief statement, Kathleen Taylor, executive director of ACLU of Washington State, said the civil rights organization was "encouraged" by the plan. But she said a court-supervised consent decree "is critical to ensure that reforms are thoroughly implemented and are sustained for the long term."

The plan's use-of-force provisions call for developing "updated, clear policies" on the use of "lethal, less-lethal and non-lethal tools available to officers." Officers would be trained annually on the policies and on "de-escalation" of "low-level encounters." Sergeants and commanders are also to be given annual training on how to investigate and document use-of-force incidents.

Seattle's Force Review Board, established after the release of the Justice Department report in December, would be given a formal role. Some form of civilian review of the board's work would be instituted.

Issues of "biased policing" are to be addressed by streamlining race-data collection related to traffic stops and initiating the collection of race data for pedestrian encounters. The University of Washington's African-American Studies Department is to be engaged to review the department's practices as related to the issue.

In New Orleans, Perricone took himself out of the federal-local negotiations on March 16 after his role as pseudonymous online commentator came to light. Mayor Landrieu said Perricone's participation had "poisoned" the negotiations, but U.S. Attorney Jim Letten insisted the removal would not cause a delay.

ACLU official Esman says the ongoing talks are "very guarded," but she expects eventual agreement on a court-supervised consent decree. "Something will come of it," Esman says. "Whether it will be enough, whether it will work is anybody's guess."

Meanwhile, another of the police forces sharply criticized in Justice Department reports last year got new leadership in late March in a move that may ease the way for reforms. Puerto Rico Gov. Luis Fortuño named former FBI official Hector Pesquera as superintendent of the commonwealth's 17,000-person police department on March 29 following the resignation of Emilio Díaz Cólon from the post.

Díaz had been superintendent for only three months when the Justice Department report was released in September. He responded by denying any constitutional violations by the force. Over the next six months, Díaz was criticized for failing to offer an anticrime program. Fortuño quoted Díaz as saying he was resigning to avoid hurting prospective reforms.[42]

OUTLOOK
Police Under Pressure

Popular trends in law enforcement push police departments in opposite directions. Police departments use high-tech tools to surveil suspects, crack down on drugs and try to spot terrorists, even as officers are being urged to get out of their cars, walk the streets and engage the public in "community policing."[43]

Along with these competing visions of good policing come financial pressures as fiscally strapped local governments cut back on police departments' staffing, pay and services. In Detroit, police precincts are open only during daytime hours, and nonemergency reports have to be made through a central call center. To save $80 million in 2011, the Los Angeles City Council cut overtime pay for cops, but the department still had to find $41 million more in savings. And police departments around the country have been dealing with layoffs by taking reports on many property crimes over the phone instead of sending officers to investigate.[44]

The financial pressures lead police consultant Scott to worry about cutbacks in the training needed to ensure that officers live up to professional standards. "Law enforcement is not training its personnel the way it should," the former police chief says. "This is where I see many, many lawsuits that could be avoided if we as a public demanded to have better trained police officers."

Police accountability is being enhanced, however, by new technology, such as the video cameras now installed on many police cars to record officer-suspect encounters. "The way to encourage police reform and police accountability is [with] sunlight," says University of Baltimore professor Kane, "making these practices known to the public."

Technology at the same time increases the potential for police abuse of individual privacy and safety. Civil liberties groups complain that local police now are using cell phone tracking routinely and aggressively, often without much judicial oversight. Tasers, once seen as a non-lethal alternative to firearms for subduing suspects, are linked by the human rights group Amnesty International to hundreds of deaths of suspects — a risk that the manufacturer acknowledges but calls exaggerated.[45]

The high-power, high-tech weaponry provided to SWAT teams, especially for drug raids, is viewed disapprovingly, even by police-friendly experts. "In some cases, you've got this hypercoercion being used in situations that don't require this kind of force," Kane says. "It's almost like a toy that needs to be played with."

Even without high-power weaponry, the risk of unnecessary and excessive force, sometimes lethal, persists in police-civilian encounters. Review procedures in place, as in Albuquerque, often find officers' conduct justifiable, even as outside groups and victims' families disagree. But national police organizations appear to devote little attention to the subject. In assuming the presidency of the International Association of Chiefs of Police in November

2011, Quincy, Fla., Police Chief Walter McNeil said the group's highest priority would be "to continue a comprehensive violence-against-police-officers reduction strategy." McNeil did not address the issue of excessive force against civilians, nor has he mentioned the issue in his monthly column in the association's magazine despite the spate of critical Justice Department reports in December.[46]

Walker, the veteran of police accountability issues, worries that the post-9/11 emphasis on homeland security has been a setback for best police practices. "Your primary focus is not community policing, which tells you that the major things we have to do is work with people in the community," he says. And he worries about the impact of budget-imposed layoffs. "If the economy worsens," Walker says, "things could be very, very worse."

Still, Walker believes that excessive force and racial profiling are not intractable problems. "If these problems are persisting, it's just because [police leaders] are not paying attention," Walker says. "We have a much clearer picture of possible things we can do. It's just finding the will do to do them."

NOTES

1. Account drawn primarily from coverage by Brendan McCarthy in *The Times-Picayune* (New Orleans): "Raid details show focus on weed," March 10, 2012, p. A1; "Man killed by cops was not armed," March 9, 2012, p. A1. Some other information drawn from other *Times-Picayune* articles, most of them by McCarthy.

2. Johnson, Shorty quoted in McCarthy, *ibid.*, March 10.

3. The New Orleans report is available on the Justice Department's website: www.justice.gov/crt/about/spl/nopd.php. A complete list of Special Litigation Section cases and matters, including "Conduct of Law Enforcement Agencies Investigations" and "Conduct of Law Enforcement Agencies Complaints," is found here: www.justice.gov/about/spl/findsettle.php.

4. Diaz quoted in Mike Carter, Steve Miletich, and Jennifer Sullivan, "City faces possibility of court intervention," *The Seattle Times*, Dec. 17, 2011, p. A1;

Gallo's retirement reported in Denise Buffa and Josh Kovner, "Chief Steps Down," *Hartford Courant* (Conn.), Jan. 31, 2012, p. A1; Quoted in J. J. Hensley, "Negotiations between MCSO, DOJ fall apart," *The Arizona Republic* (Phoenix), April 4, 2012, p. A1.

5. For previous coverage, see these *CQ Researcher* reports: Kenneth Jost, "Policing the Police," March 17, 2000, pp. 209-240; Sarah Glazer, "Police Corruption," Nov. 24, 1995, pp. 1041-1064; Richard L. Worsnop, "Police Brutality," Sept. 6, 1991, pp. 633-656; and earlier reports in *CQ Researcher-plus Archives*.

6. See Brendan McCarthy and Laura Maggi, "NOPD deeply defective, report says," *The Times-Picayune*, March 18, 2011, p. A1; Brendan McCarthy, "Reforms in place, Serpas says," *ibid.*, March 24, 2011, p. B1. See also Laura Maggi, " 'Clear pattern' of excessive force cited," *ibid.*, March 18, 2011, p. A14.

7. See Brendan McCarthy, "Judge imposes stiff sentences on 5 NOPD officers convicted in Danziger shootings," nola.com, April 4, 2012, www.nola.com/crime/index.ssf/2012/04/judge_imposes_sentences_on_5_n.html. The defendants and their sentences are Robert Faulcon Jr., 65 years; Kenneth Bowen, 40 years; Robert Gisevius Jr., 40 years; Anthony Villavaso II, 38 years; Arthur "Archie" Kaufman, six years. For an overview of the case in advance of the trial, see Brendan McCarthy and Laura Maggi, "Federal prosecutors allege civil rights abuses," *The Times-Picayune*, June 19, 2011, A1; for a post-verdict account, see Katie Urbaszewski and Brendan McCarthy, "Danziger evidence outweighed chaos theory," *ibid.*, Aug. 23, 2011, p. A1.

8. "Taking Stock: Report from the 2010 Roundtable on the State and Local Law Enforcement Police Pattern or Practice Program (42 USC § 14141)," National Institute of Justice, September 2011, https://ncjrs.gov/pdffiles1/nij/234458.pdf.

9. Quoted in Jerry Markon, "Justice Dept. is policing the police," *The Washington Post*, Sept. 18, 2011, p. A3.

10. See "Highlights of AP's probe into NYPD intelligence operations," http://ap.org/media-center/nypd/investigation.

11. See "Investigation of the Seattle Police Department," U.S. Department of Justice, Civil Rights Division/ U.S. Attorney's Office, Western District, Washington, Dec. 16, 2011, www.justice.gov/crt/about/spl/ documents/spd_findletter_12-16-11.pdf. The letter requesting the investigation is on the ACLU's website: www.aclu-wa.org/re-request-investigate-pattern-or-practice-misconduct-seattle-police-department. For initial coverage of Williams' death, see Sara Jean Green and Steve Miletich, "Police have questions about shooting by cop," *The Seattle Times*, Sept. 1, 2010, p. A1.

12. "Police Use of Force in America," International Association of Chiefs of Police, 2001, www.theiacp.org/Portals/0/pdfs/Publications/2001useofforce.pdf; "Police Use of Force," National Institute of Justice, www.nij.gov/topics/law-enforcement/officer-safety/use-of-force/welcome.htm#note2 (modified January 2012).

13. The decisions are *Tennessee v. Garner*, 471 U.S. 1 (1985); *Graham v. Connor*, 490 U.S. 386 (1989).

14. William Terrill, Eugene A. Paoline III and Jason Ingram, "Final Technical Report Draft: Assessing Police Use of Force Policy and Outcomes," National Institute of Justice, February 2012, p. 159, www.ncjrs.gov/pdffiles1/nij/grants/237794.pdf.

15. Matthew Kauffman, "In Traffic Stops, Police Tougher on Blacks, Hispanics," *Hartford Courant* (Connecticut), Feb. 26, 2012, p. A1.

16. New Orleans data cited in Kenneth Jost, " 'Black on Black' Racial Profiling: Why?" *Jost on Justice* (blog), March 11, 2011; Justice Department findings on Maricopa County, www.justice.gov/crt/about/spl/mcso.php; East Haven; and www.justice.gov/crt/about/spl/documents/easthaven_findletter_12-19-11.pdf.

17. Figures from the New York Civil Liberties Union cited in Sean Gardiner, "Stop-and-Frisks Hit Record in 2011," *The Wall Street Journal*, Feb. 14, 2012, p. A21.

18. Gitta Laasby, "Flynn addresses inquiry into strip searches," *Journal Sentinel* (Milwaukee), March 23, 2012, p. B1. Background on Mucha drawn from past coverage by Gina Barton: "Gun Case Falls Apart With Cop's Testimony," *ibid.*, Aug. 8, 2010, p. A1; "Forceful Impact: Suspects have accused Sgt. Jason Mucha 10 times of beating them or planting drugs. He wasn't disciplined, but courts took notice," *ibid.*, Sept. 29, 2007, p. A1.

19. Anthony Cormier and Matthew Doig, "Unfit for Duty," *Herald-Tribune* (Sarasota, Fla.), December 2011 (nine parts), http://cops.htcreative.com/; Gina Barton, "At least 93 Milwaukee police officers have been disciplined for violating the law," *Journal Sentinel*, Oct. 23, 2011 (1st of 3 parts), www.jsonline.com/watchdog/watchdogreports/at-least-93-milwaukee-police-officers-have-been-disciplined-for-violating-law-132268408.html.

20. Background drawn in part from Samuel Walker and Charles M. Katz, *Police in America: An Introduction* (5th ed., 2005), chapter 2 (pp. 23-58). The sixth edition (2011) was not available for use before deadline.

21. *Ibid.*, pp. 33-34.

22. The major cases are *Brown v. Mississippi*, 297 U.S. 278 (1936); *Miranda v. Arizona*, 384 U.S. 436 (1966); *Mapp v. Ohio*, 367 U.S. 463 (1960). For background, see David G. Savage, Guide to the U.S. Supreme Court (5th ed., 2011), pp. 740-748 (confessions), 725-726 (exclusionary rule).

23. For an official assessment, see "LEAA/OJP Retrospective: 30 Years of Federal Support for State and Local Criminal Justice," U.S. Department of Justice, Office of Justice Programs, July 11, 1996, p. 3, www.ncjrs.gov/pdffiles1/nij/164509.pdf.

24. For background, see Glazer, *op. cit.*; Peter Maas, *Serpico* (1973), and the cinemazation of the same title, also 1973, with Al Pacino in the title role.

25. "14th Annual Report," City of New York Commission to Combat Police Corruption, February 2012, www.nyc.gov/html/ccpc/downloads/pdf/14th_annual_report.pdf.

26. See Tina Daunt and Jim Newton, "City OKs Police Reform Pact With U.S.," *Los Angeles Times*, Nov. 3, 2000.

27. See Ryan J. Reilly, "Report Delivers Hard Numbers on Bush Civil Rights Division," Main Justice, Dec. 7, 2009, www.mainjustice.com/2009/12/07/report-delivers-hard-numbers-on-bush-civil-rights-division/.

28. See David A. Fahrenthold, "U.S. Faults D.C. Police Use of Force in the '90s," *The Washington Post*, June 14, 2001, p. B1; "Findings Letter re Use of Force by the Washington Metropolitan Police Department," U.S. Department of Justice, June 13, 2001, www.justice.gov/crt/about/spl/documents/dcfindings.php; M.L. Erlick and Ben Schmitt, "U.S. Demand to Detroit: Stop Police Abuses Now," *Detroit Free-Press*, June 13, 2003; "Investigation of the Detroit Police Department" (technical assistance letters, 2002), U.S. Department of Justice, www.justice.gov/crt/about/spl/documents/dpd/detroit_cover.php; Jamie Stockwell and Ruben Castaneda, "Pr. George's Agrees to Curb Excessive Force by Police," *The Washington Post*, Jan. 23, 2004, p. A1; U.S. Department of Justice, "Investigation of the Prince George's County Police Department," Jan. 22, 2004, www.justice.gov/crt/about/spl/documents/pgpd/pgpd_cover.php.

29. "Investigation of the Orange County Sheriff's Office Use of Conducted Energy Devices," U.S. Department of Justice, Aug. 20, 2008, www.justice.gov/crt/about/spl/documents/orangecty_ta_ltr.pd.

30. Andrew Ramonas, "Senate Confirms Tom Perez," Main Justice, Oct. 6, 2009, www.mainjustice.com/2009/10/06/senate-confirms-tom-perez/. For a profile, see Jerry Zremski, "Former area man takes top civil rights post," *Buffalo News*, Nov. 14, 2009, p. A1.

31. Perez quoted in Markon, *op. cit.*

32. Quoted in Sarah Te Slaa, "Group Calls for Federal Investigation Into Police Department," KMTV (Omaha), March 13, 2012, www.kmtv.com/news/local/142578935.html. See also Roseann Moring, "Groups seek federal probe of Omaha police," *Omaha World-Herald*, March 14, 2012.

33. The statement is cited in full in "Police Respond to Complaint," WOWT, March 13, 2012, www.wowt.com/home/headlines/Police_Respond_to_Complaint_142541525.html?storySection=story.

34. See Jeff Proctor, "Cop Payments to Stop," *Albuquerque Journal*, March 30, 2012, p. A1; and earlier coverage by same reporter. For national coverage, see Manny Fernandez and Dan Frosch, "Payments to Albuquerque Officers Are Called a 'Bounty System,' " *The New York Times*, March 25, 2012, p. A20.

35. See Russell Contreras, "Albuquerque activists seek federal probe of police," The Associated Press, March 27, 2012. Some other background drawn from article.

36. See "Law Enforcement Management and Administrative Statistics, 2000," Bureau of Justice Statistics, April 2004, pp. 31, 32, http://bjs.ojp.usdoj.gov/content/pub/pdf/lema001a.pdf.

37. See Lynn Safranek, "Future of police auditor post under review," *Omaha World-Herald*, Oct. 31, 2006, p. 1B.

38. Liz Dorland, "Ernie Chambers Requests Federal Investigation Into Omaha Police Department," KMTV, Sept. 7, 2011, www.kmtv.com/news/local/129429963.html.

39. Jeff Proctor, "Fired Cop Cleared in Death of Vet," *Albuquerque Journal*, March 30, 2012, p. 41.

40. See "SPD 20/20: A Vision for the Future," City of Seattle, www.seattle.gov/mayor/media/PDF/SPD2020.pdf. For coverage, see Mike Carter, "Seattle mayor announces broad initiative to improve police force," *The Seattle Times*, March 29, 2012; Sara Jean Green, "Mayor's initiatives seem to address complaints of biased policing," *ibid.*

41. See Michelle Krupa and Gordon Russell, "Prosecutor bows out of NOPD talks," *The Times-Picayune*, March 17, 2012, p. A9.

42. "Former FBI director named Puerto Rico police chief," The Associated Press, March 29, 2012.

43. For background, see Richard L. Worsnop, "Community Policing," *CQ Researcher*, Feb. 5, 1993, pp. 97-120.

44. See Joe Rossiter, "Godbee: Virtual police precinct plan to go into effect Monday," *Detroit Free Press*, Jan. 31, 2012, p. A7; Kate Linthicum, "L.A. council cuts millions from budget," *Los Angeles Times*, May 19, 2011, p. AA1; Kevin Johnson, "Home burglarized? Fill out a form," *USA Today*, Aug. 25, 2010, p. 1A.

45. On use of cell phone tracking, see Eric Lichtblau, "Police Are Using Phone Tracking as Routine Tool," *The New York Times*, April 1, 2012, p. A1; on Tasers,

see CBS News, "Taser: An officer's weapon of choice," 60 Minutes (David Martin, correspondent; Mary Walsh, producer), Nov. 13, 2011, www .cbsnews.com/8301-18560_162-57323531/taser-an-officers-weapon-of-choice/.

46. See Walter A. McNeil, "The Year Ahead," *Police Chief*, November 2011, www.policechiefmagazine .org/magazine/index.cfm?fuseaction=display_ arch&article_id=2519&issue_id=112011.

BIBLIOGRAPHY

Books

Delattre, Edwin J., *Characters and Cops: Ethics in Policing* (6th ed.), AEI Press, 2011.
A professor of philosophy, emeritus, at Boston University and an adjunct scholar at the American Enterprise Institute combines two decades of studying police behavior to examine a full range of ethics issues for law enforcement. Includes detailed notes, short bibliography.

Kane, Robert J., and Michael D. White, *Jammed Up: Bad Cops, Police Misconduct, and the New York City Police Department*, New York University Press, 2012 (forthcoming: Nov. 19).
The book examines the causes of — and responses to — alleged police misconduct based on unprecedented, complete access to the confidential files of more than 1,500 New York Police Department officers over a 20-year period. Includes detailed notes, bibliography. Kane is an associate professor at the University of Baltimore's School of Criminal Justice, White an associate professor at Arizona State University's School of Criminology and Criminal Justice. For an earlier article on their findings, see Robert J. Kane and Michael D. White, "Bad Cops: A study of career-ending misconduct among New York City police officers," *Criminology and Public Policy*, Vol. 8, No. 4 (November 2009), pp. 737-769. The issue includes three other policy essays on police misconduct.

Roberg, Roy, Kenneth Novak, and Gary Cordner, *Police & Society* (3d ed.), Roxbury Publishing, 2005.
The college textbook includes lengthy chapters on "Behavior and Misconduct," "Force and Coercion" and "Accountability and Ethics." Each chapter includes notes, suggested websites for further study. The book

also comes with an interactive student study guide. The authors are professors, respectively, at San Jose State University, University of Missouri-Kansas City and Eastern Kentucky University.

Walker, Samuel, and Charles M. Katz, *Police in America: An Introduction* (6th ed.), McGraw-Hill, 2011.
The college textbook includes overviews of the history and current structure of U.S. law enforcement and individual chapters on police corruption and accountability, plus chapter notes, a glossary and an interactive student study guide. Walker is a professor of criminal justice, emeritus, at the University of Nebraska-Omaha and a longtime expert on police issues; Katz is an associate professor at Arizona State University's School of Criminology and Criminal Justice.

Walker, Samuel, *The New World of Police Accountability*, SAGE, 2005.
The book synthesizes major developments in police accountability over the previous decade. For an earlier account, see *Police Accountability: The Role of Citizen Oversight* (Thomson Learning, 2001). Walker maintains an informative website on police accountability issues, including a page covering developments in New Orleans (http://samuelwalker.net/). His other books include *Popular Justice: A History of American Criminal Justice* (2d ed.) (Oxford University Press, 1998); and *A Critical History of Police Reform: The Emergence of Professionalism* (Lexington, 1977).

Articles

Kocher, Charles, *et al.*, "Sustaining Police Operations at an Efficient and Effective Level under Difficult Economic Times," *Police Chief*, March 2012, www .policechiefmagazine.org/magazine/index.cfm?fuse action=display&article_id=2621&issue_id=32012.
The article, co-authored by a retired deputy Camden, N.J., police chief, in the monthly magazine of the International Association of Chiefs of Police examines the need for adapting police department structures and operations in times of layoffs, cutbacks and consolidated services.

Reynolds, Dawn, "Coast to Coast — the Public and the Justice Department is Demanding More Accountability," National Association of Civilian Oversight of Law Enforcement, spring 2012,

www.nacole.org/sites/default/files/NACOLE_
Review_Spring2012.pdf.
The article in the association's quarterly newsletter
reviews the Justice Department's reports on Seattle;
Maricopa County, Ariz., and East Haven, Conn.

Reports and Studies

"Taking Stock: Report from the 2010 Roundtable on
the State and Local Law Enforcement Police Pattern
or Practice Program (42 USC § 14141)," National
Institute of Justice, September 2011, https://ncjrs
.gov/pdffiles1/nij/234458.pdf.
The report includes a 10-page summary of the views
expressed at a roundtable convened to assess the impact

of the Justice Department's pattern or practice of police
misconduct program. The report includes notes, a list of
all participants and a list of settlements and investigations as of July 2010.

Weisburd, David, Rosann Greenspan, Edwin E.
Hamilton, Kellie A. Bryant and Hubert Williams,
"The Abuse of Police Authority: A National Study of
Police Officers' Attitudes," Police Foundation, 2001,
www.policefoundation.org/pdf/AOANarrative.pdf.
The first-ever national survey of police officers' attitudes
found that most believe extreme abuse-of-authority cases
are infrequent and that the public and the media are too
concerned with such incidents.

For More Information

American Civil Liberties Union, 125 Broad St., New York,
NY 10004; 212-549-2500; www.aclu.org. Has been active
on racial profiling, use of force and other police-practices
issues.

Fraternal Order of Police, Grand Lodge, 1410 Donelson
Pike, A-17, Nashville, TN 37217; 615-399-0900; www
.grandlodgefop.org. Largest membership organization representing rank-and-file law enforcement officers.

International Association of Chiefs of Police, 515 North
Washington St., Alexandria, VA 22314; 703-836-6767;
www.theiacp.org. Represents operating chief executives of
international, federal, state and local law enforcement agencies of all sizes.

**National Association of Civilian Oversight of Law
Enforcement**, 638 E. Vermont St., P.O. Box 1737, Indianapolis, IN 46206; 1-866-462-2653; www.nacole.org. Brings
together individuals and agencies working to establish or
improve oversight of police officers in the United States.

National Association of Criminal Defense Lawyers, 1025
Connecticut Ave., N.W., Suite 901, Washington, DC 20036;
202-872-8600; www.crimdefense.org. The largest organization exclusively representing criminal defense lawyers.

National District Attorneys Association, 44 Canal Center
Plaza, Suite 110, Alexandria, VA 22314; 703-549-9222;
www.ndaa.org. Represents criminal prosecutors in state,
district, county and city attorneys' offices.

National Sheriffs' Association, 1450 Duke St., Alexandria,
VA 22314; 1-800-424-7827; www.sheriffs.org. Represents
and assists sheriffs' offices nationwide through education,
training and information resources.

Police Foundation, 1201 Connecticut Ave., N.W., Washington, DC 20036-2636; 202-833-1460; www.policefounda
tion.org. Established by the Ford Foundation in 1970; sponsors research to support innovation and improvement in
policing.

10

Hispanic day laborers negotiate with a potential employer in Homestead, Fla. As low-skilled immigrants, many living below the poverty line, move to the South and Midwest to work in meatpacking and other industries, debate intensifies over immigration's impact on native-born Americans at the bottom of the income scale. Newly released Census data for 2006 show that 36.5 million Americans — including nearly 13 million children — lived below the federal poverty line of $20,614 in income for a family of four.

From *CQ Researcher*,
September 7, 2007 (updated April 27, 2011).

Domestic Poverty

Thomas J. Billitteri and Marcia Clemmitt

Marilyn Bezear, a 52-year-old single parent in Harlem who lost her husband to cancer, was living in run-down public housing and working two jobs last winter, cleaning offices and doing clerical work for a temp agency.

"Together, after taxes, I bring home up to $300 a week," she told a congressional panel in February. "With this I pay my rent, food, telephone and payments for the loan that I took out for my daughter to go to college." When the temp agency has no work, Bezear scrambles for ways to meet expenses, like working the late shift at a bowling alley and "getting home at 4:30 in the morning."

Bezear added: "I am just one of many who live through these struggles. . . . Wages, education, training and health care are a necessity. I hope my testimony did not fall on deaf ears."[1]

It's a hope that many of America's poorest citizens would no doubt echo. Despite a relatively stable economy, an overhaul of the welfare system a decade ago and billions spent on programs for the needy, poverty remains pervasive and intractable across the nation.

Conservatives say solutions must emphasize personal responsibility, higher marriage rates and fewer out-of-wedlock births, while liberals blame the negative effects of budget cuts for anti-poverty programs, tax cuts benefiting the wealthy and the need for more early-childhood-development programs. The Democratic Congress has made poverty a priority issue. And a number of presidential candidates are focusing either squarely on poverty or more generally on ideas to narrow the growing gap between the rich and poor.

253

South Is Most Impoverished Region

Almost all the Southern states have poverty levels exceeding the national average of 12.3 percent of residents living in poverty. Mississippi leads the nation with a poverty rate of 20.6 percent. New Hampshire has the lowest rate, 5.4 percent.

Percentage of People in Poverty by State, 2006

Source: "Historical Poverty Tables," U.S. Census Bureau, 2007

Newly released Census data for 2006 show that 36.5 million Americans — about one in eight — lived below the federal poverty line of $20,614 in income for a family of four. More than a third of them are children, and 3.4 million are 65 and older. And while the nation's poverty rate declined for the first time this decade, from 12.6 percent in 2005 to 12.3 percent last year, the number of children without health insurance rose to 11.7 percent in 2006.[2]

Indeed, among "rich" nations, the United States ranked second — behind Mexico — in poverty at the turn of the 21st century.[3]

"An astonishing number of people are working as hard as they possibly can but are still in poverty or have incomes that are not much above the poverty line," said Peter Edelman, a law professor at Georgetown University who was co-chairman of a poverty task force this year for the Center for American Progress, a Washington think tank.[4]

A number of indicators underscore the depth and breadth of American poverty:

- Those in "deep," or severe, poverty, with incomes of half or less of the official poverty threshold, number over 15 million — more than the populations of New York City, Los Angeles and Chicago combined. Severe poverty hit a 32-year high in 2005, according to McClatchy Newspapers.[5]

- The gap between rich and poor is growing. In 2005, the average income of the top 1 percent of U.S. households rose $102,000 (adjusted for inflation), but the bottom 90 percent saw incomes rise $250, according to economists Thomas Piketty and Emmanuel Saez.[6] And the top 1 percent got the biggest share of national income since 1928.[7]

- The chance an average American family will see its income plummet at least 50 percent is roughly two-and-a-half times that of the 1970s.[8]

- At some time, most Americans will live at least one year below the poverty line, according to sociologists Mark R. Rank and Thomas A. Hirschl.[9]

Such trends have helped push poverty and broader issues of inequality and economic insecurity onto the national stage in ways not seen for decades. Two years ago, televised images of squalor in post-Katrina New Orleans refocused the nation's attention — at least temporarily — on poverty. More recently, the subprime mortgage debacle, higher gas prices and spiraling medical costs have edged millions of middle-class Americans closer to economic ruin. Meanwhile, Main Street angst is growing over globalization, which has contributed to the elimination of one-sixth of U.S. factory jobs in the past six years.[10]

Jacob S. Hacker, a political scientist at Yale University and author of the 2006 book *The Great Risk Shift: The Assault on American Jobs, Families, Health Care, and Retirement — And How You Can Fight Back*, says poverty

Gap Between Rich and Poor Widened

The top 1 percent of income households earned about 20 percent of the nation's total income in 2005, its highest share since 1929. From 2004 to 2005, the average income of such earners increased by $102,000, after adjusting for inflation. By contrast, the average income of the bottom 90 percent rose by $250.

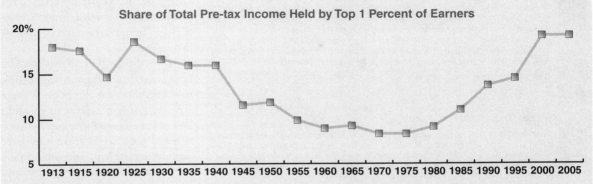

Share of Total Pre-tax Income Held by Top 1 Percent of Earners

Source: Thomas Picketty and Emmanuel Saez, based on IRS data; in Aviva Aron-Dine, "New Data Show Income Concentration Jumped Again in 2005: Income Share of Top 1% Returned to Its 2000 Level, the Highest Since 1929," Center on Budget and Policy Priorities, March 29, 2007

is on the nation's radar for reasons that go beyond high-profile events like Katrina.

"Poverty is something the middle class cares about when it looks down and sees itself poised on the financial precipice," he says. The middle class is looking up, too, at those in the top income strata, and "there's a lot more discussion about [income] inequality." And finally, many middle-class Americans "have a deep concern about the fact that we're such a rich nation, and yet children and hardworking adults who moved into the labor market after welfare reform are struggling to get by."

While politicians in both major parties have spoken to concerns about middle-class vulnerability, Democrats have been focusing squarely on poverty and inequality, blending appeals for middle-class protections with rhetoric reminiscent of the 1960s "War on Poverty."

Since assuming control of Congress in January, Democrats have held several hearings on poverty, hunger and economic threats to the needy. Rep. Charles B. Rangel, D-N.Y., chairman of the powerful House Ways and Means Committee, declared this spring that "with the exception of getting the hell out of the Middle East,

I can't think of anything more patriotic that we can do than eliminate poverty."[11]

In the 2008 presidential race, Sen. Hillary Clinton, D-N.Y., has accused the Bush administration of making the middle class and working families into "invisible Americans,"[12] while Sen. Barack Obama, D-Ill., alluding to his work as a community organizer in Chicago, has said poverty "is the cause that led me to a life of public service."[13] Former Sen. John Edwards, D-N.C., has staked his campaign on the poverty issue, calling it "the great moral issue of our time."[14]

Among other contenders, Mayor Michael Bloomberg of New York — who dropped his affiliation with the Republican Party in June — has been among the most outspoken on poverty. On Aug. 28, the billionaire founder of Bloomberg News, who is thought to be considering a third-party presidential bid, proposed a sharp expansion in the Earned Income Tax Credit (EITC), which provides tax relief to the working poor, and called on politicians of both parties to move beyond ideology to overcome poverty. Bloomberg proposed roughly doubling the number of

Democratic Candidates' Stands on Poverty

 Joseph Biden voted for the Fair Minimum Wage Act of 2007, which raised the minimum wage from $5.15 an hour to $7.25 an hour. Biden broke with his party to vote in favor of the Bankruptcy Abuse Prevention and Consumer Protection Act of 2005, which makes it harder for people to erase debt by declaring bankruptcy.

 Hillary Clinton accuses the Bush administration of turning the middle class into "invisible Americans," and says if she is elected president, "they will no longer be invisible." In 2002, Clinton was criticized by liberal groups for supporting an increase in the work requirement for welfare; she said that she supported the measure because it was tied to $8 billion in funding of day care for welfare recipients. Clinton advocated for welfare reform under her husband's administration. As a senator, Clinton voted for an increase in the federal minimum wage.

 Christopher Dodd says that one of his policy priorities influenced by Catholic social teachings and the emphasis on the common good is "creating safety nets for the disadvantaged." As a senator, one of Dodd's priorities has been helping children, and he has authored numerous child care bills. Dodd has favored increases in the federal minimum wage.

 John Edwards has made reducing poverty the signature issue of his campaign, calling it "the great moral issue of our time." He has set a goal of ending poverty in 30 years by lifting one-third of the 37 million currently impoverished Americans above the poverty line each decade through a higher minimum wage, tax cuts for low-income workers, universal health care and housing vouchers for poor families.

 Mike Gravel says America's war on drugs must end because it "does nothing but savage our inner cities and put our children at risk." Gravel proposes to help end poverty by creating a progressive tax system in which consumers of new products would be taxed at a flat rate. This would encourage Americans to save, Gravel says. This proposed system would replace the income tax and Internal Revenue Service.

 Dennis Kucinich advocates ending the war in Iraq and using the money saved to fight domestic poverty, calling homelessness, joblessness and poverty "weapons of mass destruction." In July 2007, Kucinich said that he was in favor of reparations for slavery, saying, "The Bible says we shall and must be repairers of the breach. And a breach has occurred. . . . It's a breach that has resulted in inequality in opportunities for education, for health care, for housing, for employment."

 Barack Obama In the Illinois Senate, Obama helped author the state's earned income tax credit, which provided tax cuts for low-income families. Obama has supported bills to increase the minimum wage. In *The Audacity of Hope*, Obama describes what he calls America's "empathy deficit," writing that a "stronger sense of empathy would tilt the balance of our current politics in favor of those people who are struggling in this society."

 Bill Richardson As governor of New Mexico, Richardson took steps to combat poverty in the state, one of the nation's poorest. He eliminated the tax on food and offered tax breaks to companies paying above the prevailing wage. Richardson has backed a living wage in the state and created tax credits for the creation of new jobs.

Source: This information first appeared on www.pewforum.org. Reprinted with permission from the Pew Forum on Religion & Public Life and Pew Research Center.

Americans eligible to benefit from the EITC to 19.7 million people.[15]

"We are beginning to hear a chorus of voices urging action on poverty," Rep. Jim McDermott, D-Wash., chairman of the House Ways and Means Subcommittee on Income Security and Family Support, said in April.[16]

Edelman, at the Center for American Progress, echoed the point. "There's a rising concern in the country about inequality," he said. "There's concern about giveaways to the really wealthy, and there's concern about economic insecurity. The poverty issue is embedded in that."[17]

Nevertheless, it remains unclear how far voters will go in supporting new programs for the poor. A mere 1 percent of respondents to a Gallup Poll in June ranked the "gap between rich and poor" as the most important economic problem, and only 5 percent named "poverty, hunger and homelessness" as the most important "non-economic" problem.[18]

Likewise, Edwards has trailed his rivals for the Democratic nomination and even failed to capture much support from voters who are struggling financially. In a survey of independent voters, 40 percent of respondents in households earning less than $20,000 said they would not vote for Edwards if he were the Democratic nominee.[19]

The public's fickle interest in the poor has been evident in the two years following Hurricane Katrina, which produced some of the starkest and most widely disseminated images of urban poverty in American history.

"After Katrina, with its vivid images, a lot of people who have been working in the area of poverty reduction were excited. They said, 'now we have some visible images, now people will get excited, and we can push this anti-poverty platform,'" says Elsie L. Scott, president of the Congressional Black Caucus Foundation. "That lasted a month maybe, that excitement. Now that people in New Orleans have been dispersed around the country, people want to forget about it. They don't want to admit we have this kind of poverty in the United States."

Policy experts say it would be unfortunate if Middle America fails to recognize how much poverty undermines the nation's overall well-being. Childhood poverty alone saps the United States of $500 billion per year in crime and health costs and reduced productivity, according to Harry J. Holzer, a professor of public policy at Georgetown University.[20]

Rising poverty should be a concern even among those who don't see a moral obligation to aid the poor, experts warn. "The global competitiveness of the U.S. economy suffers if workers are too poor to obtain an education and modern job skills, the government loses tax revenue and spends more on public assistance because of poverty, and communities fall victim to urban decay, crime, and unrest," notes a recent study on severe poverty in the *American Journal of Preventive Medicine*.[21]

Yet, the American public has always had a tendency to blame the poor for their ills, some poverty experts lament. "There is a common perception that the problem with the poor folks in the United States is a problem with values," said Dalton Conley, chairman of the Department of Sociology at New York University. "It's not a values deficit at all; it's really a resource deficit."[22]

And that deficit can be steep. "Most Americans would be shocked to know that full-time male workers, at the median, earned no more in 2005 than they did in 1973" after taking inflation into account, says Sheldon H Danziger, a professor of public policy at the University of Michigan. And that wage stagnation came amid a boom in productivity in the 1990s, he adds.

"There's a tendency for people to blame the poor for their own circumstances," Danziger says. "And I

Republican Candidates' Stands on Poverty

 Sam Brownback voted for the 1996 welfare reform bill that required more work for recipients and placed limits on the amount of time they could receive benefits. He says poverty can best be addressed by encouraging people to get married, get a job and not have children out of wedlock. He has promoted a "marriage development account program" to help married couples get training, buy a car, get an education or purchase a house. Brownback has voted against increasing the minimum wage.

 Rudolph Giuliani advocates requiring welfare recipients to work or engage in job training to receive benefits. New York City's welfare rolls were cut by more than half while Giuliani was mayor, and he touts his overhaul of the city's welfare system as one of his major successes. During his 2000 senate campaign, Giuliani indicated that he would support an increase in the minimum wage if studies showed it would not reduce the number of available jobs.

 Mike Huckabee says one of his priorities is to address poverty because it's "consistent with me being pro-life." He calls his desire to fight poverty a "faith position" rather than a political position. He says it is impossible to address poverty without "prioritizing stable homes and families."

 Duncan Hunter says tax cuts are the best tool for reducing poverty because they enable the poor to save and support their families. He advocates what he calls a "Fair Tax," which would replace the national income tax with a national retail sales tax. As part of his anti-poverty agenda, he supports tariffs on Chinese imports to help preserve American manufacturing jobs.

 John McCain voted for a 1996 welfare reform bill that required more work for recipients and placed limits on the amount of time they could receive benefits. Although McCain voted for a bill to increase the federal minimum wage in February 2007, he has historically voted against minimum wage increases, arguing that they can hurt small businesses.

 Ron Paul In May 2007, Paul asserted that "subsidies and welfare" only provide poor people with "crumbs," while "the military-industrial complex and the big banks" receive "the real big welfare," further impoverishing the middle class and the poor. Paul opposes foreign aid, writing that "the redistribution of wealth from rich to poor nations has done little or nothing to alleviate suffering abroad."

 W. Mitt Romney As Massachusetts governor, Romney proposed a plan requiring more people to work in order to receive state welfare benefits, bringing Massachusetts policy in line with federal welfare reforms. He supports increasing the minimum wage to match inflation but vetoed a bill to raise it in Massachusetts, saying it called for increases that were too extreme and too abrupt.

 Tom Tancredo The Colorado Congressman advocates moving from an income-based tax to a consumption-based tax, which he says would create an "explosion of job opportunities and economic growth" that would benefit all sectors of society, particularly the poor. He also supports repealing the 16th Amendment and establishing a flat, national sales tax to alleviate the burden on American companies and "put billions back into the economy."

 Fred Thompson In May the actor and former U.S. senator criticized programs that would "redistribute the income among our citizens" as "defeatist." A policy of lowering taxes, he said, would stimulate economic growth and "make the pie bigger." In 1999 he voted against an increase in the minimum wage. He also voted to reduce taxes on married couples in 2000. He has yet to officially declare his candidacy.

Source: This information first appeared on www.pewforum.org. Reprinted with permission from the Pew Forum on Religion & Public Life and Pew Research Center.

don't think anybody would blame full-time male workers."

As Congress, policy experts and presidential candidates consider what to do about poverty, here are some of the questions they are asking:

TANF Assistance on the Decline

The number of households receiving financial support through the Temporary Assistance for Needy Families (TANF) program has declined every fiscal year since 1996. A monthly average of just over 4 million households received TANF assistance in 2006, less than a third of the number of recipients 10 years earlier.

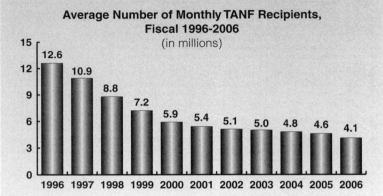

Average Number of Monthly TANF Recipients, Fiscal 1996-2006
(in millions)

Source: "2008 Budget in Brief," Department of Health and Human Services, 2007

Is extreme poverty growing?

In Savannah, Ga., not far from the lush parks and ante-bellum mansions of the city's fabled historic district, poverty runs wide and deep.

More than one-fifth of Savannah's residents live below the federal poverty line, and that's not the worst of it.* "We have six census tracts with over a 50-percent poverty rate," says Daniel Dodd, who directs a project that enlists Savannah's business community in helping the poor.

Savannah is hardly unique. At least one neighborhood of "concentrated" poverty — often defined as a place where at least 40 percent of residents live below the poverty line — exists in 46 of the nation's 50 biggest cities, according to Alan Berube, a fellow in the Metropolitan Policy Program of the Brookings Institution, a think tank in Washington.[23]

McClatchy Newspapers concluded this year that 43 percent of the nation's 37 million poor people live in severe poverty — sometimes called "extreme" or "deep" poverty. Severe poverty reflects those with incomes of less than half the federal poverty threshold — in other words, under $9,903 for a family of four and $5,080 for an individual in 2005.

"The number of severely poor Americans grew by 26 percent from 2000 to 2005," McClatchy reported. "That's 56 percent faster than the overall poverty population grew in the same period."

The rise in severe poverty extends beyond large urban counties to suburban and rural areas. "Severe poverty is worst near the Mexican border and in some areas of the South, where 6.5 million severely poor residents are struggling to find work as manufacturing jobs in the textile, apparel and furniture-making industries disappear," McClatchy noted. "The Midwestern Rust Belt and areas of the Northeast also have been hard hit as economic restructuring and foreign competition have forced numerous plant closings. At the same time, low-skilled immigrants with impoverished family members are increasingly drawn to the South and Midwest to work in meatpacking, food processing and agricultural industries."[24]

In Illinois, the rate of extreme poverty is the highest in the hard-hit Midwest, with more than 700,000 people in such straits, according to the Heartland Alliance for

---

*Many people who study domestic poverty criticize the way the government measures poverty, arguing the standard federal poverty index does not accurately count the poor. Presidential candidate John Edwards is among those who call for reform of the poverty measure. His Web site states that it "excludes necessities like taxes, health care, child care and transportation" and "fails to count some forms of aid including tax credits, food stamps, Medicaid and subsidized housing. The National Academy of Sciences has recommended improvements that would increase the count of people in poverty by more than 1 million." See also, for example, Reid Cramer, "The Misleading Way We Count the Poor: Alternatives to Our Antiquated Poverty Measure Should Consider Assets," New America Foundation, September 2003, and Douglas J. Besharov, senior scholar, American Enterprise Institute, testimony before House Subcommittee on Income Security and Family Support, "Measuring Poverty in America," Aug. 1, 2007.

Human Needs & Human Rights, an advocacy group in Chicago. A family of four living in extreme poverty in Bellevue, Ill., would have monthly expenses of $2,394 but monthly income of only $833, the group says.[25]

But some researchers see little or no evidence that severe poverty is on the rise. Robert Rector, a senior policy analyst at the conservative Heritage Foundation, said "he's seen no data that suggest increasing deprivation among the very poor," according to the McClatchy report.

Rector "questioned the growth of severe poverty, saying that census data become less accurate farther down the income ladder. He said many poor people, particularly single mothers with boyfriends, underreport their income by not including cash gifts and loans."[26]

Such skeptical views extend beyond the severely poor. "While real material hardship certainly does occur, it is limited in scope and severity," Rector told a congressional panel this year. "Most of America's 'poor' live in material conditions that would be judged as comfortable or well-off just a few generations ago. Today, the expenditures per person of the lowest-income one-fifth . . . of households equal those of the median American household in the early 1970s, after adjusting for inflation."[27]

In fact, many more consumer items are within reach of a wider segment of the population — even the poor — than they were 30 or 40 years ago, thanks in part to globalization and the spread of discount retailers. But the cost of necessities such as health care and shelter have exploded, taking a much higher proportion of income than they once did.

Indeed, while the poor may have more material goods than in the past, many analysts say poverty is much more complicated than comparisons with earlier eras might suggest.

"On the one hand, the poor have vastly more consumer goods than a generation ago — TVs, cars, washing machines, dishwashers in many cases," says Hacker of Yale University. "But at the same time, if you think about where they are relative to middle-class Americans, to say nothing of those at the top, they're much further behind."

A major portion of the spending done by poor people is for basics, especially housing, transportation, child care and health care, and the poor have had a tough time keeping up with those costs, Hacker says. What's more, "the consumption of the poor is supported by higher levels of debt that can leave them extremely vulnerable."

Step Up Savannah, one of the nation's most ambitious local anti-poverty efforts, is a collaboration of organizations from business, government, education and the nonprofit sector that helps residents of high-poverty neighborhoods become self-sufficient.

And those most vulnerable are people who live in severe poverty. From 2000 to 2004, its prevalence rose sharply. The risk of extreme poverty is significantly higher for children than adults, and it is higher for African-Americans and Hispanics than for whites or Asian-Americans, according to the study in the *American Journal of Preventive Medicine*.

"Millions of Americans, overrepresented by children and minorities, have entered conditions of extreme poverty," the study said. "After 2000, Americans subsisting under these conditions grew as a class more than any other segment of the population."[28]

Reducing severe poverty is a daunting challenge that has spurred an outpouring of policy proposals from all sides of the political spectrum.

In Savannah, Dodd's project — called Step Up, Savannah's Poverty Reduction Initiative — represents one of the nation's most ambitious local anti-poverty efforts. Formed in 2004, it is a collaboration of more than 80 organizations representing business, local government, nonprofit organizations, neighborhood groups and others. It receives donations from several major foundations as well as other sources, including businesses.

Step Up's methods include asking employers and business executives to role play for a few hours what impoverished residents experience every day. "These things are quite eye-opening for a lot of people," Dodd says. The "poverty simulation" exercise reveals "how frustrating the system is to navigate if you're making minimum wage, if you don't have the skills, and how hard it is to keep a job with what you're getting paid. There's transportation obstacles, crime," and other impediments.[29]

The exercise "provides a common frame of reference for the community and demystifies myths" about poverty, adds Dodd, who points out that welfare reform has led to a 70 percent reduction in government subsidies for the city's poor in the past seven years.[30]

Step Up's goals include expanding poor people's access to good jobs and quality health care, training them for career-level positions and expanding access to the EITC.

The effort grew from a realization that "we hadn't had a decline in poverty in 30 years," Dodd says. "People realized we'd thrown millions of dollars at this but hadn't had the impact we needed to have."

For all the project's earnestness, though, it remains unclear whether Step Up will succeed. "What I always tell people," says Dodd, "is we don't have it all figured out yet."

Has welfare reform reduced entrenched poverty?

In August 1996, President Bill Clinton's signature ended a six-decade practice of guaranteeing cash assistance to the poor. A new system required most people who get aid to work within two years of receiving it. The revised law also limited most aid to a total of five years. And it turned over to states and localities much of the control over how federal poverty money is dispensed.[31]

More then a decade later, experts are still debating whether the poor are better off.

Ron Haskins, a former Ways and Means Committee staff member who played a key role in the welfare overhaul, has written that "above all, welfare reform showed that work — even low-wage work — provides a more durable foundation for social policy than handouts."[32]

"Before welfare reform," Haskins, now a senior fellow at the Brookings Institution, said last year, "the main goal of state welfare programs was simply to give out money. But now the message families receive when they apply for welfare is that they need a job, that the 'welfare' program is there to help them find one and that they can receive cash benefits for a maximum of five years. As a result, welfare rolls plunged by over 60 percent, as many as 2 million mothers entered the labor force, earnings for females

heading families increased while their income from welfare payments fell, and child poverty declined every year between 1993 and 2000. By the late 1990s, both black child poverty and poverty among children in female-headed families had reached their lowest levels ever."

Even after four years of increased child poverty following the 2001 recession, Haskins said, the rate of child poverty was still 20 percent lower than in 1993.

Haskins went on to say that "the success of welfare reform was created both by welfare reforms itself and by the work-support programs that provided tax credits, health insurance, nutrition supplements and child care to low-income working families."[33]

Yet, despite what many see as its positive effects, welfare reform remains a mixed bag. It is not clear, for example, to what degree welfare reform itself, along with its time limits on benefits, caused poverty rates to fall and work rates to rise.

"Welfare reform, and in particular the onset of time limits, arrived in the midst of an extremely tight labor market and a flourishing economy," says Katherine Newman, a professor of sociology and public affairs at Princeton University.

"So how much the shift toward work was attributable to the pull of a growing economy and [demand for] labor is very hard to sort out," she continues. "My sense is that welfare reform had something to do with it, but it's hardly the whole story. A lot had to do with favorable market conditions."

The Center on Budget and Policy Priorities, a Washington think tank, last year noted, among other negative trends, that while child poverty declined in the 1990s, as Haskins pointed out, it nonetheless rose sharply after 2000, as did the number of children living in severe poverty.[34]

Many anti-poverty advocates say even though welfare reform put more people to work, further steps are needed to ensure that families can climb out of poverty and stay there, and that poor children are protected.

Timothy M. Smeeding, director of the Center for Policy Research at Syracuse University, says welfare reform "turned the welfare poor into the working poor. You've got more self-respect, you're earning it, but the effect on kids is mixed." He calls for a system that will "make work pay," where "you go out and you work, you show the effort, you put in 1,000 hours, and we'll find a way to make sure you've got $15,000 or $20,000 and you're not poor."

In Wisconsin — where some of the earliest efforts at welfare reform took place — the rate of growth in the number of people living in poverty was higher in 2003-2004 than in any other state.[35] Richard Schlimm, executive director of the Wisconsin Community Action Program Association, a statewide association of community-action and anti-poverty groups, says welfare reform simply "has not worked," in reducing poverty in his state.

"Certainly it was the right thing to do, to get people working," Schlimm says. "But I've always believed poor people want to work, and they prefer work over welfare.... We successfully achieved the elimination of welfare, but I maintain that we had the wrong goal. The goal was to reduce poverty, and if we kept that in our sights we would have focused a whole lot [more] funding on that than we did."

Would more government spending on poverty help?

While welfare reform encouraged work and reduced government caseloads, many experts say the fight against poverty has only begun.

Some argue that reducing poverty depends in large measure on the poor exercising greater personal responsibility. "While it is often argued that the U.S. devotes far fewer resources to social welfare spending than other rich nations, the facts show otherwise," Rector of the Heritage Foundation said. "The good news is that remaining poverty can readily be reduced further, particularly among children. There are two main reasons that American children are poor: Their parents don't work much, and fathers are absent from the home."[36]

Others say more government spending on anti-poverty programs is the key. Schlimm, at the Wisconsin Community Action Program Association, says that to reduce poverty, the nation needs political leadership coupled with "a massive investment" in affordable housing, accessible health care, education and job creation for the poor. "Let's face it, we have committed massive investments in Iraq," he says, "and [with] half of that — even a fourth of that — focused on poverty in the United States, we could make remarkable strides."

Smeeding, the Syracuse University policy researcher, says U.S. poverty could be cut by a third to a half with an outlay of $45 billion to $60 billion a year, focused on three things: child care for working mothers, guaranteed child support for mothers who have established paternity with fathers who can't or won't pay because of disability or prison, and an expansion of the EITC.

Lawrence Mead, a professor of politics at New York University, advocates a stick-and-carrot approach with low-income men. "In 2005, there were more than 7 million poor men ages 16 to 50 in the United States, and only half of them worked at all," Mead wrote. "Among black men in poverty, nearly two-thirds were idle, and their employment has fallen steadily in recent decades."

Mead proposes using the child-support and criminal-justice systems to promote work among poor males. "Right now, these institutions depress male work levels by locking men up and by garnishing their wages if they do work," he wrote. "But they could be used to promote work. For example, men in arrears on their child support could be assigned to government-run work programs, as could parolees with employment problems. These men — about 1.5 million each year — would have to show up and work regularly — on penalty of going to jail. Both groups might also receive wage subsidies. The combination might instill more regular work habits."

Mandatory work for 1.5 million men would run $2 billion to $5 billion annually, according to Mead. "In return, governments could collect more in child support and spend less on incarceration."[37]

"Everyone recognizes that men are the frontier," Mead says. The ultimate goal, he says, should be to both reward and enforce work in ways the current system doesn't do now.

While spending on new programs is one approach to fighting poverty, some argue the solution isn't more outlays for anti-poverty programs but rather a mix of free-market capitalism and charity.

"Despite nearly $9 trillion in total welfare spending since Lyndon B. Johnson declared [the] War on Poverty in 1964, the poverty rate is perilously close to where it was when we began, more than 40 years ago," wrote Michael D. Tanner, director of health and welfare studies for the conservative Cato Institute think tank.

"Clearly we are doing something wrong. Throwing money at the problem has neither reduced poverty nor made the poor self-sufficient. . . . [I]f we have learned anything by now, it is that there are limits to what

CHRONOLOGY

1950s-1960s *Many Americans enjoy a post-war economic boom, but poverty persists. Poverty rate is 22.4 percent in 1959.*

1962 Michael Harrington's book *The Other America* helps spur President Lyndon B. Johnson's War on Poverty. . . . Welfare program is renamed Aid to Families with Dependent Children (AFDC).

1964 Congress establishes permanent food stamp program. . . . Federal government develops income thresholds to define poverty in American society.

1965 Congress enacts Medicaid to provide health care to low-income people.

1967 Congress establishes the Work Incentive Program, requiring states to establish job-training programs for adults receiving welfare.

1969 President Richard M. Nixon calls hunger in America an "embarrassing and intolerable" national shame.

1970s *The energy crisis, recessions and industrial restructuring put new strains on the poor.*

1975 Congress approves Earned Income Tax Credit (EITC), partly to offset the burden of Social Security taxes on low-income families and to provide an incentive to work.

1980s *Poverty programs of the 1960s and '70s come under scrutiny from the Reagan administration.*

1981 Congress cuts cash benefits for the working poor and lets states require welfare recipients to work.

1988 President Ronald Reagan signs Family Support Act, requiring states to implement education, job training and placement programs for welfare recipients.

1990s *Clinton administration pushes Congress to pass massive welfare reforms.*

1992 Democratic presidential candidate Bill Clinton pledges to "end welfare as we know it."

1993 Clinton expands EITC.

1996 Congress ends 60-year welfare entitlement program, passing a reform law that imposes work requirements and puts time limits on cash benefits.

1997 Federal minimum wage rises to $5.15 an hour.

1997 State Children's Health Insurance Program (SCHIP) is created.

1999 The government of British Prime Minister Tony Blair introduces a plan to end child poverty in Britain by 2020, spurring calls for a similar effort in the United States.

2000s *Hurricane Katrina devastates Gulf Coast, putting spotlight on poverty.*

2000 Federal poverty rate falls to 11.3 percent, lowest since 1974.

2004 Federal appeals court upholds the "living wage" law in Berkeley, Calif., rejecting the first major challenge to civic ordinances requiring contractors to pay above-poverty wages. . . . Poverty rate climbs to 12.7 percent

Aug. 29, 2005 Hurricane Katrina hits New Orleans.

2006 Congress reauthorizes Temporary Assistance for Needy Families (TANF) as part of Deficit Reduction Act.

2007 McClatchy Newspapers analysis finds that percentage of poor Americans living in severe poverty reached a 32-year high in 2005. . . . Congress spars with the Bush administration over expansion of SCHIP. . . . House Ways and Means Committee hearings focus on poverty and inequality. . . . Democratic presidential candidate John Edwards takes a three-day, 1,800-mile "Road to One America" poverty tour. . . . Federal minimum wage rises for the first time in a decade to $5.85 an hour; it goes to $6.55 in summer 2008 and $7.25 in summer 2009. . . . Poverty rate falls to 12.3 percent.

2007 In 13 states and the District of Columbia, at least one child in five is poor. . . . Suburban poverty is growing at a faster rate than urban poverty for the first time in history.

2008 As recession begins, about 40 million Americans live in poverty, defined as annual earnings of just under $22,000 for a family of four.

2009 In the depths of the recession, the number of poor Americans rises to 43.6 million. . . . In the 100 largest metropolitan areas, unemployment rates have doubled since 2007, to an average 10.3 percent in cities and 9.3 percent in suburbs. . . . In 21 states and the District of Columbia, at least one child in five is poor. . . . Suburban poor outnumber urban poor by 1.6 million nationwide. . . .

Federal stimulus and assistance funds in the 2009 Recovery Act, such as increased unemployment benefits, help keep recession-related poverty from rising higher.

2010 By year's end, with economic recovery beginning, unemployment in major metropolitan areas drops slightly, to 9.8 percent in cities and 8.9 percent in suburbs. . . . The federal Supplemental Nutrition Assistant Program (SNAP), formerly called "food stamps," enrolls one in seven Americans.

2011 States face budget crunches as Recovery Act assistance ends. . . . Some states consider ending or limiting poverty-assistance programs such as unemployment benefits and Earned Income Tax Credits.

government programs — even reformed ones — can do to address the root causes of poverty.

"Observers have known for a long time that the surest ways to stay out of poverty are to finish school; not get pregnant outside marriage; and get a job, any job, and stick with it. That means that if we wish to fight poverty, we must end those government policies — high taxes and regulatory excess — that inhibit growth and job creation. We must protect capital investment and give people the opportunity to start new businesses. We must reform our failed government school system to encourage competition and choice. We must encourage the poor to save and invest.

"More importantly, the real work of fighting poverty must come not from the government, but from the engines of civil society. . . . [P]rivate charities are far more effective than government welfare programs."[38]

BACKGROUND

Warring on Poverty

Concerns about work, hardship and who deserves help go back to the roots of the Republic. The Virginia Assembly of 1619 decreed that a person found guilty of idleness would be forced to work under a master "til he shewe apparant signes of amendment."[39]

In the 19th century, poorhouses sprang up to accommodate a growing tide of desperate people flooding the cities from the countryside. Poverty flourished along with widespread indifference to the plight of the needy. After the Civil War the journalist and political economist Henry George called the United States a place where "amid the greatest accumulations of wealth, men die of starvation, and puny infants suckle dry breasts."[40]

Later came the first rudimentary efforts to measure poverty. In 1904 the social worker Robert Hunter set what might have been the first national poverty line — $460 per year for a five-member family in the Northern industrial states and $300 for a family in the South.[41]

In the post-World War I boom years, some Americans enjoyed unprecedented comfort and wealth, but poverty wracked much of the nation. Between 1918 and 1929, some 10 million families were poor. By 1933, in the depths of the Great Depression, a fourth of the labor force was without jobs, and an estimated 15 million families — half the American population — lived in poverty.[42]

World War II jump-started the U.S. economy, and in the 1950s and early '60s many Americans enjoyed middle-class prosperity. But not all saw their living standards rise. Poverty persisted and grew, much of it concentrated in the rural South, Appalachia and the gritty urban cores of the industrial North. Many Americans blamed the poor for their plight, dismissing racism, educational inequality and other entrenched societal ills as major factors in perpetuating poverty.

Military Families Face Financial Strain

"This spring our caseload doubled."

Meredith Leyva's work with military families recently has led her to a troubling conclusion: Poverty is growing among the ranks of deployed service members, especially those who have been seriously injured in Iraq or Afghanistan.

"This spring our caseload of both military families and wounded warriors doubled," says Leyva, who is the founder of Operation Homefront, a Santa Ana, Calif., charity that helps military families through 31 chapters nationwide. And, adds Leyva, whose husband is a Navy physician, "We saw a significant change in the types of cases. We're now seeing many more complicated and high-dollar crises that are compounded by deployment after deployment."

Meredith Leyva, founder of Operation Homefront.

Operation Homefront served approximately 1,700 families of wounded service members in 2006, Leyva says, and "over half and possibly more were living in poverty."

As for the 1.5-million-member military as a whole, however, little if any hard data exist on the extent of poverty in military families during the current conflict. Much of the government information on issues like food stamp use among military families predates the war.

Indeed, the financial health of military families can be a highly complicated and nuanced issue to analyze, even leaving aside the struggles of those dealing with catastrophic injury. "By any traditional measure of poverty..., military families are a lot better off than their civilian peers based on such things as age and education," says Joyce Raezer, chief operating officer of the National Military Family Association, a policy advocacy group in Alexandria, Va.

Still, she says some military families may be on the "financial edge," often because "they're young and financially inexperienced" and perhaps "prey for financial predators." Others may be strained by relocation demands that put them in temporary financial straits, she says.

"My sense is that you don't have folks living in poverty so that day in and day out things are inadequate," says Raezer. "But it can be episodic, where they're strapped for cash because of the military lifestyle, financial inexperience and predators."

Most military families are ineligible for food stamps because the military housing allowance puts them over the eligibility threshold, Raezer notes.

Even so, in fiscal 2006 food-stamp redemptions at military commissaries rose about $2.3 million over the previous year, to $26.2 million. While it was not clear what caused the increase, three military stores affected by Hurricane Katrina and other storms accounted for more than 80 percent of the increase.[1]

In May, U.S. Reps. James McGovern, D-Mass., and Jo Ann Emerson, R-Mo., introduced a bill that would expand

CinCHouse.com/Operation Homefront

In 1962 Michael Harrington wrote in his groundbreaking book *The Other America: Poverty in the United States:*

"There are sociological and political reasons why poverty is not seen; and there are misconceptions and prejudices that literally blind the eyes. . . . Here is the most familiar version of social blindness: 'The poor are that way because they are afraid of work. And anyway they all have big cars. If they were like me (or my father or my grandfather), they could pay their own way. But they prefer to live on the dole and cheat the taxpayers.'

"This theory," Harrington went on, "usually thought of as a virtuous and moral statement, is one of the means of making it impossible for the poor ever to pay their way. . . . [T]he real explanation of why the poor are where they are is that they made the mistake of being born to the spending for federal nutrition programs, including a provision that would exclude combat-related military pay from income calculations for food-stamp eligibility.[2]

National Guard and active-duty families can feel financial strain differently. Lt. Col. Joseph Schweikert, state family program director for the Illinois National Guard, says "there are definitely families that go through financial hardships, sometimes due to deployments. But it varies from soldier to soldier, family to family. Some make more while deployed."

Nonetheless, at least 30 percent of Guard soldiers suffer a financial loss when deployed, he says.

Because the Guard offers a college-scholarship program, many young soldiers enlist, get a degree and then enter a well-paying career field. When they are mobilized, their pay may drop sharply. "It causes the family to go through a lot of hardships," Schweikert says, especially if the soldier doesn't have savings or a spouse's income to rely on.

Still, he suggests, many Guard members can be more stable financially than active-duty troops. Guard soldiers tend to be older and to have established civilian careers. Moreover, a working spouse will not have had to uproot periodically from a job, as often happens within the active-duty forces.

"In active duty, a lot of time you have to transfer from base to base, and it's hard to establish a long-term career," Schweikert says.

Nonetheless, military families in both the Guard and regular forces may find it hard to avoid financial ruin, especially in cases of serious injury suffered in war.

When a soldier is deployed, a spouse may have to pay others to do jobs the soldier performed at home, such as

Wounded soldiers and their families attend a get-together sponsored by the Texas chapter of Operation Homefront at Brooke Army Medical Center at Fort Sam Houston.

mowing the lawn and maintaining the car, Leyva says. And if a soldier is wounded, she says, "his pay immediately drops while the expenses skyrocket." Often, a spouse takes leave from a job or quits altogether to be at the wounded soldier's bedside or to help the soldier through rehabilitation, spending long days or weeks away from home.

"Service members were never paid well," Leyva says, "but these extraordinary crises certainly overwhelm."

Leyva fears that poverty among veterans will skyrocket in the wake of the current war, as it did after the Vietnam conflict. "I think we're going to see a whole new generation of disabled veterans that are sort of the mirror images of the Vietnam veterans," she says. "It's as much about mental as physical wounds," she says, and it could lead to a new "generation of poverty."

---

[1] Karen Jowers, "Storms May Have Spurred Jump in Food-Stamp Use," *Air Force Times*, July 5, 2007, www.navytimes.com.

[2] The Feeding America's Family Act, HR 2129.

wrong parents, in the wrong section of the country, in the wrong industry or in the wrong racial or ethnic group. Once that mistake has been made, they could have been paragons of will and morality, but most of them would never even have had a chance to get out of the other America."[43]

By 1962, more than a fifth of Americans were living in poverty. Harrington's book helped spur Washington to act.[44]

A few months before his assassination, President John F. Kennedy directed his Council of Economic Advisers to study domestic poverty and recommend ways to fight it.[45]

Kennedy's successor, President Lyndon B. Johnson, followed through, declaring in his first State of the Union address, on Jan. 8, 1964, "unconditional war on poverty in America." Later that year Congress established the Office of Economic Opportunity, which attacked poverty

Did Recent Reforms Help Needy Families?

Bush administration tightened TANF work requirements.

Mention welfare reform to a political observer, and it is Bill Clinton who typically comes to mind. It was candidate Clinton who pledged to "end welfare as we know it" and President Clinton who signed the landmark welfare reform act into law in 1996.

But the Bush era also has engineered significant reforms in the welfare system, changes that could have far-reaching effects on the nation's poor.

The most important came with last year's congressional reauthorization of Temporary Assistance for Needy Families (TANF), the federal block-grant program that replaced the old welfare system.

The reauthorization strengthened work requirements and closed a loophole so that separate state-funded TANF programs have to be included in work-participation calculations.

"In effect, the Bush administration and Congress put teeth back into TANF work requirements but set difficult benchmarks for state programs that are working with adult populations experiencing many barriers to employment," Scott W. Allard, an assistant professor of political science and public policy at Brown University, noted recently.[1]

Others looking back on more than a decade of welfare reform worry the recent changes in the welfare rules could make poverty trends worse. Two analysts at the Center on Budget and Policy Priorities, Sharon Parrott, director of the center's Welfare Reform and Income Support Division, and senior researcher Arloc Sherman, argue that even though changes in TANF a decade ago "played a role in reducing poverty and raising employment rates during the 1990s, our safety net for the poorest families with children has weakened dramatically."[2]

Among the trends they pointed to: child poverty fell in the 1990s, but began rising after 2000, and the number of children in "deep" poverty rose; the number of jobless single mothers receiving no government cash assistance has risen significantly, and TANF now helps a far smaller share of families that qualify for the program than it used to help.

Last year's reauthorization could weaken the safety net even more, the two analysts suggested. Welfare reauthorization requires states to place a much bigger portion of their TANF caseloads in work activities and restricts the kind of activities that can count toward state work-participation requirements, Parrott and Sherman noted. "In many cases,

through a phalanx of new programs, from Head Start — a school-readiness effort — to Job Corps, a training program for teens and young adults.[46] Johnson's fight against poverty also included a wide range of "Great Society" programs, from the 1964 Food Stamp Act to Medicare and Medicaid.

The War on Poverty persisted under the Nixon administration, which broadened the Food Stamp program and saw the passage of the Supplemental Security Income program for disabled people, among others. Even so, President Richard M. Nixon sought to dismantle the Office of Economic Opportunity, disbursing many of its programs among various federal agencies. The office was finally closed by President Gerald R. Ford in 1975.

Under Attack

By the 1980s and the start of the Reagan administration, poverty programs were under full-scale attack. The

poverty rate, which dipped to just over 11 percent in the early 1970s, hit 15.2 percent in 1983. Conservatives, impatient with the Johnson-era philosophy of federally funded social aid for the poor, charged that the government's expensive programs were making poverty and dependence worse rather than better.

"[S]ome years ago, the federal government declared War on Poverty, and poverty won," Reagan famously said in his 1988 State of the Union address. "Today the federal government has 59 major welfare programs and spends more than $100 billion a year on them. What has all this money done? Well, too often it has only made poverty harder to escape. Federal welfare programs have created a massive social problem. With the best of intentions, government created a poverty trap that wreaks havoc on the very support system the poor need most to lift themselves out of poverty: the family."

state programs designed to address two of the biggest problems that have emerged over TANF's first decade — that parents who leave welfare for work often earn low wages and have unstable employment, and that many families with the greatest barriers to employment are being left behind — will no longer count toward states' work requirements," they wrote.

"In fact, the cheapest and easiest way for a state to meet the new work rules would simply be to assist fewer poor families, especially the families with barriers to employment who need the most help."

On top of that, the amount of basic federal block-grant funds for states has not been adjusted since 1996 and has lost 22 percent of its value to inflation, Parrott and Sherman wrote.

Some observers are more sanguine about the course of welfare reform. Writing in a "point-counterpoint" format with Parrott and Sherman, Lawrence Mead, a professor of politics at New York University and an architect of welfare reform, describes it as an "incomplete triumph." He says reform achieved its two main goals: Work levels rose sharply among poor mothers, the main beneficiaries of welfare. And caseloads plummeted.

Still, Mead says that the reform effort has had limitations. For one thing, he says, it did not create a system that promotes work on an ongoing basis through a combination of government incentives and emphasis on personal responsibility. He notes that 40 percent of those who have left welfare have not gone to work, and many welfare recipients have moved in and out of jobs.

Nor did welfare reform ensure that people leaving welfare for jobs will have enough income to live on, Mead says. "The situation has improved, but not enough."

And welfare reform did not adequately address the employment challenges among poor men, many of whom are fathers in welfare families, Mead says.

Nonetheless, Mead is hopeful the limitations of welfare reform can be addressed at least partly through engagement by the poor in the political process. Because more of the poor are working or moving toward work, they are in a stronger position to demand changes, such as payment of living wages, than they were under the old entitlement system of welfare, Mead says.

First, though, the poor must assert themselves both on the job and in the political sphere, he says.

"Finally," he writes, "what reform enforced was not work, but citizenship."[3]

---

[1] Scott W. Allard, "The Changing Face of Welfare During the Bush Administration," *Publius*, June 22, 2007.

[2] Sharon Parrott and Arloc Sherman, "Point-Counterpoint," in Richard P. Nathan, editor, "Welfare Reform After Ten Years: Strengths and Weaknesses," *Journal of Policy Analysis and Management*, Vol. 26, No. 2, 2007.

[3] Lawrence Mead, "Point-Counterpoint," in *ibid.*

The Reagan administration argued "that the social policies enacted in the 1960s and '70s had undermined the functioning of the nation's basic institutions and, by encouraging permissiveness, non-work and welfare dependence, had led to marital breakup, non-marital childbearing and the erosion of individual initiative," according to the University of Michigan's Danziger and Robert H. Haveman, a professor of economics and public affairs at the University of Wisconsin.

"The Reagan philosophy was that tax cuts and spending cuts would increase the rate of economic growth, and that the poor would ultimately benefit through the increased employment and earnings that would follow such growth," they wrote. "However, a deep recession in the early 1980s increased poverty, and the subsequent economic growth did not 'trickle down.' Although the economy expanded for many years in the 1980s, the wage rates of low- and medium-skilled male workers did not.

On the other hand, the earnings of those in the upper part of the income distribution grew rapidly."[47]

Welfare Reform

The 1980s laid the groundwork for the radical shift in anti-poverty policy that was to come during the Clinton era. In 1993 Clinton pushed through a record expansion of the Earned Income Tax Credit. Then, Clinton signed the Personal Responsibility and Work Opportunity Reconciliation Act of 1996 — otherwise known as the Welfare Reform Act.

The move to overhaul welfare outraged some. Georgetown University's Edelman resigned from the Clinton administration in protest. In a blistering critique, Edelman wrote that the measure would lead to "more malnutrition and more crime, increased infant mortality and increased drug and alcohol abuse" and "increased family violence and abuse against children and women."[48]

But others have praised the reform measure. What the Clinton bill did, a *Boston Globe* columnist opined on the act's 10th anniversary, "was end the condescending attitude that the poor were incapable of improving their situation, and that 'compassion' consisted of supplying money indefinitely to women who had children, but no husbands or jobs." The bill "replaced deadly condescension with respect."[49]

Still, while welfare caseloads plummeted, poverty persisted, even among those who joined the labor force.

"Basically, things are better than most people thought," Danziger says today. "On average, welfare recipients did much better moving from welfare to work, in part because the minimum wage was increased in 1997, the Earned Income Tax Credit expanded so much in the early '90s, states put so much into child-care subsidies, and the State Children's Health Insurance Program (SCHIP) came in. But the poverty rate among single mothers remains very high, and there's nothing new on the horizon."

Danziger noted in a 2006 paper that as many as 30 percent of single mothers who left welfare and took jobs are out of work in any given month.[50]

Advocates point out that it is possible to make real gains against poverty — and not just gains in cutting welfare caseloads. They point to big strides against child poverty in Britain, where in 1999 Prime Minister Tony Blair pledged to end child poverty by 2020.

"Elusive Dream"

But in cities and towns across America, President Johnson's 1964 pledge "not only to relieve the symptom of poverty but to cure it and, above all, to prevent it" remains an elusive dream.[51]

The loss of manufacturing jobs — and the stability and safety net they once provided — is a big reason the dream remains out of reach.

In Wisconsin, a state of 5.6 million people, the poverty rate shot from 8.2 percent to 11 percent over five years, says the Wisconsin Community Action Program Association's Schlimm. "I'm 58 and have lived in Wisconsin all my life, and it's very unusual to see those kinds of numbers," he says. It is the "loss of good jobs, manufacturing jobs" that is to blame.

"A lot of Wisconsin's good jobs support the auto industry," he continues. "And we're a paper-making state. Many of the papermakers moved. . . . When I got out of college, you could go to a paper mill, and if it didn't work

out, you could drive a couple of blocks down the street and find work with another company. In 1968 they paid $6 to $7 an hour. Now they pay $25. They're very coveted jobs. But there aren't as many of them. The economy hasn't been able to replace those very good jobs."

What matters most in the fight against poverty, many advocates contend, is leadership and political will.

The No. 1 problem is leadership, says David Bradley, executive director of the National Community Action Foundation. "We're not talking billions of dollars. We're talking receptivity to looking at ideas."

Bradley notes that the Johnson-era Office of Economic Opportunity was a laboratory for anti-poverty innovations. "For many years we've not had the federal government willing to fund and be experimental in partnering in new ideas on poverty. A lot of ideas start at the grass roots. I see incredible projects out there but no mechanism to duplicate them nationwide."

At the same time, Bradley laments that some in both political parties believe none of the ideas from the 1960s are worth keeping. "I find it frustrating that some candidates who are talking about poverty view anything that's gone on previously as not successful or not innovative or creative enough," he says. "If you're a program that started in 1964 or 1965, that doesn't mean by definition that you're still not innovative in your community."

Bradley is cautiously optimistic that a renewed commitment to fighting poverty is afoot in the nation. Political leaders in both parties are talking about the issue and the government's role in bringing about solutions, he points out.

But that will happen, Bradley says, only if solutions are not overpromised, the effort is bipartisan, innovation and creativity are part of the approach, sufficient government money is available and, "most important, if there is a general acceptance that the federal government wants to be a positive partner.

"It can be a partner that requires accountability," he says, "but a partner nevertheless."

CURRENT SITUATION

Presidential Race

It remains unclear how much traction the poverty theme will have in the 2008 presidential race. But as the campaign began moving into high gear this summer, poverty — and

Should immigration be reduced to protect the jobs of native-born poor?

YES
Steven A. Camarota
Director of Research,
Center for Immigration Studies

From testimony prepared for House Judiciary Committee, May 9, 2007

There is no evidence of a labor shortage, especially at the bottom end of the labor market where immigrants are most concentrated. . . . There is a good deal of research showing that immigration has contributed to the decline in employment and wages for less-educated natives. . . . All research indicates that less-educated immigrants consume much more in government services than they pay in taxes. Thus, not only does such immigration harm America's poor, it also burdens taxpayers. . . .

While the number of immigrants is very large . . . the impact on the overall economy or on the share of the population that is of working age is actually very small. And these effects are even smaller when one focuses only on illegal aliens, who comprise one-fourth to one-third of all immigrants. While the impact on the economy . . . may be tiny, the effect on some Americans, particular workers at the bottom of the labor market may be quite large. These workers are especially vulnerable to immigrant competition because wages for these jobs are already low, and immigrants are heavily concentrated in less-skilled and lower-paying jobs. . . .

It probably makes more sense for policymakers to focus on the winners and losers from immigration. The big losers are natives working in low-skilled, low-wage jobs. Of course, technological change and increased trade also have reduced the labor market opportunities for low-wage workers in the United States. But immigration is different because it is a discretionary policy that can be altered. On the other hand, immigrants are the big winners, as are owners of capital and skilled workers, but their gains are tiny relative to their income.

In the end, arguments for or against immigration are as much political and moral as they are economic. The latest research indicates that we can reduce immigration secure in the knowledge that it will not harm the economy. Doing so makes sense if we are very concerned about low-wage and less-skilled workers in the United States. On the other hand, if one places a high priority on helping unskilled workers in other countries, then allowing in a large number of such workers should continue.

Of course, only an infinitesimal proportion of the world's poor could ever come to this country even under the most open immigration policy one might imagine. Those who support the current high level of unskilled legal and illegal immigration should at least do so with an understanding that those American workers harmed by the policies they favor are already the poorest and most vulnerable.

NO
Gerald D. Jaynes
Professor of Economics and
African-American Studies, Yale University

From testimony before House Subcommittee on Immigration, Citizenship, Refugees, Border Security, and International Law, May 3, 2007

We can acknowledge that immigration probably hurts the employment and wages of some less-educated citizens and still conclude immigration is a net benefit for the United States. The most methodologically sound estimates of the net effects of immigration on the nation conclude that the United States, as a whole, benefits from contemporary immigration. Properly measured, this conclusion means that during a period of time reasonably long enough to allow immigrants to adjust to their new situations, they produce more national income than they consume in government services.

Confusion about this issue is caused by some analysts' failure to make appropriate distinctions between immigration's impact on specific local governments and groups and its impact on the whole nation. Although benefits of immigration — such as lower prices for consumer and producer goods and services, greater profits and tax revenues — accrue to the nation as a whole, nearly all of the costs for public services consumed by immigrants are borne by localities and specific demographic groups. . . . Even so, inappropriate methods of analysis have led some analysts to overstate the costs of immigration even at the local level. . . .

On average, Americans receive positive economic benefits from immigration, but, at least in the short run, residents of particular localities and members of certain groups may lose. . . .

Democratic concepts of justice suggest the losses of a few should not override the gains of the many. Democratic concepts of justice also demand that society's least-advantaged members should not be paying for the immigration benefits enjoyed by the entire nation. A democratic society benefiting from immigration and debating how to reshape its immigration policies should also be discussing social policies to compensate less-skilled workers through combinations of better training, relocation and educational opportunities. . . .

[T]he evidence supports the conclusion that from an economic standpoint immigration's broader benefits to the nation outweigh its costs. An assessment of the effects of immigration on the employment prospects of less-educated native-born workers is that the effect is negative but modest, and probably is significant in some specific industries and geographic locations. . . . However, it is just as likely that the relative importance of less-educated young native [workers'] job losses due to the competition of immigrants is swamped by a constellation of other factors diminishing their economic status.

what to do about it — has been high on the list of priorities among several leading Democratic candidates, most notably Edwards and Obama.

Edwards has set the ambitious goal of cutting poverty by a third within a decade and ending it within 30 years. Echoing President Johnson's Great Society program, Edwards proposes a "Working Society" where "everyone who is able to work hard will be expected to work and, in turn, be rewarded for it."

To attack poverty, Edwards is pushing more than a dozen ideas, from raising the minimum wage, fighting predatory lending and reducing teen pregnancy to creating a million temporary "stepping stone" jobs for those having difficulty finding other work.

Obama has his own long list of proposals. He also backs a transitional jobs program and a minimum-wage increase, for example, along with such steps as improving transportation access for the working poor and helping ex-prisoners find jobs.

But deeper differences exist in the two candidates' approaches. "Edwards has focused on the malignant effects of the concentration of poverty in inner cities," *The Washington Post* noted. "He has argued for dispersing low-income families by replacing public housing with a greatly expanded rental voucher program to allow families to move where there are more jobs and better schools." Obama, on the other hand, has "presented a sharply different overall objective: fixing inner-city areas so they become places where families have a shot at prospering, without having to move."[52]

Part of what is noteworthy about the Edwards and Obama proposals is that they exist at all. Many Democratic candidates, including Sen. Clinton, have focused on the plight of the middle class rather than the poor. "Since the late 1980s," the columnist E. J. Dionne Jr. noted, "Democrats have been obsessed with the middle class for reasons of simple math: no middle-class votes, no electoral victories."[53]

With the exception of recent comments by former Republican Bloomberg of New York, GOP rhetoric on poverty has not been nearly as prevalent as the Democrats'. In January, President Bush acknowledged that "income inequality is real," suggesting his administration might be poised to do more on poverty and perhaps get ahead of Democrats on the issue.[54] But more recently the administration has resisted congressional efforts to expand the SCHIP program, which benefits poor children.

Meanwhile, Republican presidential hopeful Mitt Romney echoed the longstanding conservative criticism of Democrat-backed social policies, declaring that Democrats are "thinking about big government, big welfare, big taxes, Big Brother."[55]

Anti-Poverty Proposals

In recent months several think tanks and advocacy groups have turned out policy proposals for reducing poverty. In April the liberal Center for American Progress advanced a dozen key steps to cut poverty in half in the next decade, including raising the minimum wage to half the average hourly wage, expanding the EITC and Child Tax Credit, promoting unionization, guaranteeing child-care assistance to low-income families and creating 2 million new housing vouchers "designed to help people live in opportunity-rich areas."

The center's main recommendations would cost roughly $90 billion annually — "a significant cost," it conceded, "but one that is necessary and could be readily funded through a fairer tax system." Spending $90 billion a year "would represent about 0.8 percent of the nation's gross domestic product, which is a fraction of the money spent on tax changes that benefited primarily the wealthy in recent years."

The Urban Institute estimated that four of the center's recommendations — on the minimum wage, EITC, child tax credit and child care — would cut poverty by about a fourth. Moreover, it said, both child poverty and extreme poverty would fall.[56]

A Brookings Institution proposal to "reinvigorate the fight for greater opportunity" includes seven recommendations for the next U.S. president, from strengthening work requirements in government-assistance programs, promoting marriage and funding teen pregnancy-prevention efforts to subsidizing child care for low-wage workers, increasing the minimum wage and expanding the EITC.

"We need a new generation of anti-poverty policies that focus on requiring and rewarding work, reversing the breakdown of the family and improving educational outcomes," the proposal states. The $38.6 billion per year cost should not be incurred, the authors say, unless it "can be fully covered by eliminating spending or tax preferences in other areas."[57]

Many advocates emphasize the need to help poor people build their assets, such as savings accounts and home equity, as a way of propelling them out of poverty. Also key, they say, is the need to spend more on early-childhood programs to help keep youngsters from falling into poverty in the first place.

"Universal high-quality early childhood education is the single most powerful investment we could make in insuring poverty doesn't strike the next generation," says Newman of Princeton University.

Tax Policy

Proposals to adjust federal tax policy to help lift the poor into the economic mainstream are among those getting the most attention. Much of the discussion has focused on expansion of the child and earned income tax credits.

A letter sent to members of Congress last spring by hundreds of advocacy groups urged expansion of the child credit, which can reduce the tax liability of families with children. "The current income threshold — in 2007, it is $11,750 — excludes 10 million children whose families are too poor to claim the credit," the letter stated. "The threshold keeps rising with inflation, increasing the tax burden on the poor and dropping many families from the benefit altogether."

The letter added that according to the Tax Policy Center, operated by the Urban Institute and Brookings Institution, "half of all African-American children, 46 percent of Hispanic children and 18 percent of white children received either no Child Tax Credit or a reduced amount in 2005 because their families' earnings were too low."[58]

Along with the child credit, the EITC is widely cited as ripe for expansion.

Created in 1975 to protect low-wage workers from rising payroll taxes, the credit has been expanded several times, under both Republican and Democratic administrations. More than 20 million families benefit from more than $40 billion in credits today, according to Brookings' Berube. Most of those eligible for the credit have children under age 18 living at home and earn less than $35,000, according to Berube. In 2004 the average claimant received a credit of about $1,800.[59]

While claims of abuse have been leveled at the tax credit, it has generally been popular across the political spectrum because it encourages work, helps the needy and does not levy a cost on wealthier taxpayers.[60]

But anti-poverty advocates say the tax credit could be even more effective by making it easier for families with two earners to get the credit and extending it to single workers in their late teens and early 20s.[61]

"Childless adults are the only group of working tax filers who begin to owe federal income taxes before their incomes reach the poverty line," says the letter to members of Congress. Workers in that category got an average credit of only $230 last year, the letter said. "Increasing the amount of the credit for low-income workers not living with children would increase work incentives and economic security for millions of Americans working in low-wage jobs."

Making poor people aware of the tax credit is also an obstacle that must be overcome, advocates say. Many people who are eligible for the credit don't claim it, sometimes because of language or educational barriers.

Dodd, at Step Up in Savannah, says the Internal Revenue Service said $10 million to $12 million in credits go unclaimed in his city alone.

States and Localities

As federal policymakers wrestle with the poverty issue, states and localities are making inroads of their own. Mayor Bloomberg has been promoting a plan to pay poor families in New York up to $5,000 a year to meet such goals as attending parent-teacher meetings, getting medical checkups and holding full-time jobs. Patterned after a Mexican initiative, the plan aims to help poor families make better long-range decisions and break cycles of poverty and dependence that can last generations.[62]

Other efforts are afoot in the states. A proposed bill in the California Assembly, for example, would establish an advisory Childhood Poverty Council to develop a plan to reduce child poverty in the state by half by 2017 and eliminate it by 2027.[63]

Not all such steps pan out, though. In 2004, Connecticut passed legislation committing the state to a 50 percent reduction in child poverty by 2014, but child poverty has risen since then, an official of the Connecticut Association for Community Action complained this summer, blaming the failure to enact a state-funded EITC.[64]

As states seek ways to reduce the number of poor within their borders, they also are trying to adjust to the stiffer work requirements that Congress enacted last year when it reauthorized welfare reform.[65]

The new rules are forcing some states to adapt in creative ways. In California, for example, where less than a fourth of welfare recipients work enough hours to meet federal requirements, officials are moving some teenage parents, older parents and disabled people into separate programs paid entirely by state funds so they aren't counted in federal work-participation calculations.

Arkansas, on the other hand, has been sending monthly checks to the working poor. "Arkansas eventually aims to artificially swell its welfare population from 8,000 families to as many as 11,000 and raise the work-participation rate by at least 11 percent," according to a press report. "Officials hope the extra cash will also keep the workers employed."[66]

The tougher work rules have upset poverty advocates, who argue they damage efforts to help those most vulnerable or lacking in skills to prepare for the job market. "Some of the changes made it almost impossible in some ways for people to use the system to get out of poverty," said Rep. McDermott, the Washington Democrat.[67]

But others defend the approach. "The bottom line is that the only real way to get out of poverty is to find a job," said Rep. Wally Herger, a California Republican who chaired the House subcommittee that worked on last year's reauthorization. "There's always the line, 'Well, some people can't do it.' What that's really doing is selling those people short."[68]

OUTLOOK

Ominous Signs

The outlook for real progress against domestic poverty is mixed, especially in the near term.

On one hand, concerns about poverty, income inequality and declining mobility are playing a bigger role on the national scene than they have in years. The kind of political momentum that spurred the War on Poverty in the 1960s may be emerging again — albeit in a more muted fashion and with a different set of policy proposals.

But big obstacles remain, especially funding. Congress would face difficult fiscal choices if it sought to enact any major anti-poverty program, many analysts point out. Even the Democratic majority, which has long pushed for more spending for social programs, would face major barriers.

"The Democrats have committed to pay-as-you-go budgeting, so I don't think we'll have a major push on

anti-poverty [programs] or on programs designed to help the poor and middle class" over the next four to eight years, says Yale's Hacker. "That's part of the reason for the public's frustration — we're hamstrung by the budgetary situation."

At the same time, a number of ominous developments have been occurring that suggest the poor will have an even rougher time financially than they have in recent years. The explosion in mortgage foreclosures, rising prices for basics like gasoline and milk and the ever-present threat of recession and layoffs all conspire most heavily against those with the fewest resources. Recently, job growth and expansion in the service sector have both been weaker than expected, indicating tougher times ahead for those on the economic margins.

Coupled with the uncertain economic outlook is the unresolved issue of immigration. Some analysts are less concerned about illegal immigrants taking low-paying jobs from native-born Americans as they are about the chance that immigrant groups will become mired in permanent poverty because of out-of-wedlock births and other social problems.

"In the long term," says Mead of New York University, "overcoming poverty probably does depend on restricting immigration" to 1970 levels. Curbing immigration, he says, not only would make more entry-level jobs available to native-born men — the group that Mead sees as a priority for anti-poverty action — but also help keep a new underclass from developing even as the nation struggles to reduce poverty in the established population.

As scholars and activists look ahead, some express optimism, as Lyndon Johnson once did, that poverty not only can be substantially reduced but actually eliminated. Others note that Johnson's vow to eliminate poverty raised expectations that were never satisfied.

"I think the poor are always going to be with us," says Bradley of the National Community Action Foundation. "Can we substantially reduce poverty? Yes. But the [idea] that somehow certain programs are going to eradicate poverty in America is just unrealistic."

UPDATE

Between 2008 and 2009, the deep recession that began around December 2007 increased the U.S. poverty rate from 13.2 percent to 14.3 percent, its highest level since 1994, according to the Census Bureau.[69]

Nevertheless, say some analysts, poverty might have increased even more had public programs not propped up many families. In the recession's wake, though, many such programs are threatened with severe cutbacks, even as the unemployment that plunged many people into poverty remains high.

The number of Americans living in poverty rose from just under 40 million in 2008 to about 43.6 million in 2009 — the largest number in the 51 years the government has reported poverty statistics. The poverty-rate increase related to the recession was smaller than the one that accompanied the twin recessions that ran from January 1980 through late 1982 but larger than that during the 1973-1975 recession, the Census Bureau says.[70]

Steeply rising unemployment connected to the recession helped drive the increase in poverty rates since 2007.

In the nation's 100 largest metropolitan areas, city and suburban unemployment both nearly doubled between December 2007 and December 2009, rising to 10.3 percent in the 100 largest cities and to 9.3 percent in their suburbs, according to analysts Elizabeth Kneebone and Emily Garr at the centrist Brookings Institution.[71] Furthermore, by December 2010, or 12 months after economists say that economic recovery had begun, unemployment in major metropolitan areas had dropped only slightly — to 9.8 percent in cities and 8.9 percent in suburbs.[72]

Along with rising and persistent unemployment came a telling rise in the use of government anti-poverty assistance, notably the Supplemental Nutrition Assistance Program (SNAP) — previously called "food stamps." SNAP enrolled a record 43.5 million Americans — one in seven — as of November 2010.[73] Especially in the deepest part of the recession, between January 2008 and July 2009, SNAP use "increased steeply and steadily," wrote Kneebone and Garr.[74]

The poorest Americans — those with incomes 50 percent or less of the federal poverty level, about $11,000 for a family of four — made up 6.3 percent of the entire population, some 19 million people, in 2009. That was up from 5.7 percent of the population, or 17.1 million people, in 2008, the Census Bureau says.[75]

Getty Images/Joe Raedle

A social worker displays a federal foood-assistance card. The Supplemental Nutrition Assistance Program (SNAP) enrolled a record 43.5 million Americans — one in seven — as of November 2010.

Poverty among children — the age group most likely to live in a poor household — increased because of the recession as well. Before the recession hit, 13 states and the District of Columbia had child-poverty rates of at least 20 percent or higher. But by 2009, eight more states had joined the list of those where at least one child in five lived in poverty, according to Brookings analyst Julia B. Isaacs. The largest recession-related increases in child poverty occurred in Michigan, Indiana and Ohio.[76]

Once mainly a phenomenon of cities and rural areas, poverty has increased in American suburbs over the past decade, and the trend seems to be continuing. Between 1999 and 2009, the number of people nationwide living below the federal poverty line — $21,954 in household income for a family of four in 2009 — grew by 25.6 percent. Suburbs of the nation's 100 largest metropolitan areas, however, saw their poverty rate swell by a whopping 37.4 percent. By 2009, 1.6 million more poor people lived in suburbs than in cities, "a dramatic departure from 2000 when city poor outnumbered their suburban counterparts by almost 400,000," writes Brookings analyst Kneebone.[77]

Anti-Poverty Programs

The severity of the so-called Great Recession and the steep, long-term rise in unemployment that accompanied it would have increased poverty much more, had not government programs supported Americans in the downturn, according to the Center on Budget and Policy Priorities (CBPP), a liberal think tank.

According to the Census Bureau's traditional poverty measures, the poverty rate increased by 1.1 percent between 2008 and 2009, a modest uptick given that unemployment rates had doubled in many regions and many Americans lost their homes to foreclosure. But using a new alternative measure that takes into account the poverty-ameliorating effects of tax credits and non-cash government benefits such as SNAP, the Census Bureau finds that the national poverty rate did not increase at all between 2008 and 2009, "a remarkable achievement" given the recession's severity, wrote CBPP analyst Arloc Sherman.[78]

"Poverty usually burgeons in major recessions" but did not in the most recent because of existing poverty programs and, especially, the Obama administration's 2009 stimulus legislation, said Sherman. Programs in the 2009 Recovery Act "kept more than 4.5 million people out of poverty" in that year, according to CBPP. Expansions of unemployment benefits enacted in the stimulus plan kept 1.3 million people above the poverty line; improvements in the Child Tax Credit and the Earned Income Tax Credit (EITC), 1.5 million; the Making Work Pay tax credit, 1 million; and increased benefit levels for SNAP, 700,000, Sherman estimated.[79]

In 2011, however, as Recovery Act assistance ends and states and cities struggle to trim budgets strained by recession-fueled tax-revenue losses, programs that help stave off poverty likely face substantial cuts.

Michigan, Missouri, Arkansas and Florida, for example, are among states where new limits on unemployment benefits have been proposed. In April, Republican Gov. Rick Snyder made Michigan the first state to cut the number of weeks the state will pay unemployment benefits, signing legislation to cut the benefit period from 26 weeks to 20.[80]

Michigan is one of at least 23 states where lawmakers are mulling an end to EITCs that go to the working poor; the credits are "refundable," meaning that, in some cases, recipients may get more money than they paid in income taxes. Snyder and conservative lawmakers view ending the EITC as a potentially important step to trim

a $1.8 billion state budget deficit. The credit returns an average of $432 annually to recipients, who are mostly families with children.[81]

"The $400 . . . could mean the difference between paying my . . . energy bill or not," commented Rohnalda Hollon, an Iraq War veteran and single mother of three in Beaverton, Mich.[82]

But "we cannot afford these sacred cows," said Republican state Sen. Roger Kahn, who sponsored a bill to end the credit. "Do we need it? Can we afford it? What's it worth? For the EITC the answers are no, no and not enough," Kahn said.[83]

Conservative analysts increasingly argue that government aid such as unemployment benefits and the EITC are a costly burden on taxpayers and an alarming sign that too many Americans have grown dependent on government rather than relying on their own enterprise to get through hard times.

The Heritage Foundation, a conservative think tank, for example, has repeatedly "raised concerns about the challenges that rapidly growing dependence poses to this country's republican form of government and for the broader civil society," wrote Heritage analysts William W. Beach and Patrick D. Tyrrell. "Growing dependence on government erodes the spirit of self-reliance and self-improvement," they argue.[84]

Programs such as the EITC, which provide benefits even to people who are too poor to pay income tax under current laws, are a special problem, wrote Beach and Tyrrell. "Dependence-creating programs quickly morph into political assets that policymakers readily embrace," and "voters tend to support politicians or political parties that give them higher incomes or subsidies for the essentials of life," they note. "Can this republican form of government withstand the political weight of a massively growing population of Americans who believe themselves entitled to government benefits, and who contribute little or nothing for them?" the Heritage analysts ask.[85]

NOTES

1. Testimony before House Ways and Means Subcommittee on Income Security and Family Support, "Hearing on Economic Opportunity and Poverty in America," Feb. 13, 2007.

2. Figures reflect U.S. Census Bureau data for 2006. For background, see Kathy Koch, "Child Poverty," *CQ Researcher*, April 7, 2000, pp. 281-304.

3. Timothy M. Smeeding, testimony before House Ways and Means Subcommittee on Income Security and Family Support, "Hearing on Economic Opportunity and Poverty in America," Feb. 13, 2007. The study is based on Smeeding's calculations from the Luxembourg Income Study.

4. Quoted in Bob Herbert, "The Millions Left Out," *The New York Times*, May 12, 2007, p. A25.

5. Tony Pugh, "U.S. Economy Leaving Record Numbers in Severe Poverty," McClatchy Newspapers, Feb. 22, 2007, updated May 25, 2007.

6. Aviva Aron-Dine, "New Data Show Income Concentration Jumped Again in 2005," Center on Budget and Policy Priorities, March 29, 2007, www.cbpp.org/3-29-07inc.htm.

7. David Cay Johnston, "Income Gap Is Widening, Data Shows," *The New York Times*, March 29, 2007, p. C1.

8. "Panel Study of Income Dynamics; Cross-National Equivalent File," Cornell University. Cited in John Edwards, Marion Crain and Arne L. Kalleberg, eds., *Ending Poverty in America: How to Restore the American Dream* (2007), The New Press, published in conjunction with the Center on Poverty, Work and Opportunity, University of North Carolina at Chapel Hill. Data are from Jacob S. Hacker, "The Risky Outlook for Middle-Class America," Chapter 5, p. 72.

9. Mark R. Rank, "Toward a New Understanding of American Poverty," *Journal of Law & Policy*, Vol. 20:17, p. 33, http://law.wustl.edu/Journal/20/p17Rankbookpage.pdf.

10. Steven Greenhouse, "A Unified Voice Argues the Case for U.S. Manufacturing," *The New York Times*, April 26, 2007, p. C2.

11. Katrina vanden Heuvel, "Twelve Steps to Cutting Poverty in Half," Blog: Editor's Cut, *The Nation*, April 30, 2007, www.thenation.com/blogs/edcut?pid=190867.

12. Patrick Healy, "Clinton Vows Middle Class Will Not Be 'Invisible' to Her," *The New York Times*, March 11, 2007, www.nyt.com.

13. Quoted in Alec MacGillis, "Obama Says He, Too, Is a Poverty Fighter," *The Washington Post*, July 19, 2007, p. 4A.

14. Jackie Calmes, "Edwards's Theme: U.S. Poverty," *The Wall Street Journal Online*, Dec. 28, 2006.

15. Edward Luce, "Bloomberg urges US to extend anti-poverty scheme," *FT.com* (*Financial Times*), Aug. 29, 2007.

16. "McDermott Announces Hearing on Proposals for Reducing Poverty," press release, House Ways and Means Subcommittee on Income Security and Family Support, April 26, 2007.

17. Mike Dorning, "Will Poverty Make Political Comeback?" *Chicago Tribune*, June 3, 2007, p. 4.

18. Gallup Poll, June 11-14, 2007.

19. Jon Cohen, "Despite Focus on Poverty, Edwards Trails Among the Poor," *The Washington Post*, July 11, 2007, p. 7A.

20. Testimony before House Committee on Ways and Means, "Hearing on the Economic and Societal Costs of Poverty," Jan. 24, 2007.

21. Steven H. Woolf, Robert E. Johnson and H. Jack Geiger, "The Rising Prevalence of Severe Poverty in America: A Growing Threat to Public Health," *American Journal of Preventive Medicine*, Vol. 31, Issue 4, October 2006, p. 332.

22. Quoted in "Statement of Child Welfare League of America," House Ways and Means Subcommittee on Income Security and Family Support, "Hearing on Economic Opportunity and Poverty in America," Feb. 13, 2007. According to the statement, Conley's comment came in an ABC television profile of poverty in Camden, N.J., broadcast in January 2007.

23. Testimony before House Ways and Means Subcommittee on Income Security and Family Support, Feb. 13, 2007. Berube said concentrated poverty is defined by Paul Jargowsky of the University of Texas-Dallas as neighborhoods where at least 40 percent of individuals live below the poverty line.

24. Pugh, *op. cit.*

25. Nell McNamara and Doug Schenkelberg, *Extreme Poverty & Human Rights: A Primer* (2007),

Mid-America Institute on Poverty of Heartland Alliance for Human Needs & Human Rights. For the Bellevue data, the report cites Pennsylvania State University, "Poverty in America (n.d.) Living Wage Calculator," retrieved Nov. 15, 2006, from www.livingwage.geog.psu.edu/.

26. Pugh, *op. cit.*

27. Testimony before House Ways and Means Subcommittee on Income Security and Family Support, Feb. 13, 2007.

28. Woolf, *et al.*, *op. cit.*

29. Peter Katel, "Minimum Wage," *CQ Researcher*, Dec. 16, 2005, pp. 1053-1076.

30. Sarah Glazer, "Welfare Reform," *CQ Researcher*, Aug. 3, 2001, pp. 601-632.

31. Dan Froomkin, "Welfare's Changing Face," www.Washingtonpost.com/wp-srv/politics/special/welfare/welfare.htm, updated July 23, 1998.

32. Ron Haskins, "Welfare Check," *The Wall Street Journal*, July 27, 2006, accessed at www.brookings.edu.

33. "Interview: Welfare Reform, 10 Years Later," *The Examiner*, Aug. 24, 2006, accessed at www.brookings.edu.

34. Sharon Parrott and Arloc Sherman, "TANF at 10: Program Results are More Mixed Than Often Understood," Center on Budget and Policy Priorities, Aug. 17, 2006.

35. Wisconsin Council on Children & Families, "Wisconsin Ranks First in Growth in Poverty: Census Bureau Reports," press release, Aug. 30, 2005. See also testimony of Richard Schlimm, House Ways and Means Committee, "Hearing on the Economic and Societal Costs of Poverty," Jan. 24, 2007.

36. Testimony before House Subcommittee on Income Security and Family Support, Feb. 13, 2007.

37. Lawrence Mead, "And Now, 'Welfare Reform' for Men," *The Washington Post*, March 20, 2007, p. 19A.

38. Michael D. Tanner, "More Welfare, More Poverty," *The Monitor* (McAllen, Texas), Sept. 8, 2006.

39. Proceedings of the Virginia Assembly, 1619.

40. Henry George, "Progress and Poverty," first printed in 1879. Quoted in H. B. Shaffer, "Persistence of Poverty," *Editorial Research Reports*, Feb. 5, 1964, available at *CQ Researcher Plus Archive*, www.cqpress.com.

41. Gordon M. Fisher, "From Hunter to Orshansky: An Overview of (Unofficial) Poverty Lines in the United States from 1904 to 1965-Summary, March 1994, retrieved at http://aspe.hhs.gov/poverty/papers/htrssmiv.htm.

42. *CQ Researcher*, *op. cit.*

43. Michael Harrington, *The Other America: Poverty in the United States* (1962), pp. 14-15.

44. U.S. Census data show the poverty rate for individuals was 22.2 percent in 1960; 21.9 percent in 1961; 21 percent in 1962; 19.5 percent in 1963; and 19 percent in 1964. For families the rate ranged from 20.7 percent to 17.4 percent in that period.

45. See H. B. Shaffer, "Status of War on Poverty," in *Editorial Research Reports*, Jan. 25, 1967, available at *CQ Researcher Plus Archive*, www.cqpress.com.

46. Marcia Clemmitt, "Evaluating Head Start," *CQ Researcher*, Aug. 26, 2005, pp. 685-708.

47. Sheldon H. Danziger and Robert H. Haveman, eds., *Understanding Poverty* (2001), Russell Sage Foundation and Harvard University Press, pp. 4 and 5.

48. Peter Edelman, "The Worst Thing Bill Clinton Has Done," *The Atlantic Monthly*, March 1997.

49. Jeff Jacoby, "Wefare Reform Success," *The Boston Globe*, Sept. 13, 2006, p. 9A.

50. Sheldon H. Danziger, "Fighting Poverty Revisited: What did researchers know 40 years ago? What do we know today?," *Focus*, University of Wisconsin-Madison, Institute for Research on Poverty, Spring-Summer 2007, p. 3.

51. Lyndon B. Johnson, "Annual Message to Congress on the State of the Union," Jan. 8, 1964.

52. MacGillis, *op. cit.*

53. E.J. Dionne Jr., "Making the Poor Visible," *The Washington Post*, July 20, 2007, p. A19.

54. Mary H. Cooper, "Income Inequality," *CQ Researcher*, April 17, 1998, pp. 337-360.

55. www.mittromney.com.

56. Mark Greenberg, Indivar Dutta-Gupta and Elisa Minoff, "From Poverty to Prosperity: A National Strategy to Cut Poverty in Half," Center for American Progress, April 2007, www.americanprogress.org/issues/2007/04/poverty_report.html.

57. Ron Haskins and Isabel V. Sawhill, "Attacking Poverty and Inequality," Brookings Institution, Opportunity 08, in partnership with ABC News, February 2007, www.opportunity08.org/Issues/OurSociety/31/r1/Default.aspx.

58. Coalition on Human Needs, "Nearly 900 Organizations Sign Letter to Congress in Support of Expanding Tax Credits for the Poor," May 25, 2007, www.chn.org. The letter, dated May 24, 2007, was accessed at www.chn.org/pdf/2007/ctceitcletter.pdf.

59. Alan Berube, "Using the Earned Income Tax Credit to Stimulate Local Economies," Brookings Institution, www.brookings.org.

60. Adriel Bettelheim, "The Social Side of Tax Breaks," *CQ Weekly*, Feb. 5, 2007.

61. *Ibid.*

62. Diane Cardwell, "City to Reward Poor for Doing Right Thing," *The New York Times*, March 30, 2007, p. 1B.

63. The bill is AB 1118.

64. David MacDonald, communications director, Connecticut Association for Community Action, letter to the editor of the *Hartford Courant*, June 27, 2007, p. 8A.

65. Clea Benson, "States Scramble to Adapt To New Welfare Rules," *CQ Weekly*, June 25, 2007, p. 1907.

66. *Ibid.*

67. *Ibid.*

68. *Ibid.*

69. "Income, Poverty and Health Insurance Coverage in the United States: 2009," U.S. Census Bureau, September 2010, www.census.gov/prod/2010pubs/p60-238.pdf, p. 14.

70. *Ibid.*

71. Elizabeth Kneebone and Emily Garr, "The Landscape of Recession: Unemployment and Safety Net Services Across Urban and Suburban America,"
Brookings Metropolitan Policy Program, March 2010, www.brookings.edu/papers/2010/0330_recession_kneebone.aspx, p. 1.

72. Emily Garr, The Landscape of Recession: Unemployment and Safety Net Services Across Urban and Suburban America, Brookings Metropolitan Policy Program, March 2011, www.brookings.edu/papers/2011/0331_recession_garr.aspx, p. 1.

73. *Ibid.*, p. 7.

74. Kneebone and Garr, *op. cit.*, p. 9.

75. "Income, Poverty and Health Insurance in the United States," *op. cit.*, p. 19.

76. Julia B. Isaacs, "Child Poverty During the Great Recession: Predicting State Child Poverty Rates for 2010," Brookings/First Focus, January 2011, www.brookings.edu/~/media/Files/rc/papers/2010/1209_child_poverty_isaacs/1209_child_poverty_isaacs.pdf.

77. Elizabeth Kneebone, "The Great Recession and Poverty in Metropolitan America," Brookings Metropolitan Poverty Program, October 2010, www.brookings.edu/papers/2010/1007_suburban_poverty_acs_kneebone.aspx, p. 2.

78. Arloc Sherman, "Despite Deep Recession and High Unemployment, Government Efforts — Including the Recovery Act — Prevented Poverty from Rising in 2009, New Census Data Show," Center on Budget and Policy Priorities, Jan. 5, 2011, www.cbpp.org/files/1-5-11pov.pdf.

79. *Ibid.*

80. John Gramlich, "Missouri Next to Cut Jobless Benefits," *Stateline*, April 1, 2011, http://live.stateline.org/live/details/story?contentId=564274.

81. Pamela M. Prah, "States Weigh Cuts to Earned Income Tax," *Stateline*, March 28, 2011, www.stateline.org/live/details/story?contentId=562270.

82. Quoted in *ibid.*

83. Quoted in *ibid.*

84. William W. Beach and Patrick D. Tyrrell, "The 2010 Index of Dependence on Government," Heritage Foundation, Oct. 14, 2010, http://thf_media.s3.amazonaws.com/2010/pdf/CDA_10-08.pdf.

85. *Ibid.*

BIBLIOGRAPHY

Books

Danziger, Sheldon H., and Robert H. Haveman, eds., *Understanding Poverty*, **Russell Sage Foundation and Harvard University Press**, 2001.
Writings on domestic poverty range from the evolution of anti-poverty programs to health policy for the poor. Danziger is a professor of social work and public policy at the University of Michigan, Haveman, a professor of economics and public affairs at the University of Wisconsin, Madison.

DeParle, Jason, *American Dream: Three Women, Ten Kids, and a Nation's Drive to End Welfare*, **Viking Adult**, 2004.
A reporter looks at the effort to overhaul the American welfare system through the lives of three former welfare mothers.

Edwards, John, Marion Crain and Arne L. Kalleberg, eds., *Ending Poverty in America*, **New Press**, 2007.
Co-edited and with a conclusion by Democratic presidential candidate Edwards, this collection of articles reflects a progressive economic agenda.

Haskins, Ron, *Work Over Welfare: The Inside Story of the 1996 Welfare Reform Law*, **Brookings Institution Press**, 2006.
A former Republican committee staffer and a chief architect of welfare reform, Haskins tells the story of the political debates leading up to the historic welfare overhaul.

Articles

Bai, Matt, "The Poverty Platform," *New York Times Magazine*, June 10, 2007.
Taking a close look at presidential candidate John Edwards' focus on the poor, Bai says "the main economic debate in Democratic Washington" focuses on "the tools of economic policy — taxes, trade, welfare — and how to use them."

Dorning, Mike, "Will Poverty Make Political Comeback?" *Chicago Tribune*, June 3, 2007.
Since the 1960s, Dorning notes, "leading presidential candidates generally have not focused on the plight of the poor as a central issue."

Reports and Studies

Congressional Budget Office, "Changes in the Economic Resources of Low-Income Households with Children," May 2007.
This study charts income changes among the poor from the early 1990s.

Children's Defense Fund, "The State of America's Children 2005."
Marian Wright Edelman, founder and president of the Children's Defense Fund, writes, "Far less wealthy industrialized countries have committed to end child poverty, while the United States is sliding backwards."

Greenberg, Mark, Indivar Dutta-Gupta and Elisa Minoff, "From Poverty to Prosperity: A National Strategy to Cut Poverty in Half," *Center for American Progress*, April 2007.
The think tank's Task Force on Poverty says the United States should set a goal of halving poverty over the next decade.

Harrison, David, and Bob Watrus, "On Getting Out–and Staying Out–of Poverty: The Complex Causes of and Responses to Poverty in the Northwest," *Northwest Area Foundation*, 2004.
An estimated 2 million people live in poverty in the Northwest, more than 900,000 of them in severe poverty.

McNamara, Nell, and Doug Schenkelberg, "Extreme Poverty & Human Rights: A Primer," *Heartland Alliance for Human Needs & Human Rights*, 2007.
A guidebook explains how human rights advocacy can combat both global and domestic poverty.

Meyer, Bruce D., and James X. Sullivan, "Three Decades of Consumption and Income Poverty," *National Poverty Center Working Paper Series*, September 2006.
The study examines poverty measurement in the United States from 1972 through 2004 and how poverty rates have changed over the years.

Rector, Robert, "How Poor Are America's Poor? Examining the 'Plague' of Poverty in America," *Heritage Foundation*, Aug. 27, 2007.
A senior research fellow at the conservative think tank writes that " 'the plague' of American poverty might not

be as 'terrible' or 'incredible' as candidate [John] Edwards contends."

Toldson, Ivory A., and Elsie L. Scott, "Poverty, Race and Policy," *Congressional Black Caucus Foundation*, 2006.
The four-part report explores affordable-housing policy, wealth-accumulation needs and strategies for reducing poverty and unemployment.

Woolf, Steven H., Robert E. Johnson and H. Jack Geiger, "The Rising Prevalence of Severe Poverty in America: A Growing Threat to Public Health," *American Journal of Preventive Medicine*, October 2006.
Woolf, a professor of family medicine, epidemiology and community health at Virginia Commonwealth University and lead author of this study, says the growth in severe poverty and other trends "have disturbing implications for society and public health."

For More Information

Center for American Progress, 1333 H St., N.W., 10th Floor, Washington, DC 20005; (202) 682-1611; www.americanprogress.org. A liberal think tank that issued a report and recommendations on poverty this year.

Coalition on Human Needs, 1120 Connecticut Ave., N.W., Suite 910, Washington, DC 20036; (202) 223-2532; www.chn.org. An alliance of organizations that promote policies to help low-income people and others in need.

Economic Policy Institute, 1333 H St., N.W., Suite 300, East Tower, Washington, DC 20005-4707; (202) 775-8810; www.epi.org. A think tank that studies policies related to the economy, work and the interests of low- and middle-income people.

Heritage Foundation, 214 Massachusetts Ave., N.E., Washington, DC 20002-4999; (202) 546-4400; www.heritage.org. A conservative think tank that studies poverty and other public-policy issues.

Institute for Research on Poverty, University of Wisconsin-Madison, 1180 Observatory Dr., 3412 Social Science Building, Madison, WI 53706-1393; (608) 262-6358; www.irp.wisc.edu. Studies the causes and consequences of poverty.

Mid-America Institute on Poverty, 4411 North Ravenswood Ave., Chicago, Ill. 60640; (773) 336-6084; www.hearatlan

dalliance.org. A research arm of Heartland Alliance, which provides services for low-income individuals.

National Community Action Foundation, 810 First St., N.E., Suite 530, Washington, DC 20002; (202) 842-2092; www.ncaf.org. Advocates for the nation's community-action agencies.

Step Up, Savannah's Poverty Reduction Initiative, 101 East Bay St., Savannah, GA 31401; (912) 644-6420; www.stepupsavannah.org. A coalition of more than 80 local business, government and nonprofit organizations seeking to reduce poverty.

U.S. Census Bureau, 4600 Silver Hill Road, Suitland, MD 20746; www.census.gov. Maintains extensive recent and historical data on poverty and demographics.

University of North Carolina Center on Poverty, Work and Opportunity, UNC School of Law, Van Heck-Wettach Hall, 100 Ridge Road, CB#3380, Chapel Hill, N.C. 27599-3380; (919) 962-5106; www.law.unc.edu/centers/poverty/default.aspx. A national forum for scholars, policymakers and others interested in poverty, established by presidential candidate John Edwards.

Urban Institute, 2100 M St., N.W., Washington, DC 20037; (202) 833-7200; www.urban.org. Studies welfare and low-income families among a range of issues.

11

Immigration Conflict

Kenneth Jost

Arizona residents rally in Phoenix on July 31, 2010, in support of the state's hard-hitting immigration law, which gives police new responsibilities to look for immigration law violators. Five states last year followed Arizona's lead. The U.S. Supreme Court will hear arguments on the disputed Arizona measure on April 25.

From *CQ Researcher*,
March 9, 2012.

Micky Hammon minced no words when he urged his fellow Alabama legislators to enact what would become the toughest of a batch of new state laws cracking down on illegal immigrants. "This bill is designed to make it difficult for them to live here so they will deport themselves," Hammon, leader of the Alabama House of Representatives' Republican majority, said during the April 5, 2011, debate on the bill.[1]

Immigrant-rights groups say the law, which took effect Sept. 28 after partly surviving a court challenge, is as tough as Hammon hoped — and more. "It's been pretty devastating," says Mary Bauer, legal director of the Southern Poverty Law Center in Montgomery, Alabama's capital. "Tens of thousands of people have left, and the people who remain are completely terrorized by this law."

Among other provisions, Alabama's law requires state and local law enforcement officers to determine the immigration status of anyone arrested, detained or stopped if there is a "reasonable suspicion" that the person is an alien "unlawfully present" in the United States. Failure to carry alien-registration papers is made a state crime, punishable by up to 30 days in jail for a first offense.

Alabama, with an estimated 120,000 unlawful aliens living within its borders as of 2010, was one of five states that last year followed Arizona's lead a year earlier in giving police new responsibilities to look for immigration law violators.* Republican-controlled legislatures in each of the states said they were forced to

* The others were Utah, Indiana, Georgia and South Carolina.

West Has Highest Share of Unlawful Aliens

Undocumented immigrants comprise at least 6 percent of the population of Arizona, California, Nevada and Texas and at least 3.8 percent of the population of New Mexico, Oregon and Utah. Unlawful immigrants also make up sizable percentages of several other states' populations, including New Jersey and Florida. The nationwide average is 3.7 percent.

Unauthorized Immigrants as a Share of State Population, 2010

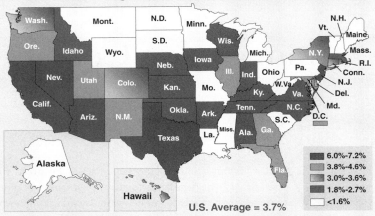

Legend:
- 6.0%-7.2%
- 3.8%-4.6%
- 3.0%-3.6%
- 1.8%-2.7%
- <1.6%

U.S. Average = 3.7%

Source: Jeffrey Passel and D'Vera Cohn, "Unauthorized Immigrant Population: National and State Trends, 2010," Pew Research Center, February 2011, p. 29, www.pewhispanic.org/files/reports/133.pdf

act because the federal government was not doing enough to control illegal immigration at the border or in U.S. workplaces. Opponents warned the laws risked profiling Latinos, including U.S. citizens and aliens with legal status.

All six of the laws are being challenged in federal court, with the "stop and check" provisions blocked except in Alabama's case. In the most important case, the Arizona measure is scheduled to be argued before the U.S. Supreme Court on April 25 after a federal appeals court struck some of the law enforcement provisions as interfering with federal immigration policy.[2]

Alabama's law includes a unique provision that prohibits unlawful aliens from entering into any "business transaction" with state or local governments. Some public utilities in the state interpreted the provision to require proof of immigration status for water or electricity service. Until a federal judge's injunction on Nov. 23, some counties were applying the law to prevent unlawful

immigrants from renewing permits for mobile homes.[3]

Once the law went into effect, school attendance by Latino youngsters dropped measurably in response to a provision — later blocked — requiring school officials to ascertain families' immigration status. The fear of deportation also led many immigrants in Alabama to seek help in preparing power-of-attorney documents to make sure their children would be taken care of in case the parents were deported, according to Isabel Rubio, executive director of the Hispanic Interest Coalition of Alabama. "You have to understand the sheer terror that people fear," Rubio says.

The law is having a palpable effect on the state's economy as well, according to agriculture and business groups. With fewer migrant workers, "some farmers have planted not as much or not planted at all," says Jeff Helms, spokesman for the Alabama Farmers Federation. Jay Reed, president of Associated Builders and Contractors of Alabama, says it has been harder to find construction workers as well.

Reed, co-chair of the multi-industry coalition Alabama Employers for Immigration Reform, wants to soften provisions that threaten employers with severe penalties, including the loss of operating licenses, for hiring undocumented workers. He and other business leaders also worry about the perception of the law outside the state's borders. "Some of our board members have expressed concern about our state's image and the effect on economic-development legislation," Reed says.

Reed says the state's Republican governor, Robert Bentley, and leaders in the GOP-controlled legislature are open to some changes in the law. But the two chief sponsors, Hammon and state Sen. Scott Beason, are both batting down any suggestions that the law will be repealed or its law enforcement measures softened.

"We are not going to weaken the law," Hammon told reporters on Feb. 14 as hundreds of opponents of the measure demonstrated outside the State House in Montgomery. "We are not going to repeal any section of the law."[4]

On the surface, Alabama seems an improbable state to take a leading role in the newest outbreak of nativist concern about immigration and immigrants. Alabama's unauthorized immigrant population has increased nearly fivefold since 2000, but the state still ranks relatively low in the proportion of unauthorized immigrants in the population and in the state's workforce.

Alabama's estimated 120,000 unauthorized immigrants comprise about 2.5 percent of the state's total population. Nationwide, the estimated 11.8 million unauthorized immigrants represent about 3.7 percent of the population. Alabama's estimated 95,000 unauthorized immigrants with jobs represent about 4.2 percent of the workforce. Nationwide, 8 million undocumented workers account for about 5.2 percent of the national workforce.[5]

Nationwide, the spike in anti-immigrant sentiment is also somewhat out of synch with current conditions. Experts and advocates on both sides of the immigration issues agree that the total unauthorized immigrant population has fallen somewhat from its peak in 2007, mainly because the struggling U.S. economy offers fewer jobs to lure incoming migrant workers.

"The inflow of illegals has slowed somewhat," says Mark Krikorian, executive director of the Center for Immigration Studies (CIS) in Washington. The center describes its stance as "low-immigration, pro-immigrant."[6]

Jobs were a major focus of the debate that led to Alabama's passage of the new law. "This is a jobs bill," Beason said as the measure, known as HB 56, reached final passage in June. "We have a problem with an illegal workforce that displaces Alabama workers. We need to put those people back to work."[7]

Today, Beason, running against an incumbent congressman for the U.S. House seat in the Birmingham area, credits the law with helping Alabama lower its

Americans Want Less Immigration

More than 40 percent of Americans say they favor a lower level of immigration, reflecting a view that has prevailed over most of the past half-century. About one in six want immigration to increase, while about one-third favor the current level.

Should immigration be kept at its present level, increased or decreased?

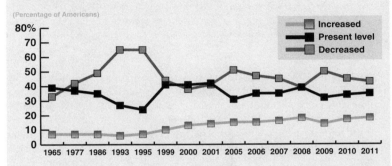

(Percentage of Americans)

Sources: Jeffrey M. Jones, "Americans' Views on Immigration Holding Steady," Gallup, June 2011, www.gallup.com/poll/148154/americans-views-immigration-holding-steady.aspx; Roger Daniels, Guarding the Golden Door, Hill and Wang Press, December 2004, p. 233

unemployment rate from 9.8 percent in September to 8.1 percent in December. "I promised that the anti-illegal immigration law would open up thousands of jobs for Alabamians, and it has done that," Beason said in a Jan. 26 statement.

A University of Alabama economist, however, doubts the law's claimed effect on unemployment. Samuel Addy, director of the university's Center for Business and Economic Research in Tuscaloosa, notes that unemployment actually has increased, rather than declined, in the four sectors in the state viewed as most dependent on immigrant labor: agriculture, construction, accommodation and food and drinking places.[8]

In a nine-page study released in January, Addy contends instead that the immigration law is likely to hurt the state's economy overall. After assuming that 40,000 to 80,000 workers leave the state, Addy calculated that the law could reduce the state's gross domestic product by $2.3 billion to $10.8 billion. State income and sales taxes could take a $56.7 million to $265.4 million hit, Addy projected, while local sales tax revenue could decline by $20.0 million to $93.1 million. Hammon dismissed the report as "baloney."[9]

Immigration Law Basics

Even experts find it confusing.

Immigrating legally to the United States is difficult at best for those who fit into categories defined in mind-numbing detail by federal law and impossible for those who do not. Here is a primer on a body of law that is complex and confusing even to immigration experts, and all the more so for would-be Americans.

The Immigration and Nationality Act — sets an overall limit of 675,000 permanent immigrants each year. The limit does not apply to spouses, unmarried minor children or parents of U.S. citizens, but the sponsoring U.S. citizen must have an income above the U.S. poverty level and promise to support family members brought to the United States.

Who gets visas — Out of the 675,000 quota, 480,000 visas are made available under family-preference rules, and up to 140,000 are allocated for employment-related preferences. Unused employment-related visas may be reallocated to the family-preference system.

The family-sponsored visas are allocated according to a preference system with numerical limits for each category. Unmarried adult children of U.S. citizens are in the first category, followed, in this order, by spouses and minor children of lawful permanent residents; unmarried adult children of lawful permanent residents; married adult children of U.S. citizens; and brothers and sisters of U.S. citizens. No other relatives qualify for a family preference. Again, the sponsor must meet financial and support requirements.

Visa categories —The employment-based preference system also sets up ranked, capped categories for would-be immigrants. The highest preference is given to "persons of extraordinary ability" in the arts, science, education, business or athletics; professors and researchers; and some multinational executives. Other categories follow in this order: persons with professional degrees or "exceptional" abilities in arts, science or business; workers with skills that are in short supply and some "unskilled" workers for jobs not temporary or seasonal; certain "special immigrants," including religious workers; and, finally, persons who will invest at least $500,000 in a job-creating enterprise that employs at least 10 full-time workers.

In addition to the numerical limits, the law sets a cap of 7 percent of the quota for immigrants from any single country. The limit in effect prevents any immigrant group from dominating immigration patterns.

Refugees — Separately, Congress and the president each year set an annual limit for the number of refugees who can be admitted based on an inability to return to their home country because of a fear of persecution. Currently, the overall ceiling is 76,000. The law also allows an unlimited number of persons already in the United States, or at a port of entry, to apply for asylum if they were persecuted or fear persecution in their home country. A total of 21,113 persons were granted asylum in fiscal 2010. Refugees and asylees are eligible to become lawful permanent residents after one year.

Debate over the rules — An immigrant who gets through this maze and gains the coveted "green card" for lawful permanent residents is eligible to apply for U.S. citizenship after five years (three years for the spouse of a U.S. citizen). An applicant must be age 18 or over and meet other requirements, including passing English and U.S. history and civics exams. About 675,000 new citizens were naturalized in 2010, down from the peak of slightly more than 1 million in the pre-recession year of 2008.

Applying for citizenship — Immigration advocates say the quotas are too low, the rules too restrictive and the waiting periods for qualified applicants too long. Low-immigration groups say the record level of legal and illegal immigration over the past decade shows the need to lower the quotas and limit the family-reunification rules.

— Kenneth Jost

Five months after it took effect, however, the law's impact may be ebbing. Police appear not to have enforced the law vigorously, perhaps stung by the nationwide embarrassment when a visiting Mercedes-Benz executive from Germany carrying only a German identification card was held after a traffic stop until he could retrieve his passport. With police enforcement lagging, some of the immigrants who left appear to be coming back. "Some people have returned," Rubio says.[10]

Meanwhile, attorneys for the Obama administration and the state were preparing for arguments on March 1 before the federal appeals court in Atlanta in the government's suit challenging the state law on grounds of federal pre-emption, the doctrine used to nullify state laws that conflict with U.S. laws and policies. The Hispanic Interest Coalition had challenged the law on broader grounds in an earlier suit, represented by the American Civil Liberties Union and other national groups.

In a massive, 115-page ruling, U.S. District Court Judge Sharon Blackburn upheld major parts of the law on Sept. 28 and then allowed the upheld parts to go into effect even as the government and civil rights groups appealed. Blackburn blocked half a dozen provisions on pre-emption grounds but found no congressional intent to prevent states from checking the immigration status of suspected unlawful aliens.[11]

With the legal challenges continuing, the political debates over immigration are intensifying. Republican presidential candidates generally agree on criticizing the Obama administration for failing to control illegal immigration even though the administration has increased the number of immigrants deported to their home countries. The Republican hopefuls disagree among themselves on the steps to deal with the problem.

For his part, Obama concedes that Congress will not approve a broad immigration overhaul in this election year. But he used his State of the Union speech to call for passage of a bill — the so-called DREAM Act — to allow legal status for some immigrants who have served in the U.S. military or completed college.

As the immigration debates continue, here are some of the major questions being considered:

Major State Immigration Laws in Court

Five states have followed Arizona's lead in giving state and local police a role in enforcing federal immigration law. With some variations, the laws authorize or require police after an arrest, detention or stop to determine the person's immigration status if he or she is reasonably suspected of being unlawfully in the United States. In legal challenges, federal courts have blocked major parts of five of the laws; the Supreme Court is set to hear arguments on April 25 in Arizona's effort to reinstate the blocked portions of its law.

State	Bill, date signed	Legal challenge
Arizona	S.B. 1070: April 23, 2010	*United States v. Arizona* Major parts enjoined; pending at Supreme Court
Utah	H.B. 497: March 15, 2011	*Utah Coalition of La Raza v. Herbert* Major parts blocked; suit on hold pending Supreme Court ruling in Arizona case
Indiana	SB 590: May 10, 2011	*Buquer v. City of Indianapolis* Major parts blocked; suit on hold pending Supreme Court ruling in Arizona case
Georgia	HB 87: May 13, 2011	*Georgia Latino Alliance v. Deal* Major parts blocked; on hold at 11th Circuit
Alabama	HB 56: June 9, 2011	*United States v. Alabama* Major parts upheld; on hold at 11th Circuit
South Carolina	S20: June 27, 2011	*United States v. South Carolina* Major parts blocked; suit on hold pending Supreme Court ruling in Arizona case

Sources: National Conference of State Legislatures, http://www.ncsl.org/issues-research/immig/omnibus-immigration-legislation.aspx; American Civil Liberties Union; news coverage.

Is illegal immigration an urgent national problem?

As the anti-illegal immigration bill HB 56 was being signed into law, Alabama's Republican Party chairman depicted the measure as needed to protect the state's taxpayers and the state's treasury. "Illegal immigrants have become a drain on our state resources and a strain on our taxpaying, law-abiding citizens," Bill Armistead declared as Republican governor Bentley signed it into law on June 9, 2011.[12]

Today, Republican officials continue to defend the law in economic terms. "Unemployment was sky high, especially in areas where there's high concentration of these undocumented workers," says Shana Kluck, the party's spokeswoman. Kluck also points to the cost on

Unlawful Immigration High Despite Dip

Despite a dip beginning in 2007, an estimated 11.2 million unauthorized immigrants live in the United States, one-third more than a decade ago (top graph). An estimated 8 million are in the civilian labor force, a 45 percent increase since 2000 (bottom graph).

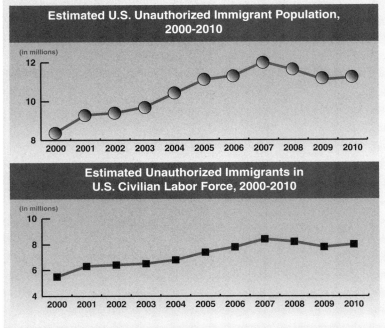

Source: Jeffrey Passel and D'Vera Cohn, "Unauthorized Immigrant Population: National and State Trends, 2010," Pew Research Center, February 2011, pp. 1, 17, www.pewhispanic.org/files/reports/133.pdf

everyone is left scrambling for crumbs at the bottom."

"The longer this economic doldrum continues, the more likely you are to see some real pushback on immigration levels as such, not just illegal immigration," says Krikorian with the low-immigration group Center for Immigration Studies. The group's research director, Steven Camarota, said if illegal immigrants are forced to go back to their home countries, there is "an ample supply of idle workers" to take the jobs freed up.[13]

Pro-immigration groups say their opponents exaggerate the costs and all but ignore the benefits of immigrant labor. "They never take into account the contributions that undocumented immigrants make," says Mary Giovagnoli, director of the American Immigration Council's Immigration Policy Center.

"We've had an economy that depends on immigration," says Ali Noorani, executive director of the National Immigration Forum. "It would be an economic and social disaster for 11 million people to pick up and leave."

Madeleine Sumption, a senior labor market analyst with the pro-immigration Migration Policy Institute in Washington, acknowledges that immigration may have what she calls a "relatively small" impact on employment and wages for citizen workers. But the costs are more than offset, she says, by the benefits to employers, consumers and the overall economy.

The benefits can be seen particularly in sectors that employ large numbers of immigrants, according to Sumption. "The United States has a large agriculture industry," she says. "Without immigration labor, it would almost certainly not be possible to produce the same volume of food in the country." The health care industry also employs a high number of immigrants, especially in low-end jobs, such as home-health aides and hospital orderlies. "These are jobs for which there is

public treasuries. "The public-assistance budgets were bursting at the seams," she says. "That's why HB 56 was necessary."

Nationally, groups favoring tighter immigration controls make similar arguments about immigrants' economic impact, especially on jobs and wages for citizen workers. "We need to slow down immigration," says Dan Stein, president of the Federation for American Immigration Reform (FAIR), pointing to the current high levels of unemployment and underemployment.

"Immigration helps to decimate the bargaining leverage of the American worker," Stein continues. "If you use a form of labor recruitment that bids down the cost of labor, that leads you to a society where a small number are very, very rich, there's nobody in the middle, and a growing demand and an expectation of an even more rapidly growing demand in the future," Sumption says.

In Alabama, Rubio with the Hispanic coalition and the leaders of the agriculture and construction groups all discount Camarota's contention that citizen workers are available to take the jobs currently being filled by immigrants. "We did not have a tomato crop [last] summer because the immigrants who pick that crop weren't there," Rubio says. "This is hard work, and many people don't want to do it."

Reed, president of the state's builders and contractors' organization, says construction companies similarly cannot find enough workers among the citizen labor force. "Traditionally, in our recruitment efforts we have unfortunately not found those that are unemployed are ready and willing to perform these kinds of jobs that require hard labor in extreme weather conditions," Helms says.

The claimed costs and benefits from immigration for public treasuries represent similarly contentious issues. Low- or anti-immigration groups emphasize the costs in government services, especially education and medical care. Pro-immigration groups point to the taxes that even unlawful aliens pay and the limits on some government benefits under federal and state laws. In an independent evaluation of the issue, the nonpartisan Congressional Budget Office in 2007 found a net cost to state and local governments but called the impact "most likely modest."[14]

The cost-benefit debates are more volatile in stressed economic times, according to David Gerber, a professor of history at the University of Buffalo and author of a primer on immigration. "People get angry when they feel that immigrants are competing for jobs of people in the United States or when they feel that immigrants are getting access to social benefits that the majority is paying for," Gerber says. "In harder times, it makes people angrier than in times of prosperity."[15]

Even so, David Coates, a professor at Wake Forest University in Winston-Salem, N.C., and co-editor of a book on immigration issues, notes that fewer undocumented workers are entering the United States now than in the peak year of 2007, and the Obama administration has been deporting unlawful aliens in significantly greater numbers than previous administrations. Asked whether illegal immigration should be less of an issue for

Republican Alabama Gov. Robert Bentley addresses lawmakers at the state capitol on June 9, 2011, before signing the state's new immigration law. Republican cosponsors of the law, Sen. Scott Beason (left), and state Rep. Micky Hammon (right), both oppose softening or repealing the law. But state business interests want to ease provisions that threaten employers with severe penalties for hiring undocumented workers. They also worry about the perception of the law outside the state.

state legislators and national politicians, Coates replies simply: "Yes, in terms of the numbers."

Should state and local police enforce immigration laws?

Alabama's HB 56 was stuffed with more provisions for state and local governments to crack down on illegal immigrants than the Arizona law that inspired it or any of the copy-cat laws passed in four other states. Along with the stop-and-check section, the law includes provisions making it a state crime for an unauthorized alien to apply for work and barring unauthorized aliens from court enforcement of any contracts. Another provision made it illegal to conceal, harbor or rent to an illegal immigrant or even to stop in a roadway to hire workers.

Opponents harshly criticized the enforcement provisions as they were signed into law. "It turns Alabama into a police state where anyone could be required to show their citizenship papers," said Cecillia Wang, director of the ACLU's Immigrant Rights Project. Noorani, with the National Immigration Forum, called the law "a radical departure from the concepts of fairness and equal treatment under the law," adding, "It makes it a crime, quite literally, to give immigrants a ride without checking their legal status."[16]

Today, even with the harboring provision and several others blocked from taking effect, opponents say the law is having the terrorizing effect that they had predicted on immigrants both legal and illegal as well as U.S. citizens of Hispanic background. "We've heard numerous accounts of people who have been stopped under very suspicious circumstances, while driving or even while walking on the street," says Justin Cox, an ACLU staff attorney in Atlanta working on the case challenging the law.

The law "has had the effect that it was intended to have," Cox says, "which was to make immigration status a pervasive issue in [immigrants'] everyday lives."

Supporters of the law are defending it, but without responding to specific criticisms. "We've seen an awful lot of illegal immigrants self-deport," House Majority Leader Hammon said as opponents rallied in Montgomery on Feb. 14. "We're also seeing Americans and legal immigrants taking these jobs."[17]

When questioned by a Montgomery television station about critical documentaries prepared for the progressive group Center for American Progress, Hammon declined to look at the films but attacked the filmmaker. "We don't need an activist director from California to come in here and tell us whether this law is good or not," Hammon said. "The people in Alabama can see it for themselves."[18]

Nationally, immigration hawks view the new state laws as unexceptionable. "They're helping the feds to enforce immigration laws," says Center for Immigration Studies executive director Krikorian. "The question is [whether] local police use immigration laws as one of the tools in their tool kit to help defend public safety."

"Every town is a border town, every state is a border state," Krikorian continues. "Immigration law has to be part of your approach, part of your strategy in dealing with some kind of a significant problem."

FAIR president Stein strongly objects to the Obama administration's legal challenges to the state laws. "It should be a massive, industrial-strength issue that the Obama administration" has attacked the laws on grounds of federal pre-emption. But Giovagnoli with the pro-immigration American Immigration Council says the state laws should be struck down. "Congress has established that immigration enforcement is a federal matter," she says. "The more states get into the mix, the more you create a real patchwork of laws that don't make sense together."

As Krikorian notes, federal law already provides for cooperative agreements between the federal government and state or local law enforcement agencies to enforce immigration laws. U.S. Immigration and Customs Enforcement (ICE), the successor agency to the Immigration and Naturalization Service, touts the so-called 287(g) program on its website as one of the agency's "top partnership initiatives." The program, authorized by an immigration law overhaul in 1996, permits the federal agency to delegate enforcement power to state or local law enforcement after officers have received training on federal immigration law.[19]

Pro-immigration groups say the training requirement distinguishes 287(g) programs from the broader roles being given state and local police by the new state laws. "State and local law enforcement officers are not trained to do this kind of work," says Cox. "Inevitably, they're going to rely on pernicious stereotypes about what an undocumented immigrant looks like." The result, Cox continues, "is a breakdown of trust between the immigrant community and law enforcement, which ultimately affects all of us. It undermines public safety."

Alabama Republicans, however, insist that the state law fulfills a 2010 campaign pledge that helped the GOP gain control of both houses of the state legislature and that it remains popular despite the criticisms and legal challenges. "We've definitely been criticized," party spokeswoman Kluck acknowledges, but she blames the criticisms on "misinformation." As for possible changes in the law, Hammon and other legislative leaders are guarding details until a bill with proposed revisions can be completed by late March.

Should Congress make it easier for illegal immigrants to become citizens?

With many Republican primary and caucus voters viewing illegal immigration as a major issue, presidential candidate and former Massachusetts Gov. Mitt Romney says he has a simple solution: Get undocumented immigrants to "self-deport" to their home countries and then get in the legal waiting line for U.S. citizenship. But one of his rivals for the Republican nomination, former House speaker Newt Gingrich, pushing stronger enforcement at the border, mocks Romney's belief that 11 million unlawful aliens will go back home voluntarily. Speaking to a Spanish-language television network in late January on the eve of the Florida presidential primary, Gingrich called Romney's plan "an Obama-level fantasy."[20]

Pro-immigration groups agree that Romney's stance is unrealistic. "It's a fantasy to think that people are going to self-deport," says the National Immigration Forum's Noorani. Unlike border-control advocates, however, Noorani and other pro-immigration advocates and experts say the solution is "a path to legal citizenship" for the undocumented.

"We need a functioning legal immigration system, a system that has the necessary legal channels for a person to immigrate here whether for a job or his family," Noorani says. "That doesn't exist here." Without "a solution," Noorani says, "the only ones who are winning are the crooked employer who is more than happy to exploit the undocumented, poor third-country worker."

Immigration hawks quickly denounce any broad legalization proposal as an "amnesty" that they say is neither workable nor deserved. "All amnesties attract future immigration," says the CIS's Krikorian. "All amnesties reward lawbreakers." As evidence, immigration critics point to the broad amnesty granted under the 1986 immigration act to some 3 million immigrants — and its evident failure within a matter of years to stem the flow of illegal immigrants from across the country's Southern borders.

As an alternative to broader proposals, pro-immigration groups are pushing narrower legislation that in its current form would grant conditional legal status to immigrants who came to the United States before age 16 and have lived in the United States for at least five years. The so-called DREAM Act — an acronym for the Development, Relief and Education for Alien Minors Act — had majority support in both chambers of the Democratic-controlled Congress in 2010 but failed to get a Senate floor vote in the face of Republican opposition.

The DREAM Act starts with the assumption that immigrants who came to the United States as children have grown up as Americans and are innocent of any intentional immigration violations. They would be eligible for a conditional permanent residency and could then earn a five-year period of temporary residency by completing two years in the U.S. military or two years in a four-year college or university.

"The intent of the DREAM Act is to provide legal status for individuals who are enlisting in our armed services or pursuing higher education," says Noorani. "Whether they came here at age 5 or 15, I think we only stand to benefit."

"It's a good way to show that if you provide legal status to folks like this, the world is not going to fall apart," says Giovagnoli with the American Immigration Council. "In fact, the country would be better off if these people were in the system."

Similar proposals have been introduced in Congress since 2001. Immigration hawks acknowledge the proposals' appeal and argue over details. "The concept that people who have been here from childhood, that it might be prudent to legalize people in that position, is a plausible one," says Krikorian. But, he adds, "As it exists, it is not a good piece of legislation."

As one change, Krikorian says the eligibility age should be lowered, perhaps to age 10 or below. "The reason they pick 16 is it legalizes more," he says. Paradoxically, Krikorian also says the bill is too narrow by allowing temporary residency only by joining the military or going to college. "What if you're not college material?" he asks.

Krikorian also dismisses the idea of absolving those who arrived as youngsters of any responsibility for immigration violations. "The parents . . . did know what they were doing," he says. The bill needs to be changed, he says, "to ensure that no parent would ever be able to benefit" under family-reunification rules.

Gingrich and some GOP lawmakers favor a narrower version of the DREAM Act that would extend legal status for serving in the military but not for going to college. Supporters oppose the narrower version. "If you read the bill carefully, it would actually allow a fewer number of immigrants to enlist in the military than the original," Noorani says. Krikorian also dismisses the alternative. He calls it "phony," adding that it would help "only a few thousand people a year."

The White House pushed hard for the bill in the Democratic-controlled Congress's lame-duck session in December 2010 but fell short in the Senate. Obama continues to speak out for the bill, most prominently in his State of the Union address. "[I]f election-year politics keeps Congress from acting on a comprehensive plan, let's at least agree to stop expelling responsible young people who want to staff our labs, start new businesses, defend this country," Obama said near the end of the Jan. 24 speech. "Send me a law that gives them the chance to earn their citizenship. I will sign it right away."[21]

BACKGROUND

Constant Ambivalence

The United States is a nation of immigrants that has been ambivalent toward immigration through most of its history. Immigrants are alternately celebrated as the source of diversity and criticized as agents of disunity. Immigrants were recruited to till the soil, build the cities and labor in the factories, but often criticized for taking jobs from and lowering wages for the citizen workforce. The federal government reflected popular sentiment in restricting immigration in the late 19th and early 20th century, only to draw later criticism for exclusionary policies. Today, the government is drawing criticism for liberalized policies adopted in the 1960s and for ineffective border enforcement from the 1980s on.[22]

African slaves were the first source of immigrant labor in America, but Congress banned importation of slaves in 1808. Otherwise, the United States maintained an open-door policy on immigration until the late 19th century. Europe's mid-century agricultural crisis drove waves of German and Irish peasants to the United States in the 1840s and '50s. Many were met by ethnic and anti-Catholic hostility, embodied in the first nativist political movement: the American or so-called Know-Nothing Party. The party carried one state in the 1856 presidential election and then faded from history.

Significant Chinese immigration began with the California Gold Rush of 1849 and increased with the post-Civil War push to complete the transcontinental railroad. Stark warnings of the "Yellow Peril" led to a series of restrictions at the federal level — most notably, the Chinese Exclusion Act of 1882, which suspended immigration of Chinese laborers and barred citizenship for those already in the United States. Significantly for present-day debates, efforts to deport those in the country or to seal the borders against new Chinese immigrants were no more than partly successful.[23]

Congress laid the basis for present-day immigration law and policy in a series of increasingly restrictive enactments from the 1890s through the early 1920s that coincided with the great waves of immigration from Europe, including regions previously unrepresented in the American polity. The Immigration Act of 1891 established the Bureau of Immigration, then under the Treasury Department, and provided for border inspections and deportation of unlawful aliens. Additional laws prescribed admission procedures, created categories of inadmissible immigrants and tightened the exclusion of immigrants from Asia.

The restrictive policies drew support from nativists worried about assimilation, pro-labor groups concerned about the impact on jobs and wages and progressive leaders fearful of the impact on the urban environment. The restrictions culminated in the passage of the first and second Quota Acts in 1921 and 1924, which established the first quantitative limitation on immigration (350,000, lowered to 150,000) and a national-origins system that favored immigrants from Northern and Western Europe. In reporting the bill in 1924, a House committee stated: "If the principle of liberty . . . is to endure, the basic strain of our population must be preserved."[24]

The Quota Acts' exception for Western Hemisphere immigrants combined with the unrest associated with the Mexican Revolution (1910-1929) to produce what Stanford historian Albert Camarillo calls "a tsunami" in immigration across the United States' Southern border. Camarillo says 1.5 million Mexicans — one-tenth of the country's population — relocated to the United States by the end of the 1930s.[25] The influx fueled ethnic prejudice embodied in the derogatory term "wetback" to refer to the Mexican immigrants, most of whom actually entered by crossing arid regions rather than fording the Rio Grande River.

During the Great Depression of the 1930s, the federal and state governments — concerned about the impact on jobs for Anglo workers — sent tens of thousands of Mexicans back to their home country, sometimes with force and little regard for due process. During World War II, however, the government worked with Mexico to establish the so-called bracero program to use temporary immigrant labor for agricultural work. The "temporary" program continued into the 1960s.

CHRONOLOGY

Before 1960 *Congress establishes immigration quotas.*

1920s Quota Act (1921), Johnson-Reed Act (1924) establish national-origins quota system, favoring Northern European immigrants over those from Southern Europe, elsewhere.

1952 McCarran-Walter Act retains national-origins system but adds small quotas for some Asian countries.

1960s *Congress opens door to immigration from outside Europe.*

1965 Immigration and Nationality Act of 1965 abolishes national-origins quota system dating from 1920s; allows dramatic increase in immigration from Central and South America, Asia.

1980s-1990s *Illegal immigration increases, becomes major public issue.*

1986 Immigration Reform and Control Act allows amnesty for many unlawful aliens, prohibits employers from employing undocumented workers; enforcement proves elusive.

1996 Illegal Immigration Reform and Immigrant Responsibility Act seeks to strengthen border security, streamline deportation proceedings; creates optional E-Verify system for employers to electronically check immigration status of workers and job applicants.

2000-Present *Illegal immigration increases; immigration reform falters in Congress; state laws to crack down on illegal immigration challenged in court.*

2001 Al Qaeda 9/11 attacks on U.S. soil underscore national security threat from failure to track potential terrorists entering United States (Sept. 11); USA Patriot Act gives immigration authorities more power to exclude suspected terrorists (Oct. 26).

2005-2006 Immigration reform measures fail in GOP-controlled Congress despite support from Republican President George W. Bush; Congress approves Secure Fence Act, to require double-layer fence on U.S.-Mexico border.

2007 Immigration reform measure dies in Senate; three motions to cut off debate fail (June 7). . . . Arizona legislature passes employer-sanctions law; companies threatened with loss of operating license for knowingly hiring undocumented aliens, required to use federal E-Verify system; signed into law by Democratic Gov. Janet Napolitano (July 2). . . . Unauthorized immigrant population in United States peaks near 12 million.

2008 Democrat Barack Obama elected president after campaign with little attention to immigration issues (Nov. 4); Obama carries Hispanic vote by 2-1 margin.

2009 Obama endorses immigration reform, but without specifics; issue takes back seat to economic recovery, health care.

2010 Arizona enacts law (S.B. 1070) to crack down on illegal immigrants; measure requires police to check immigration status if suspect or detainee is reasonably believed to be unlawful alien; makes it a crime to fail to carry alien registration papers; signed by Republican Gov. Jan Brewer (April 23); federal judge blocks parts of law (July 28). . . . DREAM Act to allow legal status for unlawful aliens who entered U.S. as minors approved by House of Representatives (Dec. 8) but fails in Senate: 55-41 vote is short of supermajority needed for passage (Dec. 18).

2011 Utah, Indiana, Georgia follow Arizona's lead in giving state, local police immigration-enforcement powers (March, May). . . . Federal appeals court upholds injunction against parts of Arizona's S.B. 1070 (April 11). . . . Supreme Court upholds Arizona's employer-sanctions law 5-3 (May 21). . . . Alabama enacts nation's toughest state law on illegal immigrants, HB 56 (June 9). . . . Federal judge blocks some parts of HB 56, allows others to take effect (Sept. 28).

2012 Immigration is flashpoint for Republican presidential candidates. . . . Obama urges passage of DREAM Act (Jan. 24). . . . Alabama, Georgia laws argued before U.S. appeals court (March 1). . . . Supreme Court to hear arguments on Arizona's S.B. 1070 (April 25); ruling due by end of June.

Journalist Reveals His Immigration Secret

"There's nothing worse than being in limbo."

When journalist-turned-immigration rights activist Jose Antonio Vargas traveled to Alabama with a documentary filmmaker, he found a Birmingham restaurant patron who strongly supported the state law cracking down on undocumented aliens. "Get your papers or get out," the patron said.

"What if I told you I didn't [have papers]?" Vargas is heard asking off camera. "Then you need you get your ass home then," the patron rejoined. [1]

Vargas says he is home — in America, where he has lived since his Filipina mother sent him, at age 12, to live in California with his grandparents in 1993. "I'm an American without papers," says Vargas, who came out as an undocumented immigrant in dramatic fashion in a 4,300-word memoir in *The New York Times Magazine* in June 2011. [2]

In the story, Vargas recounts how he learned at age 16 that he was carrying a fake green card when he applied for a driver's license. The DMV clerk let him go. Back home, Vargas confronted his grandfather, who acknowledged the forgery and told Vargas not to tell anyone else.

For the next 14 years, Vargas kept his non-status secret from all but a handful of enablers as he completed high school and college and advanced rapidly from entry-level newspaper jobs to national-impact journalism at *The Washington Post*, *Huffington Post* and glossy magazines. His one attempt at legal status ended in crushing disappointment in 2002 when an immigration lawyer told him he would have to return to the Philippines and wait for 10 years to apply to come back.

Vargas was inspired to write about his life by the example of four undocumented students who walked from Miami to Washington, D.C., in 2010 to lobby for the DREAM Act, the status-legalizing proposal for immigrants who came to the United States as minors. Vargas's story, published by *The Times* after *The Washington Post* decided not to, quickly went viral in old and new media alike.

In the eight months since, Vargas has founded and become the public face for a Web-based campaign, Define American (www.defineamerican.org). "Define American brings new voices into the immigration conversation, shining a light on a growing 21st century Underground Railroad: American citizens who are forced to fill in where our broken immigration system fails," the mission statement reads. "Together, we are going to fix a broken system."

The DREAM Act fell just short of passage in Congress in December 2010 and has gotten little traction since. Broader proposals to give legal status to some of the 11 million unlawful

Journalist Jose Antonio Vargas disclosed in *The New York Times* in June 2011 that he was an undocumented immigrant.

aliens are far off the political radar screen. Vargas is critical of Alabama's law cracking down on illegal immigration but acknowledges the states' frustration with federal policies. "At the end of the day, the federal government hasn't done anything on this issue," he says.

In the meantime, Vargas waits. "There's nothing worse than being in limbo," he says. In the story, he cited some of the hardships for the undocumented. As one example, he cannot risk traveling to the Philippines, so he has yet to meet his 14-year-old brother. But Vargas says he has no plan to "self-deport." "I love this country," he says.

— *Kenneth Jost*

[1]"The Two Faces of Alabama," http://isthisalabama.org/. The films by director Chris Weitz were prepared under the auspices of the Center for American Progress. Some comments from Vargas are from a Feb. 15, 2012, screening of the videos at the center.

[2] Jose Antonio Vargas, "Outlaw," *The New York Times Magazine*, June 26, 2011, p. 22. Disclosure: the author is a professional acquaintance and Facebook friend of Vargas.

Congress liberalized immigration law with a 1952 statute that included restrictionist elements as well and then, dramatically, with a 1965 law that scrapped the Eurocentric national-origins system and opened the gate to increased immigration from Latin America and Asia.

The 1952 law preserved the national-origins system but replaced the Chinese Exclusion Act with very small quotas for countries in the so-called Asia-Pacific Triangle. The act also eliminated discrimination between sexes. Over the next decade, immigration from European countries declined, seemingly weakening the rationale for the national-origins system. Against the backdrop of the civil rights revolution, the national-origins system seemed to many also to be antithetical to American values. The result was the Immigration Act of 1965, which replaced the national-origins system with a system of preferences favoring family reunification or to lesser extents admissions of professionals or skilled or unskilled workers needed in the U.S. workforce.

Quickly, the demographics of immigration shifted — and dramatically. Immigration increased overall under the new law, and the new immigrants came mostly from Latin America and Asia. By 1978, the peak year of the decade, 44 percent of legal immigration came from the Americas, 42 percent from Asia and only 12 percent from Europe.[26]

Cracking Down?

Immigration to the United States increased overall in the last decades of the 20th century, and illegal immigration in particular exploded to levels that fueled a public and political backlash. Congress and the executive branch tried to stem the flow of undocumented aliens first in 1986 by combining employer sanctions with an amnesty for those in the country for several years and then a decade later by increasing enforcement and deportations.

Then, in the wake of the Sept. 11, 2001, terrorist attacks on the United States, Congress and President George W. Bush joined in further efforts to tighten admission procedures and crack down on foreigners in the country without authorization.

Estimates of the number of immigrants in the United States illegally are inherently imprecise, but the general upward trend from the 1980s until a plateau in the 2000s is undisputed. As Congress took up immigration bills in the mid-1980s, the Census Bureau estimated the number of those undocumented at 3 million to 5 million; many politicians used higher figures. The former Immigration and Naturalization Service put the number at 3.5 million in 1990 and 7.0 million a decade later. Whatever the precise number, public opinion polls registered increasing concern about the overall level of immigration. By the mid-1990s, Gallup polls found roughly two-thirds of respondents in favor of decreasing the level of immigration, one-fourth in favor of maintaining the then-present level and fewer than 10 percent for an increase.[27]

The congressional proposals leading to the Immigration Reform and Control Act in 1986 sought to stem illegal immigration while recognizing the reality of millions of undocumented immigrants and the continuing need for immigrant labor, especially in U.S. agriculture. The law allowed legal status for immigrants in the country continuously since 1982 but aimed to deter unauthorized immigration in the future by forcing employers to verify the status of prospective hires and penalizing them for hiring anyone without legal status. Agricultural interests, however, won approval of a new guest worker program. Some 3 million people gained legal status under the two provisions, but illegal immigration continued to increase even as civil rights groups warned that the employer sanctions would result in discrimination against Latino citizens.

The backlash against illegal immigration produced a new strategy for reducing the inflows: state and federal laws cutting off benefits for aliens in the country without authorization. California, home to an estimated 1.3 million undocumented aliens at the time, blazed the path in 1994 with passage of a ballot measure, Proposition 187, that barred any government benefits to illegal aliens, including health care and public schooling. The education provision was flatly unconstitutional under a 1982 ruling by the U.S. Supreme Court that guaranteed K-12 education for school-age alien children.[28]

The measure mobilized Latino voters in the state. They contributed to the election of a Democratic governor in 1998, Gray Davis, who dropped the state's defense of the measure in court in his first year in office. In the meantime, however, Congress in 1996 had approved provisions — reluctantly signed into law by President Bill Clinton — to deny unauthorized aliens most federal benefits, including food stamps, family assistance and Social Security. The law allows states to deny state-provided benefits

A Maricopa County deputy arrests a woman following a sweep for illegal immigrants in Phoenix on July 29, 2010. The police operation came after protesters against Arizona's tough immigration law clashed with police hours after the law went into effect. Although the most controversial parts of the law have been blocked, five other states — Utah, Indiana, Georgia, Alabama and South Carolina — last year enacted similar laws.

as well; today, at least a dozen states have enacted such further restrictions.

The centerpieces of the 1996 immigration law, however, were measures to beef up enforcement and toughen deportation policy. The Illegal Immigration Reform and Immigrant Responsibility Act authorized more money for the Border Patrol and INS, approved more funding for a 14-mile border fence already under construction and increased penalties for document fraud and alien smuggling. It sought to streamline deportation proceedings, limit appeals and bar re-entry of any deportee for at least five years. And it established an Internet-based employer verification system (E-Verify) aimed at making it easier and more reliable for employers to check legal status of prospective hires. The law proved to be tougher on paper, however, than in practice. The border fence remains incomplete, deportation proceedings backlogged and E-Verify optional and — according to critics — unreliable. And illegal immigration continued to increase.

The 9/11 attacks added homeland security to the concerns raised by the nation's porous immigration system. In post-mortems by immigration hawks, the Al Qaeda hijackers were seen as having gained entry into the United States with minimal scrutiny of their visa

applications and in many cases having overstayed because of inadequate follow-up.[29] The so-called USA Patriot Act, enacted in October 2001 just 45 days after the attacks, gave the INS — later renamed the U.S. Citizenship and Immigration Service and transferred to the new Department of Homeland Security — greater authority to exclude or detain foreigners suspected of ties to terrorist organizations. The act also mandated information-sharing by the FBI to identify aliens with criminal records. Along with other counterterrorism measures, the act is viewed by supporters today as having helped prevent any successful attacks on U.S. soil since 2001. Illegal immigration, however, continued to increase — peaking at roughly 12 million in 2007.

Getting Tough

Congress and the White House moved from post-9/11 security issues to broader questions of immigration policy during Bush's second term, but bipartisan efforts to allow legal status for unlawful aliens fell victim to Republican opposition in the Senate. As a presidential candidate, Democrat Obama carried the Hispanic vote by a 2-1 margin over Republican John McCain after a campaign with limited attention to immigration issues. In the White House, Obama stepped up enforcement in some respects even as he urged Congress to back broad reform measures. The reform proposals failed with Democrats in control of both the House and the Senate and hardly got started after Republicans regained control of the House in the 2010 elections.

Bush lent support to bipartisan reform efforts in the Republican-controlled Congress in 2005 and 2006 and again in the Democratic-controlled Congress in his final two years in office. Congress in 2006 could agree only on authorizing a 700-mile border fence after reaching an impasse over a House-passed enforcement measure and a Senate-approved path-to-citizenship bill. Bush redoubled efforts in 2007 by backing a massive, bipartisan bill that would have allowed "earned citizenship" for aliens who had lived in the United States for at least eight years and met other requirements. As in the previous Congress, many Republicans rejected the proposal as an unacceptable amnesty. The bill died on June 7 after the Senate rejected three cloture motions to cut off debate.[30]

Immigration played only a minor role in the 2008 presidential campaign between Obama and McCain,

Senate colleagues who had both supported reform proposals. Both campaigns responded to growing public anger over illegal immigration by emphasizing enforcement when discussing the issue, but the subject went unmentioned in the candidates' three televised debates. McCain, once popular with Hispanics in his home state of Arizona, appeared to have paid at the polls for the GOP's hard line on immigration. Exit polls indicated that Obama won 67 percent of a record-size Hispanic vote; McCain got 31 percent — a significant drop from Bush's 39 percent share of the vote in 2004.[31]

With Obama in office, Congress remained gridlocked even as the president tried to smooth the way for reform measures by stepping up enforcement. The congressional gridlock had already invited state lawmakers to step into the vacuum. State legislatures passed more than 200 immigration-related laws in 2007 and 2008, according to a compilation by the National Conference on State Legislatures; the number soared to more than 300 annually for the next three years.[32]

The numbers included some resolutions praising the country's multi-ethnic heritage, but most of the new state laws sought to tighten enforcement against undocumented aliens or to limit benefits to them. Among the earliest of the new laws was an Arizona measure — enacted in June 2007, two weeks after the Senate impasse in Washington — that provided for lifting the business licenses of companies that knowingly hired illegal aliens and mandated use of the federal E-Verify program to ascertain status of prospective hires. Business and labor groups, supported by the Obama administration, challenged the law on federal preemption grounds. The Supreme Court's 5-3 decision in May 2011 to uphold the law prompted several states to enact similar mandatory E-Verify provisions.[33]

The interplay on immigration policy between Washington and state capitals is continuing. In Obama's first three years in office, the total number of removals increased to what ICE calls on its website "record levels." Even so, Arizona lawmakers and officials criticized federal enforcement as inadequate in the legislative debate leading to SB 1070's enactment in April 2010. Legal challenges followed quickly — first from a Latino organization; then from a broad coalition of civil rights and civil liberties groups; and then, on July 6, from the Justice Department. The most controversial parts of the law have been blocked, first by U.S. District Court Judge Susan Bolton's injunction later that month and then by the Ninth Circuit's decision affirming her decision in April 2011. The legal challenges did not stop five other states — Utah, Indiana, Georgia, Alabama and South Carolina — from enacting similar laws in spring and early summer 2011. Civil rights groups and the Justice Department followed with similar suits challenging the new state enactments.

As the 2012 presidential campaign got under way, immigration emerged as an issue between Republican candidates vying for the party's nomination. The issue posed difficulties for the GOP hopefuls as they sought to appeal to rank-and-file GOP voters upset about illegal immigration without forfeiting Latino votes in the primary season and in the general election. Presumed frontrunner Mitt Romney took a hard stance against illegal immigration in early contests but softened his message in advance of winning the pivotal Jan. 31 primary in Florida with its substantial Hispanic vote.

Despite differences in details and in rhetoric, the three leading GOP candidates — Romney, Newt Gingrich and Rick Santorum — all said they opposed the DREAM Act in its present form even as Obama called for Congress to pass the bill in his State of the Union speech.

CURRENT SITUATION

Obama's Approach

The Obama administration is claiming success in increasing border enforcement and removing unlawful aliens while injecting more prosecutorial discretion into deportation cases. But the mix of firm and flexible policies is resulting in criticism from both sides of the issue.

U.S. Immigration and Customs Enforcement (ICE) counted a record 396,906 "removals" during fiscal 2011, including court-ordered deportations as well as administrative or voluntary removals or returns. The number includes a record 216,698 aliens with criminal convictions.[34]

Meanwhile, Homeland Security Secretary Janet Napolitano says illegal border-crossing attempts have decreased by more than half in the last three years. In a Jan. 30 speech to the National Press Club in Washington, Napolitano linked the decline to an increase in the number of Border Patrol agents to 21,000, which she said was more than double the number in 2004.

"The Obama administration has undertaken the most serious and sustained actions to secure our borders in our nation's history," Napolitano told journalists. "And it is clear from every measure we currently have that this approach is working."[35]

Immigration hawk Krikorian with the Center for Immigration Studies gives the administration some, but only some, credit for the removal statistics. "They're not making up the numbers," Krikorian says. But he notes that immigration removals increased during the Bush administration and that the rate of increase has slowed under Obama.

In addition, Krikorian notes that new figures compiled by a government information tracking service indicate the pace of new immigration cases and of court-processed deportations slowed in the first quarter of fiscal 2012 (October, November and December 2011). A report in early February by Syracuse University's Transactional Records Access Clearinghouse (TRAC) shows 34,362 court-ordered removals or "voluntary departures" in the period, compared to 35,771 in the previous three months — about a 4 percent drop.

A separate TRAC report later in the month showed what the service called a "sharp decline" in new ICE filings. ICE initiated 39,331 new deportation proceedings in the nation's 50 immigration courts during the first quarter of fiscal 2012, according to the report, a 33 percent decline from the 58,639 new filings in the previous quarter.[36]

"The people in this administration would like to pull the plug on enforcement altogether," Krikorian complains. "They refuse to ask for more money for detention beds and then plead poverty that they can't do more."

From the opposite perspective, some Latino officials and organizations have been critical of the pace of deportations. When Obama delivered a speech in favor of immigration reform in El Paso, Texas, in May 2011, the president of the National Council of La Raza tempered praise for the president's position with criticism of the deportation policy.

"As record levels of detention and deportation continue to soar, families are torn apart, innocent youth are being deported and children are left behind without the protection of their parents," Janet Murguía said in a May 10 press release. "Such policies do not reflect American values and do little to solve the problem. We can do better."[37]

Latinos disapprove of the Obama administration's handling of deportations by roughly a 2-1 margin, according to a poll by the Pew Hispanic Center in December 2011. Overall, the poll found 59 percent of those surveyed opposed the administration's policy while 27 percent approved. Disapproval was higher among foreign-born Latinos (70 percent) than those born in the United States (46 percent).[38]

Napolitano and ICE Director John Morton are both claiming credit for focusing the agency's enforcement on the most serious cases, including criminal aliens, repeat violators and recent border crossers. Morton announced the new "prosecutorial discretion" policy in an agency-wide directive in June 2011.[39]

TRAC, however, questions the claimed emphasis on criminal aliens. The 39,331 new deportation filings in the first quarter of fiscal 2012 included only 1,300 against aliens with convictions for "aggravated felonies," as defined in immigration law. "Even this small share was down from previous quarters," the Feb. 21 report states. Aliens with aggravated felony convictions accounted for 3.3 percent of deportations in the period, compared to 3.8 percent in the previous quarter.[40]

The administration is also being questioned on its claim — in Obama's El Paso speech and elsewhere — to have virtually completed the border fence that Congress ordered constructed in the Secure Fence Act of 2006.[41] The act called for the 652-mile barrier to be constructed of two layers of reinforced fencing but was amended the next year — with Bush still in office — to give the administration more discretion in what type of barriers to use.

As of May 2011, the barrier included only 36 miles of double-layer fencing, according to PolitiFact, the fact-checking service of the *Tampa Bay Times*. The rest is single-layer fencing or vehicle barriers that critic Krikorian says are so low that a pedestrian can step over them. PolitiFact calls Obama's claim "mostly false."[42]

Meanwhile, the administration is preparing to extend nationwide its controversial "Secure Communities" program, which tries to spot immigration law violators by matching fingerprints of local arrestees with the database of the Department of Homeland Security (DHS). A match allows U.S. Immigration and Customs Enforcement (ICE)

Should Congress pass the DREAM Act?

YES
Walter A. Ewing
Senior Researcher, Immigration Policy Center American Immigration Council

Written for *CQ Researcher*, March 2012

The Development, Relief and Education for Alien Minors Act is rooted in common sense. To begin with, it would benefit a group of unauthorized young people who, in most cases, did not come to this country of their own accord. Rather, they were brought here by their parents. The DREAM Act would also enable its beneficiaries to achieve higher levels of education and obtain better, higher-paying jobs, which would increase their contributions to the U.S. economy and American society. In short, the DREAM Act represents basic fairness and enlightened self-interest.

More than 2 million young people would benefit from the DREAM Act, and their numbers grow by roughly 65,000 per year. They came to the United States before age 18, many as young children. They tend to be culturally American and fluent in English. Their primary ties are to this country, not the countries of their birth. And the majority had no say in the decision to come to this country without authorization — that decision was made by the adult members of their families. Punishing these young people for the actions of their parents runs counter to American social values and legal norms. Yet, without the DREAM Act, these young people will be forced to live on the margins of U.S. society or will be deported to countries they may not even know.

Assuming they aren't deported, the young people who would benefit from the DREAM Act face enormous barriers to higher education and professional jobs because of their unauthorized status. They are ineligible for most forms of college financial aid and cannot work legally in this country. The DREAM Act would remove these barriers, which would benefit the U.S. economy.

The College Board estimates that over the course of a working lifetime, a college graduate earns 60 percent more than a high school graduate. This higher income translates into extra tax revenue flowing to federal, state and local governments.

The DREAM Act is in the best interest of the United States both socially and economically. It would resolve the legal status of millions of unauthorized young people in a way that is consistent with core American values. And it would empower these young people to become better-educated, higher-earning workers and taxpayers. Every day that goes by without passage of the DREAM Act is another day of wasted talent and potential.

NO
Mark Krikorian
Executive Director, Center for Immigration Studies

Written for *CQ Researcher*, March 2012

The appeal of the DREAM Act is obvious. People brought here illegally at a very young age and who have grown up in the United States are the most sympathetic group of illegal immigrants. Much of the public is open to the idea of amnesty for them.

But the actual DREAM Act before Congress is a deeply flawed measure in at least four ways:

• Rather than limiting amnesty to those brought here as infants and toddlers, it applies to illegal immigrants who arrived before their 16th birthday. But if the argument is that their very identity was formed here, age 7 would be a more sensible cutoff. That is recognized as a turning point in a child's psychological development (called the "age of reason" by the Catholic Church, hence the traditional age for First Communion). Such a lower-age cutoff, combined with a requirement of at least 10 years' residence here, would make a hypothetical DREAM Act 2.0 much more defensible.

• All amnesties are vulnerable to fraud, even more than other immigration benefits. About one-fourth of the beneficiaries of the amnesty granted by Congress in 1986 were liars, including one of the leaders of the 1993 World Trade Center bombing. But the DREAM Act specifically prohibits the prosecution of anyone who lies on an amnesty application. So you can make any false claim you like about your arrival or schooling in America without fear of punishment. A DREAM Act 2.0 would make clear that any lies, no matter how trivial, will result in arrest and imprisonment.

• All amnesties send a signal to prospective illegal immigrants that, if you get in and keep your head down, you might benefit from the next amnesty. But the bill contains no enforcement provisions to limit the need for another DREAM Act a decade from now. That's why a serious proposal would include measures such as electronic verification of the legal status of all new hires, plus explicit authorization for state and local enforcement of immigration law.

• Finally, all amnesties reward illegal immigrants — in this case including the adults who brought their children here illegally. A credible DREAM Act 2.0 would bar the adult relatives of the beneficiaries from ever receiving any immigration status or even a right to visit the United States. If those who came as children are not responsible, then those who are responsible must pay the price for their lawbreaking.

to issue a so-called detainer against violators, sending their cases into the immigration enforcement system. The administration touts the program as "a simple and common sense" enforcement tool. Critics note, however, that it has resulted in wrongful detention of U.S. citizens in a considerable but unknown number of cases. One reason for the mistakes: The DHS database includes all immigration transactions, not just violations, and thus could show a match for an immigrant with legal status.[43]

Supreme Court Action

All eyes are on the Supreme Court as the justices prepare for arguments on April 25 in Arizona's effort to reinstate major parts of its trend-setting law cracking down on illegal immigrants.

The Arizona case is the furthest advanced of suits challenging the six recently enacted state laws that give state and local police responsibility for enforcing federal immigration laws. After winning an injunction blocking major parts of the Arizona law, the Obama administration filed similar suits against Alabama's HB 56 as well as the Georgia and South Carolina measures.

The ACLU's Immigrants Rights Project, along with Hispanic and other civil rights groups, has filed separate challenges on broader grounds against all six laws. Federal district courts have blocked parts of all the laws, though some contentious parts of Alabama's law were allowed to take effect.

District court judges in the Indiana, South Carolina and Utah cases put the litigation on hold pending the Supreme Court's decision in the Arizona case. Alabama and Georgia asked the Eleventh U.S. Circuit Court of Appeals to postpone the scheduled March 1 arguments in their cases, but the court declined.

Judge Charles R. Wilson opened the Atlanta-based court's March 1 session, however, by announcing that the three-judge panel had decided to withhold its opinion until after the Supreme Court decides the Arizona case. "Hopefully, that information will help you in framing your arguments today," Wilson told the assembled lawyers.[44]

Wilson and fellow Democratic-appointed Circuit Judge Beverly B. Martin dominated the questioning during the three hours of arguments in the cases. Both judges pressed lawyers defending Alabama and Georgia on the effects of their laws on the education of children, the ability of

illegal aliens to carry on with their lives while immigration courts decided their cases and what would happen if every state adopted their approach to dealing with immigration violations. The third member of the panel, Richard Voorhees, a Republican-appointed federal district court judge, asked only three questions on technical issues.

Opening the government's argument in the Alabama case, Deputy Assistant U.S. Attorney General Beth Brinkmann said the state's law attempts to usurp exclusive federal authority over immigration. "The regulation of immigration is a matter vested exclusively in the national government," Brinkman said. "Alabama's state-specific regulation scheme violates that authority. It attacks every aspect of an alien's life and makes it impossible for the alien to live."

Alabama Solicitor General John C. Neiman Jr. drew sharp challenges from Wilson and Martin even before he began his argument. Wilson focused on the law's Section 10, which makes it a criminal misdemeanor for an alien unlawfully present in the United States to fail to carry alien registration papers.

"You could be convicted and sent to jail in Alabama even though the Department of Homeland Security says, 'You're an illegal alien, but we've decided you're going to remain here in the United States?' " Wilson asked.

Neiman conceded the point. "If the deportation hearing occurred after the violation of Section 10, then yes," Neiman said. "Someone could be held to be in violation of Section 10 and then later be held not removable."

Wilson also pressed Neiman on the potential effects on the federal government's ability to control immigration policy if states enacted laws with different levels of severity. "These laws could certainly have the effect of making certain states places where illegal aliens would be likely to go," the state's attorney acknowledged.

Representing the ACLU in the separate challenge, Immigrants Rights Project director Wang sharply attacked the motive behind the Alabama law. The law, she said, was written to carry out the legislature's stated objective "to attack every aspect of an illegal immigrant's life so that they will deport themselves."*

---

*The appeals court on March 8 issued a temporary injunction blocking enforcement of two provisions, those prohibiting unlawful aliens from enforcing contracts in court or entering into business transactions with state or local government agencies.

In Washington, lawyers for Arizona filed their brief with the Supreme Court defending its law, SB 1070, in early February. Among 20 *amicus* briefs filed in support of Arizona's case is one drafted by the Michigan attorney general's office on behalf of 16 states similarly defending the states' right to help enforce federal immigration law. A similar brief was filed by nine states in the Eleventh Circuit in support of the Alabama law.

The government's brief in the Arizona case is due March 19. Following the April 25 arguments, the Supreme Court is expected to decide the case before the current term ends in late June.

Meanwhile, legal challenges to other parts of the state's law are continuing in federal court in Arizona. In a Feb. 29 ruling, Bolton blocked on First Amendment grounds a provision prohibiting people from blocking traffic when they offer day labor services on the street.[45]

OUTLOOK

A Broken System

The immigration system is broken. On that much, the pro- and low-immigration groups agree. But they disagree sharply on how to fix it. And the divide defeats any attempts to fix it even if it can be fixed.

Pro-immigration groups like to talk about the "three-legged stool" of immigration reform: legal channels for family- and job-based immigration; a path to citizenship for unlawful aliens already in the United States; and better border security. Low-immigration groups agree on the need for better border controls but want to make it harder, not easier, for would-be immigrants and generally oppose legal status for the near-record number of unlawful aliens.

Public opinion is ambivalent and conflicted on immigration issues even as immigration, legal and illegal, has reached record levels. The nearly 14 million new immigrants, legal and illegal, who came to the United States from 2000 to 2010 made that decade the highest ever in U.S. history, according to the low-immigration Center for Immigration Studies. The foreign-born population reached 40 million, the center says, also a record.[46]

Some public opinion polls find support for legal status for illegal immigrants, especially if the survey questions specify conditions to meet: 66 percent

supported it, for example, in a Fox News poll in early December 2011. Three weeks earlier, however, a CNN poll found majority support (55 percent) for concentrating on "stopping the flow of illegal immigrants and deporting those already here" instead of developing a plan for legal residency (42 percent).[47]

Other polls appear consistently to find support for the laws in Arizona and other states to crack down on illegal immigrants — most recently by a 2-1 margin in a poll by Quinnipiac University in Connecticut.[48] "Popular sentiment is always against immigration," says Muzaffar Chishti, director of the Migration Policy Institute's office at New York University School of Law and himself a naturalized U.S. citizen who emigrated from his native India in 1974.

Pro-immigration groups say the public is ahead of the politicians in Washington and state capitals who are pushing for stricter laws. State legislators "have chosen to scapegoat immigration instead of solving tough economic challenges," says Noorani with the National Immigration Forum. "There are politicians who would rather treat this as a political hot potato," he adds, instead of offering "practical solutions."

From the opposite side, the Federation for American Immigration Reform's Stein says he is "pessimistic, disappointed and puzzled" by what he calls "the short-sighted views" of political leaders. Earlier, Stein says, "politicians all over the country were touting the virtues of engagement in immigration policy." But now he complains that even Republicans are talking about "amnesty and the DREAM Act," instead of criticizing what he calls the Obama administration's "elimination of any immigration enforcement."

Enforcement, however, is one component of the system that, if not broken, is at least completely overwhelmed. In explaining the new prosecutorial discretion policy, ICE director Morton frankly acknowledged the agency "has limited resources to remove those illegally in the United States."[49] The nation's immigrant courts have a current backlog of 300,225 cases, according to a TRAC compilation, double the number in 2001.[50]

Employers' groups say the system's rules for hiring immigrants are problematic at best. In Alabama, Reed with the contractors' group says employers do their best to comply with the status-verification requirements but find the procedures and paperwork difficult. The farm federation's Helms says the same for the rules for temporary guest workers. "We're working at the national level to have a more effective way to hire legal migrant workers to do those jobs that it's hard to find local workers to do," he says.

The rulings by the Supreme Court on the Arizona law will clarify the lines between federal and state enforcement responsibilities, but the Center for Immigration Studies' Krikorian says the decision is likely to increase the politicization of the issue. A ruling to uphold the law will encourage other states to follow Arizona's lead, he says, but would also "energize the anti-enforcement groups." A ruling to find the state laws pre-empted, on the other hand, will mobilize pro-enforcement groups, he says.

The political and legal debates will be conducted against the backdrop of the nation's rapidly growing Hispanic population, attributable more to birth rates than to immigration.[51] "Whoever the next president is, whoever the next Congress is, will have to address this issue," says Giovagnoli with the American Immigration Council. "The demographics are not going to allow people to ignore this issue.

"I do believe we're going to reform the immigration system," Giovagnoli adds "It's going to be a lot of work. Even under the best of circumstances, it's a lot of work."

NOTES

1. Quoted in Kim Chandler, "Alabama House passes Arizona-style immigration bill," *The Birmingham News*, April 6, 2011, p. 1A.

2. The case is *Arizona v. United States*, 11-182. Background and legal filings compiled on SCOTUSblog, www.scotusblog.com/case-files/cases/arizona-v-united-states/?wpmp_switcher=desktop.-

3. See Human Rights Watch, "No Way to Live: Alabama's Immigration Law," December 2011, www.hrw.org/news/2011/12/13/usalabama-no-way-live-under-immigrant-law.

4. Quoted in David White, "Hundreds rally at State House seeking immigration law repeal," *The Birmingham News*, Feb. 15, 2012, p. 1A.

5. See "Unauthorized Immigrant Population: State and National Trends, 2010," Pew Hispanic Center, Feb. 1, 2011, pp. 23, 24, www.pewhispanic.org/files/reports/133.pdf. The U.S. Department of Homeland Security estimates differ slightly; for 2010, it estimates nationwide unauthorized immigrant population at 10.8 million.

6. For previous *CQ Researcher* coverage, see: Alan Greenblatt, "Immigration Debate," pp. 97-120, updated Dec. 10, 2011; Reed Karaim, "America's Border Fence," Sept. 19, 2008, pp. 745-768; Peter Katel, "Illegal Immigration," May 6, 2005, pp. 393-420; David Masci, "Debate Over Immigration," July 14, 2000, pp. 569-592; Kenneth Jost, "Cracking Down on Immigration," Feb. 3, 1995.

7. Quoted in David White, "Illegal immigration bill passes," *The Birmingham News*, June 3, 2011, p. 1A.

8. See Dana Beyerle, "Study says immigration law has economic costs," *Tuscaloosa News*, Jan. 31, 2012, www.tuscaloosanews.com/article/20120131/news/120139966. For Beason's statement, see http://scottbeason.com/2012/01/26/beason-statement-on-the-impact-of-hb-56-on-alabama-unemployment-rate/.

9. Samuel Addy, "A Cost-Benefit Analysis of the New Alabama Immigration Law," Center for Business and Economic Research, Culverhouse College of Commerce and Business Administration, University of Alabama, January 2012, http://cber.cba.ua.edu/New%20AL%20Immigration%20Law%20-%20Costs%20and%20Benefits.pdf; Hammon quoted in Brian Lyman, "Studies, surveys examine immigration law's impact," *The Montgomery Advertiser*, Feb. 1, 2012.

10. See Alan Gomez, "Immigrants return to Alabama," *USA Today*, Feb. 22, 2012, p. 3A; Jay Reeves, "Immigrants trickling back to Ala despite crackdown," The Associated Press, Feb. 19, 2012.

11. The decision in *United States v. Alabama*, 2:11-CV-2746-SLB, U.S.D.C.-N.D.Ala. (Sept. 28, 2011), is available via *The New York Times*: http://graphics8.nytimes.com/packages/pdf/national/112746memopnentered.pdf. For coverage, see Brian Lyman, "Judge allows key part of immigration

law to go into effect," *The Montgomery Advertiser*, Sept. 29, 2011; Brian Lawson, "Judge halts part of immigration law," *The Birmingham News*, Sept. 29, 2011, p. 1A. The Alabama Office of the Attorney General has a chronology of the legal proceedings: www.ago.state.al.us/Page-Immigration-Litigation-Federal.

12. Quoted in Eric Velasco, "Immigration law draws praise, scorn," *The Birmingham News*, June 10, 2011, p. 1A.

13. Steven A. Camarota, "A Need for More Immigrant Workers?," Center for Immigration Studies, June 2011, http://cis.org/no-need-for-more-immigrant-workers-q1-2011.

14. "The Impact of Unauthorized Immigrants on the Budgets of State and Local Governments," Congressional Budget Office, Dec. 6, 2007, p. 3, /www.cbo.gov/sites/default/files/cbofiles/ftp docs/87xx/doc8711/12-6-immigration.pdf.

15. David Gerber, *American Immigration: A Very Short Introduction* (2011).

16. Quoted in Velasco, *op. cit.*

17. Quoted in White, *op. cit.* Hammon's office did not respond to several *CQ Researcher* requests for an interview.

18. "Alabama's Illegal Immigration Law Gets Hollywood's Attention," WAKA/CBS8, Montgomery, Feb. 21, 2012, www.waka.com/home/top-stories/Alabamas-Illegal-Immigration-Law-Gets-Attention-From-Hollywood-139937153.html. The four separate videos by Chris Weitz, collectively titled "Is This Alabama?" are on an eponymous website: http://isthisalabama.org/.

19. See "Delegation of Immigration Authority 287(g) Immigration and Nationality Act," www.ice.gov/287g/ (visited February 2012).

20. See Sandhya Somashekhar and Amy Gardner, "Immigration is flash point in Fla. Primary," *The Washington Post*, Jan. 26, 2012, p. A6.

21. Text available on the White House website: www.whitehouse.gov/the-press-office/2012/01/24/remarks-president-state-union-address.

22. General background drawn from Gerber, *op. cit.*; Otis L. Graham Jr., *Unguarded Gates: A History of America's Immigration Crisis* (2004). Some country-by-country background drawn from Mary C. Waters and Reed Ueda (eds.), *The New Americans: A Guide to Immigration Since 1965* (2007).

23. Roger Daniels, *Guarding the Golden Door: American Immigration Policy and Immigrants Since 1882* (2004), pp. 19-22.

24. Quoted in Graham, *op. cit.*, p. 51.

25. Albert M. Camarillo, "Mexico," in Waters and Ueda, *op. cit.*, p. 506.

26. Figures from *INS Statistical Yearbook*, 1978, cited in Daniels, *op. cit.*, p 138.

27. Polls cited in Daniels, *op. cit.*, p. 233.

28. See *Plyler v. Doe*, 452 U.S. 202 (1982).

29. See Graham, *op. cit.*, Chap. 17, and sources cited therein.

30. "Immigration Rewrite Dies in Senate," *CQ Almanac 2007*, pp. 15-9 — 15-11, http://library.cqpress.com/cqalmanac/cqal07-1006-44907-2047763.

31. See Julia Preston, "Immigration Cools as Campaign Issue," *The New York Times*, Oct. 29, 2008, p. A20, www.nytimes.com/2008/10/29/us/politics/29immig.html; Mark Hugo Lopez, "How Hispanics Voted in the 2008 Election," Pew Hispanic Research Center, Nov. 5, 2008, updated Nov. 7, 2008, http://pewresearch.org/pubs/1024/exit-poll-analysis-hispanics.

32. "Immigration Policy Report: 2011 Immigration-Related Laws and Resolutions in the States (Jan. 1-Dec. 7, 2011)," National Conference of State Legislatures, www.ncsl.org/issues-research/immigration/state-immigration-legislation-report-dec-2011.aspx.

33. The decision is *Chamber of Commerce v. Whiting*, 563 U.S. — (2011). For coverage, see Kenneth Jost, *Supreme Court Yearbook 2010-2011*, http://library.cqpress.com/scyb/document.php?id=scyb10-1270-72832-2397001&type=hitlist&num=0.

34. See "ICE Removals, Fiscal Years 2007-2011," in Mark Hugo Lopez, *et al.*, "As Deportations Rise to Record Levels, Most Latinos Oppose Obama's Policy," Pew Hispanic Center, Dec. 28, 2011, p. 33, http://pewresearch.org/pubs/2158/

latinos-hispanics-immigration-policy-deportations-george-bush-barack-obama-administration-democrats-republicans. The report notes that ICE's statistics differ somewhat from those released by DHS, its parent department.

35. "Secretary of Homeland Security Janet Napolitano's 2nd Annual Address on the State of America's Homeland Security: Homeland Security and Economic Security," Jan. 30, 2012, www.dhs.gov/ynews/speeches/napolitano-state-of-america-homeland-security.shtm.

36. "Share of Immigration Cases Ending in Deportation Orders Hits Record Low," *TRAC Reports*, Feb. 7, 2012, http://trac.syr.edu/immigration/reports/272/; "Sharp Decline in ICE Deportation Filings," Feb. 21, 2012, http://trac.syr.edu/immigration/reports/274/. For coverage, see Paloma Esquivel, "Number of deportation cases down by a third," *Los Angeles Times*, Feb. 24, 2012, p. AA2, http://articles.latimes.com/2012/feb/24/local/la-me-deportation-drop-20120224.

37. Text of La Raza statement, www.nclr.org/index.php/about_us/news/news_releases/janet_murgua_president_and_ceo_of_nclr_responds_to_president_obamas_speech_in_el_paso_texas/. For coverage of the president's speech, see Milan Simonich, "In El Paso, President Obama renews national immigration debate, argues humane policy would aid national economy," *El Paso Times*, May 11, 2011.

38. Lopez, *op. cit.*, p. 16.

39. U.S. Immigration and Customs Enforcement: Memorandum, June 17, 2011, www.ice.gov/doclib/secure-communities/pdf/prosecutorial-discretion-memo.pdf. For coverage, see Susan Carroll, "ICE memo urges more discretion in immigration changes," *Houston Chronicle*, June 21, 2011, p. A3.

40. "Sharp Decline," *op. cit.*

41. For background, see Reed Karaim, "America's Border Fence," *CQ Researcher*, Sept. 19, 2008, pp. 745-768.

42. "Obama says the border fence is 'now basically complete,'" PolitiFact, www.politifact.com/truth-o-meter/statements/2011/may/16/barack-obama/obama-says-border-fence-now-basically-complete/.

The original rating of "partly true" was changed to "mostly false" on July 27, 2011.

43. See "Secure Communities," on the ICE website: www.ice.gov/secure_communities/; Julia Preston, "Immigration Crackdown Snares Americans," *The New York Times*, Dec. 14, 2011, p. A20, www.nytimes.com/2011/12/14/us/measures-to-capture-illegal-aliens-nab-citizens.html?pagewanted=all.

44. Coverage of the hearing by contributing writer Don Plummer. For additional coverage, see Brian Lawson, "11th Circuit won't rule on Alabama/Georgia laws until after Supreme Court rules on Arizona," *The Huntsville Times*, March 2, 2012; Jeremy Redmon, "Court to rule later on Georgia, Alabama anti-illegal immigrant laws," *The Atlanta Journal-Constitution*, March 2, 2012.

45. See Jacques Billeaud, "Judge blocks day labor rules in AZ immigration law," The Associated Press, March 1, 2012.

46. Steven A. Camarota, "A Record-Setting Decade of Immigration, 2000-2010," Center for Immigration Studies, October 2011, www.cis.org/articles/2011/record-setting-decade.pdf.

47. Fox News poll, Dec. 5-7, 2011, and CNN/ORC International poll, Nov. 18-20, 2011, cited at www.PollingReport.com/immigration.htm.

48. Quinnipiac University poll, Feb. 14-20, 2011, cited *ibid.*

49. ICE memo, *op. cit.*

50. "Immigration Court Backlog Tool," Transactional Records Access Clearinghouse, http://trac.syr.edu/phptools/immigration/court_backlog/ (visited March 2012).

51. "The Mexican-American Boom: Births Overtake Immigration," Pew Hispanic Center, July 24, 2011, www.pewhispanic.org/files/reports/144.pdf. The report depicts the phenomenon as "especially evident" among Mexican-Americans; it notes that Mexican-Americans are on average younger than other racial or ethnic groups and that Mexican-American women have more children than their counterparts in other groups. For background, see David Masci, "Latinos' Future," *CQ Researcher*, Oct. 17, 2003, pp. 869-892.

BIBLIOGRAPHY

Books

Coates, David, and Peter M. Siavelis (eds.), *Getting Immigration Right: What Every American Needs to Know*, **Potomac, 2009.**
Essays by 15 contributors representing a range of backgrounds and views examine, among other issues, the economic impact of immigration and proposed reforms to address illegal immigration. Includes notes, two-page list of further readings. Coates holds a professorship in Anglo-American studies at Wake Forest University; Siavelis is an associate professor of political science there.

Daniels, Roger, *Guarding the Golden Door: American Immigration Policy and Immigrants Since 1882*, **Hill and Wang, 2004.**
A professor of history emeritus at the University of Cincinnati gives a generally well-balanced account of developments and trends in U.S. immigration policies from the Chinese Exclusion Act of 1882 through the immediate post-9/11 period. Includes detailed notes, 16-page bibliography.

Gerber, David, *American Immigration: A Very Short Introduction*, **Oxford University Press, 2011.**
A professor of history at the University of Buffalo gives a compact, generally positive overview of the history of immigration from colonial America to the present. Includes two-page list of further readings.

Graham, Otis L. Jr., *Unguarded Gates: A History of America's Immigration Crisis*, **Rowman & Littlefield, 2004.**
A professor emeritus at the University of California-Santa Barbara provides a critical account of the United States' transition from an open-border policy with relatively small-scale immigration to a system of managed immigration that he views today as overwhelmed by both legal and illegal immigration. Includes notes.

Reimers, David M., *Other Immigrants: The Global Origins of the American People*, **New York University Press, 2005.**
A New York University professor of history emeritus brings together new information and research about the non-European immigration to the United States, emphasizing the emergence of "a new multicultural society" since 1940. Individual chapters cover Central and South America, East and South Asia, the Middle East, "new black" immigrants and refugees and asylees. Includes extensive notes, six-page list of suggested readings.

Waters, Mary C., and Reed Ueda (eds.), *The New Americans: A Guide to Immigration Since 1965*, **Harvard University Press, 2007.**
The book includes essays by more than 50 contributors, some covering broad immigration-related topics and others providing individual portraits of immigrant populations by country or region of origin. Includes detailed notes for each essay, comprehensive listing of immigration and naturalization legislation from 1790 through 2002. Waters is a professor of sociology at Harvard University, Ueda a professor of history at Tufts University.

Articles

"Reap What You Sow," *This American Life*, **Jan. 27, 2012, www.thisamericanlife.org/radio-archives/episode/456/reap-what-you-sow.**
The segment by reporter Jack Hitt on the popular public radio program found that Alabama's law to encourage undocumented immigrants to self-deport was having unintended consequences.

Kemper, Bob, "Immigration Reform: Is It Feasible?," *Washington Lawyer*, **October 2011, p. 22, www.dcbar .org/for_lawyers/resources/publications/washington_lawyer/october_2011/immigration_reform.cfm.**
The article gives a good overview of recent and current immigration debates, concluding with the prediction that any "permanent resolution" will likely prove to be "elusive."

Reports and Studies

"No Way to Live: Alabama's Immigrant Law," **Human Rights Watch, December 2011, www.hrw.org/reports/2011/12/14/no-way-live-0.**
The highly critical report finds that Alabama's law cracking down on illegal immigrants has "severely affected" the state's unlawful aliens and their children, many of them U.S. citizens, as well as "the broader community linked to this population."

Baxter, Tom, "Alabama's Immigration Disaster: The Harshest Law in the Land Harms the State's Economy

and Society," Center for American Progress, February 2012, www.americanprogress.org/issues/2012/02/pdf/alabama_immigration_disaster.pdf.

The critical account by journalist Baxter under the auspices of the progressive Center for American Progress finds that Alabama's anti-illegal immigration law has had "particularly harsh" social and economic costs and effects.

Passel, Jeffrey S., and D'Vera Cohn, "Unauthorized Immigrant Population: National and State Trends, 2010," Pew Hispanic Center, Feb. 1, 2011, www.pewhispanic.org/files/reports/133.pdf.

The 32-page report by the Washington-based center provides national and state-by-state estimates of the unauthorized immigrant population and the number of unauthorized immigrants in the workforce.

For More Information

American Civil Liberties Union, Immigrant Rights Project, 125 Broad St., 18th floor, New York, NY 10004; 212-549-2500; www.aclu.org/immigrants-rights. Seeks to expand and enforce civil liberties and civil rights of immigrants.

American Immigration Council, 1331 G St., N.W., 2nd floor, Washington, DC 20005; 202-507-7500; www.americanimmigrationcouncil.org. Supports sensible and humane immigration policies.

America's Voice, 1050 17th St., N.W., Suite 490, Washington, DC 20036; 202-463-8602; http://americasvoiceonline.org/. Supports "real, comprehensive immigration reform," including reform of immigration enforcement practices.

Center for Immigration Studies, 1522 K St., N.W., Suite 820, Washington, DC 20005-1202; 202-466-8185; www.cis.org. An independent, nonpartisan research organization that supports what it calls low-immigration, pro-immigrant policies.

Define American, www.defineamerican.com/. Founded by journalist and undocumented immigrant Jose Antonio Vargas, the web-based organization seeks to fix what it calls a "broken" immigration system.

Federation for American Immigration Reform, 25 Massachusetts Ave., N.W., Suite 330, Washington, DC 20001; 202-328-7004; www.fairus.org. Seeks "significantly lower" immigration levels.

Migration Policy Institute, 1400 16th St., N.W., Suite 300, Washington, DC 20036; 202-266-1940; www.migrationpolicy.org. A nonpartisan, nonprofit think tank dedicated to analysis of the movement of people worldwide.

National Council of La Raza, 1126 16th St., N.W., Suite 600, Washington, DC 20036-4845; 202-785-1670; www.nclr.org. The country's largest national Hispanic advocacy and civil rights organization.

National Immigration Forum, 50 F St., N.W., Suite 300, Washington, DC 20001; 202-347-0040; www.immigrationforum.org. Advocates for the values of immigration and immigrants to the nation.

Pew Hispanic Center, 1615 L St., N.W., Suite 700, Washington, DC 20036; 202-419-4300; www.pewhispanic.org/. Seeks to improve understanding of the U.S. Hispanic population and to chronicle Latinos' growing impact on the nation.

12

Child Poverty

Peter Katel

Impoverished Los Angeles residents queue up for free food, household items and toys at the Miracle in South Central event on Dec. 13, 2008. The national poverty rate is 15.1 percent — the highest in 28 years. More than a third of the 46.2 million people living below the poverty line are children.

From *CQ Researcher*, October 28, 2011.

J ason Barnett and his two brothers have better reason than many kids to welcome Friday afternoons. That's when they open a special backpack full of donated food that Jason brings home from his elementary school in Belen, N.M.

Inside are plastic-wrapped single servings of peanut butter and jelly, crackers, raisins, milk, juice and other healthy items. "You should see their eyes," says the boys' mother, Shannon Barnett. "There's usually cereal in it, which helps with breakfast over the weekend. If they're still hungry, I'm able to give them another bowl."

The Roadrunner Food Bank, New Mexico's major food charity, started the program 11 years ago after school officials in Albuquerque said some students went hungry on weekends. Now, demand is booming throughout the state, where 40 percent of New Mexicans — 806,000 out of a total population of 2 million — missed meals last year, according to a Roadrunner study.[1]

How many children went hungry isn't known. But children make up one-fourth of the population of New Mexico, which has a child-poverty rate of 30 percent, second only to Mississippi's (33 percent).[2]

Jason, 7, and his brothers — Andrew, 5, and Elias, 11 — weren't in danger of missing meals until about three years ago, their mother says. The family lives on about $15,000 a year that Paul Barnett earns at a building-supply company. That's well below the government's poverty threshold of $26,023 for a family of five with three children.[3]

305

Parental Unemployment Fuels Child Poverty

More than 12 percent of children in 14 states — including two of the biggest, California and Florida — have at least one unemployed parent, a factor that experts say contributes significantly to child poverty. In another dozen states, including New York and Texas, between 8 and 9 percent of children have at least one jobless parent. The national poverty rate has risen to 15.1 percent as unemployment hovers above 9 percent because of the recent recession.

Percentage of Children With At Least One Unemployed Parent, 2010

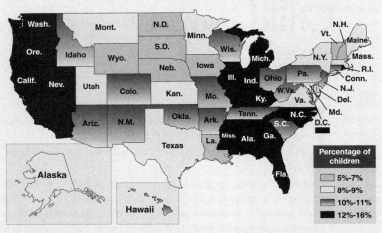

Source: "America's Children, America's Challenge," Annie E. Casey Foundation, 2011, www.aecf.org/~/media/Pubs/Initiatives/KIDS COUNT/123/2011KIDSCOUNT DataBook/2011KCDB_FINAL_essay.pdf

The Barnetts had managed to scrape by with the help of food stamps, a federal housing subsidy and a federal income-tax credit for low-income families. But about three years ago, when gas and food prices rose sharply, the family sought help: monthly baskets from the food bank, and the backpack for the boys.[4]

"I just kind of suck in my pride and just get help," Paul Barnett says. "I was kind of embarrassed at first. But a lot of my friends are in a lot worse shape."

Indeed, millions of Americans are in dire financial straits. The national poverty rate, 15.1 percent, is the highest in 28 years. In 1983 it hit 15.2 percent.[5]

The picture is even bleaker for children, who make up a fourth of the U.S. population and more than a third of the 46.2 million people living below the poverty threshold. Over all, one in five U.S. children lives below

the poverty line, a far higher rate than adults (13.7 percent) and the elderly (9 percent).[6]

It has been 52 years since the United States suffered a sustained bout of poverty as bad as the current one. In 1959, the rate hit 22.4 percent, concentrated among whites in isolated Appalachian mountain hollows and blacks in squalid urban ghettos and the rural South. The era spawned a spate of reform efforts, culminating in President Lyndon B. Johnson's War on Poverty program, which centered on providing welfare benefits to low-income families with children.

But by the mid-1990s, conservatives and some liberals alike were arguing that many of the Johnson-era reforms had created a culture of dependency on government aid. In 1996 Congress overhauled the welfare system, imposing work requirements and putting time limits on cash payments to the needy.

Welfare rolls plunged in the aftermath of the reforms. But the economic crisis, which began in 2007 and has pushed the national unemployment rate above 9 percent, has forced millions of families to seek government or private aid, or both. In response, Congress has expanded the welfare caseload, but only by 13 percent — not enough, advocates argue, to keep millions of children out of poverty. They are urging renewal of an emergency fund that Congress created in 2009 through the so-called economic stimulus bill — with an expiration date of Sept. 30, 2010.[7]

Child poverty arouses special concern because its effects can last a lifetime. "Children who are reared in poor families are more likely to fail in school, drop out of school, get arrested," says Ron Haskins, co-director of the Center on Children and Families at the Brookings Institution, a centrist think tank in Washington. "And the earlier the poverty starts, and the more years that a kid is reared in a household in poverty, the more likely those bad things are to happen."

Experts on both sides of the liberal-conservative divide agree that child poverty is causing the gap between rich and poor to widen. But they disagree on why more than 16 million Americans under age 18 live below the poverty line — and on how to improve the situation.

For conservatives skeptical of government anti-poverty projects, child poverty above all is a behavioral issue — a reflection of the growing tendency to have children out of wedlock. A report last year by the National Center for Health Statistics shows that unwed mothers — a growing number of them in their 20s — accounted for 40 percent of U.S. births in 2008, the most recent year for which data are available. That rate has risen steadily over two decades. It was 26 percent in 1988 and 33 percent in 1998.[8]

And last year, children below the poverty line in single-mother households outnumbered poor children in married-couple families, by 8.6 million to 5.8 million.[9]

"Our society is bifurcating into one of upper-middle-class children raised by college-educated couples who are married and children born out of marriage to . . . women who have an overwhelming probability of being poor and remaining poor," says Robert Rector, a senior research fellow at the Heritage Foundation, a conservative think tank in Washington.

But liberal poverty experts, while acknowledging a link between single motherhood and poverty, reject the notion that out-of-wedlock childbearing is either the main cause of child poverty or the key to its solution. "People are poor because they don't have enough income," says LaDonna Pavetti, vice president for

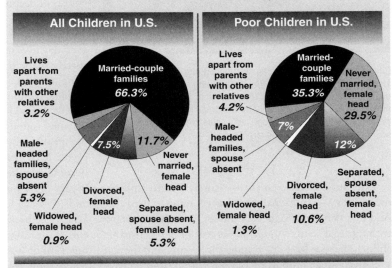

Poverty Most Prevalent in Single-Parent Families

More than half of poor children in the U.S. come from households with single mothers — whether divorced, separated, widowed or never having married — compared with one-fourth for all children. Two-thirds of all children live in families headed by married couples. Only about one-third of children in poverty come from such families.

Family Living Arrangements for All Children and Poor Children, 2009

All Children in U.S.

- Lives apart from parents with other relatives 3.2%
- Married-couple families 66.3%
- Male-headed families, spouse absent 5.3%
- Widowed, female head 0.9%
- Divorced, female head 7.5%
- Separated, spouse absent, female head 5.3%
- Never married, female head 11.7%

Poor Children in U.S.

- Lives apart from parents with other relatives 4.2%
- Male-headed families, spouse absent
- Married-couple families 35.3%
- Never married, female head 29.5%
- Widowed, female head 1.3%
- Divorced, female head 10.6%
- 7%
- Separated, spouse absent, female head 12%

* Poverty measures are based on families' annual pre-tax income. In 2009, the threshold for a family consisting of a single mother with one child was $14,787; with two children it was $17,285. The poverty line for a married couple with one child was $17,268; with two children it was $21,756.

** Percentages do not total 100 because of rounding.

Source: Thomas Gabe, "Welfare, Work, and Poverty Status of Female Headed Families With Children: 1987-2009," Congressional Research Service, July 2011, digitalcommons.ilr.cornell.edu/cgi/viewcontent.cgi?article=1852&context=key_workplace

family-income support policy at the liberal Center on Budget and Policy Priorities. "There is also a problem of people not having the skills to qualify for jobs that will move them out of poverty."

That problem is especially acute among Hispanics, who account for the single biggest number of children in poverty of any ethnic or racial group — 6.1 million. Non-Hispanic whites account for 5 million poor children and African-Americans for 4.4 million.[10]

Children of homeowners facing eviction in Long Beach, Calif., eat Thanksgiving dinner on Nov. 24, 2010, during a protest outside a bank. The economic crisis has forced millions of families to seek government or private aid, or both. Congress has expanded welfare benefits, but not enough, advocates argue, to keep millions of children out of poverty.

Educational achievement — closely tied to employment skills — traditionally has lagged among Hispanics. And that deficiency is greatest among immigrants, many without legal status. About 68 percent of poor Hispanic children have at least one immigrant parent. And though a relatively small proportion of poor Latino children have unemployed parents — about 19 percent — that proportion has risen significantly, from about 12 percent, in 2007.[11]

Anti-poverty activists want the federal government to boost spending on programs aimed at helping millions of people climb the socioeconomic ladder. Conservatives, on the other hand, contend that Washington already spends billions on such programs.

"I have no doubt that we have more people in poverty," says Michael Tanner, a senior fellow at the Cato Institute, a libertarian think tank in Washington. "But we're spending more money fighting poverty than ever before."

Conservatives also complain that in calculating the poverty rate, the government doesn't count food stamps, medical care, housing subsidies and other benefits for the poor. (The Census Bureau is studying how to devise a new poverty-calculation method that would include the value of benefits.)[12]

But anti-poverty advocates argue that including the benefits would simply show that while the government safety net is keeping some people from the severest levels of need, many more Americans are sliding beneath the poverty threshold.

"If you try various ways of correcting the data, you find fewer people in the most extreme forms of poverty," says Arloc Sherman, a senior researcher at the Center on Budget and Policy Priorities. "That has a bigger effect on counts of deeply poor people than on counts of the poor overall."

Such policy debates can seem far removed from the everyday lives of children living in poverty, but they ultimately shape the economic trajectory of families struggling to make ends meet.

Jane Trujillo and her husband, both deaf, have been unable to find jobs in Belen and can't afford to commute 60 miles roundtrip to Albuquerque.

Speaking by phone through a sign-language interpreter, Mrs. Trujillo says the backpack-food program has become essential to ensuring that her 6-year-old son and 9-year-old daughter don't go to bed hungry on weekends. "I have had to restrict the amount of milk," she says. "The backpack really helps, particularly toward the end of the month. We get $300 a month in food stamps, but $300 is not enough. Toward the end of the month, when food is tight, the kids eat first. They're more important than we are."

As policy advocates, lawmakers and anti-poverty groups seek solutions to the nation's child-poverty problem, here are some of the issues they are discussing:

Should Congress expand welfare funding?

When Congress overhauled the welfare system in 1996, it made a major change in the way Washington disburses welfare funds to the states. Under the old system, the government made annual appropriations that Congress adjusted according to need, as reflected in the number of eligible applicants in each state. Under the new system, states receive fixed amounts in the form of "block grants" that they then use to make monthly payments to the poor.[13]

Conservatives hail block-grant funding because it limits the expansion of a program that many of them distrust. But liberals complain that it leaves states with little or no flexibility to expand welfare rolls when economic disaster hits and poverty rises.

Total outlays to the states under the block-grant program — called Temporary Assistance to Needy Families (TANF) — have remained unchanged since 1996, at $16.5 billion per year. In addition, states contribute a total of $10.4 billion to TANF and related programs for the needy. That amount also has remained the same since 1996.[14]

But inflation eroded the value of the federal block grants by 28 percent from 1997 through last January, the nonpartisan Congressional Research Service calculated.[15]

A safety mechanism created by Congress when it switched to the block-grant approach provided $63 million, divided among 16 of the hardest-hit states, in fiscal 2010.[16] A separate "emergency contingency fund" created by the American Recovery and Reinvestment Act of 2009 — the "stimulus" law — gave states another $5 billion for TANF programs, including job-subsidy payments to employers, in fiscal 2009 and 2010.[17]

But critics say those measures haven't done nearly enough to keep millions of Americans from falling out of the middle class or sliding deeper into poverty.

"It used to be the case that TANF and its predecessor" — Aid to Families with Dependent Children (AFDC), the old welfare program Congress eliminated in 1996 —"kept millions of people above the poverty line and responded during recessions," says Sherman of the Center on Budget and Policy Priorities. "Now, having dwindled to a fraction of the previous real [inflation-adjusted]

Poverty Highest Among Minorities

Some 46 million Americans — 15.1 percent of the U.S. population — lived below the poverty line in 2010, including more than one-fourth of blacks and Hispanics. About one-fifth of those younger than 18 and a third of families headed by a single mother lived below the poverty threshold.

Percentage of People and Families in Poverty, 2010

Race	
White	22.9%
Black	27.4%
Asian	12.1%
Hispanic (any race)	26.6%
Age	
Under 18	22.0%
18 to 64	13.7%
65 and older	9.0%
Family type	
Married couple	6.2%
Female head, no husband present	31.6%
Male head, no wife present	15.8%
Total	**15.1%**

Source: "People and Families in Poverty By Selected Characteristics: 2009 and 2010," U.S. Census Bureau, March 2011, www.census.gov/hhes/www/poverty/data/incpovhlth/2010/table4.pdf

funding level, it is protecting many fewer people from recession and bouts of joblessness."

Indeed, argue Sherman and other critics, the TANF caseload has grown only modestly compared with the scale of the recession and what they see as the true level of need. In September 2010, the caseload stood at 1.9 million families — representing 4.4 million people, three-fourths of them children. That was only 200,000 more families than in July 2008, when the worst of the economic crisis began to grip the nation.[18] Yet, between 2009 and 2010, the number of people below the poverty line rose by 2.6 million — including 900,000 more children.[19]

Critics such as Sherman look to another program for needy families — food stamps — as a better approach than TANF for adjusting benefits during hard times. Unlike TANF, food-stamp allocations rise and fall according to need. "When the unemployment rate soared, the food stamp program responded," Sherman says.

The number of food-stamp recipients increased by nearly 82 percent, from 24.9 million to 45.3 million people, from July 2006 to July of this year, according to the nonprofit Food Research and Action Center, an advocacy organization. During that period, the nation's unemployment rate rose from 4.7 percent to 9.1 percent.[20]

But conservative policy analysts cite the food-stamp increase for a different reason than proof of flexibility. They point to it as evidence that the welfare system as a whole has been steadily expanding, not contracting.

One in Seven Households Is Short of Food

Nearly 15 percent of U.S. households lack enough food to meet their needs. Those with low food security have enough to avoid disrupting eating patterns if they turn to such strategies as dieting, using food stamps or visiting food pantries. Households with very low food security lack adequate income or other resources to obtain food and must periodically reduce their food intake.

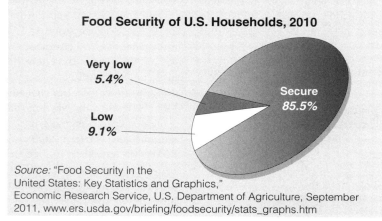

Food Security of U.S. Households, 2010

Very low
5.4%

Low
9.1%

Secure
85.5%

Source: "Food Security in the United States: Key Statistics and Graphics," Economic Research Service, U.S. Department of Agriculture, September 2011, www.ers.usda.gov/briefing/foodsecurity/stats_graphs.htm

Along with TANF cash payments and food stamps, they also cite continuing funding increases in medical assistance for the poor, child development programs such as Head Start, subsidized housing and other programs.[21] In this context, says the Heritage Foundation's Rector, TANF "only supplies 10 percent of assistance given to families with children."

As for expanding TANF funding, Rector argues, "I can't think of anything more foolish to do, and I can't think of anything more unpopular with the public than resurrecting an entitlement program for single parents. It would put a Band-Aid on the problem of single parenthood while ignoring the causes of poverty and the ever-increasing problem of dependency and poverty."

Some liberal poverty experts acknowledge that TANF is no panacea. "No one gets out of poverty by receiving cash assistance," says Elizabeth Lower-Basch, senior policy analyst for the Center for Law and Social Policy (CLASP), an advocacy organization in Washington. But, she says, welfare payments have been effective at lifting or keeping people out of extreme poverty. "One of the places where you see the weakness of TANF showing up is the growth of extreme child poverty."

Lower-Basch argues that the TANF emergency fund of 2009 provides a worthy model of how to extend the program's reach. But she acknowledges that the outlook for increasing anti-poverty funding in general is poor. "Not having things become worse feels like an accomplishment," she says.

The views expressed in September by Rep. Geoff Davis, R-Ky., chairman of the House Ways and Means Committee's Subcommittee on Human Resources, suggest that the priority of the House Republican majority, at least, is to tighten work requirements and curb reported abuses by recipients rather than expand funding.

"Not enough adults on welfare are working or preparing for work today," Davis said at a hearing he called on welfare-to-work rules and enforcement. He cited a July report by the Department of Health and Human Services that said only about one-fourth of "work-eligible adults" were meeting work requirements under TANF.[22]

Davis did say that "TANF can and should be strengthened to help more low-income families support themselves." But his remarks focused on what he said are abuses by state administrators. "Instead of the state helping more adults prepare for and begin work," he said, "they scour their books to uncover more spending they can credit to the TANF program and thereby reduce the number of people they have to engage in work activities."[23]

Are poor children now in elementary school a lost generation?

Experts of all political orientations agree that the longer children spend in poverty, the less their chances for bettering themselves as they grow up.

Researchers for Child Trends, a nonpartisan Washington think tank, wrote in 2009 that 10 studies found strong links between child poverty and poor academic performance, especially during early childhood. A host of social, emotional and behavioral problems are associated with child poverty as well, the researchers noted. One possible cause, they said, is that poor families are more likely to live in single-parent households, often under less supervision and amid more turmoil.[24]

"Studies find that those who experienced persistent poverty as children are much more likely to be poor as adults than those who were not poor during childhood," the researchers wrote. That trend runs more strongly in the black than the white population, they added, with 33 percent of African-Americans who were poor as children remaining in poverty as young adults. Among their white counterparts, only 7 percent were poor in their mid-20s.[25]

Haskins, the Brookings Institution scholar, disputes the notion that a generation of young people living through today's economic woes has, on the whole, lost its chance at advancement. But he says their circumstances are cause for "great concern."

"We want people to have an equal chance," he said. "That's been the whole idea of the country — and they don't."

Nevertheless, the possibility of upward mobility still exists, Haskins says. "If kids from the bottom get to college, they increase their odds of making it to the top by a factor of four."

Yet, college is not a sure ticket to stability or upward mobility. Linda Gonzales, 63, of Corrales, N.M., who helps take care of her 4- and 12-year-old grandchildren, is questioning her son's decision to pursue a college degree in civil engineering. "A lot of people are wanting to go back to school because they'll get better jobs, but I don't think the jobs are there," says Gonzales, who lost her nursing-care business last year. Gonzales says her son's part-time job selling hot tubs may not have much of a future either.

Joseph T. Jones, president and CEO of the Center for Urban Families, a Baltimore nonprofit that runs job-training and "responsible fatherhood" projects, argues that very young poor children may have better prospects than present conditions indicate. "Elementary-school students have a better shot at the economy turning around" by the time they are in their teens, he says.

But teenagers in poverty are in danger, Jones says. Speaking after meeting with African-American high-school students in Louisville, Ky., he says, "We are really at risk of saying to them, 'We don't care how much effort you put into education, once you graduate we don't have a darn thing for you.'"

Sherman of the Center on Budget and Policy Priorities argues strongly against the idea that poverty is an immovable obstacle to poor children's futures. Early-childhood education programs alone, he says, "deliver huge impacts on academic achievement and behavior even decades later."

In general, Sherman says, disadvantages that come with poverty are not immutable. "Successful interventions enable children to get the stimulation they need to grow," he says. At the same time, policies such as the Earned Income Tax Credit for poor families, or employment opportunities for struggling parents, can go a long way toward "removing the strains of poverty on the rest of the family, which might otherwise interfere with a child having a nurturing home environment," he says.

But analysts who contend that poverty is a cultural phenomenon more than an economic one offer a grimmer prognosis for today's poor young people. "Certainly a generation of kids who are going to struggle through a host of social problems — very poor school performance, marginal work ethic when they get out of school, drugs, a lot of criminal behavior — they're likely to repeat those problems when they become adults," says Rector of the Heritage Foundation.

He argues that government programs, especially those that involve boosting income, miss the point. "We clearly are not going to make any progress until we deal with the real causes of why families are poor," he says. Chief among them, he says, is the growing number of single-mother families.

Is single motherhood a bigger cause of child poverty than the low-wage economy?

A striking increase in out-of-wedlock births is adding fuel to a debate that's been running for decades — or, by some lights, for more than a century: To what extent does single motherhood lead to child poverty?

The two trends clearly are connected. The latest U.S. Census report on poverty notes that the poverty rate for children in single-mother households was 47 percent, but 11.6 percent in married-couple households. Overall, 31.6 percent of single-mother households were below the poverty line, compared with only 6.2 percent of married-couple families.[26]

Reuters/Lucy Nicholson

Children from homeless shelters walk to an after-school program at the South Los Angeles Learning Center on March 16, 2011. School on Wheels runs the program, which uses volunteers to tutor children in shelters, parks and motels around the city, as well as at two centers.

In Mississippi, 48 percent of children lived in single-parent families.[27]

Academics and advocates have been studying links between single motherhood and child poverty for decades. James Heckman, a Nobel laureate economist at the University of Chicago who specializes in social inequality, has written that the consequences of growing up in poverty can be deep and far-reaching. "There are large gaps in cognitive stimulation and emotional support at early ages," between children in two-parent and those in single-parent households, he wrote this year. But he went on to argue that early-childhood programs can compensate for some of the disadvantages.[28]

As Heckman noted, the issue has taken on greater urgency because childbirth by married women is on the decline. Among African-Americans, 72 percent of births are to single women. The statistic stands out given the disproportionate extent of poverty in the black population: 27.4 percent of African-Americans live below the poverty line. In the white, non-Hispanic population, the rate is about 10 percent.[29]

For conservative poverty experts, the trends indicate that unmarried motherhood is by far the greatest cause of child poverty. "Those women have an overwhelming probability of being poor and remaining poor," says the Heritage Foundation's Rector. "In general, being married reduces the probability of poverty by about 80 percent."

Rector acknowledges that joblessness caused by the recession has put more families below the poverty line. "But when the recession goes away," he says, "we'll have the same child poverty we had before it began. The reality of this debate is that it is politically incorrect to ever discuss why people are actually poor. This factor — marriage — is more important than dropping out of high school, but we never tell anyone."

Nevertheless, few dispute that households headed by married couples are less vulnerable to poverty. Jones, of the Center for Urban Families, says, "We shouldn't be shy about talking about the institution of marriage. It's pretty clear that children who are raised in two-parent households, particularly if they are married households, fare better than their counterparts in single-parent families."

But Jones — who fathered a son out of wedlock before settling down to married life, and another son, with another woman — warns that single-minded focus on marriage as the cure for poverty is potentially dangerous. Single parenthood should not be a reason for excluding people from benefits, he argues. "We should not be so rigid as to say you are not worthy of support if you are not on a path to marriage," Jones says.

Yet no other way to significantly reduce single parenthood may exist other than curtailing benefits, says Tanner of the Cato Institute. "You can't go on just giving people money for having kids," he says. Such a move undoubtedly would cause personal crises for any number of women — and their children — he acknowledges, adding that private charities could soften some of the blows. But, he says, "Without crises you're not going to get behavioral changes."

Unlike Rector, Tanner says he doesn't believe that single parenthood outranks all other poverty-generating factors. But, he says, it's important enough for policymakers to zero in on. "Having a child out of wedlock is a pretty good guarantee of being in poverty," he says.

Haskins of Brookings argues that unemployment outranks unmarried motherhood on the list of poverty's causes. In a recent paper, he cited a 30 percent decrease in poverty among single mothers and their children, from 47 percent in 1991 to 33 percent in 2000.[30] During that period — just before and after the 1996 welfare overhaul —"we saw a 40 percent increase in work rates of never-married mothers," he says. "Poverty fell like a rock for single-parent families to its lowest level ever."

Nevertheless, Haskins says, marriage — along with education — is almost as important as work in reducing child poverty. "If we don't do something about reducing the proportion of kids in female-headed families and don't do something about getting kids through at least two years of post-secondary school or vocational training," he says, "we are not going to have an impact on poverty."

BACKGROUND

Focus on Children

Children have been the main concern of U.S. anti-poverty efforts since such endeavors began in systematic fashion in the early 1900s. Until the last years of the 20th century, government's emphasis was on ensuring that mothers raising children on their own wouldn't have to enter the workplace.[31]

Likewise, officials wanted to ensure that orphans and poverty-stricken children could be raised in families rather than institutions. In 1909, the White House Conference on the Care of Dependent Children, presided over by President Theodore Roosevelt, led to establishment of a federal Children's Bureau and a foster-care system designed to place children in homes rather than orphanages.[32]

State governments, meanwhile, were making their own efforts to keep needy children at home. At a time when nearly all families depended on a father's paycheck, a movement to establish widows' pensions scored its first victory when Missouri enacted a pension law in 1911.

In reality, the promise of subsidized child care was not always kept, historians write. Payments were small enough that widows and divorced or abandoned women had to supplement them with paid work. In Philadelphia, 84 percent of pension recipients held jobs. In Chicago the rate was 66 percent and in Los Angeles 57 percent. County pension administrators worried that more substantial payments would encourage wives to walk out on their husbands, or husbands to desert their families.[33]

President Lyndon B. Johnson greets a resident during a tour of the impoverished Appalachia region in June 1964. Widespread poverty in Appalachian mountain hollows, urban ghettos and the rural South spawned a spate of reform efforts, culminating in Johnson's War on Poverty program, which targeted low-income families with children.

Lyndon Baines Johnson Library & Museum

An even greater weakness of the state pension laws was that counties didn't have to participate. In 1931, the Children's Bureau reported that half of the nation's counties had not established pension systems.

At that point, the widespread misery of the Great Depression had created enormous demand for a comprehensive nationwide system of providing for children whose families had fallen on hard times. Part of the New Deal package of social legislation pushed through Congress by President Franklin D. Roosevelt's administration was the Aid to Dependent Children (ADC) program, created by the Social Security Act of 1935.

Under ADC, the federal government contributed to states' pension programs. Payments to families, which by the law's language were intended to help provide a "reasonable subsistence compatible with decency and health," were capped at $18 a month for the first child and $12 monthly for subsequent children.[34]

Nearly all the child beneficiaries lived with widowed mothers. Women who had been abandoned, or were divorced, accounted for most of the remaining pensioners. Only 2 percent of the children in the program lived with mothers who had given birth out of wedlock.

The overall population of households headed by unwed mothers was greater than the number who received government assistance. State ADC administrators tended to

CHRONOLOGY

1909-1935 Early welfare goals include keeping widowed mothers from having to join the workforce.

1909 President Theodore Roosevelt calls first White House Conference on Care of Dependent Children.

1911 Missouri passes nation's first pension for widows, to free them from working.

1931 Nearly all states have widows' pensions, but half the counties don't participate.

1935 New Deal's Social Security Act includes first federal welfare system, Aid to Dependent Children.

1960s *Democratic president launches biggest package of domestic social programs since New Deal.*

1962 President John F. Kennedy praises new book, The Other America, documenting widespread poverty. . . . Aid to Dependent Children is renamed Aid to Families with Dependent Children (AFDC).

1964 Democratic President Lyndon B. Johnson declares War on Poverty, which sparks a number of federal initiatives, including Head Start.

1965 The Negro Family: A Case for National Action, by Labor Department staffer Daniel Patrick Moynihan, argues for jobs for men over welfare, expresses concern at the growth in single-mother black households.

1967 In an early effort to link welfare to work, Congress establishes voluntary Work Incentive (WIN) program to encourage AFDC recipients to obtain job training and jobs.

1971-1987 Welfare opponents argue AFDC fosters dependency.

1971 Congress makes WIN mandatory but doesn't fully fund revamped program.

1972 Children in single-mother families account for 50 percent of all children below poverty line.

1981 Congress lets states use welfare funds to subsidize job training.

1986 President Ronald Reagan decries "welfare culture" marked by family breakdown.

1988 Family Support Act requires AFDC recipients to log 20 hours a week of job training or employment.

1992-2010 *Democratic president oversees major transformation of welfare system.*

1992 Vowing to "end welfare as we know it," Democratic presidential candidate Bill Clinton promises to revamp the system into a "second chance, not a way of life."

1995 New Republican House majority introduces welfare-revamping Work Opportunity Act, which passes both houses.

1996 President Clinton vetoes the bill. . . . White House negotiations with both parties produce Personal Responsibility and Work Opportunity Reconciliation Act, with stiff work requirements for welfare recipients.

1999 Work rate of never-married mothers on welfare rises to 66 percent, up from 46.5 percent in 1995.

2000 Poverty among single mothers and their children falls to all-time low of 33 percent of population.

2008 Forty percent of U.S. births are to unmarried mothers.

2009 "Stimulus" law creates $5 billion emergency fund for national welfare system.

2010 Poverty rate grows to 15.1 percent, with population below poverty line growing by 2.6 million to 46.2 million in one year.

2011 Agriculture Department reports nearly 15 percent of population, including 16.2 million children, lives in "food-insecure" households. . . . Florida and three other states require drug tests for welfare applicants.

bar support to families of unmarried women, who were considered far outside the bounds of respectability and traditional morality. During the 1950s, at least 19 states adopted policies that prohibited aid to children who were born to unwed mothers after they had begun receiving welfare.[35]

ADC gave state officials considerable power in setting eligibility standards. Under rules that were struck down by courts in 1960, states could require that aid go only to children living in so-called "suitable homes." In practice, that provision was used to block aid to unmarried mothers as well as many black mothers.[36]

Distinctions between categories of single mothers were reinforced by a change to the Social Security law in 1939. A separate Social Security benefit was created for widows and their surviving children. The effect was to divide beneficiaries of government support between the children of women whose husbands had died and the offspring of mothers who had divorced, been abandoned or had never married.

By 1961 nearly all families headed by widowed mothers were receiving Society Security benefits, while only 7.7 percent of families receiving ADC funds were headed by widows.

War on Poverty

President John F. Kennedy's inauguration in 1961 followed a campaign in which poverty surfaced as a national issue for the first time since the 1930s.

Kennedy's campaign visit to impoverished Appalachian communities in West Virginia made an obvious impression on the candidate and received wide media coverage. One year after becoming president, Kennedy praised a new book, *The Other America*, by writer and political activist Michael Harrington, who reported on and denounced the extent of poverty in a rich nation.[37]

Harrington's book also influenced Kennedy's successor, Lyndon Johnson.

Providing children the opportunity to rise from poverty was one of the threads running through Johnson entire War on Poverty — the name he gave to a collection of social programs passed during his administration — and the main idea animating Head Start, an early-childhood education program still operating today.

Specifically, Head Start owed its existence to data presented to Johnson's poverty czar, Sargent Shriver.

Shriver's researchers told him that half of the nation's 30 million poor were children, most of them under age 12. "It was clear that it was foolish to talk about a 'total war against poverty,' the phraseology the president was using, if you were doing nothing about children," Shriver told associates.[38]

The "war," in combination with the social and political changes that rocked the country during the 1960s, helped shape welfare policy and law during the decades that followed.

One way it did so was by spurring a notable expansion in welfare rolls. The federal family-support program — renamed Aid to Families with Dependent Children (AFDC) in 1962 — saw beneficiaries more than double, from 3.5 million in 1962 to 7.4 million in 1970.[39]

Poverty itself didn't double in that period. But, encouraged by a welfare-recipients movement that considered benefits a right, not a privilege, low-income citizens became more likely to apply for welfare. During the 1960s, an estimated 33 percent of eligible families received assistance. By 1971, more than 90 percent of eligible households were on the welfare rolls.

Also promoting welfare expansion were U.S. Supreme Court decisions that overturned state welfare rules limiting eligibility. They included so-called "man in the house" policies that barred or stopped payments when adult males were found in recipients' or applicants' homes. Another court decision eliminated long-term residency requirements for recipients.

By 1971, a backlash was already under way. *U.S. News & World Report*, the most conservative of the three national newsweeklies, published a piece reporting that welfare spending threatened to "bankrupt the States and cities, and to drain the U.S. Treasury with chronic federal deficits."[40]

The magazine pointed to one development in particular: the growth in mother-headed households. AFDC child recipients whose fathers had deserted or whose mothers had never wed accounted for 80 percent of young beneficiaries, up from 60 percent a few years earlier, the magazine reported (without specifying the number of years).[41]

While some may have viewed *U.S. News*'s take on the issue as political spin, there was no question that female-headed households were becoming more common, especially in the poor population. In 1960, children in such

States to Welfare Seekers: Drug Test Comes First

"Taxpayers deserve to know money is being used for its intended purpose."

As the bad economy drives up demand for welfare and employment aid, some state governments are imposing a controversial new condition for assistance: drug screening.

This year alone:

- Florida required welfare applicants to pay for — and pass — a drug test. They are reimbursed the $25 to $35 fee unless they fail. However, a federal judge in late October temporarily blocked enforcement of the new law on constitutional grounds.
- Missouri authorized drug testing of welfare recipients suspected of drug use — a step Arizona took two years ago. Those who test positive lose benefits unless they sign up for treatment.
- Indiana required aid recipients applying for job training to be tested for drugs. A positive result for drug use bars an applicant from training for 90 days, or for one year after a second positive result.

And legislators in some 35 other states have introduced similar drug-testing measures.[1]

"The taxpayers deserve to know that the money they are spending is being used for its intended purpose," said Joe Follick, a spokesman for the Florida Department of Children and Families. "If a family receiving [cash assistance] includes someone who has a substance-abuse problem, the odds of that money being used for purposes other than helping that family increases."[2]

But the American Civil Liberties Union (ACLU) won the first round in a legal challenge to the lawsuit when U.S. District Judge Mary Scriven of Orlando ruled that the new law was unlikely to survive a lawsuit that claims the law violates the Fourth Amendment's protection against unreasonable search and seizure. Scriven was appointed by President George W. Bush.

The judge said the state had failed to show a "special need" warranting exemption from the requirement to show probable cause or reasonable suspicion. "If invoking an interest in preventing public funds from potentially being used to fund drug use were the only requirement to establish a special need," she wrote, "the state could impose drug testing as an eligibility requirement for every beneficiary of every government program." The injunction she granted suspending the law remains in effect pending a full hearing, not yet scheduled.[3]

The ACLU sued on behalf of Luis Lebron, a 35-year-old Navy veteran who is caring for his 4-year-old son and disabled mother while studying accounting at the University of Central Florida. Responding to Scriven's order, he said he was "happy that the judge stood up for me and my rights and said the state can't act without a reason or suspicion."[4]

The lawsuit's Fourth Amendment argument echoed a federal court decision in 2000 that threw out a similar drug-test law in Michigan.

Drug testing of individuals not suspected of a crime is constitutionally permissible only where public safety is concerned, the court said, citing testing of people whose work requires them to carry a gun. "In this instance, there is no indication of a concrete danger to public safety which demands departure from the Fourth Amendment's main rule and normal requirement of individualized suspicion," the ruling said.[5]

Despite the resistance from civil-liberties advocates, however, conservative politicians and lawmakers see drug testing as a way to avoid channeling welfare money to people they view as undeserving of it.

In advocating for Florida's law, Republican Gov. Rick Scott asserted that drug abuse is more common among welfare recipients. "Studies show that people that are on welfare are higher users of drugs than people not on welfare," Scott said in a CNN interview in June. "Our taxpayers don't want to subsidize somebody else's drug addiction."[6]

The results from the first batch of about 1,000 tests didn't bear out Scott's impression, however. About 2 percent of applicants tested positive for drug use, the state's Department of Children and Families announced. Another 2 percent did not complete the application process, including the drug test for unspecified reasons. Test supporters said the abstainers knew they would fail the drug exam. Opponents said the walkaways couldn't afford to advance the drug test fee or couldn't reach a testing facility.[7]

By comparison, in 2010 just under 9 percent of the population age 12 and above reported using illicit drugs in the preceding month, according to the Department of Health and Human Services.[8]

Like Florida's governor, Rep. Geoff Davis, R-Ky., chairman of the House Ways and Means Human Resources Subcommittee, has spoken approvingly of drug tests for welfare applicants.

"In a world where many employers require drug testing to ensure workers are clean and sober, neither taxpayers nor welfare recipients are helped if we have a lower standard for those collecting welfare benefits designed to help them enter work," Davis said.

He spoke at a recent hearing on the federal welfare law, Temporary Assistance for Needy Families (TANF). Passed in 1996 with bipartisan support, the law imposed work requirements, put time limits on cash payments to the needy and authorized drug tests as a condition of aid.

But others in Congress are questioning whether money spent on drug testing might divert funds from the poor.

"Do you think it's a better investment, given the limited nature of the resources that we have, to drug test everyone?" Rep. Joseph Crowley, D-N.Y., asked Scott Wetzler, chief of psychology at New York's Montefiore Hospital, who runs a treatment program for welfare recipients with histories of drug abuse.[9]

"It would be a huge, huge, practical problem to actually drug test everybody," said Wetzler, whose program tests only people in drug treatment. "And it's not clear that you actually would be able to have the treatment capacity to receive all those people into treatment. So it's not clear what you even do with that information if you had it."[10]

— *Peter Katel*

Republican Gov. Rick Scott of Florida contends that drug abuse is more common among welfare recipients and that "our taxpayers don't want to subsidize somebody else's addiction."

"Missouri Legislature approves drug tests for welfare recipients," *St. Louis Post-Dispatch*, May 11, 2011, www.stltoday.com/news/local/govt-and-politics/article_953196cf-8104-5758-8198-60e151debe90.html; Amy B. Wang, "Welfare recipients face drug tests," *Arizona Republic*, Nov. 25, 2009, www.azcentral.com/arizonarepublic/local/articles/2009/11/25/20091125urinetesting1125.html.

[2] Quoted in Catherine Whittenburg, "Welfare drug-testing yields 2% positive results," *Tampa Bay Online*, Aug. 24, 2011, www.tbo.com/news/politics/2011/aug/24/3/welfare-drug-testing-yields-2-percent-positive-res-ar-252458/.

[3] Quoted in Rebecca Catalenello, "Florida's welfare drug testing halted by federal judge," *The Miami Herald*, Oct. 25, 2011, www.miamiherald.com/2011/10/24/2470519/florida-welfare-drug-testing-halted.html.

[4] Quoted in Schneider and Kennedy, *op. cit.*

[5] *Marchwinski v. Howard*, 113 F.Supp.2d 1134, www.aclufl.org/pdfs/Marchwinski.pdf.

[6] Aaron Sharockman, "Rick Scott Says Welfare Recipients Are More Likely to Use Illicit Drugs," *St. Petersburg Times*, June 9, 2011.

[7] Whittenburg, *op. cit.*; Kelli Kennedy, "Nearly 1,600 welfare applicants decline drug test," The Associated Press, Oct. 11, 2011.

[8] "Results from the 2010 National Survey on Drug Use and Health: Summary of National Findings," Health and Human Services Department, September 2011, http://oas.samhsa.gov/NSDUH/2k10NSDUH/2k10Results.htm#Fig7-1.

[9] "Hearing of the House Ways and Means Committee, 'Improving Work and Other Welfare Reform Goals, Focusing on Reauthorization of the Temporary Assistance for Needy Families Program,'" Federal News Service, Sept. 8, 2011.

[10] *Ibid.*

[1] A.G. Sulzberger, "States Adding Drug Test as Hurdle for Welfare," *The New York Times*, Oct. 11, 2011, www.nytimes.com/2011/10/11/us/states-adding-drug-test-as-hurdle-for-welfare.html?ref=us; Mike Schneider and Kelli Kennedy, "Florida Welfare Drug Testing Law Blocked by Federal Judge," The Associated Press, Oct. 24, 2011, www.huffingtonpost.com/2011/10/24/rick-scott-drug-testing-welfare-florida_n_1029332.html; Tom Coyne, "Indiana the first state to require drug tests for job training," The Associated Press, *Chesterton Tribune* (Indiana), July 11, 2011, http://chestertontribune.com/Business/indiana_the_first_state_to_requi.htm; Rebecca Berg,

Child Poverty Most Prevalent in South

Mississippi has the nation's highest child-poverty rate, with one in three residents under age 18 below the poverty threshold. Three other Southern states — Alabama, Arkansas and Louisiana — are in the top five. New Mexico ranks second, with 30 percent of children in poverty. California far outpaces other states in the total number of children in poverty, at slightly more than 2 million.

Percentage and Number of Children Under 18 in Poverty
(by state, 2010)

State	Percent	Number	State	Percent	Number
United States	**22%**	**15,749,000**	Illinois	19%	600,000
Mississippi	33%	242,000	Pennsylvania	19%	522,000
New Mexico	30%	154,000	Rhode Island	19%	42,000
Alabama	28%	311,000	Wisconsin	19%	250,000
Arkansas	28%	193,000	Delaware	18%	37,000
Louisiana	27%	300,000	Kansas	18%	131,000
Kentucky	26%	263,000	Maine	18%	48,000
South Carolina	26%	278,000	Nebraska	18%	82,000
Tennessee	26%	377,000	South Dakota	18%	36,000
Texas	26%	1,751,000	Washington	18%	284,000
Georgia	25%	611,000	Colorado	17%	211,000
North Carolina	25%	560,000	Vermont	17%	21,000
Oklahoma	25%	227,000	Iowa	16%	115,000
West Virginia	25%	96,000	North Dakota	16%	24,000
Arizona	24%	392,000	Utah	16%	136,000
Florida	23%	924,000	Minnesota	15%	192,000
Michigan	23%	539,000	Hawaii	14%	41,000
Ohio	23%	624,000	Massachusetts	14%	201,000
California	22%	2,013,000	New Jersey	14%	295,000
Indiana	22%	342,000	Virginia	14%	265,000
Nevada	22%	144,000	Wyoming	14%	19,000
Oregon	22%	184,000	Alaska	13%	24,000
Missouri	21%	291,000	Connecticut	13%	103,000
New York	21%	901,000	Maryland	13%	173,000
Montana	20%	44,000	New Hampshire	10%	28,000
Idaho	19%	80,000			

Source: "Data Across States," Annie E. Casey Foundation, 2011, datacenter.kidscount.org/data/acrossstates/Default.aspx

households accounted for 9.2 percent of all children and 23.7 percent of all poor children. By 1972, children in single-mother families represented 14.2 percent of all children and more than 50 percent of poor children.[42]

Families in Crisis

Single motherhood was especially prevalent among African-Americans, who were also disproportionately represented on welfare rolls. As early as 1965, Daniel Patrick Moynihan, a liberal New Deal-style Democrat who was then a staff member of the Labor Department's Office of Policy Planning and Research, zeroed in on that trend. In a report titled, "The Negro Family: The Case for National Action," he argued that employment of fathers was far more valuable than welfare payments in lifting families out of poverty.[43]

"In the beginning, the number of AFDC families in which the father was absent because of desertion was less than a third of the total," Moynihan wrote. "Today it is two-thirds." He linked paternal abandonment to persistent joblessness for black men. "Negro unemployment, with the exception of a few years during World War II and the Korean War, has continued at disaster levels for 35 years."[44]

Initially, Moynihan's report was greeted positively by African-American leaders, including the Rev. Martin Luther King Jr., many of whom had also expressed alarm at a growing number of black households headed by single mothers. They were echoing concerns of earlier generations of black leaders. W. E. B. DuBois, the most prominent African-American scholar and intellectual activist of the 20th century, had condemned the single-motherhood trend as far back as 1899.[45]

Nevertheless, applause for Moynihan's report faded quickly. Reactions among black leaders and white liberals turned hostile, guided by the view that Moynihan was holding African-Americans entirely responsible for black poverty.

To some extent, that response may have been inspired less by Moynihan's paper than by the favorable reception that the report got from conservatives. They took it, wrote

John McWhorter, a present-day analyst of race-related issues, "as a statement rather than as a 'case for action.' "

Nonetheless, McWhorter argued that the decades that followed provided evidence that Moynihan had focused accurately on one element of the poverty equation in the country's most disproportionately poverty-stricken population: "Multigenerational welfare dependency and all-but-fatherless neighborhoods became a norm in poor black communities," McWhorter wrote. "Surely the burden of proof is upon those who would argue that this was unconnected with the relaxation of eligibility rules for AFDC benefits in the 1960s."[46]

Other scholars argue from a more liberal perspective that Moynihan's emphasis on male employment discouraged efforts to raise AFDC payments or provide well-paying jobs for welfare mothers. At the same time, liberals contend, the report strengthened efforts to require AFDC mothers to get jobs. "Requiring welfare recipients to work, the argument went, might put pressure on mothers and fathers to stay together or not have children in the first place," three historians wrote in a history of welfare.[47] As debate swirled over the Moynihan report, its examination of the links between family structure, economics and poverty may have influenced the first War on Poverty-era congressional efforts to promote employment for welfare recipients.

In 1967, Congress established the Work Incentive (WIN) program, which required states to provide training and employment programs for "appropriate" AFDC beneficiaries. And to encourage recipients to work, some of what they earned — the first $30, plus one-third of the remaining amount — wouldn't be counted against their welfare payments. (A similar, smaller program set up in 1961 had stricter incentives for recipients to find employment.)[48]

Overall, the welfare-law amendment that created WIN marked a shift in attitude, notes Thomas Gabe, a social policy analyst for the Congressional Research Service. The law replaced requirements that services to recipients be "rehabilitative" and "competence-enhancing." Instead, the law now emphasized practical, job-finding assistance, such as job and training referral.[49]

Requiring Work

The WIN program only hinted at the transformation ahead. Discontent with the idea of paying people who

Seven-year-old Jayla gets ready for her weekly tutoring session last March 16 at the shelter in Los Angles where she lives with her mother. One in five U.S. children lives below the poverty line, a far higher rate than adults (13.7 percent) and the elderly (9 percent).

Reuters/Lucy Nicholson

didn't work, even if they were single mothers, was increasing both in Washington policy circles and in the states.[50]

In 1971, Congress changed WIN from a voluntary program to one in which welfare recipients were required to participate if they had no preschool-age children at home or other special circumstances. However, the practical effects of the new requirement were limited because the program wasn't fully funded.

Similarly, in 1971, California's Republican governor, Ronald W. Reagan, promoted a new approach to welfare that he dubbed "workfare." The legislature authorized a pilot program that required welfare recipients to get jobs. The program never got fully off the ground, however. A 1976 study by the state Employment Development Department concluded that it was badly designed, but a legislative sponsor said that counties ignored the project.[51]

Still, the appeal of requiring welfare recipients to work continued to grow. In 1981, during the first year of Reagan's presidency, Congress granted states the power to tailor WIN programs as they saw fit. States also gained

Food Banks Support Many in New Mexico

"We always ate, but sometimes just a little."

On a sunny morning in late September, 75 mothers and children, mostly Spanish-speaking Mexican immigrants, lined up in the parking lot of a mobile home community in the dusty South Valley of Albuquerque, N.M.

The crowd waited in line to fill baskets with cucumbers, onions, jalapeño chilies, cartons of long-life milk, dry pasta and other supplies from the Roadrunner Food Bank.

In the days before the monthly food deliveries started, "We always ate," says Laura Sánchez, the mother of a 4-month-old girl and two older children, "but sometimes just a little." Her husband works construction, earning about $350 a week when there's work, but often there is none.

"We started to see this two years ago," says Guillermo Yelo, pastor of Camino de Vida (Pathway of Life) church, who organized the food distribution. "A lot of people here don't have jobs. It made me realize the need for help."

A few hours later and about 10 miles north, another group gathered in a school gym in Corrales, a village that began as an 18th-century land grant by the Spanish crown.[1]

Among them was Lynette Bratvold, a homeowner who works two clerical jobs to support her husband and 3-year-old son. "My husband stays home with our child so that we don't have to pay outrageous child-care costs," she says. "So we need assistance with food."

Her husband, a high-school graduate, worked as a security guard when he was employed — earning at most $10 an hour. "I'm working 50-60 hours a week, and it's still not enough," she says.

As more people, even those working full time, needed assistance, the food bank, the state's main food charity, saw its distribution rise to about 24 million pounds in fiscal 2010-11 — a 10 percent increase over the previous year, says spokeswoman Sonya Warwick.

Nationally, food banks served 5.7 million a week in 2009 (the latest numbers available), a 27 percent increase since 2005, according to Feed America, a national alliance of food charities.[2]

Now, Feed America is warning Roadrunner and other food operations in New Mexico of a looming cutback in the free food it receives from the U.S. Department of Agriculture, which contributes about 20 percent of Roadrunner's stock. "We've been told to expect a reduction of 40 percent to 50 percent of that food," Warwick says. "We are trying to make sure we have various food sources so that when the cuts hit we don't have a crisis."

In fact, New Mexico is a state with two distinct populations, and one already is in crisis. Affluent New Mexicans, those who support the state's international reputation as an artists' haven, skiing destination and nuclear research center, are doing just fine, on the whole.

But the other New Mexico has been suffering a slow-motion crisis for several years. The state's 30 percent child-poverty rate is exceeded only by Mississippi's 33 percent.[3] And while the unemployment rate of 6.6 percent is lower than the national average of 9.1 percent, the state's 18.2 percent poverty rate in 2009 is significantly higher than the latest national rate of 15.1 percent. A longtime prevalence of low-wage work, compounded by the scarcity of regular employment in parts of the state, including the New Mexico portion of the Navajo Nation (most of which is in

authority to use federal welfare funds to subsidize on-the-job training.

States got further encouragement to step up work requirements from a 1986 report by the private, non-profit Manpower Demonstration Research Corp. (MDRC), a think tank on poverty-related issues. After studying reorganized welfare-to-work programs in eight states, Manpower concluded that they could increase

employment and be cost-effective — though not to an extraordinary extent.

In his 1986 State of the Union address, Reagan called for changing the welfare system, arguing that it should be judged by how many recipients left the program because they no longer needed support. "In the welfare culture, the breakdown of the family, the most basic support system, has reached crisis proportions — in female and

Arizona), explain the disparity between relatively low joblessness and high poverty.

"We have chunks of counties where people just aren't in the formal economy," says Gerry Bradley, research director at New Mexico Voices for Children, a nonprofit advocacy group.

"We're sort of bouncing along the bottom," Bradley says. He adds, citing 0.9 percent employment growth during the 12 months ending last August, "Maybe we're starting to turn around."[4]

New Mexico is a so-called "majority minority" state, with a population that's 46 percent Hispanic (both citizens and immigrants) and 9 percent Native American, a white, non-Hispanic population of 40 percent, plus small percentages of black, Asian and multi-racial people. The state ranks fourth from the bottom nationwide in a composite score of child-development indicators assembled by Voices for Children that includes the percentages of low-birth-weight babies and households with no stable employment.[5]

Hispanic New Mexicans tend to be concentrated in occupations that require less education — construction, above all. And construction, Bradley says, was "hammered by the recession."

Echoing Bradley's conclusion are the mothers gathered for food in South Valley.

"My husband works sometimes for two days, sometimes for a couple of weeks," says Soledad Murillo, a 47-year-old grandmother of six and mother of three daughters, none married. A 15-year New Mexico resident who comes from Durango, Mexico, Murillo says that jobs used to be far easier to find.

Linda Aguayo, who fled the ultraviolent Mexican border town of Ciudad Juárez three years ago, then returned, then fled again five months ago, says her husband fixes refrigerator cases and other store appliances. "But it's not stable work," she says. "Whatever he makes just pays the rent."

Roadrunner Food Bank

The Roadrunner Food Bank's Mobile Food Pantry helps struggling families throughout New Mexico. The program served 85,000 children and 127,500 adults last year.

Without the donated food, she says, "We'd be eating less."

— *Peter Katel*

[1] "Brief History of Corrales," Corrales Historical Society, 2004, www.corraleshistory.com/html/morehistory.html.

[2] "Hunger in America: Key Findings," 2010, http://feedingamerica.org/hunger-in-america/hunger-studies/hunger-study-2010/key-findings.aspx.

[3] "Children in Poverty (Percent) — 2010," Kids Count Data Center, Annie E. Casey Foundation, undated, http://datacenter.kidscount.org/data/acrossstates/Rankings.aspx?ind=43.

[4] *Ibid.*

[5] "Early Childhood Supports in New Mexico," New Mexico Voices for Children, updated 2010, www.nmvoices.org/attachments/ece-supports-2010-update.pdf.

child poverty, child abandonment, horrible crimes and deteriorating schools," Reagan declared. He announced that his domestic-policy council would develop a new approach to aiding the poor.[52]

By the following year, Congress took another step toward making work a condition of welfare. The Family Support Act of 1988 obliged AFDC recipients, unless specifically exempted, to enroll in job training or find employment.

That goal was reflected in the name given to related state programs, Job Opportunities and Basic Skills Training (JOBS). Because recipients who could not obtain child care were exempt from the new standard, Congress stepped up funding for that service. JOBS participants were required to work or train for 20 hours a week.

But by the standards of those who hoped that the 1988 law would transform the welfare system, actual changes were modest. The General Accounting Office (now the Government Accountability Office) reported in 1995 that about 20 percent of eligible AFDC recipients participated in some JOBS activity each month, though not all of them for the mandated 20 hours a week.

But the law set a new tone concerning welfare recipients and what was expected of them. Politicians took note that those expectations reflected attitudes among a broad swath of voters in both parties.

Accordingly, Democratic presidential candidate Bill Clinton vowed during his 1992 campaign to "end welfare as we know it." Elaborating, Clinton said in a campaign commercial: "Those who are able must go to work. . . . It's time to make welfare what it should be — a second chance, not a way of life."[53]

Slightly more than two years later, newly triumphant Republicans who had overturned longtime Democratic control of the House introduced the Work Opportunity Act of 1995. The bill reflected Republicans' campaign pledge, laid out in their "Contract With America" political platform, to "achieve what some 30 years of massive welfare spending has not been able to accomplish: reduce illegitimacy, require work and save taxpayers money."[54]

As debate over welfare intensified, Clinton vetoed two Republican-crafted bills that he said were too harsh in their treatment of welfare mothers. He pointed to their failure to provide adequately for child care and medical care for AFDC recipients entering the job market.[55]

For a Democratic president, welfare was politically tricky. Clinton's party was divided between so-called "neoliberals" (like himself), who strongly supported replacing the old welfare system, and traditional Democrats, who found more to support than to oppose in AFDC.[56]

In 1996, intense negotiations between Clinton and Republican leaders, and between Clinton and his fellow Democrats, produced the Personal Responsibility and Work Opportunity Reconciliation Act of 1996.

Hailed as the most significant piece of social legislation since the War on Poverty, the law required that recipients of what had become TANF go to work within two years of receiving aid and that aid be limited to five years. Moreover, the welfare-funding system was changed to fixed "block grants," replacing need-gauged appropriations.[57]

In the context of the economic boom of the late 1990s, the new law showed some remarkable results. The work rate of never-married mothers shot up from 46.5 percent of their total population in 1995 to 66 percent in 1999, an increase of about 40 percent in four years.[58]

As a result, Haskins of Brookings reported in a study last summer that poverty among single mothers and their children decreased from a 1991 peak of 47.1 percent to 33 percent in 2000 — the lowest level ever for that group.[59]

When the full force of the recession hit in 2009, however, another feature of the new welfare system became apparent. The block-grant funding scheme had the effect of limiting expansion of welfare rolls, the Congressional Research Service reported. "The fixed nature of TANF funding imposes some financial risk on states," it said. "Generally states bear the risk of increased costs from a cash welfare-caseload rise."[60]

CURRENT SITUATION
Budget Worries

Poverty experts worry that deficit-reduction efforts could shortchange funding for medical care for poor children and their families. Up to now, they say, the medical system for the poor has been responding effectively to the nation's worsening economic conditions.

While the number of poor children has grown in recent years, the population of those not covered by medical insurance declined — from 7.9 million in 2007 to 7.3 million in 2010, the Census Bureau reported. During that period, the number of children covered by Medicaid — the state- and federally funded medical-care system for the poor — grew from 20.9 million to 26 million.[61]

Medicaid and the Children's Health Insurance Program (CHIP) "stepped into the void," says Bruce Lesley, president of First Focus, a child-policy advocacy organization in Washington. CHIP provides low-cost medical care to children whose family incomes are low but above the poverty line.

But advocates have grounds for concern. Decisions by the Joint Committee on Deficit Reduction — the so-called congressional "super committee" charged this fall with proposing measures to reduce federal deficits by $1.5 trillion over 10 years — could lead to an erosion of medical care for the poor.[62]

And the Obama administration, as part of its own deficit-reduction proposal, has recommended cutting

AT ISSUE

Should mothers who have children out of wedlock be denied welfare?

YES
Michael D. Tanner
Senior Fellow, Cato Institute

NO
LaDonna A. Pavetti
Vice President for Family Income-Support Policy, Center on Budget and Policy Priorities

Written for *CQ Researcher*, October 2011

Since Lyndon Johnson declared a War on Poverty in 1965, the federal government has spent roughly $18 trillion fighting poverty, almost $700 billion this year alone, on some 107 separate programs. Yet, the poverty rate stands at 15.1 percent. While this number may be partially inflated because of the poor economy, it is important to realize that, despite trillions in spending, we have never gotten the poverty rate below 11 percent. Clearly we are doing some things wrong.

One is perpetuating government programs that create an incentive for behavior that is likely to lead to poverty. In particular, our welfare programs continue to provide benefits to women who give birth out of wedlock.

The concern over this trend is not about personal morality. Having a child out of wedlock often means a lifetime of poverty. Children living with single mothers are almost six times more likely to be poor than those living with two parents. More than 20 percent of welfare recipients start on welfare because they have an out-of-wedlock birth. They also tend to stay on welfare longer than other recipients.

The trend is even worse among unwed teenage mothers. Half go on welfare within one year of the birth of their first child; 75 percent are on welfare within five years of the child's birth. Women who started on welfare because of an out-of-wedlock birth average more than nine years on welfare and make up roughly 40 percent of all recipients who are on welfare for 10 years or longer.

While there are many factors behind the rise in out-of-wedlock births, the availability of welfare is one. Of the more than 20 major studies of the issue, more than three-quarters show a significant link between benefit levels and out-of-wedlock childbearing.

Obviously no one gets pregnant to get welfare. But by softening the immediate as opposed to the long-term economic consequences of out-of-wedlock births, welfare has removed a major incentive to avoid them. As Charles Murray, a political scientist at the American Enterprise Institute, put it, "The evil of the modern welfare state is not that it bribes women to have babies — wanting to have babies is natural — but that it enables women to bear children without the natural social restraints."

A good start to a welfare policy that might actually reduce poverty would be to set a date — say nine months from today — after which an out-of-wedlock birth would no longer make one eligible for welfare.

Written for *CQ Researcher*, October 2011

The case for rejecting a policy that would deny cash assistance to mothers who have children out of wedlock was compelling in 1996, when Congress created Temporary Assistance for Needy Families (TANF) — the current welfare law — and it's even more compelling now.

For starters, such a policy would deny support to children who bear no responsibility for their parents' actions. With growing evidence that poverty among young children reduces their chances of success throughout their lives, we should do everything we can to make sure that all children have the support they need to become productive adults.

A recent article by University of California, Irvine, education professor Greg J. Duncan and University of Wisconsin, Madison, professor of social work Katherine Magnuson provides all the evidence we need. Duncan is one of the most respected academic researchers on the consequences of childhood poverty, and he has always been particularly cautious in drawing policy conclusions from academic research. Two key points from the article stand out:

- Income matters for young, low-income children's learning;
- Poverty in early childhood may reduce earnings much later in life.

The authors recommend that states avoid TANF policy changes that threaten the well-being of young children. Indeed, we should be seeking more ways to remediate deep and persistent poverty in early childhood — not fewer.

Besides, although TANF provides an important safety net for single-parent families, it is not the main source of support for families with out-of-wedlock children. So, denying them these benefits will play no role in changing societal behavior. In the late 1990s, when the economy was strong, record numbers of single parents entered the labor force, reaching a high of 83 percent by 2000. Even in the current economy, 74 percent of them still work. In contrast, only 27 families for every 100 in poverty receive TANF benefits. And, TANF benefits are meager: In the median state in 2011, a family of three received $429 per month; in 14 states, such a family received less than $300.

In 1968, the Supreme Court ruled that children born to unmarried parents could not be punished for their parents' actions. The question we should be answering is: How can we make investments in our children that guarantee bright and productive futures for all of them? The answers matter not only for our children, but for all of us.

Eight-year-old Briana, left, and her sister, Daneen, 9, watch as their mother asks for a Thanksgiving turkey at the "banquet in a box" food-distribution event held by the Denver Rescue Mission in Colorado on Nov. 23, 2010. In 2009 food banks served 5.7 million people a week in the United States (the latest figure available), according to Feed America, a national alliance of food charities.

$72 million from Medicaid. "The Medicaid cuts in the president's proposal shift the burden to states and ultimately onto the shoulders of seniors, people with disabilities and low-income families who depend on the program as their lifeline," Ronald F. Pollack, executive director of Families USA, an organization that advocates for expanded health-care coverage, told *The New York Times*.[63]

As evidence of subsidized health care's vulnerability, Lower-Basch of the Center for Law and Social Policy (CLASP) cites lawmakers' reluctance to make sharp cuts in Social Security and Medicare, plus Obama's aim of raising $1.5 trillion over 10 years largely by raising taxes on high earners and cutting subsidized health programs.

"The president commented that 'it's not class warfare, it's math,'" Lower-Basch says. "At some point there are, mathematically, only a certain number of things to cut. Particularly if you take Social Security and Medicare off the table, that doesn't leave a lot of targets" besides food stamps and Medicaid, she says.

The political mechanics of deficit reduction also work in favor of cutting Medicaid funding because most Americans don't understand the technical language surrounding entitlements, Lower-Basch says. "Part of what we worry about is the process of getting to these very high-level procedural issues that are abstract," she says.

"People don't know what they mean, and what they mean is cuts in critical programs for low-income families."

Alarm among liberal advocates has stepped down a notch since earlier in the year, when Rep. Paul Ryan, R-Wis., a top Republican deficit hawk, proposed a federal budget in which Medicaid would be funded by fixed block grants to the states. The Center on Budget and Policy Priorities calculated that the proposal would have reduced Medicaid funding by at least 25 percent, based on 2009 budget figures.[64]

Obama and congressional Democrats would firmly oppose any such move, advocates say. But Haskins of the Brookings Institution suggests that the logic behind the block-grant idea remains plausible. He says, in fact, that he would support a Medicaid block grant if it came with annual funding increases.

Citing the growing costs of Medicaid and Medicare, Haskins says, "We've got to get hold of that or it's going to bankrupt us."

But Haskins adds, "If you gave a block grant with no mechanism for increasing funding, or just an increase with the rate of inflation, states would either have to cut services or spend more, and they can't spend more."

Child Support

For some poverty experts, enforcement of child-support payments is an anti-poverty tool that gets too little attention.

"We've actually reduced our investment in child-support enforcement," says Lesley of First Focus. "If we think that fathers should have responsibility for their kids, one way to address that is enforcement."

Federal "incentive" grants had been awarded to states that showed enforcement results, but those grants were eliminated by deficit-reduction legislation in 2005. The grants, which supplied from 6 percent to 39 percent of state enforcement budgets, were restored for 2009 and 2010 by the "stimulus" bill at the beginning of the Obama administration.[65]

"In 2008, 625,000 children would have been poor if they had not received child support, increasing child poverty by 4.4 percent," Elaine Sorensen of the Urban Institute, a centrist think tank in Washington, wrote last year in laying out the case for strengthening enforcement efforts. In that year, by her calculation, child-support payments aided 17 million children, ranking second to Medicaid, whose child caseload was 22.8

million — in the number of young people who received support.[66]

Sorensen also noted that among poor families with children, child support represents an average of 10 percent of family income — marginally more than the 9 percent that welfare payments represented.[67]

Nevertheless, the high and persistent joblessness that dominates the economy is having an effect on child support. The Government Accountability Office (GAO), Congress's nonpartisan investigative arm, reported in a study early this year that child-support collections had decreased for the first time in 2009, by $641 million.[68]

"Obtaining collections from a noncustodial parent with a limited ability to pay, such as those whose employment or earnings have been affected by the economic recession, is more difficult," the GAO noted.[69]

Some anti-poverty advocates point to a finding in the GAO study that they believe supports their view that enforcement is useful to only a minority of poor families, at least in present economic circumstances. The GAO found that only a third of families eligible for child-support and welfare payments actually received child-support money.[70]

Child-support payments "make a huge difference to families that receive it," says Lower-Basch of CLASP. But, she adds, most fathers of children who live under the poverty line with their mothers aren't in any position to provide significant support. "People talk about deadbeat dads, then figured out that many of them are dead broke, not deadbeat. They have minimal incomes themselves."

Jones of the Center for Urban Families warns that child-support enforcement laws, if not written with an eye to the realities that dominate families who live in poverty, can end up making matters worse. Maryland law authorizes the state to claim 65 percent of a worker's take-home pay for child support, he notes.[71]

"You take 65 percent from somebody who makes less than $10,000 a year," Jones says, and "you're setting someone up to live in the underground economy: 'I'm not going to take a legal job because I can't afford to have my money taken.' And when I become a senior citizen, I have no Social Security to draw on."

Cartoon Debate

The increase in child poverty may not have gotten much notice from politicians. Over on "Sesame Street,"

though, the development has prompted a new Muppet to join the cast for a special program. Lily, a purple-faced girl in a denim jumper, was created to represent the 16.2 million children who live in what the U.S. Agriculture Department calls "food-insecure" households.[72]

These are families who don't have guaranteed access at all times to nutritious food — a condition affecting nearly 15 percent of the U.S. population, according to the Agriculture Department.[73]

Lily appeared on a one-hour Public Broadcasting System special in early October, "Growing Hope Against Hunger." "While collecting foods at a food drive and from a community garden, the Sesame friends meet Lily, a new character whose family has an ongoing struggle with hunger," the show's production company, "Sesame Workshop," said in a press release. "The Sesame characters learn how their simple actions, such as planting a seed, can make a world of difference to others. . . . The special reassures children that they are not alone: There are people who care and can help."[74]

At a time when poverty and related issues have generated little political debate, the addition of Lily to the "Sesame Street" cast prompted sniping in some conservative media.

"I just don't understand why this Muppet is hungry," Andrea Tantaros, co-host of a Fox News talk show, "The Five," said on her Oct. 7 show. "Obama has expanded Medicaid by $60 billion, he's expanded food stamps, he's expanded WIC — Women's, Infants and Children (nutrition). . . . Why is Lily hungry? Bob, should Lily be taken away from her parents? . . . There's so much money out there to feed these kids."[75]

Tantaros was echoing a theme sounded by conservative analysts, who point to the expanded food-stamp program and other anti-poverty programs as evidence of liberal mischaracterization of U.S. poverty as severe deprivation.

Nevertheless, another school of conservative commentary takes poverty indicators at face value to criticize Obama's presidency. "With a record number of Americans on food stamps, increased debt and record poverty, Sesame Street will introduce a poor, starving muppet to educate on the growing number of starving children in Obama's America," Jim Hoft, a conservative blogger, wrote at his site, "Gateway Pundit."[76]

Hoft's comment was circulated on the left side of the blogosphere by "Media Matters for America," which monitors conservative media for a liberal audience. In the same way, another liberal site, *Crooks and Liars*, posted a clip of the Fox News discussion.[77]

Liberals, for their part, have been applauding "Sesame Street" for tackling the hunger issue. "Good they're doing it, sad it's necessary," wrote Laura Clawson, a contributor to the *Daily Kos.*[78]

OUTLOOK

Needed: Poverty Target

If the poor and the well-off occupy different spheres of reality, so do poverty policy experts of opposing political views. Their differences run far deeper than disagreements over specific policies.

Lesley of First Focus, for instance, insists that the political establishment — Democrats and Republicans alike — is neglecting the issue of poverty. "What we really need in this country is something like a poverty-reduction target," he says. "Every year you would have the target, and the administration would be required to come up with its agenda on how to address the problem. If we had a conversation among Republicans and Democrats about who is not doing enough about child poverty, I would retire."

For now, despite the Census Bureau poverty statistics that got policy experts talking, politicians have taken a pass, Lesley says. "The conversations are among advocates and think tanks. There's 22 percent of children in poverty — where's Barack Obama? [House Speaker John] Boehner, where's his agenda?"

Rector of the Heritage Foundation dismisses the idea that poverty is being ignored. "That's just a ploy," he says. "Programs are growing like crazy. The sky is always falling from their perspective. There's been a gargantuan expansion of welfare spending that's not going to go down when the recession ends," he says.

Rector and two colleagues wrote in 2009 that welfare spending aimed at poor and low-income people had grown thirteen-fold, after adjusting for inflation, to more than $700 billion, since President Johnson launched the War on Poverty in 1964.[79]

At the same time, Rector sees no end to the growth in out-of-wedlock births — the major source, in his view, of poverty. "We're on a trajectory where the working-class white family is slowly disintegrating. That creates an automatic poverty population."

Liberal analysts raise their own fear about changes in the social structure. "It's widely thought in the United States that we're the land of opportunity," says Gerry Bradley, research director at New Mexico Voices for Children, an Albuquerque-based advocacy group. "But we're getting to the point where it's more difficult for people to move out of their income group than it is in European countries that are thought to be more stratified."

The likelihood of Congress cutting benefit programs that help lower-income people afford higher education will worsen the picture, Bradley argues. "Cutting these programs is going to ensure that we have a more rigid class structure than we already do."[80]

Jones of the Center for Urban Families sounds a guardedly optimistic note. "I have to believe that in 10 years the economy will be better," he says. But he's less certain about the level of national leadership.

"Our democracy depends on our political system to make the necessary recalibration to respond to circumstances," he says. "Unless the people in control change, or our system changes, we will be worse off than we are now. I think the American people are going to have rise up and say to policy makers, 'You've got to stop the ideological warfare.'"

On another note of tempered optimism, Jane Trujillo and Shannon Barnett of Belen, N.M., are both counting the value of education. Trujillo is studying for an associate's degree in nursing. Barnett vows to do likewise.

"I didn't finish school, so I've now started classes for my GED," Barnett says. "As soon as I'm done with that I'm going to try to get into nursing school. I'm hoping that once that happens we won't be struggling so much. I am just focusing on my education."

NOTES

1. "Missing Meals in New Mexico," Roadrunner Food Bank, December 2010, www.rrfb.org/wp-content/uploads/2011/02/Executive-Summary-Version-2.pdf; "New Mexico QuickFacts," U.S. Census Bureau, updated June 3, 2011, http://quickfacts.census.gov/qfd/states/35000.html.

2. "Children in Poverty (Percent) — 2010," Kids Count Data Center, Annie E. Casey Foundation, undated, http://datacenter.kidscount.org/data/acrossstates/Rankings.aspx?ind=43.

3. "Poverty thresholds," U.S. Census Bureau, updated Sept. 13, 2011, www.census.gov/hhes/www/poverty/data/threshld/index.html.

4. Increases in food and gasoline prices in 2009-2011 are major reasons that U.S. incomes have fallen in value, a study by two former Census Bureau professionals concluded. See Robert Pear, "Recession Officially Over, U.S. Incomes Kept Falling," *The New York Times*, Oct. 10, 2011, www.nytimes.com/2011/10/10/us/recession-officially-over-us-incomes-kept-falling.html?_r=1&hp.

5. Carmen DeNavas-Walt, *et al.*, "Poverty Status of People by Family Relationship, Race, and Hispanic Origin: 1959 to 2010," U.S. Census Bureau, updated Sept. 13, 2011, p. 62, www.census.gov/hhes/www/poverty/data/historical/people.html. For background, see Thomas J. Billitteri, "Domestic Poverty," *CQ Researcher*, Sept. 7, 2007, pp. 721-744, updated April 27, 2011.

6. "Income, Poverty, and Health Insurance Coverage in the United States: 2010," U.S. Census Bureau, September 2011, p. 17, www.census.gov/prod/2011pubs/p60-239.pdf.

7. Gene Falk, "The TANF Emergency Contingency Fund," Congressional Research Service, Dec. 22, 2010, Summary page, www.fas.org/sgp/crs/misc/R41078.pdf.

8. Joyce A. Martin, *et al.*, "Births: Final Data for 2008," National Vital Statistics Reports, National Center for Health Statistics, Dec. 8, 2010, p. 44, www.cdc.gov/nchs/data/nvsr/nvsr59/nvsr59_01.pdf; "U.S. Births Rise for First Time in Eight Years," Family Planning Perspectives, Guttmacher Institute, September-October 2000, www.guttmacher.org/pubs/journals/3226300.html; Current Trends in Fertility and Infant and Maternal Health — United States, 1980-1988," Centers for Disease Control, June 14, 1991, www.cdc.gov/mmwr/preview/mmwrhtml/00014440.htm; Stephanie J. Ventura, "Changing Patterns of Nonmarital Childbearing in the United States," National Center for Health

Statistics, May 2009, www.cdc.gov/nchs/data/databriefs/db18.pdf.

9. "Related Children Under 18 by Householder's Work Experience and Family Structure: 2010," Current Population Survey, U.S. Census Bureau, Labor Department, updated Sept. 13, 2011, www.census.gov/hhes/www/cpstables/032011/pov/new21_100_01.htm.

10. Mark Hugo Lopez and Gabriel Velasco, "Childhood Poverty Among Hispanics Sets Record, Leads Nation," Pew Hispanic Center, Sept. 28, 2011, p. 4, http://pewhispanic.org/files/reports/147.pdf.

11. *Ibid.*, pp. 11-14; "Educational Attainment: Better Than Meets the Eye, But Large Challenges Remain," Pew Hispanic Center, January 2002, http://pewhispanic.org/files/factsheets/3.pdf.

12. See Kathleen S. Short, "The Supplemental Poverty Measure: Examining the Incidence and Depth of Poverty in the U.S. Taking Account of Taxes and Transfers," U.S. Census Bureau, June 30, 2011, www.census.gov/hhes/povmeas/methodology/supplemental/research.html.

13. "A Brief History of the AFDC Program," Health and Human Services Department, June 1998, http://aspe.hhs.gov/hsp/afdc/afdcbase98.htm.

14. Gene Falk, The Temporary Assistance for Needy Families (TANF) Block Grant: Responses to Frequently Asked Questions," Congressional Research Service, May 4, 2011, www.workforceatm.org/assets/utilities/serve.cfm?path=/sections/pdf/2011/TheTemporaryAssistanceforNeedyFamiliesTANFBlockGrantResponsestoFrequentlyAskedQuestions3.pdf.

15. *Ibid.*, p. 6.

16. *Ibid.*, pp. 1, 3, 7.

17. *Ibid.*, p. 2.

18. *Ibid.*, p. 9; "Caseload Data 2011," Administration for Children and Families, Health and Human Services Department, updated July 25, 2011, www.acf.hhs.gov/programs/ofa/data-reports/caseload/caseload_current.htm#2011.

19. Sabrina Tavernise, "Soaring Poverty Casts Spotlight on 'Lost Decade,' " *The New York Times*, Sept. 13, 2011, www.nytimes.com/2011/09/14/us/14census

.html?pagewanted=1&_r=1&sq=census%20 2010%20poverty&st=cse&scp=2; DeNavas-Walt, *op. cit.*, pp. 14, 17.

20. "Supplemental Nutrition Assistance Program: Number of Persons Participating," Food Research and Action Center, updated monthly, http://frac .org/wp-content/uploads/2011/03/snapdata2011_ july.pdf; "Labor Force Statistics from the Current Population Survey," U.S. Bureau of Labor Statistics, updated regularly, http://data.bls.gov/timeseries/ LNS14000000.

21. Robert Rector, *et al.*, "Obama to Spend $10.3 Trillion on Welfare," Heritage Foundation, Sept. 16, 2009, www.heritage.org/Research/Reports/2009/09/ Obama-to-Spend-103-Trillion-on-Welfare- Uncovering-the-Full-Cost-of-Means-Tested- Welfare-or-Aid-to-the-Poor.

22. "Hearing of the House Ways and Means Committee, 'Improving Work and Other Welfare Reform Goals, Focusing on Reauthorization of the Temporary Assistance for Needy Families Program," Federal News Service, Sept. 8, 2011; "Engagement in Additional Work Activities and Expenditures for Other Benefits and Services, a TANF Report to Congress," March 2011, (no page numbers), www .acf.hhs.gov/programs/ofa/data-reports/cra-report- to-congress/cra_report-to-congress.html#_Toc29 8161525.

23. Hearing, *ibid.*

24. Kristin Anderson Moore, *et al.*, "Children in Poverty: Trends, Consequences, and Policy Options," Child Trends, April 2009, www .childtrends.org/files/child_trends-2009_04_07_ rb_childreninpoverty.pdf.

25. *Ibid.*

26. DeNavas-Walt, *et al.*, *op. cit.*, pp. 17-18, 74.

27. "2011 Kids Count Data Book," Annie E. Casey Foundation, 2011, p. 62, http://datacenter.kids- count.org/databook/2011/OnlineBooks/2011 KCDB_FINAL.pdf; Vanessa R. Wight, *et al.*, "Who are America's Poor Children?," National Center for Children in Poverty, Columbia University, March 2011, www.nccp.org/publications/pub_1001 .html.

28. James J. Heckman, "The Economics of Inequality," *American Educator*, Spring 2011, p. 33, www.aft .org/pdfs/americaneducator/spring2011/Heckman .pdf.

29. "Income, Poverty, and Health Insurance Coverage," *op. cit.*, p. 15.

30. Ron Haskins, "Fighting Poverty the American Way," Brookings Institution, June 20, 2011, p. 32, www .brookings.edu/~/media/Files/rc/papers/2011/ 0620_fighting_poverty_haskins/0620_fighting_ poverty_haskins.pdf.

31. Except where otherwise indicated, this subsection is drawn from Premilla Nadasen, *et al.*, *Welfare in the United States: A History With Documents 1935-1996* (2009); Thomas Gabe, "Welfare, Work and Poverty Status of Female-Headed Families With Children: 1987-2009, Congressional Research Service, July 15, 2011, http://digitalcommons.ilr.cornell.edu/cgi/ viewcontent.cgi?article=1852&context=key_work place; for background, see Kathy Koch, "Child Poverty," *CQ Researcher*, April 7, 2000, pp. 281-304.

32. Jennifer Michael and Madeleine Goldstein, "Reviving the White House Conference on Children," Children's Voice, Child Welfare League of America, January-February 2008, www.cwla.org/ voice/0801whconf.htm.

33. Nadasen, *et al.*, *op. cit.*, pp. 15-16.

34. Quoted in Susan W. Blank and Barbara B. Blum, "A Brief History of Work Expectations for Welfare Mothers," *Future of Children* (Journal), Spring 1997, p. 30, www.princeton.edu/futureofchildren/publica tions/docs/07_01_02.pdf.

35. *Ibid.*, p. 30.

36. Blank and Blum, *op. cit.*, p. 30.

37. Richard B. Drake, *A History of Appalachia* (2001), p. 173; Maurice Isserman, "Michael Harrington: Warrior on Poverty," *The New York Times*, June 19, 2009, www.nytimes.com/2009/06/21/books/ review/Isserman-t.html. Except where otherwise indicated, this subsection is drawn from Gabe, *op. cit.*

38. Quoted in Edward Zigler and Susan Muenchow, *Head Start: The Inside Story of America's Most Successful Educational Experiment* (1992), p. 3.

39. "Trends in the AFDC Caseload since 1962," U.S. Health and Human Services Department, undated, p. 15, http://aspe.hhs.gov/hsp/afdc/baseline/2caseload.pdf.

40. Report included in Nadasen, *et al.*, p. 169.

41. *Ibid.*

42. Gabe, *op. cit.*, p. 69.

43. Daniel Patrick Moynihan, "The Negro Family: The Case for National Action," U.S. Department of Labor, March 1965, www.dol.gov/oasam/programs/history/webid-meynihan.htm.

44. *Ibid.*

45. Nadasen, *et al.*, *op. cit.*, pp. 45-46; John McWhorter, "Legitimacy at Last," *The New Republic*, April 16, 2010, www.tnr.com/book/review/legitimacy-last.

46. *Ibid.*

47. Nadasen, *et al.*, *op. cit.*, p. 47.

48. Gabe, *op. cit.*, pp. 59-60.

49. *Ibid.*, p. 60.

50. For background, see Peter Katel, "Straining the Safety Net," *CQ Researcher*, July 31, 2009, pp. 645-668. Except where otherwise stated, this subsection draws on Blank and Blum, *op. cit.*

51. Katel, *ibid.*

52. "Address Before a Joint Session of the Congress Reporting on the State of the Union," Feb. 4, 1986, http://reagan2020.us/speeches/state_of_the_union_1986.asp.

53. Quoted in Richard L. Berke, "Clinton: Getting People Off Welfare," *The New York Times*, Sept. 10, 1992, www.nytimes.com/1992/09/10/us/the-1992-campaign-the-ad-campaign-clinton-getting-people-off-welfare.html.

54. Quoted in Gabe, *op. cit.*, p. 8.

55. "Fact Sheet, The Personal Responsibility and Work Opportunity Reconciliation Act of 1996," Health and Human Services Dept., September 1996, http://aspe.hhs.gov/hsp/abbrev/prwora96.htm; "Interview: Welfare reform, 10 years later (with Ron Haskins)," Brookings Institution, Aug. 24, 2006, www.brookings.edu/interviews/2006/0824welfare_haskins.aspx.

56. *Ibid.*, Haskins; Ronald Brownstein, "A Stormy Debate Is Brewing Within GOP Over Clinton's Big Lead in Polls," *Los Angeles Times*, Sept. 9, 1996, p. A5.

57. *Ibid.*

58. Ron Haskins, "Fighting Poverty the American Way," Brookings Institution, June 20, 2011, pp. 4, 32, www.brookings.edu/~/media/Files/rc/papers/2011/0620_fighting_poverty_haskins/0620_fighting_poverty_haskins.pdf.

59. *Ibid.*

60. Gene Falk, "The Temporary Assistance for Needy Families (TANF) Block Grant: Responses to Frequently Asked Questions," Congressional Research Service, Jan. 21, 2009, p. 1, http://stuff.mit.edu/afs/sipb/contrib/wikileaks-crs/wikileaks-crs-reports/RL32760.pdf.

61. "Income, Poverty, and Health Insurance . . . ," *op. cit.*, p. 82.

62. "Joint Select Committee on Deficit Reduction," undated, www.deficitreduction.gov/public.

63. Quoted in Robert Pear, "In Cuts to Health Programs, Experts See Difficult Task in Protecting Patients," *The New York Times*, Sept. 20, 2011, www.nytimes.com/2011/09/21/us/politics/wielding-the-ax-on-medicaid-and-medicare-without-wounding-the-patient.html.

64. Edwin Park and Matt Broaddus, "What if Ryan's Medicaid Block Grant Had Taken Effect in 2000," Center on Budget and Policy Priorities, April 12, 2011, www.cbpp.org/cms/index.cfm?fa=view&id=3466.

65. "Child Support Enforcement," Government Accountability Office, January, www.gao.gov/new.items/d11196.pdf.

66. Elaine Sorensen, "Child Support Plays an Increasingly Important Role for Poor Custodial Families," Urban Institute, December 2010, p. 1, www.urban.org/publications/412272.html.

67. *Ibid.*, p. 3.

68. "Child Support Enforcement," *op. cit.*, p. 11.

69. *Ibid.*, p. 14.

70. *Ibid.*, p. 14.

71. "Department of Human Resources, Child Support," Maryland state government, undated, www.dhr.state.md.us/csea/download/EMPLOYERJOBAID.doc.

72. Dave Itzkoff, " 'Sesame Street' Special on Hunger Introduces New Muppet Character," *The New York Times*, ArtsBeat blog, Oct. 3, 2011, http://artsbeat.blogs.nytimes.com/2011/10/03/sesame-street-special-on-hunger-introduces-new-muppet-character; "Food Security in the United States," U.S. Agriculture Department, updated Sept. 7, 2011, www.ers.usda.gov/Briefing/FoodSecurity/stats_graphs.htm.

73. *Ibid.*

74. "Project Overview, growing hope against hunger," Sesame Workshop, Oct. 4, 2011, www.s2.cinemagnetics.com/press-release/english.html.

75. "Sign of the Times: Poverty-Stricken Muppet," "The Five" transcript, Oct. 7, 2011, www.foxnews.com/on-air/the-five/transcript/sign-times-poverty-stricken-muppet.

76. Melody Johnson, "Strings Attached: Right-Wing Media Take Shots At New Poverty-Stricken Sesame Street Character," Media Matters for America, Oct. 6, 2011, http://mediamatters.org/blog/201110060010.

77. "Fox Panel Attacks Sesame Street for Wanting to Educate Children About Poverty," *Crooks and Liars*, Oct. 8, 2011, http://videocafe.crooksandliars.com/heather/fox-panel-attacks-sesame-street-wanting-ed.

78. Laura Clawson, "This week in the War on Workers: The hungry Muppet," *Daily Kos*, Oct. 8, 2011, http://labor.dailykos.com.

79. Robert Rector, Katherine Bradley, Rachel Sheffield, "Obama to Spend $10 trillion on Welfare," Heritage Foundation, Sept. 16, 2009, p. 1, www.heritage.org/research/reports/2009/09/obama-to-spend-103-trillion-on-welfare-uncovering-the-full-cost-of-means-tested-welfare-or-aid-to-the-poor.

80. For background, see Marcia Clemmitt, "Student Debt," *CQ Researcher*, Oct. 21, 2011, pp. 877-900.

BIBLIOGRAPHY

Books

Mead, Lawrence M., *Expanding Work Programs for Poor Men*, AEI Press, 2011.
A leading conservative poverty-policy expert lays out a case for requiring low-income men to work, following the example of the 1996 welfare law and its demands on largely female welfare recipients. Poor children would benefit, he writes, as child-support payments increased.

Nadasen, Premilla, Jennifer Mittelstadt and Marisa Chappell, *Welfare in the United States: A History With Documents, 1935-1996*, Routledge, 2009.
Three historians chronicle and analyze welfare history from a pro-welfare recipients' perspective.

Articles

Alderman, Lesley, "Government Helps to Insure Children, Even Above the Poverty Line," *The New York Times*, Oct. 9, 2010, p. B6, www.nytimes.com/2010/10/09/health/09patient.html.
Successful results are reported for the federal-state health coverage program for low-income children.

Crary, David, *et al.*, "Behind the poverty numbers: real lives, real pain," The Associated Press, Sept. 19, 2011.
In a series of profiles from across the country, AP correspondents report on the hardships faced by growing numbers of families.

D'Innocenzio, Anne, and Dena Potter, "Food-stamp shoppers buy at midnight across the country," *The Washington Post*, Oct. 24, 2010, p. A8, www.washingtonpost.com/wp-dyn/content/article/2010/10/23/AR2010102300179.html.
The Post uncovers a nationwide trend of families racing to stock up on food as soon as their electronic food-stamp cards are recharged once a month at midnight.

Davey, Monica, "Families Feel Sharp Edge of State Budget Cuts," *The New York Times*, Sept. 7, 2011, p. A22, www.nytimes.com/2011/09/07/us/07states.html?pagewanted=all.
Hard-pressed states are reducing aid to poor families, a correspondent reports from the Midwest.

Egger, Robert, "5 Myths about hunger in America," *The Washington Post*, Nov. 21, 2010, p. B2, www.washingtonpost.com/wp-dyn/content/article/2010/11/19/AR2010111906872.html.
The founder of a Washington food-preparation business argues that hunger and poor nutrition are far bigger problems than generally recognized.

Gordey, Cynthia, "Welfare, Fathers and Those Persistent Myths," *The Root*, June 17, 2011, www.theroot.com/views/welfare-fathers-and-those-persistent-myths.
A writer for an online magazine on African-American issues reports on the growing recognition of fathers' importance for children growing up in mother-headed households.

Reports and Studies

Falk, Gene, "The Temporary Assistance for Needy Families (TANF) Block Grant: Responses to Frequently Asked Questions," *Congressional Research Service*, Feb. 16, 2011, www.naswa.org/assets/utilities/serve.cfm?gid=231C9E08-41AA-4283-9E35-7625F0575B4E.
A social-policy expert for Congress' nonpartisan research arm provides a wealth of basic information on the welfare system.

Gabe, Thomas, "Welfare, Work, and Poverty Status of Female-Headed Families with Children: 1987-2009," *Congressional Research Service*, July 15, 2011, http://digitalcommons.ilr.cornell.edu/cgi/viewcontent.cgi?article=1852&context=key_workplace.
Another CRS specialist provides a detailed, data-rich analysis of one of the most long-running issues in anti-poverty policy.

Haskins, Ron, "Fighting Poverty the American Way," *Brookings Institution*, June 2011, www.brookings.edu/papers/2011/0620_fighting_poverty_haskins.aspx.
A key figure in the 1996 welfare overhaul examines welfare policy against the backdrop of American political culture.

DeNavas-Walt, Carmen, *et al.*, "Income, Poverty, and Health Insurance Coverage in the United States: 2010," *U.S. Census Bureau*, September 2011, www.census.gov/prod/2011pubs/p60-239.pdf.
Census Bureau experts marshal enormous quantities of data to illustrate ongoing trends in income and well-being.

Rector, Robert, *et al.*, "Obama to Spend $10.3 Trillion on Welfare," *Heritage Foundation*, Sept. 16, 2009, www.heritage.org/research/reports/2009/09/obama-to-spend-103-trillion-on-welfare-uncovering-the-full-cost-of-means-tested-welfare-or-aid-to-the-poor.
Analysts for a leading conservative think tank present a case for extreme skepticism about government anti-poverty programs.

Seith, David, and Courtney Kalof, "Who Are America's Poor Children?" *National Center for Children in Poverty*, Columbia University, July 2011, www.nccp.org/publications/pdf/text_1032.pdf.
Researchers for a leading child-poverty think tank analyze the defining characteristics of children in poverty.

For More Information

Center for Urban Families, 2201 North Monroe St., Baltimore, MD 21217; 410-367-5691; http://cfuf.org/index. Develops and runs training programs in job skills and fatherhood.

Center on Budget and Policy Priorities, 820 First St., N.E., Suite 510, Washington, DC 20002; 202-408-1080; www.cbpp.org. Research and advocacy organization specializing in legislative and policy analysis.

CLASP, 1200 18th St., N.W., Washington, DC 20036; 202-906-8000; www.clasp.org. Advocacy organization focusing on children and family law and policy.

Feeding America, 35 East Wacker Drive, Chicago, IL 60601; 800-771-2303; http://feedingamerica.org. National alliance of food banks that provides information on hunger, nutrition conditions and relevant laws and policies.

Heritage Foundation, 214 Massachusetts Ave., N.E., Washington, DC 20002-4999; 202-546-4400; www.heritage.org/Issues/Poverty-and-Inequality. Conservative think tank that conducts research on poverty and related issues.

National Center for Children in Poverty, 215 W. 125th St., 3rd Floor, New York, NY 10027; 646-284-9600; www.nccp.org. Columbia University think tank providing data-analysis tools on poverty and health.

U.S. Census Bureau, 4600 Silver Hill Road, S.E., Washington, DC 20233; 301-763-4636; www.census.gov/hhes/www/poverty/poverty.html. Federal agency providing a vast amount of current and historical information on poverty.